European Accountancy Yearbook 1992/93

Managing Editor
Ellen Rocco

Editor
John Leslie

Published by
Graham & Trotman
A member of Wolters Kluwer Academic Publishers
LONDON/DORDRECHT/BOSTON

Sterling House, 66 Wilton Road, London SW1V 1DE, United Kingdom
Telephone: 071-821 1123 Telex: 298878 Gramco G Facsimile: 071-630 5229

First edition published in 1992 by
Graham & Trotman Ltd
Sterling House, 66 Wilton Road
London SW1V 1DE

Graham & Trotman Ltd is a member of the

DPA
DIRECTORY PUBLISHERS
ASSOCIATION
ASSOCIATE MEMBER

British Library Cataloging in Publication Data

Library of Congress CIP data is available from the publisher

ISBN 1 85333610 6
ISSN 0963-0538

Concept and Editorial by:
Ellen Rocco Directory Consultancy
38 Northolme Road, London N5 2UU

Computer typeset by Graham & Trotman Ltd
Printed and bound in Great Britain by Hartnolls Ltd, Bodmin, Cornwall

Foreword

If 1992 was ever expected to mark the culmination of the process of European harmonisation, even the most dedicated idealist must have abandoned such a belief by now.

Despite the enormous progress that has been made, the achievements of the past decade are overshadowed by the work which remains to be completed before Europe can function as a fully integrated community.

In that sense, 1992 is only a transitional phase – a waypoint on the route towards an effective single market. In another sense, however, 1992 is a fulcrum; the point at which a unified Europe passes from concept to reality.

Until now, the European effort has been a matter of pushing against the gradient to achieve necessary reform. From now on, it may be more a question of checking the pace of change, ensuring that control and co-ordination are kept.

If Europe is to maintain control and realise its aims, communication and information will become increasingly vital. For the accountancy profession there are specific challenges: to develop and mature the rapidly expanding pan-European networks of both large and smaller firms; to capitalise effectively on the progress towards mutual recognition of professional qualifications; but most of all to provide the best advice on the practical impact of the various company directives and fiscal harmonisation measures.

THE EUROPEAN ACCOUNTANCY YEARBOOK has an important part to play in the process of building the information base without which the EC cannot hope to progress. While of obvious importance to the accountancy profession itself, the *YEARBOOK* will play an even more significant role among the myriad companies and businesses, large and small, which are now attuning their operations to the European single market.

The accountancy profession's role in guiding and facilitating the development of industry and commerce is already well established. The challenge now facing the profession is to ensure that its own structure, expansion and communication across Europe will always be ready to meet the ever-growing needs of its clientele.

I look forward to *THE EUROPEAN ACCOUNTANCY YEARBOOK*'s contribution towards an ever better and better-informed profession serving an ever more demanding and challenging business market.

Edouard Salustro
President
Fédération des Experts Comptables Européens

Contents

Introduction

This first edition of *THE EUROPEAN ACCOUNTANCY YEARBOOK* reflects the current trend in European accountancy – that of harmonisation and cross-border co-operation in almost every area of the profession.

The trend is intimately linked to the growing requirements of client companies – for tax, legal and economic information and overall advice on setting up trade into new European countries, and for locally based accountancy services once the new venture has been established.

Competition has never been greater within the profession itself, and this has also had an impact on the development of alliances between practices. The largest accountancy firms, already international in outlook, have adopted energetic policies of acquisition and merger to ensure they offer full local representation across Europe. Their networks are now increasingly mirrored by associations, alliances and networks of medium-sized and smaller firms seeking to offer a similar level of cross-border services without the firms losing their character as smaller independent practices.

Such developments are taking place against a backdrop of rapidly developing EC harmonisation legislation affecting company law, audit requirements, taxation and most recently mutual recognition of professional qualifications. The effect of all this is to open still further the market for pan-European accountancy services; and to ensure that commercial companies have a widening range of choice from which to select their professional advisors.

It is hoped that *THE EUROPEAN ACCOUNTANCY YEARBOOK,* the first directory to list European accountancy firms in one dedicated volume, will assist both client companies and accountants themselves by charting the movement towards one Europe.

The heart of the Yearbook is the extensive listing of accountancy practices country by country, and the separate section listing networks, groups and associations with their principal national offices in each country.

Details are included of over 3,700 accountancy firms and companies, covering all 17 EC and EFTA countries as well as eight additional tax havens and other financially important and geographically compatible countries (it was decided to exclude Eastern Europe from this edition of the Yearbook due to the fluid political situation and the still relatively undeveloped state of the profession in the former Eastern bloc countries). The number of firms listed in each country broadly reflects the size of the practising profession there; the UK section lists the greatest number of firms, followed by the Netherlands, Germany and France.

In addition to the listings, the Yearbook includes eight specially-commissioned articles on topical issues; country-specific information on taxation, general economic indicators and the structure of the profession; and a guide to the leading European professional accountancy bodies by country.

Every listing in the Yearbook has been compiled from original information verified by the accountancy practice or group itself. The extent of the information differs in accordance with regulations about advertising and promotion in the country concerned, each practice's individual rules, and the group or network's philosophy on disclosure. A minority of practices have been unable or unwilling to provide verified information, and have not been included in this edition.

Practices are eligible for inclusion (free of charge) regardless of their size, if they have an existing capacity for and interest in providing cross-border services, as evidenced by ▷

membership of an international or European accountancy group or network (most but not all firms listed belong to a network), registration with a national chamber of commerce or professional body, or a direct request to be included within the Yearbook. Client services listed are those provided within the accountancy practice; divisions providing non-accountancy services (eg management consultancy or legal advice) are not included.

Notes on using the directory

There are two main sections: *'European Accountancy Groups'*, and *'European Accountancy Firms by Country'*.

The *Accountancy Groups* section lists 45 groups, networks and affiliations in alphabetical order. Use this section to find out about the central organisation, size and structure of a group; and also to look up the principal national offices of the group in any particular country. Expanded information about national offices is given in the *Accountancy Firms by Country* section.

The *Accountancy Firms by Country* section provides detailed entries for the firms practising in each country, listed alphabetically by the name of the principal national office (allowing easy cross-reference to and from the *Accountancy Groups* section). Some 270 of the firms listed in this section are not affiliated to or members of any international group or network.

Under each principal office is a list of its regional offices, affiliates or correspondents in that country. Only basic contact information is given for subsidiary offices; see the main listing for greater detail, including European affiliation (where appropriate), numbers of staff, fee income, client services, industry specialisations and major clients. The total offices figure (where shown) is the total of all offices in that country (some of which may not be listed) as stated by the firm itself.

Addresses and telephone numbers have been presented following a consistent style within each country concerned. Telephone and fax numbers give:

- the country code, preceded by a ' + ' (eg +43 for Austria)
- the area code, in brackets (in some countries such as France and Luxembourg, no area code is used)
- the customer number.

When dialling from outside the country, the appropriate international code (eg 010 from the UK) should be dialled before the country code. When dialling from within the country, the country code should be omitted; an additional digit (usually '9' or '0') may be required before the area code shown.

Tax data provided on the country divider pages is in most cases updated to 1 January 1992. It is by its nature subject to frequent change, and should always be verified before making any decision based on its authenticity.

We have used the greatest care in compiling *THE EUROPEAN ACCOUNTANCY YEARBOOK*. However, if you find any inaccuracy we would greatly appreciate being told. We would equally welcome any observations on the content and structure or ideas on how the Yearbook could be of even greater use to you in future.

The Editors

by Julie Blyth

Based on a recent research project by Precepta Group, this summary looks at developments in the role and structure of accountancy in Europe, and changes yet to come.

Battle for market share

The European accountancy sector is currently undergoing a period of change, as a reaction to the restructuring of European industry, the implication of regulatory changes, and the recent fluctuations in general economic activity. As the battle for market share intensifies in a relatively unstable environment, firms are being forced to re-evaluate their European strategies for the 1990's and beyond.

The European market, which is estimated to account for about 40% of worldwide revenue, has grown steadily over the last decade. Average annual growth rates of between 20% and 40% have been common in the case of the larger firms. While the UK and the Netherlands' markets have reached a stage of maturity, the Southern European countries, such as Spain, Portugal and Italy, are showing strong growth and this is likely to continue throughout the 1990's.

A number of economic and legislative changes have combined to create a significant stimulus to demand for accountancy services. The EC Fourth Directive, implemented in all EC member states over the last ten years, has greatly extended the statutory audit requirement to all but small, private companies, creating new opportunities in the firms' core business. This, combined with the Seventh and Eighth Directives, has gone some way towards harmonising accounting systems. In addition, the development and restructuring of European industry in the run up to 1992 will lead to an increasing number of opportunities for accountancy firms.

The market is regarded as being highly concentrated in the hands of a few large firms and is therefore characterised by a high degree of competitive rivalry. An analysis of the *Financial Times* Top 500 European companies in 1990 shows that 83% were audited by the 'Big Six'. However, this compares favourably with the mature US market where a similar study revealed that 98% of the leading companies were audited by the 'Big Six'. Recently some undesirable elements of competition have become more common, for example price wars, which have left the industry less stable and profitable. The fact that the market for auditing and accountancy services is exhibiting slower growth is encouraging firms to vie more strongly for market share.

The high level of merger and acquisition activity in the last few years, including the 'mega-mergers' of 1989, has been both a cause and a consequence of this intense competitive rivalry. Many firms consider mergers and acquisitions to be a path to faster growth and increased profits. In order to achieve the advantages of economies of scale in the short term, firms cannot necessarily rely on organic growth, but instead seek partners who can contribute the resources to strengthen the merged firm both geographically and in product/service lines.

Pan-European networks

The increasing internationalisation of business in Europe, and the subsequent need for comparable financial information in each country, has driven firms to establish pan-European networks in order that they may serve their multinational clients in all countries in which they are present. Consequently, the sector has been characterised by a regrouping of firms into different international networks capable of serving an international client base. Firms have also positioned themselves to achieve wider market access by establishing greenfield operations (BDO in Eastern Europe), by merging with national firms (Price Waterhouse with Befec in France), and by establishing joint ventures (Coopers and Lybrand with the Magyar Hitel Bank in Hungary).

As their traditional core auditing and accounting markets begin to show slower growth rates, firms have reacted by developing new services and expanding into new markets, such as management consultancy, tax advice, corporate finance, and even personal financial planning and investment advice, where the potential for growth is greater. This has also occurred in response to the demands of their clients for informed advice on a wide range of issues. Many companies see advantages in having all their business service needs satisfied by one firm which already has an intimate knowledge of their business. Although firms are unlikely to face competition over their entire range of services ▷

from any one source, they may face threats in particular areas of business. In consultancy, for example, the firms are competing strongly with the specialist management consultancy firms; in the area of tax advice, accountants face competition from the legal profession; and in corporate finance work, the firms are increasingly competing in the same market as the merchant banks, for example, in M&A work and management buy-outs.

While most of the leading firms now offer a highly diversified range of services, many firms compete by focusing on a particular client segment, for example, companies of a particular size or in a particular industry (Horwath International specialises in the tourism and leisure sector). There are a number of advantages in serving a specific target group, particularly in terms of the experience and knowledge which helps the firm to become more efficient in serving that group.

A three-tier alignment

The market is made up of three different strategic groups. Firstly, the 'Big Six' with their predominantly 'Anglo-Saxon' background, have grown significantly over the last few decades to establish a dominant position in the accountancy sector worldwide. The firms' size alone differentiates them from their closest competitors. They have extensive international networks, which are continually being extended to take advantage of growth opportunities in new markets (for example, Eastern Europe). The firms also have a substantial resource base which allows them to diversify in order to maintain revenue growth. Most national firms operate under the name of the international firm in order to take advantage of 'brand image' and reputation.

The second tier are major firms in their own right. Although smaller than the 'Big Six', they are able to offer a complete range of services to their clients. Their competitive strategy is based on a number of factors. They are positioning themselves for access to a wider market by incorporating new firms into their networks, particularly in the faster growing markets. The firms differentiate themselves through quality of service and close relationships between partners and clients. The staff/partner ratio therefore tends to be lower in this group. The firms are in a position to benefit from economies of scale but allow each national member firm to retain a high degree of independence and flexibility to react to opportunities as they arise in their home markets.

The final group is characterised by associations of small and medium-sized firms which have grouped together mainly as a defensive move against the threat of possible takeover. The networks are either national (France Defi) or international (Inpact) and are mainly based on referral work between the independent members and shared resources and expertise. Although lacking the size and geographic presence of the 'Big Six' and second tier, they are able to differentiate their services through close personal contact and the provision of a specialised service to clients.

The driving forces for change

The growing need for the independent and objective provision of financial information will remain an important driving force behind the future development of the sector. The users of this information, however, have gradually begun to see the accountants as being responsible for the detection of fraud and other irregularities in the accounts. The role of the accountant is likely to become more risky in the future, with a growing number of lawsuits being filed against the firms.

Another major impetus behind the development of the profession is the response of the firms to the increasingly sophisticated demands of business. Many have proved themselves to be flexible enough to react to new opportunities, as demonstrated by the continual diversification into new services. It is possible that in the future auditing and accounting will begin to play a smaller part in the work of accountancy practices and will be replaced by consultancy based services. In addition, firms will face a threat of substitution in accounting and book-keeping from sophisticated financial software products. This is likely to be a particularly important threat in the future with the introduction of pan-European accounting and software systems.

Accountancy firms must react swiftly to new market opportunities. Although growth potential remains strong in the Southern European markets at least, firms must continually look to exploit new market opportunities. The democratisation of Eastern European countries and their transition to market economies, for example, will require a ▷

great deal of assistance in the form of financial and management expertise from Western accountancy firms.

Apart from reacting to the demands of clients for new services and exploiting new markets, what factors will differentiate the winners from the losers in today's accountancy market? One of the key success factors will undoubtedly be the ability to improve productivity, particularly in view of the impending scarcity of high quality recruits. The growth potential of accountancy firms is highly dependent on the availability of new recruits, but due to the declining teenage population the demand is likely to exceed the supply over the next few years. As a result, there will have to be increased spending on recruitment, training and the remuneration of staff.

Harnessing the new technology

Increased spending on information technology will also be required in order to increase productivity and subsequently profitability. New technology has the capacity to influence developments in auditing and accounting methodologies and procedures, as well as the organisation and staffing of firms in the future. Computerising the market makes each individual more productive, and also de-skills many tasks so that less qualified (and therefore less costly) support staff may carry out these tasks instead.

Other important success factors for firms will be marketing and providing a high quality of service. Firms will be required to research consumer demand and to react to this by improving existing services and developing new ones, the ultimate objective being to provide the services required for each client at a price which provides value for money. In addition, quality of service is one of the principal ways of differentiating a firm's product/service from those of its competitors. This can be judged by the speed and efficiency of the reaction to clients' requests, for example, or the ability to take initiative in recommending ideas or solutions to problems.

The future scenario for the accountancy profession will largely be determined by the interaction of a number of external and internal forces. Economic prosperity and the continued internationalisation of world markets, for example, will undoubtedly represent an opportunity to accountancy firms. Further progress is required, however, on the issue of harmonisation and the creation of a single European market for accountancy services; only then can firms truly consider themselves to be 'pan-European'. Firms must also be prepared to respond to international opportunities, not just in Eastern Europe but in regions such as the Far East and South America.

One of the main threats facing firms in the future is not an external one but is posed by the firms themselves. Complacency, and an inability to react swiftly to changes in the business, could potentially be the biggest hazard facing the firms during the 1990's. In the long term, the success of a firm will be largely dependent on the ability to adapt new skills in response to the changing demands of clients and to balance professional and commercial acumen. Firms which lack the flexibility to react swiftly to the changing demands of the business will ultimately be at a disadvantage in facing the considerable challenges of the coming years.

Julie Blyth is a Researcher working with Precepta Group.

Precepta Group is a Paris-based research and consultancy company. It has become, in a few years, one of the major European companies specialising in competitive and strategic analyses of industrial and service sectors, on a pan-European scale. Precepta is at 85 rue La Fayette, 75009 PARIS (Tel: +33 (1) 48 78 80 40) and at 4 Cromwell Place, LONDON SW7 2JJ (Tel: +44 (71) 584 5757).

LOCATION, INCENTIVES AND TAXATION: Far reaching strategic implications

by WP Vossen and ES van Herwaarden

A decision on location can literally make or break a new project, but is too often given little importance. We offer a guide to some of the most critical factors to be taken into account.

Get it right first time

Many companies are now reconsidering their strategies, faced with the wide range of challenges and opportunities presented by the integration in 1993 of the 12 countries of the European Community (EC), and the dramatic changes in Central and Eastern Europe.

Operational structures are being reviewed to take advantage of the benefits resulting from the elimination of transport quotas, the minimisation of border controls, the harmonisation and recognition of standards and professional or academic qualifications, and the liberalisation of telecommunications and financial services. New projects are being conceived to penetrate markets which, until recently, were part of state-controlled economies.

In the course of corporate restructuring and expansion, the location of existing and new facilities is an important, but often underestimated, issue. The choice of a new site or building has far-reaching strategic implications. It will play a decisive role in the overall success of a venture. Moreover, the location decision is irreversible. Whilst bad decisions on engineering, equipment or product design can often be reversed, pressure on companies for investment in fixed assets, human resources, and financing is so large that no room is left to reverse a location decision once it has been implemented.

Besides the important financial implications, in the increasingly competitive business environment, an inadequate location and resulting project failure will often lead to loss of market share to competing companies. Companies cannot overestimate the strategic implications of a location decision. They have no choice but to get it right the first time.

Not only the impact, but also the complexity of location decision-making is often overlooked. A large number of factors determine whether a site or building offers optimum conditions for a business's investment and operations. Selecting a location requires careful evaluation of such elements as labour availability, infrastructure, telecommunications, wages and social security regulations, corporate and personal income tax incentives, social climate and living conditions.

Overlooked complexity

As a result, when comparing alternative locations, decision makers are faced with an intricate set of interrelated and often incomparable elements. In addition, the task of acquiring the necessary technical and economic data is far from easy. To identify the best location, trade-offs and compromises must inevitably be made.

Few companies are fully prepared for solving this problem. Many simply go by the impressions of their top management or review locations on the basis of one element only. The debris resulting from such an approach can be found around Europe. A region south of Brussels, for example, hosts a manufacturing facility belonging to a renowned multinational company. The site was selected by the company's CEO, who enjoyed the living conditions of the area. The factory now stands idle as the question of social climate had not been fully addressed.

In other cases, businesses have been attracted by favourable incentives only to close down their factories later because high transport costs made their products uncompetitive. Many similar cases only serve to reinforce the need for an organised, methodical approach.

The elements that businesses need to take into account when assessing alternative locations can be grouped into two categories:

- intangible factors, including the physical-technical factors.
- cost elements

Intangibles and cost elements

Intangible elements cannot be expressed in monetary terms. They relate to the qualitative aspects of a location and determine whether a location is viable from an operational point of view. Typical intangibles include labour availability, social climate, infrastructure, proximity to airports or highways, living conditions, and economic and political stability. This list is certainly not all-embracing.

Cost elements relate to the cost structure of a location. They determine the profitability that a project can achieve in a given area and include: land cost, construction costs, wages, transport costs, utility costs and financing costs. Two elements in particular - incentives and taxation - call for special attention.

The relevance of these elements will vary from company to company. Location decision makers should carefully analyse what their project requires in terms of operational environment, and what its elasticity is with respect to alternative cost structures. A clear project definition is imperative. Neglecting this analysis has been the cause of many unsuccessful locations and consolidations.

It is in a company's clear interest to seek maximum incentives and optimal tax rates in locations where it can physically operate. Experience shows that schemes and regulations dealing with these fields are far from transparent.

Incentives and location

Incentives, for instance, can mean a reduction of fixed asset investment, or reduced operating costs in the early years after start-up. A company may obtain incentives from regional or national authorities and, in some cases, successfully apply for an EC-sponsored scheme. In many countries there is a legal limit to the amount that may be granted under a special scheme. When no standard amounts are specified, companies must negotiate to obtain the highest amount possible for their project.

Adequate project definition will allow a business to focus on those schemes which are really relevant to it. For example, when locating a chemical processing plant, cash grants related to investment in equipment will have a far greater impact on the project's profitability than a reduction of its land price. Labour intensive projects, such as packaging or electronic assembly, should select locations where the company can obtain training grants, or exemption from employer's social security payments.

The importance of tax considerations, like incentives, varies from project to project. As a rule, however, a low corporate tax rate should be preferred to a high rate mitigated by offsetting factors, because experience shows that low rates tend to be more permanent than deductions and tax incentives. In practice, tax authorities in the EC have lumbered location decision makers with a wide variety of tax rates and related incentive schemes. These rates will not be harmonised in 1992 and there is little likelihood that either corporate or individual rates will be harmonised in the forseeable future.

However, non-tax factors may require that a project be located in a high-tax country or region. Even then, there are ways to keep profit under control. For production operations 'contract manufacturing' may allow it to maintain profit as a percentage of costs. A distribution centre, in turn, should seek to obtain 'cost centre' status in high-tax areas, generating no profit for itself. As a third example, a central sales office offering management, logistical and financial support to local sales forces should not be located in a high-tax environment.

In all cases, the local tax aspects of a location should be evaluated in the broader context of the company's overall tax planning.

Negotiations with local and national authorities start once the analysis of intangible and cost elements has identified a short list of four to five locations. The objective of this step is to obtain firm official commitment concerning, for example, required permits, incentives, and tax deductions.

After the analysis: negotiations

Experience shows that important financial benefits can be obtained since there is fierce competition between regions and countries where the attraction of inward investment is concerned. Such was the recent case of a US$50 million European distribution centre. The initial analysis identified a possible reduction of fixed asset investment of 14% in location A, and 17% in location B. After negotiations with authorities eager to attract this prestigious project, and optimisation of possible tax structures, the net present value of possible savings amounted to 68% and 22% of fixed asset investment for locations A and B respectively.

However, the temptation of possible benefits should not detract from the extreme caution companies must exercise during such negotiations. For one thing, over-zealous officials may exceed their brief when awarding grants and tax reductions. Even the highest national authorities may be forced to back down on their commitments. On several occasions, EC Commission officials have forced national authorities to demand repayment of cash grants and other incentives. For example, Beaulieu, the Belgian textile multinational, has been ordered to repay the amount it obtained, on the grounds of non-compliance with EC regulations.

Once the location has been selected and the initiatives and possible tax exemptions assured, steps must be taken to start up the new facilities and, in the case of consolidation, to reorganise the company's structures and operations.

Consider, for instance, a consolidation of several national headquarters into a new European headquarters. Prime concerns relate to the project itself, for example in obtaining the necessary building and operating permits, setting up the legal and tax structure, and starting application procedures. Yet companies must also give attention to personnel in terms of new housing, removals, finance, insurance, and schooling. The company must ensure that the transfer of personnel is accomplished as efficiently as possible without causing unnecessary disturbances.

Starting up and closing down

Closing down facilities in the course of a consolidation exercise is another delicate task. Improper handling not only increases the cost of the closures but also increases the start-up cost of the new operation. A hasty withdrawal also damages a company's image in the country where a facility is closed. It can lead to strained relations with the authorities, and possible loss of market share. In this context, a major French company entered into lengthy and costly legal battles over indemnity payments with government authorities and unions after it decided overnight to close down its plant, making over 1,000 workers redundant. These complications could have been avoided by more careful planning of its withdrawal.

Whether for headquarters, distribution centres, central sales units, plants, R&D centres, or any other type of facility, the location decision has far-reaching strategic implications. The selected site or building not only determines the degree to which a company can physically and technically operate, it also determines the potential profitability of the venture.

Sound decision-making is therefore required when locating new operations or relocating existing ones in the course of a consolidation. This calls for careful analysis and expertise in a variety of areas, ranging from social geography and industrial engineering, to international tax planning and logistics. The complexities of a location decision, involving the difficult evaluation of both cost and intangible factors, including the often non-transparent issues related to incentives and tax, are frequently underestimated.

Too often, locations are selected on the basis of a brief scan, resulting in only partial success or outright failure. Clearly such situations must be avoided. Location decisions have to be right first time.

WP Vossen is Managing Director of Plant Location International (PLI) and Price Waterhouse partner for location studies.

ES van Herwaarden is a PLI Senior Consultant.

PLI specialises in location studies for plants, distribution centres, R&D, headquarters and other facilities. Brussels-based, it has operated worldwide since 1960. PLI is a member firm of Price Waterhouse.

THE ROLE OF THE MAJOR FIRMS: Local needs with global strategy

by Nigel Moore

For accountancy firms as well as companies, the ride into the new Europe can be a bumpy one. Based on Ernst & Young's experience, though, a widespread network offering quality and size, driven by clients' needs rather than internal forces, offers multinational companies invaluable advice and guidance.

Threat and opportunity

As the Single European Market draws steadily nearer, the concept of Europe is central to the consciousness of the accountancy profession, no longer a distant dream but something real and immediate. Very few business decisions can now be reached without an awareness of Europe. In the deliberations which created Ernst & Young, the probable consequences of 1992 swiftly emerged into an issue of paramount importance.

The birth of Ernst & Young is, of course, ancient history. We live in a world of large-scale mergers among professional firms, in which the motivating principle is often sheer self-aggrandisement. But the decision to create one of the world's largest accountancy firms was not taken simply for considerations of size. Rather it was client-focused, taken because the firm was convinced that its clients would be better served in this rapidly changing business environment by the enhanced level of services and the greater geographical coverage which such a merger would provide.

Nowhere is this principle more apparent than in the crucible of Europe, where two significant existing presences were brought together to form an unparalleled professional network. At present Ernst & Young has offices in 29 European countries and a complement of nearly 24,000 staff. Co-ordinating and deploying this mass of people and resources naturally requires disciplined organisation. So while executive control over the workings of Ernst & Young Europe remains in the hands of national senior partners, strategy and planning is administered by the Chairman's office, run from Brussels by three experienced partners.

This arrangement has several advantages: it allows the firm to make key decisions very quickly; it allows it to respond to client needs immediately; and it allows it to do so from an administrative base located at the very heart of European decision-making.

Constructing a network

There are, of course, various ways of constructing a European network. You can install your own employees in the target market and hope that they are sufficiently attuned to its challenges, or you can find a local practice to form an association with (bearing in mind that many of your competitors will probably be on the same track). Alternatively, you can buy outright. Ernst & Young's approach combines each of these strategies, a pragmatism based on the vital principle that Europe, as a commercial environment, is far from homogeneous.

Though Europe might be fast becoming a single entity, at present many of its constituent parts are markedly dissimilar and the European player needs to cultivate a flexible approach. This, after all, is the *new* Europe: inchoate, its outlines barely discernible. To march into it with a rigid set of prejudices and an unshakeable conviction that there is only one way of doing things is to store up trouble – for your clients as much as yourself.

Despite these pitfalls, the scope for the international accountancy firm in meeting client needs in Europe is very great. Opportunities for pan-European work vary from discipline to discipline, but the general outlook is bright.

Comprehensive advice

Inevitably at this point the 'small-is-beautiful' argument tends to raise its head. Surely, the occasional critic asserts, with such a large and diverse organisation the needs of the client will only be swamped beneath a tide of bureaucracy. The answer is that being a niche player is all very well, but the complexities, the very scale, of the new Europe demand something more. The large multinational companies who operate in it, organisations whose financial arrangements extend across national boundaries and jurisdictions, need comprehensive professional advice – capable, for example, of examining reporting requirements in the UK, Dutch tax law and government grants in the Algarve; not in isolation but as part of a wider, corporate strategy.

This need is markedly apparent in the rapidly emerging markets of Eastern Europe. Here, faced with what is virtually virgin territory, currency difficulties and a host of cultural and linguistic challenges, large international companies require maximally effective professional advice. Assistance to multinational clients operating in this unfamiliar environment takes several forms, embracing privatisation and restructuring work as well as traditional accountancy disciplines. As the process of galvanising moribund Eastern European industries and bringing them to the point where they can compete with the West gathers pace, rapid expansion in the area can only continue.

Question of strategy

At the heart of this entry into the new Europe, whether of the Eastern bloc or the Single Market, lies the question of strategy. Here there is a symbiosis between the accountancy firm's interests and those of its clients: the decisions which accountancy firms have had to face in conjunction with the new Europe are no different to those faced by any large organisation. What emerges from them are two over-riding needs – for our response to Europe to be planned and thought through, and for us to take decisions ourselves, in our own time, instead of being forced to comply with other people's decisions as a consequence of our own negligence and timidity.

For whatever the ultimate result of the Single Market, one thing is certain: many of the players limbering up for the race to future prosperity will not survive. In the next ten years we are likely to see a weeding out of the unfit and the inefficient quite unprecedented in European business history.

Our experience in Europe has demonstrated to us that those firms who were first in developing an effective and sustainable European network will become the leaders in the new marketplace which will come rapidly into existence after 1992. Its touchstone is the need to demonstrate the strength of your firm's resources.

Niche players may flatter themselves on their ability to perform specific tasks, yet it is our experience that new work is frequently obtained by professional service firms simply because they are perceived to have the necessary resources. Naturally, size will never replace quality of service, but size added to quality of service is a powerful inducement to potential clients with, for example, operations in six European countries, some of them a thousand miles apart, and whose staff speak half-a-dozen different languages.

Meeting clients' needs

This emphasis is crucial. The successful professional services firms of the next decade will be client-focused. One of the greatest problems of the new European environment, full of competing networks, is to maintain quality control – ensuring, for example, that referred work is properly carried out and that the firm's attitudes to client services are developing in a way that will suit the clients' needs. Networks inevitably create bureaucracies with their own internal pressures and motivating forces. The temptation to devise business systems based on policies which will suit the firm's internal arrangements rather than those which respond to the needs of customers is very strong. It has to be resisted.

But however well prepared the professional services firm imagines itself to be for 1992 and the opening up of Eastern Europe, the future remains uncertain. Amid an atmosphere of constant change, in which threat and opportunity have continually to be disentangled, the most forward looking accountant has no way of predicting the European situation a decade hence.

Organise and plan

All we can do is to organise and plan ahead, ensuring that it is we, through our foresight and initiative, who take the decisions about our future. The journey towards the new Europe has been described by one commentator as: 'An expedition undertaken in not very reliable transport, over increasingly unpromising terrain, with considerable disagreement over the actual route, but with the hope of lasting reward'. It is up to us to take that hope and, through planning, determination and our own expertise, convert it into certainty.

Nigel Moore is Regional Managing Partner of Ernst & Young Eastern Europe.

EUROPEAN ANNUAL REPORTS: Promoting your image

by Peter Clifton

Annual reports define the company's personality for a wide and important readership. We review what's good – and not so good – in the presentation of recent European reports.

The worth of good design

Common European accountancy standards are emerging for annual reports, but there are wide variations in how the major European companies exploit the publication of the report as a promotional tool. Most successful European companies recognise that the report has high visibility, influencing shareholders, financiers, potential investors, the employees, and even the critics of the company. Accountants and financial directors should be encouraged to recognise the worth of investing in good design and professional copywriting, because the look and feel of a report can convey as much about a company as the figures.

Peter Prowse Associates analyse the top 50 European companies' reports annually for content, presentation and appearance. In 1990, there were over 25 British companies rated as in the top 50 European companies by the *Sunday Times,* as well as 6 French companies, 3 each from Sweden and Germany, 2 from the Netherlands, and 1 each from Denmark, Belgium and Ireland. All but three of the reports were in English, and there was only one case of a poor translation *(Trelleborg).* These companies were mostly first-class in self presentation, generally as international companies, and all but one of them *(GUS),* we judge, used professional services for a large part of the task of designing and compiling their reports. Some of the trends we observed in making our analysis are described in this article.

Magazine-style reports

The general standard of the reports is like that of the best consumer magazines: matching the best business magazines in the standard of the writing, in layout, in photographs and in editing. The best of the bunch of fifty Europe-wide reports that we read came from *Thorn EMI,* and we described it as 'a good read'. *Tesco* provided a good example of the use of magazine-style headlines, and *British Telecom* went further than any other company in adopting the magazine style. We feel that the trend will be towards this type of presentation.

The report that is a 'good read' will influence the reader with the message that you want to convey more than the dull document that is scanned by the uninterested reader. The output of *Hoffman-La Roche* and *Glaxo* are two examples of very earnest reports that are over-written and tedious, and *SmithKline Beecham* is in such contrast, with a lively and interesting report, that it is difficult to believe that it is in the same industry.

Elements of design

The general style adopted by the top 50 companies is 'businesslike'. That means that business graphics – bar-charts in particular – are sometimes used on the cover to convey a picture of growth *(BET* and *BOC),* as well as inside, where they were particularly well-employed by *L'Air Liquide* and *LVMH.* We found that an absence of bar-charts in a report can actually mean there was a bad year.

Most of the best reports have excellent covers, conveying the company identity unmistakably (*ICI* is outstanding). Some experiments with broad-brush graphics in colour, however, don't seem to come off. *MD Foods,* the Danish company, went for an impressionistic, cheerful style based on marigold yellow and greens, which looks inappropriate. The intrusive *Kingfisher* logotype makes for an unsuccessful experiment in our view. But it is *Sears* who went furthest along the route of mixing text, water-colour graphics and photographs, and their report is summed up as 'second-rate'. Too much stylistic variety can be messy.

Whether intended or not, every company report conveys an image of the company concerned. Does it really want to appear to be boring, impersonal or scarcely distinguishable from any other company?

The main way to convey a corporate character is by the use of photographs. The company can choose to show parts of its business that are people-driven and stress the role of the employees in businesses in which we tend to forget the worker (eg *BT, Opel*); it can stress its work for health, although much of what it does might seem to threaten the environment (*Solvay, ICI*); it can virtually ignore controversial points of its product-offer to stress other business (*BAT, BTR*); it can produce an impression of sturdy coherence across a conglomerate by careful selection of subjects (*Hanson* with pictures of heavy machinery).

Showing a caring face

Boots is an excellent example of the use of photographs to show a caring face, by giving pictures of a variety of customers. Two Scandinavian companies, *MD* and *Trelleborg*, achieve a feeling of cheerfulness by showing smiling faces. Photos are the primary way of getting character across to the reader.

The best company reports have one striking common characteristic: they look as if the authors of the report want to impress you that they are indeed the best, with more details rather than less, better photographs, 'perfect' binding, glossier covers, and with a truly world-wide coverage.

A very detailed discussion of problems, allied to statements on a company's strategy, is not always appropriate: but some argument about the company's direction marks the best report. This is not a statement of mission: it is more like the exposition and illustration of a plan. Thus for *Guinness*, the problems associated with alcoholism are acknowledged: a policy of encouraging consumers not to buy more, but to buy better products is explained at the end of the Chairman's report. The report also illustrates the company's policies of being well-represented around the world, and its concentration on core businesses, as it proceeds.

SmithKline Beecham shows the same logic, this time setting out its strategy in numbered headings, and then illustrating the objectives and the decisions taken to achieve them. *Allied-Lyons* sets out several headings for its mission, and shows how these are being achieved.

Tackling major issues

Most of these companies are international, and they take pains to show that they are. Companies that come over as having a very British horizon – even if they have interests abroad – include *Marks & Spencer, Tesco, British Allied-Lyons* and *Boots*.

It is particularly the other countries of the EC that have outward-directed company statements. The events of 1989 in Eastern Europe were referred to by *Solvay* and *Peugeot* in particular, *Solvay* pledging itself to be active in markets lost since the advent of Communism and *Peugeot* announcing investment plans. The Swedish companies looked forward to getting Sweden into the European Community. Two of the most interesting discussions of the new Europe are to be found in *Daimler-Benz* and *Lafarge Coppée.* The fact that 35 companies addressed the issues connected with the environment shows its increasing importance in company policies and politics.

ICI, in its American-styled report, shows greenness even in its cover, which has a satellite picture of Europe. Even the retail chain *Marks & Spencer* makes a statement about 'green issues'. Put next to the way that these companies handle the issues, the silence of companies like *RTZ, BOC* and *Trelleborg* on the environment seems unnecessary.

Address your audience

There isn't enough space in an article like this to cover all the requisites of the good European company report, but it will be appreciated that the best reports do not neglect any part of the audience they think important. *Marks & Spencer* make a particularly impressive statement about their employee policies, and *British Telecom* is obviously concerned with the small investor. We found that there are companies which are self-obsessed, and companies that, sensibly, set out each year to teach readers new to their company all about their markets, products and plans.

When you consider the ability of a company like *Tesco* to appear in a completely different league to *GUS*, though they are both in the same broad line of business and both successful, you will realise the importance of the annual report as a promotional tool.

Peter Clifton is a Senior Consultant at Peter Prowse Associates. A graduate in economics from Oxford University, his professional experience includes nine years as Market Research Manager with ITT Europe in Brussels.

Peter Prowse Associates is a consultancy specialising in corporate communications and international marketing. In addition to advising companies on their annual reports and media relations, the consultancy helps a number of European regional agencies to attract international investment. *Information and copies of the Company Report* Report *are available from Peter Prowse Associates, The Coach House, 24 Bridge Street, Leatherhead, Surrey KT22 8BZ. Tel 0372 363386. Fax 0372 363359.*

MANAGEMENT CONSULTANCY: Boosting your European management team

by Paul Batchelor

Now in the 'big business' league, European consultancy firms have played a fundamental part in changing the business climate over the past decade. Why is consultancy so attractive to increasing numbers of companies?

Staggering growth rate

Fees paid to consulting firms in Europe in 1990 were estimated at over $8bn, a sixth of which were generated in the UK. By any standards, this figure illustrates that management consultancy is big business and has now developed into a well established profession.

The current size of the market is the result of a staggering growth rate in the last decade. It is generally accepted that the market will continue to show an increase of around 10% or more per year throughout the 1990s although competitive pressures will intensify. Many factors have helped to fuel this expansion but primarily it is because of three main trends:

- changes in the business, competitive and technological environment in most markets
- an increase in the tendency to buy in specialist services in order to foster lean and mean corporate structures
- increased market penetration in less mature markets

The accounting firms are major players in the consultancy marketplace although their degree of dominance varies greatly between markets. There is no doubt that the established network of European practices has enabled 'The Big Six' to steal a lead on many other management consultancy firms, despite the fact that many of them entered the market as a whole much later than some of the independent consulting firms. We estimate that more than 18,000 consultants are now employed by the major accounting firms, generating fees of about $2.5bn across Europe.

Most of the accountancy firms provide services across a broad range of management consulting skills. Experts are most usually sought for consulting on information technology (IT), accounting systems and financial management and many of the services have developed out of the traditional accounting practices. However, consultancy has now matured into other areas of expertise such as manufacturing, strategy, marketing, human resource management and business economics.

The development of specific types of skills has been followed by an increase in the offering of industry or sector specialisms which provide an effective basis for integrating functional skills. Many firms will now, for example, offer teams which concentrate on providing services to government or the banking and insurance sectors.

What is management consulting?

The Institute of Management Consultants, the professional body for the industry in the UK, describes it as 'the service provided to business, public and other undertakings by an independent and qualified person in identifying and investigating problems concerned with policy, organisation, procedures and methods, recommending appropriate action and helping to implement those recommendations'. If any consultant used that description to a potential client when selling his services, the chances of making a sale would be pretty slim.

Consulting is not a substitute for good management. At its best, it is about assisting management to achieve change so that the new situation is in some way better than it was before the consultant was engaged. Although consulting is a diverse discipline, it is useful to consider a typical assignment as progressing through five stages. The key aspects of each stage are:

- evaluate current position
- assess needs and readiness for change
- build commitment to change
- carry out change and maintain commitment
- stabilise change.

What can consultants offer?

Many companies find they benefit from buying the specialist advice that consultants provide. Few businesses nowadays can afford to retain a large in-house capability to meet all of their various needs. Many companies therefore supplement their leaner corporate structures by buying in expertise as and when it is required.

But consultants offer more than specialist knowledge. Consultants can bring to a problem their experience of having seen that situation in a variety of guises before. This is particularly true for consultants with specialist sector knowledge.

Consultants should also bring a high degree of objectivity to a particular situation. They have no axe to grind and are not personally affected when they provide their advice. This is particularly important where issues are strategic or affect individuals personally. Good consultants are skilled at working with management both in handling issues sensitively and in providing an objective view of what is best for the client.

In other situations, company management find that they do not have the resources or expertise available in-house; management time is so scarce that it is often highly cost effective to use consultants to analyse a particular business opportunity. Increasingly, though, management chooses to work with its selected consultants as part of a joint team in order to maximise the transfer of techniques and to achieve early commitment to any changes which need to be made.

Management consultants have been a fundamental part of business development and change, particularly during the last decade. They have also been key contributors to the public sector reforms which have taken place (particularly in the UK), over recent years and which are now evident in Eastern Europe.

All the world's a stage

Although the UK and Germany are currently the biggest European markets for consultancy work, many other European countries are demonstrating rapidly growing demand for these services. This has accelerated as businesses in Europe adapt their international structures to respond to new customer needs and adjust to the different levels of development and competitiveness between one country and another.

But the single biggest influence on the development of European management consultancy has been the impending creation of the world's largest single market. The breakdown of trade barriers and impact of potential global competition from Japan and the US; the growth in technology; and massive political changes have all brought forward the need for businesses to call upon the expertise of outside consultants.

Businesses have been compelled to look at increasing the amount of 'cross border' commercial activity they conduct and have turned to their professional services firms to advise on how to approach this. Advice on joint ventures, trade regulation and potential investments has now become a common part of many companies' briefs to their consultants.

Not just a single profession

Despite the changes and growth, management consultancy is still very different from one country to the next. Whilst it has been a recognised profession in the UK for over 30 years, in France it has been established for around 15 years and in many others for less. Historically, in the accounting firms this is due to differences in the restrictions placed on auditors. In the UK, auditors have been seen as business advisers for many years, whereas in other European countries audit services to clients have been governed by stricter legal requirements. These have traditionally inhibited the growth of additional services offering broader advice. However, this is now changing as businesses become more complex in their demands. Another important key to the development of the management consultancy business in Europe is people mobility. As changes affect organisations at different times in different countries, the movement of resources and deployment of experienced consultants to the place of need is essential. This is of course balanced with the development of local expertise. At Coopers & Lybrand, one of the largest firms of management consultants in Europe, a European staff exchange programme encourages the exporting of skills and cultures and a network of centres of excellence facilitates the cross-border deployment of specialist skills.

Management consultancy feeds on change. As long as companies and governments experience change, there will be a need for consultancy. The 1980s saw some of the biggest changes in recent economic and political history; the 1990s will see the evolution of many more. As the globe 'shrinks', the stage for the management consultant expands and the demands for help from the big consultancy firms are sure to increase.

Paul Batchelor is Executive Partner in Charge of MCS Europe at Coopers & Lybrand Europe.

CROSS-BORDER ACCOUNTING: Transfer of skills

by John Williams

The new EC directive allowing accountants to set up in practice outside their native states signals the profession's direction for the 1990's. We look at the directive in practice, and the movement towards a wider GATS.

Mutual recognition

The EC mutual recognition directive together with the proposed General Agreement on Trade in Services (GATS) form the basis upon which the accountancy profession will go forward to face the challenges of the final decade of the century. Liberalisation of professional services offers dramatic new opportunities for accountants to expand into new markets although at the same time it will present them with increased competition at home. How will the structure of the European and worldwide profession be affected by these new developments?

The EC mutual recognition directive came into force in all twelve member-states on 4 January 1991, but to date only Germany, Denmark, Portugal, the Republic of Ireland and the United Kingdom have implemented the necessary national legislation for the accountancy profession.

In simple terms, mutual recognition means that an EC national who is a member of a profession in one member-state is entitled to practise that profession in another member-state without having to requalify. Moreover, migrant accountants have an automatic right of admission to the professional bodies in other member-states and to the use of their titles. Thus, a British *chartered accountant* is able to become a *Wirtschaftsprüfer* in Germany and a French *expert comptable* can become a *chartered accountant* here.

To safeguard the public, the directive stipulates that professionals moving from one member-state to another can be required to make good any deficiencies in their qualifications and the professional qualifications in the member-state in which they wish to practise. While differences in terms of length of education and training will not be significant within the accountancy profession, content may vary substantially.

The directive accordingly provides that, where differences in content are evident, migrants may choose whether to take an aptitude test to show that they have the necessary knowledge or to undergo an adaptation period of supervised practical experience in the host member-state. The directive further provides that, if the practice of a profession requires precise knowledge of national law and involves providing advice on national law as a constant and essential aspect of professional activity, then a member-state may specify which route the migrant shall follow. At the time of writing it seems likely that all the member-states will rule that the accountancy profession should be included within the definition of a 'legal' profession, and that migrants should take an aptitude test.

Aptitude tests

Where an aptitude test is imposed, the competent authorities in the member-states concerned are required to compare their education and training requirements and identify any deficiencies in subjects which are essential for practice in the host member-state. 'Practice' in this context may also include employment in commerce and industry, in education or in other spheres of work. Migrants will then be tested in the essential areas of difference; they may also be required to pass a test in the professional rules relating to the practice of the profession in the member-state concerned.

Over the past year The Institute of Chartered Accountants in England and Wales, The Institute of Chartered Accountants of Scotland and The Institute of Chartered Accountants in Ireland, have jointly conducted bilateral negotiations with accountancy bodies in most of the other EC member-states and have exchanged detailed information on examination syllabuses in order to facilitate the development of appropriate aptitude tests.

The three Institutes have notified their 2,000 members living or working elsewhere in the EC of their right of access to the local professions under the terms of the directive, and already considerable interest has been shown by members.

Inevitably, with an initiative of such major influence, there will be some teething troubles. These have appeared so far in the form of delays in many member-states in passing the legislation necessary for the implementation of the directive. Chartered accountants seeking to take advantage of the provisions of the directive in a number of member-states have had their applications refused on the grounds that the local legislation is not yet in place.

Teething troubles

The view of the EC Commission is that, as Community law takes precedence over national law, the directive must be deemed to have been implemented in all member-states since 4 January 1991, whether or not appropriate national legislation has been implemented. The principle of the supremacy of EC law has been confirmed by a recent decision of the European Court in the case of *Irene Vlassopoulou v. Ministerium für Justiz, bundes- und Europäer-gelegenheiten, Baden-Württemberg*.

Migrant accountants who are frustrated in their attempts to gain access to the local accountancy profession in another member-state are advised by the EC Commission to keep them informed (Directorate General III), to advise their appropriate government department (the Department of Trade and Industry in the United Kingdom) and to consider taking the matter to the administrative court in the member-state where they have been refused.

The EC Commission sees the mutual recognition directive as a vital element in the competition of the 1992 Single Market and, therefore, began infringement proceedings in September last year against any member-states which had failed to implement the directive or had not done so correctly.

Finally, it is important to note that the directive provides only for the mutual recognition of qualifications when professional people actually move to other EC member-states in order to live and work there. It does not cover the situation of the cross-border provision of services (on a visiting basis), nor does it extend to the mutual recognition of firms. Liberalisation in both of these areas is essential before there will be a completely open market for professional services.

The accountancy profession in the United Kingdom and in other EC member-states, as well as the *Fédération des Experts Comptables Européens* (the European regional accountancy organisation), is continuing to press the EC Commission for further liberalisation in these areas.

GATT, the General Agreement on Tariffs and Trade, was set up at the end of the Second World War – jointly with the International Monetary Fund and the World Bank – to guide the world towards post-war reconstruction. It laid the basis for the liberalisation and expansion of world trade in goods which made possible the significant economic growth which has been a feature of the second half of this century: it contributed to this by providing mechanisms to avoid the pitfalls of protectionism.

GATS – a broader front

The 'Uruguay round' of negotiations was launched in 1986 and included, for the first time, a call for the liberalisation of trade in services, including accountancy. The aim of the Uruguay round is to establish a multilateral framework of principles and rules with a view to encouraging an expansion of trade in financial and other services, so promoting the economic growth of all the trading partners which are signatories to the agreement.

The benefits which would flow from the international liberalisation of professional practice rights have produced a determination by many national officials responsible for negotiating the General Agreement on Trade in Services (GATS) under the Uruguay round not to allow their efforts to be frustrated by the antics of the 'farming lobby' which has threatened, and still threatens, to block progress towards an agreement on services.

There was at one time a real danger that, unless agreement was reached by the end of 1990, the Uruguay round negotiations would come to an end and there would be nothing to show for the four years of hard bargaining.

The three Institutes of Chartered Accountants in the United Kingdom and Ireland have consistently advocated the right of professional people to offer their services anywhere in the world, free of artificial barriers of a protectionist nature.

At the same time, they have continued to maintain that, while liberalisation is a desirable end, the protection of the public interest is paramount and should not be jeopardised by anything in the GATS. Liberalisation is not the same thing as deregulation, and the maintenance of national regulations which protect the public interest is both legitimate and desirable. This approach has been supported by the United Kingdom government and by the European

Commission, and has been their official line in the GATS negotiations.

Freedom of choice

If growth in world trade is to be sustained, it is essential that the GATT system should be extended. The decision of the United States Congress in May this year to continue negotiations is therefore to be welcomed. The onus is now firmly on the official negotiators to make real progress towards an agreement. Modern technology in travel and communications has made the world small. The globalisation of business has made it even smaller.

It is in the interests of the accountancy profession, the clients in commerce and industry whom it serves, and the general public, that artificial barriers preventing freedom of choice in the appointment of professional advisers should be eliminated. The accountancy profession in the United Kingdom and Ireland therefore welcomes the moves in this direction which are promised by the mutual recognition directive and the Uruguay round negotiations.

John Williams is Director of International Affairs at The Institute of Chartered Accountants in England and Wales (ICAEW). He is responsible to the recently-established Joint International Committee of the ICAEW, ICAS and ICAI for the international interests of the three Institutes of Chartered Accountants in the United Kingdom and Ireland. He is also staff adviser to the United Kingdom representatives on the Councils of the International Federation of Accountants (IFAC) and of the Fédération des Experts Comptables Européens (FEE).

THE SMALLER FIRMS' NETWORK: Pooled expertise with personal service

by Simon Noakes

Membership of a European or international network allows the smaller firm to offer its clients a broader range of services than before without losing the firm's personal style and independence.

Business links with Europe

During the 1970's and 1980's, the large international firms expanded over the globe to such an extent that it seemed that the few giants would take over most of the accountancy world.

Initially, the smaller firms did not worry too much, concentrating on providing services to their traditional client base of small business and family firms. About ten years ago, however, a new threat began to be realised – the Single European Market. Not many small firms at that time were equipped to deal with the new business links with Europe.

The approach of 1992, combined with the increasing number of clients developing interests in Europe (whether acquiring businesses or buying a holiday home), spurred on a number of smaller practices to set about establishing more formal links in European countries.

For Beavis Walker, a single office practice based in London, the catalyst was a conference in Copenhagen, which the firm was attending as an observer, of lawyers who had already formed European networks. At the conference, discussions started with Lau Lauritsen of Copenhagen accountancy practice S. A. Christensen & W. Kjaerulff I/S. Both firms realised that action was necessary if they were to thrive in the new Europe.

As Lau Lauritsen points out: 'We could see great potential for ourselves and our clients if our existing European contacts could be expanded. We were also spurred on by the fear that, in the absence of suitable contact firms, we would have to refer clients to the offices of the major firms'.

Keeping independent status

At the same time as recognising the need for some form of co-operation, the two were determined to retain their independent status. For this reason the idea of linking in with one of the major firms was quickly dismissed. It was not an acceptable idea, not least because clients were used to the personal style of a smaller firm, more familiar with servicing the needs of the smaller client.

The answer was to set up a network of like-minded firms, starting with existing contacts. Without such a network, they would be unable to satisfy the growing demand from clients wishing to take advantage of the opportunities offered by the single market in Europe.

INPACT, the International Network of Professional Accountants, started life with sixteen member firms and now has fifty-five in twenty-two countries.

The member firms of INPACT have no formal legal relationship. A constitution was drawn up to outline basic rules and safeguard the interests of members, but the informal structure is well suited to the type of association. There is a board of directors that meets quarterly to discuss and progress ideas. The chairmanship rotates annually and the chairman is host to the conference. Copenhagen was the location for the 1991 conference and, perhaps symbolically, Brussels is the venue for 1992.

Developing national networks

When INPACT was founded, there was one member firm in each country. Since then, INPACT members in some countries have been developing their own networks of associate firms. A particularly strong network exists in the UK with fifteen firms, and Italy has eleven associate firms. The French are also developing a network and the Spanish have plans to do so within the next year.

The principal benefit of a network of small firms throughout Europe has been to broaden the geographical base covered by each member. The members are in a position to refer clients to firms they know personally and in which they have confidence. Furthermore, as the member firms are all of a similar size, they understand the types of business dealt with. With the assistance of network members, technical queries on overseas tax and other such matters can be answered without expensive and time consuming research.

Experience so far has already shown that the support of a European network has meant that member firms are able to retain clients with overseas connections that might otherwise have been lost to the major international practices. 'If being a member of INPACT has meant that one client has stayed with me to benefit from INPACT contacts, then it is well worth the membership fee', says Jos Cappelle from Bureau Fiduciaire Lerminiaux et Cie SA, Brussels.

International co-operation

Referrals of business between firms is of obvious financial benefit, but there are also other plus points such as the sharing of marketing costs. Another important benefit is the pooling of expertise and the educational value of visiting practices abroad. 'Clients are amazed that I can be in telephone contact with a partner in twenty-two countries' says Laurent Ginet of SODIP, Paris.

One example of co-operation between INPACT firms is the accountancy service provided by a UK firm for a client of the Paris firm – a hotel chain with hotels in the UK and in France. A more unusual example is the case of a client in York in the North of England who wished to dispose of a diamond. The associate in York contacted our associate in Amsterdam who put the client in touch with a diamond broker who acquired the gem.

Membership of a network often leads to development in other areas. Two INPACT member firms, Cavells of Bristol and Farrell, Grant, Sparks in Dublin, have recently formed a joint partnership specialising in insolvency work. Partner Pearse Farrell says 'Being part of such a network has given us access to a wider client base and share of expertise'.

A wider range of services

During the past three years, members of INPACT have found that clients, quite rightly, expect a wider range of business services these days – wider than just accountancy, and with barriers coming down across Europe, wider geographically too.

The small firm network enables its members to provide a comprehensive service to such clients with international aspirations, whilst at the same time preserving the independence of the firms involved.

Simon Noakes is International Director of INPACT, and senior partner of Beavis Walker.

INPACT, the International Network of Professional Accountants, has 55 like-minded member firms in twenty-two countries.

by Martin Ben-Nathan

Introducing the EEIG (or 'Earwig') – an innovative business structure devised by the EC to solve the problems of cross-border trading partnerships. How well does it work?

A new business entity

A European Economic Interest Grouping (EEIG – or 'Earwig' as it is affectionately known in the UK) is a new form of pan-European business entity. It has some of the characteristics of both a partnership and a company, but differs significantly from either type of business structure in certain key areas. Its purpose is to facilitate the promotion of trade between member states by providing a transnational vehicle for cross-border economic co-operation.

The framework for EEIGs – explained in more detail below – was originally laid down in an EC Council Regulation of July 1985, which required member states to set up the necessary domestic machinery by July 1989.

The structure which has resulted provides a good illustration of many aspects of the wider European debate. The concepts and ideals are noble and grand, as indeed is the language. But when it comes down to looking at the details of how things will work, many questions remain unanswered.

Framework of an EEIG

Before looking at the opportunities, and the problems, presented by EEIGs, it may be helpful to summarise their main characteristics:

Constitution: An EEIG is constituted by a contract of formation between its members who must be either companies, firms or other legal bodies formed under the law of an EC member state with registered offices and central administration within the EC, or else individuals carrying on business within the Community.

Purpose: The purpose of an EEIG must be to facilitate or develop the economic activities *of its members*. This means that, although an EEIG can trade and may make incidental profits, its operations cannot exist in isolation – only in conjunction with and ancillary to the main economic activities of its members. It is not allowed to exercise management or supervisory powers over any of its members' activities nor is it allowed to hold shares in any of its members.

Restrictions: A number of other restrictions apply. An EEIG may not employ more than 500 persons; it may not be used to circumvent certain legal restrictions on loans to directors; it may not be a member of another EEIG; and it may not invite investment from the public.

Ownership & Management: There is a two-tier ownership/management structure. In return for financial contributions, members have voting and profit participation rights akin to those of shareholders in a company; but liability for an EEIG's debts is both unlimited and on a 'joint and several liability' basis (as in UK partnerships). The members appoint managers who, like the directors of a company, represent the EEIG and contract with third parties.

Registration: An EEIG is registered in the member state where its official address is located. Prescribed particulars must be published in the official gazette of that member state covering events such as a change in composition of the EEIG or in its contract of formation, the appointment or removal of a manager, or of liquidation or winding up.

Relocation: The official address, which determines the country of registration and thus inter alia which system of national law applies to an EEIG, may be transferred from one member state to another relatively freely, subject to certain formalities.

Taxation: The EEIG structure is intended to be tax transparent – that is, it is intended that each member should be taxed on its own share of profit or capital gains. However the position is not so simple – see below.

Economic co-operation

The raison d'etre for such a business entity is set out in its founding EC regulation as being to address 'legal, fiscal or psychological difficulties' which might impair effective cross-border economic co-operation between member states. It was therefore looked upon by its founding fathers as a business co-ordinator and catalyst; others may find defter uses, for example in the field of off-balance sheet finance.

THE FUTURE OF THE EEIG: Practical problems for new entity

To date EEIGs have in practice proved quite popular with lawyers who use them to overcome certain inhibitions on their ability to enter into international partnerships. In this way national partnerships or firms can work together under the umbrella of an EEIG in circumstances where a full partnership is not appropriate.

Another field where EEIGs may have scope to develop is as a medium for EC government agencies to combine their efforts in Eastern Europe or the Third World. Co-ordination and marketing will generally be the natural domain of the EEIG.

Practical difficulties

So far so good. But difficulties and questions start to creep in when the global principles of the EC Regulation are superimposed onto the legal and taxation systems of a particular member state.

For example, within the UK such a structure would be best recognised as a partnership; yet it is not governed by the Partnership Act 1890, but instead by parts of the Companies Act 1985 and the Insolvency Act 1986. Other parts of the Companies Act do not apply, however – for example there are no statutory accounting or audit requirements – and there is some legal debate as to exactly which parts of the Insolvency Act do apply and which do not.

Taxation also presents ambiguities and difficulties in practice. For taxation purposes Article 40 of the EC Regulation states that profits or losses resulting from the activities of an EEIG's members shall be taxable only in the hands of its members.

Such simplicity flatters to deceive. For example, overseas members of a non-UK registered EEIG carrying on a trade through its UK establishment will not themselves be liable to UK tax on profits or capital gains associated with the UK activity. However, in certain circumstances the UK member or members could be liable for UK tax on their behalf, as agents of their EC brothers.

And the concept of fiscal transparency may not necessarily apply to taxes on payments of interest or royalties. If withholding taxes apply, to which jurisdiction will the EEIG or its member account and under which law will any withholding tax be determined? If relief under double taxation treaties is sought, which treaty should a third party look to for protection – its national treaty with the country of registration of the EEIG, or its national treaties with the respective countries of its various members?

VAT and transfer duties are also areas of difficulty. The view of the UK Customs authorities appears to be that VAT could apply to 'in house' transactions between the EEIG and its members, while stamp duty may be applicable to transfers of assets. Moreover, a non-resident individual's interest in an EEIG incorporated in the UK will constitute property sited in the UK for Inheritance Tax purposes.

Valuable function

Of course there will be a number of circumstances in which EEIGs may in due course perform a valuable function in encouraging enterprises in different parts of the Community to work together and promote their mutual interests. But these few thoughts show just how difficult it can be to create a pan-European entity which fits comfortably into the complex legislative frameworks of many different states.

Martin Ben-Nathan is a senior tax partner at Casson Beckman, a leading firm of chartered accountants and business advisers based in London at Hobson House, 155 Gower St, London WC1E 6BJ (Telephone + 44 (71) 387 2888).

by Aaron A Rubenstein

Although a single EC-wide tax structure is still many years away, national taxes are already converging, and a layer of EC regulations is coming into force. It is not too soon to start planning for the changes ahead.

Freeing the tax barriers

As Europe gets closer to completing its internal market and embarks on the difficult task of creating a single currency, the likelihood that it will one day have a single, uniform tax system stretching from the south of Portugal to the northern tip of Denmark seems as remote as ever. Despite the distance of this reality, the 12-nation grouping of the EC is actually proceeding quite rapidly to a convergence or *'approximation'*, of its different tax systems, scheduled to take place in the mid-1990s.

These efforts fall short of complete harmonisation but they are aimed at producing a European-wide tax system that does not inhibit businesses from treating Europe as one big internal market. By removing existing tax barriers to the free movement of capital and finance around Europe, the EC is seeking to encourage cross-border mergers and investments, and ultimately, a single European economy.

For businesses based in Europe and beyond, these developments on the EC tax front have two major implications, according to Lieven Denys, an international tax partner in KPMG Brussels and the chairman of KPMG's 1992 Tax Network. 'First of all, although there will continue to be differences in tax rules from country to country, there will be an important layer of EC-wide tax regulations,' he says. 'And secondly, though this may all sound complicated, it also creates opportunities for re-examining a company's entire tax position in Europe and finding ways of taking advantage of the new situation to lower tax liability.'

A flurry of initiatives

Since 1990 in particular, the EC has unleashed a flurry of new initiatives in the tax field. These initiatives, especially two newly-published tax directives, will eventually be converted into national law by the 12 separate EC member states. Even so, there could still be nuances in interpretation and implementation from country to country, requiring companies to make a careful examination of these differences in doing their future tax planning.

Caution is an important watchword in the run-up to greater tax convergence. Not only are parts of the directives open to different interpretations, the directives are also silent on a number of critical issues. Not surprisingly, tax has always been a crucial element in hopes for – and progress towards – European integration: the challenge of creating common rules has confronted the EC partners since they signed the Treaty of Rome in 1958. For years, the expressed goal on tax was a full harmonisation of tax rates and tax rules.

But since 1990 it has become clear that diversity will remain for some time to come, largely because it has proved difficult, if not impossible, to get EC-wide agreement on direct taxes. Rather than pushing for harmonisation, the EC Commission has decided to let itself be guided by the concept of *subsidiarity*. In effect, this means that the Commission will not get involved in every aspect of Europe's economy but that it will do its best to reach well-defined goals that have been set by the member states. In practical terms, this implies that income tax rates will certainly continue to differ from country to country, as will systems imposing corporate tax rates, which are of critical concern to any business with operations in Europe.

Lord Cockfield, the former EC Commissioner and a current consultant for KPMG on European Community affairs, predicts that the EC will have a single corporate tax someday, but he stresses that this is very much a long-term prospect. 'A European corporate tax system will only come when you've not only completed the single market but also the single currency, and there will then be time to tackle it.'

Single tax system 'a dream'

Robert Kramer, an international tax partner at Meijberg, the Dutch KPMG tax firm also says that a single corporate tax should be regarded as a 'dream', at least for the time being and probably for the next 20 years as well.

Ironically, perhaps, corporate tax rates have started to converge anyway around the EC, with 35% the most common average figure. Kramer believes this development is not so much an EC initiative as a 'Reagan initiative', referring to the tax reforms and tax cuts introduced by the former US president in the mid-1980s. These US cuts spurred many European countries to follow suit.

Though harmonisation of direct taxes, such as corporate tax, is certainly a distant prospect at best, indirect taxes throughout the EC stand a much better chance of being brought into line with one another in the near future.

At the moment, value-added tax and other indirect taxes, such as excise duties on tobacco and alcohol, vary enormously from one country to the other. The problem of finding a common VAT rate has excited much political debate and tedious negotiations, but recently a compromise was reached, with agreement on a minimum standard EC-wide rate of 15%.

For businesses in Europe, the most important, practical consequence of VAT changes is not the level of VAT itself but the way in which the system is administered. During the transitional period up to the end of 1996, there will be a far-reaching shift in responsibility for administering VAT, with companies being made responsible for the proper functioning of the whole system for the first time.

Simplification of VAT on exports

At the moment, it's still the case that VAT export administration is done by customs officials who stamp papers and documents at the border. It's going to be up to companies to keep track of VAT. That carries the risk that part of the circuit will disappear. In 1997 however, the system is scheduled to become simpler and more transparent. The exporter will charge VAT to his foreign customer and pay it to the tax authorities at home. The customer in, say, Italy will be able to deduct his VAT payment from his Italian tax. A 'clearing house' will then settle these intra-EC VAT flows.

Unfortunately, from the point of view of business, there will be no such simplicity about corporate tax or other taxes such as capital gains. But provisions are being made to create an EC tax system which makes mergers and cross-border investments fiscally 'neutral', and the EC has made great strides forward in trying to fashion a tax system which does not penalise or reward a company for deciding to establish operations in one country rather than in another.

Much of the progress so far is contained in two path-breaking EC directives, one on the tax relationship between parent and subsidiary companies in Europe and the other on the tax implications of cross-border mergers and demergers. Two other draft directives have been prepared but are not yet approved. The first deals with the tax treatment of a company's losses in another EC country, while the other calls for the abolition of withholding taxes on inter-group interest and royalty payments. The EC has also drawn up an arbitration convention designed to prevent double taxation resulting from transfer pricing adjustments made by a company that is active in two or more member states. However, the status of the draft convention is different from that of a directive, making the directives of more immediate interest to business people.

Directive on group companies

The parent-subsidiary directive is revolutionary because it abolishes the right of member states to levy withholding taxes on profits distributed by a subsidiary company located in one EC country to a parent or holding company in another EC country. This is an important development on the road to harmonisation of taxes across Europe, though partial and temporary exemptions will be granted to – Germany, Greece and Portugal.

The directive seems simple enough at first glance, but KPMG tax experts such as Kramer caution: 'You only need to scratch the surface gently and problems start jumping out at you very rapidly'. Two immediate problems are, firstly, that the directive applies only to limited types of companies as enumerated in the directive and, secondly, that these companies must be subject to ordinary corporate tax in their home country of establishment.

With these conditions in mind, several complications quickly emerge. In Germany, for instance, it is common for businesses – even major multinational businesses – to be legally organised as partnerships, raising the question of whether or how they will be treated for tax purposes. One implication of this problem – and it is an implication which is true, too, of other EC tax initiatives – is that companies may want (or need) to change their legal forms and structures in order to take advantage of the new tax rules and thereby lower their overall European tax bill.

The stipulation in the directive that companies must pay domestic corporate tax could prove to be a problem for Dutch statutory investment companies such as Robeco, the large, Rotterdam-based investment fund group, which is not liable to Dutch corporate tax.

'Treaty shopping' lives on

Implementation of the new parent-subsidiary rules would mark a great step forward but, again, the new system will not do away with all national tax differences. In 1992 and beyond, companies active in Europe will still go 'treaty shopping' to give themselves the best possible location for tax purposes. Belgium is well known for its favourable tax treatment of European 'coordination centres', Ireland for its preferential tax treatment of manufacturing companies and the Netherlands for its treaty provisions on double taxation and participatory interests.

Despite the general trend towards greater tax convergence brought about by the parent-subsidiary directive, these treaties can still be harnessed in different ways for tax purposes.

One example is the case of a German parent company which has two subsidiaries in Europe, one in the Netherlands and the other in France. Knowing that it wants to sell the French subsidiary eventually, the German company decides to make the Dutch subsidiary a holding company which then, in turn, owns the French company and later sells it. Because Dutch tax laws are attractive for foreign companies to set up holding companies, the capital gains on the transaction, which would otherwise have been liable to tax in Germany, will be exempt from tax in the Netherlands.

The second innovation in EC tax rules, the merger directive, will also have major implications for a company's structure and its investments across Europe. The directive, due to go into effect by January 1992 in all Member States except Portugal, is designed to encourage merger activity across Europe by providing tax relief to European companies for transactions which meet conditions laid down in the document.

This will be done by deferring tax on capital gains arising from a reorganisation, giving companies the freedom to transfer tax-exempt provisions and reserves, as well as permitting the carrying forward of tax losses.

Mergers and de-mergers

Denys points out that, despite its name, the merger directive also applies in particular to 'de-mergers' – the splitting up of a company, perhaps as a prelude to a joint venture between part of the original company and another European company. One potential problem, he argues, is that the tax treatment of mergers and de-mergers will require that changes be made first to domestic legislation on company laws. This is in itself a highly complicated task because the EC is currently trying to harmonise company laws across Europe.

'But starting in 1992, the directive could certainly be applied to two other types of cross-border transactions – the transfer of branches of activities in exchange for shares and the exchange of shares as part of a stock merger or de-merger,' Denys says. 'As always, the directive does not cover all eventualities. It does not explicitly cover, for instance, the tax treatment of taxed reserves, tax incentives or tax deferrals. In general, there are still some open issues. In our advice to clients, we will need to incorporate possible EC-wide legislation in our domestic corporate advice.'

Planning is needed now

The need for careful tax-planning will increase rather than decrease with the approach of greater convergence in Europe's tax systems. If companies are to benefit fully from the changes ahead, they will have to re-examine their entire tax position throughout Europe and probe it for adjustments to take advantage of the country-by-country implementation of EC directives.

Though the directives have yet to be translated into national law, it is not too early to start preparing for the impending changes. One important reason for early planning is that the parent-subsidiary directive stipulates a two-year holding period before the tax benefits can be realised.

Clearly, the implications of tax changes in Europe are tremendous, and solutions will need to be found which are tailor-made to individual companies' circumstances.

Aaron A Rubenstein is Partner-in-Charge of the KPMG International Tax Centre, Amsterdam.

Affiliated Conference of Practising Accountants International (ACPA)

European Executive Office
Acre House, 11-15 William Road, LONDON NW1 3ER, United Kingdom
Tel: + *44* (71) 388 7000
Fax: + *44* (71) 380 4900

European partners:	214
Professional staff:	752
Non-professional staff:	515
Total staff:	**1,481**

MEMBER FIRMS

European firms:	31
Number of Countries:	14

PRINCIPAL NATIONAL OFFICES

Austria
AWIT ALLGEMEINE WIRTSCHAFTSTREUHAND GmbH
Capistrangasse 4/9, 1060 VIENNA
PRODINGER & PARTNER
Auerspergstrasse 8, 5700 ZELL/SEE
Total Offices: 2

Belgium
WALKIERS & COMPANY
Eglantierlaan 5, 2020 ANTWERP
Total Offices: 1

Denmark
OTTO HOUD STATSAUTORISEREDE REVISORER A/S
Hammerensgade 6, 1267 COPENHAGEN K
Total Offices: 1

France
COFINGEC
16 rue Mollien, 92100 BOULOGNE SUR SEINE, Paris
LECLERCQ ET ASSOCIÉS
92 rue Saint-Brice, B.P. 128, 28003 CHARTRES CEDEX
CLAUDINE VERGNOLLE-CHARANSONNET
12 place des Victoires, 75002 PARIS
Total Offices: 3

Germany
HAAG, HAAG & PARTNERS
Max Beckmann Strasse 53, 6000 FRANKFURT AM MAIN 70
W. HARTMANN - W. BEERMANN
Matthiasstrasse 6, 4440 RHEINE 1
PLATZ & VON OERTZEN GmbH
Grafenberger Allee 32, 4000 DUSSELDORF
DR. KARL RÜDIGER STEEB
Ismaninger Strasse 106, 8000 MUNICH 80
Total Offices: 6

Republic of Ireland
McGRATH & CO
Kildress House, Pembroke Row, Lower Baggot Street, DUBLIN 2
Total Offices: 1

Italy
STUDIO VECCHIETTI MASSACCI
Viale Carducci 19, 40125 BOLOGNA
Total Offices: 1

Luxembourg
FIDUCIAIRE LEX BENOY
13 rue Bertholet, B.P. 618, 2016 LUXEMBOURG
Total Offices: 1

The Netherlands
ESHUIS GROEP
Twentelaan 5, 7600 RE ALMELO
JOORE (REGISTERACCOUNTANTS)
Ringbaan Noord 179, 5046 AA TILBURG
Total Offices: 3

Norway
HUBERT & CO
Holbergsgt. 19, 0166 OSLO 1
Total Offices: 1

Spain
A.T.D. AUDITORES SA
Claudio Coello 20, 2ºD, 28001 MADRID
FAURA-CASAS SL AUDITORS-CONSULTORS
Casp 31, 2º 1ª, 08010 BARCELONA
Total Offices: 5

Sweden
PER STRANDINS REVISIONSBYRÅ
Svämpvagen 7, 191 51 SOLLENTUNA
GUNNAR THORENS REVISIONSBYRÅ AB
Sveavägen 155, 113 46 STOCKHOLM
Total Offices: 2

Switzerland
ANCA FIDUCIAIRE SA
Rue de Lausanne 43, 1211 GENEVA 2
MAAG, MÜLLI, SCHÖB & PARTNER AG
Bellerivestrasse 59, 8034 ZURICH
Total Offices: 2

United Kingdom
H.W. FISHER & COMPANY
11-15 William Road, LONDON NW1 3ER
Total Offices: 2

HISTORY & STRUCTURE

The Affiliated Conference of Practising Accountants International (ACPA) has grown and prospered since its founding in 1978. Today, our member firms have more than 80 offices in 25 countries throughout the world. In addition to growth in numbers our members have adapted and expanded the range of services they offer to meet the changing needs of the business community they serve. ACPA provide traditional accounting, auditing and tax services and the full spectrum of management advisory services ▷

required in today's challenging business environment. The guiding principle of ACPA is an unwavering dedication to the delivery of quality client services. All of our member firms subscribe to this principle.

Alliott Peirson International

International Office
96 High Street, GUILDFORD, Surrey GU1 3DL, United Kingdom
Tel: + *44* (483) 33119
Fax: + *44* (483) 37339

International Contact: David Almond

EUROPEAN PERSONNEL
Chairman: Barry R. Jamison
Secretary: David W. Almond
Management Committee: Wim Borrie
Management Committee: Arno Meyer
Management Committee: Alan Wilson
Management Committee: Per Winther
Management Committee: J. Vern Williams
Vice Chairman: Christian Mayer
Administrator: Brenda Dale

European partners:	147
Professional staff:	600
Non-professional staff:	245
Total staff:	**992**

EUROPEAN FEE INCOME

Year End: 31.12.90	**US$**
Total:	**105,000,000**

MEMBER FIRMS

European firms:	62
Number of Countries:	15

PRINCIPAL NATIONAL OFFICES

Austria
GAIER, MAYER & COMP GmbH
Brucknerstrasse 4, 1041 VIENNA
Total Offices: 1

Belgium
TAX CONSULT SA
Avenue Charles Woestelaan 257 B1, 1050 BRUSSELS
VAN CAKENBERGHE
Leopoldstraat 37, 2000 ANTWERP
Total Offices: 3

Denmark
LOPS & BRANDT A/S
Finsenvej 80, 2000 FREDERIKSBERG, Copenhagen
Total Offices: 2

France
B.E.S.C.
100 rue Martre, 92110 CLICHY, Paris
D.G.R. CONSEIL
100 rue Martre, 92110 CLICHY, Paris
NICE AUDIT GESTION CONSEIL
Transit Centre, 16 avenue Thiers, 06000 NICE
SOCIÉTÉ CIVILE DHINAUN FAYSSE, PETIT
2 rue de la Claire, 69009 LYON
Total Offices: 4

Germany
OBERBAYERISCHE TREUHAND UND REVISIONS GmbH
Landsberger Strasse 478, 8000 MUNICH 60
PROF. DR. ERWIN POUGIN GmbH
Hohenstaugenring 62, 5000 COLOGNE 1
Total Offices: 4

Republic of Ireland
DONNELLY & CO
Taney Hall, Eglinton Terrace, Dundrum, DUBLIN 14
Total Offices: 1

Italy
FIDERCONSULT/AUDIREVI
Via Birmania 81, 00144 ROME
SOFIRESA
Via dei Bossi 7, 20122 MILAN
Total Offices: 2

Liechtenstein
CONFIDA TRUSTEE & AUDITING COMPANY
Heilligkreuz 8, Postfach 40, 9490 VADUZ
Total Offices: 1

The Netherlands
BORRIE & CO
P.O. Box 8565, 3009 AN ROTTERDAM
Total Offices: 3

Norway
AUDINOR A/S
Postboks 1363, 1401 SKI
Total Offices: 2

Portugal
AUDITE - AUDITORIAS CONTABILISTICAS METÅDOS E ORGANIZACAO LDA
Rua Tomas Ribeiro 41, 4º Esq, 1000 LISBON
Total Offices: 1

Spain
ALBERT & ASOCIADOS, ABOGADOS
GESCONTROL AUDITORES SA
Espalter 13, 2º izqda, 28014 MADRID
FIDEM AUDITORS SA
Mallorca 260, atica, 08008 BARCELONA
Total Offices: 2

Sweden
FÖRENADE REVISORER I ALINGSÅS AB
Tomasgårdsvägen 19, 441 39 ALINGSÅS
FÖRENADE REVISORER I GÖTEBORG AB
Viktoriagatan 3, 411 25 GOTHENBURG
REVISIONSKOMPANIET REKO AB
Engelbrektsgatan 7, 203 13 MALMÖ
REVISUM REVISIONSBYRÅ HB
Rehnsgatan 5, 113 57 STOCKHOLM
Total Offices: 5

▷

Switzerland
EGLOFF FIDUCIARIA E REVISIONI SA
Via Motta 1, 6900 LUGANO
RFF REVISION FISCALITÉ FIDUCIAIRE SA
Chemin Rieu 12, 1211 GENEVA 17
TREUHANDVEREINIGUNG AG
Ziegelrain 29, 5001 AARAU
Total Offices: 6

United Kingdom
ALLIOTT PEIRSON ASSOCIATES
5th Floor, 9 Kingsway, LONDON WC2B 6XF
Total Offices: 23

HISTORY & STRUCTURE
Alliott Peirson International is an international group of independent accounting firms with members throughout the world. The group was formed in 1979 and in 1989 was ranked 19th in the world. All members offer the basic services of accounting, audit and taxation. Most members also specialise in other areas such as legal services, acquisitions, investment advice, computer and management consultancy and executive search.

Arthur Andersen Worldwide

European Executive Office
1 Surrey Street, LONDON WC2R 2PS,
United Kingdom
Tel: *+44* (71) 438 3000
Fax: *+44* (71) 831 1133

International Contact: Manuel Soto

EUROPEAN PERSONNEL
Marketing Director: Francis H. Quinlan

European partners:	568
Professional staff:	14,812
Non-professional staff:	4,165
Total staff:	**19,548**

EUROPEAN FEE INCOME

Year End: 1991	**US$**	**%**
Accountancy & Audit:	681,000,000	37.0
Consultancy:	907,500,000	49.0
Tax:	259,400,000	14.0
Total:	**1,847,900,000**	

MEMBER FIRMS

European firms:	88
Number of Countries:	19

PRINCIPAL NATIONAL OFFICES

Austria
AUDITOR TREUHAND GmbH
Börsegebäude, Wipplingerstrasse 34, 1010 VIENNA
Total Offices: 1

Belgium
ARTHUR ANDERSEN & CO
Avenue des Arts 56, 1040 BRUSSELS
Total Offices: 2

Channel Islands
ARTHUR ANDERSEN & CO
40 The Esplanade, ST HELIER, Jersey JE4 8NN
Total Offices: 1

Cyprus
CHRYSANTHOU & CHRISTOFOROU
3 Homer Avenue, Flat 310, NICOSIA
Total Offices: 1

Denmark
ARTHUR ANDERSEN & CO
Grønningen 17, 1012 COPENHAGEN K
Total Offices: 2

Finland
ARTHUR ANDERSEN & CO
Ruoholahdenkatu 8, 00180 HELSINKI
Total Offices: 1

France
ARTHUR ANDERSEN & CO
Tour GAN - CEDEX 13, 92082 PARIS LA DÉFENSE 2
Total Offices: 4

Germany
ARTHUR ANDERSEN & CO
Friedrich-Ebert-Anlage 2-14, Postfach 11 01 12, 6000 FRANKFURT AM MAIN 11
Total Offices: 13

Greece
ARTHUR ANDERSEN & CO
Syngrou Avenue 377, 175 64 ATHENS
Total Offices: 1

Republic of Ireland
ARTHUR ANDERSEN & CO
Andersen House, International Financial Servs Ctr, DUBLIN 1
Total Offices: 1

Italy
ARTHUR ANDERSEN & CO
Via Campania 47, 00187 ROME
Total Offices: 12

Luxembourg
ARTHUR ANDERSEN & CO
672 rue de Neudorf, 2220 LUXEMBOURG
Total Offices: 1

The Netherlands
ARTHUR ANDERSEN & CO
Zwaansvliet 20, 1081 AP AMSTERDAM
Total Offices: 4

Norway
ARTHUR ANDERSEN & CO
Drammensveien 134, 0212 OSLO 2
Total Offices: 4

Portugal
ARTHUR ANDERSEN & CO
Amoreiras Torre 1, 15, 1000 LISBON
Total Offices: 2

▷

Spain
ARTHUR ANDERSEN & CO
Raimundo Fernández Villaverde 65, Edificio Windsor, 28003 MADRID
Total Offices: 16

Sweden
ARTHUR ANDERSEN & CO
Sveavägen 155, Box 23501, 104 35 STOCKHOLM
Total Offices: 6

Switzerland
ARTHUR ANDERSEN & CO
Lavaterstrasse 93, Postfach 71, 8027 ZURICH
Total Offices: 5

United Kingdom
ARTHUR ANDERSEN & CO
1 Surrey Street, LONDON WC2R 2PS
Total Offices: 10

HISTORY & STRUCTURE

Arthur Andersen are committed to meeting and exceeding clients' expectations by delivering services with a strong industry focus, superb technical competence and a commitment to the professional values of integrity and objectivity. Arthur Andersen offers its clients audit and business advisory services, tax services and corporate speciality services. Arthur Andersen serves the market through a fully integrated organization comprising separate practice entities organized under the laws of the country in which they are based - a unique structure that assures every client of consistent high quality and timely service.

ATD International

European Executive Office
Hogarth House, 31 Sheet Street, WINDSOR, Berkshire SL4 1BY, United Kingdom
Tel: +44 (753) 831525
Fax: +44 (753) 831352

International Contact: Martin Goddard

EUROPEAN FEE INCOME

Year End: 31.12.90	%
Accountancy & Audit:	30.0
Insolvency:	10.0
Consultancy:	40.0
Tax:	20.0

MEMBER FIRMS

European firms:	19
Number of Countries:	14

PRINCIPAL NATIONAL OFFICES

Austria
WIRTSCHAFTSPRÜFER DR. PETER WOLF
Lehargasse 3a, 1060 VIENNA
Total Offices: 1

Belgium
A.L. BELLEKENS
Avenue de Broquevillelaan 270/10, 1200 BRUSSELS
Total Offices: 1

Channel Islands
NORMAN ALLPORT & CO
P.O. Box 781, ST HELIER, Jersey JE4 8ZZ
Total Offices: 1

Denmark
REVISIONSFIRMÆT J. ANDERSEN
Strandpromendaden 27, 2100 COPENHAGEN Ø
Total Offices: 1

France
DSA
22 place du Général-Catroux, 75017 PARIS
Total Offices: 2

Germany
WIDMANN UND PARTNER
Kriegstrasse 81, 7500 KARLSRUHE
Total Offices: 1

Republic of Ireland
GORMAN & ASSOCIATES
66 Lower Baggott Street, DUBLIN 2
Total Offices: 1

Italy
METODO
Foro Buonaparte 69, 20121 MILAN
Total Offices: 1

The Netherlands
MASMAN BOSMAN & CO
Laan Copes van Cattenburch 92, 2585 GE 's GRAVENHAGE, The Hague
Total Offices: 2

Norway
REVISJONSFIRMÆT VEEL, KARLSEN & CO
Fr. Nansens Plass 9, 0160 OSLO
Total Offices: 1

Spain
BUFETE DIAZ ARIAS
Plaza de las Cortes 4-10, 28014 MADRID
Total Offices: 2

Sweden
DAHLSTRÖM & HOLMBERG REVISIONSBYRÅ AB
Birger Jarlsgatan 26, 1tr, 114 34 STOCKHOLM
Total Offices: 1

Switzerland
TUREVA TREUHAND AG
Splügenstrasse 10, 8002 ZURICH
Total Offices: 2

United Kingdom
AUCKLAND GODDARD HAMPSON & SWAIN
Hogarth House, 31 Sheet Street, WINDSOR, Berkshire SL4 1BY
Total Offices: 2

▷

HISTORY & STRUCTURE
Almost all ATD International's member firms were founded by former partners and managers of "Big Six" accounting firms committed to providing a commercially directed, high quality, personal service to their clients. They have learned that providing a viable alternative to the "Big Six" has an appeal to both privately owned entrepreneurial businesses and public groups. ATDI members also assist other members' clients with business support through introductions to professionals in complementary disciplines and by business-to-business introductions. ATDI is committed to recruiting further members which will enhance its coverage without prejudicing the overall quality and professional standards of its membership.

A.E.E. International

International Office
212 boulevard Bineau, 92200 NEUILLY, France
Tel: +*33* (1) 47 82 65 13
Fax: +*33* (1) 47 60 91 63

European Executive Office
Seestrasse 5, 8002 ZURICH, Switzerland
Tel: +*41* (1) 202 65 25

EUROPEAN PERSONNEL
Chairman: P.F. Autef
Managing Partner: R.H. Kleiner
Accountancy (General): R.H. Kleiner
Audit: B. Hoffman
Corporate Finance: P.F. Autef
Tax (Corporate): P. Canonn
Tax (International): S.A. Corner

European partners:	120
Professional staff:	1,010
Non-professional staff:	150
Total staff:	**1,280**

EUROPEAN FEE INCOME

Year End: 31.12.90	**US$ (000)**	%
Accountancy & Audit:	31,200,000	40.0
Consultancy:	27,300,000	35.0
Tax:	15,600,000	20.0
Other:	3,900,000	5.0
Total:	**78,000,000**	

MEMBER FIRMS

European firms:	16
Number of Countries:	10

PRINCIPAL NATIONAL OFFICES

Austria
BILANZ-DATA
Karlsplatz 3, 1010 VIENNA
Total Offices: 1

Denmark
FAURUM & JORGENSEN
Læderstræde 22, 1201 COPENHAGEN K
Total Offices: 1

France
P.F. AUTEF
23 boulevard de la Saussaye, 92200 NEUILLY
Total Offices: 5

Germany
R.& K. TREUHANDGESELLSCHAFT mbH
Hessenring 99b, 6380 BAD HOMBURG
G. ULRICHS
Hohe Bleichen 5, 2000 HAMBURG 36
Total Offices: 2

Republic of Ireland
ORPEN FRANKS
28-30 Burlington Road, DUBLIN 4
Total Offices: 1

Italy
PROREVI, SOCIETA PROFESSIONALE DI REVISIONE E CERTIFICAZIONE
Via C. Battisti 8, 20122 MILAN
Total Offices: 1

Portugal
TECHNOPLANO
Avenida Joa Crisostomo 66, 4 E, 1000 LISBON
Total Offices: 1

Spain
RAIMON CASANELLAS SL
Valencia 362, ent 1ª, 08009 BARCELONA
Total Offices: 1

Switzerland
E.N. BURKE
Schaffhauserstrasse 351, 8050 ZURICH
Total Offices: 1

United Kingdom
GERALD EDELMAN
25 Harley Street, LONDON W1N 2BR
Total Offices: 2

HISTORY & STRUCTURE
AEE International, a network of independent legal, accountancy and financial firms throughout the world, was formed to provide clients with recognised high standards of business, accounting and tax services. The strength of AEE lies in the strength of each national and independent member firm which has joined voluntarily in mutual association, signing a common exclusive agreement for work referral, standards and exchange of technical experience.

BDO Binder

International Office
Boulevard de la Woluwe 60, 1200 BRUSSELS, Belgium
Tel: +*32* (2) 77 18 30 4
Fax: +*32* (2) 77 14 44 3

International Contact: Guy Anthony Riegels ▷

European Accountancy Groups

EUROPEAN PERSONNEL

International Secretary: Paul W. M. Van Elten

European partners:	617
Professional staff:	4,634
Non-professional staff:	1,557
Total staff:	**6,808**

EUROPEAN FEE INCOME

Year End: 31.12.91	**US$**	**%**
Accountancy & Audit:	296,651,997	59.0
Consultancy:	35,104,577	7.0
Tax:	114,165,743	23.0
Other:	58,604,290	11.0
Total:	**504,526,607**	

MEMBER FIRMS

European firms:	190
Number of Countries:	22

PRINCIPAL NATIONAL OFFICES

Austria
BDO BINDER GmbH
Stock im Eisen-Platz 3, 1010 VIENNA 1
Total Offices: 7

Belgium
BDO HILLEN
Boulevard de la Woluwe 60, 1200 BRUSSELS
Total Offices: 2

Channel Islands
BDO CARNABY BARRETT
Seaton House, Seaton Place, ST HELIER,
Jersey BDO READS
Commerce House, ST PETER PORT, Guernsey
Total Offices: 2

Cyprus
BDO IOANNOU & CHRISTODOULIDES
Office 403, Galaxias Comm Cntr, 4th Floor,
Corner 33 Makarios III Avenue, &
36 Ayias Elenis Street, NICOSIA
Total Offices: 2

Denmark
BDO SCANREVISION AKTIESELSKAB
Strandgade 12, 1401 COPENHAGEN K
Total Offices: 22

Finland
FINNAUDIT OY
Kansakoulukuja 1A, 00100 HELSINKI 10
Total Offices: 2

France
BDO-3G - GROUPE GUY GENDROT
24 quai Carnot, 92210 PARIS-SAINT-CLOUD
Total Offices: 9

Germany
BDO DEUTSCHE WARENTREUHAND AG
Ferdinandstrasse 59, 2000 HAMBURG 1
Total Offices: 30

Greece
YANNES G. YAMARELLOS SA
Agiou Konstantinou Street 4, 104 31 ATHENS
Total Offices: 1

Isle of Man
BDO BINDER
Ragnall House, 18 Peel Road, DOUGLAS
Total Offices: 1

Republic of Ireland
BDO BINDER
Setanta Centre, Nassau Street, DUBLIN 2
Total Offices: 1

Italy
SALA SCELSI FARINA BDO
Piazza del Liberty 4, 20121 MILAN
Total Offices: 2

Liechtenstein
REVIKON REVISIONS-UND BERATUNGS AG
Städtle 35, 9490 VADUZ
Total Offices: 1

Luxembourg
BDO BINDER (LUXEMBOURG) SARL
17 rue des Pommiers, 2343 LUXEMBOURG
Total Offices: 1

Malta
BDO ATTARD BUTTIGIEG PSAILA & CO
136 St Christopher Street, VALLETTA
Total Offices: 1

The Netherlands
BDO CAMPSOBERSGROEP
Central Services, Fellenoord 240, 5611 ZC
EINDHOVEN
Total Offices: 19

Norway
BDO LORANGE OG BRÆNDE & CO
Rådhusgt. 17, 0158 OSLO 1
Total Offices: 1

Portugal
BARROSO, DA SILVA, DIAS,
CASAVAO & ASOCIADOS
Avenida da República 50, 10th Floor, 1000 LISBON
Total Offices: 2

Spain
BDO BINDER SA
Serrano 85, 28006 MADRID
Total Offices: 2

Sweden
BDO REVISION AB
Klarabergsviadukten 70, 107 24 STOCKHOLM
Total Offices: 26

Switzerland
NEUTRA GRUPPE
Löwenstrasse 56, 8023 ZURICH
Total Offices: 34

▷

United Kingdom
BDO BINDER HAMLYN
20 Old Bailey, LONDON EC4M 7BH
Total Offices: 26

HISTORY & STRUCTURE

BDO Binder was founded in Europe during 1963 and remains the most European of all the large international accountancy organisations with more than 50% of its fee income generated in Europe. Its International Office is in Brussels. From its European roots, BDO Binder has developed to be the seventh largest international accounting and consulting organization with a network of member firms in 62 countries and total fees of over US$1.1 billion. BDO Binder has over 400 offices around the world, employing some 16,000 partners and staff. BDO Binder has correspondents in another 23 countries. BDO Binder's international organisation is structured around a council which includes a representative from each member firm. The council elects a policy board, which is supported by the international office and technical committees.

BKR International

European Executive Office
2 Bloomsbury Street, LONDON WC1B 3ST, United Kingdom
Tel: +*44* (71) 413 5100
Fax: +*44* (71) 413 5101

International Contact: Charles Tucker

EUROPEAN PERSONNEL
Chairman: Walter Hoffman
Secretary: Charles Tucker

European partners:	146
Professional staff:	1,172
Non-professional staff:	337
Total staff:	**1,655**

EUROPEAN FEE INCOME

Year End: 30.06.91	**£**	**%**
Accountancy & Audit:		50.0
Insolvency:		5.0
Consultancy:		24.0
Tax:		21.0
Total:	**60,000,000**	

MEMBER FIRMS

European firms:	60
Number of Countries:	15

PRINCIPAL NATIONAL OFFICES

Austria
NEUNER + HENZL TREUHAND GmbH
Garnisongasse 20, 1096 VIENNA
Total Offices: 4

Belgium
CALLENS PIRENNE & CO
Van Eycklei 17, Boite 5, 2018 ANTWERP
Total Offices: 4

Channel Islands
STRACHANS
Sommerville House, Phillips Street, ST HELIER, Jersey
Total Offices: 1

Cyprus
DAMIANOU & CO
5 Hitron Street, NICOSIA
Total Offices: 1

Denmark
RIR - REVISION
Himmelev Bygade 70, 4000 ROSKILDE
Total Offices: 3

France
GUÉRARD VIALA
125 rue de Montreuil, 75011 PARIS
Total Offices: 11

Germany
RHEINREVISION GmbH
Wilhelm-Strausse-Strasse 45-47, 4050 MÖNCHENGLADBACH 2, Dusseldorf
TREUHAND UNION FINK & PARTNER GmbH
Burgermeister-Smidt Strasse 59/61, 2800 BREMEN 1
TREUHAND-GESELLSCHAFT "HANSA" mbH
Kajen 6, 2000 HAMBURG 11
Total Offices: 4

Liechtenstein
EUROCOUNT WIRTSCHAFTSBERATUNG ANSTALT
Altenbach 8, 9490 VADUZ
Total Offices: 1

Luxembourg
CALLENS PIRENNE
boulevard d'Avranches 12-14, 1012 LUXEMBOURG
Total Offices: 1

Malta
MANGION MERCIECA & CO
21 Mannario Road, BIRKIRKARA
Total Offices: 1

The Netherlands
KOOIJ & PARTNERS
Maliesingel 26, 3581 BH UTRECHT
Total Offices: 1

Spain
AUDIT SA
Calle Josep Tarradellas 147, 2º 1a, 08029 BARCELONA
Total Offices: 9

Sweden
VERNER & PARTNERS
Birger Jarlsgatan 33, V, 111 45 STOCKHOLM
Total Offices: 1

▷

European Accountancy Groups

Switzerland
RST REVISIONS AG
Peter Merian-Strasse 54, 4002 BASLE
Total Offices: 3

United Kingdom
BAKER TILLY
2 Bloomsbury Street, LONDON WC1B 3ST
Total Offices: 15

HISTORY & STRUCTURE
BKR Group was founded in 1982, part of the worldwide 'BKR International', an association of some 50 independent accountancy firms co-operating in the international field and linked by the common philosophy to give the highest standard of service to clients.

The Channel International Association

International Office
27-31 Blandford Street, LONDON W1H 3AD, United Kingdom
Tel: +*44* (71) 935 7755
Fax: + *44* (71) 935 9172

International Contact: Peter Galloway

EUROPEAN PERSONNEL
Chairman: Patrick Aubart
Secretary: Pamela Walker

European partners:	35
Professional staff:	300
Non-professional staff:	50
Total staff:	**385**

MEMBER FIRMS

European firms:	7
Number of Countries:	6

PRINCIPAL NATIONAL OFFICES

France
SEECF/UNF
197 boulevard Malesherbes, 75017 PARIS
Total Offices: 1

Germany
EVERS, POHL & REISCHER GmbH
Widenmayerstrasse 36, 8000 MUNICH 22
KIEFFER STUBBEN
Morsenbroicher Weg 200, 4000 DUSSELDORF 30
Total Offices: 2

Republic of Ireland
BASTOW CHARLETON
Marine House, Clanwilliam Court, DUBLIN 2
Total Offices: 1

Italy
STUDIO TRAVIA
Via Gesu 13, 20121 MILAN
Total Offices: 1

Spain
COC SERVICIOS
Paseo de Gracia 120, 08008 BARCELONA
Total Offices: 1

United Kingdom
LEIGH CARR
27-31 Blandford Street, LONDON W1H 3AD
Total Offices: 1

HISTORY & STRUCTURE
The Channel International Association was formed by Peter Galloway (London) and Patrick Aubart (Paris). The Association has eight full members from the EC and Cyprus. Representatives of member firms meet once every three months. The objective of all members is to provide, for those clients who require it, a service throughout the EC which is comparable with the service received in their home country. It is intended to expand the Association sufficiently to ensure cover in most business centres throughout the EC but, at the same time, keep it small enough so that the personal touch is retained.

Clark Kenneth Leventhal

International Office
25 New Street Square, LONDON EC4A 3LN, United Kingdom
Tel: +*44* (71) 353 1577
Fax: + *44* (71) 583 3691

International Contact: Nicholas C. Blake

EUROPEAN PERSONNEL
Chairman: Rod Evans
Vice-Chairman: James Gemmell
Executive Committee: Howard Gilmour
Executive Committee: Peter Grote
Executive Committee: Irving Kroll
Executive Committee: Julio Pilon
Executive Committee: Guillaume de Saint-Gérand
Executive Committee: Günter von Bremen

European partners:	221
Professional staff:	1,350
Non-professional staff:	404
Total staff:	**2,055**

EUROPEAN FEE INCOME

Year End: 30.06.91	**US$**
Total:	**172,000,000**

MEMBER FIRMS

European firms:	103
Number of Countries:	17

PRINCIPAL NATIONAL OFFICES

Austria
CONSULTATIO mbH
Holzmeistergasse 9, 1210 VIENNA
Total Offices: 1

▷

Belgium
C.V. CLAEYS DE MAEYER & CO SC
Rue de L'Autonomie 9, 1070 BRUSSELS
Total Offices: 1

Channel Islands
CLARK WHITEHILL LONG
Borough House, Rue du Pré, ST PETER PORT, Guernsey
Total Offices: 1

Cyprus
AFXENTIOU & PHILLIPPIDES
Afemia House, 3rd Floor, 70 Makarios Avenue, NICOSIA
Total Offices: 1

Denmark
ALSØ & BREINHOLT A/S
Roskildevej 39, 2000 COPENHAGEN F
Total Offices: 3

France
JEAN ARTHUIS ET ASSOCIÉS
208 rue Raymond-Losserand, 75014 PARIS
M.B.B.R.
208 rue Raymond-Losserand, 75014 PARIS
Total Offices: 2

Germany
BACHEM, FERVERS, JANSSEN & MEHRHOFF
Hohenzollernring 57-63, 5000 COLOGNE 1
DUSSELDORFER TREUHAND-GESELLSCHAFT ALTENBURG & TEWES AG
Am Wehrhahn/Worringer Strasse 2-4, 4000 DUSSELDORF 1
"FIDES" TREUHANDGESELLSCHAFT REINFENRATH & CO
Contrescarpe 97, 2800 BREMEN 1
GOUTIER, KNOPF, TULLOCH & PARTNER
Holzhausenstrasse 25, 6000 FRANKFURT
M.B.B.R. (ET ASSOCIÉS)
Plank Strasse 7, 3010 MAGDEBURG
DR. BOHN WEGNER & PARTNER
Beethovenstrasse 8, 8000 MUNICH 2
WIRTSCHAFTSTREUHAND GmbH
Herdweg 18, 7000 STUTTGART 1
Total Offices: 16

Isle of Man
CLARK WHITEHILL
7th Floor, Victory House, Prospect Hill, DOUGLAS
Total Offices: 1

Republic of Ireland
V.F. NATHAN & CO
Christchurch Square, DUBLIN 8
Total Offices: 2

Italy
S.E.R.C.A.
Via XX Settembre 19, 25121 BRESCIA
Total Offices: 3

Luxembourg
INTERFIDUCIAIRE & INTERAUDIT
121 avenue de la Faïencerie, 1511 LUXEMBOURG
Total Offices: 2

The Netherlands
DE ROO & VAN DER VEEN GROEP
Noordsingel 208-210, 3032 BM ROTTERDAM
Total Offices: 3

Norway
BIRKELAND OG UVHOLTS REVISJONSBYRÅ
Schwensenagt. 7, 0170 OSLO 1
Total Offices: 1

Spain
AUDISERVICIOS SATORRA Y PLANAS SRC
Muntaner 261, 4º 2ª, 08021 BARCELONA
Total Offices: 2

Sweden
SVEN JOSEFSONS REVISIONSBYRÅ AB
Huvudstagatan 1, 17 158 SOLNA, Stockholm
Total Offices: 1

Switzerland
MEGA FIDUCIARIA SA
Corso San Gottardo 32, 6830 CHIASSO

OFISA
Chemin des Charmettes 7, 1003 LAUSANNE

TREUHAND-UND REVISIONSGESELLSCHAFT ZURICH
Schaffhauserstrasse 18, 8023 ZURICH
Total Offices: 5

United Kingdom
CLARK WHITEHILL
25 New Street Square, LONDON EC4A 3LN
Total Offices: 58

HISTORY & STRUCTURE

Clark Kenneth Leventhal (CKL) is an association of separate and independent accounting firms worldwide. Each member operates under its own local or national name and, therefore, remains autonomous. Individual members are all firms of high standing in their own countries and many rank in the top 15 firms in the accounting profession in those countries. The association dates back to 1973.

Coopers & Lybrand Europe

European Executive Office
European Community Office, Avenue de Tervuren 2, Boite 3, 1040 BRUSSELS, Belgium
Tel: *+32* (2) 73 59 06 5
Fax: *+32* (2) 73 36 61 8

EUROPEAN PERSONNEL

Executive Partner: Willem L.J. Bröcker
Planning & Marketing: Sydney Richardson
US Liaison: Frank A. Bodie Jr.

European Accountancy Groups

Tax Services: Martin van Rooijn
Information Technology: Ian Buckingham
Financial Management: Clive Pyne
Manufacturing & Logistics: James Warner
Commerce & Industry: Hans-Gunther Bollig
Marketing & Communications: Suzanne Harris
Management Consultancy: Paul Batchelor
Total staff: 30,000 +

EUROPEAN FEE INCOME

Year End: 1991	**US$ (million)**
Total:	**2,300**

MEMBER FIRMS

European firms:	350
Number of Countries:	25

PRINCIPAL NATIONAL OFFICES

Austria
COOPERS & LYBRAND GmbH / INTER-TREUHAND mbH
Berggasse 31, 1090 VIENNA
Total Offices: 1

Belgium
COOPERS & LYBRAND JACOBS EECKHOUT THIRIFAY & CO
Avenue Marcel Thiry 216, 1200 BRUSSELS
Total Offices: 3

Channel Islands
COOPERS & LYBRAND DELOITTE
La Motte Chambers, ST HELIER, Jersey JE2 4SY
Total Offices: 2

Cyprus
COOPERS & LYBRAND/IOANNOU ZAMPELAS & CO
Julia House, 3 Them. Dervis Street, NICOSIA
Total Offices: 5

Denmark
K.G. JENSEN COOPERS & LYBRAND
16-28 Lyngbyveij, COPENHAGEN
Total Offices: 32

Finland
SALMI VIRKKUNEN & HELENIUS OY/ COOPERS & LYBRAND
Keskuskatu 3, 00100 HELSINKI
Total Offices: 14

France
COOPERS & LYBRAND
56 rue de Ponthieu, 75008 PARIS
Total Offices: 18

Germany
COOPERS & LYBRAND/TREUHAND VEREINIGUNG AG
Wöhlerstrasse 6-10, 6000 FRANKFURT 1
TREUARBEIT AG
Bockenheimer Anlage 15, 6000 FRANKFURT 1
Total Offices: 45

Gibraltar
COOPERS & LYBRAND
ICC Building, Casemates Square, GIBRALTAR
Total Offices: 1

Greece
COOPERS & LYBRAND
Abacus House, 9 Semitelou Street, 115 28 ATHENS
Total Offices: 3

Greenland
K.G. JENSEN REVISIONSAKTIESELSKAB GREENLAND
P.O. Box 144, 3920 QAQORTOQ, (Julianehåb)
Total Offices: 3

Iceland
ENDURSKODUNARMIDSTÖDIN HF - N. MANSCHER/COOPERS & LYBRAND
Höfdabakki 9, 112 REYKJAVIK
Total Offices: 5

Isle of Man
COOPERS & LYBRAND
12 Finch Road, DOUGLAS
Total Offices: 1

Republic of Ireland
COOPERS & LYBRAND
Fitzwilliam House, Wilton Place, DUBLIN 2
Total Offices: 6

Italy
COOPERS & LYBRAND SAS
Via Vittor Pisani 20, 20124 MILAN
Total Offices: 12

Liechtenstein
COOPERS & LYBRAND AKTIENGESELLSCHAFT
Pflugstrasse 20, VADUZ
Total Offices: 1

Luxembourg
COOPERS & LYBRAND
16 Rue Eugène Ruppert, 2453 LUXEMBOURG
Total Offices: 1

Malta
COOPERS & LYBRAND/ZAMMIT TABONA BONELLO & CO
167 Merchants Street, VALLETTA
Total Offices: 1

The Netherlands
COOPERS & LYBRAND DIJKER VAN DIEN
Prins Bernhardplein 200, 1097 JB AMSTERDAM
Total Offices: 31

Norway
COOPERS & LYBRAND A/S
Havnelageret, 0150 OSLO 1
Total Offices: 20

Portugal
COOPERS & LYBRAND LDA
Av Antonio José D'Almeida SF 2c, 1000 LISBON
Total Offices: 2

▷

Spain

COOPERS & LYBRAND SA

Rosario Pino 14-16, planta 16, 28020 MADRID

Total Offices: 15

Sweden

ÖHRLINGS REVEKO AB

Tegeluddsvägen 31, 115 41 STOCKHOLM

Total Offices: 100

Switzerland

COOPERS & LYBRAND AG

St. Jakobs-Strasse 25, 4052 BASEL

Total Offices: 16

United Kingdom

COOPERS & LYBRAND DELOITTE

Plumtree Court, LONDON EC4A 4HT

Total Offices: 41

HISTORY & STRUCTURE

Coopers & Lybrand Europe, formed in 1989 to co-ordinate the Coopers & Lybrand network established in Europe for over 30 years, is an association of Coopers & Lybrand firms in Europe. Through Coopers & Lybrand Europe our strong national firms are committed to develop and implement common strategies to meet client needs, to fund joint operations and services and to invest collectively in new areas of activity to provide a high level of service to our international and national clients. This is accomplished through the dedicated resources in our Executive Office which reports directly to the European Board Council of Senior Partners. Coopers & Lybrand have 30,000 people in Europe, trained to internationally agreed standards with offices in every Western European country and an established presence in Eastern and Central Europe and in the Soviet Union. They offer the following business advisory services across Europe: Audit, Management Consultancy, International Tax, Corporate Finance, and European Community Affairs.

CPA Associates Inc

European Executive Office

Greenwood House, 4/7 Salisbury Court, LONDON EC4 8BT

Tel: +44 (71) 583 7575

Fax: +44 (71) 583 2081

International Contact: Peter Scolding

EUROPEAN PERSONNEL

Chairman: J.F. Flynn

MEMBER FIRMS

European firms:	14
Number of Countries:	8

PRINCIPAL NATIONAL OFFICES

Channel Islands

McFADYEN, SCOTT-WARREN & MORRIS

Broadcasting House, Rouge Bouillon, ST HELIER, Jersey

Total Offices: 1

France

C.M.S. EXPERTS ASSOCIÉS

149 boulevard Malesherbes, 75017 PARIS

Total Offices: 2

Germany

BERND RODL & PARTNER

Erlenstegenstrasse 10, 8500 NUREMBERG 20

Total Offices: 1

Greece

Total Offices: 1

Republic of Ireland

O'SULLIVAN KEOGH

OSK House, 29 Lower Baggot Street, DUBLIN 2

Total Offices: 1

Spain

CORTÉS, PERÉZ Y CIA AUDITORES

5 Gutenberg 3-13, 5º A, TERRASSA (Barcelona)

Total Offices: 2

Switzerland

Total Offices: 1

United Kingdom

HUGHES ALLEN

Greenwood House, 4/7 Salisbury Court, LONDON EC4Y 8BT

Total Offices: 5

HISTORY & STRUCTURE

Founded in 1957, CPA Associates Inc. is an international association of independent CPA firms which provide clients with professional accounting, audit, tax and management advisory services. Each member preserves its autonomy and yet has access to a variety of member services and the combined professional strengths and widespread geographic locations of all the member firms. Programs conducted for the benefit of members include annual seminars, video tape library for in-housing training, consulting services for accounting, audit, tax and practice management, peer review programs, reference guide listing each member's expertise, information central data bank, five client newsletters, directory, member surveys, fax network and discount on a variety of products. ▷

European Accountancy Groups

DFK International

European Executive Office
Russell Square House, 10/12 Russell Square,
LONDON WC1B 5LF, United Kingdom
Tel: *+44* (71) 436 6722
Fax: *+44* (71) 436 6606

International Contact: John W. Powell

EUROPEAN PERSONNEL
President: Claude Gengoux
Administrator: Rene Harwood

European partners:	207
Professional staff:	1,130
Non-professional staff:	337
Total staff:	**1,674**

EUROPEAN FEE INCOME

Year End: 31.12.91	**US$**
Total:	**130,525,000**

MEMBER FIRMS

European firms:	82
Number of Countries:	18

PRINCIPAL NATIONAL OFFICES

Austria
IB INTERBILANZ WIRTSCHAFTSTREUHAND GmbH
Gusshausstrasse 4, 1040 VIENNA
Total Offices: 1

Belgium
DEGREZ, MERCKEN, ROUVROY & CO SCC
Avenue Jules César 9, 1150 BRUSSELS
Total Offices: 4

Cyprus
A. CHRYSANTHOU & CO
El Greco House, 20 Queen Frederica Street, Office 303, NICOSIA
N. CONSTANTINOU & CO
Rega Ferou Street, Limassol Centre, Block B, Office 508, LIMASSOL
Total Offices: 2

Finland
OLLI WESAMAA HTM TILINTARKASTUSRYHMÄ OY/AUDIT GROUP LTD
Pohjoisesplanadi 27 C, 00100 HELSINKI
Total Offices: 1

France
DFK FRANCE
33 rue Daru, 75008 PARIS
Total Offices: 23

Germany
DFK GERMANY
Maria-Theresia Strasse 5, 8000 MUNICH 80
Total Offices: 7

Gibraltar
CLINTONS
Suites 2 & 3, Gibraltar Heights, 215 Main Street, P.O. Box 239, GIBRALTAR
Total Offices: 1

Greece
I.J. ANDRONIS
28 Kapodistrou Street, 106 82 ATHENS
Total Offices: 1

Iceland
SAMEINADA ENDURSKODUNARSKRIFSTOFAN H/F
Armuli 10, 108 REYKJAVIK
Total Offices: 1

Republic of Ireland
McQUILLANS - DFK
Drury Court, 56-58 Drury Street, DUBLIN 2
Total Offices: 2

Italy
DFK ITALIA SNC
Via Visconti di Modrone 38, 20122 MILAN
Total Offices: 1

The Netherlands
FOEDERER GROEP ACCOUNTANTS NV
Zernikestraat 10, 5612 HZ EINDHOVEN
Total Offices: 13

Norway
REVINOR A/S
Storgaten 37, 0182 OSLO
Total Offices: 12

Portugal
CIC CENTRO DE INFORMATICA E CONTABILIDADE LDA
Rua Conde de Sabugosa 15, 2º-A, 1700 LISBON
Total Offices: 1

Spain
DFK ESPAÑA SA
Rambla de Catalunya 135 'pral, 08008 BARCELONA
Total Offices: 4

Sweden
SVEREV - DFK INTERNATIONAL (SWEDEN)
Sveavägen 13-15 VII, 111 57 STOCKHOLM
Total Offices: 12

Switzerland
DFK (SUISSE) SA GENEVE
Route de Frontenex 62, 1211 GENEVA 6
Total Offices: 7

United Kingdom
CHANTREY VELLACOTT
Russell Square House, 10/12 Russell Square, LONDON WC1B 5LF
Total Offices: 7

▷

HISTORY & STRUCTURE

DFK International is committed to meeting the needs of businesses and individuals with interests in more than one country. Its members are accounting firms which intend to remain independent national practices. It was formed in 1962 and was incorporated, with limited liability, in 1982. All member firms are members of and parties to an agreement with the corporation. The members appoint a multinational Board of Directors, which appoints the President, the Executive Committee and the Executive Director who are responsible for management and development. DFK International is divided into three regions of the World, one of which covers Europe.

DRM Internationally

International Office
186 City Road, LONDON EC1V 2NU,
United Kingdom
Tel: +44 (71) 251 1644
Fax: +44 (71) 250 0801

European Executive Office
Avenue des Arts 44, 1040 BRUSSELS, Belgium
Tel: +32 (2) 51 45 03 8
Fax: +32 (2) 51 45 70 5

International Contact: David Maxwell

EUROPEAN PERSONNEL

European Director: David Maxwell
Information Manager: Hervé Pierret

European partners:	230
Professional staff:	1,402
Non-professional staff:	558
Total staff:	**2,190**

MEMBER FIRMS

European firms:	87
Number of Countries:	20

PRINCIPAL NATIONAL OFFICES

Austria
NOEWP - NIEDEROESTERR
WIRTSCHAFTSPRUEFUNGS
Riemerschmidgasse 9, 2344 MARIA ENDZERSDORF
Total Offices: 2

Belgium
S.P.R.L. NEVENS
Boulevard Saint Michel 27, 1040 BRUSSELS
Total Offices: 1

Channel Islands
READS & CO
Wellington House, Union Street, ST HELIER, Jersey
Total Offices: 2

Cyprus
T.C. SHAKALLIS & CO
Acropolis Centre, 3rd Floor, Gladstone Street, LIMASSOL
Total Offices: 1

Denmark
CHRISTIANSEN & ENGELBRECHTSEN REVISIONS-FIRMA
Adelgade 15, 1304 COPENHAGEN K
Total Offices: 6

France
SALUSTRO REYDEL
65 rue de Courcelles, 75008 PARIS
Total Offices: 16

Germany
ADVISOR TREUHAND GmbH
Tulpenhofstrasse 18, 6050 OFFENBACH AM MAIN 1
AWT AUDITRON WIRTSCHAFTS-TREUHAND GmbH
Willy-Lessing Strasse 12, 8600 BAMBERG
HAARMANN, HEMMELRATH & PARTNER
Effnerstrasse 38, 8000 MUNICH 81
Total Offices: 8

Greece
ATHOS STYLIANOU ASSOCIATES EPE
Ethnikis Antistaseos 84, 152 31 ATHENS
Total Offices: 1

Isle of Man
READS & CO
Meghraj Centre, Upper Church Street, DOUGLAS
Total Offices: 1

Republic of Ireland
KIERAN CORRIGAN & CO
41 Fitzwilliam Place, DUBLIN 2
Total Offices: 1

Italy
STUDIO TRIBUTARIO VINCENZO CAFIERO
Via G. Carducci 4, 00187 ROME
SOCIETA GENERALE DI REVISIONE E CERTIFICAZIONE
Via XX Settembre 1, 00187 ROME
Total Offices: 3

Luxembourg
REVILUX SARL
15 boulevard Roosevelt, 2450 LUXEMBOURG
Total Offices: 1

Malta
DIAMANTINO, MIZZO & CO
Valletta Buildings, South Street, VALLETTA
Total Offices: 1

The Netherlands
SCHADÉ HARKEMA & PARTNERS
Reimersbeek 2, 1082 AG AMSTERDAM
Total Offices: 4

Norway
DYBWAD REVISION A/S
Bygdøy Allé 23, 0262 OSLO
Total Offices: 1

Portugal
PATRICIO, MIMOSO E MENDES JORGE
Rua Nogueira e Sousa 8, 1º, 1100 LISBON
Total Offices: 2

Spain
P.B. AUDITORES SL
Avenida Diagonal 598, 08021 BARCELONA
SOCIEDAD FIDUCIARIA ESPAÑOLA
Diputacion 239, 08007 BARCELONA
Total Offices: 3

Sweden
RANBY ODHAM REVISORER AB
Första Långgatan 30, 400 32 GOTHENBURG
Total Offices: 5

Switzerland
METROPOLITAN FIDUCIAIRE SA
100 Rue du Rhône, 1211 GENEVA 3
TESTOR TREUHAND AG
Rittergasse 35, 4001 BASLE
Total Offices: 5

United Kingdom
JONES PETERS & COMPANY
6 Church Street, BANBRIDGE, Co Down BT32 4AA
ROBSON RHODES
186 City Road, LONDON EC1V 2NU
SCOTT OSWALD & CO
1 Royal Terrace, EDINBURGH EH7 5AD
Total Offices: 23

HISTORY & STRUCTURE

DRM is an international organisation of independent national firms operating in approximately 60 countries worldwide. It was established in the mid-1960s.

DRT International

European Executive Office
185 avenue Charles-de-Gaulle, 92200 NEUILLY SUR SEINE, Paris, France
Tel: +33 (1) 40 88 28 00
Fax: +33 (1) 40 88 28 28

International Contact: Thomas Presby

EUROPEAN PERSONNEL

Chairman: Jacques Manardo
Director of Communications: David Read

European partners:	1,220
Professional staff:	11,980
Non-professional staff:	3,800
Total staff:	**17,000**

EUROPEAN FEE INCOME

Year End: 30.09.90	**US$**
Total:	**1,300,000,000**

MEMBER FIRMS

European firms:	21
Number of Countries:	21

PRINCIPAL NATIONAL OFFICES

Austria
DANUBIA TREUHAND-UND BERATUNGSGES mbH
Rotenturmstrasse 1, 1010 VIENNA
Total Offices: 1

Belgium
TINNEMANS, POURBAIX, VAES & CO
Brussels Airport Park, Berkenlaan 6, 1831 DIEGEM
Total Offices: 2

Channel Islands
TOUCHE ROSS & CO
66-68 Esplanade, ST HELIER, Jersey JE2 3QB
Total Offices: 2

Cyprus
DELOITTE & TOUCHE
256 Makarios Avenue, LIMASSOL
Total Offices: 3

Denmark
SCHØBEL & MARHOLT REVISIONAKTIESELSKAB
H.C. Andersens Boulevard 2, 1553 COPENHAGEN V
Total Offices: 26

Finland
TILINTARKASTAJIEN OY - REVISORERNAS AB
Kaivokatu 8, 00100 HELSINKI
Total Offices: 11

France
DELOITTE ROSS TOMMATSU
185 avenue Charles de Gaulle, 92201 NEUILLY SUR SEINE, Paris
Total Offices: 5

Germany
WOLLERT-ELMENDORFF DEUTSCHE INDUSTRIE-TREUHAND GmbH
Bahnstrasse 16, 4000 DUSSELDORF 1
Total Offices: 14

Greece
DELOITTE & TOUCHE
P.O. Box 75195, Kallithea, 176 10 ATHENS
Total Offices: 3

Isle of Man
TOUCHE ROSS & CO
Bank of Scotland House, Prospect Hill, DOUGLAS
Total Offices: 1

Republic of Ireland
DELOITTE & TOUCHE
Deloitte & Touche House, Earlsfort Centre, Earlsfort Terrace, DUBLIN 2
Total Offices: 3

Italy
DELOITTE & TOUCHE
Via Monte di Pieta 24, 20121 MILAN
Total Offices: 12

▷

Luxembourg
FIDUCIAIRE GÉNÉRALE DE LUXEMBOURG
3 route d'Arlon, 8009 STRASSEN
Total Offices: 2

Malta
MANDUCA, MERCIECA & CO
21 Archbishop Street, VALLETTA
Total Offices: 2

The Netherlands
TRN GROEP
Admiraliteitskade 50, 3063 ED ROTTERDAM
Total Offices: 60

Norway
FORUM TOUCHE ROSS
Pilestredet 75C, OSLO 3
Total Offices: 9

Portugal
DELOITTE ROSS TOHMATSU
Avenida das Descobertas, Galerias Alto da Barra, Piso 3, 2780 OEIRAS
Total Offices: 3

Spain
DELOITTE & TOUCHE
Torre Picasso, planta 38, 28020 MADRID
Total Offices: 13

Sweden
TRG REVISION AB
Arenavägen 55, 121 26 STOCKHOLM-GLOBEN
Total Offices: 55

Switzerland
DELOITTE & TOUCHE
Zollikerstrasse 228, 8008 ZURICH
Total Offices: 2

United Kingdom
TOUCHE ROSS & CO
Peterborough Court, 133 Fleet Street, LONDON EC4A 2TR
Total Offices: 27

HISTORY & STRUCTURE

DRT International is one of the world's largest providers of professional services with a worldwide fee income of US$4.6 billion. Created from Deloitte Haskins and Sells and Touche Ross International, DRT International offers a balanced service geographically, occupying leading positions in Europe, North America and Asia Pacific, and in the range and strength of services it offers to clients in audit and accounting, management consulting and tax. DRT International in Europe, as elsewhere, works closely with clients to help them to achieve their objectives. WDRT understand their businesses, and the issues such as markets and competition that affect their future in Europe and worldwide. DRT operate from over 250 offices throughout Europe to ensure that professionals are available in every major business centre in the region, and practises as one firm, in order to deliver a more consistent service to all clients wherever they are.

Ernst & Young Europe

European Executive Office
Avenue Marcel Thiry 204, 1200 BRUSSELS, Belgium
Tel: +32 (2) 774 91 11
Fax: +32 (2) 774 96 90

International Contact: Dan Newman

EUROPEAN PERSONNEL
Chairman: Henk Neeleman
Managing Partner: Jules Muis

European partners:	782
Professional staff:	19,004
Non-professional staff:	5,555
Total staff:	**25,341**

EUROPEAN FEE INCOME

Year End: 30.09.90	**US$**
Total:	**1,853,000,000**

MEMBER FIRMS

European firms:	289
Number of Countries:	23

PRINCIPAL NATIONAL OFFICES

Austria
SÜD-OST TREUHAND AG
Praterstrasse 23, 1021 VIENNA
Total Offices: 8

Belgium
ERNST & YOUNG
Avenue Marcel Thiry 204, 1200 BRUSSELS
Total Offices: 8

Channel Islands
ERNST & YOUNG
14 New Street, ST PETER PORT, Guernsey
ERNST & YOUNG
Le Gallais Chambers, 54 Bath Street, ST HELIER, Jersey JE4 8YD
Total Offices: 2

Cyprus
ERNST & YOUNG
Nicosia Tower Centre, 36 Byron Avenue, 162 NICOSIA
Total Offices: 2

Denmark
ERNST & YOUNG A/S
Tagensvej 82, 2200 COPENHAGEN N
Total Offices: 15

Finland
TILINTARKASTAJIEN OY / OY ERNST & YOUNG AB
Aleksanterinkatu 48A (to May 92), Kaivokatu 8 (from May 92), 00100 HELSINKI
Total Offices: 13

▷

European Accountancy Groups

France
ERNST & YOUNG
Tour Manhattan, CEDEX 21, 6 Place de l'Iris, 92095 PARIS LA DEFENSE 2
Total Offices: 11

Germany
SCHITAG SCHWÄBISCHE TREUHAND AG
Jägerstrasse 26, 7000 STUTTGART 10
Total Offices: 32

Gibraltar
ERNST & YOUNG
Suite 5, International House, Bell Lane, GIBRALTAR
Total Offices: 1

Greece
ERNST & YOUNG
Athens Tower, 23rd Floor, 2 Messogion Street, 115 27 ATHENS
Total Offices: 1

Iceland
ENDURSKODUN & RADGJOF HF
Skeifan 11a, 108 REYKJAVIK
Total Offices: 1

Isle of Man
ERNST & YOUNG
Derby House, Athol Street, DOUGLAS
Total Offices: 3

Republic of Ireland
ERNST & YOUNG
Stephen Court, 18/21 St Stephens Green, DUBLIN 2
Total Offices: 6

Italy
RECONTA ERNST & YOUNG
Via Torino 68, 20123 MILAN
Total Offices: 32

Luxembourg
ERNST & YOUNG
6 avenue Emile Reuter, B.P. 351,
2013 LUXEMBOURG
Total Offices: 1

Monaco
SOMODECO
Immeuble Les Lys, 3 rue Louis Auréglia,
98000 MONACO
Total Offices: 1

The Netherlands
MORET ERNST & YOUNG
G.H. Betzweg 1, 3068 AZ ROTTERDAM
Total Offices: 54

Norway
ERNST & YOUNG
Stenersgt. 10, 0184 OSLO 1
Total Offices: 29

Portugal
ERNST & YOUNG & CIA
Avda Antonio Augusto de Aguiar 21, 3º E,
1000 LISBON
Total Offices: 4

Spain
ERNST & YOUNG
Alberto Alcocer 24, 28036 MADRID
Total Offices: 17

Sweden
ERNST & YOUNG
Adolf Fredriks Kyrkogata 2, 103 62 STOCKHOLM
Total Offices: 63

Switzerland
ATAG ERNST & YOUNG
Bleicherweg 21, 8002 ZURICH
Total Offices: 24

United Kingdom
ERNST & YOUNG
Becket House, 1 Lambeth Palace Road,
LONDON SE1 7EU
Total Offices: 31

HISTORY & STRUCTURE
Ernst & Young, the world's leading integrated professional services firm, was created in 1989 from the merger of Ernst & Whinney and Arthur Young.

Eura-Audit International

International Office
8 rue de Turin, 75008 PARIS, France
Tel: +33 (1) 42 93 82 12
Fax: +33 (1) 43 87 91 49

International Contact: Jean Martin

EUROPEAN PERSONNEL
Secretary-General: Gilbert Michel
President: Jean Martin
Vice-President: Jean Bernard Buchs
Total staff: **3,500**

EUROPEAN FEE INCOME

Year End: 1990	**FFr (000)**	%
Accountancy & Audit:	200,000,000	77.0
Consultancy:	60,000,000	33.0
Total:	**260,000,000**	

MEMBER FIRMS
European firms: 39
Number of Countries: 5

PRINCIPAL NATIONAL OFFICES

Belgium
TYTGAT-ARCELIN & CO
77 Avenue de la Toison d'Or, Boite 10,
1060 BRUSSELS

▷

CABINET DE REVISION VERCRUYSSE, DELPLACE, MORTIER & CO
Passage de la Poste 4, Boite 120, 7700 MOUSCRON
Total Offices: 2

France
AEC CONSULTANTS
allée des Sapins, B.P. 443, 44474 CARQUEFOU CEDEX
AUDIT RÉVISION ET CONTROLE (ARC)
Le Mercure C, Zone Industrielle des Milles, 13851 AIX EN PROVENCE CEDEX 3
BCD CONSULTANTS
102 rue Vauban, B.P. 3208, 68064 MULHOUSE CEDEX
DELARUE-HEDIEU
63 boulevard Côte Blatin, 63000 CLERMONT FERRAND
DMV - EUREXCO
57 rue de Gand, 59800 LILLE
EURA-AUDIT INTERNATIONAL SARL
8 rue de Turin, 75008 PARIS
EXPERTS COMPTABLES ASSOCIÉS
138 avenue de Castres, 31500 TOULOUSE
SA FIDEURAF
8 rue de Turin, 75008 PARIS
DIDIER REMY
29 rue Labbottière, 33000 BORDEAUX
CABINET SBC CIRON
108 bis, cours du Médoc, 33000 BORDEAUX
SOCIÉTÉ FIDUCIAIRE DE CONTROLE ET DE RÉVISION
32 bis, avenue Félix-Faure, 69007 LYONS
SOFICO FRANCE
Centre d'Affaires de Metz, 1 place du Pont à Seille, 57000 METZ
Total Offices: 31

Germany
ALL-AUDIT REVISION UND TREUHAND GmbH
Grossherzog Friedrich Strasse 40, 6600 SAARBRÜCKEN
CONFIDA AG
Rathausstrasse 12, 2000 HAMBURG 1
INTRACONSULT TREUHAND GmbH
Windmühlstrasse 2, 6000 FRANKFURT
JÄGER
Konigstrasse 62, 6000 STUTTGART 1
Total Offices: 4

Switzerland
FIDUCIAIRE VERIFID SA
Rue du Rhône 100, Case Postale 908, 1211 GENEVA 3
Total Offices: 1

United Kingdom
THE CHARTERGROUP PARTNERSHIP LTD
Orbital House, 85 Croydon Road, CATERHAM, Surrey CR3 6PD
Total Offices: 58

HISTORY & STRUCTURE
Eura-Audit was founded in 1986 for the purpose of advising and assisting clients in all of the major European and African business centres. Its members grew quickly from 11 to about 50 representing more than 100 major towns in Europe and Africa. It works closely with an English group, The CharterGroup Partnership. The Group offers services in auditing, international taxation, data processing, research and training. There is an African and Eastern Europe committee which carefully follows the evolution of the profession in those areas. A monthly digest informs the members of internal news. Another newsletter, written in French, German and English, provides current financial, legal and commercial information on international subjects like taxation, financial law etc.

GMN International

European Executive Office
42 Upper Berkeley St, LONDON W1H 8AB, United Kingdom
Tel: *+44* (71) 723 7293
Fax: *+44* (71) 724 3488

International Contact: Michael Cannon

EUROPEAN PERSONNEL
Administration: Elisabeth Tham

European partners:	175
Total staff:	**1,300**

EUROPEAN FEE INCOME

Year End: 30.06.91	**ECU**
Total:	**67,900,000**

MEMBER FIRMS

European firms:	44
Number of Countries:	12

PRINCIPAL NATIONAL OFFICES

Austria
VICTORIA WIRTSCHAFTSTREUHAND GmbH
Prinz-Eugen-Strasse 16, 1040 VIENNA
Total Offices: 2

Belgium
PIRENNE & CO
Marcel Grünerstraat 13, 1080 BRUSSELS
Total Offices: 1

Channel Islands
ALEX PICOT & CO
Paragon House, 95-97 Halkett Place, ST HELIER, Jersey JE1 1BX
Total Offices: 1

Cyprus
L. DEMETRIOU
4-6 Romanos Street, Office 103, NICOSIA
Total Offices: 1

▷

Denmark
INTEG-GROUP
Solvang 20, 3450 ALLERØD, Copenhagen
Total Offices: 12

France
FCC AUDIT ET CONSEIL
8 boulevard Berthier, 75838 PARIS
Total Offices: 4

Germany
DR. DORNBACH & PARTNER
Markenbildchenweg 20, 5400 KOBLENZ
Total Offices: 3

Republic of Ireland
MERRY, MULLEN & CO
6 Gardiner Place, DUBLIN 1
Total Offices: 1

The Netherlands
LUITEN BRAET
Meent 24, 4141 AC LEERDAM
Total Offices: 4

Spain
ESPAUDIT - GABINETE DE AUDITORIA SA
Serrano 78, piso 6 dcha, 28006 MADRID
Total Offices: 4

Sweden
PREVISOR REVISIONSBURÅ AB
Karlbergsvägen 16, 113 27 STOCKHOLM
Total Offices: 2

United Kingdom
NASH BROAD WESSON
42 Upper Berkeley Street, LONDON W1H 8AB
Total Offices: 16

HISTORY & STRUCTURE

GMN Europe is one of the regional groups of GMN International which was founded in 1977. The member firms, though quite independent of each other, maintain close working links in an endeavour to provide professional advice and services for their respective corporate and private clients on an immediate and personal basis. The European group meets twice a year. The other groups are called the North American and the Pacific Groups. The essence of GMN is not to become one of the 'Big 6' or an international accounting firm but to be a strong, independent, regional group of firms able to service all of its clients' needs.

Grant Thornton International

International Office
Grant Thornton House, Melton Street, Euston Square, LONDON NW1 2EP, United Kingdom
Tel: + *44* (71) 383 5100
Fax: + *44* (71) 383 4334

European partners:	559
Professional staff:	3,911
Non-professional staff:	1,406
Total staff:	**5,876**

EUROPEAN FEE INCOME

Year End: 30.06.91	**US$**
Total:	**343,000,000**

MEMBER FIRMS

European firms:	156
Number of Countries:	21

PRINCIPAL NATIONAL OFFICES

Austria
JONASCH & PLATZER
Henckellgasse 19, 1140 VIENNA
Total Offices: 1

Belgium
VAN POYER & CO
Avenue Roger Vandendriessche 41, 1150 BRUSSELS
Total Offices: 3

Cyprus
COSTOURIS, MICHAELIDES & CO
"Cosmo" Building, Corner, Grivas Dighenis & Dem Severis Av., NICOSIA
Total Offices: 2

Denmark
GROTHEN & PERREGAARD A/S
Stockholmsgade 45, 2100 COPENHAGEN 0
Total Offices: 1

Finland
TILINTARKASTUSTOIMISTO YRJO TUOKKO KY
Lautturinkuja 2, 00570 HELSINKI
Total Offices: 7

France
EXCO FRANCE
6 square de l'Opera Louis-Jouvet, 75009 PARIS
Total Offices: 23

Germany
GRANT THORNTON GmbH
Kastanienallee 9/11, 2900 OLDENBURG
Total Offices: 9

Gibraltar
CLINTONS
Units 2 & 3 (2nd floor), Gibraltar Heights, 215 Main Street, GIBRALTAR
Total Offices: 1

Greece
COSTOURIS, MICHAELIDES & CO
64 Kifisias Avenue, 2nd Floor, 151 25 MAROUSI, Athens
Total Offices: 1

Republic of Ireland
GRANT THORNTON
Kinnear Court, Cumberland Street South, DUBLIN 2
Total Offices: 2

▷

Italy
ITALAUDIT SPA
Via Durini 18, 20122 MILAN
Total Offices: 6

Liechtenstein
ERNST NIGG
Lettstrasse 10, 9490 VADUZ
Total Offices: 1

Luxembourg
REVISION ET CONSEILS ASSOCIÉS
33 bld Grand Duchesse Charlotte,
1331 LUXEMBOURG
FIDUCIAIRE RUTLEDGE & WILSON SA
7 rue Pierre d'Aspelt, 1142 LUXEMBOURG
Total Offices: 2

Malta
BONELLO, GAUCI & MICALLEF
Grant Thornton House, Princess Elizabeth Street,
TA'XBIEX
Total Offices: 1

The Netherlands
ARENTHALS CHAUDRON
Buitenveldertselaan 158, 1081 AB AMSTERDAM
Total Offices: 9

Norway
GRANT THORNTON NORGE A/S
Wesselsgate 8, 0165 OSLO
Total Offices: 1

Portugal
GRANT THORNTON & KENNARD LDA
Avenue Miguel Bombarda 21, 3º esq, 1000 LISBON
Total Offices: 1

Spain
UNIAUDIT SA
Edificio Barcino, Tuset 20-24, 08006 BARCELONA
Total Offices: 10

Sweden
LINDEBERGS REVISIONSBYRÅ AB
Sveavägen 34, Box 3061, 103 61 STOCKHOLM
Total Offices: 18

Switzerland
GRANT THORNTON SA
26 Rue de la Corraterie, Case postale 45,
1211 GENEVA 11
Total Offices: 10

United Kingdom
GRANT THORNTON
Grant Thornton House, Melton Street, Euston Square, LONDON NW1 2EP
Total Offices: 52

HISTORY & STRUCTURE

The European network is part of Grant Thornton International, a worldwide federation of national accounting firms employing over 17,000 people in more than 500 offices with a combined turnover exceeding $1 billion. Grant Thornton International, which was founded in 1980, is particularly dedicated to helping growth orientated owner-managed businesses expand their international operations successfully. The philosophy of the group is that wherever a company operates, the best advice can only be provided by professionals who are part of the local business community. The member firms share a commitment to provide a coordinated service of the highest quality to their clients. The firms work together to keep up-to-date with the latest developments in their fields. This involves continuing joint development of methodology and related software so as to ensure that the resources throughout the group are available to any client.

Growth & Progress Challenge

European Executive Office
53 avenue des Perdrix, 94201 LA VARENNE, St Hilaire
Tel: +33 (1) 48 85 86 89
Fax: +33 (1) 48 85 89 30

International Contact: Constantin Rapti

MEMBER FIRMS
European firms: 11
Number of Countries: 6

PRINCIPAL NATIONAL OFFICES

Belgium
BERNARD ET CIE ACC
Parc de la Cense Rouge, Rue du Bois Saint-Jean 20, 4102 OUGREE
JEAN CLAUDE HARDY
Betgne 9, 4052 SPRIMONT DOLEMBREUX
Total Offices: 2

France
FRANCE EXPERTISE ASSOCIÉS (F.E.A.)
122 boulevard Malesherbes, 75017 PARIS
PROGESTION
122 boulevard Malesherbes, 75017 PARIS
CONSTANTIN RAPTI
53 avenue des Perdrix, 94210 LA VARENNE, Saint Hilaire
Total Offices: 3

Germany
HEINZELMANN & PARTNERS
Babenhäuserstrasse 31, 6057 DIETZENBACH, Frankfurt
HANS LUDWIG SCHMITZ
Tivolistrasse 46, 5160 DUREN
RODERICH CORNELIUS SIEGERT
Dingolfinger Strasse 2, 8000 MUNICH 80
Total Offices: 4

▷

Italy
STUDIO RENATO CINELLI
Via Colona 12, 33170 PORDENONE
Total Offices: 1

Spain
ELISARDO SANCHEZ Y ASESORES ASOCIADOS SA
Alameda de Colono 28, 29001 MALAGA
Total Offices: 1

United Kingdom
BREBNER, ALLEN & TRAPP
The Quadrangle, 180 Wardour Street,
LONDON W1V 3AA
Total Offices: 1

HLB

HLB International

European Executive Office
Spectrum House, 20/26 Cursitor Street, LONDON
EC4A 1HY, United Kingdom
Tel: *+44* (71) 405 2088
Fax: *+44* (71) 405 5548

International Contact: Peter J. Frost

EUROPEAN PERSONNEL
Chairman: Peter J. Frost
Administrator: Carolina Carmona
Marketing Co-ordinator: Sandra Dalmeijer

European partners:	395
Professional staff:	2,180
Non-professional staff:	742
Total staff:	**3,317**

EUROPEAN FEE INCOME

Year End: 30.09.91	**US$**
Total:	**217,872,000**

MEMBER FIRMS

European firms:	129
Number of Countries:	16

PRINCIPAL NATIONAL OFFICES

Austria
INTERCONTROL GmbH
Bergasse 16, 1090 VIENNA
Total Offices: 1

Belgium
PEETERS, DEJAEGHERE, DUPONT & PARTNERS
Sint Jansvliet 2, 2000 ANTWERP
Total Offices: 4

Channel Islands
JACKSON FOX
Union House, Union Street, ST HELIER,
Jersey JE4 8TZ
Total Offices: 1

Cyprus
KYPRIANIDES & STYLIANOU
6 Ayas Elenis Street, Saint Helen Tower, 2nd Floor,
No. 21, NICOSIA
Total Offices: 1

Denmark
MORTENSEN & BEIERHOLM
Vester Søgade 10, 1601 COPENHAGEN V
Total Offices: 9

France
GROUPE FRANCE AUDIT
138 boulevard Haussmann, 75008 PARIS
Total Offices: 39

Germany
HLB TREUHAND GmbH
Hofkamp 24, 5600 WUPPERTAL 1
Total Offices: 14

Greece
ELEKTIKI-LOGISTIKI-FOROTECHNIKI LTD
19 Akadimias Street, 106 71 ATHENS
Total Offices: 1

Republic of Ireland
DUIGNAN & CO/KIDSONS IMPEY
84 Northumberland Road, Ballsbridge, DUBLIN 4
Total Offices: 1

Italy
HODGSON LANDAU BRANDS SAS
Piazza Velasca 5, 20122 MILAN
Total Offices: 5

Malta
FALZON & FALZON
Casa Floriana, Pietro Floriani Street, FLORIANA
Total Offices: 2

The Netherlands
HLB NEDERLAND ACCOUNTANTS &
CONSULTANTS
Cronenburg 73, 1081 GM AMSTERDAM
Total Offices: 13

Norway
REVICO SANDVIKA A/S
Hamangskogen 60, 1300 SANDVIKA
Total Offices: 6

Spain
BOVE MONTERO Y CIA
Mariano Cubi 7 & 9, atico 2ª, 08006 BARCELONA
Total Offices: 2

Switzerland
FIREL & MANDACO SA
9 rue Charles-Humbert, 1205 GENEVA
OSTSCHWEIZERISCHE
TREUHANDGESELLSCHAFT AG
Selnaustrasse 15, 8002 ZURICH
Total Offices: 6

▷

United Kingdom
KIDSONS IMPEY
Spectrum House, 20/26 Cursitor Street,
LONDON EC4A 1HY
Total Offices: 42

HISTORY & STRUCTURE
HLB International is a worldwide organisation of professional accounting firms, each providing clients with a comprehensive and personal service relating to auditing, taxation, accounting and general financial and management advice. Formed in 1969, it has member firms in 56 countries and correspondents in a further 16. Its annual fee income from members is in excess of US$370 million, generated by 6,400 partners and staff in more than 240 offices worldwide. HLB members are well established practices of high local stnding, capable of handling international assignments in all the main business centres and experienced in co-ordinating activities between countries.

Horwath International

European Executive Office
8 Baker Street, LONDON W1M 1DA, United Kingdom
Tel: +44 (71) 486 5888
Fax: +44 (71) 487 3686

International Contact: Phillip Sober

EUROPEAN PERSONNEL
Chairman: Paul A. Hipps

European partners:	403
Professional staff:	2,779
Non-professional staff:	743
Total staff:	**3,925**

EUROPEAN FEE INCOME

Year End: 31.12.90	**US$**	%
Accountancy & Audit:	192,000,000	69.0
Insolvency:	9,442,000	3.0
Consultancy:	48,883,000	18.0
Tax:	27,815,000	10.0
Total:	**278,140,000**	

MEMBER FIRMS

European firms:	127
Number of Countries:	20

PRINCIPAL NATIONAL OFFICES

Andorra
HORWATH ANDORRA SA
Bonaventura Armengol 15, 5º 3º, ANDORRA LA VELLA
Total Offices: 1

Austria
IB INTERFIDES
Grungasse 16, 1052 VIENNA
Total Offices: 1

Belgium
C.V. BLANCKAERT, MISSORTEN, SPAENHOVEN & CO - S.C.
Meiseselaan 71, 1020 BRUSSELS
Total Offices: 2

Channel Islands
FEATHERSTONE TOOLE & CO
16 Dumaresq Street, ST HELIER, Jersey
Total Offices: 1

Cyprus
P. KALOPETRIDES & CO
2 Christ Sozos Street, Eiffel Tower, 3rd & 6th Floors, NICOSIA
Total Offices: 4

Denmark
ASKGAARD OLESEN HORWATH
Stoltenbergsgade 9, 1576 COPENHAGEN K
Total Offices: 4

Finland
JÄGERHORN, LINDBERG, ALMQVIST OY AB
Mannerheimvägen 76b, 00250 HELSINKI
Total Offices: 2

France
CCAS/HORWATH FRANCE
12 rue de Madrid, 75008 PARIS
Total Offices: 5

Germany
HHG HORWATH & HORWATH GmbH
Alexanderstrasse 12, 7000 STUTTGART 10
Total Offices: 7

Greece
ALEXANDER, YOUNG & CO
5-7 Filellinon Street, 185 36 PIRAEUS
Total Offices: 1

Iceland
LÖGGILTIR ENDURSKODENDUR HF
Suóurlandsbraut 32, 108 REYKJAVIK
Total Offices: 1

Republic of Ireland
SIMPSON XAVIER
20 Merchants Quay, DUBLIN 8
Total Offices: 2

Italy
HORWATH & HORWATH ITALIA SAS
Via Calabrian 7, 00187 ROME
Total Offices: 5

The Netherlands
WALGEMOED GROEP
Weerdestein 117, 1083 GH AMSTERDAM
Total Offices: 20

Norway
REVISOR-KONTORET A/S
Sandakervn 35b, Torshov, 0402 OSLO 4
Total Offices: 1

▷

Portugal
HORWATH CONSULTING (TURISMO) LDA
Rua Joao da Silva, Lote 33, 1900 LISBON
Total Offices: 1

Spain
GASSO Y CIA AUDITORES
Ronda General Mitre 126, 6º 2º, 08021 BARCELONA
Total Offices: 10

Sweden
TÖNNERVIK HORWATH AB
Tingsgatan 9, 372 37 RONNEBY
Total Offices: 26

Switzerland
CURATOR & HORWATH
Freigutstrasse 27, 8039 ZURICH
Total Offices: 6

United Kingdom
STOY HAYWARD
8 Baker Street, LONDON W1M 1DA
Total Offices: 11

HISTORY & STRUCTURE

Horwath International (HI) is an international network of independent accounting and management consulting firms. More than 70 partner and correspondent firms with over 270 offices throughout the world serve their clients internationally with HI's coordination and support. Each member firm is well established as a leader in the national business community and is staffed by nationals, guaranteeing a knowledge of local laws and customs which is important to clients undertaking new ventures or expanding into other countries. Quality professional services (accounting, auditing, tax and consulting) are basic to HI member firms' global operations. While each member firm assumes full and exclusive responsibility for its professional services, common operating standards for international work have been developed and are monitored continuously through a system of quality controls. Activities and engagements are coordinated in Headquarters in New York, under direction of the Chief Executive Officer Werner E. Rotach. Regional directors are responsible for coordinating activities in Europe, Asia, North and Latin America.

IAG International

International Office
Boulevard Auguste Reyers 103, 1040 BRUSSELS, Belgium
Tel: +32 (2) 73 69 05 7
Fax: +32 (2) 73 36 21 3
International Contact: Tom Hens

EUROPEAN PERSONNEL
Chairman: Hans Hoegen Dijkhof
Vice-Chairman: Hans-Rudolf Staiger
Secretary: Robert Rakison

MEMBER FIRMS
European firms: 14
Number of Countries: 7

PRINCIPAL NATIONAL OFFICES

France
CONSEIL & EXPERTISE
21/23 boulevard Richard-Lenoir, 75011 PARIS
Total Offices: 3

Germany
BUSE, KOCH, GORSLER, NESSELHAUF, MOERCHEN
Abteistrasse 57, 2000 HAMBURG 13
MEYER-SIEVERS, OPITZ, KILIAN
Petersweg 1a, 2100 HAMBURG 90
Total Offices: 3

Monaco
CORPORATE DATA SERVICES
18 boulevard des Moulins, 98000 MONACO
Total Offices: 1

The Netherlands
HAAGSE ACCOUNTANTS GROEP
Lange Voorhout 14, 2514 ED 's-GRAVENHAGE
HOEGEN DIJKHOF & VAN BRAKEL
Wilhelminapark 24, 3581 NE UTRECHT
Total Offices: 3

Spain
BLACKSTONE FRANKS plc
Daoiz y Velarde 6, Edificio Beneco 2a y 3a, Apartado de Correos 159, 29640 FUENGIROLA (Malaga)
Total Offices: 1

United Kingdom
BILLIMORIA, BRACE, HAMBLIN, WILLIAMS
7th Floor, Queens House, 2 Holly Road, TWICKENHAM, Middlesex TW1 4EG
BLACKSTONE FRANKS
Barbican House, 26-34 Old Street, LONDON EC1V 9HL
Total Offices: 3

HISTORY & STRUCTURE

Integrated Advisory Group (IAG) International is a pan-European multidisciplinary group of professional and independent lawyers, tax lawyers and accountants with offices throughout Europe. As well as providing responsive high quality advice to other member firms and their clients throughout Europe, its members aim at as much integration as possible with a view to providing a truly transnational service in cross border transactions. IAG International was formed in 1989 by 16 well-known and established European firms of lawyers, tax advisers and accountants. As at 22 April 1991, the Group had 38 members, with offices in 46 cities throughout Western and Eastern Europe. ▷

Independent Accountants International

European Executive Office
1 Park Place, Canary Wharf, LONDON E14 4HJ, United Kingdom
Tel: *+44* (71) 987 5030
Fax: *+44* (71) 987 9707

International Contact: Ian Frazer

EUROPEAN PERSONNEL
Executive Director: Arthur Goessel

EUROPEAN FEE INCOME

Year End: 1990	**US$**	**%**
Accountancy & Audit:	35,300,000	59.0
Consultancy:	9,000,000	15.0
Tax:	15,570,000	26.0
Total:	**59,870,000**	

MEMBER FIRMS

European firms:	30
Number of Countries:	15

PRINCIPAL NATIONAL OFFICES

Austria
INTEREXPERT-TREUHAND GmbH & CO OHG
Gierstergasse 6, 1120 VIENNA
Total Offices: 1

Belgium
DOMS ELPERS & CO
Rue de Pacale 33, 1040 BRUSSELS
Total Offices: 1

Cyprus
P.G. ECONOMIDES & CO
Doma Building, 227 Archbishop Makarios III Avenue, LIMASSOL
Total Offices: 1

Denmark
REVISIONSFIRMÆT BAYER
Stengade 48, 3000 HELSINGØR
REVISIONSFIRMÆT CARL JOHAN NIELSEN A/S
Herslebsgade 1, 7100 VEJLE
Total Offices: 3

France
AUDITEC AQUITAINE
Z.I. de Chanteloiseau, 33140 VILLENAVE D'ORNON
SECFI
23 rue d'Anjou, 75008 PARIS
Total Offices: 3

Germany
DR. HANS-UWE EHLERS
Brahmsallee 18, 2000 HAMBURG 13
DRS. R. MATZENBACH & W. THIER
Corneliusstrasse 4, 6000 FRANKFURT 1
DIPL-KFM GERHARD SLAMAL
Franz-Vaahsen-Weg 5a, 4000 DUSSELDORF 31
Total Offices: 3

Greece
KYPRIS AND COMPANY
293 Kifissia Avenue, Kifissia, 145 61 ATHENS
Total Offices: 1

Iceland
HAGSKIL H.F.
Furugerdi 5, 108 REYKJAVIK
Total Offices: 3

Republic of Ireland
CAPLIN MEHAN
Adelaide House, 19/20 Adelaide Road, DUBLIN 2
Total Offices: 1

Italy
GIANCARLO PAGLIARINI SOCI SAS
Via G.B. Morgagni 11, 20129 MILAN
Total Offices: 2

The Netherlands
BLÖMER & CO
Krÿtwal 1-3, 3430 AA NIEUWEGEIN
Total Offices: 1

Portugal
EUGÉNIO BRANCO - GESTAO E SERVIÇOS SA
Praça Francisco Sâ Carneiro 293, 1º, 4200 PORTO
Total Offices: 2

Spain
IVC AUDITORES SA
Felix Boix 14, entreplanta dcha, 28036 MADRID
Total Offices: 3

Switzerland
TREUREVA AG
Stampfenbachstrasse 153, 8035 ZURICH 6
Total Offices: 3

United Kingdom
ARMSTRONG WATSON & CO
15 Victoria Place, CARLISLE CA1 1EW
DOWNHAM TRAIN EPSTEIN
The Hollins, Hollins Lane, Unsworth, BURY, Lancashire BL9 8AT
LITTLEJOHN FRAZER
1 Park Place, Canary Wharf, LONDON E14 4HJ
WEEKS GREEN
College Keep, 4-12 Terminus Terrace, SOUTHAMPTON SO1 1XJ
Total Offices: 20

HISTORY & STRUCTURE

Independent Accountants International (IA) was founded in 1978. It currently has just over 100 member firms worldwide and situated in most major cities. It is divided into four regions, North American, Europe and Africa, Asia Pacific and Latin America. There are offices in all European Community countries and more recently representative offices have been opened in Budapest and Prague. All IA members have to meet pre-determined standards and are inspected before acceptance for membership. They are then subject to a peer review every 3-5 ▷

European Accountancy Groups

years. They are all full service firms offering a personal service to all corporate and private clients.

INPACT - International Network of Professional Accountants

International Office
14 Southampton Place, LONDON WC1A 2AJ, United Kingdom
Tel: + *44* (71) 430 1111
Fax: + *44* (71) 831 0439

International Contact: Simon Noakes

EUROPEAN PERSONNEL
Chairman: Jos Cappelle
Director (England): Simon Noakes
Director (Ireland): Pearse Farrell
Director (France): Laurent Ginet
Director (Germany): Michael Tille
Director (Denmark): Lau Lauritsen
Director (Italy): Giuseppe Verna
Director (Belgium): Jos Cappelle
International Co-Ordinator: Sally-Ann Whittaker

European partners:	200
Professional staff:	1,600
Total staff:	**1,800**

EUROPEAN FEE INCOME

Year End: 31.12.90	**£**
Total:	**44,563,600**

MEMBER FIRMS

European firms:	64
Number of Countries:	21

PRINCIPAL NATIONAL OFFICES

Austria
DR WERNER FRITSCH
Goldschmiedgasse 10, 1010 VIENNA
DKFM HERBERT F. MAIER
Walfishchgasse 5/8, 1015 VIENNA
Total Offices: 2

Belgium
BUREAU FIDUCIAIRE LERMINIAUX ET CIE SA
84 Rue Renkin, 1030 BRUSSELS
PEETERS V., VINCKE, MELS & CO
Avenue des Croix de Guerre, 1120 BRUSSELS
Total Offices: 3

Channel Islands
GRAEME LE ROSSIGNOL & CO
6 Hilgrove Street, ST HELIER, Jersey
Total Offices: 1

Cyprus
EMILIOS KALLENOS
Demitas Tower, 14 Michalakopoulou, NICOSIA
Total Offices: 1

Denmark
REVISIONSFIRMÆT S.A. CHRISTENSEN & W. KJÆRULFF I/S
St Kongensgade 68, P.O. Box 9015, 1022 COPENHAGEN
P'F GRANNSKODARAVIRKID JOGVAN SUNDSTEIN
R.C. Effersøsgøta 26, P.O. Box 191, 110 TORSHAVN
Total Offices: 2

Finland
TILINTARKASTUSRENGAS OY
Paasivuorenkatu 2 C, 00530 HELSINKI
Total Offices: 1

France
AUDIT DE FRANCE - SODIP
12 cours Louis Lumière, 25 bis, avenue du Petit-Parc, 94306 VINCENNES CEDEX
Total Offices: 3

Germany
UWP UNITREU GmbH
Arndtstrasse 39, 6000 FRANKFURT/MAIN
Total Offices: 5

Gibraltar
BROWNE CRAINE & CO
Don House, 37 Line Wall Road, GIBRALTAR
Total Offices: 1

Isle of Man
BROWNE CRAINE & CO
Burleigh Manor, Peel Road, DOUGLAS
Total Offices: 1

Republic of Ireland
FARRELL, GRANT, SPARKS & CO
Molyneux House, 67/69 Bride Street, DUBLIN 8
Total Offices: 1

Italy
STUDIO ASSOCIATO DI CONSULENZA BERNELLI MASSOLO E SCHIESARI
Via C. Colombo 1, 10128 TURIN
STUDIO COMMERCIALISTA CORTELLAZZO & SOATTO
Via Porciglia 14, PADUA
COSTAGUTA & SALMONI
Via C.R. Ceccardi 4/42, 16121 GENOA
STUDIO FIRMA
Via Palladio 29/a, 37136 VERONA
STUDIO GIANNONE PROFESSIONISTI E ASSOCIATI
Corso Garibaldi 148, 84100 SALERNO
STUDIO GAETANO NAPOLITANO
Via delle Coppelle 35, 00186 ROME
STUDIO PROTO
Via Regina Margherita 28, 88074 CROTONE
STUDIO SEMERIA DOTTORI ANTONIO
Via Gioberti 29, 18038 SAN REMO ▷

STUDIO VERNA
Via Cesare Battisti 21, 20122 MILAN
Total Offices: 9

Luxembourg
FIDUCIAIRE ALBERT HUBERTY
49 boulevard Royal, 2449 LUXEMBOURG
Total Offices: 1

Monaco
FRANÇOIS JEAN BRYCH
2 avenue Saint Charles, 98000 MONTE CARLO
Total Offices: 1

The Netherlands
VAN DEN REEK & ASSOCIATES
President Rooseveltlaan 4a, 5707 GD HELMOND
Total Offices: 1

Norway
REVISJONSFIRMAET KETIL ELLEFSEN
Tollbugt. 21, Postboks 2063, 3003 DRAMMEN, Oslo
Total Offices: 1

Portugal
A.M. CALADO CORTES
Third Floor, Rua de Crucifixo 28, 1100 LISBON
Total Offices: 1

Spain
A.E.A. AUDITORES DE EMPRESAS ASOCIADOS SA
Alfonso XII 18, 20, 28014 MADRID
ALCAIN Y RIBA AUDITORES SA
Plaza Francesc Macia 3, 2-1, 08021 BARCELONA
AUDITORIA Y CONSULTA SA
Paeso de las Delicias 3, 4º izqda, 41001 SEVILLE
Total Offices: 3

Sweden
EKONOMIGRUPPEN AB
Hälsingegatan 47, 100 31 STOCKHOLM
Total Offices: 1

Switzerland
CAMINADA TREUHAND AG ZUG
Baarerstrasse 112, 6300 ZUG
CAMINADA TREUHAND AG ZURICH
Zollikerstrasse 27, 8032 ZURICH
Total Offices: 2

United Kingdom
BARRON & BARRON
Bathurst House, 86 Micklegate, YORK YO1 2HN
BEAVIS WALKER
14 Southampton Place, LONDON WC1A 2AJ
CAVELLS
Bridge House, 7-9 Church Road, Lawrence Hill, BRISTOL BS5 9JJ
CHADWICK & CO
Bridgewater House, 60 Whitworth Street, MANCHESTER M1 6LX
CONDIE & CO
11 Alva Street, EDINBURGH EH2 4PH
FRANCIS CLARK
23 Devon Square, NEWTON ABBOT, Devon TQ12 2HU
J.R. HAWORTH & CO
1 Stanley Street, ACCRINGTON, Lancashire BB5 6PD
HAYLES & PARTNERS
39 Castle Street, LEICESTER LE1 5WN
KANAS & PARTNERS
Bridgewater House, 60 Whitworth Street, MANCHESTER M1 6LX
McCRACKENS
Hanover House, 117-119 Cleethorpe Road, GRIMSBY, South Humberside DN31 3ET
MOFFAT & CO
5 Clarendon Place, LEAMINGTON SPA, Warwickshire CV32 5QL
MOORE FLETCHER & CO
26 Paradise Square, SHEFFIELD S1 1TU
HENRY MURRAY & CO
23 Church Place, LURGAN, Co Armagh
THOBURN & CHAPMAN
Milburn House, Dean Street, NEWCASTLE-UPON-TYNE NE1 1NR
Total Offices: 23

HISTORY & STRUCTURE

INPACT, the International Network of Professional Accountants, is a European association of 60 independent accountancy firms. In the two years since its inauguration, INPACT has developed as a significant force providing clients with the strength of a major network of like-minded small and medium-sized accountancy firms. By providing a sophisticated range of quality services, the INPACT network can help the smaller enterprise secure a niche in an increasingly global marketplace. United by the same professional philosophy based on personal contact and quality, clients can be confident that they will receive a service of the highest expertise, whenever and wherever they are referred to an INPACT member.

International Association of Practising Accountants (IAPA)

International Office
7th Floor, Victoria House, Victoria Road, ALDERSHOT, Hampshire GU11 1JJ, United Kingdom
Tel: +44 (252) 27666
Fax: +44 (252) 310890

International Contact: David A. Turnbull

MEMBER FIRMS

European firms:	18
Number of Countries:	6

▷

European Accountancy Groups

PRINCIPAL NATIONAL OFFICES

Austria
OMIKRON
Markgraf, Rudigerstrasse 8, 1150 VIENNA
Total Offices: 1

Belgium
ACCOUNTANTSKANTOOR DIRK VERMEIREN & CO NV
Dascottelei 120, 2100 DEURNE (Antwerp)
Total Offices: 1

The Netherlands
EBBEN SLAATS DE JONGE
Bovendonk 9, 4707 ZH ROOSENDAAL
Total Offices: 2

Spain
AUDIT NETWORK SA
Paseo San Juan 140, pral 1ª, 08037 BARCELONA
Total Offices: 12

United Kingdom
THE UK 200 GROUP OF PRACTISING CHARTERED ACCOUNTANTS
7th Floor, Victoria House, Victoria Road, ALDERSHOT, Hampshire GU11 1JJ
Total Offices: 1

HISTORY & STRUCTURE

The UK 200 Group of Practising Accountants is a group of independent firms of chartered accountants, practising in approximately 200 towns and cities throughout the UK. Members provide a personal service of high standards for all its clients. By combining resources and with readily available expert consultants who are employed by the Group, member firms provide the specialist services normally associated with the largest firms of accountants. Working links have been recently established with professional contacts in Europe, America and other major business areas worldwide.

The International Group of Accounting Firms Ltd (IGAF)

European Executive Office
102 Friar Gate, DERBY DE1 1FH, United Kingdom
Tel: +44 (332) 200772
Fax: +44 (332) 295600

International Contact: Jens Christian Aarup

EUROPEAN FEE INCOME

Year End: 31.12.90	**US$**
Total:	**150,000,000**

MEMBER FIRMS

European firms:	50
Number of Countries:	12

PRINCIPAL NATIONAL OFFICES

Austria
TREUHAND UNION
Breyerstrasse 9, 2500 BADEN
Total Offices: 1

Channel Islands
WOOLFORD & CO
Dixcart House, Sir William Place, ST PETER PORT, Guernsey
Total Offices: 1

Denmark
PARTNER REVISION STATSAUTORISEREDE REVISORER A/S
Industrivej Nord 15, Birk, 7400 HERNING
REVISIONSFIRMÆT P.J. ÅRUP
Norre Farimagsgade 15, 1364 COPENHAGEN K
Total Offices: 3

France
ALPHA AUDIT
51 rue Blanche, 75009 PARIS
AUDIT FRANCE ASSOCIÉS
Residence "Le Grand Pavois", boulevard de Lattre de Tassigny 2, B.P. 100, 03204 VICHY CEDEX
COGEP
route D'Orleans, 18230 ST DOULCHARD
GROUPE ECAF
333 boulevard Président-Wilson, 33200 BORDEAUX-CAUDERAN
SOREGOR
18 rue Bouche-Thomas, B.P. 244, 49002 ANGERS CEDEX
SOVEC
Le Concorde, 48 boulevard Georges-Pompidou, 00500 GAP, Hautes Alpes
Total Offices: 10

Germany
BAYERN-REVISION GmbH
Agnes-Bernauer-Strasse 90, Postfach 21 05 29, 8000 MUNICH 21
FRANZ X. KIRSCHNER E-CONSULTING GmbH
Schlosspark Gern, 8330 EGGENFELDEN
Total Offices: 4

Republic of Ireland
JOY McNABOLA MURRAY
17 Earlsfort Terrace, DUBLIN 2
Total Offices: 1

Italy
GUISEPPE BROGI
Via Landino 5, FLORENCE
STUDIO CHLODI
Via B. Bosco 57-9, 16121 GENOA
PROF. GIROLAMO DELL'OLIO & ASSOCIATI
Argiro 29, 70122 BARI
STUDIO PASCUCCI
Via F. Caracciolois, 80122 NAPLES
Total Offices: 5

▷

The Netherlands
CROP, DE KLEUVER & CO
Johan van Oldenbarneveltlaan 34, 3818 HB
AMERSFOORT
Total Offices: 6

Norway
ELIASSEN & ALMVANG ANS
Tollbugaten 28, 0157 OSLO
Total Offices: 1

Sweden
GOTEBORGS FORETAGS REVISION AB
Prinsgatan 12, 413 05 GOTHENBURG
LANDINS REVISIONSBYRÅ AB
Box 1236, 171 24 SOLNA
Total Offices: 2

Switzerland
ROBERTO BASSI & PARTNERS
Piazza Monte Ceneri 13, 6901 LUGANO
INTERCONSULTA, ACCOUNTANTS AND TRUSTEES
Nordstrasse 190, Postfach 801, 8037 ZURICH
Total Offices: 3

United Kingdom
COOPER-PARRY, WATSON, SOWTER & CO
102 Friar Gate, DERBY DE1 1FH
JEFFREY CRAWFORD & CO
25 Castle Terrace, EDINBURGH EH1 2ER
CREASEYS
12 Lonsdale Gardens, TUNBRIDGE WELLS, Kent TN1 1PA
GRUBER LEVINSON FRANKS
Peter House, Oxford Street, MANCHESTER M1 5AB
LEVY GEE
100 Chalk Farm Road, LONDON NW1 8EH
NICHOLS FULFORD & CO
7 Donegal Square East, BELFAST BT1 5HD
THOMAS, WESTCOTT & GILLARD
42 New Street, HONITON, Devon EX14 8BU
WILSON KINNAIR
Hutton House, Sandyford Road, NEWCASTLE-UPON-TYNE NE2 1QU
WOOLFORD & COMPANY
Suite 22, Bridge House, Bridge Street, WALTON-ON-THAMES, Surrey KT12 1AL
Total Offices: 13

HISTORY & STRUCTURE

The International Group of Accounting Firms Ltd. (IGAF) is approximately the 17th largest worldwide grouping of accounting firms with 89 members in 35 countries worldwide. IGAF has over 3,500 personnel generating over US$ 280,000,000 in annual revenue from serving over 70,000 clients. IGAF was founded by 10 US and Canadian firms in 1977 to provide a multi-national capability for local and regional firms and is now one of the largest associations of independent firms in the world.

InterContinental Consultants (ICC)

Administrative Office
67 Carleton Road, LONDON N7 0ET,
United Kingdom
Tel: + *44* (71) 607 4924
Fax: + *44* (71) 700 0213

International Contact: Deirdre Jones

EUROPEAN PERSONNEL
President: Rex W.N. Barrett
Director: Keith A. Wilson
Director: Andrew S. Roy

MEMBER FIRMS

European firms:	46
Number of Countries:	12

PRINCIPAL NATIONAL OFFICES

Channel Islands
CHANNEL TRUST LIMITED
Albert House, South Esplanade, ST PETER PORT, Guernsey
Total Offices: 1

Denmark
REVIONSFIRMÆT PREBEN RASMUSSEN AS
Thorsgade 59, 3, 2200 COPENHAGEN
Total Offices: 1

France
GROUPE FIDETA
61 avenue Kléber, 75116 PARIS
Total Offices: 25

Germany
DR. KARL WALTER BACH
Maximilianstrasse 20, 8000 MUNICH 22
TREUPLAN GmbH
Gleueler Strasse 303-313, 5000 COLOGNE 41 (Deckstein)
DR. VONDERRECK UND SCHULTE
Marktstrasse 61-63, 4200 OBERHAUSEN 1
Total Offices: 3

Gibraltar
CHALBRIDGE MANAGEMENT LTD
Suite G, Second Floor, Eurolife Building, 1 Corral Road, GIBRALTAR
Total Offices: 1

Isle of Man
BENNETT ROY & CO
Viking House, Nelson Street, DOUGLAS
Total Offices: 2

Republic of Ireland
FITZGERALD & ASSOCIATES
11 Anglesea Street, DUBLIN 2
Total Offices: 2

Italy
STUDIO PICCINELLI
Via Pontida 3, 25121 BRESCIA

European Accountancy Groups

DI LUIGI STAFFICO & CO

Corso Venezia 16, 20121 MILAN

Total Offices: 2

The Netherlands

VAN DER HOEK EN LENGTON BV

Singel 197, 3311 KR DORDRECHT

Total Offices: 2

Spain

INTERSER-INTERMEDIACION Y SERVICIOS INTERNACIONALES SA

Gurtubay 6, 28001 MADRID

Total Offices: 3

Switzerland

ANSBACHER (SWITZERLAND) LTD

Mühlebachstrasse 32, 8032 ZURICH

COMINS SARL

7 Avenue Pictet de Rochemont, 1207 GENEVA

Total Offices: 2

United Kingdom

COMINS & CO

22 St Andrew Street, LONDON EC4A 3AN

FREEDA, MILSTON, CEDAR, BAKER

Hathaway House, Popes Drive, Finchley, LONDON N3 1QF

Total Offices: 3

HISTORY & STRUCTURE

InterContinental Consultants (ICC) was conceived in 1970 by Rex W.N. Barrett who was Senior Partner of Comins & Co from 1971 to 1990. Initiated by an awareness of the establishment of the European Common Market, he felt that international associations of firms were vital in order to provide an approved quality of service to clients. Gradually, the group has developed to have representatives in 26 countries. The Group meets once a year with an annual conference in a different international venue. A parallel Lawyers Group started in 1984. The two groups are run separately but share an annual conference. The Accountant Group is a Limited Company with each member firm of accountants being a shareholder of a nominal 100 shares. The objectives of the network are threefold: to provide an improved service to clients of member firms, to expand knowledge and awareness of firms and business practices in other countries and to afford an opportunity of cross-border trade. It should be noted that ICC Inter-Continental Consultants Accountant Group is a worldwide network and not only a European one.

Jeffreys Henry International

European Executive Office
The Old Vicarage, Glasson Dock, Nr LANCASTER LA2 0BZ
Tel: +*44* (524) 751498
Fax: +*44* (524) 751498

Administrative Office
EUROPEAN BUSINESS CENTRE, Avenue de Tervueren 84-B4, 1040 BRUSSELS
Tel: +*32* (2) 73 57 22 6
Fax: +*32* (2) 73 51 70 5

Administrative Office
EUROPEAN REGISTERED OFFICE, Talstrasse 80, 8021 ZURICH
Tel: +*41* (1) 211 38 33
Fax: +*41* (1) 211 48 82
Mailing address: Case postale 614, 8021 ZURICH

International Contact: Peter Quick

EUROPEAN PERSONNEL
Chairman: Yitz Jaffe

European partners:	226
Professional staff:	856
Total staff:	**1,081**

EUROPEAN FEE INCOME

Year End: 30.09.90	**US$**
Total:	**130,000,000**

MEMBER FIRMS

European firms:	47
Number of Countries:	14

PRINCIPAL NATIONAL OFFICES

Austria
HANS BAUMGARTNER WIRTSCHAFTSTREUHAND GmbH
Leopoldsgasse 6, 1020 VIENNA
Total Offices: 1

Belgium
TOELEN CATS & CO
Avenue de Tervueren 84, 1040 BRUSSELS
Total Offices: 4

Denmark
REVISIONSFIRMAET ERIC NIELSEN & N.H. CHRISTENSEN
Hasseris Bymidte 6, P.O. Box 9, 9100 ÅLBORG
Total Offices: 1

France
RÉVISION ET CONTROLE
88 avenue Niel, 75017 PARIS
Total Offices: 3

Germany
WESTDEUTSCHE REVISIONS + TREUHAND GmbH
Schottweg 3, 2000 HAMBURG 76
Total Offices: 5

▷

Isle of Man
L. THOMPSON & CO
Wellington House, Market Street, DOUGLAS
Total Offices: 1

Republic of Ireland
POWER & HUNTER
48 Fitzwilliam Square, DUBLIN 2
Total Offices: 1

Italy
STUDIO BERNONI
Piazza Filippo Meda 3, 20121 MILAN
STUDIO RAMONDELLI
Via Lucrezio Caro 7A, 00193 ROME
Total Offices: 2

Luxembourg
UNIVERSALIA (FIDUCIAIRE) SA
3b boulevard de Prince Henri, 1724 LUXEMBOURG
Total Offices: 1

The Netherlands
STEENS & PARTNERS
Thomas Mannplaats 311, 3009 GD ROTTERDAM
Total Offices: 1

Spain
CORTES Y CIA
Rosellon 255, 5º, 08008 BARCELONA
Total Offices: 3

Sweden
A & C REVISIONSBYRÅ HB
Holmgatan 4, 211 45 MALMÖ
REVISIONSBYRAN PRÖÖM WESTMANN ÖSTERBERG AG
Fleminggatan 62b, 100 28 STOCKHOLM
Total Offices: 2

Switzerland
VISURA TREUHAND-GESELLSCHAFT
Talstrasse 80, 8021 ZURICH
Total Offices: 19

United Kingdom
BARTON, COTSEN
1st Floor, Dominions House North, Dominions Arcade, CARDIFF CF1 4AR
DOWNHAM & CO
Northern Assurance Buildings, Albert Square, 9-21 Princess Street, MANCHESTER M2 4DN
GERBER, LANDA & GEE
54/56 Berkeley Street, GLASGOW G3 7DS
HAYSOM SILVERTON & PARTNERS
145 Queensway, Bletchley, MILTON KEYNES MK2 2DY
JEFFREYS HENRY
Finsgate, 5/7 Cranwood Street, LONDON EC1V 9EE
Total Offices: 5

HISTORY & STRUCTURE

Jeffreys Henry International (JHI) is an association of independent accountants spread throughout the world. Founded in 1975, JHI has grown steadily and there are currently over fifty members in twenty five countries. It is the aim of JHI to be represented in every major country. Regional Groups have been formed in large geographical areas such as Europe, North America and the Pacific Rim - each with its own administration. This enables members in each region to exchange technical information so vital to international business. The European Region has a Business Centre in Brussels which provides information on EC matters to members.

KPMG

International Office
KPMG Building, Burg. Rijnderslaan 20, 1185 MC AMSTELVEEN, The Netherlands
Tel: *+31* (20) 6566700
Fax: *+31* (20) 6566777
Mailing address: International Office, P.O. Box 74111, 1070 BC AMSTERDAM, The Netherlands

International Contact: Steve Butler

EUROPEAN PERSONNEL
Chairman: Johan Steenmeijer
Administrator: Michael Speer
Marketing: Peter Zimmermann

European partners:	2,506
Professional staff:	24,800
Non-professional staff:	8,214
Total staff:	**35,520**

EUROPEAN FEE INCOME

Year End: 30.09.91	**US$**
Total:	**3,081,000,000**

MEMBER FIRMS

European firms:	337
Number of Countries:	22

PRINCIPAL NATIONAL OFFICES

Austria
KPMG ALPEN-TREUHAND GmbH
Kolingasse 19, 1090 VIENNA
Total Offices: 13

Belgium
KPMG
Neerveldstraat 101-103, 1200 BRUSSELS
Total Offices: 4

Channel Islands
KPMG PEAT MARWICK
10 Lefebvre Street, ST PETER PORT, Guernsey
Total Offices: 2

▷

European Accountancy Groups

Cyprus
KPMG PEAT MARWICK
10 Mnasiadou Street, NICOSIA
Total Offices: 5

Denmark
KPMG C. JESPERSEN
Borups Allé 177, 2000 FREDERIKSBERG, Copenhagen
Total Offices: 17

Finland
KPMG WIDENIUS, SEDERHOLM & SOMERI OY
Mannerheimintie 20 B, 00100 HELSINKI
Total Offices: 15

France
FIDAL
2 bis, rue de Villiers, 92309 LEVALLOIS-PERRET
KPMG FIDUCIAIRE DE FRANCE
2 bis, rue de Villiers, 92309 LEVALLOIS-PERRET
KPMG PEAT MARWICK SA
Tour Fiat, Cedex 16, 92084 PARIS/LA DEFENSE
Total Offices: 110

Germany
KPMG DEUTSCHE TREUHAND GRUPPE
Beethovenstrasse 8-10, 6000 FRANKFURT 1
Total Offices: 35

Gibraltar
KPMG PEAT MARWICK
Suite C, 3rd Floor, Regal House, Queensway, GIBRALTAR
Total Offices: 2

Greece
KPMG PEAT MARWICK KYRIACOU
15 Mesoghion Avenue, Ambelokipi, 115 26 ATHENS
Total Offices: 1

Iceland
KPMG ENDURSKODUN HF
Sudurlandsbraut 18, 108 REYKJAVIK
Total Offices: 8

Isle of Man
KPMG PEAT MARWICK
Heritage Court, 41 Athol Street, DOUGLAS
Total Offices: 1

Republic of Ireland
KPMG STOKES KENNEDY CROWLEY
1 Stokes Place, St Stephen's Green, DUBLIN 2
Total Offices: 5

Italy
KPMG FIDES FIDUCIARIA SPA
Via Vittor Pisani 25, 20124 MILAN
KPMG PEAT MARWICK FIDES SNC
Via Vittor Pisani 25, 20124 MILAN
KPMG PEAT MARWICK SNC
Via Vittor Pisani 25, 20124 MILAN
STUDIO ASSOCIATO TARGA-DI PACO-PAGANI-VICHI
Via Vittor Pisani 27, 20124 MILAN
Total Offices: 35

Luxembourg
KPMG PEAT MARWICK INTER-REVISION
283 route d'Arlon, 1150 LUXEMBOURG
Total Offices: 1

The Netherlands
KPMG KLYNVELD
Burgemeester Rijnderslaan 10-20, KPMG Building, 1185 MC AMSTELVEEN
Total Offices: 102

Norway
KPMG PEAT MARWICK A/S
Brynsveien 12, 0611 OSLO
Total Offices: 14

Portugal
KPMG PEAT MARWICK
Avenida da República 24, 1000 LISBON
Total Offices: 3

Spain
KPMG PEAT MARWICK Y CIA
Edificio Torre Europa, Paseo de la Castellana 95, 28046 MADRID
Total Offices: 12

Sweden
KPMG BOHLINS REVISIONSBYRÅ AB
Tegelbacken 4, 103 23 STOCKHOLM
Total Offices: 100

Switzerland
KPMG FIDES PEAT
Pflanzschulstrasse 2, 8026 ZURICH
MAYO ASSOCIATES SA
Avenue Pictet de Rochemont 7, 1207 GENEVA
Total Offices: 19

United Kingdom
KPMG PEAT MARWICK
1 Puddle Dock, Blackfriars, LONDON EC4V 3PD
Total Offices: 49

HISTORY & STRUCTURE

KPMG was formed in 1987 by the merger of two major international public accounting and consulting firms: Klynveld Main Goedeler (KMG), dominant in Continental Europe, and Peat Marwick International (PMI), a leading Anglo-American firm. KPMG has also further strengthened its KPMG practices in the Asia/Pacific region, thus creating the most geographically balanced professional services firm in the world. KPMG now has 125 national practices with offices in more than 800 cities that combine local market knowledge with global standards of professionalism, ethics and technical quality. International activities in the areas of professional practice, human resources and industry specialisation are coordinated through ▷

KPMG's international headquarters in Amsterdam, The Netherlands.

Kreston International

International Office
Kreston House, 66 Broomfield Road, CHELMSFORD CM1 1SW, United Kingdom
Tel: +44 (245) 26444
Fax: +44 (245) 490682

International Contact: Chris Flint

EUROPEAN PERSONNEL
Chairman: Chris Benbow
Marketing Director: Torben Bjerre-Poulsen

European partners:	180
Professional staff:	1,120
Non-professional staff:	290
Total staff:	**1,590**

EUROPEAN FEE INCOME

Year End: 31.12.91	**US$**
Total:	**90,100,000**

MEMBER FIRMS

European firms:	15
Number of Countries:	2

PRINCIPAL NATIONAL OFFICES

Isle of Man
FINNIE & CO
Kreston House, 6 Goldie Terrace, DOUGLAS
Total Offices: 1

United Kingdom
FINNIE & CO
Kreston House, 8 Gate Street, LONDON WC2A 3HJ
Total Offices: 15

HISTORY & STRUCTURE

Kreston International is a worldwide association of autonomous and independent national accountancy firms, with members in the Americas, Eastern and Western Europe, the Middle East, Asia and Australia. Kreston was originally formed in 1971 and was established to provide an effective service to international clients. Although independent, each firm promotes uniformly high standards of service. A full-time partner is responsible for client contact, tailoring service to client needs. Multinational assignments, co-ordinated by the member firm in the country of origin, are handled by nationals of the relevant countries. As well as providing accounting, auditing, taxation, investigating and management consultancy services, in some countries legal and property advice is also available.

K.S. International

European Executive Office
Devonshire House, 146 Bishopsgate, LONDON EC2M 4JX, United Kingdom
Tel: +44 (71) 377 8888
Fax: +44 (71) 247 7048

International Contact: Martin Burchmore

EUROPEAN PERSONNEL
Chairman: Michael Snyder
Administartor: Martin Burchmore

European partners:	73
Professional staff:	381
Non-professional staff:	137
Total staff:	**591**

EUROPEAN FEE INCOME

Year End: 1991	**£**
Total:	**24,500,000**

MEMBER FIRMS

European firms:	25
Number of Countries:	8

PRINCIPAL NATIONAL OFFICES

Belgium
VANACKER GOVAERTS & PARTNERS NV
St Maartenplein 3, 8000 BRUGGE
Total Offices: 1

Cyprus
TIMENIDES & EVANGELI
10 Dimitsanis, NICOSIA
Total Offices: 1

Denmark
AUDIREVISION APS
Falkoner Allé 53, 3, 2000 FREDERIKSBERG, Copenhagen
Total Offices: 8

France
ORCOM CENTRE
2 avenue de Paris, 45056 ORLEANS
CABINET SOREL
59 rue la Boetie, 75008 PARIS
Total Offices: 2

Germany
Dipl-Kfm H. WILLMS GmbH
Hansaallee 201, 4000 DUSSELDORF
Total Offices: 1

Republic of Ireland
FAULKNER ORR
1 Adelaide Court, Adelaide Road, DUBLIN 2
Total Offices: 1

Italy
COREVI LOMBARDIA SAS
Viale Campania 46, 20133 MILAN
Total Offices: 5

▷

United Kingdom
KINGSTON SMITH
Devonshire House, 146 Bishopsgate, LONDON
EC2M 4JX
Total Offices: 6

HISTORY & STRUCTURE

K.S. International, formed in 1990 as a network of independent accountancy firms in Europe with associates throughout the world, serves companies with international operations or business interests by being able to provide a full range of services. Its range of clients varies from quoted public companies to small businesses and individuals. One of the group's particular strengths is the ability to serve owner-managed businesses i.e. entrepreneurs, family firms and partnerships. All members of the group pride themselves in having a personal approach to their clients and ensure that good business sense always comes first.

Midsnell International

European Executive Office
Secretariat, Ibex House, Baker Street, WEYBRIDGE, Surrey KT13 8AH
Tel: *+44* (932) 853393
Fax: *+44* (932) 8543232

International Contact: Stephen Yeates

EUROPEAN PERSONNEL
Administrator: Stephen Yeates

European partners:	102
Professional staff:	639
Total staff:	**741**

EUROPEAN FEE INCOME

Year End: 1990	**US$**
Total:	**52,000,000**

MEMBER FIRMS

European firms:	45
Number of Countries:	16

PRINCIPAL NATIONAL OFFICES

Austria
PROF DKFM DR SCHUSTER & DKFM WALTER TÜRKE, MAG. PETER GROTSCHAR
Kaiserstrasse 37, 1070 VIENNA
Total Offices: 1

Belgium
HENDRICKX, VAN WOENSEL & CO
Frankrijklei 133, 2000 ANTWERP
Total Offices: 2

Cyprus
GREGORIOU & CO
Greg Tower, 7 Florina Street, NICOSIA
Total Offices: 1

Denmark
REVISIONSFIRMA BUSCH-SØRENSEN
Europaplads 2, 8100 ÅRHUS
FAURUM & SCHIØLER
Kronprinsensgade 5, 2, 1114 COPENHAGEN K
Total Offices: 4

Finland
AURECO OY
Hatanpäänvaltatie 4 A 5, 33100 TAMPERE
TILINTARKASTUSTOIMISTO KALERVO ARILUOMA KY
Mannerheimintie 16 A 3, 00100 HELSINKI
Total Offices: 2

France
FIDUCIAIRE COMPTABLE DU NORD
90 avenue Ledru-Rollin, 75011 PARIS
FIDUCIAIRE VIDOR SA
1 rue Damrémont, 75018 PARIS
Total Offices: 19

Germany
DR. HUPPERTZ, WALTER, WIRTZ GmbH
Josefstrasse 53, 4054 NETTETAL 1
MERCATORPRUFUNG GmbH
Am Buchenbaum 28, 4100 DUISBERG 1
DIPL.-KFM. DR. H.-J. SCHMIDT-WILKE
Am Holzgraben, 3000 HANNOVER 1
Total Offices: 3

Isle of Man
MOORE SNELLING
Victory House, Prospect Hill, DOUGLAS
Total Offices: 1

Republic of Ireland
COPSEY, MURRAY & CO
Charter House, 5 Pembroke Row, DUBLIN 2
Total Offices: 1

Italy
DR. GOFFREDO CAVERNI
Via 2 Settembre 14, 56100 PISA
STUDIO DE LEONE
Via Ampère 47, 20122 MILAN
Total Offices: 2

Liechtenstein
ADVISA TREUHAND-ANSTALT
Heiligkreuz 42, 9490 VADUZ
Total Offices: 1

The Netherlands
SPRINGELING AND VERSTEGEN REGISTERACCOUNTANTS
Koningin Emmaplein 10, 3016 AB ROTTERDAM
Total Offices: 2

Portugal
ANTONIO ALMEIDA, BERNARDO E MURALHA
Rua Tomas Ribeiro 41, 3º dtº, 1000 LISBON
Total Offices: 1

▷

Sweden
REVISIONSBYRÅN LUNDBERG & CO AB
Aniaraplatsen 2, 191 23 SOLLENTUNA
Total Offices: 3

Switzerland
BUDLIGER TREUHAND AG
Postfach 8059, Waffenplatzstrasse 64,
8002 ZURICH
FIDUCIAIRE VIDOR SA
Boulevard de Grancy 7, 1006 LAUSANNE
Total Offices: 3

United Kingdom
DUNCAN SHEARD GLASS
Castle Chambers, 43 Castle Street,
LIVERPOOL L2 9TL
FRASER GORDON & CO
Station House, 15 Station Road, ST IVES,
Cambridgeshire PE17 4BH
HOMER GITTINS
402/403 Stourport Road, KIDDERMINSTER,
Worcestershire DY11 7BG
LANHAM & FRANCIS
60 Princes Street, YEOVIL, Somerset BA20 1HL
MIDGLEY, SNELLING & CO
6th Floor, 9 Kingsway, LONDON WC2B 6XF
O'BRIEN & JAMES
Llanover Road, PONTYPRIDD,
Mid Glamorgan CF37 4LB
RICKARD KEEN & CO
9 Nelson Street, SOUTHEND-ON-SEA,
Essex SS1 1EH
WATSON WOOD
York House, 249 Manningham Lane, BRADFORD,
West Yorkshire BD8 7EW
WENHAM MAJOR
89 Cornwall Street, BIRMINGHAM B3 3BY
J. WILD & CO
Lancaster House, Blackburn Street, Radcliffe,
MANCHESTER M26 9TS
Total Offices: 14

HISTORY & STRUCTURE

Midsnell International is an association of independent firms of public accountants linked together for the benefit of members and all their clients. It grew from the associations of the United Kingdom firm of Midgley Snelling & Co, which had been developed since 1947. Midsnell International has more than 90 members with more than 160 offices located in excess of 60 countries. Members comprise a variety of large, medium and small firms. The primary objective of Midsnell International is to provide international assistance for clients and member firms who wish to expand or trade beyond their own country and to provide the benefit of access to international information to member firms and their clients. The Association believes that local accounting firms in each country committed to the highest professional standards can best provide the services required by other firms and their clients. Each member is solely responsible for their own work. However, before being admitted to the Association, all firms are visited and are subject to a quality control review to ensure their standards of knowledge, quality control and adherence to standards of professional service are those expected within the Association.

Moore Stephens

International Office
St Paul's House, Warwick Lane, LONDON
EC4P 4BN, United Kingdom
Tel: +*44* (71) 248 4499
Fax: +*44* (71) 248 3408

European Executive Office
Community Office, Avenue Louise 207-209, Boite 8,
1050 BRUSSELS
Tel: +*32* (2) 64 83 78 4
Fax: +*32* (2) 64 05 34 3

International Contact: Paul Stockton

EUROPEAN PERSONNEL
Chairman: Guiseppe Barranco
Administrator: Paul Stockton

European partners:	307
Professional staff:	1,772
Non-professional staff:	636
Total staff:	**2,715**

EUROPEAN FEE INCOME

Year End: 31.12.90	**US$**
Total:	**198,300,000**

MEMBER FIRMS

European firms:	102
Number of Countries:	21

PRINCIPAL NATIONAL OFFICES

Austria
FISCHER, KROS & COMP
P.O. Box 112, Auhofstrasse 1-3, 1130 VIENNA
Total Offices: 2

Belgium
MOORE STEPHENS
Avenue Louise 207-209, Boite 8, 1050 BRUSSELS
Total Offices: 1

Channel Islands
MOORE STEPHENS
First Island House, Peter Street, ST HELIER,
Jersey JE4 8SG
MOORE STEPHENS
Town Mills South, La Rue du Pré, ST PETER PORT,
Guernsey
Total Offices: 2

▷

European Accountancy Groups

Cyprus
MOORE STEPHENS
Iris Tower, 6th Floor, Makarios Avenue & Agapinor Street, NICOSIA
Total Offices: 1

Denmark
MOORE STEPHENS APS
Åboulevard 56, 2200 COPENHAGEN N
Total Offices: 8

France
GROUP CONCORDE, CONCORDE SA
15 rue Bertin-Poirée, 75001 PARIS
Total Offices: 13

Germany
MS BERATUNGS-UND-TREUHAND-UNION GmbH
Hildesheimer Strasse 9, 3000 HANNOVER 1
Total Offices: 18

Gibraltar
MOORE STEPHENS
Suite 34, Victoria House, 26 Main Street, GIBRALTAR
Total Offices: 1

Greece
MOORE STEPHENS
93 Akti Miaouli, 185 38 PIRAEUS
Total Offices: 2

Isle of Man
MOORE STEPHENS
P.O. Box 25, Clinch's House, Lord Street, DOUGLAS
Total Offices: 1

Republic of Ireland
MOORE STEPHENS
6 Fitzwilliam Place, DUBLIN 2
Total Offices: 1

Italy
CONCORDE EUROFIDUCIARIA SRL
Via Cosimo del Fante 16, 20122 MILAN
MOORE STEPHENS & CO SAS
Via Cosimo del Fante 16, 20122 MILAN
Total Offices: 4

Malta
R.S. ATTARD & CO
P.O. Box 324, 46 Timber Wharf, MARSA
Total Offices: 2

Monaco
MOORE STEPHENS SERVICES SAM
L'Estoril, avenue Princesse Grace,
98000 MONTE CARLO
Total Offices: 1

The Netherlands
MOORE STEPHENS NETHERLANDS
Noordhollandstraat 71, 1081 AS AMSTERDAM
Total Offices: 3

Norway
BAKKE & HJELMAASLARSEN
Billingstadsletta 19a, Postboks 66,
1312 SLEPENDEN
Total Offices: 1

Portugal
MOORE STEPHENS
Av Freimiguel Contreiras 54, 10º, 1700 LISBON
Total Offices: 2

Spain
MOORE STEPHENS & SANTACANA GRUP SA
Avenida Diagonal 476, 4º 2ª, 08006 BARCELONA
Total Offices: 8

Sweden
LARS BOCK & CO REVISIONSBYRÅ AB
Sergels Torg 12, 12th Floor, 111 57 STOCKHOLM
Total Offices: 4

Switzerland
MOORE STEPHENS AG
Kanal Strasse 9, 8152 GLATTBRUGG, Zurich
Total Offices: 3

United Kingdom
MOORE STEPHENS
St Paul's House, Warwick Lane,
LONDON EC4P 4BN
Total Offices: 37

HISTORY & STRUCTURE

Moore Stephens' first office was opened in London in 1907. In the late 1950's, the firm began to develop an international accounting group to service its many clients in the world shipping industry. Since then the firm's client base has broadened so that today it serves every sector in the international business community. From the 1960's onwards, the international group spread across the world with substantial development in Australia, The East, India, The Middle East, North and South America and Europe. In Europe, member firms are grouped under a regional partnership, Moore Stephens Europe, having 107 offices Europe-wide in total.

Moores Rowland International

European Executive Office
Place Rouppe 16, 1000 BRUSSELS, Belgium
Tel: +32 (2) 51 03 24 3
Fax: +32 (2) 51 03 33 3

International Contact: Jérôme Adam

EUROPEAN PERSONNEL

Chairman: Victor Clements

European partners:	521
Professional staff:	2,939
Non-professional staff:	996
Total staff:	**4,456**

▷

EUROPEAN FEE INCOME
Year End: 31.12.91 ECU
Total: 255,000,000

MEMBER FIRMS
European firms: 185
Number of Countries: 21

PRINCIPAL NATIONAL OFFICES

Austria
ATTESTA WIRTSCHAFTSTREUHAND GmbH
Weimarerstrasse 32, 1180 VIENNA
Total Offices: 1

Belgium
BOEYE, GEDDES VAN GULCK & CO
Place Rouppe 16, 1000 BRUSSELS
FIDUCIAIRE MOORES ROWLAND SA
Place Rouppe 16, 1000 BRUSSELS
Total Offices: 22

Channel Islands
LINCE SALISBURY
Avenue House, St Julian's Avenue, ST PETER PORT, Guernsey
MOORES ROWLAND
Broadcasting House, Rouge Bouillon, ST HELIER, Jersey
MOORES ROWLAND
Barclays Bank Chambers, Grand Rue, ST MARTIN, Guernsey
Total Offices: 3

Cyprus
PETRIDES & MODINOS
3rd Floor, Loucaides Building, St Andrew & Archbishop Kyprianou, LIMASSOL
Total Offices: 1

Denmark
CITY REVISION A/S
Blegdamsvej 60, 2100 COPENHAGEN Ø
Total Offices: 1

France
FIDUCIAIRE DE STRASBOURG
5 Rue du Dôme, 67000 STRASBOURG
FIDULOR
81 boulevard de Stalingrad, B.P. 1215, 69611 VILLEURBANNE-LYON
Total Offices: 20

Germany
DR. BREIDENBACH - DR. GÜLDENAGEL & PARTNER
Hofave 95, Postfach 13 23 64, 5600 WUPERTAL-ELBERFELD
DR. CLARENZ - DR ZACHARIAS
Kaiser-Wilhelm-Ring 24, 5000 COLOGNE 1
FALK & CO GmbH
Slevogtstrasse 6, 6900 HEIDELBERG
DR. GENAUST-BÖTTCHER-BÜCHL
Mittelweg 118, Ecke Alsterchaussee, 2000 HAMBURG 13
GTW - TREUHAND GmbH
Briennerstrasse 16, 8000 MUNICH 2
HANSABERATUNG GmbH
Wachtstrasse 17-24, Postfach 10 51 44, 2800 BREMEN 1
DR. KLEINERTZ UND PARTNER GmbH
Benrather Schlossallee 49-53, 4000 DUSSELDORF 13 (Benrath)
TREUHANDPARTNER PLENKER JÄGER, FINKEN, WELLING GmbH
Eichendorffstrasse 46, 4150 KREFELD
RÖVER & PARTNER
Douglasstrasse 18, 1000 BERLIN 33
RTS REVISION, TREUHAND GmbH
Faktoreistrasse 4, 6600 SAARBRÜCKEN
VERHULSDONK & PARTNER GmbH
Elisabethstrasse 16, 4000 DUSSELDORF 1
Total Offices: 17

Gibraltar
OLIVERO & DODWELL
12/3 George's Lane, P.O. Box 417, GIBRALTAR
Total Offices: 1

Greece
CONSTANTIN SIGALAS DIPL. KAUFMANN
Syngrou Avenue 76, 117 42 ATHENS
Total Offices: 1

Isle of Man
MOORES ROWLAND
Finch House, 24 Finch Road, DOUGLAS
Total Offices: 1

Republic of Ireland
JOHN WOODS & CO
Woods House, BLACKROCK, Co Dublin
Total Offices: 1

Italy
BOMPANI AUDIT SAS
Viale Monte Rosa 3, 20149 MILAN
Total Offices: 3

Luxembourg
FIDUCIAIRE CENTRALE DU LUXEMBOURG
4 rue Henri Schnadt, 2530 LUXEMBOURG
Total Offices: 1

Malta
ANTON CHETCUTI-GANADO
2 Merchants Street, VALLETTA 5
Total Offices: 1

Monaco
MOORES ROWLAND CORPORATE SERVICES
2 avenue de Monte-Carlo, B.P. 343, 98006 MONACO
Total Offices: 1

The Netherlands
P & H GROEP
Calandstraat 41, 3016 CA ROTTERDAM
Total Offices: 21

▷

European Accountancy Groups

Norway
REVISOR-GRUPPEN NORGE A/S
Holtegt. 22, 0355 OSLO 3
Total Offices: 8

Portugal
ALVES, COSTA & ASSOCIADOS SROC
Avenida da Republica 48, 1000 LISBON
JOHN DE LAROQUE
Vivenda do Alto da Bonita, Rua do Alto da Bonita, Ranholas, 2710 SINTRA
Total Offices: 2

Sweden
LRF REVISION AB
Karlbergsvägen 77-81, 100 31 STOCKHOLM
Total Offices: 12

Switzerland
MOORES & ROWLAND AG
Seefeldstrasse 45, Postfach 335, 8034 ZURICH
USHER & CO
Place des Eaux Vives 6, 1207 GENEVA
Total Offices: 3

United Kingdom
ALLEN, SYKES
1 Cockton Hill Road, BISHOP AUCKLAND, Co Durham DL14 6EN
BRACE WHINCUP
National Westminster Bank Buildings, 113 Bute Street, CARDIFF CF1 6EQ
FORRESTER BOYD
26 South St Mary's Gate, GRIMSBY, South Humberside DN31 1LW
GARBUTT & ELLIOTT
Sherburn House, 41 Ings Road, LEEDS LS9 9EJ
GILCHRIST, TASH
Cleveland Buildings, Queen's Square, MIDDLESBROUGH, Cleveland TS2 1PA
ALBERT GOODMAN & CO
Mary Street House, Mary Street, TAUNTON, Somerset TA1 3NW
HAWSONS
Pegasus House, 463a Glossop Road, SHEFFIELD S10 2QD
HAZLEWOODS
Windsor House, Bayshill Road, CHELTENHAM, Gloucestershire GL50 3AT
HILTON, SHARP & CLARKE
30 New Road, BRIGHTON BN1 1BN
HONEY BARRETT & CO
51-55 Gildredge Road, EASTBOURNE, East Sussex BN21 4SF
HOWARTH HAWSONS
37 Stramongate, KENDAL, Cumbria LA9 4BH
JACKSON ANDREWS
Andras House, 60 Great Victoria Street, BELFAST BT2 7ET
LOVEWELL BLAKE
102 Prince of Wales Road, NORWICH NR1 1NY
MANN, JUDD, GORDON
26 Lewis Street, STORNOWAY, Isle of Lewis PA87 2JF
MOORES ROWLAND
Clifford's Inn, Fetter Lane, LONDON EC4A 1AS
PORTER, MATTHEWS & MARSDEN
Oakmount, 6 East Park Road, BLACKBURN BB1 8BW
RITSON, SMITH & PARTNERS
16 Carden Place, ABERDEEN AB9 1XF
SPAIN BROTHERS & CO
Falcon House, 73 College Road, MAIDSTONE, Kent ME15 6RW
TAYLOR HAWSONS
Albion House, 6 Albion Place, South Parade, DONCASTER, South Yorkshire DN1 2EG
WHITLEY, STIMPSON & PARTNERS
Penrose House, Oxford Road, BANBURY, Oxfordshire OX16 7AB
Total Offices: 65

HISTORY & STRUCTURE

Moores Rowland International (MRI) is a group of leading independent accounting practices. MRI presently ranks 9th in size worldwide and brings together 107 firms with 1,400 partners in 370 offices with 10,000 staff in 60 countries. With a comparatively high ratio of partners to staff, a partner of a member firm is readily available to provide personalised service. MRI is under the supervision of a multinational Executive Committee. It has three regional groups, Moores Rowland Europe, Moores Rowland North America and Moores Rowland Asia Pacific.

Morison International

International Office
805 Salisbury House, 31 Finsbury Circus, LONDON EC2M 5SQ, United Kingdom
Tel: +44 (71) 628 2040
Fax: +44 (71) 628 7531

International Contact: Martin Silverman

EUROPEAN PERSONNEL
Chairman: Martin Silverman
Vice-Chairman: Rene de Vries
Marketing: Gillian Angel
Administrator: Sarah Donne

European partners:	85
Professional staff:	620
Non-professional staff:	178
Total staff:	**883**

EUROPEAN FEE INCOME

Year End: 31.12.91	**US$**
Total:	**61,000,000**

▷

MEMBER FIRMS
European firms: 24
Number of Countries: 8

PRINCIPAL NATIONAL OFFICES

Belgium
VB BIJNENS, DEGEEST & CO
Muntelbeekstraat 42, 3500 HASSELT
Total Offices: 2

Denmark
KROGH & RONALD
Vestergade 11-17, P.O. Box 409, 8100 ÅRHUS C
Total Offices: 3

France
APLITEC
44 quai de Jemmapes, 75010 PARIS
CABINET BOYER
66 rue Saint Jacques, 13006 MARSEILLE
Total Offices: 2

Germany
BEISEL, HAFELE, VOLL, ZWEIFEL & PARTNER
Gartenstraße 46, 6000 FRANKFURT AM MAIN 70
FISCHER + PARTNER KG
Flachsland 29-31, 2000 HAMBURG 76
Total Offices: 4

Republic of Ireland
BUTLER, FITZPATRICK, CAVANAGH, DONNELLY
90 Ranelagh Road, DUBLIN 6
Total Offices: 1

The Netherlands
VAN DER HOEK EN BLOK
Rosestraat 1033, 3008 AD ROTTERDAM
WITLOX ADVIES
Kempenlandstraat 1, 5262 CA VUGHT
Total Offices: 8

Spain
ALVAREZ, MOLINERO & CIA
Ferraz 28, 3 izqda, 28008 MADRID
Total Offices: 1

United Kingdom
MORISON STONEHAM
805 Salisbury House, 31 Finsbury Circus, LONDON EC2M 5SQ
Total Offices: 4

HISTORY & STRUCTURE

Morison International's strong regional members provide representation in the major European commercial centres. The Group's aim is to give clients practical professional advice and contacts for doing business in Europe. Members are independent business advisors, each of whom has been carefully selected for their commitment to providing the highest level of cost-effective, personal service and professional advice. Services offered internationally by the Group include accounting, audit, taxation, legal, mergers and acquisitions, grants, funding and consultancy. All members are regularly working together and in close touch, ensuring a common approach which gives confidence to clients and members alike.

NEXIA
INTERNATIONAL

Nexia International

International Office
2 rue Paul-Cézanne, 75008 PARIS, France
Tel: +33 (1) 40 76 60 60
Fax: +33 (1) 42 89 26 25

European Executive Office
Koningslaan 30, 1075 AD AMSTERDAM
Tel: +31 (20) 6769955
Fax: +31 (20) 6764478

EUROPEAN PERSONNEL
International Chairman: Patrice de Maistre
International Executive Director: Nigel Hodges
International Manager: Simon Tesh
International General Secretary: Martine Agopian
European Chairman: Eppo Horlings
European Assistant: Ingrid Kromheer

European partners: 280
Total staff: 2,800

EUROPEAN FEE INCOME
Year End: 31.10.91 US$
Total: 168,000,000

MEMBER FIRMS
European firms: 87
Number of Countries: 17

PRINCIPAL NATIONAL OFFICES

Austria
EWB REVISIONS-UND TREUHAND GmbH
Am Modenapark 10, 1030 VIENNA
Total Offices: 1

Belgium
ANDRÉ HOSTE & ASSOCIÉS
Avenue Château de Walzin 10, 1180 BRUSSELS
Total Offices: 1

Channel Islands
MICHAEL FORREST & PARTNERS
Langtry House, 40 La Motte Street, ST HELIER, Jersey
Total Offices: 1

Cyprus
PAVLOU, POYIADJIS & CO
2 Sophouli Street, Chanteclair House, NICOSIA
Total Offices: 1

▷

European Accountancy Groups

Denmark
REVISIONSFIRMÆT PREBEN LARSEN
Overgaden Neden Vandet 9C,
1023 COPENHAGEN K
Total Offices: 5

France
GROUPE CALAN ROMOLINO
2 rue Paul-Cézanne, 75008 PARIS
Total Offices: 15

Germany
BTR BERATUNG UND TREUHAND RING GmbH
BTR Secretariat, Hansa-Allee 201, 4000
DUSSELDORF 11
Total Offices: 17

Greece
KOLOKOTRONIS - PAPAKYRIACOU & CO
Veritas House, 27-31 Hatzikyriacou Avenue,
185 38 PIRAEUS
Total Offices: 1

Republic of Ireland
OLIVER FREANEY & COMPANY
45 Northumberland Road, DUBLIN 4
Total Offices: 1

Italy
CONSULAUDIT SAS
3 Via XX Settembre, 10121 TURIN
Total Offices: 5

Luxembourg
FIDUCIAIRE FERNAND FABER
15 boulevard Roosevelt, 2450 LUXEMBOURG
Total Offices: 1

Malta
MIZZI SCERRI SAID & CO
Fifth Floor, Airways House, 6-10 High Street,
SLIEMA
Total Offices: 1

The Netherlands
HORLINGS, BROUWER & HORLINGS
Koningslaan 30, 1075 AD AMSTERDAM
Total Offices: 2

Portugal
CONSULTEAM/INTERAUDIT
Rua Tomás Ribeiro 50, 1º, 1000 LISBON
Total Offices: 2

Spain
AUDIHISPANA
Avenida Pau Casals 13-15, 08021 BARCELONA
Total Offices: 10

Switzerland
EXPERTA GROUP
Am Schanzengraden 23, 8002 ZURICH
Total Offices: 8

United Kingdom
NEVILLE RUSSELL
246 Bishopsgate, LONDON EC2M 4PB
Total Offices: 20

HISTORY & STRUCTURE

Nexia International has been an international organisation for over 25 years, now with a new name following the merger between NR International and Spicer & Oppenheim International. The international group is represented in over 55 countries throughout the world. Its well-established national member firms have together some 300 offices. Worldwide around 8,000 people work in the network. Each member firm is managed and staffed by nationals of the country concerned and can provide clients with a comprehensive range of services relating to auditing, accounting, tax, consulting and financial and management advice. Co-ordination of common standards and objectives throughout the member firms is maintained by the International Board of Directors and a number of specialised committees under the overall authority of the International Council.

Pannell Kerr Forster Worldwide

International Office
New Garden House, 78 Hatton Garden, LONDON
EC1N 8JA, United Kingdom
Tel: *+44* (71) 405 7393
Fax: *+44* (71) 405 6736

International Contact: Claude Brown

EUROPEAN PERSONNEL

Chairman: Claude Brown

European partners:	306
Professional staff:	2,361
Non-professional staff:	571
Total staff:	**3,238**

EUROPEAN FEE INCOME

Year End: 30.06.91	**US$**	**%**
Accountancy & Audit:	132,446,880	62.0
Insolvency:	12,817,470	6.0
Consultancy:	29,907,430	14.0
Tax:	38,452,410	18.0
Total:	**213,624,190**	

MEMBER FIRMS

European firms:	84
Number of Countries:	16

PRINCIPAL NATIONAL OFFICES

Austria
AAC
Gluckgasse 1, 1010 VIENNA 1
Total Offices: 1

Belgium
LIPPENS, MARTEYN & RABAEY
Gentsesteenweg 1154, 1080 BRUSSELS
Total Offices: 2

Channel Islands
PANNELL KERR FORSTER
Suites 13 & 15, Sarnia House, Le Truchot, ST PETER PORT, Guernsey
Total Offices: 1

Cyprus
SAVVIDES & PARTNERS/PANNELL KERR FORSTER
4th, 5th & 7th Floor Meliza Court, 229 Archbishop Makarios III Avenue, LIMASSOL 255
Total Offices: 3

Denmark
PANNELL KERR FORSTER DENMARK AS
Frederiksgade 1, 1265 COPENHAGEN K
Total Offices: 4

France
FIDUCIAIRE EXPERTISES CONSEILS (F.E.C.)
rue du Faubourg-Saint-Honoré 237, 75008 PARIS
Total Offices: 3

Germany
PANNELL KERR FORSTER GmbH
Jungfernstieg 7, 2000 HAMBURG 36
Total Offices: 15

Isle of Man
PANNELL KERR FORSTER
Exchange House, 54-58 Athol Street, DOUGLAS
Total Offices: 3

Republic of Ireland
PANNELL KERR FORSTER
17 Percy Place, DUBLIN 4
Total Offices: 1

Italy
SINTEA SAS
Corso Buenos Aires 23, 20124 MILAN
Total Offices: 2

The Netherlands
WALLAST & STAM
Karrepad 2, 2623 AP DELFT
Total Offices: 5

Norway
SAMARBEIDENDE REVISORER A/S
Strandgt. 17, 2801 GJØVIK
Total Offices: 4

Spain
PANNELL KERR FORSTER
Travessera de Gracia Forster 29, 08021 BARCELONA
Total Offices: 3

Sweden
SET - SVENSSON, ERIKSON & TJUS REVISIONSBYRÅ HB
Kungsgatan 6, 211 49 MALMÖ
Total Offices: 8

Switzerland
FIDUCIAIRE OFOR SA
1 Place Saint-Gervais, 1211 GENEVA 1

PANNELL KERR FORSTER AG
Postfach 375, 8027 ZURICH
Total Offices: 4

United Kingdom
PANNELL KERR FORSTER
New Garden House, 78 Hatton Garden, LONDON EC1N 8JA
Total Offices: 33

HISTORY & STRUCTURE

Pannell Kerr Forster (PKF) is an international firm of business advisers with 200 offices staffed by over 5,000 professionals with worldwide fees in excess of US$400 million. PKF operates in over 75 countries throughout the world, embracing Europe, North America, East and West Africa, The Caribbean, Central and South America, Southern Asia, China and the Far East, Australia and New Zealand.

Price Waterhouse

European Executive Office
No 1 London Bridge, LONDON SE1 9QL, United Kingdom
Tel: +44 (71) 939 3000
Fax: +44 (71) 403 5265

International Contact: Anne Wolfe

EUROPEAN PERSONNEL
Chairman: Sir Jeffery Bowman
Marketing: Robert Brooke

European partners:	863
Professional staff:	10,235
Non-professional staff:	4,108
Total staff:	**15,206**

EUROPEAN FEE INCOME

Year End: 30.06.90	**SFr**	**%**
Accountancy & Audit:	772,000,000	51.0
Insolvency:	42,000,000	3.0
Consultancy:	357,000,000	23.0
Tax:	342,000,000	23.0
Total:	**1,513,000,000**	

MEMBER FIRMS

European firms:	145
Number of Countries:	22

PRINCIPAL NATIONAL OFFICES

Austria
PRICE WATERHOUSE AG
Prinz Eugen Strasse 72, 1040 VIENNA
Total Offices: 5

Belgium
PRICE WATERHOUSE
Boulevard de la Woluwe 62, 1200 BRUSSELS
Total Offices: 4

▷

European Accountancy Groups

Channel Islands
PRICE WATERHOUSE
Eagle House, Don Road, ST HELIER, Jersey
Total Offices: 1

Cyprus
PRICE WATERHOUSE
Kermia House, 4 Diagoras Street, NICOSIA
Total Offices: 4

Denmark
PRICE WATERHOUSE/SEIER-PETERSEN
Tuborg Boulevard 1, 2900 HELLERUP
Total Offices: 3

Finland
PRICE WATERHOUSE
Kansakoulukuja 1, 4th Floor, 00100 HELSINKI
Total Offices: 2

France
PRICE WATERHOUSE
98 rue de Courcelles, 75017 PARIS
Total Offices: 9

Germany
PRICE WATERHOUSE GmbH
Gervinusstrasse 17, 6000 FRANKFURT
Total Offices: 10

Gibraltar
PRICE WATERHOUSE
9th, Floor Suite 6, International Commercial Centre, Casemates Square, GIBRALTAR
Total Offices: 1

Greece
PRICE WATERHOUSE
Tower of Athens, 16th Floor, 2 Messogion Avenue, 115 27 ATHENS
Total Offices: 2

Isle of Man
PRICE WATERHOUSE
Target House, 1 & 3 Upper Church Street, DOUGLAS
Total Offices: 1

Republic of Ireland
PRICE WATERHOUSE
Gardner House, Wilton Place, DUBLIN 2
Total Offices: 3

Italy
PRICE WATERHOUSE
Corso Europa 2, 20122 MILAN
Total Offices: 14

Luxembourg
PRICE WATERHOUSE
24 avenue de la Liberté, 1930 LUXEMBOURG
Total Offices: 1

Malta
NAUDI, GIORGIO, LEONE GANADO & CO
Villa Mauramy, Mgr A. Mifsud Street, TA'XBIEX
Total Offices: 2

The Netherlands
PRICE WATERHOUSE
Hofplein 19, 3032 AC ROTTERDAM
Total Offices: 4

Norway
PRICE WATERHOUSE A/S
Stensberggt. 26, 0110 OSLO 1
Total Offices: 3

Portugal
PRICE WATERHOUSE
Avenida Eng. Duarte Pacheco 19, 8º, 1000 LISBON
Total Offices: 4

Spain
EDIFICIO PRICE WATERHOUSE
Paseo de la Castellana 43, 28046 MADRID
Total Offices: 17

Sweden
PRICE WATERHOUSE
Regeringsgatan 66, 111 87 STOCKHOLM
Total Offices: 12

Switzerland
REVISUISSE PRICE WATERHOUSE
Stampfenbachstrasse 109, 8035 ZURICH
Total Offices: 22

United Kingdom
PRICE WATERHOUSE
Southwark Towers, 32 London Bridge Street, LONDON SE1 9SY
Total Offices: 21

HISTORY & STRUCTURE

Founded in London in 1849, Price Waterhouse is one of the world's largest international organisations of accountants, business advisers and management consultants. It has grown principally by establishing offices around the world in response to client needs and following capital flows. Price Waterhouse Europe is a combination under which member firms work closely together to provide integrated services from 140 offices throughout Europe. Worldwide, the organisation consists of a network of firms with over 49,000 staff in approximately 460 offices in 110 territories.

Russell Bedford International

European Executive Office
Russell Bedford House, City Forum, 250 City Road, LONDON EC1V 2QQ, United Kingdom
Tel: *+44* (71) 490 7766
Fax: *+44* (71) 490 5102

International Contact: Geoffrey Goodyear

EUROPEAN PERSONNEL
Chairman: Stanley Prashker
Administrator: Katrin Voss

▷

European partners:	95	
Professional staff:	190	
Non-professional staff:	533	
Total staff:	**818**	

EUROPEAN FEE INCOME

Year End: 31.12.90	**£**	**%**
Accountancy & Audit:	6,280,000	30.0
Insolvency:	1,570,000	10.0
Consultancy:	10,990,000	30.0
Tax:	12,560,000	30.0
Total:	**31,400,000**	

MEMBER FIRMS

European firms:	23
Number of Countries:	12

PRINCIPAL NATIONAL OFFICES

Austria
REVISIONSTREUHAND
Margaretenstrasse 78, 1050 VIENNA
Total Offices: 2

Belgium
GHYOOT, KOEVOETS, ROSIER, VAN SANDE & CO
Amerikalei 108, 2000 ANTWERP
Total Offices: 3

Channel Islands
LUBBOCK FINE
Suite 11, Queensway House, Queen Street, ST HELIER, Jersey JE4 8TZ
Total Offices: 1

Denmark
REVISORSHUSET A/S
Buddingevej 289, P.O. Box 52, 2860 SØBORG
Total Offices: 1

Finland
TILINTARKSTUSTOIMISTO SELINHEIMO KY
Peltolantie 21, 013 00 VANTAA
Total Offices: 1

France
EXPERTS FRANCE
10 rue de Laborde, 75008 PARIS
SODAREX - SOCIÉTÉ D'ANALYSES, DE RÉVISION ET D'EXPERTISES COMPTABLES
cours Journu-Auber 50, 33300 BORDEAUX
Total Offices: 2

Germany
BEEH & HAPPICH
Praunheimer Landstrasse 32, 6000 FRANKFURT AM MAIN 90
JESSEN & PARTNER
Geffckenstrasse 21, 2000 HAMBURG 20
DIPL-KFM CLAUS SECURS
Achenbachstrasse 8, 4000 DUSSELDORF 1
Total Offices: 3

Italy
STUDIO LAURI ED ASSOCIATI
Viale dell'Esperanto 10, 00144 ROME
Total Offices: 1

The Netherlands
DE ZEEUW & DE KEIZER REGISTERACCOUNTANTS
Jacob Obrechtstraat 56, 1071 KN AMSTERDAM
Total Offices: 4

Spain
MTR Y ASOCIADOS
Plaza Francesc Macia 5, 1º 1ª, 08021 BARCELONA (Cataluna)
Total Offices: 1

Sweden
REVISORSRINGEN SVERIGE AB
Karlsbergsvägen 77-81, 100 31 STOCKHOLM
Total Offices: 15

United Kingdom
LUBBOCK FINE
Russell Bedford House, City Forum, 250 City Road, LONDON EC1V 2QQ
Total Offices: 1

HISTORY & STRUCTURE

Founded in 1983 by Lubbock Fine in association with French and German practices, the Russell Bedford International network (RBI) now extends to over 40 firms in more than 20 countries worldwide with over 200 partners and 1,500 supporting staff. Its goal is to make available to the international business community a full network of financial services, auditing, accountancy and taxation facilities - based on leading independent firms in each country. Each member is required to maintain high standards of both technical and personal services so ensuring that the same facilities are available to our clients worldwide. Particularly active areas are capital markets, international taxation and audit. RBI is increasingly involved in such specific activities as creating efficient organisational structures, financial planning and financing, mergers and acquisitions, valuations and investigations.

S & W International

International Office
No. 1 Riding House Street, LONDON W1A 3AS, United Kingdom
Tel: *+44* (71) 637 5377
Fax: *+44* (71) 631 0741

International Contact: John McCagney

European partners:	100
Professional staff:	780
Non-professional staff:	180
Total staff:	**1,060**

▷

EUROPEAN FEE INCOME

Year End: 31.12.91	£	%
Accountancy & Audit:	27,000,000	34.0
Insolvency:	7,000,000	8.0
Consultancy:	9,000,000	11.0
Other:	38,000,000	47.0
Total:	**81,000,000**	

MEMBER FIRMS

European firms: 35
Number of Countries: 13

PRINCIPAL NATIONAL OFFICES

Belgium
VOF VAN GEET, DERICK & CO
Kerkstraat 2, 9200 DENDERMONDE
Total Offices: 3

Denmark
DSR
Helsingforsgade 27, 8200 ÅRHUS
VANLOSE REVISION APS
Limfjordsvej 45 A, 2720 VANLOSE, Copenhagen
Total Offices: 2

Finland
JORMA WAINIO OY
Satamakatu 4, 00160 HELSINKI
Total Offices: 1

France
S & W ASSOCIÉS
47 rue de Chaillot, 75116 PARIS
Total Offices: 2

Germany
DIPL-KFM KARL BERG GmbH
Rheinberger Strasse 2, 4000 DUSSELDORF 30
Total Offices: 1

Republic of Ireland
CREMIN, MCCARTHY & CO
28 Harcourt Street, DUBLIN 2
Total Offices: 1

Italy
DR. CORRADO CASSINIS
Via Mascheroni 29, 20145 MILAN
Total Offices: 1

The Netherlands
FERNHOUT, STRUIJK & VAN DER VEKEN ACCOUNTANTS BV
Korte Steigerstraat 6, 5301 CE ZALTBOMMEL
Total Offices: 4

Norway
OTTERSTADS REVISJONSKONTOR A/S
Henrik Ibsensgt. 7, 0179 OSLO 1
Total Offices: 1

Spain
HERREROS Y DE LA FUENTE
Calvo Sotelo 11, SANTANDER 39002
S & W AUDIT GROUP
Bailen 188, 08037 BARCELONA
Total Offices: 2

Sweden
OSSERS REVISIONSBYRÅ AB
Drivhjulsvägen 28, 126 30 HÄGERSTEN, Stockholm
Total Offices: 3

Switzerland
ANDREAS BAUMANN & CO
Zürichstrasse 27 B, 8134 ADLISWIL
MULTIFIDUCIARE SA
Rue Faucigny 5, 1700 FRIBOURG
TREFIMA INC
Atlantis Building, Zurcherstrasse 65, 9500 WIL 1, Zurich
Total Offices: 10

United Kingdom
SMITH & WILLIAMSON
No. 1 Riding House Street, LONDON W1A 3AS
Total Offices: 6

HISTORY & STRUCTURE

S & W International, founded in 1981, is an association of independent firms of accountants organised for the purpose of giving a more comprehensive international service to clients. All the member firms provide a full range of professional services for auditing, accounting, taxation, reports for company reconstructions, acquisitions and mergers, corporate finance and financial planning for individuals and companies. In addition, some member firms offer specialised services such as investment management, banking and pension advice.

SC International

International Office
Fairfax House, Fulwood Place, Gray's Inn,
LONDON WC1V 6UB, United Kingdom
Tel: +44 (71) 405 2828
Fax: +44 (71) 405 7887

International Contact: Michael W. Dawson

EUROPEAN PERSONNEL

Administrator: Nicholas Kelsey
Marketing: H. Davis

European partners: 102
Professional staff: 700
Total staff: 802

EUROPEAN FEE INCOME

Year End: 31.12.90	US$
Total:	**75,000,000**

MEMBER FIRMS

European firms: 27
Number of Countries: 14

▷

PRINCIPAL NATIONAL OFFICES

Austria
LIBERTAS INTERCOUNT REVISIONS-UND BERATUNGSGESELLSCHAFT
Teinfaltstrasse 4, 1010 VIENNA
Total Offices: 1

Channel Islands
SAFFERY CHAMPNESS
La Tonnelle House, Les Banques, ST SAMPSON, Guernsey
Total Offices: 1

Cyprus
KITTIS-TROKOUDES
Anemomylos Offices, Suite 104, 8M Karaolis Street, NICOSIA 162
Total Offices: 1

Denmark
LUNDGAARD ANDERSEN & GLUD AS
Peter Bangs Vej 24, 2000 FREDERIKSBERG
Total Offices: 1

France
CONSULTAUDIT SA
134 rue Legendre, 75017 PARIS
Total Offices: 2

Germany
DR. EBNER, DR. STOLZ UND PARTNER GmbH
Stiftstrasse 5, 7000 STUTTGART 1
Total Offices: 5

Republic of Ireland
HAYDEN BROWN
Grafton Buildings, 34 Grafton Street, DUBLIN 2
Total Offices: 1

Italy
STUDIO MAURIZIO GORDOL
Cia Senato 20, MILAN
Total Offices: 1

Monaco
CLAUDE L.R. TOMATIS
7 rue de l'Industrie, 98000 MONACO
Total Offices: 1

The Netherlands
OVERGAAUW & VAN DER SPEK BV
Bongerd 2, 2900 AS CAPELLE A/D IJSSEL
Total Offices: 1

Spain
CLEMARES Y CIA SRC
Sagasta 16, 4º deha, 28004 MADRID
ECHEVERRIA, SEGURA ILLA Y CIA
Roger de Lluria 36, atico, 08009 BARCELONA
SANCHEZ ANDRES Y CIA
C/Diputación 4, bis 2º, 48009 BILBAO
Total Offices: 4

Sweden
REVIDENTIA HB
Sibyllegatan 43-45, 114 42 STOCKHOLM
Total Offices: 1

Switzerland
INTERNATIONALE TREUHAND AG
Hirzbodenweg 103, 4020 BASLE
Total Offices: 3

United Kingdom
SAFFERY CHAMPNESS
Fairfax House, Fulwood Place, Gray's Inn, LONDON EC1V 6UB
Total Offices: 7

HISTORY & STRUCTURE

SC International (SCI) is a world wide Association of Accountants and Business Consultants, which has been developed in order to provide a better service to the growing number of clients requiring a truly international approach to their affairs. Since its formation in May 1986, the Association has developed into an organisation represented by member firms represented in 60 offices around the world with approximately 1,500 partners and staff earning an annual fee income in excess of US$100m. In addition, there is a continuing process of meeting new members in countries where SCI is already represented, as well as expanding into new areas, and thus strengthening the coverage of the organisation.

Summit International Associates Inc

European Executive Office
Hobson House, 155 Gower Street, LONDON WC1E 6BJ, United Kingdom
Tel: *+44* (71) 387 2888
Fax: *+44* (71) 388 0600

International Contact: Peter Catto

European partners:	174
Professional staff:	1,380
Non-professional staff:	527
Total staff:	**2,081**

EUROPEAN FEE INCOME

Year End: 30.06.91	**US$**
Total:	**143,000,000**

MEMBER FIRMS

European firms:	77
Number of Countries:	19

PRINCIPAL NATIONAL OFFICES

Austria
UNIVERSALE REVISIONS-UND TREUHAND GmbH
Lichtenfelsgasse 5, 1010 VIENNA 1
Total Offices: 1

Belgium
C.V. HALLER, JOOS, WAETERLOOS & PARTNERS
Martelaarslaan 80, 9000 GHENT
Total Offices: 2

European Accountancy Groups

Cyprus
PROIOS & CO
6 Neoptolemos Street, NICOSIA
Total Offices: 1

Denmark
REVISIONSFIRMÆT KNUD E. RASMUSSEN
Slotsgade 21, 5100 ODENSE C
Total Offices: 3

Finland
IMMONEN, KARTTUNEN, LAUKKANEN & CO KY
Hietalahdenkatu 2 B 20, 00180 HELSINKI
Total Offices: 3

France
AMYOT AUDITEURS ET CONSEILS
2 rue Washington, 75008 PARIS
Total Offices: 5

Germany
ALLREVISION GmbH
Widenmayerstrasse 5, 8000 MUNICH 22
DR. H. CLAUSS - DR. E. PAAEL
Achtermannstrasse 11, 4400 MÜNSTER
DORNHOF KLOSS UND PARTNER GmbH
Mönckebergstrasse 18, Domhof, 2000 HAMBURG 1
DR. HARZEM & PARTNER GmbH
Godesberger Allee 125-127, 5300 BONN 2
Total Offices: 18

Greece
E. HELLINAKIS & CO
95 Timotheou Street, 16231 ATHENS
Total Offices: 1

Isle of Man
NOBLE & CO
Abacus House, Mona Street, DOUGLAS
Total Offices: 1

Republic of Ireland
CHAPMAN FLOOD & CO
Mount Herbert Court, 34 Upper Mount Street, DUBLIN 2
Total Offices: 2

Luxembourg
FIDUCIAIRE CONTINENTALE
allée Marconi 16, 2012 LUXEMBOURG
Total Offices: 1

Malta
MERCIECA & ASSOCIATES
International House, Naxxar road, SAN GWANN
Total Offices: 1

The Netherlands
KROESE WEVERS & CO
Auke Vleerstraat 5, 7521 PE ENSCHEDE
VEKEMANS & BERK
Maliebaan 74, 3581 CV UTRECHT
Total Offices: 13

Norway
GRIMSRUD & CO
Drammensveien 21, 0255 OSLO 2
Total Offices: 1

Portugal
CACHUDO NUNES & ASSOCIADOS CONSULTORES DE GESTAO E INVESTIMENTO LDA
Rua Sampaio e Pina 58, 2º dto, 1000 LISBON
Total Offices: 2

Spain
SOLER, SAIZ, HOPEWELL SCP
Paseo de la Habana 54, 5th Floor, 28036 MADRID
Total Offices: 2

Sweden
WAHLBERGS REVISIONSBYRÅ AB
Kungsgatan 8, Fourth Floor, 111 43 STOCKHOLM
Total Offices: 3

Switzerland
OBT TREUHAND AG
Rorschacher Strasse 63, 9003 ST GALLEN
SOCIÉTÉ DE CONTROLE FIDUCIAIRE SA
Rue Ami-Lullin 4, 1211 GENEVA 3
Total Offices: 14

United Kingdom
CASSON BECKMAN
Hobson House, 155 Gower Street, LONDON WC1E 6BJ
Total Offices: 3

HISTORY & STRUCTURE

Summit International is an association of leading independent accounting firms located in major financial centres. It is one of the world's largest, most prestigious and highly ranked accounting groups. Through our membership in Summit, we offer our clients a global network of more than 60 local and regional firms. Each Summit firm is committed to providing the highest level of professional service. Each is a leader in its market area and enjoys an established reputation for excellence. In addition to broad geographical coverage, Summit member firms are able to offer comprehensive services in accounting, auditing and tax, as well as systems and business consulting to clients in virtually every industry. ▷

TEG (The European Group of Accounting & Auditing Firms)

International Office
1910 South Highland Avenue, Suite 210,
LOMBARD, Illinois 60148, USA
Tel: + 1 (708) 916 0300
Fax: + 1 (708) 916 0868

MEMBER FIRMS

European firms:	9
Number of Countries:	7

PRINCIPAL NATIONAL OFFICES

Belgium
DELVAUX, BOVIJN, FRONVILLE & CO SC
Boulevard L. Schmidt 32, 1040 BRUSSELS
Total Offices: 1

France
CADERAS MARTIN
76 rue de Monceau, 75008 PARIS
Total Offices: 2

Germany
G.R.T. GESELLSCHAFT FÜR REVISION UND TREUHAND mbH
Brönerstrasse 11, 6000 FRANKFURT
Total Offices: 2

Italy
FIDIREVISA ITALIA SRL
Via Senato 12, 20121 MILAN
Total Offices: 2

The Netherlands
BARNVELD SCHEVERS
P.O. Box 409, Rietgors 10, 3430 NIEUWEGEIN
Total Offices: 1

United Kingdom
DIXON WILSON
P.O. Box 900, Rotherwick House, 3 Thomas More Street, LONDON E1 9YX
Total Offices: 1

TGI International

International Office
Aldwych House, 79/91 Aldwych, LONDON
WC2B 4HN, United Kingdom
Tel: + 44 (71) 242 2444
Fax: + 44 (71) 242 1117

International Contact: Ken Clarke

MEMBER FIRMS

European firms:	37
Number of Countries:	14

PRINCIPAL NATIONAL OFFICES

Austria
HALPERN & PRINZ
Wasagasse 4, 1090 VIENNA
Total Offices: 1

Cyprus
N. A. YAMAKIS
Regaena House, Regaena Street 4, P.O. Box 1082, NICOSIA
Total Offices: 1

Denmark
REVISORGAARDEN I KØBENHAVN AS
Kattesundet 14, P.O. Box 2084,
1013 COPENHAGEN
Total Offices: 1

France
BRIGGS - TRONEL
35 avenue Victor-Hugo, 75116 PARIS
Total Offices: 3

Germany
HANS ESCHER
Zeil 29-31, 6000 FRANKFURT AM MAIN 1
FRÜCHTNICHT UND PARTNER
Amelungstrasse 5, 2000 HAMBURG 36
DR. HERBERT LINK
Im Birkets 15, 6942 MÖRLENBACH-WEIHER
FRANZ REISSNER TREUHANDGESELLSCHAFT mbH
Prinz-Georg-Strasse 15, 4000 DUSSELDORF 30
ROOLF & PARTNER GmbH
Kennedyallee 55, 6000 FRANKFURT AM MAIN 70
DR. WAHL & PARTNER GmbH
Prinzregentenstrasse 54, 8000 MUNICH 22
WEHNER-ZIMMER & PARTNER GmbH
Benesisstrasse 8-12, 5000 COLOGNE 1
DR. WOLTER & PARTNER mbH
Postfach 6066, Luisenstrasse 4, 3000 HANNOVER 1
Total Offices: 9

Isle of Man
K.J. ROSIER ASSOCIATES
1 Crosby Terrace, DOUGLAS
Total Offices: 1

Republic of Ireland
RYAN GLENNON & CO.
Trinity House, Charleston Road, Ranelagh, DUBLIN 6
Total Offices: 1

Italy
CHARTERED SAS
Via Ugo Foscolo 4, 20121 MILAN
Total Offices: 1

The Netherlands
JOANKNECHT & VAN ZELST
Dr. Berlagelaan 22, P.O. Box 263,
5600 AG EINDHOVEN
Total Offices: 2

Norway
REVISIONSFIRMÆT ÅSVANG & CO A/S
Storgaten 13, P.O. Box 334, 3101 TØNSBERG
Total Offices: 1

▷

Spain
SOLER, SAIZ, HOPEWELL SCP
Paseo de la Habana No. 54-5º Dcha, 28036 MADRID
Total Offices: 2

Sweden
OSBORNE JOHNSONS REVISIONSBYRÅ AB
Kammakargatan 7, 11140 STOCKHOLM
Total Offices: 3

Switzerland
TRIGEMA AG
Lessingstrasse 5, Postfach, 8059 ZURICH
Total Offices: 1

United Kingdom
CLEMENT KEYS RABJOHNS
Nettleton House, Calthorpe Road, Edgbaston, BIRMINGHAM B15 1RL
COOPER LANCASTER
Aldwych House, 79/91 Aldwych, LONDON WC2B 4HN
Total Offices: 11

Urbach Hacker Young International

International Office
St Alphage House, 2 Fore Street, LONDON EC2Y 5DH, United Kingdom
Tel: +44 (71) 588 3611
Fax: +44 (71) 638 2159

International Contact: Arthur Harverd

EUROPEAN PERSONNEL
Chairman: Frank Stansil
Administrator: Vanessa Gunn
Marketing: Arthur D. Harverd

MEMBER FIRMS
European firms: 57
Number of Countries: 15

PRINCIPAL NATIONAL OFFICES

Austria
BURGER, MAYER-SCHÜTZ & PALFFY WIRTSCHAFTSPRÜFUNGS GmbH
Brucknerstrasse 8, 1040 VIENNA
Total Offices: 3

Belgium
HERMANT-DODEMONT & CO
Avenue Adolphe-Lacomblelaan 69-71, Boite 5, 1040 BRUSSELS
Total Offices: 5

Denmark
HANSEN & SORENSEN
Vestergade 48 H, P.O. Box 422, 8100 ÅRHUS C
INFO:REVISION A/S
Sorgenfrivej 18, 2800 LYNGBY, Copenhagen
NØRGAARD & FALK HANSEN
Skulkenborg 2, 5100 ODENSE C
Total Offices: 4

France
GUYOT, VARONA ET ASSOCIÉS
8 rue de Florence, 75008 PARIS
Total Offices: 2

Germany
LAUER & DILLER
Maximilianplatz 12, 8000 MUNICH 2
DR. LEFEVRE & SCHMIDT
Eulenkrugpfad 2, 2000 HAMBURG 67
DR. LEYH & DR. KOSSOW
Weidenweg 9, 5060 BERGISCH GLADBACH, Cologne
Total Offices: 9

Gibraltar
CARUANA & CO
Imossi House, 1/5 Irish Town, GIBRALTAR
Total Offices: 1

Greece
C.D. TZAVELLAS & CO
192b Alexandras Avenue, 115 21 ATHENS
Total Offices: 1

Republic of Ireland
O'CONNOR, LEDDY & HOLMES
Century House, Harold's Cross Road, DUBLIN 6
Total Offices: 1

Italy
FIDALTA
Piazza della Repubblica 9, 20121 MILAN
Total Offices: 2

The Netherlands
GOVERS ACCOUNTANTS/CONSULTANTS
Geldropseweg 26, 5611 SJ EINDHOVEN
Total Offices: 4

Portugal
CCA - CAIANO PEREIRA, CONSULTORES ASSOCIADOS, LDA
Rua David de Sousa 10, r/c Esq, 1000 LISBON
Total Offices: 1

Spain
CONSULTOR SA
Ronda General Mitre 160, 3º, 08006 BARCELONA
Total Offices: 10

Sweden
IDEKO REVISIONSBYRÅ AB
Västra Hamngatan 12, 411 17 GOTHENBURG
LARS NORBERG & CO AB
Södra Förstadsgatan 13, 200 10 MALMÖ
LEIF R. WAHLBERG REVISION AB
Herserudsvägen 3, 181 23 LIDINGÖ
Total Offices: 3

Switzerland
BALMER-ETIENNE TREUHAND AG
Kauffmannweg 4, 6003 LUCERNE
Total Offices: 2

▷

United Kingdom
HACKER YOUNG
St Alphage House, 2 Fore Street,
LONDON EC2Y 5DH
Total Offices: 10

HISTORY & STRUCTURE

Urbach Hacker Young International was formed five years ago and now embraces independent accounting firms in 30 different countries and 77 cities. Further expansion of the association is planned. As well as representation in most European countries, there are member firms in the Americas, Pacific Rim countries, the Middle East and Asia. Whilst the majority of the clients of UHYI are medium-sized enterprises, many firms have developed in depth specialisation in selected commercial sectors and professional activities.

Austria

Area: 83,850 sq km (32,389 sq miles)
Population: 7,576,300 (1987 estimate)
Density: 90.3 per sq km
Capital: Vienna

GDP: Sch. 9 trn, US$174 bn (1991 forecast)
GDP per head: US$22,850 (1991 forecast)
Inflation: 1990 - 3.3%
1991 - 3.6% (forecast)

Official and Spoken Language: Official language is German; local variations occur. English, French and Italian spoken by many

Time: GMT (in Summer GMT + 2)
Telephone Dialling Code: +43

Currency: Schilling (Sch) = 100 groschen
Banking Hours: 0800-1230 and 1330-1500 Monday-Friday, except Thursdays, 0800-1230 and 1330-1730. Hours may vary locally. Head offices do not close for the break
Professional accountancy body: Kammer der Wirtschaftstreuhander (Chamber of Accountants)

Corporate Tax Data

Information supplied by Richard Citron, international tax partner of Stoy Hayward.

The tax year; nature and rates of tax
The tax year is the calendar year.

The corporation tax (Koerperschaftsteuer) is levied at a rate of 30% (on both distributed and undistributed income).

Residence and territoriality
Companies resident in Austria are liable to corporation tax on their worldwide income and gains.

A company incorporated in Austria is resident there as is a company incorporated elsewhere but whose activities are directed from Austria.

The tax base
Method of calculation. Taxable profits are calculated on an increase in net worth basis, by comparing net assets at the beginning and end of the accounting year.

Disallowable items. The main disallowable items are: most entertainment expenses, most transfers to reserves, 50% of supervisory board (Aufsichtsrat) members' fees, expenses relating to non-taxable items, corporation tax itself.

Exempt income/special deductions. Dividends received from Austrian companies and foreign companies qualifying for the affiliation privilege (see below) are exempt.

Interest paid. Normally deductible on the accruals basis. Disallowed interest includes interest on borrowings used to acquire a shareholding qualifying for the affiliation privilege, interest on long term borrowings (for trade tax purposes only) and interest in excess of arm's length rates paid to connected persons. ▷

Stock. Stock and work in progress is valued at the lower of cost or "going concern" value.

Depreciation. Mostly straight line basis only, within a range of acceptable rates for different types of asset. Book depreciation usually matches tax depreciation. There is no pooling of assets. Many assets qualify in addition for an investment allowance of up to 20% in the year of acquisition.

Treatment of dividends received and paid

Dividends received from Austrian companies. Exempt from tax.

Dividends received from foreign companies. Taxable, except where the Austrian company's holding in the paying company is 25% or more throughout the entire fiscal year, in which case the "affiliation privilege" (Beteiligungsertragsbefreiung) generally exempts the dividend from tax.

Dividends paid to Austrian and non-resident shareholders. Withholding tax of 25% must be deducted from dividends paid except where paid: (1) to Austrian resident companies holding 25% or more of the equity; (2) on liquidation distributions and (3) to non-residents covered by a tax treaty specifying a different rate, in which case an application for a refund or the reduced rate should be made.

Anti-avoidance measures

Austrian law recognises the general fraus legis (or abus de droit) principle, whereby transactions that are regarded as an abuse of the statutes can be nullified. There are also thin-capitalisation provisions.

Treatment of losses

Current period. Trading losses and capital losses may be set off against both trading profits and capital gains of the same period (there is no carry-back).

Carry forward. Losses may be carried forward (to the extent that they remain unrelieved in the current period) against future profits for a maximum of seven years.

Treatment of capital gains

Treatment. Capital gains are treated as income.

Computation. The gain (or loss) is computed by deducting depreciated cost from sale proceeds. There is no allowance for inflation.

Rollover. There is no general rollover or deferral (except on the disposal of a fixed asset held for at least seven years the sale proceeds of which are used to acquire other assets located in Austria).

Special treatment for shares. Gains from disposals of shares in foreign companies qualifying for the affiliation privilege are exempt.

Groups of companies

There is no general "fiscal unity" concept, so each member of a group of companies is treated separately, with no facility for pooling profits and losses or tax free transfers of assets. However, there is an exception for "integrated companies" (Organschaften), which may file consolidated tax returns. To qualify, subsidiaries must inter alia be financially, organisationally and economically integrated with the parent company, which must hold at least 75% of the shares in each subsidiary.

Treatment of branches

An Austrian branch of a foreign resident company is treated for tax purposes exactly as if it were an Austrian resident company. There is no special branch profits tax and no withholding tax on remittances of profits from the branch to head office. Branches are also liable to the trade tax and the net worth tax (see below).

Other taxes

Other taxes include:

Taxes on income and gains. There is a trade tax (Gewerbesteuer) levied as a local business income tax. The trade tax payable is deductible in calculating the trade tax itself, as is the net worth tax (see below), but the corporation tax is not. The rate of the tax is fixed by the province itself. It is about 13% of income before tax.

Taxes on capital. Companies are subject to a net worth tax (Vermoegensteuer) at a rate of 1% on 90% of the value of net assets worldwide although some assets are excluded. A 0.5% surcharge may also be payable if the shares are held by another company.

Subject to a double tax treaty, Austrian branches of foreign companies are liable to the tax on their assets situated in Austria, except shareholdings in Austrian companies. Where the shares in the company are owned by another company, a further tax ("Erbschaftssteuera equivalent" - substitute inheritance tax) may be levied at 0.5%.

Turnover taxes. There is a value added tax (Mehrwertsteuer) of 20%, with a reduced rate of 10% and a luxury rate of 32%. Exports are zero rated.

Payroll and social security taxes. There is a payroll tax (Lohnsummensteuer) of about 4.5% of gross salaries, on a monthly basis. There are also employers' social security contributions and a separate local payroll tax.

Transaction taxes. There is a share capital duty of 2% on new share issues (based on proceeds and not par value), a loan capital duty of 0.8%, stamp duties on share transfers and other conveyances and a land transfer tax of 3.5%.

AAC

Gluckgasse 1, 1010 VIENNA 1
Tel: + *43* (1) 51 21 88 7
Fax: + *43* (1) 51 20 29 6

European Affiliation: Pannell Kerr Forster Worldwide

International Contact: Mag. Monika Janska

ATTESTA WIRTSCHAFTSTREUHAND GmbH

Weimarerstrasse 32, 1180 VIENNA
Tel: + *43* (1) 47 01 99 7
Fax: + *43* (1) 47 01 99 722

European Affiliation: Moores Rowland International

International Contact: Melitta Kabele

AUDITOR TREUHAND GmbH

Börsegebäude, Wipplingerstrasse 34, 1010 VIENNA
Tel: + *43* (1) 53 13 3
Fax: + *43* (1) 53 31 95 9

European Affiliation: Arthur Andersen Worldwide

International Contact: Günter Cerha

AWIT ALLGEMEINE WIRTSCHAFTSTREUHAND GmbH

Capistrangasse 4/9, 1060 VIENNA
Tel: + *43* (1) 58 77 13 1
Fax: + *43* (1) 58 71 63 8

European Affiliation: Affiliated Conference of Practising Accountants International (ACPA)

International Contact: Dr. Udo Stalzer

Partners:	1
Professional staff:	3
Non-professional staff:	5
Total Staff:	**9**

FEE INCOME

Year End: 1990	%
Accountancy & Audit:	60.0
Tax:	40.0

CONTACT INFORMATION

Chairman & Managing Partner: Dr. Udo Stalzer
Audit & Tax: Dr. Gottfried Wirth
Audit & Tax: Christian Kogelgruber
Accountancy & Tax: Michael Karglmayer

CLIENT SERVICES

Accountancy (General), Audit, Value for Money Studies, Taxation (Corporate), Taxation (International)

HANS BAUMGARTNER WIRTSCHAFTSTREUHAND GmbH

Leopoldsgasse 6, 1020 VIENNA
Tel: + *43* (1) 33 44 70
Fax: + *43* (1) 21 62 82 0

European Affiliation: Jeffreys Henry International

International Contact: Andreas Baumgartner

BDO BINDER GmbH

Stock im Eisen-Platz 3, 1010 VIENNA 1
Tel: + *43* (1) 51 27 62 1
Fax: + *43* (1) 51 34 26 9

European Affiliation: BDO Binder

International Contact: Dr. Wolfgang Forster

Partners:	20
Professional staff:	200
Non-professional staff:	40
Total Staff:	**260**

FEE INCOME

Year End: 1990	%
Accountancy & Audit:	50.0
Insolvency:	5.0
Consultancy:	5.0
Tax:	35.0
Other:	5.0

CONTACT INFORMATION

Chairman: Dr. Wolfgang Gassner
Managing Partner: Siegbert Jaköncic
Accountancy (General): Anton Weber
Corporate Finance: Dr. Wolfgang Houska
Management Consultancy: Dr. Bernhard Gröhs
Administration: Elisabeth Pointner
Tax (Corporate): Dr. Johann Perthold
Tax (International): Dr. Eduard Lechner
Audit & Public Sector: Siegbert Jaköncic
Office Director: Monica Stadler
Marketing: Wolfgang Riedl

CLIENT SERVICES

Accountancy (General), Audit, Corporate Finance Advice, Insolvency & Corporate Restructuring, Litigation/Legal Services, Management & Business Advice, Management Buy-outs, Mergers & Acquisitions, Pensions Planning, Value for Money Studies, Taxation (Corporate), Taxation (International), Trust Settlement & Estates

Industry Specialisations: Contractors, Electricity, Airlines, Communities, Chemicals & Fibres, Food Stores, Machinery, Beverages

MAJOR CLIENTS

AEG, Austria Tabak Werke, Austrian Airlines, Austrian Industries, Die Erste Österr Spar Casse, Girozentrale, Lenzing AG, Maschinenfabrik Andritz, Julius Meinl AG, Metallwerk Plansee, Österr Länderbank AG, Philips (Daughter Firms), Pols, Porr AG, Siemens (Daughter Firms), J.M. Voith AG

OTHER OFFICES

ÖSTERREICHISCHE WIRTSCHAFTSBERATUNG INTERNATIONALE TREUHAND GmbH
Rosentaler Strasse 5/8, 9020 KLAGENFURT
Tel: + *43* (463) 55 91 0 *Fax:* + *43* (463) 51 44 29
Contact: Dr. Johann Neuner

ASSOCIATED FIRMS

AUDIT SALZBURG WIRTSCHAFTSPRÜFUNGS GmbH
Mildenburggasse 6, 5020 SALZBURG
Tel: + *43* (662) 28 57 10 *Fax:* + *43* (662) 23 09 1

EIDOS WIRTSCHAFTSBERATUNG GmbH
Stock im Eisen-Platz 3, 1010 VIENNA 1
Tel: + *43* (1) 51 27 62 1 *Fax:* + *43* (1) 51 34 26 9
Contact: Dr. Wolfgang Gassner

MAG. ALFRED RIEDL & COMPANY KG
Schubertstrasse 8, 3430 TULLN
Tel: + *43* (2272) 35 30 *Fax:* + *43* (2272) 35 30 22

Total Number of Offices: 7

▷

BILANZ-DATA
Karlsplatz 3, 1010 VIENNA
Tel: + *43* (1) 50 53 11 7

European Affiliation: A.E.E. International

International Contact: E. Baier

CLIENT SERVICES
All Services

BURGER, MAYER-SCHÜTZ & PALFFY WIRTSCHAFTSPRÜFUNGS GmbH
Brucknerstrasse 8, 1040 VIENNA
Tel: + *43* (1) 50 54 80 1
Fax: + *43* (1) 50 54 80 172

European Affiliation: Urbach Hacker Young International

International Contact: Dr. Ernst Burger

Partners:	4
Professional staff:	30
Non-professional staff:	5
Total Staff:	**39**

FEE INCOME

Year End: 1990	%
Accountancy & Audit:	40.0
Insolvency:	5.0
Consultancy:	5.0
Tax:	40.0
Other:	10.0

CONTACT INFORMATION
Chairman: Dr. Ernst Burger
Managing Partner: Martin Palffy
Managing Partner: Stefan Gruber

CLIENT SERVICES
All Services

OTHER OFFICES

DR MAYER-SCHÜTZ WIRTSCHAFTSPRÜNGS GmbH
Karl-Wiser-Strasse 1, 4020 LINZ
Tel: + *43* (732) 66 16 11 *Fax:* + *43* (732) 58 68 1
Contact: Dr. Wolfgang Mayer-Schütz

DR MARTIN PALFFY
Schloss Sighartstein, 5202 NEUMARKT
Tel: + *43* (6216) 25 1 *Fax:* + *43* (6216) 73 09
Contact: Dr. Martin Palffy

Total Number of Offices: 3

CONSULTATIO mbH
Holzmeistergasse 9, 1210 VIENNA
Tel: + *43* (1) 38 76 32 240
Fax: + *43* (1) 38 76 32 279

European Affiliation: Clark Kenneth Leventhal

International Contact: Gerhard Pichler

Partners:	3
Professional staff:	62
Non-professional staff:	12
Total Staff:	77

FEE INCOME

Year End: 1990	%
Accountancy & Audit:	42.2
Tax:	22.7
Other:	35.1

CLIENT SERVICES
Accountancy (General), Audit, Corporate Finance Advice, Insolvency & Corporate Restructuring, Management & Business Advice, Taxation (Corporate), Taxation (International)

COOPERS & LYBRAND GmbH/INTER-TREUHAND mbH
Berggasse 31, 1090 VIENNA
Tel: + *43* (1) 31 37 70
Fax: + *43* (1) 31 37 76
Mailing Address: Postfach 161, 1092 VIENNA

European Affiliation: Coopers & Lybrand Europe

International Contact: Walter Mahr

Total Staff: **150**

CONTACT INFORMATION
Managing Partner: Walter Mahr
Corporate Finance: Hans Wessely
Management Consultancy: Stefan Sabadello
Tax: Helmut Knotzinger

CLIENT SERVICES
All Services

Industry Specialisations: Banking, Insurance, Automotive, Pharmaceuticals, Food & Drink, Communications

DANUBIA TREUHAND-UND BERATUNGSGES mbH
Rotenturmstrasse 1, 1010 VIENNA
Tel: + *43* (1) 53 38 81 5
Fax: + *43* (1) 53 38 84 0

European Affiliation: DRT International

International Contact: Andreas Palatin

Total Staff: **50**

CLIENT SERVICES
All Services

MAJOR CLIENTS
Amada, Arab Bank, Boehringer Mannheim, Gaskoks, General Motors Acceptance Corporation, General Motors Corporation, Group Honeywell Bull, Hoerbiger Group, Intercont, Man-Öaf, Man-SNF, Merril Lynch, Procter & Gamble Company, Quester Baustoffhandel, Tandon Computers Corporation, Tektronix, Tel Mineralwolle, Viennatone, Waagner-Biro

EWB REVISIONS-UND TREUHAND GmbH
Am Modenapark 10, 1030 VIENNA
Tel: + *43* (1) 71 29 99 1
Fax: + *43* (1) 71 29 99 130

European Affiliation: Nexia International

Partners:	2
Professional staff:	12
Non-professional staff:	6
Total Staff:	**20**

FEE INCOME

Year End: 31.12.91	Sch	%
Accountancy & Audit:		25.0
Insolvency:		5.0
Consultancy:		15.0
Tax:		55.0
Total:	**20,000,000**	

▷

CONTACT INFORMATION
Chairman: Dr. V. Hammerle
Managing Partner: Hartwig Reinold

CLIENT SERVICES
Accountancy (General), Audit, Insolvency & Corporate Restructuring, Management & Business Advice, Management Buy-outs, Mergers & Acquisitions, Taxation (Corporate), Taxation (International)

Industry Specialisations: Tourism, Publishing

FISCHER, KROS & COMP

P.O. Box 112, Auhofstrasse 1-3, 1130 VIENNA
Tel: + 43 (1) 87 73 90 00
Fax: + 43 (1) 87 73 90 030

European Affiliation: Moore Stephens

International Contact: Jurgen Fischer

Total Number of Offices: 2

DR. WERNER FRITSCH

Goldschmiedgasse 10, 1010 VIENNA
Tel: + 43 (1) 53 34 51 1
Fax: + 43 (1) 53 34 51 141

European Affiliation: INPACT - International Network of Professional Accountants

International Contact: Dr. Werner Fritsch

GAIER, MAYER & COMP GmbH

Brucknerstrasse 4, 1041 VIENNA
Tel: + 43 (1) 50 53 79 50
Fax: + 43 (1) 50 53 79 540
Mailing Address: P.O. Box 108, 1041 VIENNA

European Affiliation: Alliott Peirson International

International Contact: Christian Mayer

HALPERN & PRINZ

Wasagasse 4, 1090 VIENNA
Tel: + 43 (1) 34 66 91
Fax: + 43 (1) 34 66 91 20

European Affiliation: TGI International

International Contact: Dr. Gerhard Prinz

IB INTERBILANZ WIRTSCHAFTSTREUHAND GmbH

Gusshausstrasse 4, 1040 VIENNA
Tel: + 43 (1) 50 54 31 3
Fax: + 43 (1) 50 54 57 013

European Affiliation: DFK International

International Contact: Fritz Himmer

Partners:	8
Professional staff:	28
Non-professional staff:	4
Total Staff:	**40**

FEE INCOME

Year End: 1991	%
Accountancy & Audit:	60.0
Consultancy:	10.0
Tax:	30.0

CONTACT INFORMATION
Chairman: Fritz Himmer
Administration: E. Schwartz
Tax (International): Martin Wagner
Accountancy & Tax (Corporate): Marco Egger
Audit & Corporate Finance: Fritz Himmer
Public Sector & Consultancy: Arnold Steffens

CLIENT SERVICES
Accountancy (General), Audit, Corporate Finance Advice, Management Buy-outs, Mergers & Acquisitions, Taxation (Corporate), Taxation (International), Management Consultancy

Industry Specialisations: Automotive (Wholesale & Retail), Machinery

IB INTERFIDES

Grungasse 16, 1052 VIENNA
Tel: + 43 (1) 588 33
Fax: + 43 (1) 588 33 88

European Affiliation: Horwath International

International Contact: Dr. Günther Halvax

INTERCONTROL GmbH

Bergasse 16, 1090 VIENNA
Tel: + 43 (1) 31 26 01 0
Fax: + 43 (1) 31 26 01 20

European Affiliation: HLB International

INTEREXPERT-TREUHAND GmbH & CO OHG

Gierstergasse 6, 1120 VIENNA
Tel: + 43 (1) 83 56 15
Fax: + 43 (1) 83 56 15 18

European Affiliation: Independent Accountants International

International Contact: Hubert Cussigh
Dr. Peter Hammerschmidt

Partners:	2
Professional staff:	15
Non-professional staff:	12
Total Staff:	**29**

FEE INCOME

Year End: 31.01.91	**Sch**	%
Accountancy & Audit:		60.0
Consultancy:		10.0
Tax:		20.0
Other:		10.0
Total:	**25,000,000**	

CONTACT INFORMATION
Partner: Hubert Cussigh
Partner: Dr. Peter Hammerschmidt

CLIENT SERVICES
Accountancy (General), Audit, Corporate Finance Advice, Insolvency & Corporate Restructuring, Management & Business Advice, Taxation (Corporate), Taxation (International)

Industry Specialisations: Joint Ventures in Eastern Europe

JONASCH & PLATZER

Henckellgasse 19, 1140 VIENNA
Tel: + 43 (1) 94 42 56
Fax: + 43 (1) 94 51 35 13

▷

European Affiliation: Grant Thornton International

International Contact: Dr. Walter Platzer

Partners:	6
Professional staff:	17
Non-professional staff:	4
Total Staff:	**27**

CONTACT INFORMATION

Managing Partner: Dr. Walter Platzer
Tax (Corporate): Dr. Franz Schiessel
Tax (International): Dr. Andreas Köninger
Accountancy & Audit: Josef Toglhofer
Corporate Finance & Administration: Dr. Walter Platzer

CLIENT SERVICES

Accountancy (General), Audit, Corporate Finance Advice, Insolvency & Corporate Restructuring, Litigation/Legal Services, Management & Business Advice, Management Buy-outs, Mergers & Acquisitions, Taxation (Corporate), Taxation (International)

KPMG

KPMG ALPEN-TREUHAND GmbH

Kolingasse 19, 1090 VIENNA
Tel: + 43 (1) 31 33 20
Fax: + 43 (1) 31 33 25

European Affiliation: KPMG

International Contact: Georg Edlinger

Partners:	33
Professional staff:	298
Non-professional staff:	143
Total Staff:	**474**

FEE INCOME

Year End: 30.09.91	**Sch**	**%**
Accountancy & Audit:	266,076,000	58.0
Consultancy:	24,789,000	26.0
Tax:	118,944,000	5.0
Other:	50,331,000	11.0
Total:	**460,140,000**	

CONTACT INFORMATION

Managing Partner: Paul Hassler
Corporate Finance: Anton W. Knott
Management Consultancy: Franz Wojda
Accountancy & Audit: Martin Wagner
Tax: Thomas Kozich

CLIENT SERVICES

Accountancy (General), Audit, Corporate Finance Advice, Insolvency & Corporate Restructuring, Management & Business Advice, Management Buy-outs, Mergers & Acquisitions, Pensions Planning, Taxation (Corporate), Taxation (International)

Industry Specialisations: Banking, Insurance, Electrical, Mining & Metals, Brewing, Tyres, Construction & Building Materials

MAJOR CLIENTS

Asea Brown Boveri, BAWAG Bank für Arbeit und Wirtschaft AG, BAWAG Verischerungs-AG, Brau AG, Creditanstalt-Bankverein, EA-General AG, EVN, Genossenschaftliche Zentralbank AG, Interunfall-RAS Versicherungs-Aktiengesellschaft, Landis & Gyr, Metallgesellschaft Austria AG, OKA, Osterreichische Brau AG, Osterreichische Philips Industrie GmbH, Semperit Reifen AG, Siemens AG Osterreich, Universale Bau AG, Wiener Allianz Versicherung AG, Wiener Stadtische Versicherung, Wienerberger Baustoffindustrie AG

OTHER OFFICES

KPMG ALPEN-TREUHAND GmbH
Kudlichstrasse 43, 4020 LINZ
Tel: + 43 (732) 66 40 61 *Fax:* + 43 (732) 66 40 61
Contact: Gerd-Dieter Mirtl

KPMG ALPEN-TREUHAND GmbH
Glacisstrasse 27, 8010 GRAZ
Tel: + 43 (732) 66 40 61 *Fax:* + 43 (732) 66 4061245
Contact: Johannes Haider

KPMG AUSTRIA WIRTSCHAFTSPRÜFUNGS GmbH
Kolingasse 19, 1090 VIENNA
Tel: + 43 (1) 31 33 20 *Fax:* + 43 (1) 31 99 28 3
Contact: Georg Edlinger

KPMG KÄRNTNER TREUHAND GmbH
Krassniggstrasse 36, 9020 KLAGENFURT
Tel: + 43 (463) 51 28 20 *Fax:* + 43 (463) 51 28 20
Contact: Ernst Kohlführt

KPMG KÄRNTNER TREUHAND GmbH
Bahnhofstrasse 18, 9800 SPITTAL/DRAU
Tel: + 43 (4762) 40 01 *Fax:* + 43 (4762) 40 01 18
Contact: Hans Malliga

KPMG KÄRNTNER TREUHAND GmbH
Gerbergasse 13, 9500 VILLACH
Tel: + 43 (4242) 22 92 0 *Fax:* + 43 (4242) 22 92 020
Contact: Hans Malliga

KPMG GmbH
Grosse Mohrengasse 1, 1020 VIENNA
Tel: + 43 (1) 21 66 87 0 *Fax:* + 43 (1) 21 66 87 0
Contact: Franz Wojda

MUNDUS TREUHAND GmbH
Reichenhallerstrasse 6-8, 5020 SALZBURG
Tel: + 43 (662) 84 45 95 *Fax:* + 43 (662) 84 45 95
Contact: Otto Troyer

Total Number of Offices: 13

LIBERTAS INTERCOUNT REVISIONS- UND BERATUNGSGESELLSCHAFT

Teinfaltstrasse 4, 1010 VIENNA
Tel: + 43 (63) 94 16 0
Fax: + 43 (63) 94 16 20

European Affiliation: SC International

International Contact: Cornelius Kodrnja

DKFM HERBERT F. MAIER

Walfishchgasse 5/8, 1015 VIENNA
Tel: + 43 (1) 51 38 36 2
Fax: + 43 (1) 51 34 86 4

European Affiliation: INPACT - International Network of Professional Accountants

International Contact: Herbert Maier

Partners:	1
Professional staff:	1

CLIENT SERVICES

All Services

Industry Specialisations: Leisure, Arts

Total Number of Offices: 2

NEUNER + HENZL TREUHAND GmbH

Garnisongasse 20, 1096 VIENNA
Tel: + *43* (1) 40 39 52 8
Fax: + *43* (1) 40 87 84 5

European Affiliation: BKR International

International Contact: Michael Neuner

Partners:	3
Professional staff:	19
Non-professional staff:	10
Total Staff:	**32**

FEE INCOME

Year End: 1990	**Sch**	**%**
Accountancy & Audit:		48.0
Consultancy:		3.0
Tax:		46.0
Other:		3.0
Total:	**44,451,000**	

CONTACT INFORMATION

Chairman: Kurt Neuner
Managing Partner: Pipin Henzl
Management Consultancy: Kurt Neuner
Administration: Pipin Henzl
Audit & Corporate Tax: Richard Plessin
Audit & Tax (Corporate): Michael Neuner
Audit & Tax (International): Ursula Neuner

CLIENT SERVICES

Accountancy (General), Audit, Computer Installation, Insolvency & Corporate Restructuring, Management & Business Advice, Mergers & Acquisitions, Taxation (Corporate), Taxation (International)

MAJOR CLIENTS

Arlberg Straßentunnel AG, Autobahnen-und Schnellstraßen AG, BEGAS-Burgenländische Erdgasversorgungs-AG, Brenner Autobahn AG, Burgenland Holding AG, Burgenländische Elektrizitäts-wirtschafts-AG, Chemie-Holding AG, Koenig & Bauer AG, Langbein-Pfanhauser-Werke Beteil AG, Nestlé AG, OKGT Hungarian Oil and Gas Trust, ÖMV AG, Österreichische Elektrizitätswirtschafts AG, Österreichische Nationalbank, Österreichischer Rundfunk, Pyhrn Autobahn AG, Salzburger Kredit - und Wechsel - Bank AG, Tauernautobahn AG, Vorarlberger Kraftwerke AG, Wiener Bundesstraßen AG

OTHER OFFICES

NEUNER + HENZL TREU-MANDAT
Garnisongasse 20, 1096 VIENNA
Tel: + *43* (1) 40 39 52 8 *Fax:* + *43* (1) 40 87 84 5

REVIDATA EDV-BERATUNG GmbH
Garnisongasse 20, 1096 VIENNA
Tel: + *43* (1) 40 39 52 8 *Fax:* + *43* (1) 40 87 84 5

DR. ROSENKRANZ BERATUNGSGESELLSCHAFT
Garnisongasse 20, 1096 VIENNA
Tel: + *43* (1) 40 39 52 8 *Fax:* + *43* (1) 40 87 84 5

Total Number of Offices: 4

NOEWP - NIEDEROESTERR WIRTSCHAFTSPRUEFUNGS

Riemerschmidgasse 9, 2344 MARIA ENDZERSDORF
Tel: + *43* (2236) 24 20 60
Fax: + *43* (2236) 25 99 5

European Affiliation: DRM Internationally

International Contact: Dr. W. Egger

Partners:	5
Professional staff:	9
Non-professional staff:	16
Total Staff:	**30**

CONTACT INFORMATION

Managing Partner: Dr. A. Egger
Accountancy & Audit: Dr. A. Egger
Tax: G. Schellmann

CLIENT SERVICES

Accountancy (General), Audit, Corporate Finance Advice, Insolvency & Corporate Restructuring, Management & Business Advice, Management Buy-outs, Mergers & Acquisitions, Pensions Planning, Value for Money Studies, Taxation (Corporate), Taxation (International), Trust Settlement & Estates

ASSOCIATED FIRMS

EXACTA TREUHAND-UND BERATUNGSGESELLSCHAFT mbH
Bösendorferstrasse 1, 1010 VIENNA
Tel: + *43* (1) 50 11 40 *Fax:* + *43* (1) 50 11 46 0
Contact: Dr. Peter Zeinler

Total Number of Offices: 2

OMIKRON

Markgraf, Rudigerstrasse 8, 1150 VIENNA
Tel: + *43* (1) 95 65 81
Fax: + *43* (1) 95 65 84 25

European Affiliation: International Association of Practising Accountants (IAPA)

International Contact: Peter Rosenstingel
Anna Maria Dreher

Partners:	2
Professional staff:	8
Non-professional staff:	13
Total Staff:	**23**

CONTACT INFORMATION

Partner: Peter Rosenstingl
Tax Consultant: Anna Maria Dreher

CLIENT SERVICES

Accountancy (General), Corporate Finance Advice, Management & Business Advice, Mergers & Acquisitions, Taxation (Corporate), Trust Settlement & Estates

PRICE WATERHOUSE AG

Prinz Eugen Strasse 72, 1040 VIENNA
Tel: + *43* (1) 71 34 56
Fax: + *43* (1) 71 34 56

European Affiliation: Price Waterhouse

Partners:	6
Professional staff:	100
Non-professional staff:	20
Total Staff:	**126**

FEE INCOME

Year End: 30.06.91	**%**
Accountancy & Audit:	55.0
Consultancy:	5.0
Tax:	40.0

CONTACT INFORMATION

Managing Partner: Günther Robol
Accountancy (General): Friedrich Rödler
Corporate Finance: Friederike Berghold
Insolvency: Wolfram Steiner
Administration: Josef Koppensteiner
Public Sector: Christian Kraetschmer
Audit & Management Consultancy: Günther Robol
Tax: Friedrich Rödler
Financial Services: Friederike Berghold
Information Systems: Aslan Milla

CLIENT SERVICES

Accountancy (General), Audit, Corporate Finance Advice, Insolvency & Corporate Restructuring, Management & Business Advice, Management Buy-outs, Mergers & Acquisitions, Taxation (Corporate), Taxation (International), Management Consultancy

Industry Specialisations: Banking, Advertising Agencies, Manufacturing, Pharmaceutical, Eastern Europe

OTHER OFFICES

GRT LEITNER, LENNERT & CO
Ottensheimer Strasse 32, 4040 LINZ
Tel: + 43 (732) 23 64 46 0 *Fax:* + 43 (732) 23 64 4634
Contact: Reinhard Leitner

GRT REVISIONS-UND TREUHANDGESELLSCHAFT mbH
Riedergasse 10a, 6900 BREGENZ
Tel: + 43 (1) 58 82 00
Contact: Günter Robol

GRT SALZBURG
Nonntaler Hauptstrasse 55, 5020 SALZBURG
Tel: + 43 (662) 82 54 70 *Fax:* + 43 (662) 82 54 7013
Contact: Manfred Laubichler

GRT & PARTNER
Kempfstrasse 23, 9021 KLAGENFURT
Tel: + 43 (463) 51 62 81 *Fax:* + 43 (463) 56 58 82 0
Contact: Dr. Hubert Huber

Total Number of Offices: 5

PRODINGER & PARTNER

Auerspergstrasse 8, 5700 ZELL/SEE
Tel: + 43 (6542) 36 61
Fax: + 43 (6542) 36 61 14

European Affiliation: Affiliated Conference of Practising Accountants International (ACPA)

International Contact: Dr. Erwin Prodinger

REVISIONSTREUHAND

Margaretenstrasse 78, 1050 VIENNA
Tel: + 43 (1) 56 55 61 0
Fax: + 43 (1) 56 55 61 40

European Affiliation: Russell Bedford International

International Contact: Dr. Wolfgang Wiesner
Mag. Johann Pokorny

OTHER OFFICES

REVISIONSTREUHAND
Reichenhallerstrasse 10a, 5020 SALZBURG
Tel: + 43 (662) 84 22 90 *Fax:* + 43 (662) 84 99 37

Total Number of Offices: 2

PROF DKFM DR SCHUSTER & DKFM WALTER TÜRKE, MAG. PETER GROTSCHAR

Kaiserstrasse 37, 1070 VIENNA
Tel: + 43 (1) 93 66 01
Fax: + 43 (1) 96 48 83

European Affiliation: Midsnell International

International Contact: W. Türke

SÜD-OST TREUHAND AG

Praterstrasse 23, 1021 VIENNA
Tel: + 43 (1) 21 17 00
Fax: + 43 (1) 21 62 07 7
Mailing Address: P.O. Box 290, 1021 VIENNA

European Affiliation: Ernst & Young Europe

International Contact: Alexius Göschl

OTHER OFFICES

ERNST & YOUNG GmbH
Praterstrasse 23, 1021 VIENNA
Tel: + 43 (1) 21 17 00 *Fax:* + 43 (1) 21 62 07 7

EUROPÄISCHE TREUHAND GmbH
Helferstorferstrasse 4, 1010 VIENNA
Tel: + 43 (1) 53 31 70 4 *Fax:* + 43 (1) 53 54 56 540
Contact: Johannes Marenzi

SÜD-OST TREUHAND
Landstrasse 49/III, 4020 LINZ
Tel: + 43 (732) 27 32 55 *Fax:* + 43 (732) 28 30 12
Contact: Erich Abpurg

SÜD-OST TREUHAND
Lichtenfelsgasse 17, 8010 GRAZ
Tel: + 43 (316) 36 97 8 *Fax:* + 43 (316) 36 97 83 1
Contact: Friedrich Spritzey

SÜD-OST TREUHAND
Evangelische Kirchengasse 4, 7400 OBERWART
Tel: + 43 (3352) 23 83 *Fax:* + 43 (3352) 23 83 21
Contact: Hans Roth

SÜD-OST TREUHAND
Nonntaler Hauptstrasse 49/II, 5020 SALZBURG
Tel: + 43 (662) 82 07 93 *Fax:* + 43 (662) 82 07 9319
Contact: Paul Huber

SÜD-OST TREUHAND
Service Department, Prinz-Eugen-Strasse 34, 1041 VIENNA
Tel: + 43 (1) 50 12 1 *Fax:* + 43 (1) 50 56 04 0
Contact: Walter Wundsam

Total Number of Offices: 8

TREUHAND UNION

Breyerstrasse 9, 2500 BADEN
Tel: + 43 (2252) 43350
Fax: + 43 (2252) 42919

European Affiliation: The International Group of Accounting Firms Ltd (IGAF)

International Contact: Jost Lehner

UNIVERSALE REVISIONS-UND TREUHAND GmbH

Lichtenfelsgasse 5, 1010 VIENNA 1
Tel: + 43 (1) 43 37 18
Fax: + 43 (1) 43 88 45

▷

European Affiliation: Summit International Associates Inc

International Contact: Wolfgang Dittrich

Partners:	4
Professional staff:	7
Non-professional staff:	3
Total Staff:	**14**

FEE INCOME

Year End: 31.12.90	**Sch**	**%**
Accountancy & Audit:	3,760,000	40.0
Tax:	2,820,000	30.0
Other:	2,820,000	30.0
Total:	**9,400,000**	

CONTACT INFORMATION
Managing Partner: Bruno Grosschedl
Administration: Renate Jordan
Accountancy & Audit: Bruno Grosschedl
Insolvency & Tax (Corporate): Guntram Mathis
Public Sector & Tax (International): Wolfgang Dittrich
Valuation of Enterprise & Utilities: Wolfgang Dittrich
Utilities (Consumer Price): Gerhard Grabner

CLIENT SERVICES
Accountancy (General), Audit, Insolvency & Corporate Restructuring, Management & Business Advice, Management Buy-outs, Mergers & Acquisitions, Taxation (Corporate), Taxation (International), Cost Controlling Electricity Price, Valuation of Enterprise

Industry Specialisations: Railways, Aluminium, Chemical, Agriculture, Banking, Paper, Auto, Construction, Trading, Hospitals

VICTORIA WIRTSCHAFTSTREUHAND GmbH

Prinz-Eugen-Strasse 16, 1040 VIENNA
Tel: + *43* (1) 50 57 83 60
Fax: + *43* (1) 50 55 51 1

European Affiliation: GMN International

International Contact: Dr. Alfred Schreder

Total Number of Offices: 2

WIRTSCHAFTSPRÜFER DR. PETER WOLF

Lehargasse 3a, 1060 VIENNA
Tel: + *43* (1) 58 77 26 0
Fax: + *43* (1) 58 77 26 0

European Affiliation: ATD International

International Contact: Dr. Peter Wolf

Belgium

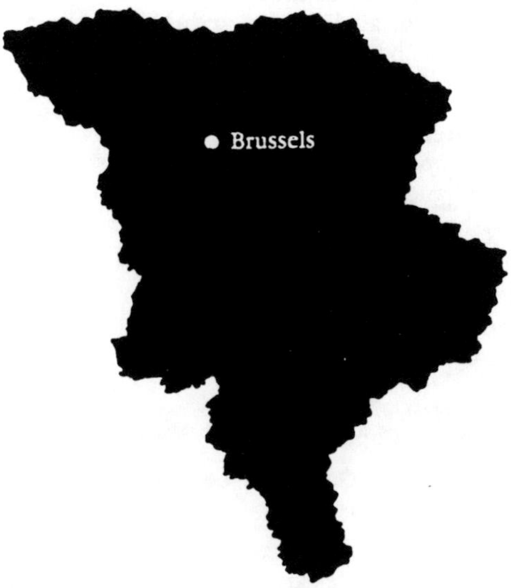

Area: 30,513 sq km (11,781 sq miles)
Population: 9,875,716 (1987 estimate)
Density: 323 per sq km
Capital: Brussels

GDP: BFr6.9 trn, US$210 bn
GDP per head: US$21,230
Inflation: 1990 - 3.0%
1991 - 2.8% (forecast)

Official and Spoken Language: Flemish and French

Time: GMT + 1 (in Summer GMT + 2)
Telephone Dialling Code: + 32

Currency: Belgian Franc (BFr) = 100 centimes
Banking Hours: 0900-1200 and 1400-1600 Monday to Friday
Professional accountancy bodies: Institut des Reviseurs d'Enterprises (IRE)
Institut des Experts Comptables (IEC)

Corporate Tax Data

Information supplied by Richard Citron, international tax partner of Stoy Hayward.

The tax year; nature and rates of tax

The tax year is the calendar year. The tax year is that in which an accounting period ends, if not 31 December.

The corporation tax (impôt des sociétés; vennootschapsbelasting) applies at a standard rate of 39% for the tax year 1992 (41% for 1991) on both distributed and undistributed income. There are lower rates for profits below BFr 13,000,000. Some capital gains are taxed at 19.5%.

Special regimes. Special taxation treatment is accorded to Belgian based administration or liaison offices of foreign companies, including the "coordination centre". Briefly, a coordination centre:

(1) Is part of an international group, with certain minimum consolidated equity and consolidated turnover requirements with subsidiaries in at least four different countries;
(2) Employs at least 10 persons in Belgium at the end of its second year of operations;
(3) Is engaged in activities such as advertising, information, centralisation of administration, accounting or financing operations and not commercial activities.

Coordination centre advantages:

(1) Liability to corporation tax is based on a notional percentage (negotiable but usually 4% to 10%) of certain expenses (excluding financial and salary costs) incurred (with certain lower limits).
(2) Dividends paid by coordination centres are not subject to withholding tax.

Belgium

Corporate residence rules and territoriality

Companies resident in Belgium are liable to corporation tax on worldwide profits or gains.

Companies incorporated in Belgium are resident there as are companies having their principal place of management in Belgium.

The tax base

Method of calculation. Taxable profits are based on total profits reported in the annual accounts.

Disallowable items. These include 50% of entertainment expenses, 25% of most costs related to motor cars, some reserves and certain accruals. Limits are placed on bad debt provisions.

Exempt income and special deductions. Certain dividend income is exempt (see below). Investment allowances are deductible.

Interest paid. Interest is normally deductible on an accruals basis. A withholding tax of 10% (25% if the loan predates 1 March 1990) is deductible from interest payments unless made to Belgian financial institutions, the Belgian state or to non-residents for whom a tax treaty prescribes a different rate.

Stock. Stock and work in progress is valued at the lower of cost and market value.

Depreciation. Either the straight line or the reducing balance basis may be used with a generally accepted range of values for different types of asset (ie. 3% for office buildings; 4% for factories and up to 33% for computers and tools). Many assets qualify in addition for an investment allowance of between 3% and 10% of cost (for 1991).

Treatment of dividends received and paid

Dividends received from Belgian companies. Under a participation exemption, 95% of the gross amount is exempted from tax. If a withholding has been suffered, it may be set against the recipient company's corporate tax liability and refunded where appropriate.

Dividends received from abroad. The same treatment applies as for Belgian source dividends although there are anti-abuse provisions limiting the scope of the exemption, eg the exemption is not available for dividends distributed by investment companies such as Luxembourg's SICAVs. Otherwise, the dividend is liable to corporation tax.

Dividends paid. No withholding tax is levied on dividends paid to a Belgian or other EC company provided that certain conditions are met, ie a participation of 25% has been held for at least one year. Otherwise a withholding of 25% is applied reduceble by double tax treaty.

Anti-avoidance measures

There are certain limits on deductible loan interest if not paid to banks or financial institutions. Transfer pricing rules also exist.

Treatment of losses

Current period. Losses may be offset against all income and gains of the current period (there is no carry-back).

Future periods. Losses may be carried forward to set off against future income and gains indefinitely although limited to the greater of BF 20 million and 50% of taxable income per year.

Treatment of capital gains

Treatment. Capital gains are treated as income.

Computation. Gains are computed by deducting cost from sale proceeds.

Roll-over. Roll-over exists for a wide variety of assets, but the rules are complicated and depend on length of ownership.

Special treatment of shares. Capital gains realised on the disposal of shares in either Belgian or foreign companies qualifying for the participation exemption are exempt from tax. Where shares were written down for tax purposes (this is no longer possible for accounting periods ending after 24 July 1991), any corresponding gain is taxed at the full corporation tax rate.

Treatment of groups

There is no concept of fiscal unity, so every company in a group must be treated separately.

Treatment of branches

A Belgian branch of a non-resident company is taxed on the same basis as a Belgian resident company although it suffers income tax at the rate of 43%. This is reduced by virtue of the operation of double tax treaties in many cases to 39%. The branch tax rate is 42.05% where the head office is France, the Netherlands or Luxembourg. Roll-over of capital gains is available to branches.

Other taxes

Taxes on capital. There is a variable real estate tax levied at the communal, provincial and national levels on all property situated in Belgium.

Turnover taxes. There is a value added tax with a standard rate of 19%, reduced rates of 6% and 17% and luxury rates of 25% and 33%. Exports are zero rated.

Transaction taxes. A capital duty of 0.5% is levied on capital contributions to companies. A registration tax of 12.5% is payable by the purchaser of immovable property.

Payroll taxes. A social security tax is payable on gross salaries at a minimum rate of 34%.

AGNEESSENS, VERSCHELDEN & PARTNERS BV - CV

L. Schmidtlaan 119, 1040 BRUSSELS
Tel: +32 (2) 73 24 44 0
Fax: +32 (2) 73 24 74 0

International Contact: Emmanuel Agneessens

Partners:	3
Professional staff:	12
Non-professional staff:	5
Total Staff:	**20**

FEE INCOME

Year End: 31.12.90	**BFr**	**%**
Accountancy & Audit:	26,000,000	82.0
Consultancy:	3,000,000	9.0
Tax:	3,000,000	9.0
Total:	**32,000,000**	

OTHER OFFICES

AGNEESSENS, VERSCHELDEN & PARTNERS BV-CV
Leeuw Van Vlaanderenlaan 33, 8500 KORTRIJK
Tel: +32 (56) 22 02 06 *Fax:* +32 (56) 22 02 93
Contact: Geert Lingier

AGNEESSENS, VERSCHELDEN & PARTNERS BV-CV
Thonetlaan 110, 2050 ANTWERP
Tel: +32 (3) 21 97 67 6 *Fax:* +32 (3) 21 98 27 9
Contact: Frans Verschelden

Total Number of Offices: 3

ARTHUR ANDERSEN & CO

Avenue des Arts 56, 1040 BRUSSELS
Tel: +32 (2) 51 04 21 1
Fax: +32 (2) 51 34 40 0

European Affiliation: Arthur Andersen Worldwide

International Contact: Marcel R. Asselberghs

CONTACT INFORMATION

Audit: Marcel R. Asselberghs
Tax (Corporate): Germain J. Vantieghem

CLIENT SERVICES

Accountancy (General), Audit, Computer Installation, Corporate Finance Advice, Insolvency & Corporate Restructuring, Litigation/Legal Services, Management & Business Advice, Management Buy-outs, Mergers & Acquisitions, Pensions Planning, Value for Money Studies, Taxation (Corporate), Taxation (International), Company Secretarial Services, Executive Renumeration, Personal Financial Planning

OTHER OFFICES

ARTHUR ANDERSEN & CO
Desguinlei 92, 2018 ANTWERP
Tel: +32 (3) 21 64 88 0 *Fax:* +32 (3) 23 73 68 7

Total Number of Offices: 2

BDO HILLEN

Boulevard de la Woluwe 60, 1200 BRUSSELS
Tel: +32 (2) 77 19 91 6
Fax: +32 (2) 77 15 65 6

European Affiliation: BDO Binder

Partners:	3
Professional staff:	44
Non-professional staff:	9
Total Staff:	**56**

FEE INCOME

Year End: 31.12.90	**BFr**	**%**
Accountancy & Audit:	100,000,000	83.0
Tax:	20,000,000	17.0
Total:	**120,000,000**	

CONTACT INFORMATION

Managing Partner: Frans J. Samyn
Accountancy (General): Rolf Adriaenssens
Accountancy (General): André Sempels
Audit: Frans J. Samyn
Audit: Luc Annick
Tax (Corporate): Patrik van Cauter
Tax (International): Martine Timmerman

CLIENT SERVICES

Accountancy (General), Audit, Management & Business Advice, Taxation (Corporate), Taxation (International)

OTHER OFFICES

BDO HILLEN
Uitbreidingstraat 66, 2600 ANTWERP
Mailing Address: Boite 13, 2600 ANTWERP
Tel: +32 (3) 23 05 84 0 *Fax:* +32 (3) 21 84 51 5
Contact: Rolf Adriaenssens

Total Number of Offices: 2

A.L. BELLEKENS

Avenue de Broquevillelaan 270/10, 1200 BRUSSELS
Tel: +32 (2) 77 00 91 8
Fax: +32 (2) 77 01 45 1

European Affiliation: ATD International

International Contact: Alfons Bellekens

Partners:	1
Professional staff:	6
Non-professional staff:	1
Total Staff:	**8**

FEE INCOME

Year End: 31.12.90	**%**
Accountancy & Audit:	65.0
Consultancy:	5.0
Tax:	20.0
Other:	10.0

CLIENT SERVICES

Accountancy (General), Audit, Corporate Finance Advice, Management & Business Advice, Taxation (Corporate)

BERNARD ET CIE ACC

Parc de la Cense Rouge, Rue du Bois Saint-Jean 20, 4102 OUGREE
Tel: +32 (41) 67 71 60
Fax: +32 (41) 67 90 03

European Affiliation: Growth & Progress Challenge

International Contact: J.C. Hardy

Partners:	3
Professional staff:	1
Non-professional staff:	1
Total Staff:	**5**

FEE INCOME

Year End: 30.06.90	**%**
Accountancy & Audit:	85.0
Tax:	15.0

▷

CONTACT INFORMATION
Chairman: Daniel Bernard
Managing Partner: D. Bernard

CLIENT SERVICES
Accountancy (General), Audit

MAJOR CLIENTS
Assimil - Editions Nelis SA, Ero Electronic Benelux SA, Good Night SA

C.V. BLANCKAERT, MISSORTEN, SPAENHOVEN & CO - SC

Meiseselaan 71, 1020 BRUSSELS
Tel: +*32* (2) 26 80 83 5
Fax: +*32* (2) 26 83 98 7

European Affiliation: Horwath International

International Contact: Prof. Dr. W. Missorten

Partners:	3
Professional staff:	13
Non-professional staff:	5
Total Staff:	**21**

FEE INCOME

Year End: 30.06.91	%
Accountancy & Audit:	94.0
Tax:	6.0

CONTACT INFORMATION
Audit: D. Blanchart
Audit: G. Spaenhoven
Audit & Tax: Prof. Dr. W. Missorten

CLIENT SERVICES
Audit, Taxation (Corporate), Taxation (International)

Industry Specialisations: Banking, Financial services

MAJOR CLIENTS
Beaulieu, Dr Beers Group, Mitsubishi Bank Group, Pacuro Group, Sheraton Hotel Group

OTHER OFFICES

C.V. BLANCKAERT, MISSORTEN, SPAENHOVEN & CO - SC
de Merodelei 4, 2600 BIRCHEM/ANTWERP
Tel: +*32* (3) 23 93 82 3 *Fax:* +*32* (3) 21 88 32 5
Contact: D. Blanchart

Total Number of Offices: 2

BOEYE, GEDDES VAN GULCK & CO

Place Rouppe 16, 1000 BRUSSELS
Tel: +*32* (2) 51 33 89 3
Fax: +*32* (2) 51 41 74 8

European Affiliation: Moores Rowland International

International Contact: John A. Geddes

OTHER OFFICES

BOEYE, GEDDES VAN GULCK & CO
Herentalsebaan 71-75, 2100 ANTWERP (Deurne)
Tel: +*32* (3) 32 23 86 0 *Fax:* +*32* (3) 32 23 85 8
Contact: Antoon Boeye

BOEYE, GEDDES VAN GULCK & CO
President Kennedypark 4, Bus 2, 8500 KORTRIJK
Tel: +*32* (56) 22 20 37 *Fax:* +*32* (56) 22 25 83
Contact: Dirk De Keyser

BOEYE, GEDDES VAN GULCK & CO
Bedrijfsstraat 2, 3500 HASSELT
Tel: +*32* (11) 22 01 68 *Fax:* +*32* (11) 22 01 83
Contact: Jean Vanderhaegen

BOEYE, GEDDES VAN GULCK & CO
Place St Jacques 11, Boite 21, 4000 LIEGE
Tel: +*32* (41) 22 90 86
Contact: Georges Finamore

BOEYE, GEDDES VAN GULCK & CO
Residentie Torensbos, Parklaan 55/25, 2300 TURNHOUT
Tel: +*32* (14) 42 07 21
Contact: Eddy Loots

Total Number of Offices: 6

CALLENS PIRENNE & CO

Van Eycklei 17, Boite 5, 2018 ANTWERP
Tel: +*32* (3) 23 11 56 8
Fax: +*32* (3) 23 35 10 2

European Affiliation: BKR International

International Contact: Boudewijn Callens

OTHER OFFICES

CALLENS PIRENNE & CO
Avenue Louise 207-209, Boite 22, 1050 BRUSSELS
Tel: +*32* (2) 64 04 67 8 *Fax:* +*32* (2) 64 98 21 0

CALLENS PIRENNE & CO
Centrum Createc, Kennedypark 1, P.O. Box 1, 8500 COURTRAY
Tel: +*32* (56) 23 55 75 *Fax:* +*32* (56) 23 55 01
Contact: Willy Vrijghem

CALLENS PIRENNE & CO
Chaussee de Theux 32, 4802 VERVIERS (LIEGE)
Tel: +*32* (87) 22 19 21
Contact: André Bruls

Total Number of Offices: 4

R. CARDOEN & CO BVBA

Stationsstraat 47, 1740 TERNAT
Tel: +*32* (2) 58 20 71 5
Fax: +*32* (2) 58 22 53 3

International Contact: Raymond Cardoen

Partners:	2
Professional staff:	4
Non-professional staff:	2
Total Staff:	**8**

FEE INCOME

Year End: 31.12.90	%
Accountancy & Audit:	60.0
Consultancy:	20.0
Tax:	15.0
Other:	5.0

CONTACT INFORMATION
Managing Partner: Raymond Cardoen

CLIENT SERVICES
Accountancy (General), Audit, Corporate Finance Advice, Insolvency & Corporate Restructuring, Management & Business Advice, Management Buy-outs, Mergers & Acquisitions, Taxation (Corporate), Trust Settlement & Estates

Industry Specialisations: Construction, Meat, Textiles

C.V. CLAEYS DE MAEYER & CO SC

Rue de L'Autonomie 9, 1070 BRUSSELS
Tel: +*32* (2) 52 14 52 5
Fax: +*32* (2) 52 08 23 2

European Affiliation: Clark Kenneth Leventhal

International Contact: Ivo Claeys

▷

Partners:	2
Professional staff:	18
Non-professional staff:	2
Total Staff:	**22**

FEE INCOME

Year End: 1990	%
Accountancy & Audit:	70.0
Tax:	30.0

CLIENT SERVICES

Accountancy (General), Audit, Corporate Finance Advice, Insolvency & Corporate Restructuring, Management & Business Advice, Taxation (Corporate), Taxation (International)

COOPERS & LYBRAND JACOBS EECKHOUT THIRIFAY & CO

Avenue Marcel Thiry 216, 1200 BRUSSELS
Tel: +*32* (2) 77 44 21 1
Fax: +*32* (2) 77 44 29 9

European Affiliation: Coopers & Lybrand Europe

International Contact: Georges F. Jacobs

Partners:	25
Professional staff:	340
Non-professional staff:	110
Total Staff:	**475**

CONTACT INFORMATION

Managing Partner: Georges F. Jacobs

CLIENT SERVICES

Accountancy (General), Audit, Computer Installation, Corporate Finance Advice, Insolvency & Corporate Restructuring, Life & Risk Assurance, Litigation/Legal Services, Management & Business Advice, Management Buy-outs, Mergers & Acquisitions, Pensions Planning, Value for Money Studies, Taxation (Corporate), Taxation (International), Trust Settlement & Estates, US Tax Consulting

OTHER OFFICES

COOPERS & LYBRAND EUROPE
European Community Office, Avenue de Tervuren 2, Boite 3, 1040 BRUSSELS
Tel: + *32* (2) 73 59 06 5 *Fax:* + *32* (2) 73 36 61 8

COOPERS & LYBRAND JACOBS EECKHOUT THIRIFAY & CO
Empire Building, Appelmanstraat 29, 2018 ANTWERP
Tel: + *32* (3) 22 43 61 1 *Fax:* + *32* (3) 23 17 51 7
Contact: Walter Caers

Total Number of Offices: 3

BEDRIJFSREVISOREN DE MEY EN CO BVBA

Kapellendries 29, 9230 WETTEREN
Tel: +*32* (91) 69 21 87
Fax: + *32* (91) 69 43 60

Partners:	1
Professional staff:	6
Non-professional staff:	1
Total Staff:	**8**

FEE INCOME

Year End: 31.12.90	**BFr**	%
Accountancy & Audit:	4,000,000	67.0
Consultancy:	1,000,000	17.0
Tax:	1,000,000	16.0
Total:	**6,000,000**	

CONTACT INFORMATION

Managing Partner: Willy de Mey

CLIENT SERVICES

Accountancy (General), Audit, Computer Installation, Corporate Finance Advice, Management Buy-outs, Mergers & Acquisitions, Value for Money Studies, Taxation (Corporate), Trust Settlement & Estates, Management Consultancy

MAJOR CLIENTS

de Clerck NV, Libeco NV, Paleis Voor Schone Kunsten, Prabel NV, Sitra NV, Van Guyse BVBA, Weverij Standaert

DEGREZ, MERCKEN, ROUVROY & CO SCC

Avenue Jules César 9, 1150 BRUSSELS
Tel: +*32* (2) 76 32 05 0
Fax: + *32* (2) 76 31 74 2

European Affiliation: DFK International

International Contact: Maurice Degrez

Partners:	4
Professional staff:	6
Non-professional staff:	3
Total Staff:	**13**

FEE INCOME

Year End: 31.12.90	%
Accountancy & Audit:	40.0
Consultancy:	20.0
Tax:	40.0

CONTACT INFORMATION

Managing Partner: Maurice Degrez
Accountancy (General): Thierry Hocepied
Management Consultancy: Maurice Degrez
Insolvency & Administration: Lucette Schouffler
Tax (Corporate & International): Johan Dens

CLIENT SERVICES

Accountancy (General), Audit, Corporate Finance Advice, Litigation/ Legal Services, Management & Business Advice, Mergers & Acquisitions, Taxation (Corporate), Taxation (International)

OTHER OFFICES

DEGREZ & CO SPRL
Oude Tervuursebaan 78, 3060 BERTEM
Tel: + *32* (16) 48 04 21
Contact: Lucette Schouffler

DEGREZ, MERCKEN, ROUVROY & CO SCC
Rue de France 29, 6340 PHILIPPEVILLE
Tel: + *32* (71) 66 77 88 *Fax:* + *32* (71) 66 65 14
Contact: André Rouvroy

JURIBEL SA
'De Wilde Zee', Wiegstraat 19, 2000 ANTWERP
Tel: + *32* (3) 23 22 32 8 *Fax:* + *32* (3) 23 40 98 6
Contact: Johan Dens

Total Number of Offices: 4

DELVAUX, BOVIJN, FRONVILLE & CO SC

Boulevard L. Schmidt 32, 1040 BRUSSELS
Tel: +*32* (2) 73 64 06 4
Fax: + *32* (2) 73 69 85 6

European Affiliation: TEG (The European Group of Accounting & Auditing Firms)

International Contact: Edward van Rijswijck

▷

DOMS ELPERS & CO

Rue de Pacale 33, 1040 BRUSSELS
Tel: +*32* (2) 23 10 87 5
Fax: +*32* (2) 23 03 14 2

European Affiliation: Independent Accountants International

International Contact: W.L.J. Doms

ERNST & YOUNG

Avenue Marcel Thiry 204, 1200 BRUSSELS
Tel: +*32* (2) 77 49 11 1
Fax: +*32* (2) 77 49 09 0

European Affiliation: Ernst & Young Europe

International Contact: Eric de Lembre

OTHER OFFICES

ERNST & YOUNG ACCOUNTANTS
Nationalestraat 5, Boite 35, 2000 ANTWERP
Tel: +*32* (3) 23 33 25 6 *Fax:* +*32* (3) 23 34 78 2
Contact: Mark De Vos

ERNST & YOUNG BEDRIJFSREVISOREN (AUDIT)
J. Englishstraat 54, 2140 BORGERHOUT
Tel: +*32* (3) 21 71 20 0 *Fax:* +*32* (3) 23 53 14 5
Contact: Gust Herrewijn

ERNST & YOUNG BEDRIJFSREVISOREN (AUDIT)
Residentie 'Lieven Bauwens', Martelaarslaan 53-55, 9000 GHENT
Tel: +*32* (91) 23 80 05 *Fax:* +*32* (91) 23 69 76
Contact: Paul Rappe

ERNST & YOUNG BEDRIJFSREVISOREN (AUDIT)
Luikersteenweg 185A, 3500 HASSELT
Tel: +*32* (11) 27 31 72 *Fax:* +*32* (11) 27 58 47
Contact: Hugo C.M. Joossens

ERNST & YOUNG REVISEURS D'ENTERPRISES (AUDIT)
Rue J. d'Outremeuse 91, 4020 LIEGE
Tel: +*32* (41) 42 65 62 *Fax:* +*32* (41) 41 71 57
Contact: Henri Kowalski

ERNST & YOUNG TAX CONSULTANTS
J. Englishstraat 54, 2140 BORGERHOUT
Tel: +*32* (3) 21 71 25 0 *Fax:* +*32* (3) 23 53 14 5
Contact: Paul Op de Beeck

ERNST & YOUNG TAX CONSULTANTS
Residentie 'Lieven Bauwens', Martelaarslaan 53-55, 9000 GHENT
Tel: +*32* (91) 23 80 05 *Fax:* +*32* (91) 23 69 76
Contact: Luc Cappelle

Total Number of Offices: 8

FRANSOLET VAN PASSEL & CO

38 Rue des Vennes, 4020 LIEGE
Tel: +*32* (41) 41 00 64
Fax: +*32* (41) 41 51 04

GHYOOT, KOEVOETS, ROSIER, VAN SANDE & CO

Amerikalei 108, 2000 ANTWERP
Tel: +*32* (3) 23 84 01 5
Fax: +*32* (3) 23 83 68 1

European Affiliation: Russell Bedford International

International Contact: Jean-Paul Koevoets

OTHER OFFICES

GHYOOT, KOEVOETS, ROSIER, VAN SANDE & CO
Avenue du Congo 11, 1050 BRUSSELS
Tel: +*32* (2) 64 98 51 9 *Fax:* +*32* (2) 64 88 82 3

GHYOOT, KOEVOETS, ROSIER, VAN SANDE & CO
Fraikinstraat 7, 2200 HERENTALS
Tel: +*32* (14) 21 04 63 *Fax:* +*32* (14) 23 11 34

Total Number of Offices: 3

C.V. HALLER, JOOS, WAETERLOOS & PARTNERS

Martelaarslaan 80, 9000 GHENT
Tel: +*32* (91) 24 11 59
Fax: +*32* (91) 33 10 68

European Affiliation: Summit International Associates Inc

International Contact: Gaston Haller
Martine Buysse
Paul van Kerk Hove

Partners:	7
Professional staff:	17
Non-professional staff:	16
Total Staff:	**40**

CONTACT INFORMATION

Managing Partner: Gaston Haller
Managing Partner: Hugo Waeterloos
Managing Partner: Luc H. Joos
Tax (Corporate & International): Marcel Brouckaert

CLIENT SERVICES

Accountancy (General), Audit, Corporate Finance Advice, Insolvency & Corporate Restructuring, Management & Business Advice, Mergers & Acquisitions, Taxation (Corporate), Taxation (International), Management Consultancy

OTHER OFFICES

C.V. HALLER, JOOS, WAETERLOOS & PARTNERS
Avenue De Tervueren 62, 1040 BRUSSELS
Tel: +*32* (2) 73 50 05 8
Contact: Gaston Haller

Total Number of Offices: 2

JEAN CLAUDE HARDY

Betgne 9, 4052 SPRIMONT DOLEMBREUX

European Affiliation: Growth & Progress Challenge

International Contact: Jean Claude Hardy

HENDRICKX, VAN WOENSEL & CO

Frankrijklei 133, 2000 ANTWERP
Tel: +*32* (3) 22 60 47 6
Fax: +*32* (3) 23 26 32 3

European Affiliation: Midsnell International

International Contact: Felix Hendrickx

OTHER OFFICES

HENDRICKX, VAN WOENSEL & CO
Avenue de la Toisin, Boite 20, 1060 BRUSSELS
Tel: +*32* (2) 53 92 64 1 *Fax:* +*32* (2) 53 43 50 1
Contact: Felix Hendrickx

Total Number of Offices: 2

HERMANT-DODEMONT & CO

Avenue Adolphe-Lacomblelaan 69-71, Boite 5, 1040 BRUSSELS
Tel: +*32* (2) 73 54 32 5
Fax: +*32* (2) 73 64 81 7

▷

European Affiliation: Urbach Hacker Young International

International Contact: Jean Dodemont

Partners:	7
Professional staff:	46
Non-professional staff:	13
Total Staff:	**66**

FEE INCOME

Year End: 1990	**BFr (000)**	**%**
Accountancy & Audit:	91,500	61.0
Tax:	58,000	39.0
Total:	**149,500**	

CONTACT INFORMATION

Managing Partner: Jean Dodemont
Accountancy (General): Daniel van Preht
Audit: J.P. Vandaele
Tax (Corporate): Paul Delestinne

CLIENT SERVICES

Accountancy (General), Audit, Corporate Finance Advice, Litigation/ Legal Services, Management & Business Advice, Management Buy-outs, Mergers & Acquisitions, Taxation (Corporate), Taxation (International), Management Consultancy

OTHER OFFICES

HERMANT-DODEMONT & CO
Oosterveldaau 102, 2610 ANTWERP
Tel: + *32* (3) 44 00 05 4 *Fax:* + *32* (3) 44 07 90 9
Contact: Ludo van Montfort

HERMANT-DODEMONT & CO
H. Consciencestraat 10, 8500 KORTRIJK
Tel: + *32* (5) 22 49 87 *Fax:* + *32* (5) 20 21 67
Contact: Daniel van Praet

HERMANT-DODEMONT & CO
Rue Forgeuz 4, 4000 LIEGE
Tel: + *32* (41) 23 67 25 *Fax:* + *32* (41) 25 58 16
Contact: Christian Grimmonprez

SEFICA
Faubourg de Bruxelles, 6200 CHARLEROI
Tel: + *32* (71) 35 74 73 *Fax:* + *32* (71) 35 83 12
Contact: Joseph Bourtier

Total Number of Offices: 5

ANDRÉ HOSTE & ASSOCIÉS

Avenue Château de Walzin 10, 1180 BRUSSELS
Tel: + *32* (2) 34 72 50 0
Fax: + *32* (2) 34 70 64 9

European Affiliation: Nexia International

International Contact: Dominic Rousselle

CONTACT INFORMATION

Partner: Catherine Dienst
Partner: André Hoste
Partner: Christian Sorel

KPMG

Neerveldstraat 101-103, 1200 BRUSSELS
Tel: + *32* (2) 77 34 30 0
Fax: + *32* (2) 77 34 39 9

European Affiliation: KPMG

Partners:	43
Professional staff:	423
Non-professional staff:	76
Total Staff:	**542**

FEE INCOME

Year End: 30.06.91	**BFr**	**%**
Accountancy & Audit:	1,081,000,000	73.0
Consultancy:	74,000,000	5.0
Tax:	296,000,000	20.0
Other:	30,000,000	2.0
Total:	**1,481,000,000**	

CONTACT INFORMATION

Chairman: A. Vanderveren
Audit: A. Vanderveren
Management Consultancy: A. Bruijs
Tax (Corporate): L. Denys

CLIENT SERVICES

Accountancy (General), Audit, Corporate Finance Advice, Management & Business Advice, Management Buy-outs, Mergers & Acquisitions, Taxation (Corporate), Taxation (International)

OTHER OFFICES

KPMG
Jan van Rijswijcklaan 162, 2020 ANTWERP
Tel: + *32* (3) 21 64 97 0 *Fax:* + *32* (3) 21 64 98 4
Contact: Peter P. Berger

KPMG
Belfaststraat 11, 8500 KORTRYK
Tel: + *32* (56) 20 25 76 *Fax:* + *32* (56) 22 49 52
Contact: Paul Behets

Total Number of Offices: 4

D. LEBRUN ET ASSOCIÉS SPRL

Rue de Jumet 76, 6041 GOSSELIES (Charleroi)
Tel: + *32* (71) 37 03 13
Fax: + *32* (71) 37 01 39

International Contact: Daniel Lebrun

Partners:	4
Professional staff:	4
Non-professional staff:	2
Total Staff:	**10**

CONTACT INFORMATION

Chairman: Daniel Lebrun
Managing Partner: Jean-Marie Joaris
Audit: Daniel Lebrun
Management Consultancy: Philippe Leemans
Administration: Jean-Marie Joaris
Accountancy & Public Sector: Chantal Stilman
Corporate Finance & Public Aids: Xavier Davoye
Tax: Thierry Lejuste

CLIENT SERVICES

Accountancy (General), Audit, Corporate Finance Advice, Insolvency & Corporate Restructuring, Management Buy-outs, Mergers & Acquisitions, Taxation (Corporate), Taxation (International), Management Consultancy

Industry Specialisations: Aeronautics, Hospitals, Public Sector

MAJOR CLIENTS

Donnay SA, Sonaca SA, S.I.T.A. SC

▷

BUREAU FIDUCIAIRE LERMINIAUX ET CIE SA

84 Rue Renkin, 1030 BRUSSELS
Tel: +32 (2) 24 52 41 0
Fax: +32 (2) 21 67 58 9

European Affiliation: INPACT - International Network of Professional Accountants

International Contact: Ernest Lerminiaux

CONTACT INFORMATION

Partner: Josiane Lerminiaux-Vincke
Partner: Jos Cappelle

LIPPENS, MARTEYN & RABAEY

Gentsesteenweg 1154, 1080 BRUSSELS
Tel: +32 (2) 46 90 10 0
Fax: +32 (2) 46 90 96 9

European Affiliation: Pannell Kerr Forster Worldwide

International Contact: Marc E. Marteyn

OTHER OFFICES

LIPPENS, MARTEYN & RABAEY
Onderbergen 13, 9000 GHENT
Tel: +32 (91) 24 35 83 *Fax:* +32 (91) 24 28 45
Contact: Jan Lippens

Total Number of Offices: 2

MOORE STEPHENS

Avenue Louise 207-209, Boite 8, 1050 BRUSSELS
Tel: +32 (2) 64 83 78 4
Fax: +32 (2) 64 05 34 3

European Affiliation: Moore Stephens

International Contact: Christopher Thubron

FIDUCIAIRE MOORES ROWLAND SA

Place Rouppe 16, 1000 BRUSSELS
Tel: +32 (2) 51 03 21 1
Fax: +32 (2) 51 26 58 6

European Affiliation: Moores Rowland International

International Contact: Andrew R. Gemmell

OTHER OFFICES

FIDUCIAIRE MOORES ROWLAND SA
Herentalsebaan 71-75, 2100 ANTWERP
Tel: +32 (3) 36 61 41 5 *Fax:* +32 (3) 36 61 76 7
Contact: Willy Jacobs

FIDUCIAIRE MOORES ROWLAND SA
Gistelsesteenweg 138, 8200 BRUGGE
Tel: +32 (50) 38 89 46 *Fax:* +32 (50) 38 86 47
Contact: Gery Misschaert

FIDUCIAIRE MOORES ROWLAND SA
Boulevard Devreux 11, Boites 36/38, 6000 CHARLEROI
Tel: +32 (71) 32 74 78 *Fax:* +32 (71) 33 18 55
Contact: Pierre Dandoy

FIDUCIAIRE MOORES ROWLAND SA
Jubileumlaan 35, 9000 GHENT
Tel: +32 (91) 23 13 09 *Fax:* +32 (91) 33 04 51
Contact: Robert Amouts

FIDUCIAIRE MOORES ROWLAND SA
Walenstraat 86, 3500 HASSELT
Tel: +32 (11) 22 97 31 *Fax:* +32 (11) 24 16 23
Contact: Luc Rijckalts

FIDUCIAIRE MOORES ROWLAND SA
President Kennedypark 4, 8500 KORTRIJK
Tel: +32 (56) 22 06 95 *Fax:* +32 (56) 20 29 31
Contact: Jaak Vandendriessche

FIDUCIAIRE MOORES ROWLAND SA
Ambachtenlaan 21, Bus 1A, 3001 LEUVEN (Haasrode)
Tel: +32 (16) 20 83 83 *Fax:* +32 (16) 22 22 64
Contact: René de Groof

FIDUCIAIRE MOORES ROWLAND SA
Place Saint Jacques 11, Boite 021, 4000 LIEGE
Tel: +32 (41) 22 90 44 *Fax:* +32 (41) 22 91 56
Contact: Paul Ferrand

FIDUCIAIRE MOORES ROWLAND SA
Rue des Marcottes 1, 7000 MONS
Tel: +32 (65) 35 26 43 *Fax:* +32 (65) 34 67 55
Contact: Jacques Mathy

FIDUCIAIRE MOORES ROWLAND SA
Place Josephine Charlotte 3, 5100 NAMUR
Tel: +32 (81) 30 40 12 *Fax:* +32 (81) 30 62 82
Contact: Paul Ferrand

FIDUCIAIRE MOORES ROWLAND SA
Meensesteenweg 332, 8800 ROESELARE
Tel: +32 (51) 22 05 26 *Fax:* +32 (51) 22 71 25
Contact: Dirk Clarysse

FIDUCIAIRE MOORES ROWLAND SA
Hofstraat 50/54, 9100 SINT NIKLAAS
Tel: +32 (3) 77 75 48 0 *Fax:* +32 (3) 77 79 90 2
Contact: Martin Meul

FIDUCIAIRE MOORES ROWLAND SA
Place Crombez 25, 7500 TOURNAI
Tel: +32 (69) 22 91 82 *Fax:* +32 (69) 22 91 81
Contact: Jacques Mathy

FIDUCIAIRE MOORES ROWLAND SA
Residentie Torensbos, Bus 17, Parklaan 55, 2300 TURNHOUT
Tel: +32 (14) 43 77 01 *Fax:* +32 (14) 42 55 29
Contact: Marcel Cuypers

FIDUCIAIRE MOORES ROWLAND SA
Keukeldamstraat 92, 8790 WAREGEM
Tel: +32 (56) 61 10 37 *Fax:* +32 (56) 61 03 56
Contact: Jaak Vandendriessche

Total Number of Offices: 16

PEETERS V., VINCKE, MELS & CO

Avenue des Croix de Guerre, 1120 BRUSSELS
Tel: +32 (2) 26 85 83 3
Fax: +32 (2) 26 86 02 3
Mailing Address: Boite 9, 1120 BRUSSELS

European Affiliation: INPACT - International Network of Professional Accountants

International Contact: J.P. Vincke

OTHER OFFICES

PEETERS V., VINCKE, MELS & CO
Arthur Matthijslaan, 41 Bus 8, 2140 ANTWERP
Tel: +32 (3) 23 69 63 6 *Fax:* +32 (3) 27 10 95 9

Total Number of Offices: 2

PEETERS, DEJAEGHERE, DUPONT & PARTNERS

Sint Jansvliet 2, 2000 ANTWERP
Tel: +32 (3) 22 62 21 6
Fax: +32 (3) 22 50 69 7
Mailing Address: Boite 4, 2000 ANTWERP

▷

European Affiliation: HLB International

International Contact: Leo Peeters

Partners:	6
Professional staff:	15
Non-professional staff:	8
Total Staff:	**29**

CONTACT INFORMATION

All Services (Antwerp): Leo Peeters
All Services (Brussels): Thierry Dupont
All Services (Brussels): Gilbert Janssens
All Services (Izegem): Jean Pierre Dejaeghere
All Services (Torbout): Hedwig van der Donckt

CLIENT SERVICES

All Services

OTHER OFFICES

PEETERS, DEJAEGHERE, DUPONT & PARTNERS
Burg. Vandenbogaerdelaan 25, 8870 IZEGEM
Tel: + *32* (51) 30 98 99 *Fax:* + *32* (51) 31 46 60
Contact: Jean Pierre Dejaeghere

PEETERS, DEJAEGHERE, DUPONT & PARTNERS
Vorstlaan 207, Boite 8, 1160 BRUSSELS
Tel: + *32* (2) 67 53 39 0 *Fax:* + *32* (2) 67 53 50 9
Contact: Thierry Dupont

PEETERS, DEJAEGHERE, DUPONT & PARTNERS
Elisabethlaan 2, 8820 TORHOUT
Tel: + *32* (50) 21 44 49 *Fax:* + *32* (50) 21 33 25
Contact: Hedwig Van der Donckt

Total Number of Offices: 4

PIRENNE & CO

Marcel Grünerstraat 13, 1080 BRUSSELS
Tel: + *32* (2) 42 67 22 8
Fax: + *32* (2) 42 42 39 8
Mailing Address: Boite 6, 1080 BRUSSELS

European Affiliation: GMN International

International Contact: Jozef Pirenne

Partners:	2
Professional staff:	11
Non-professional staff:	2
Total Staff:	**15**

CONTACT INFORMATION

Corporate Finance: Dirk Walgraeve
Accountancy & Administration: Alain van Esse
Corporate Finance, Tax & Insolvency: Jozef Pirenne

CLIENT SERVICES

Accountancy (General), Audit, Insolvency & Corporate Restructuring, Management & Business Advice, Mergers & Acquisitions, Taxation (Corporate), Taxation (International)

Industry Specialisations: Belgian Court, Belgian Ministry

PRICE WATERHOUSE

Boulevard de la Woluwe 62, 1200 BRUSSELS
Tel: + *32* (2) 77 31 21 1
Fax: + *32* (2) 77 01 92 5

European Affiliation: Price Waterhouse

International Contact: Paul Pauwels

OTHER OFFICES

PAUWELS & PARTNERS - REVISEURS D'ENTERPRISES/ BEDRIJFSREVISOREN
Boulevard de la Woluwe 62, 1200 BRUSSELS
Tel: + *32* (2) 77 31 21 1 *Fax:* + *32* (2) 77 03 24 9

PRICE WATERHOUSE
Antwerp Tower-15th Floor, De Keyserlei 5-Bus 11B, 2018 ANTWERP
Tel: + *32* (3) 23 31 85 0 *Fax:* + *32* (3) 23 11 96 9
Contact: Alaister Mackay

PRICE WATERHOUSE EC SERVICES
Place St Lambert 14, 1200 BRUSSELS
Tel: + *32* (2) 77 34 91 1 *Fax:* + *32* (2) 76 25 10 0
Contact: Kevin Casey

Total Number of Offices: 4

S.P.R.L. NEVENS

Boulevard Saint Michel 27, 1040 BRUSSELS
Tel: + *32* (2) 73 52 40 0
Fax: + *32* (2) 73 53 63 6

European Affiliation: DRM Internationally

International Contact: Jacques Nevens

CONTACT INFORMATION

Managing Partner: Jacques Nevens

TAX CONSULT SA

Avenue Charles Woestelaan 257 B1, 1050 BRUSSELS
Tel: + *32* (2) 42 52 57 5
Fax: + *32* (2) 42 58 04 9

European Affiliation: Alliott Peirson International

International Contact: Liliane M. Vissers-Van Bever

OTHER OFFICES

TAX CONSULT SA
Ave Maurice 1 B16, 1050 BRUSSELS
Tel: + *32* (2) 64 78 33 9 *Fax:* + *32* (2) 64 90 74 6
Contact: Jean-Marie Leclercq

Total Number of Offices: 2

TINNEMANS, POURBAIX, VAES & CO

Brussels Airport Park, Berkenlaan 6, 1831 DIEGEM
Tel: + *32* (2) 71 89 60 0
Fax: + *32* (2) 71 89 89 0

European Affiliation: DRT International

International Contact: Clarence Steininger

Partners:	18
Professional staff:	225
Non-professional staff:	35
Total Staff:	**278**

CLIENT SERVICES

Accountancy (General), Audit, Computer Installation, Corporate Finance Advice, Insolvency & Corporate Restructuring, Litigation/Legal Services, Management & Business Advice, Mergers & Acquisitions, Taxation (Corporate), Taxation (International)

Total Number of Offices: 2

▷

TOELEN CATS & CO

Avenue de Tervueren 84, 1040 BRUSSELS
Tel: +32 (2) 73 58 14 6
Fax: +32 (2) 73 51 70 5

European Affiliation: Jeffreys Henry International

International Contact: L. Toelen

Partners:	7
Professional staff:	27
Non-professional staff:	7
Total Staff:	**41**

FEE INCOME

Year End: 30.06.91	**BFr**	**%**
Accountancy & Audit:	60,200	56.0
Consultancy:	8,900	8.3
Tax:	38,300	35.7
Total:	**107,400**	

CONTACT INFORMATION
Managing Partner: L. Toelen
Managing Partner: J.F. Cats
Managing Partner: E. Riske
Accountancy (General): L. Toelen
Management Consultancy: J.P. Victor
Public Sector: J.F. Cats
Tax: L. Roose
Legal Services: W. Coppens

CLIENT SERVICES
Accountancy (General), Audit, Computer Installation, Corporate Finance Advice, Insolvency & Corporate Restructuring, Litigation/Legal Services, Management & Business Advice, Management Buy-outs, Mergers & Acquisitions, Value for Money Studies, Taxation (Corporate), Taxation (International)

OTHER OFFICES

BUREAU D'ETUDES FISCALES ET JURIDIQUES SPRL
Brand Whitlocklaan 85, 1200 BRUSSELS
Tel: +32 (2) 73 59 12 0 *Fax:* +32 (2) 73 52 72 5
Contact: Dr. Luc Roose

RISKÉ & CO
Kipdorpvest 40 B24, 2000 ANTWERP
Tel: +32 (3) 23 15 26 4 *Fax:* +32 (3) 23 23 75 8

RISKÉ & CO
Monnikenwerve 17-19 B5, 8000 BRUGGE
Tel: +32 (50) 31 67 90 *Fax:* +32 (50) 32 01 28
Contact: E. Riské

Total Number of Offices: 4

TYTGAT-ARCELIN & CO

77 Avenue de la Toison d'Or, Boite 10, 1060 BRUSSELS
Tel: +32 (2) 53 75 32 7
Fax: +32 (2) 53 70 95 5

European Affiliation: Eura-Audit International

International Contact: G. Arcelin

VAN CAKENBERGHE

Leopoldstraat 37, 2000 ANTWERP
Tel: +32 (3) 23 43 51 0
Fax: +32 (3) 22 63 14 4

European Affiliation: Alliott Peirson International

International Contact: Rik van Cakenberghe

VAN POYER & CO

Avenue Roger Vandendriessche 41, 1150 BRUSSELS
Tel: +32 (2) 77 00 30 6
Fax: +32 (2) 77 01 88 5

European Affiliation: Grant Thornton International

International Contact: Guy van Hoye

Partners:	8
Professional staff:	41
Non-professional staff:	11
Total Staff:	**60**

FEE INCOME

Year End: 1990	**BFr**	**%**
Accountancy & Audit:	92,920,000	64.0
Tax:	51,680,000	36.0
Total:	**144,600,000**	

CONTACT INFORMATION
Accountancy (General): Joseph Sonnet
Audit: Roland van Cutsem
Administration: Etienne Lacroix
Tax (Corporate): Etienne Drion du Chapois
Tax (International): Jean Matton

CLIENT SERVICES
Accountancy (General), Audit, Computer Installation, Litigation/Legal Services, Management Buy-outs, Mergers & Acquisitions, Taxation (Corporate), Taxation (International)

MAJOR CLIENTS
Alexander Proudfoot, Atochem - CECA, Bayer, Carion (Scansped), Charmeuse, Dolfus Meig, Engrais Rosier, Etam, Evian, Mecar, Promodata, Renault, Rhône Poulenc, Roche Bobois, Saupiquet, Savour Club, Schlumberger Technol, Seiko, Sema Group, Stenval - BSN

OTHER OFFICES

VAN POYER & CO
Rue Fabry 18, 4000 LIEGE
Tel: +32 (41) 52 20 77 *Fax:* +32 (41) 52 25 07
Contact: Maurice Lerusse

VAN POYER & CO
Marathonstraat 17, 9000 GHENT
Tel: +32 (91) 21 11 53
Contact: Guy van Hoye

Total Number of Offices: 3

VANACKER GOVAERTS & PARTNERS NV

St Maartenplein 3, 8000 BRUGGE
Tel: +32 (50) 34 17 37
Fax: +32 (50) 33 78 43

European Affiliation: K.S. International

International Contact: Johan van Haeverbeke

Partners:	4
Total Staff:	**40**

CLIENT SERVICES
Accountancy (General), Litigation/Legal Services, Fiscal Department, Wages Department, Joint Venture with Software Company

---

VB BIJNENS, DEGEEST & CO

Muntelbeekstraat 42, 3500 HASSELT
Tel: +32 (11) 27 27 24
Fax: +32 (11) 27 56 42

▷

European Affiliation: Morison International

International Contact: Filip Vyncke

Partners:	3
Professional staff:	80
Non-professional staff:	17
Total Staff:	**100**

FEE INCOME

Year End: 31.12.90	**BFr**
Total:	**250,000,000**

CONTACT INFORMATION
Managing Partner: François Degeest
Audit, Investigation & Consultancy: Jos Bijnens
Senior Partner: Jos Bijnens
Tax: Filip Vyncke
Audit & Investigation: François Degeest
Litigation Support & Legal Services: Elly Smets
Corporate Finance & Grants: Jos Bijnens
Corporate Finance & Grants: François Degeest
Systems/Computers: Simons Briers

CLIENT SERVICES
All Services

Industry Specialisations: Leisure, Transport, Food, Building

OTHER OFFICES
VB BIJNENS, DEGEEST & Co
Jacques Sermonlaan 38, 1080 BRUSSELS
Tel: + *32* (2) 42 57 11 4 *Fax:* + *32* (2) 42 51 54 1
Contact: François Degeest

Total Number of Offices: 2

VENNOTEN VAN HALLER, JOOS, WAETERLOOS & PARTNERS CV
Martelaarslaan 80, 9000 GHENT
Tel: + *32* (91) 25 87 88
Fax: + *32* (91) 33 10 68

International Contact: Luc H. Joos

CABINET DE REVISION VERCRUYSSE, DELPLACE, MORTIER & CO
Passage de la Poste 4, Boite 120, 7700 MOUSCRON
Tel: + *32* (56) 34 77 46
Fax: + *32* (56) 34 66 91

European Affiliation: Eura-Audit International

International Contact: L. Delplace
A. Mortier
M. Vercruysse

ACCOUNTANTSKANTOOR DIRK VERMEIREN & CO NV
Dascottelei 120, 2100 DEURNE (Antwerp)
Tel: + *32* (3) 32 21 98 0
Fax: + *32* (3) 32 26 08 5

European Affiliation: International Association of Practising Accountants (IAPA)

Partners:	1
Professional staff:	2
Non-professional staff:	8
Total Staff:	**11**

FEE INCOME

Year End: 30.06.91	**BFr**
Accountancy & Audit:	20,000,000
Consultancy:	1,000,000
Tax:	5,000,000
Total:	**26,000,000**

CONTACT INFORMATION
Chairman: Dirk Vermeiren
Accountancy (General): Anita Verhoeven
Tax: Dirk Vermeiren

CLIENT SERVICES
Accountancy (General), Audit, Corporate Finance Advice, Management & Business Advice, Taxation (Corporate), Taxation (International)

VOF VAN GEET, DERICK & CO
Kerkstraat 2, 9200 DENDERMONDE
Tel: + *32* (52) 22 22 88
Fax: + *32* (52) 22 23 19

European Affiliation: S & W International

International Contact: Hugo van Geet

OTHER OFFICES
VOF VAN GEET, DERICK & CO
Jan Welterslan 13-15, 2100 DEURNE, Antwerp
Tel: + *32* (33) 26 14 00 *Fax:* + *32* (33) 26 12 15

Total Number of Offices: 3

WALKIERS & COMPANY
Eglantierlaan 5, 2020 ANTWERP
Tel: + *32* (3) 83 00 41 5
Fax: + *32* (3) 83 04 45 5

European Affiliation: Affiliated Conference of Practising Accountants International (ACPA)

International Contact: Emile Walkiers

CONTACT INFORMATION
Managing Partner: Emile Walkiers
Managing Partner: Eric J.A. Vandenhouten

WOOD, APPLETON, OLIVER & CO LTD
Avenue Louise 207-209, Boite 8, 1050 BRUSSELS
Tel: + *32* (2) 64 00 79 6
Fax: + *32* (2) 64 05 34 3

International Contact: Joseph Oliver
Christopher Thubron

▷

Area: 43,092 sq km (16,638 sq miles)
Population: 5,129,254 (1988 estimate)
Density: 119.0 per sq km
Capital: Copenhagen

GDP: DKr848 bn, US$140 bn
GDP per head: US$27,320
Inflation: 1990 - 2.8%
1991 - 3.5% (forecast)

Official and Spoken Languages: Danish, English, French and German widely spoken

Time: GMT + 1 (in Summer GMT + 2)
Telephone Dialling Code: +45

Currency: Danish Krone (DKr) = 100 ore
Banking Hours: 0930-1600 Monday-Friday except Thursdays, 0930-1800
Professional accountancy body: Foreningen af Statsautoriserede Revisorer (FSR)

Corporate Tax Data

Information supplied by Richard Citron, international tax partner of Stoy Hayward.

The tax year; nature and rates of tax
The tax year is the year ending 31 March.
Companies pay corporate income tax (indkomstskat af aktieselskaber) at a flat rate of 38% on distributed and undistributed income.

Residence and territoriality
Danish resident companies pay tax on their worldwide income. A Danish registered limited company (A/S) or private limited company (ApS), or an association or other similar body engaged in commercial activities where the majority of its committee members and its head office are domiciled in Denmark will be resident in Denmark for tax purposes.

The tax base
Method of calculation. Taxable profits are based on the profit reported in the accounts.

Disallowable items. The major disallowable items are formation expenses, 75% of entertainment expenses and provisions for unquantifiable anticipated losses.

Exempt income and special deductions. For dividends, see below. A foreign trading relief applies. The tax liability on a company's total income is reduced by 50% of the tax attributable to the foreign trading income (including income from a foreign branch and from a share in a foreign partnership). It is also given even where the income is actually exempt from Danish tax under the terms of a treaty.

Interest paid. Interest is deductible on an accruals basis, but where payable to connected persons, is limited to arm's length rates. ▷

Stock. Stocks may be valued either at market value at the end of the accounting period, gross purchase price or cost of production. A limited form of stock relief is available.

Depreciation. Different rules apply.

(1) Plant and machinery. All plant forms one pool for depreciation purposes to which is applied the rate of depreciation (the maximum being 30%). Plant costing less than DKr5,000 (adjusted annually) and plant with a useful life of less than three years may be written off in the year of purchase, up to an overall limit of DKr 200,000 annually.
(2) Buildings. Generally a maximum of 6% on cost until 60% has been written down; 2% thereafter. Office buildings in general do not qualify.
(3) Other rates apply for various types of asset (eg patent rights, scientific research).

Treatment of dividends

Dividends received from Danish companies.

(1) Where less than 25% is held in the paying company, the dividend received is taxable at an effective rate of 25%, achieved by taxing only 66% of the dividend received at the full 38% rate.
(2) Where 25% or more is held (a substantial participation), dividends are exempt provided shares have been owned for the whole year in which the dividends are received.

Dividends received from abroad. Dividends from substantial participations are similarly exempt, provided that the tax system of the paying country is not substantially different from Denmark's.

Dividends paid. A withholding tax of 30% is deductible from dividends paid to resident and non-resident shareholders, unless the recipient is a parent company exempt from tax on the dividend under the substantial participation rule.

Anti-avoidance measures

Transfer pricing rules operate and Denmark recognises a substance over form doctrine to look through shell companies etc.

Treatment of losses

Current period. Trading losses may be set off against income and gains of the current period (there is no carry-back).

Future periods. Trading losses may be carried forward for a maximum of five years.

Treatment of capital gains

Treatment. Capital gains are generally treated as part of the company's income and are computed by deducting cost (or depreciated net book value) from sale proceeds (special rules apply to plant and machinery). Gains from immovable business property disposed of after seven years or more are exempt.

Rollover. There is no deferral of capital gains on reinvestment in new assets.

Special treatment for shares. Where shares have been held for three years or more, the gain is usually exempt from tax. However, restrictions apply to the exemption for shares in foreign companies (ie where they were held with a speculative or tax avoidance motive).

Treatment of groups

A parent company together with its 100% directly or indirectly owned subsidiaries (including foreign subsidiaries) may opt for joint taxation of profits and losses.

The 100% ownership rule however is relaxed where the law of the foreign country insists on a minimum home country participation. Joint taxation of foreign subsidiaries means that losses incurred by foreign subsidiaries can be set off against Danish source income and gains and that foreign tax credits can be more effectively used. Furthermore, the foreign trading relief (see 'The tax base' above) is also available and extends to the whole of the subsidiary's income.

Dividends received from subsidiaries within a group are exempt from Danish corporate income tax, unless received from subsidiaries resident in tax havens.

Treatment of branches

A Danish branch of a non-resident company is effectively treated as if it were a Danish resident company. There is no withholding tax on remittances of profits from the branch.

Other taxes

There is a local property tax of between approximately 1% and 2.5%.

Turnover taxes. A value added tax applies at a single rate of 22%. Exports are exempt. There is also a labour market contribution of 2.5% on the value of goods and services, charged on the same basis as VAT.

Transaction taxes. There is a capital duty of 1% on additional capital subscriptions in a Danish company and stamp duty on various transactions such as share transfers (1%) and property sales (1.2%).

Payroll taxes. There are no payroll taxes on the employer.

ALSØ & BREINHOLT A/S

Roskildevej 39, 2000 COPENHAGEN F
Tel: + *45* 36 44 20 66
Fax: + *45* 36 44 20 88

European Affiliation: Clark Kenneth Leventhal

International Contact: Bent Alsø

Partners:	7
Professional staff:	38
Non-professional staff:	10
Total Staff:	**55**

FEE INCOME

Year End: 1990	%
Accountancy & Audit:	70.0
Tax:	15.0
Other:	15.0

CLIENT SERVICES

Accountancy (General), Audit, Corporate Finance Advice, Insolvency & Corporate Restructuring, Management & Business Advice, Taxation (Corporate), Taxation (International)

OTHER OFFICES

REVISIONSAKTIESELSKABET JØHNK & ANDERSEN
Køgevej 40, 2630 TÅSTRUP
Tel: + *45* 42 99 78 22 *Fax:* + *45* 42 99 02 66
Contact: Verner Jøhnk

ASSOCIATED FIRMS

REVISIONSAKTIESELSKABET ARNT SØRENSEN
Ringgade 6, 6300 GRÅSTEN
Tel: + *45* 74 65 23 23 *Fax:* + *45* 74 65 12 78
Contact: Arnt Sørensen

Total Number of Offices: 3

REVISIONSFIRMÆT J. ANDERSEN

Strandpromendaden 27, 2100 COPENHAGEN Ø
Tel: + *45* 31 18 64 44
Fax: + *45* 31 18 65 85

European Affiliation: ATD International

International Contact: Peter Wordahl

Partners:	2
Professional staff:	20
Non-professional staff:	4
Total Staff:	**26**

CONTACT INFORMATION

Managing Partner: Jan Andersen

CLIENT SERVICES

Accountancy (General), Audit, Corporate Finance Advice, Insolvency & Corporate Restructuring, Management & Business Advice, Management Buy-outs, Mergers & Acquisitions, Taxation (Corporate), Taxation (International)

ARTHUR ANDERSEN & CO

Grønningen 17, 1012 COPENHAGEN K
Tel: + *45* 33 11 15 44
Fax: + *45* 33 11 23 37

European Affiliation: Arthur Andersen Worldwide

International Contact: Torgny Pahle

CONTACT INFORMATION

Audit: Torgny Pahle
Tax (Corporate): Jørgen Skou

CLIENT SERVICES

Accountancy (General), Audit, Computer Installation, Corporate Finance Advice, Insolvency & Corporate Restructuring, Litigation/Legal Services, Management & Business Advice, Management Buy-outs, Mergers & Acquisitions, Pensions Planning, Value for Money Studies, Taxation (Corporate), Taxation (International), Company Secretarial Services, Executive Remuneration, Financial Planning

OTHER OFFICES

ARTHUR ANDERSEN & CO
H.H. Seedorfs Straede 3-5, 8000 ÅRHUS C
Tel: + *45* 86 19 55 55 *Fax:* + *45* 86 19 59 37

Total Number of Offices: 2

ASKGAARD OLESEN HORWATH

Stoltenbergsgade 9, 1576 COPENHAGEN K
Tel: + *45* 33 11 74 00
Fax: + *45* 33 11 74 34

European Affiliation: Horwath International

International Contact: Jørgen Borresen

OTHER OFFICES

ASKGAARD OLESEN HORWATH
Frederiks Allé 26, 8000 ÅRHUS C
Tel: + *45* 86 13 83 00 *Fax:* + *45* 86 13 82 69
Contact: Søren Andersen

ASKGAARD OLESEN HORWATH
Sondre Allé 5, 4600 KØGE
Tel: + *45* 53 65 74 00 *Fax:* + *45* 53 65 83 00
Contact: Lars Gyrn

ASKGAARD OLESEN HORWATH
Allehelgensgade 22, 4000 ROSKILDE
Tel: + *45* 42 36 26 00 *Fax:* + *45* 42 36 26 88
Contact: Lars Søndergaard

Total Number of Offices: 4

AUDIREVISION APS

Falkoner Allé 53, 3, 2000 FREDERIKSBERG, Copenhagen
Tel: + *45* 38 34 11 66
Fax: + *45* 38 33 18 40

European Affiliation: K.S. International

International Contact: Ruth Sloth Frederiksen

Partners:	9
Professional staff:	32
Non-professional staff:	8
Total Staff:	**49**

FEE INCOME

Year End: 31.12.90	**DKr**
Total:	**20,800,000**

CONTACT INFORMATION

Partner: Mogens Andersen
Partner: Eskild Schjerning
Partner: Bjarne Walther
Partner: Johnny Osmark
Partner: Ib Østlund
Partner: Kristian Silversleth
Partner: Otto Bonke
Partner: Erik Henriksen
Partner: Ruth Sloth Frederiksen

CLIENT SERVICES

All Services

▷

Denmark

ASSOCIATED FIRMS

REVISIONSFIRMÆT CARL H. ANDERSEN
Falkoner Alle 53, 3, 2000 FREDERIKSBERG, Copenhagen
Tel: + 45 38 34 11 66 *Fax:* + 45 38 33 18 40
Contact: Erik Henriksen

REVISIONSFIRMÆT OTTO BONKE
Præstegårdsvej 52, 4330 HVALSO
Tel: + 45 42 40 86 86 *Fax:* + 45 42 40 82 33
Contact: Otto Bonke

GREVE REVISION A/S
Hundige Strandvej 42, 2670 GREVE
Tel: + 45 42 90 31 63 *Fax:* + 45 42 69 31 63
Contact: Mogens Andersen

REVISIONSFIRMÆT JOHNNY OSMARK
Torvet 21c, 4600 KØGE
Tel: + 45 56 63 03 00 *Fax:* + 45 56 63 01 82
Contact: Johnny Osmark

REVISIONSFIRMÆT IB OSTLUND A/S
Gammel Kongevej 85, 1850 FREDERIKSBERG, Copenhagen
Tel: + 45 31 24 46 11 *Fax:* + 45 31 24 41 50
Contact: Ib Ostlund

REVISIONSFIRMÆT ESKILD SCHJERNING
Strandvejen 6, 2100 COPENHAGEN
Tel: + 45 31 29 25 94 *Fax:* + 45 39 27 14 85
Contact: Eskild Schjerning

REVISIONSFIRMÆT BJARNE WALTHER
Kiplings Allé 48, 2860 SØBORG
Tel: + 45 31 67 15 22 *Fax:* + 45 31 67 00 34
Contact: Bjarne Walther

Total Number of Offices: 8

REVISIONSFIRMÆT BAYER

Stengade 48, 3000 HELSINGØR
Tel: + 45 49 21 41 11
Fax: + 45 49 21 43 44

European Affiliation: Independent Accountants International

International Contact: Hans Chr. Bayer

Partners:	1
Professional staff:	0
Non-professional staff:	7
Total Staff:	**8**

CLIENT SERVICES
All Services

BDO SCANREVISION AKTIESELSKAB

Strandgade 12, 1401 COPENHAGEN K
Tel: + 45 32 96 11 00
Fax: + 45 32 96 11 01

European Affiliation: BDO Binder

International Contact: Morten Schneider

Partners:	68
Professional staff:	368
Non-professional staff:	125
Total Staff:	**561**

FEE INCOME

Year End: 31.12.90	%
Accountancy & Audit:	55.0
Consultancy:	25.0
Tax:	15.0
Other:	5.0

CONTACT INFORMATION
Chairman: Ole Jensen
Managing Partner: Peter Sandal Jeppesen
Management Consultancy: Lars Zäll
Accountancy & Audit: Steen Christensen
Tax (Corporate & International): Flemming Jacobsen

CLIENT SERVICES
All Services

Industry Specialisations: Textiles, Fish, Hotels, Schools, Housing Societies, Supermarkets, Slaughterhouses

OTHER OFFICES

BDO SCANREVISION AKTIESELSKAB
Storegade 5, 7330 BRANDE
Tel: + 45 97 18 33 88 *Fax:* + 45 97 18 35 36
Contact: Henning Hejboll Sorensen

BDO SCANREVISION AKTIESELSKAB
Nygade 34, 9700 BRØNDERSLEV
Tel: + 45 98 82 42 11 *Fax:* + 45 98 80 01 22
Contact: Svend Erik Andersen

BDO SCANREVISION AKTIESELSKAB
Østergade 12, 7361 EJSTRUPHOLM
Tel: + 45 75 77 24 55 *Fax:* + 45 75 77 23 80
Contact: Henning Hejboll Sorensen

BDO SCANREVISION AKTIESELSKAB
Assensvej 4, 5600 FÅBORG
Tel: + 45 62 61 78 18 *Fax:* + 45 62 61 94 84
Contact: Niels Erik Jorgensen

BDO SCANREVISION AKTIESELSKAB
Rimmensalle 89, 9900 FREDERIKSHAVN
Tel: + 45 98 42 02 22 *Fax:* + 45 98 43 20 59
Contact: Poul-Erik Markfoged

BDO SCANREVISION AKTIESELSKAB
Markedspladsen 2, 7400 HERNING
Tel: + 45 97 12 33 88 *Fax:* + 45 97 22 47 46
Contact: Fleming Wohlk

BDO SCANREVISION AKTIESELSKAB
Jorgen Fibigersgade 16, 9850 HIRTSHALS
Tel: + 45 98 94 33 11 *Fax:* + 45 98 94 19 56
Contact: Ole Rimmen

BDO SCANREVISION AKTIESELSKAB
Norrebro 15, 9800 HJØRRING
Tel: + 45 98 92 25 11 *Fax:* + 45 98 91 19 96
Contact: Villy Steen

BDO SCANREVISION AKTIESELSKAB
Nytorv 12, 9500 HOBRO
Tel: + 45 98 52 25 11 *Fax:* + 45 98 51 03 25
Contact: Kaj Mikkelsen

BDO SCANREVISION AKTIESELSKAB
Saturnvej 1, 7430 IKAST
Tel: + 45 97 15 33 88 *Fax:* + 45 97 25 07 13
Contact: Niels Erik Bach

BDO SCANREVISION AKTIESELSKAB
Kongegade 24, 5800 NYBORG
Tel: + 45 65 31 03 53 *Fax:* + 45 65 30 11 76
Contact: Lars Ove Hansen

BDO SCANREVISION AKTIESELSKAB
Pantheonsgade 10, 5100 ODENSE C
Tel: + 45 66 11 92 22 *Fax:* + 45 66 14 71 22
Contact: Peter Sandal Jeppesen

BDO SCANREVISION AKTIESELSKAB
Lejrvej 8, 6330 PADBORG
Tel: + 45 74 67 25 40 *Fax:* + 45 74 67 25 47
Contact: Hans Peter Alnor

▷

BDO SCANREVISION AKTIESELSKAB
Provstegården, Provstegade 10, 8900 RANDERS
Tel: + 45 86 43 31 11 *Fax:* + 45 86 41 95 05
Contact: Christian Lassen

BDO SCANREVISION AKTIESELSKAB
Sæbygårdvej 25, 9300 SÆBY
Tel: + 45 98 46 33 55 *Fax:* + 45 98 46 45 09
Contact: Karl Aage Brasted

BDO SCANREVISION AKTIESELSKAB
Østergade 11, 8600 SILKEBORG
Tel: + 45 86 82 17 33 *Fax:* + 45 86 82 04 74
Contact: Niels Hvid Enevoldsen

BDO SCANREVISION AKTIESELSKAB
Ole Romersvej 4, 9870 SINDAL
Tel: + 45 98 93 43 11 *Fax:* + 45 98 93 43 23
Contact: Anton Madsen

BDO SCANREVISION AKTIESELSKAB
EC Center, Ole Romersvej 4, 9870 SINDAL
Tel: + 45 98 93 43 11 *Fax:* + 45 98 93 43 23
Contact: Annemarie Kvistgaard

BDO SCANREVISION AKTIESELSKAB
Spliidsvej 25 A, 9990 SKAGEN
Tel: + 45 98 44 45 11 *Fax:* + 45 98 45 02 34
Contact: John Kristiansen

BDO SCANREVISION AKTIESELSKAB
Sofiendalsvej 1, 9000 ÅLBORG
Tel: + 45 98 18 52 11 *Fax:* + 45 98 18 54 23
Contact: Birger Rasmussen

BDO SCANREVISION AKTIESELSKAB
Åboulevarden 11-13, 8000 ÅRHUS C
Tel: + 45 86 19 55 11 *Fax:* + 45 86 19 59 69
Contact: Torleif Vodsgaard

Total Number of Offices: 22

REVISIONSFIRMA BUSCH-SØRENSEN

Europaplads 2, 8100 ÅRHUS
Tel: + 45 86 12 97 66
Fax: + 45 86 12 94 37
Mailing Address: P.O. Box 202, 8100 ÅRHUS

European Affiliation: Midsnell International

International Contact: Ove Hartvigsen

OTHER OFFICES

REVISIONSFIRMA BUSCH-SØRENSEN
Dagmar Centret 1, 8660 SKANDERBORG
Mailing Address: P.O. Box 572, 8660 SKANDERBORG
Tel: + 45 86 52 53 66 *Fax:* + 45 86 52 47 22
Contact: Anders Christiansen

Total Number of Offices: 2

REVISIONSFIRMÆT S.A. CHRISTENSEN & W. KJÆRULFF I/S

St Kongensgade 68, P.O. Box 9015, 1022 COPENHAGEN
Tel: + 45 33 13 15 15
Fax: + 45 33 13 19 91

European Affiliation: INPACT - International Network of Professional Accountants

International Contact: Lau H. Lauritsen
Mogens Stern

CHRISTIANSEN & ENGELBRECHTSEN REVISIONS-FIRMA

Adelgade 15, 1304 COPENHAGEN K
Tel: + 45 33 14 87 82
Fax: + 45 33 14 83 25

European Affiliation: DRM Internationally

International Contact: Michael Palitzsch

Partners:	17
Professional staff:	88
Non-professional staff:	20
Total Staff:	**125**

FEE INCOME

Year End: 31.12.90	**DKr (million)**
Total:	**76,000,000**

CONTACT INFORMATION

Managing Partner: Ole Byrgesen
Accountancy (General): Svend Therchilsen
Audit: Søren Danielsen
Administration: Erik Olsen
Tax (Corporate): Sven-Åge Sørensen
Insolvency & Public Sector: Jens Jørgensen
Corporate Finance & Consultancy: Michael Palitzsch

CLIENT SERVICES

Accountancy (General), Audit, Corporate Finance Advice, Insolvency & Corporate Restructuring, Management & Business Advice, Management Buy-outs, Mergers & Acquisitions, Pensions Planning, Taxation (Corporate), Taxation (International)

Industry Specialisations: Real Estate, Shipping, Transport, Chemicals, Medical, Plastics, Banks, Tools, Farming, Hotels, Restaurants

MAJOR CLIENTS

Bech-Hansen & Studsgaard, Esselte, Hempel, Paints, Jack Saws, Large Pension Funds, Lawyers & Economist Association, Leo, Pharmaceuticals, Magasin du Nord, SIF - Shipping, World Radio & Television Handphones

OTHER OFFICES

CHRISTIANSEN & ENGELBRECHTSEN
Banevaenget 5, 4930 MARIBO
Tel: + 45 53 88 44 55 *Fax:* + 45 53 88 45 66
Contact: Hevrik Drachmann

CHRISTIANSEN & ENGELBRECHTSEN
Vejlegade 35, 4900 NAKSKOV
Tel: + 45 53 92 25 00 *Fax:* + 45 53 92 88 89
Contact: Niels Bruhn

CHRISTIANSEN & ENGELBRECHTSEN
Rosenvaenget 23, 4800 NYKOEBING F
Tel: + 45 54 86 04 44 *Fax:* + 45 54 82 20 83
Contact: Dav Kôfoed

CHRISTIANSEN & ENGELBRECHTSEN
Snellemark 16, 3700 ROENNE
Tel: + 45 53 95 10 66 *Fax:* + 45 53 95 91 66
Contact: Svend-Erik Larsen

CHRISTIANSEN & ENGELBRECHTSEN
Torvegade 5, 7100 VEJLE
Tel: + 45 75 82 51 00 *Fax:* + 45 75 82 51 53
Contact: Egon Evers

Total Number of Offices: 6

▷

Denmark

CITY REVISION A/S

Blegdamsvej 60, 2100 COPENHAGEN Ø
Tel: + 45 35 28 03 33
Fax: + 45 35 28 03 34

European Affiliation: Moores Rowland International

International Contact: Poul Erik Vennekilde

Partners:	11
Professional staff:	98
Non-professional staff:	10
Total Staff:	**119**

FEE INCOME

Year End: 30.04.91	**DKr**
Total:	**64,000,000**

CONTACT INFORMATION
Chairman: Poul Erik Vennekilde
Managing Partner: Carsten Gottschalk
Audit: Stig Chr. Göte
Tax (Corporate): Peter Skov Hansen

CLIENT SERVICES
Accountancy (General), Audit, Corporate Finance Advice, Insolvency & Corporate Restructuring, Management Buy-outs, Taxation (Corporate), Taxation (International)

DSR

Helsingforsgade 27, 8200 ÅRHUS
Tel: + 45 86 10 11 11
Fax: + 45 86 16 64 20

European Affiliation: S & W International

International Contact: Ejgil Jensen

Partners:	6
Professional staff:	40
Non-professional staff:	10
Total Staff:	**56**

CONTACT INFORMATION
Tax (International): John Bygholm
Accountancy & Audit: Erling Hansen
Accountancy & Audit: Chr. Aggerholm
Accountancy & Audit: Keld Brabrand
Accountancy & Audit: Torben Maehlissen

CLIENT SERVICES
Accountancy (General), Audit, Computer Installation, Corporate Finance Advice, Insolvency & Corporate Restructuring, Management & Business Advice, Taxation (Corporate), Taxation (International)

Total Number of Offices: 2

ERNST & YOUNG A/S

Tagensvej 82, 2200 COPENHAGEN N
Tel: + 45 35 82 48 48
Fax: + 45 35 82 48 00

European Affiliation: Ernst & Young Europe

International Contact: Teddy Wivel

Partners:	82
Professional staff:	568
Non-professional staff:	60
Total Staff:	**710**

FEE INCOME

Year End: 31.12.90	**DKr**
Total:	**326,000,000**

CONTACT INFORMATION
Chairman: Teddy Wivel
Managing Partner: Mogens Lundin
Managing Partner: Søren Hedemand
Corporate Finance: Anker Nielsen
Insolvency: B.L. Rasmussen
Management Consultancy: Anker Nielsen
Administration: Søren Hedemand
Public Sector: Jan Franck
Accountancy & Audit: Hans-Ole Reichardt
Tax: Niels Chr. Steen
Health Care: Lise Aagaard
Information Technology: Finn Hindkjær Pedersen

CLIENT SERVICES
Accountancy (General), Audit, Corporate Finance Advice, Insolvency & Corporate Restructuring, Management & Business Advice, Management Buy-outs, Mergers & Acquisitions, Taxation (Corporate), Taxation (International), Privatization, Quality Management, Information Technology

Industry Specialisations: Health Care

MAJOR CLIENTS
Ålborg Portland, ABB Denmark, Burmeister & Wain, Danisco, Danish Fur Auctions, Dansk Alfa Laval, World Turist Wagon-Lits, Siemens Denmark, Incentive, Jens Villadsens Fab., Jensen Group, Lego Gruppen, Novo Nordisk, Peder P. Hedegaard, Rockwool International, Schur International, Sterling Airways, Stora Papyrus, Toyota Denmark, Tulip International

OTHER OFFICES

ERNST & YOUNG A/S
Østergade 38, 5610 ASSENS
Tel: + 45 64 71 42 00 *Fax:* + 45 61 71 42 03
Contact: Flemming Olsen

ERNST & YOUNG A/S
Frodesgade 70, 6700 ESBJERG
Tel: + 45 75 13 61 11 *Fax:* + 45 75 13 37 37
Contact: H.C. Fejring

ERNST & YOUNG A/S
Østergade 13, 8450 HAMMEL
Tel: + 45 86 96 91 00 *Fax:* + 45 86 96 96 03
Contact: Hans Kristian Caroe

ERNST & YOUNG A/S
Helsingørgade 63, 3400 HILLERØD
Tel: + 45 42 25 35 00 *Fax:* + 45 42 26 58 33
Contact: Carsten Nyrup Jorgensen

ERNST & YOUNG A/S
Pakhustorvet 2, 6000 KOLDING
Tel: + 45 75 54 26 22 *Fax:* + 45 75 54 28 95
Contact: Knud Beer

ERNST & YOUNG A/S
Farvergade 15, 4700 NÆSTVED
Tel: + 45 53 72 77 88 *Fax:* + 45 55 77 13 88
Contact: Jorgen Smith

ERNST & YOUNG A/S
Torvet 2, 4800 NYKØBING FALSTER
Tel: + 45 54 86 00 88 *Fax:* + 45 54 82 24 77
Contact: P. Riemann Rasmussen

ERNST & YOUNG A/S
Thomas B. Thriges Gade 30, 5100 ODENSE C
Tel: + 45 66 11 95 00 *Fax:* + 45 66 91 25 11
Contact: Bent Banke

ERNST & YOUNG A/S
Østergade 11, 4000 ROSKILDE
Tel: + 45 42 35 00 35 *Fax:* + 45 42 36 00 54
Contact: Alfred Grinderslev

▷

ERNST & YOUNG A/S
Ellegårdsvej 25, 6400 SØNDERBORG
Tel: + 45 74 42 35 36 *Fax:* + 45 74 42 38 13
Contact: Michael Herschend

ERNST & YOUNG A/S
Spikergade 19, 6270 TØNDER
Tel: + 45 74 72 55 66 *Fax:* + 45 74 72 03 10
Contact: Bjarne Bruun Sorensen

ERNST & YOUNG A/S
Damhaven 3C, 7100 VEJLE
Tel: + 45 75 83 28 88 *Fax:* + 45 75 82 88 23
Contact: Knud Steffensen

ERNST & YOUNG A/S
Boulevarden 28-30, 9000 ÅLBORG
Tel: + 45 98 12 33 44 *Fax:* + 45 98 11 55 10
Contact: Scott Steen Jensen

ERNST & YOUNG A/S
Søren Frichs Vej 38A, 8230 ÅBYHØJ - ÅRHUS
Tel: + 45 86 15 99 44 *Fax:* + 45 86 15 76 33
Contact: Willy Friis

Total Number of Offices: 15

FAURUM & JORGENSEN

Læderstræde 22, 1201 COPENHAGEN K
Tel: + 45 01 32 40 33
Fax: + 45 01 12 04 39

European Affiliation: A.E.E. International

International Contact: L. Faurum

FAURUM & SCHIØLER

Kronprinsensgade 5, 2, 1114 COPENHAGEN K
Tel: + 45 33 32 40 33
Fax: + 45 33 12 04 39

European Affiliation: Midsnell International

International Contact: Leif Faurum

OTHER OFFICES

FARUM & SCHIØLER
Frederiksgade 19, 1265 COPENHAGEN
Tel: + 45 33 15 25 33 *Fax:* + 45 33 91 25 33
Contact: Jacob Schiøler

Total Number of Offices: 2

P'F GRANNSKODARAVIRKID JOGVAN SUNDSTEIN

R.C. Effersøsgøta 26, P.O. Box 191, 110 TORSHAVN
Tel: + 45 29 81 47 00
Fax: + 45 29 81 38 15

European Affiliation: INPACT - International Network of Professional Accountants

International Contact: Jogvan Joensen

GROTHEN & PERREGAARD A/S

Stockholmsgade 45, 2100 COPENHAGEN 0
Tel: + 45 31 42 48 44
Fax: + 45 31 42 29 11

European Affiliation: Grant Thornton International

International Contact: J. Frank Jakobsen

Partners:	9
Professional staff:	85
Non-professional staff:	18
Total Staff:	**112**

CONTACT INFORMATION

Chairman: Svend Jensen
Managing Partner: J. Frank Jakobsen

CLIENT SERVICES

Accountancy (General), Audit, Management & Business Advice, Taxation (Corporate), Taxation (International), Company Formation, Computer Consultancy

HANSEN & SORENSEN

Vestergade 48 H, P.O. Box 422, 8100 ÅRHUS C
Tel: + 45 86 13 90 00
Fax: + 45 86 13 91 13

European Affiliation: Urbach Hacker Young International

OTTO HOUD STATISAUTORISEREDE REVISORER A/S

Hammerensgade 6, 1267 COPENHAGEN K
Tel: + 45 33 11 00 47
Fax: + 45 33 32 21 30

European Affiliation: Affiliated Conference of Practising Accountants International (ACPA)

International Contact: Carsten Stohn

Partners:	5
Professional staff:	30
Non-professional staff:	5
Total Staff:	**40**

CONTACT INFORMATION

Chairman: Gunnar Andersen

CLIENT SERVICES

Accountancy (General), Audit, Corporate Finance Advice, Management & Business Advice, Management Buy-outs, Mergers & Acquisitions, Value for Money Studies, Taxation (Corporate), Taxation (International)

INFO:REVISION A/S

Sorgenfrivej 18, 2800 LYNGBY, Copenhagen
Tel: + 45 45 93 23 00
Fax: + 45 45 93 20 80

European Affiliation: Urbach Hacker Young International

International Contact: Hans Wilhelm Christensen

Partners:	5
Professional staff:	40
Non-professional staff:	5
Total Staff:	**50**

FEE INCOME

Year End: 31.12.90	**DKr**
Total:	**25,000,000**

CLIENT SERVICES

Accountancy (General), Audit, Corporate Finance Advice, Management & Business Advice, Management Buy-outs, Mergers & Acquisitions, Pensions Planning, Value for Money Studies, Taxation (Corporate) ▷

INTEG-GROUP

Solvang 20, 3450 ALLERØD, Copenhagen
Tel: + 45 42 27 57 77
Fax: + 45 42 27 22 08

European Affiliation: GMN International

International Contact: Leith Olsen

Partners:	53
Professional staff:	261
Non-professional staff:	83
Total Staff:	**397**

FEE INCOME

Year End: 31.12.90	**DKr**	**%**
Accountancy & Audit:	53,000,000	35.0
Consultancy:	45,000,000	30.0
Tax:	52,000,000	35.0
Total:	**150,000,000**	

CONTACT INFORMATION

Chairman: Jens Vetlov
Taxation: Gitte Skouby

CLIENT SERVICES

All Services

Industry Specialisations: Small and Medium-sized Companies

ASSOCIATED FIRMS

REVISIONSFIRMÆT E. BAGGER-PETERSEN I/S
Gammelmosevej 46, 2820 GENTOFTE
Tel: + 45 45 93 22 99 *Fax:* + 45 45 93 14 34
Contact: John Bagger-Petersen

JENSEN & RATH
Skagensvej 147, P.O. Box 319, 9800 HJØRRING
Tel: + 45 98 92 82 11 *Fax:* + 45 98 92 82 11
Contact: Kaj Kristensen

JF-REVISION APS
Algade 27, 4000 ROSKILDE
Tel: + 45 42 36 50 50 *Fax:* + 45 42 36 49 15
Contact: John Formsgaard

JYSK REVISOR-INTERESSENTSKAB
Åboulevarden 21, 8100 ÅRHUS C
Tel: + 45 86 19 15 44 *Fax:* + 45 86 18 34 60
Contact: Poul Eskerod

REVISIONSFIRMÆT NIELS KRISTIAN LADEFOGED
Kastanie Allé 1, 6400 SØNDERBORG
Tel: + 45 74 42 13 25 *Fax:* + 45 74 43 03 46
Contact: Niels Kristian Ladefoged

NEJSTGAARD & VETLOV
Solvang 20, 3450 ALLERØD
Tel: + 45 42 27 57 77 *Fax:* + 45 42 27 22 08
Contact: Jens Vetlov

OESTERGAARD & KOCH A/S
Sofiendalsvej 3, 9200 ÅLBORG SV
Tel: + 45 98 18 70 00 *Fax:* + 45 98 18 75 44
Contact: Erling Andersen

REVISIONSFIRMÆT KAJ OLSEN
Dalbygade 42, 6000 KOLDING
Tel: + 45 75 50 56 00 *Fax:* + 45 75 52 22 25
Contact: Steffen Knudsen

REVISIONSFIRMÆT LEO OLSEN
Hunderupvej 116, 5230 ODENSE M
Tel: + 45 66 11 36 00 *Fax:* + 45 65 91 34 03
Contact: Leith Olsen

RV REVISION, VIBORG
Fabrikvej 11, 8800 VIBORG
Tel: + 45 86 62 63 33 *Fax:* + 45 86 62 16 53
Contact: Jens Henrik Jensen

REVISIONSFIRMÆT TORBEN OXBØLL
Hoegevej 21, 6705 ESBJERG O
Tel: + 45 75 14 12 11 *Fax:* + 45 75 14 34 84
Contact: Peter Gammelvind

Total Number of Offices: 12

K.G. JENSEN COOPERS & LYBRAND

16-28 Lyngbyveij, COPENHAGEN
Tel: + 45 39 27 31 13
Fax: + 45 39 27 27 72
Mailing Address: P.O. Box 2152, 1016 COPENHAGEN K

European Affiliation: Coopers & Lybrand Europe

International Contact: Kurt Nielson
Total Staff: **1,025**

CONTACT INFORMATION

Chairman: Kurt Nielson
Managing Partner: Torben Haaning
Corporate Finance: Per Vaerndal
Management Consultancy: John Lucas
Tax: Gunver Maltesen

CLIENT SERVICES

Accountancy (General), Audit, Computer Installation, Corporate Finance Advice, Insolvency & Corporate Restructuring, Life & Risk Assurance, Litigation/Legal Services, Management & Business Advice, Management Buy-outs, Mergers & Acquisitions, Pensions Planning, Value for Money Studies, Taxation (Corporate), Taxation (International), Trust Settlement & Estates, Total Quality Management, Management Consultancy

Industry Specialisations: Banking, Insurance, Automotive, Pharmaceuticals, Food & Drink, Communication

OTHER OFFICES

K.G. JENSEN COOPERS & LYBRAND
Østergade 11-13, 9690 FJERRITSLEV
Tel: + 45 98 21 18 11 *Fax:* + 45 98 21 30 57
Contact: Lars Johansen

K.G. JENSEN COOPERS & LYBRAND
Smedevænget 8, 7000 FREDERICIA
Tel: + 45 75 92 72 00 *Fax:* + 45 75 93 16 92
Contact: Lars Baek

K.G. JENSEN COOPERS & LYBRAND
Østergade 3, 3600 FREDERIKSSUND
Tel: + 45 42 31 35 40 *Fax:* + 45 42 31 36 97
Contact: Per Paakjær

K.G. JENSEN COOPERS & LYBRAND
Gefionsvej 2, 3000 HELSINGØR
Tel: + 45 49 21 36 66 *Fax:* + 45 49 21 37 98
Contact: Arne Aaen

K.G. JENSEN COOPERS & LYBRAND
Herlev Hovedgade 127, 2730 HERLEV
Tel: + 45 44 94 83 66 *Fax:* + 45 44 94 14 84
Contact: Bent Rasmussen

K.G. JENSEN COOPERS & LYBRAND
Hafniahus, Fredensgade 18, 7400 HERNING
Mailing Address: P.O. Box 122, 7400 HERNING
Tel: + 45 97 22 10 99 *Fax:* + 45 97 22 10 82
Contact: Anker Stensig Andersen

▷

K.G. JENSEN COOPERS & LYBRAND
Algade 61, 4300 HOLBÆK
Mailing Address: P.O. Box 300, 4300 HOLBÆK
Tel: + 45 53 43 35 40 *Fax:* + 45 53 44 20 72
Contact: Vagn Bysøe

K.G. JENSEN COOPERS & LYBRAND
Hjaltesvej 16, 7500 HOLSTEBRO
Mailing Address: P.O. Box 1443, 7500 HOLSTEBRO
Tel: + 45 97 42 19 88 *Fax:* + 45 97 42 18 64
Contact: Torben Haaning

K.G. JENSEN COOPERS & LYBRAND
Vænget 17, 4400 KALUNDBORG
Tel: + 45 53 51 35 40 *Fax:* + 45 53 51 00 76
Contact: Jorgen Eghoff

K.G. JENSEN COOPERS & LYBRAND
Hollændervej 4, 6000 KOLDING
Tel: + 45 75 52 65 11 *Fax:* + 45 75 50 15 67
Contact: Poul Roest

K.G. JENSEN COOPERS & LYBRAND
Langelandsvej 3, 5500 MIDDELFART
Tel: + 45 64 41 02 34 *Fax:* + 45 64 41 01 34
Contact: Kenneth Brønlund

K.G. JENSEN COOPERS & LYBRAND
Torvet 2, 4800 NYKØBING F
Tel: + 45 54 85 10 55 *Fax:* + 45 54 85 14 84
Contact: Jorgen Kristensen

K.G. JENSEN COOPERS & LYBRAND
Jerbanegade 2, 7900 NYKØBING MORS
Tel: + 45 97 72 23 00 *Fax:* + 45 97 72 29 85
Contact: Jesper Andreassen

K.G. JENSEN COOPERS & LYBRAND
Algade 47b, 4500 NYKØBING S
Tel: + 45 53 41 35 40 *Fax:* + 45 53 41 01 58
Contact: Hans Erik Glüsing

K.G. JENSEN COOPERS & LYBRAND
Axeltorv 5, 4700 NÆSTVED
Tel: + 45 53 72 35 40 *Fax:* + 45 53 73 59 81
Contact: Ole Brand

K.G. JENSEN COOPERS & LYBRAND
Tinghusgården 30, Albanigade, 5100 ODENSE C
Mailing Address: P.O. Box 1249, 5100 ODENSE C
Tel: + 45 66 12 60 50 *Fax:* + 45 66 14 85 25
Contact: Flemming Petersen

K.G. JENSEN COOPERS & LYBRAND
Slotscentret, 8900 RANDERS
Tel: + 45 86 42 63 22 *Fax:* + 45 86 42 52 05
Contact: Olaf Mathiassen

K.G. JENSEN COOPERS & LYBRAND
I.C. Christensens Allé 5, 6950 RINGKØBING
Tel: + 45 97 32 05 55 *Fax:* + 45 97 32 19 98
Contact: Peter Eeg

K.G. JENSEN COOPERS & LYBRAND
Nørretorv 14, 4100 RINGSTED
Mailing Address: P.O. Box 50, 4100 RINGSTED
Tel: + 45 53 61 45 40 *Fax:* + 45 53 61 18 20
Contact: Kurt Bülow

K.G. JENSEN COOPERS & LYBRAND
Torvegade 4, 9870 SINDAL
Mailing Address: P.O. Box 16, 9870 SINDAL
Tel: + 45 98 93 67 66 *Fax:* + 45 98 93 67 88
Contact: Henrik Christiansen

K.G. JENSEN COOPERS & LYBRAND
Resenvej 81, 7800 SKIVE
Tel: + 45 97 52 30 22 *Fax:* + 45 97 52 89 90
Contact: Peter H. Christensen

K.G. JENSEN COOPERS & LYBRAND
Østergade 40, 6900 SKJERN
Tel: + 45 97 35 02 66 *Fax:* + 45 97 35 37 53
Contact: Jens Hvid

K.G. JENSEN COOPERS & LYBRAND
Merkurvej 2, 4200 SLAGELSE
Mailing Address: P.O. Box 264, 4200 SLAGELSE
Tel: + 45 53 52 37 30 *Fax:* + 45 53 10 07 30
Contact: Bertel Erichsen

K.G. JENSEN COOPERS & LYBRAND
Bredgade 3, 7600 STRUER
Tel: + 45 97 85 07 22 *Fax:* + 45 97 84 04 15
Contact: Jørn Møller Pederson

K.G. JENSEN COOPERS & LYBRAND
Enghavevej 2, 7100 VEJLE
Mailing Address: P.O. Box 439, 7100 VEJLE
Tel: + 45 75 82 55 99 *Fax:* + 45 75 84 09 87
Contact: Finn Ladefoged Jensen

K.G. JENSEN COOPERS & LYBRAND
Bredgade 10, 6920 VIDEBÆK
Tel: + 45 97 17 29 00 *Fax:* + 45 97 17 32 90
Contact: Niels Jørgen Lodahl

K.G. JENSEN COOPERS & LYBRAND
Algade 59, 4760 VORDINGBORG
Tel: + 45 53 77 35 40 *Fax:* + 45 53 77 15 40
Contact: Preben Pedersen

K.G. JENSEN COOPERS & LYBRAND
Skelagervej 1a, 9100 ÅLBORG
Mailing Address: P.O. Box 69, 9100 ÅLBORG
Tel: + 45 98 18 87 99 *Fax:* + 45 98 18 87 44
Contact: Poul Østergaard Andersen

K.G. JENSEN COOPERS & LYBRAND
Vestergade 28, 9620 ÅLESTRUP
Tel: + 45 98 64 17 33 *Fax:* + 45 98 64 30 41
Contact: Annette Mindegaard

K.G. JENSEN COOPERS & LYBRAND
Lille Torv 6, 8000 ÅRHUS C
Tel: + 45 86 13 72 00 *Fax:* + 45 86 18 37 50
Contact: Benni Hansen

K.G. JENSEN COOPERS & LYBRAND
Department of Administration, Holsted Erhversomrade 15b, 4700 NÆSTVED
Tel: + 45 53 73 35 40 *Fax:* + 45 53 73 37 67
Contact: Aage Hijorth

Total Number of Offices: 32

KPMG

KPMG C. JESPERSEN
Borups Allé 177, 2000 FREDERIKSBERG, Copenhagen
Tel: + 45 38 18 30 00
Fax: + 45 38 18 30 45
Mailing Address: P.O. Box 250, 2000 FREDERIKSBERG

European Affiliation: KPMG

International Contact: Ib Eriksen
Ole Haslund
Ole Koefoed

Partners:	170
Professional staff:	800
Non-professional staff:	270
Total Staff:	**1,240**

▷

Denmark

FEE INCOME

Year End: 31.12.91	**DKr**	**%**
Accountancy & Audit:	309,000,000	53.0
Consultancy:	198,000,000	34.0
Tax:	70,000,000	12.0
Other:	6,000,000	1.0
Total:	**583,000,000**	

CONTACT INFORMATION

Managing Partner: John Gath
Managing Partner: Aksel Runge Johansen
Managing Partner: J.O. Burch Pedersen
Corporate Finance: Finn L. Meyer
Insolvency: Poul Erik Olsen
Management Consultancy: Stig Due
Public Sector: Tage Rossen-Jørgensen
Accountancy & Audit: Arne Nielsen
Tax: Niels Mou Jakobsen
EDP Audit: Carsten Heilbuth
M & A: Find Smidt

CLIENT SERVICES

Accountancy (General), Audit, Computer Installation, Corporate Finance Advice, Insolvency & Corporate Restructuring, Management & Business Advice, Management Buy-outs, Mergers & Acquisitions, Pensions Planning, Taxation (Corporate), Taxation (International)

Industry Specialisations: Banking, Insurance, Construction, Food & Beverages, Manufacturing, Wholesale/Retail Trade, Transport

MAJOR CLIENTS

Baltica, Carlsberg, Danfoss, Den Danske Bank, East Asiatic Company, Glutenberghus, Hafnia, ISS, J. Lautitzen, Magasin, MD Foods, A.P. Moller, NKT, SAS, F.L. Smidth, Sophus Berendsen, Superfos, Topdanmark, Tulip International, Unibank

OTHER OFFICES

KPMG C. JESPERSEN
Randersvej 38, 6700 ESBJERG
Tel: + *45* 75 18 08 22 *Fax:* + *45* 75 45 11 81

KPMG C. JESPERSEN
Torvegade 51, 7323 GIVE
Mailing Address: P.O. Box 18, 7323 GIVE
Tel: + *45* 75 73 50 22 *Fax:* + *45* 75 73 56 12

KPMG C. JESPERSEN
Jomfrustien 6-8, 6100 HADERSLEV
Tel: + *45* 74 52 32 13 *Fax:* + *45* 74 53 12 05

KPMG C. JESPERSEN
The Nielsens Gade 92, 7400 HERNING
Mailing Address: P.O. Box 360, 7400 HERNING
Tel: + *45* 97 12 61 11 *Fax:* + *45* 97 21 41 17

KPMG C. JESPERSEN
Søndergade 22, 8700 HORSENS
Tel: + *45* 75 62 88 22 *Fax:* + *45* 75 62 88 26

KPMG C. JESPERSEN
Phønixhuset, Østergade 1 A, 7430 IKAST
Tel: + *45* 97 15 44 55 *Fax:* + *45* 97 23 13 46

KPMG C. JESPERSEN
Pakhstorvat 16, 6000 KOLDING
Mailing Address: P.O. Box 205, 6000 KOLDING
Tel: + *45* 75 53 11 22 *Fax:* + *45* 75 53 10 69

KPMG C. JESPERSEN
Børstenbindervej 6, 5230 ODENSE M
Tel: + *45* 66 15 86 86 *Fax:* + *45* 66 15 46 86

KPMG C. JESPERSEN
Niels Brocks Gade 12, 8900 RANDERS
Mailing Address: P.O. Box 236, 8900 RANDERS
Tel: + *45* 97 32 19 00 *Fax:* + *45* 97 32 49 80

KPMG C. JESPERSEN
Østergade 9, 6950 RINGKØBING
Tel: + *45* 97 32 19 00 *Fax:* + *45* 97 32 49 80

KPMG C. JESPERSEN
Hafniahus, Toldbodvej 13 B, 5700 SVENDBORG
Tel: + *45* 62 21 36 12 *Fax:* + *45* 62 22 82 66

KPMG C. JESPERSEN
Sundsmarkvej 12, 6400 SØNDERBORG
Tel: + *45* 74 42 10 77 *Fax:* + *45* 74 42 50 55

KPMG C. JESPERSEN
Brummersvej 2, 7100 VEJLE
Mailing Address: P.O. Box 70, 7100 VEJLE
Tel: + *45* 75 82 56 22 *Fax:* + *45* 75 82 28 95

KPMG C. JESPERSEN
Skibbroagade 27, 6200 ÅBENRÅ
Tel: + *45* 74 62 63 22 *Fax:* + *45* 75 62 04 55

KPMG C. JESPERSEN
Nyhavnsgade 9, 9100 ÅLBORG
Mailing Address: P.O. Box 1533, 9100 ÅLBORG
Tel: + *45* 98 12 66 22 *Fax:* + *45* 98 16 85 22

KPMG C. JESPERSEN
Clemenstorv 8, 8100 ÅRHUS
Mailing Address: P.O. Box 330, 8100 ÅRHUS C
Tel: + *45* 86 12 92 00 *Fax:* + *45* 86 19 24 21

Total Number of Offices: 17

KROGH & RONALD

Vestergade 11-17, P.O. Box 409, 8100 ÅRHUS C
Tel: + *45* 86 12 32 55
Fax: + *45* 86 76 09 60

European Affiliation: Morison International

International Contact: Per Krogh Petersen

Partners:	5
Professional staff:	62
Non-professional staff:	15
Total Staff:	**82**

FEE INCOME

Year End: 31.12.90	**DKr**
Total:	**30,000,000**

CONTACT INFORMATION

Managing Partner: A. Ronald Hansen
Managing Partner: Per Krogh Petersen
Corporate Finance: Per Krogh Petersen
Management Consultancy: A. Ronald Hansen
Accountancy & Audit: S. Groenbaek Hansen
Tax: B. Bertelsen

CLIENT SERVICES

Accountancy (General), Audit, Computer Installation, Corporate Finance Advice, Management & Business Advice, Management Buy-outs, Mergers & Acquisitions, Pensions Planning, Taxation (Corporate), Taxation (International), Trust Settlement & Estates

Industry Specialisations: Transport, Shipping

Total Number of Offices: 3

LOPS & BRANDT A/S

Finsenvej 80, 2000 FREDERIKSBERG, Copenhagen
Tel: + *45* 31 87 99 11
Fax: + *45* 31 87 61 04

European Affiliation: Alliott Peirson International

International Contact: Per Winther

OTHER OFFICES

LOPS & BRANDT A/S
Torvet 19, 4600 KØGE
Tel: + *45* 53 65 52 52 *Fax:* + *45* 53 65 94 52
Contact: Ove Brandt

Total Number of Offices: 2

LUNDGAARD ANDERSEN & GLUD A/S

Peter Bangs Vej 24, 2000 FREDERIKSBERG
Tel: + *45* 38 33 34 00
Fax: + *45* 38 33 33 34
Mailing Address: P.O. Box 201, 2000 FREDERIKSBERG, Copenhagen

European Affiliation: SC International

International Contact: Henning O. Olsen

MOORE STEPHENS APS

Åboulevard 56, 2200 COPENHAGEN N
Tel: + *45* 31 39 36 00
Fax: + *45* 31 39 35 00

European Affiliation: Moore Stephens

International Contact: Jan Ole Edelbo

OTHER OFFICES

REVISIONSFIRMÆT EDELBO & DALGAARD A/S
Kastanievej 3, 5230 ODENSE M
Tel: + *45* 66 14 77 66 *Fax:* + *45* 65 91 44 66
Contact: Niels E. Thrane

REVISIONSFIRMÆT EDELBO & DALGAARD A/S
Torvet 2, 5900 RUDKØBING
Tel: + *45* 62 51 38 30 *Fax:* + *45* 62 51 45 45
Contact: Ebbe Baek

REVISIONSFIRMÆT EDELBO & DALGGARD A/S
Kongensgade 18, 5960 MARSTAL
Tel: + *45* 62 53 18 30 *Fax:* + *45* 62 53 21 35
Contact: Jan A. Mortensen

CORRESPONDENT FIRMS

REVISIONSFIRMÆT BRANDT & SIGSTEN PEDERSEN
Bytorvet 34, 7730 HANSTHOLM
Tel: + *45* 97 96 10 55 *Fax:* + *45* 97 96 25 43
Contact: Ole Sprogøe

REVISIONSFIRMÆT BRANDT & SIGSTEN PEDERSEN
Møllevaenget 17, 7760 HURUP
Tel: + *45* 97 95 18 22 *Fax:* + *45* 97 95 26 80

REVISIONSFIRMÆT BRANDT & SIGSTEN PEDERSEN
Limfjordsvej 42, 7900 NYKØBING MORS
Tel: + *45* 97 72 32 44 *Fax:* + *45* 97 72 33 12
Contact: Anders Borg

REVISIONSFIRMÆT BRANDT & SIGSTEN PEDERSEN
Thyparken 10, 7700 THISTED
Tel: + *45* 97 91 11 11 *Fax:* + *45* 97 91 05 71

Total Number of Offices: 8

MORTENSEN & BEIERHOLM

Vester Søgade 10, 1601 COPENHAGEN V
Tel: + *45* 33 12 68 11
Fax: + *45* 33 32 37 73

European Affiliation: HLB International

International Contact: Finn E. Nielsen

Partners:	37
Professional staff:	170
Non-professional staff:	54
Total Staff:	**261**

CONTACT INFORMATION

Chairman: Mogens Andersen
Managing Partner: Jan C. Nielsen
Audit: Mogens Nyhegn
Management Consultancy: Hans Møllegaard
Tax (Corporate): Karin Hald

CLIENT SERVICES

Accountancy (General), Audit, Computer Installation, Corporate Finance Advice, Insolvency & Corporate Restructuring, Management Buy-outs, Mergers & Acquisitions, Taxation (Corporate), Taxation (International)

Industry Specialisations: Banking, Fishing, Air & Ground Transportation, Freight Forwarding

OTHER OFFICES

MORTENSEN & BEIERHOLM
Vørgårdvej 2, 9200 ÅLBORG
Tel: + *45* 98 18 72 00 *Fax:* + *45* 98 18 81 18
Contact: Erik S. Christensen

MORTENSEN & BEIERHOLM
Guldsmedgade 3, 8000 ÅRHUS C
Tel: + *45* 86 18 53 00 *Fax:* + *45* 86 18 54 51
Contact: Anders C. Sørensen

MORTENSEN & BEIERHOLM
Gåskærgade 32-34, 6100 HADERSLEV
Tel: + *45* 74 52 18 12 *Fax:* + *45* 74 53 32 32
Contact: Jørn Petersen

MORTENSEN & BEIERHOLM
Ringvejen 2 A, 9560 HADSUND
Tel: + *45* 98 57 24 44 *Fax:* + *45* 98 57 45 01
Contact: Erik Dethlefsen

MORTENSEN & BEIERHOLM
Bregentvedvej 22, 4690 HASLEV
Tel: + *45* 56 31 27 90 *Fax:* + *45* 56 31 61 61
Contact: Henrik Bøgh Nielson

MORTENSEN & BEIERHOLM
Læsøvej 5A, 9800 HJØRRING
Tel: + *45* 98 92 18 11 *Fax:* + *45* 98 92 10 73
Contact: Lars Poulsen

MORTENSEN & BEIERHOLM
Smedevej 1 B, 9500 HOBRO
Tel: + *45* 98 52 09 99 *Fax:* + *45* 98 52 05 12
Contact: Peter Sørensen

MORTENSEN & BEIERHOLM
Ringvejen, 8800 VIBORG
Tel: + *45* 86 61 18 11 *Fax:* + *45* 86 62 88 32
Contact: Mogens Andersen

Total Number of Offices: 9

Denmark

REVISIONSFIRMAET ERIC NIELSEN & N.H. CHRISTENSEN

Hasseris Bymidte 6, P.O. Box 9, 9100 ÅLBORG
Tel: + 45 98 18 33 33
Fax: + 45 98 18 09 08

European Affiliation: Jeffreys Henry International

International Contact: Gustav Hedeager

Partners:	14
Total Staff:	**107**

FEE INCOME

Year End: 1990	**US$**	**%**
Accountancy & Audit:		63.0
Tax:		30.0
Other:		7.0
Total:	**6,500,000**	

REVISIONSFIRMÆT CARL JOHAN NIELSEN A/S

Herslebsgade 1, 7100 VEJLE
Tel: + 45 75 82 48 77
Fax: + 45 75 83 57 57
Mailing Address: P.O. Box 14, 7100 VEJLE

European Affiliation: Independent Accountants International

International Contact: Ejler Jørgensen

Partners:	5
Professional staff:	19
Non-professional staff:	7
Total Staff:	**31**

FEE INCOME

Year End: 1990	**%**
Accountancy & Audit:	82.0
Consultancy:	6.0
Tax:	12.0

CONTACT INFORMATION
Chairman: Sven Alversig
Managing Partner: Finn Lindgaard

CLIENT SERVICES
Accountancy (General), Audit, Computer Installation, Corporate Finance Advice, Insolvency & Corporate Restructuring, Life & Risk Assurance, Litigation/Legal Services, Management & Business Advice, Management Buy-outs, Mergers & Acquisitions, Pensions Planning, Value for Money Studies, Taxation (Corporate), Taxation (International), Trust Settlement & Estates, Bookkeeping, Financial Planning, EDP

NØRGAARD & FALK HANSEN

Skulkenborg 2, 5100 ODENSE C
Tel: + 45 66 12 14 77
Fax: + 45 66 13 75 66

European Affiliation: Urbach Hacker Young International

Partners:	2
Professional staff:	13
Non-professional staff:	2
Total Staff:	**17**

FEE INCOME

Year End: 31.12.90	**%**
Accountancy & Audit:	60.0
Consultancy:	30.0
Tax:	10.0

CONTACT INFORMATION
Managing Partner: Preben Nørgaard
Managing Partner: Leib Falk Hansen

OTHER OFFICES
NØRGAARD & FALK HANSEN
Østergade 5, 5610 ASSENS
Tel: + 45 64 71 56 77 *Fax:* + 45 64 71 46 77
Contact: Leib Falk Hansen

Total Number of Offices: 2

PANNELL KERR FORSTER DENMARK A/S

Frederiksgade 1, 1265 COPENHAGEN K
Tel: + 45 33 11 88 11
Fax: + 45 42 94 34 90

European Affiliation: Pannell Kerr Forster Worldwide

International Contact: Christopher Spencer

OTHER OFFICES
PANNELL KERR FORSTER DENMARK AS
Turbinevej 13, 2730 HERLEV, Copenhagen
Tel: + 45 44 94 32 44 *Fax:* + 45 44 94 34 90

Total Number of Offices: 3

PARTNER REVISION STATSAUTORISEREDE REVISORER A/S

Industrivej Nord 15, Birk, 7400 HERNING
Tel: + 45 97 12 50 22
Fax: + 45 97 21 37 88

European Affiliation: The International Group of Accounting Firms Ltd (IGAF)

International Contact: Aksel Boegh

OTHER OFFICES
PARTNER REVISION STATSAUTORISEREDE REVISORER A/S
Thrigesvej 3, 7430 IKAST
Tel: + 45 97 15 40 22 *Fax:* + 45 97 25 10 04
Contact: Thorkild Lundsgaard

Total Number of Offices: 2

REVISIONSFIRMÆT PREBEN LARSEN

Overgaden Neden Vandet 9C, 1023 COPENHAGEN K
Tel: + 45 32 96 20 00
Fax: + 45 32 96 20 40
Mailing Address: P.O. Box 1930, 1023 COPENHAGEN K

European Affiliation: Nexia International

International Contact: Peter W. Viereck

Partners:	15

FEE INCOME

Year End: 31.12.90	**DKr 000**	**%**
Accountancy & Audit:	26,500	55.0
Insolvency:	500	1.0
Consultancy:	14,000	29.0
Tax:	7,200	15.0
Total:	**48,200**	

CONTACT INFORMATION
Managing Partner: Per Otto Bech
Accountancy (General): Ole Møller Andreasen
Public Sector: Søren Jensen
Tax (Corporate): Marianne Bratholm
Tax (International): Carsten Ploug Thomsen

Corporate Finance & Insolvency: Peter Viereck
Audit & Administration: Knud Otto Jørgensen

CLIENT SERVICES
Accountancy (General), Audit, Computer Installation, Corporate Finance Advice, Insolvency & Corporate Restructuring, Management & Business Advice, Management Buy-outs, Mergers & Acquisitions, Value for Money Studies, Taxation (Corporate), Taxation (International), Trust Settlement & Estates

Industry Specialisations: Construction

MAJOR CLIENTS
B & W - Energi, Faxe Bryg Holding AS, T.H. Olesen AS, Ove Arkil A/S, Schulstad Gruppen A/S, Stelton A/S, Thrige Tilon A/S

OTHER OFFICES

REVISIONSFIRMÆT PREBEN LARSEN
Helsingørvej 1, P.O. Box 139, 3480 FREDENSBORG
Tel: + 45 42 28 48 80 *Fax:* + 45 42 28 23 08
Contact: Henning Nielsen

REVISIONSFIRMÆT PREBEN LARSEN
Storegade 86, P.O. Box 296, 6100 HADERSLEV
Tel: + 45 74 53 08 11 *Fax:* + 45 74 53 08 14
Contact: Poul P. Møller

REVISIONSFIRMÆT PREBEN LARSEN
Vestergade 11, 5000 ODENSE C
Tel: + 45 66 12 11 12 *Fax:* + 45 65 91 26 45
Contact: Jan Grevelund

REVISIONSFIRMÆT PREBEN LARSEN
Frederiksgade 76, 8000 ÅRHUS C
Tel: + 45 86 19 36 11 *Fax:* + 45 86 20 21 41
Contact: Bodil Flyvbjerg Hansen

Total Number of Offices: 5

REVIONSFIRMÆT PREBEN RASMUSSEN A/S

Thorsgade 59, 3, 2200 COPENHAGEN
Tel: + 45 31 81 88 22
Fax: + 45 35 82 28 20

European Affiliation: InterContinental Consultants (ICC)

International Contact: Per Krogh Rants
Flemming Rasmussen

PRICE WATERHOUSE/SEIER-PETERSEN

Tuborg Boulevard 1, 2900 HELLERUP
Tel: + 45 39 47 00 00
Fax: + 45 39 47 00 10
Mailing Address: P.O. Box 129, 2900 HELLERUP

European Affiliation: Price Waterhouse

International Contact: Noel M. Drew

Partners:	27
Professional staff:	293
Non-professional staff:	85
Total Staff:	**405**

FEE INCOME

Year End: 30.06.91	**DKr**	**%**
Accountancy & Audit:		66.0
Consultancy:		20.0
Tax:		14.0
Total:	**251,000,000**	

CONTACT INFORMATION
Chairman: Noel M. Drew
Corporate Finance: Carsten Gerner
Management Consultancy: Hans Dydensborg
Administration: Neils Møller
Private Sector & Privatisation: Morten Iversen
Accountancy & Audit: Aubrey Garner
Tax: Torben Wolsted

CLIENT SERVICES
All Services

MAJOR CLIENTS
A/S Cheminova, A/S Dansk Shell, Baltica Holding A/S, Bang & Olufsen A/S, BRF Kredit, Carlsberg AS, Copenhagen Airport A/S, Dansk Supermarked A/S, LM Ericsson A/S, Giro Bank A/S, IBM Danmark A/S, Jyske Holding A/S, Novo Nordisk A/S, Nykredit, Pensam, Phønix Contractors A/S, Saint Gobain Glass A/S, Skandinavisk Holding A/S, Tele Danmark A/S, Tellus Ejendomsinvest A/S

OTHER OFFICES

PRICE WATERHOUSE/SEIER PETERSEN
Åboulevarden 70, 8000 ÅRHUS
Tel: + 45 89 32 00 00 *Fax:* + 45 89 32 00 10
Contact: Jorgen Dissing

PRICE WATERHOUSE/SEIER PETERSEN
Rådhustorvet 11, 8700 HORSENS
Tel: + 45 75 62 18 55 *Fax:* + 45 75 62 27 06
Contact: Kaj Atzen

Total Number of Offices: 3

REVISIONSFIRMÆT KNUD E. RASMUSSEN

Slotsgade 21, 5100 ODENSE C
Tel: + 45 66 14 14 40
Fax: + 45 66 14 14 44

European Affiliation: Summit International Associates Inc

International Contact: Peter Schak Larsen

Partners:	9
Professional staff:	69
Non-professional staff:	6
Total Staff:	**84**

FEE INCOME

Year End: 31.12.90	**DKr**	**%**
Accountancy & Audit:		55.0
Insolvency:		5.0
Consultancy:		15.0
Tax:		15.0
Other:		10.0
Total:	**35,100,000**	

CONTACT INFORMATION
Managing Partner: Flemming Heden Knudsen
Insolvency: Erik Ramsland
Management Consultancy: Niels Sloth
Tax (Corporate): Flemming Heden Knudsen
Tax (International): Peter Schak Larsen
Accountancy & Audit: Klaus Kold
Computer Services: Helge Munk

CLIENT SERVICES
All Services

OTHER OFFICES

REVISIONSFIRMÆT KNUD E. RASMUSSEN/A. MATHIASEN
Vendersgade 20, 7000 FREDERICIA
Tel: + 45 75 92 49 11 *Fax:* + 45 75 92 49 87
Contact: Knud-Ove Jeppesen

▷

STEEN SOMMER/KNUD E. RASMUSSEN
Østergade 1, 1100 COPENHAGEN K
Tel: + 45 33 14 80 22 *Fax:* + 45 33 14 86 22
Contact: Steen Sommer

Total Number of Offices: 3

REVISORGAARDEN I KØBENHAVN AS

Kattesundet 14, P.O. Box 2084, 1013 COPENHAGEN
Tel: + 45 33 93 22 33
Fax: + 45 33 93 22 23

European Affiliation: TGI International

International Contact: Jesper Lind Hansen

REVISORSHUSET A/S

Buddingevej 289, P.O. Box 52, 2860 SØBORG
Tel: + 45 31 67 25 00
Fax: + 45 31 67 11 19

European Affiliation: Russell Bedford International

International Contact: Hans Jørn Lindeskov

RIR - REVISION

Himmelev Bygade 70, 4000 ROSKILDE
Tel: + 45 42 36 60 00
Fax: + 45 42 36 07 70

European Affiliation: BKR International

International Contact: Per Buch Hansen

Partners:	9
Professional staff:	30
Non-professional staff:	10
Total Staff:	**49**

CONTACT INFORMATION

Administration: Hanne Brødsgaard
Accountancy & Audit: Kurt Nielsen
Tax: André Helin

CLIENT SERVICES

Accountancy (General), Audit, Computer Installation, Corporate Finance Advice, Insolvency & Corporate Restructuring, Management & Business Advice, Management Buy-outs, Mergers & Acquisitions, Pensions Planning, Value for Money Studies, Taxation (Corporate), Taxation (International)

Industry Specialisations: Privatisation, Auditing &, Management Consultancy in Poland

OTHER OFFICES

RIR - REVISION
Frederiksgade 9, 1265 COPENHAGEN K
Tel: + 45 33 15 44 15 *Fax:* + 45 33 15 03 10
Contact: Palle Thaisen

RIR - REVISION
Smedelundsgade 18, 4300 HOLBÆCK
Tel: + 45 53 43 81 00 *Fax:* + 45 53 43 81 91
Contact: Hans Henrik Hansen

Total Number of Offices: 3

SCHØBEL & MARHOLT REVISIONAKTIESELSKAB

H.C. Andersens Boulevard 2, 1553 COPENHAGEN V
Tel: + 45 33 15 68 98
Fax: + 45 33 12 41 53

European Affiliation: DRT International

International Contact: Bent Hansen

Total Staff: 1,400

CLIENT SERVICES

All Services

MAJOR CLIENTS

Ålborg Portland, Carl Allers Etablissement, Bikoben, Commercial Leasing, Danisco, Danish Crown, Dansk Landbrugs Grovvareselsk, GN Store Nord, Gonlands Hjemmestyre, Grundfos International, ISS International Service System, Rasmussen & Schiotz, Skandinavisk Holding, Smidth & Co F.L., Steff Houlberg, Superfos, Tele Danmark, Topdanmark, Tryg Nykredit, Unibank

Total Number of Offices: 26

VANLOSE REVISION APS

Limfjordsvej 45 A, 2720 VANLOSE, Copenhagen
Tel: + 45 31 19 77 77
Fax: + 45 31 86 77 60

European Affiliation: S & W International

International Contact: Martin Berkowitz

REVISIONSFIRMÆT P.J. ÅRUP

Norre Farimagsgade 15, 1364 COPENHAGEN K
Tel: + 45 33 15 87 27
Fax: + 45 33 15 84 26

European Affiliation: The International Group of Accounting Firms Ltd (IGAF)

International Contact: Henning Lund Thomsen

K.G. JENSEN REVISIONSAKTIESELSKAB GREENLAND

P.O. Box 144, 3920 QAQORTOQ, (Julianehåb)
Tel: + 299 38391
Fax: + 299 38891

European Affiliation: Coopers & Lybrand Europe

International Contact: Kaj Vahlkvist

OTHER OFFICES

K.G. JENSEN REVISIONSAKTIESELSKAB GREENLAND
Bycentret, 3900 NUUK
Mailing Address: P.O. Box 319, 3900 NUUK (Godthab)
Tel: + 299 23133 *Fax:* + 299 23066
Contact: Flemming Bolding Christiansen

K.G. JENSEN REVISIONSAKTIESLSKAB GREENLAND
P.O. Box 90, 3912 MANIITSOQ (Sukkertoppen)
Tel: + 299 13433 *Fax:* + 299 13077
Contact: Erik Hvejsel Larsen

Total Number of Offices: 3

Finland

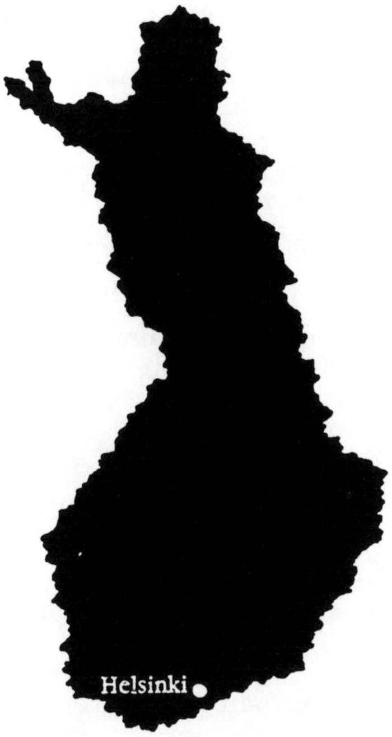

Area: 338,145 sq km (130,559 sq miles)
Population: 4,938,602 (1987 estimate)
Density: 14.6 per sq km
Capital: Helsinki

GDP: Fm577 bn, US$150 bn
GDP per head: US$30,070
Inflation: 1990 - 6.3%
1991 - 5.5% (forecast)

Official and Spoken Languages: Finnish. English is first foreign language. Swedish also spoken.

Time: GMT + 2 (in Summer GMT + 3)
Telephone Dialling Code: + 338

Currency: Markka (Fm) = 100 penni
Banking Hours: 0915-1615 Monday-Friday
Professional accountancy body: KHT-Yhdistys Foreningen CGR

Corporate Tax Data

Information supplied by Richard Citron, international tax partner of Stoy Hayward.

The tax year; nature and rates of tax

The tax year is the calendar year.

Companies are liable to national income tax (valtion tulovero) at a flat rate of 19%on both distributed and undistributed income. Lower rates are charged for taxable profits of below FMK 100,000. Local taxes are also payable on income.

Residence and territoriality

Finnish resident companies are taxable on their worldwide income. A company is resident in Finland if it is registered there or if its central management and control is exercised in Finland.

The tax base

Method of calculation. Taxable profits are based on the profit reported in the accounts. Income is calculated separately according to its source.

Disallowable items. Entertaining expenses are non-deductible if "unreasonable" in relation to turnover; local and church taxes are not deductible. The deductibility of charitable donations is limited.

Exempt income/special deductions. For dividends, see below. A non-specific doubtful debt reserve, of up to 2% of trade debtors, may be established. Contributions to an operating reserve up to a maximum of 30% of payroll are also tax deductible.

Interest paid. Loan interest is deductible on an accruals basis but where paid to affiliates or shareholders must be a genuine loan. Interest paid to non-residents is generally not subject to withholding tax.

Stock. Stock is valued at the lower of cost and market value. An inventory reserve of up to 25% may in certain instances be deductible. ▷

Depreciation. Different methods are prescribed for different types of asset. (1) Buildings are depreciable on the reducing balance basis at rates of between 5% and 20%. (2) Machinery and plant is also depreciable on a reducing balance basis at rates of up to 30%. Machinery and plant is pooled and sale proceeds deducted from the pool value. (3) Intangible assets are depreciable on the straightline basis at rates of between 10% and 20%.

Treatment of dividends

Dividends received from Finnish companies. These carry a tax credit of 2/3 of the net dividend (based on an approximate combined national, local and church tax liability of 40%). The excess tax credit is repayable if the total tax due on the company is less than 40%.

Dividends received from abroad. These are generally exempt under treaty, but where there is no treaty, the dividend, grossed up by the foreign tax paid, is included in taxable income. The foreign tax paid is available as a tax credit.

Dividends payable to residents. Dividends payable to residents of Finland carry a tax credit of 2/3 of the net dividend.

Dividends payable to non-residents. Non-residents of Finland are not entitled to the tax credit. A withholding tax of 25% is deductible instead.

Anti-avoidance measures

Thin capitalisation rules are operated with regard to Finnish subsidiaries of foreign companies.Transfer pricing rules are also applied to transactions (including interest payments) with foreign affiliates.

Treatment of losses

Current period. There is no set off of losses in the current period because of the "schedular" system. If the aggregate profits and losses from all sources amount to a loss, the aggregate loss is carried forward (there is no carry-back).

Future periods. The aggregate loss can be carried forward and set off against total taxable profits for national income tax purposes or profits from that source for local income tax purposes for a maximum of five years (ten years for new businesses).

Treatment of capital gains

Treatment. Capital gains are treated as income.

Computation. The rules are complicated. Broadly:

(1) Real property or shares held for business purposes. If the property has been owned for at least ten years (or shares for five years), the gain is computed by deducting the book value from 60% of the net sale proceeds. Where the property or shares have been owned for less than ten (or five, as the case may be) years, the profit is taxed in full.

(2) Real property or shares not used for business purposes. The gain is computed by deducting the greater of cost and 50% of the sale proceeds from the sale proceeds. Where the property has been held for at least ten years (five for shares), the gain is further reduced by an allowance of FMk 220,000 and the taxable gain is 50% of the resulting figure.

Non-residents are generally not liable to tax on capital gains arising from the sale of shares in a Finnish company.

Rollover. There are no rollover provisions as such, but a replacement reserve can be established with the gain from disposal of a building, so deferring the gain.

Treatment of groups

A tax group may be formed by a holding company and its 90% or more subsidiaries, all of which must be resident in Finland, for the purpose of shifting profits and losses around the group by means of tax-deductible contribution payments (taxable in the hands of the recipient).

Treatment of branches

A branch of a non-resident company would be subject to income tax. It would also be liable to national net worth tax, unless exempted by treaty. There is no withholding tax on remittances of profit abroad.

Other taxes

Local income tax. Levied on a similar base to national income tax. The rates vary between 14% and 19.5%. There is also a church tax of between 1% and 2% on the local income tax base.

Taxes on capital. Non-resident companies are in principle liable to national net worth tax, at 1% on the net value of assets situated in Finland.

Turnover taxes. There is a sales tax of 18.05% on the sale price of goods and certain services, inclusive of the tax itself (an effective rate of 22%). Exports are not subject to the tax.

Transaction taxes. A duty of 6% is payable on the transfer of real property and a1.6% duty is payable on a share transfer. This duty is not payable on a transfer between non-residents.

Social security. Employers pay contributions of between 23% and 25% of payroll. In addition, statutory holiday pay of 14%-17% is payable.

ARTHUR ANDERSEN & CO

Ruoholahdenkatu 8, 00180 HELSINKI
Tel: +*358* (0) 694 0411
Fax: +*358* (0) 693 1210

European Affiliation: Arthur Andersen Worldwide

International Contact: Hannu Vänskä

CONTACT INFORMATION

Audit: Hannu Vänskä
Tax (Corporate): Ara Tähtinen

CLIENT SERVICES

Accountancy (General), Audit, Computer Installation, Corporate Finance Advice, Insolvency & Corporate Restructuring, Litigation/Legal Services, Management & Business Advice, Management Buy-outs, Mergers & Acquisitions, Pensions Planning, Value for Money Studies, Taxation (Corporate), Taxation (International)

AURECO OY

Hatanpäänvaltatie 4 A 5, 33100 TAMPERE
Tel: +*358* (31) 236 733
Fax: +*358* (31) 233 722

European Affiliation: Midsnell International

International Contact: Risto Koivisto

Partners:	2
Professional staff:	2
Total Staff:	4

FEE INCOME

Year End: 28.02.91	%
Accountancy & Audit:	45.0
Consultancy:	40.0
Tax:	5.0
Other:	10.0

CONTACT INFORMATION

Chairman: Risto Koivisto
Managing Partner: Ravno Werner

CLIENT SERVICES

Accountancy (General), Audit, Corporate Finance Advice, Insolvency & Corporate Restructuring, Management & Business Advice, Management Buy-outs, Mergers & Acquisitions, Value for Money Studies, Taxation (Corporate), Taxation (International)

FINNAUDIT OY

Kansakoulukuja 1A, 00100 HELSINKI 10
Tel: +*358* (0) 694 6900
Fax: +*358* (0) 694 3276

European Affiliation: BDO Binder

Partners:	2
Professional staff:	6
Non-professional staff:	1
Total Staff:	9

CONTACT INFORMATION

Managing Partner: André Kumlander

CLIENT SERVICES

Audit, Management & Business Advice, Management Buy-outs, Mergers & Acquisitions, Taxation (Corporate), Taxation (International)

OTHER OFFICES

TILINTARKASTUSTOIMISTO KALLINEN ET HYYTIÄINEN KY
Kirkkokatu 37 A, 70100 KUOPIO
Tel: +*358* (71) 125 033
Contact: Reino Hyytiainen

Total Number of Offices: 2

IMMONEN, KARTTUNEN, LAUKKANEN & CO KY

Hietalahdenkatu 2 B 20, 00180 HELSINKI
Tel: +*358* (0) 648 717
Fax: +*358* (0) 607 876

European Affiliation: Summit International Associates Inc

International Contact: Jouko Karttunen

Partners:	5
Professional staff:	45
Total Staff:	**50**

FEE INCOME

Year End: 1990	**FIM**	%
Accountancy & Audit:		95.0
Insolvency:		1.0
Consultancy:		3.0
Tax:		1.0
Total:	**11,000,000**	

CONTACT INFORMATION

Managing Partner: Jouko Karttunen
Audit: Seppo Laukkanen
Corporate Finance: Erkki Immonen
Management Consultancy: Kari Immonen
Administration: Tuula Hakamies
Tax (Corporate): Jouko Karttunen
Accountancy, Audit & Administration: Jouko Karttunen
Computer Installation: Seppo Laukkanen
Computer Installation: Kari Immonen
Wholesale Distribution: Erkki Immonen

CLIENT SERVICES

Accountancy (General), Audit, Computer Installation, Corporate Finance Advice, Insolvency & Corporate Restructuring, Management & Business Advice, Management Buy-outs, Mergers & Acquisitions, Taxation (Corporate), Special Audit in Bankrupt Cases

Industry Specialisations: Wholesale and Distribution, Research and Development, Construction

OTHER OFFICES

IMMONEN, KARTTUNEN, LAUKKANEN & CO KY
Kirkkokatu 1, 48100 KOTKA
Tel: +*358* (52) 181 54 *Fax:* +*358* (52) 154 43
Contact: Airi Pihljerta

IMMONEN, KARTTUNEN, LAUKKANEN & CO KY
Mannerheiminkatu 1 B, 06100 PORVOO
Tel: +*358* (15) 131 022 *Fax:* +*358* (15) 173 564
Contact: Pirjo Vaittinen

Total Number of Offices: 3

JÄGERHORN, LINDBERG, ALMQVIST OY AB

Mannerheimvägen 76b, 00250 HELSINKI
Tel: +*358* (0) 491 711
Fax: +*358* (0) 491 933

European Affiliation: Horwath International

International Contact: Harry Lindberg

Partners:	6
Professional staff:	3
Non-professional staff:	1
Total Staff:	**10**

▷

FEE INCOME

Year End: 31.12.90	**FIM**	**%**
Accountancy & Audit:		60.0
Consultancy:		20.0
Tax:		20.0
Total:	**452,000,000**	

CONTACT INFORMATION

Chairman: Reginald Jägerhorn
Managing Partner: Sune Almqvist
Accountancy (General): Sune Almqvist
Audit & Management Consultancy: Reginald Jägerhorn
Tax: Harry Lindberg

CLIENT SERVICES

Accountancy (General), Audit, Corporate Finance Advice, Insolvency & Corporate Restructuring, Management & Business Advice, Management Buy-outs, Mergers & Acquisitions, Value for Money Studies, Taxation (Corporate), Taxation (International)

Industry Specialisations: Small & Medium-sized Companies

OTHER OFFICES

JÄGERHORN, LINDBERG, ALMQVIST OY AB
Strandgatan 29, 65120 VASA
Tel: + *358* (61) 173 620

Total Number of Offices: 2

TILINTARKASTUSTOIMISTO KALERVO ARILUOMA KY

Mannerheimintie 16 A 3, 00100 HELSINKI
Tel: + *358* (0) 209 595
Fax: + *358* (0) 642 348

European Affiliation: Midsnell International

International Contact: Kalervo Ariluoma

KPMG WIDENIUS, SEDERHOLM & SOMERI OY

Mannerheimintie 20 B, 00100 HELSINKI
Tel: + *358* (0) 693 931
Fax: + *358* (0) 693 9399
Mailing Address: PL 1037, 00101 HELSINKI

European Affiliation: KPMG

International Contact: Hannu Niilekselä

Partners:	37
Professional staff:	174
Non-professional staff:	30
Total Staff:	**241**

FEE INCOME

Year End: 30.09.91	**FIM**
Accountancy & Audit:	73,150
Consultancy:	15,343
Tax:	2,744
Other:	897
Total:	**92,134**

CONTACT INFORMATION

Chairman: Eric Haglund
Managing Partner: Eric Haglund
Insolvency: Aimo Silventoinen
Management Consultancy: Pekka Mäkelä
Administration: Leena von Geeich
Tax (Corporate): Mauri Palvi
Tax (International): Bengt Nyholm
Accountancy & Audit: Heikki Koskelainen

CLIENT SERVICES

Audit, Insolvency & Corporate Restructuring, Management & Business Advice, Management Buy-outs, Mergers & Acquisitions, Taxation (Corporate), Taxation (International)

MAJOR CLIENTS

Ahlström A Osakeyhtiö, Eka-yhtymä Osuuskunta, Huhamäki Oy, Kemira Oy, Kymmene Oy, Metra Oy Ab, Nokia-yhtymä, Partek Oy Ab, Rautaruukki Oy, Sampo-yhtiöt, Suomen Yhdyspankki Oy, Valmet-Konserni

Total Number of Offices: 15

OLLI WESAMAA HTM TILINTARKASTUSRYHMÄ OY/AUDIT GROUP LTD

Pohjoisesplanadi 27 C, 00100 HELSINKI
Tel: + *358* (0) 604 204
Fax: + *358* (0) 664 136

European Affiliation: DFK International

International Contact: Olli Wesamaa

PRICE WATERHOUSE

Kansakoulukuja 1, 4th Floor, 00100 HELSINKI
Tel: + *358* (0) 694 4499
Fax: + *358* (0) 694 3375

European Affiliation: Price Waterhouse

Partners:	3
Professional staff:	31
Non-professional staff:	6
Total Staff:	**40**

FEE INCOME

Year End: 30.06.91	**FIM**
Accountancy & Audit:	6,000,000
Consultancy:	1,000,000
Tax:	4,500,000
Total:	**11,500,000**

CONTACT INFORMATION

Managing Partner: Anders Landelius
Audit: Hannele Selesvuo
Corporate Finance: Anders Landelius
Management Consultancy: Martti Vuorio
Tax: Raimo Pallonen

CLIENT SERVICES

Accountancy (General), Audit, Corporate Finance Advice, Management Buy-outs, Mergers & Acquisitions, Taxation (Corporate), Taxation (International)

OTHER OFFICES

PRICE WATERHOUSE
Kehräsaari, 33200 TAMPERE
Tel: + *358* (31) 242 8658 *Fax:* + *358* (31) 122 987
Contact: Esa Vuorenpää

Total Number of Offices: 2

SALMI VIRKKUNEN & HELENIUS OY/ COOPERS & LYBRAND

Keskuskatu 3, 00100 HELSINKI
Tel: +*358* (0) 658 044
Fax: +*358* (0) 174 102
Mailing Address: PL 1015, 00101 HELSINKI

European Affiliation: Coopers & Lybrand Europe

International Contact: Antti Helenius

Partners:	25
Professional staff:	150
Non-professional staff:	30
Total Staff:	**205**

CONTACT INFORMATION
Chairman: Antti Helenius
Managing Partner: Tauno Haataja
Management Consultancy: Antti Sääskilahti
Tax (International): Ilkka Kajas

CLIENT SERVICES
Accountancy (General), Audit, Management & Business Advice, Mergers & Acquisitions, Taxation (Corporate), Taxation (International)

Industry Specialisations: Banking, Insurance, Automotive, Forestry, Pharmaceutical, Food & Drink, Communications

OTHER OFFICES
SALMI VIRKKUNEN & HELENIUS OY/COOPERS & LYBRAND
Asematie 1, 68600 PIETARSAARI
Tel: +*358* (67) 234 774 *Fax:* +*358* (67) 230 893

SALMI VIRKKUNEN & HELENIUS OY/COOPERS & LYBRAND
Rovakatu 38 A 16, 96200 ROVANIEMI
Tel: +*358* (60) 312 780 *Fax:* +*358* (60) 318 086

SALMI VIRKKUNEN & HELENIUS OY/COOPERS & LYBRAND
PL 810, Strömberginkatu 2, 65101 VAASA
Tel: +*358* (61) 155 866 *Fax:* +*358* (61) 155 552

SALMI VIRKKUNEN & HELENIUS OY/COOPERS & LYBRAND
Vuorikatu 26 A, 70100 KUOPIO
Tel: +*358* (71) 115 780 *Fax:* +*358* (71) 118 825

SALMI VIRKKUNEN & HELENIUS OY/COOPERS & LYBRAND
Kauppakatu 61, 53100 LAPPEENRANTA
Tel: +*358* (53) 503 16 *Fax:* +*358* (53) 503 63

SALMI VIRKKUNEN & HELENIUS OY/COOPERS & LYBRAND
Aurakatu 14 B, 20100 TURKU
Tel: +*358* (21) 510 801 *Fax:* +*358* (21) 518 323

TILINTARKASTUSTOIMISTO JOKELA JA VÄISÄNEN OY
Kauppatori 1, 57130 SAVONLINNA
Tel: +*358* (57) 244 74 *Fax:* +*358* (57) 514 838

Total Number of Offices: 14

TILINTARKASTAJIEN OY - REVISORERNAS AB

Kaivokatu 8, 00100 HELSINKI
Tel: +*358* (0) 622 1233
Fax: +*358* (0) 622 1323

European Affiliation: DRT International

International Contact: Mikael Paul

Total Staff: **126**

CLIENT SERVICES
All Services

MAJOR CLIENTS
ABB Stromberg, Elaeke - Varma, C.J. Hartman, HOK, KWH - Yhtyma, Luhta, Meira, Orion, Post & Telecommunications of Finland, SOK, Sponsor, Starck-Johann-Telko, Suomen GM, Teboil, Teollisuudem Voima, Tietotehdas, Union Bank of Finland, Veitsiluoto

Total Number of Offices: 11

TILINTARKASTAJIEN OY / OY ERNST & YOUNG AB

Aleksanterinkatu 48A (to May 92), Kaivokatu 8 (from May 92), 00100 HELSINKI
Tel: +*358* (0) 172 771
Fax: +*358* (0) 622 1377

European Affiliation: Ernst & Young Europe

International Contact: Carl Gustav af Hällström

Total Number of Offices: 13

TILINTARKASTUSRENGAS OY

Paasivuorenkatu 2 C, 00530 HELSINKI
Tel: +*358* (0) 718 211
Fax: +*358* (0) 701 8855

European Affiliation: INPACT - International Network of Professional Accountants

International Contact: Arto Kuusiola

TILINTARKSTUSTOIMISTO SELINHEIMO KY

Peltolantie 21, 013 00 VANTAA
Tel: +*358* (0) 857 3711
Fax: +*358* (0) 857 3755

European Affiliation: Russell Bedford International

International Contact: Juhani Selinheimo

TILINTARKASTUSTOIMISTO YRJO TUOKKO KY

Lautturinkuja 2, 00570 HELSINKI
Tel: +*358* (0) 684 9122
Fax: +*358* (0) 684 9407

European Affiliation: Grant Thornton International

International Contact: Yrjo Tuokko

Partners:	6
Professional staff:	13
Non-professional staff:	5
Total Staff:	**24**

FEE INCOME

Year End: 1990	**FIM (million)**
Total:	**13,276**

CONTACT INFORMATION
Managing Partner: Yrjo Tuokko

CLIENT SERVICES
Audit, Insolvency & Corporate Restructuring, Management & Business Advice, Mergers & Acquisitions, Taxation (Corporate), Taxation (International), Company Formation

OTHER OFFICES
TILINTARKASTUSTOIMISTO YRJO TUOKKO KY
Tellervonkatu 14-16 C28, 40200 JYVASKYLA
Tel: +*358* (41) 617 800 *Fax:* +*358* (41) 617 888

TILINTARKASTUSTOIMISTO YRJO TUOKKO KY
Porrassalmenkatu 15 B 36, 50100 MIKKELI
Tel: + *358* (55) 362 177 *Fax:* + *358* (55) 151 207

TILINTARKASTUSTOIMISTO YRJO TUOKKO KY
Gallen-Kallelankatu 9 A 18, 28100 PORI
Tel: + *358* (39) 338 487 *Fax:* + *358* (39) 338 467

TILINTARKASTUSTOIMISTO YRJO TUOKKO KY
Hallituskatu 26, 96100 ROVANIEMI
Tel: + *358* (60) 314 493 *Fax:* + *358* (60) 311 408

TILINTARKASTUSTOIMISTO YRJO TUOKKO KY
Kauppakatu 6A5, 60100 SEINÄJOKI
Tel: + *358* (64) 134 320 *Fax:* + *358* (64) 134 310

TILINTARKASTUSTOIMISTO YRJO TUOKKO KY
Pitkamaenkatu 4, 20250 TURKU
Tel: + *358* (21) 548 007

Total Number of Offices: 7

JORMA WAINIO OY

Satamakatu 4, 00160 HELSINKI
Tel: + *358* (0) 176 351
Fax: + *358* (0) 176 521
Mailing Address: PL 209, 00160 HELSINKI

European Affiliation: S & W International
National Affiliation: OSSERS INTERNATIONAL

International Contact: Jorma M. Wainio

Partners: 1

FEE INCOME

Year End: 31.12.90	%
Accountancy & Audit:	90.0
Tax:	5.0
Other:	5.0

CONTACT INFORMATION

Managing Partner: Jorma Wainio

CLIENT SERVICES

All Services

MAJOR CLIENTS

Aazet Oy, Amargo Oy, Chorus Productions Oy, City-Boy Oy, Creart Oy Ab, Cronimo Oy Ab, Helsinki Automatic Center Oy, Hydrosuprex Oy, Kaivopuiston Kirjapaino Oy, Lekoair Liikelennot Oy, Miva-Car Oy, Nimike Oy Ab, Parttipuoti Oy, Polarmusic Oy, Reproteekki Oy, Stepup Oy, Studiorakennus Oy, Tair Oy, Timberco Oy Ltd, Tuontipojat Oy

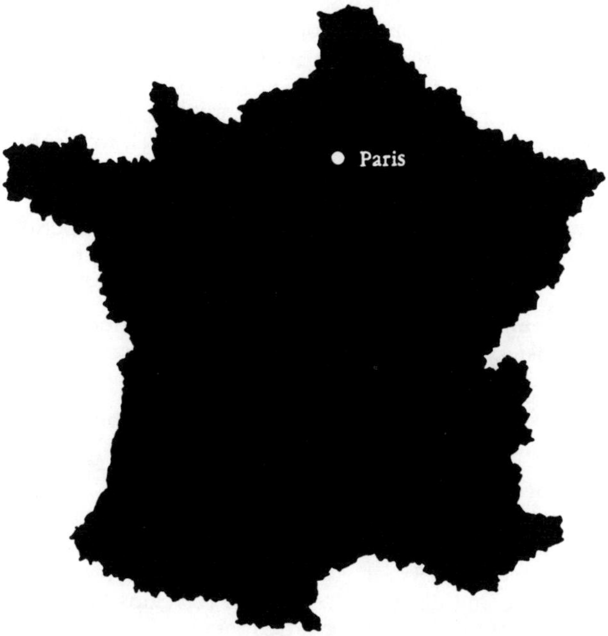

Area: 543,965 sq km (210,026 sq miles)
Population: 55,632,000 (1987)
Density: 102.3 per sq km
Capital: Paris

GDP: FFr6.52 trn, US$1.21 trn
GDP per head: US$22,420
Inflation: 1990 - 3.5%
1991 - 3.7% (forecast)

Official and Spoken Language: French. Many regional dialects. Some English spoken

Time: GMT + 1 (in Summer GMT + 2)
Telephone Dialling Code: +33

Currency: French Franc (FFr) = 100 centimes
Banking Hours: 0900-1600 Monday-Friday and closed either Saturday or Monday. Close at 1200 before bank holidays, may close all or part of the day after. May also close 1200-1400 for lunch.
Professional accountancy bodies: Ordre des Experts Comptables Agréés (DECCA)
Compagnie Nationale des Commisaires aux Comptes (CNCC)

Corporate Tax Data

Information supplied by Richard Citron, international tax partner of Stoy Hayward.

The tax year; nature and rates of tax

The tax year is the financial year of the company, but at least one return must be filed within a calendar year.

Corporate income tax (impôt sur les sociétés) is charged at 34%, whether the income is undistributed or not, subject to a minimum of FF5,000. A reduced rate is payable on long term capital gains.

Residence and territoriality

French resident companies pay corporate income tax on all income arising in France. Most foreign income (and capital gains) is exempt. A company is resident in France if it is incorporated under French law or its central control and management are found in France.

The tax base

Method of calculation. The taxable profit is based on the profit reported in the accounts.

Disallowable items. The major disallowable items are: transfers to the general and statutory reserve (réserve légale), costs of providing certain benefits to employees and excessive charitable donations.

Exempt income/special deductions. Profits from foreign branches are exempt. Contributions to pension schemes are deductible as are certain dividends on new shares. Formation expenses may be deducted in the period in which they are incurred or amortised over a period of five years. Contributions by companies to the compulsory profit sharing plan are deductible.

▷

Interest paid. Interest is deductible under either an accruals or a paid basis.

Stock. Stock and work in progress are valued at the lower of cost and market value. A measure of stock relief is available.

Depreciation. Tax depreciation may be calculated on either a straightline or a reducing balance basis, at rates fixed by the tax authorities (eg. industrial buildings 5%, residential buildings 1-2% and motor vehicles 20-25%). Land is not normally depreciable.

Treatment of dividends

Dividends received from French companies. An imputation system operates in France, under which dividends paid carry a tax credit (avoir fiscal) of 50% of the net dividend. This is transferred to the recipient company's own shareholders when it pays a dividend.

Dividends paid to residents. There is now only one rate of corporation tax for distributed or undistributed profits and the equalisation tax (pré-compte mobilier) which often used to be on the payment of dividends is no longer due. Credit is given for foreign tax suffered.

Dividends paid to non-residents. Non-residents of France are in general not entitled to the avoir fiscal. A withholding tax of 25% (reduced where appropriate by treaty) is deductible from the dividend.

Anti-avoidance measures

Thin capitalisation rules are applied where interest is paid to foreign lenders. There are also controlled foreign company measures. In certain circumstances, French companies with an interest of 25% or more in a foreign company established in a territory with a "low tax" regime may be required to include their corresponding share of the foreign company's profits. There are also transfer pricing rules.

Treatment of losses

Current period. Trading losses may be set against income and capital gains of the same period.

Past periods. Trading losses may be carried back against undistributed income or gains of the three preceding years.

Future periods. Where not used in the current or in past periods losses may be carried forward against taxable income for up to five years. Losses corresponding to the depreciation of fixed assets may be carried forward indefinitely.

Treatment of capital gains

Treatment. Capital gains are subject to corporate income tax, but at reduced rates in certain cases.

(1) Short term gains (including inter alia the gain on an asset held for less than two years) less appropriate losses are taxable at the full rate of corporate income tax.
(2) Long term gains are broadly gains on assets held for at least two years. They are taxable at a reduced rate of 18%. When distributed to shareholders they are added back to taxable income and taxed at the full rate, with a credit for the tax paid.
(3) Net short term losses in any accounting period may be carried forward as an ordinary trading loss.

Computation. Gains are computed by deducting the cost (or net book value where depreciation has been claimed) from sale proceeds.

Rollover. There is no rollover against the cost of replacement assets.

Special treatment of shares. Where a non-resident makes a capital gain on disposal of shares in a French company, the gain is taxed at 19% if the holding has exceeded 25% at any time in the five years preceding disposal. Exemption for gains on shares is conferred by most tax treaties.

Treatment of groups

A French parent company and any of its 95% subsidiaries may elect for group treatment. Transfers of assets may be made tax free and dividends paid free of tax within a group.

Treatment of branches

French branches of non-resident companies are liable for corporate income tax in the same manner as French resident companies. There is also a 25% withholding tax on branch profits but this may be reduced or eliminated under a tax treaty.

Other taxes

A *local tax* known as "taxe professionnelle" is levied at varying rates (maximum 4%) on 18% of gross salaries (including fringe benefits) and the annual rental value of the company's property. A number of local property taxes apply.

Turnover taxes. There is a value added tax on the supply of goods and services. The standard rate is 18.6% and there is a reduced rate of 5.5% and a luxury rate of 22%.

Transaction taxes. There are various taxes on the transfer of assets and on capital subscriptions.

Payroll taxes. Employers' social security contributions of approximately 39% are payable as is a special residential housing levy of 0.65% on payroll and an apprenticeship tax of 0.6% of payroll and a salary tax and training levy.

AEC CONSULTANTS
allée des Sapins, B.P. 443, 44474 CARQUEFOU CEDEX
Tel: +*33* 40 68 20 20
Fax: +*33* 40 93 78 20

European Affiliation: Eura-Audit International

International Contact: J-Y. Gourdon
J-Y. Fortun

OTHER OFFICES
AEC CONSULTANTS
rue Watt, B.P. 383, 85010 LA ROCHE/YON CEDEX
Tel: +*33* 51 37 44 17 *Fax:* +*33* 51 37 88 58
Contact: D. Girard

AEC CONSULTANTS
6 rue de la Rigourdière, 35510 CESSON SEVIGNÉ
Tel: +*33* 99 83 87 88 *Fax:* +*33* 99 83 23 70
Contact: D. Vrignaud

Total Number of Offices: 3

ALPHA AUDIT
51 rue Blanche, 75009 PARIS
Tel: +*33* (1) 48 73 69 91
Fax: +*33* (1) 40 16 11 74

European Affiliation: The International Group of Accounting Firms Ltd (IGAF)

International Contact: M. Leo Jegard

Total Number of Offices: 4

AMYOT AUDITEURS ET CONSEILS
2 rue Washington, 75008 PARIS
Tel: +*33* (1) 42 89 18 27
Fax: +*33* (1) 42 89 30 75

European Affiliation: Summit International Associates Inc

International Contact: Daniel Kurkdjian

Partners:	17
Professional staff:	77
Non-professional staff:	16
Total Staff:	**110**

FEE INCOME

Year End: 30.09.91	%
Accountancy & Audit:	77.0
Consultancy:	8.0
Tax:	15.0

CONTACT INFORMATION
Chairman: Hratchia Tchoulakian
Accountancy (General): Arthur Kotchian
Audit: Jean-Pierre Debenoit
Corporate Finance: Michael Cohen
Administration: Hratchia Tchoulakian
Tax: Bernard Alexandre
Mergers & Acquisitions: Pierre Grafmeyer
Legal Services: Jean Nadal

CLIENT SERVICES
Accountancy (General), Audit, Computer Installation, Litigation/Legal Services, Management & Business Advice, Mergers & Acquisitions, Value for Money Studies, Taxation (Corporate), Taxation (International)

Industry Specialisations: Construction, Engineering, Water Treatment, Software

OTHER OFFICES
AMYOT ANDRES ET ASSOCIÉS
51 boulevard de Chateaudun, 45000 ORLEANS
Tel: +*33* 38 54 35 89 *Fax:* +*33* 38 54 81 49
Contact: Gilbert Le Pironnec

AMYOT AUDITEURS ET CONSEILS
6 rue Amyot, 75005 PARIS
Tel: +*33* (1) 43 31 86 92 *Fax:* +*33* (1) 43 37 19 63
Contact: Michael Cohen

AMYOT AUDITEURS ET CONSEILS
3 rue Anizon, 44000 NANTES
Tel: +*33* 40 69 21 18 *Fax:* +*33* 40 69 21 15
Contact: Pascal Duault

AMYOT AUDITEURS ET CONSEILS RHONE-ALPES
14 chemin de la Pomme, 69811 TASSIN B.P. 20, LYON CEDEX
Tel: +*33* 78 34 28 25 *Fax:* +*33* 78 34 77 78
Contact: Pierre Grafmeyer

Total Number of Offices: 5

APLITEC
44 quai de Jemmapes, 75010 PARIS
Tel: +*33* (1) 40 40 38 38
Fax: +*33* (1) 40 40 38 98

European Affiliation: Morison International

International Contact: Jean-Pierre Larroze

Partners:	9
Professional staff:	73
Non-professional staff:	10
Total Staff:	**92**

FEE INCOME

Year End: 31.12.90	**FFr**	%
Accountancy & Audit:		85.0
Consultancy:		5.0
Tax:		10.0
Total:	**42,000,000**	

CONTACT INFORMATION
Chairman: Gérard Leplé
Managing Partner: André Chopineau
Accountancy (General): Gérard Decaux
Audit: Jacques Vais
Corporate Finance: Hervé Lobry
Administration: André Chopineau
Public Sector: Gérard Leplé
Tax (Corporate): Bernard Girodroux-Lavigne
Tax (International): Jean-Pierre Larroze
Management Consultancy & EDP: Pierre Laot

CLIENT SERVICES
Accountancy (General), Audit, Computer Installation, Corporate Finance Advice, Litigation/Legal Services, Management & Business Advice, Management Buy-outs, Mergers & Acquisitions, Taxation (Corporate), Taxation (International), Trust Settlement & Estates, Mutual Funds

Industry Specialisations: Prêt-à-Porter, Fashion, Newspaper, Data Processing, Engineering, Advertising, Transport, Real Estate

MAJOR CLIENTS
Banque Saga (SICAV - FCP), BTP Banque, Conté, Financière Atlas (SICAV - FCP), Go Voyages, Group Bernard Krief, Groupe Metrologie International, Groupe Orca, Groupe Socpresse (Figaro - France Soir), La Cinq, LBO - France, Ofivalmo (SICAV - FCP), Saunier Duval Eau Chaude Chauffage, Société Nouvelle D'Exploitation de La Tour Eiffel, Sofretu (Subsidiary of RATP), Spontex, Subsidiary of Groupe Calberson, TASQ International, Thierry Mugler, Union Normande Investments

Total Number of Offices: 2

JEAN ARTHUIS ET ASSOCIÉS

208 rue Raymond-Losserand, 75014 PARIS
Tel: +33 (1) 40 44 44 04
Fax: +33 (1) 40 44 40 61

European Affiliation: Clark Kenneth Leventhal

International Contact: Guillaume de Saint-Gérand

Partners:	10
Professional staff:	67
Non-professional staff:	17
Total Staff:	**94**

FEE INCOME

Year End: 1990	**%**
Accountancy & Audit:	83.0
Other:	7.0

CLIENT SERVICES
Accountancy (General), Audit, Corporate Finance Advice, Insolvency & Corporate Restructuring, Management & Business Advice, Taxation (Corporate)

CONTACT INFORMATION
Chairman: Jean-Jacques Mesmin
Accountancy (General): Gérard Prigent
Audit: Raymond Cornu
Insolvency: Georges Spandonis
Administration: Dominiques Chatelain
Public Sector: Alain Vignaud
Tax (Corporate): Yves Chaumet

CLIENT SERVICES
All Services

OTHER OFFICES

CCI CONSEILS
46 rue Président-Edouard-Herriot, 69002 LYON
Tel: +33 78 38 15 07 *Fax:* +33 78 42 78 17
Contact: Marcel Larose

SOFIA
Forum d'Orvault, 34 rue Jules-Verne, 44700 ORVAULT NANTES
Tel: +33 40 63 70 33 *Fax:* +33 40 63 38 80
Contact: Christian Bouchon

Total Number of Offices: 3

ARTHUR ANDERSEN & CO

Tour GAN - CEDEX 13, 92082 PARIS LA DÉFENSE 2
Tel: +33 (1) 42 91 06 06
Fax: +33 (1) 42 91 06 59

European Affiliation: Arthur Andersen Worldwide

International Contact: Georges Barthès de Ruyter

CONTACT INFORMATION
Audit: Georges Barthès de Ruyter
Tax (Corporate): Xavier de Sarrau

CLIENT SERVICES
Accountancy (General), Audit, Computer Installation, Corporate Finance Advice, Insolvency & Corporate Restructuring, Litigation/Legal Services, Management & Business Advice, Management Buy-outs, Mergers & Acquisitions, Pensions Planning, Value for Money Studies, Taxation (Corporate), Taxation (International)

OTHER OFFICES

ARTHUR ANDERSEN & CO
Tour Crédit Lyonnais 129, rue Servient, 69431 LYON CEDEX 03
Tel: +33 78 63 72 00 *Fax:* +33 78 95 46 47

ARTHUR ANDERSEN & CO
Tour Europe, 20 place des Halles, 6700 STRASBOURG
Tel: +33 88 75 63 23 *Fax:* +33 88 22 20 67

Total Number of Offices: 4

AUDIT DE FRANCE - SODIP

12 cours Louis Lumière, 25 bis, avenue du Petit-Parc,
94306 VINCENNES CEDEX
Tel: +33 49 57 51 51
Fax: +33 49 57 51 60

European Affiliation: INPACT - International Network of Professional Accountants

International Contact: Laurent Ginet

Partners:	18
Professional staff:	125
Non-professional staff:	21
Total Staff:	**164**

FEE INCOME

Year End: 30.09.90	**FFr**
Total:	**6,418,000**

AUDIT FRANCE ASSOCIÉS

Residence "Le Grand Pavois", boulevard de Lattre de Tassigny 2,
B.P. 100, 03204 VICHY CEDEX
Tel: +33 70 31 39 52
Fax: +33 70 98 43 77

European Affiliation: The International Group of Accounting Firms Ltd (IGAF)

International Contact: Jacques Rozan

Total Number of Offices: 6

AUDIT RÉVISION ET CONTROLE (ARC)

Le Mercure C, Zone Industrielle des Milles,
13851 AIX EN PROVENCE CEDEX 3
Tel: +33 42 60 01 69
Fax: +33 42 34 37 16

European Affiliation: Eura-Audit International

International Contact: A. Rougier

AUDITEC AQUITAINE

Z.I. de Chanteloiseau, 33140 VILLENAVE D'ORNON
Tel: +33 56 75 33 93
Fax: +33 56 75 39 20

European Affiliation: Independent Accountants International

International Contact: Patrick Varron

Partners:	2
Professional staff:	20
Non-professional staff:	4
Total Staff:	**26**

CONTACT INFORMATION
Accountancy (General): Edmond Caubraque
Audit: Patrick Varron

CLIENT SERVICES
All Services

Industry Specialisations: Textile (Manufacture of Garments), Foods Manufacturing ▷

P.F. AUTEF
23 boulevard de la Saussaye, 92200 NEUILLY
Tel: +33 (1) 47 47 40 37
Fax: +33 (1) 47 38 13 58

European Affiliation: A.E.E. International

International Contact: P.F. Autef

CLIENT SERVICES
Accountancy (General), Litigation/Legal Services, Taxation (Corporate), Taxation (International), Management Consultancy, Financial Consultancy

ASSOCIATED FIRMS
J.P. DELSOL
38 rue de la Barrière, B.P. 138, 19004 TULLE CEDEX
Tel: +33 55 26 49 97
Contact: J.P. Delsol

AUDIT ET ASSISTANCE INTERNATIONALE A. LAGOUTTE
130 boulevard Delebecque, 59503 DOUAI
Tel: +33 27 87 69 56
Contact: A. Lagoutte

H. NEGREVERGNE
44 allées de Tourny, 33000 BORDEAUX
Tel: +33 56 44 76 60 *Fax:* +33 56 44 33 84
Contact: H. Negrevergne

A. PALMER
1029 boulevard Blaise-Doumerc, 82000 MONTAUBAN
Tel: +33 63 66 15 49

Total Number of Offices: 5

BCD CONSULTANTS
102 rue Vauban, B.P. 3208, 68064 MULHOUSE CEDEX
Tel: +33 89 45 26 73
Fax: +33 89 56 51 48

European Affiliation: Eura-Audit International

International Contact: J.G. Cottin

OTHER OFFICES
BCD CONSULTANTS
5 rue Baldner, 67000 STRASBOURG
Contact: J.P. Buyat

Total Number of Offices: 2

BDO-3G - GROUPE GUY GENDROT
24 quai Carnot, 92210 PARIS-SAINT-CLOUD
Tel: +33 (1) 46 02 70 07
Fax: +33 (1) 47 71 17 00

European Affiliation: BDO Binder

International Contact: Guy Gendrot

Partners:	20
Professional staff:	200
Non-professional staff:	20
Total Staff:	**240**

FEE INCOME

Year End: 1990	**FFr**	**%**
Accountancy & Audit:		80.0
Consultancy:		5.0
Tax:		10.0
Other:		5.0
Total:	**120,000,000**	

CONTACT INFORMATION
Accountancy (General): Patrick Gifaux
Audit: Jean-Claude Boutier
Corporate Finance: Pascal Gendrot
Management Consultancy: Philippe Canel
Tax (Corporate): Stephane Beaumont

CLIENT SERVICES
Accountancy (General), Audit, Corporate Finance Advice, Litigation/Legal Services, Management & Business Advice, Management Buy-outs, Mergers & Acquisitions, Taxation (Corporate), Taxation (International)

MAJOR CLIENTS
Arjomari, Banque San Paolo, Banque Vernes, Banque Worms, Citroen, Financière Strafor, Mines Depotasse d'Alsace, Mors, Moulinex, Perrier, V.A.P.

OTHER OFFICES
BDO-3G - GROUPE GUY GENDROT
37 rue Buffon, 84007 AVIGNON
Mailing Address: B.P. 139, 84007 AVIGNON
Tel: +33 90 85 59 07 *Fax:* +33 90 82 96 25
Contact: Guy Gendrot

BDO-3G - GROUPE GUY GENDROT
68 boulevard du Général-de-Gaulle, 59100 ROUBAIX
Tel: +33 20 73 47 05 *Fax:* +33 20 73 33 47
Contact: Guy Gendrot

BDO-3G - GROUPE GUY GENDROT
79 rue Francois-Mermet, 69160 TASSIN-LA-DEMI-LUNE
Tel: +33 78 34 19 54 *Fax:* +33 78 34 26 66
Contact: Jean Gaudin

BDO-3G - GROUPE GUY GENDROT
15 rue de Verdun, 68100 MULHOUSE
Tel: +33 89 65 53 65 *Fax:* +33 89 64 09 00
Contact: Guy Gendrot

BDO-3G - GROUPE GUY GENDROT
7 rue d'Athenes, 44085 NANTES CEDEX
Mailing Address: B.P. 218, 44085 NANTES CEDEX
Tel: +33 40 93 05 05 *Fax:* +33 40 93 15 87
Contact: Marc Dupe

BDO-3G - GROUPE GUY GENDROT
42 rue de la l'ère Armée, 67000 STRASBOURG
Tel: +33 88 25 10 17
Contact: Guy Gendrot

BDO-3G - GROUPE GUY GENDROT
60 boulevard Carnot, 31000 TOULOUSE
Tel: +33 61 62 28 39 *Fax:* +33 61 62 42 27
Contact: Guy Gendrot

ASSOCIATED FIRMS
BDO-3G - FIDUCIAIRE AIXOISE
7 avenue du Maréchal-Lyautey, 13100 AIX-EN-PROVENCE
Tel: +33 42 26 27 28 *Fax:* +33 42 26 58 99
Contact: Guy Gendrot

Total Number of Offices: 9

B.E.S.C.
100 rue Martre, 92110 CLICHY, Paris
Tel: +33 (1) 47 31 16 92
Fax: +33 (1) 42 70 11 79

European Affiliation: Alliott Peirson International

International Contact: Christian Berat

CABINET BOYER
66 rue Saint Jacques, 13006 MARSEILLE
Tel: +33 91 37 55 75
Fax: +33 91 37 27 04

▷

European Affiliation: Morison International

International Contact: Bernard Skrhak

Partners:	5
Professional staff:	14
Non-professional staff:	4
Total Staff:	**23**

FEE INCOME

Year End: 31.12.90	**FFr**
Total:	**6,506,000**

CONTACT INFORMATION

Managing Partner: Andrée Boyer
Managing Partner: Bernard Skrhak
Managing Partner: Jean Jouve
Accountancy (General): Marc Vigorito
Audit: Andrée Boyer
Corporate Finance: Bernard Skrhak
Insolvency: Jean Jouve
Management Consultancy: Bernard Skrhak
Tax (Corporate): Lionel Yvant
Tax (International): Renaud Belnet
Litigation Support: Albert Hini
Computer Systems: Lionel Yvant

CLIENT SERVICES

All Services

Industry Specialisations: Professional Associations, Food, Building, Public Works, Engineering, Electronics, Private Hospitals

---

BRIGGS - TRONEL

35 avenue Victor-Hugo, 75116 PARIS
Tel: +33 (1) 45 00 64 14
Fax: +33 (1) 45 01 69 98

European Affiliation: TGI International

International Contact: Bernard Tronel

OTHER OFFICES

A. GERING-BRIGGS
51 avenue Raymond-Poincaré, 75116 PARIS
Tel: +33 (1) 45 53 44 55 *Fax:* +33 (1) 45 53 58 23
Contact: Annette Gering-Briggs

B. TRONEL & ASSOCIÉS SA
34 avenue Victor-Hugo, 75116 PARIS
Tel: +33 (1) 45 00 64 14 *Fax:* +33 (1) 45 01 69 98
Contact: Bernard Tronel

Total Number of Offices: 3

CLAUDE BROSSELIN

1 bis, rue du Printemps, 78230 LE PECQ
Tel: +33 (1) 39 76 69 92
Fax: +33 (1) 39 76 77 92

International Contact: Claude Brosselin

Partners:	1
Professional staff:	5
Total Staff:	**6**

FEE INCOME

Year End: 31.12.90	**FFr**	**%**
Accountancy & Audit:	1,300,000	87.0
Consultancy:	200,000	13.0
Total:	**1,500,000**	

CLIENT SERVICES

Accountancy (General), Audit, Computer Installation, Life & Risk Assurance, Litigation/Legal Services, Management & Business Advice, Taxation (Corporate), International Consolidated Accounts

OTHER OFFICES

CLAUDE BROSSELIN
1 villa des Fleurs, 93130 NOILY LE SEC
Tel: +33 (1) 48 02 21 91 *Fax:* +33 (1) 48 02 21 91

Total Number of Offices: 2

CADERAS MARTIN

76 rue de Monceau, 75008 PARIS
Tel: +33 (1) 42 94 07 08
Fax: +33 (1) 42 94 93 29

European Affiliation: TEG (The European Group of Accounting & Auditing Firms)

International Contact: François Martin

OTHER OFFICES

GROUP EXCEL-OUEST
1 quai de la Jonelière, 44072 NANTES CEDEX 03
Tel: +33 40 74 51 61
Contact: Alain Pantecouteau

Total Number of Offices: 2

GROUPE CALAN ROMOLINO

2 rue Paul-Cézanne, 75008 PARIS
Tel: +33 (1) 40 76 60 60
Fax: +33 (1) 42 89 26 25

European Affiliation: Nexia International

International Contact: Patrice de Maistre

Partners:	35
Professional staff:	370
Non-professional staff:	30
Total Staff:	**435**

FEE INCOME

Year End: 31.12.91	**FFr**	**%**
Accountancy & Audit:		65.0
Insolvency:		20.0
Consultancy:		10.0
Tax:		5.0
Total:	**211,000,000**	

CONTACT INFORMATION

Chairman: Gilles de Calan
Management Consultancy: Yves Labat
Public Sector: Antoine Martial-Couvreur
Accountancy & Audit: Gilles de Calan
Computer Audit: Jean-Marc Lumet
Tax: Chantal Roisne-Megard

CLIENT SERVICES

Accountancy (General), Audit, Corporate Finance Advice, Litigation/Legal Services, Management & Business Advice, Mergers & Acquisitions, Taxation (Corporate), Taxation (International), Privatisations, Cash Management, Local Authority Consultancy, IT & Management Consultancy

Industry Specialisations: Communication, Banking & Finance, Transportation, Insurance, Printing, Real Estate, Steel Industry

MAJOR CLIENTS

AXA, Beghin Say, Crédit Agricole, Crédit Commercial de France, GAN, Groupe de la Cité, Groupe San Paolo, Lucia, NRJ, RSCG, Sagem, SAT, SFPI, Snecma, Sucres et Denrées, Auguste Thouard ▷

OTHER OFFICES

GROUPE CALAN RAMOLINO
334 avenue du Général-Leclerc, 44150 ANCENIS
Tel: + *33* 40 96 14 24
Contact: Jean-Pierre Blot

GROUPE CALAN RAMOLINO
81 rue des Ponts de Cé, 49000 ANGERS
Tel: + *33* 41 47 02 76 *Fax:* + *33* 41 44 24 00
Contact: Eric Groud

GROUPE CALAN RAMOLINO
45 Cours Médoc, 33300 BORDEAUX
Tel: + *33* 47 81 02 50 *Fax:* + *33* 57 81 02 70
Contact: Didier Fabre

GROUPE CALAN RAMOLINO
avenue du Président-Wilson, B.P. 44, 44110 CHATEAUBRIANT
Tel: + *33* 40 81 21 11 *Fax:* + *33* 40 28 01 77
Contact: Bernard Baudot

GROUPE CALAN RAMOLINO
39 rue du Docteur-Roux, B.P. 1982, 49319 CHOLET CEDEX
Tel: + *33* 41 49 10 59 *Fax:* + *33* 41 49 10 50
Contact: Christian Lepicier

GROUPE CALAN RAMOLINO
29 Z.E. de Puymoyen, 16400 LA COURONNE
Tel: + *33* 45 61 34 02 *Fax:* + *33* 45 61 49 85
Contact: Nicole Duvent

GROUPE CALAN RAMOLINO
5 & 7 avenue de la Préfecture, 72000 LE MANS
Tel: + *33* 43 23 74 94
Contact: Maryvonne Janvier

GROUPE CALAN RAMOLINO
220 rue Paul-Bellamy, 44000 NANTES
Tel: + *33* 40 94 44 45
Contact: Didier Allain Dupré

GROUPE CALAN RAMOLINO
12 rue du Soleil, 79000 NIORT
Tel: + *33* 49 24 15 00 *Fax:* + *33* 49 24 55 42
Contact: Louis d'Haussy

GROUPE CALAN RAMOLINO
55 rue de l'université, 'Le pavé neuf', Villa d'entreprise C3, 93191 NOISY LE GRAND
Tel: + *33* (1) 45 92 90 80 *Fax:* + *33* (1) 43 03 15 33
Contact: Gérard Sauzet

GROUPE CALAN RAMOLINO
2 boulevard de la Tour d'Auvergne, 35000 RENNES
Tel: + *33* 99 35 00 35
Contact: Geoffroy de Rudelle

GROUPE CALAN RAMOLINO
10 quai Rouget de l'Isle, 67100 STRASBOURG
Tel: + *33* 88 37 94 94 *Fax:* + *33* 88 37 37 10
Contact: Serge Hugel

GROUPE CALAN RAMOLINO
60 rue Rabelais, 79100 THOUARS
Tel: + *33* 49 66 26 23 *Fax:* + *33* 49 66 52 55
Contact: Loic Cottineau

Total Number of Offices: 15

CCAS/HORWATH FRANCE

12 rue de Madrid, 75008 PARIS
Tel: + *33* (1) 43 87 11 40
Fax: + *33* (1) 45 22 78 87

European Affiliation: Horwath International

International Contact: René Amirkhanian

Partners:	17
Professional staff:	123
Non-professional staff:	35
Total Staff:	**175**

FEE INCOME

Year End: 31.08.91	**FFr**	**%**
Accountancy & Audit:	54,000,000	60.0
Consultancy:	18,000,000	20.0
Tax:	9,000,000	10.0
Other:	9,300,000	10.0
Total:	**90,300,000**	

CONTACT INFORMATION

Chairman: Ferdinand Angleys
Managing Partner: Dominique Gagnard
Accountancy (General): Robert Moreno
Audit: Xavier Urrutibehety
Insolvency: René Amirkhanian
Management Consultancy: Christian Laporte
Administration: Ferdinand Angleys
Tax (International): Dominique Gagnard

CLIENT SERVICES

Accountancy (General), Audit, Computer Installation, Corporate Finance Advice, Management & Business Advice, Mergers & Acquisitions, Pensions Planning, Taxation (Corporate), Taxation (International), Strategic Planning, Organisation Consulting, Management Information Systems

Industry Specialisations: Leisure, Tourism, Press, Media, Fashion, Oil & Mining

OTHER OFFICES

CCAS REVIFRANCE
54 avenue Marceau, 75008 PARIS

CCAS SA
27 cours Pierre-Puget, 13006 MARSEILLE

CCAS SA
102 avenue Jean-Rieux, 31008 TOULOUSE

Total Number of Offices: 5

C.M.S. EXPERTS ASSOCIÉS

149 boulevard Malesherbes, 75017 PARIS
Tel: + *33* (1) 47 66 20 15
Fax: + *33* (1) 43 80 03 98

European Affiliation: CPA Associates Inc

International Contact: Philippe Clément

Partners:	7
Professional staff:	28
Non-professional staff:	3
Total Staff:	**38**

FEE INCOME

Year End: 1990	**FFr**	**%**
Accountancy & Audit:	6,000,000	55.0
Consultancy:	2,000,000	18.0
Tax:	2,000,000	18.0
Other:	1,000,000	9.0
Total:	**11,000,000**	

CONTACT INFORMATION

Chairman: Stéphane Sznajderman
Managing Partner: Claude Mittelette
Accountancy (General): Jean Michel Lamour
Audit: Claude Mittelette
Corporate Finance: Alain Topolinski
Management Consultancy: Stéphane Sznajderman

▷

France

Administration: Martine Krajenska
Public Sector: Christophe Grosselin
Tax (Corporate): Philippe Clement

CLIENT SERVICES

Accountancy (General), Audit, Computer Installation, Corporate Finance Advice, Management & Business Advice, Management Buy-outs, Mergers & Acquisitions, Value for Money Studies, Taxation (Corporate)

OTHER OFFICES

C.M.S. EXPERTS ASSOCIÉS
16 avenue de Friedland, 75008 PARIS

Total Number of Offices: 2

COFINGEC

16 rue Mollien, 92100 BOULOGNE SUR SEINE, Paris
Tel: +33 (1) 46 03 91 86
Fax: +33 (1) 46 04 08 74

European Affiliation: Affiliated Conference of Practising Accountants International (ACPA)

International Contact: Delphine Taghian

CONTACT INFORMATION

Managing Partner: Philippe Pelade

COGEP

route D'Orleans, 18230 ST DOULCHARD
Tel: +33 48 24 51 00
Fax: +33 48 96 31 30

European Affiliation: The International Group of Accounting Firms Ltd (IGAF)

International Contact: Henri Roy

GROUP CONCORDE, CONCORDE SA

15 rue Bertin-Poirée, 75001 PARIS
Tel: +33 (1) 42 33 26 10
Fax: +33 (1) 42 33 26 73

European Affiliation: Moore Stephens

International Contact: Jean-Philippe Teytaut

ASSOCIATED FIRMS

AUDIT CONSEIL ENTERPRISE SERVICES
83 rue de la Victoire, 75009 PARIS
Tel: +33 (1) 45 26 33 43 *Fax:* +33 (1) 45 26 34 18
Contact: Jean-Pierre Lecorcier

AUDIT SA
21 bis, rue Lord-Byron, 75008 PARIS
Tel: +33 (1) 60 65 72 53

COGEED SA
107 rue de l'Université, 75007 PARIS
Tel: +33 (1) 47 05 77 35 *Fax:* +33 (1) 47 53 94 55
Contact: Dominique Leveque

CONCORDE EUROPÉENNE AUDIT - FRANCE
21 bis, rue Lord-Byron, 75008 PARIS
Tel: +33 (1) 43 59 58 73 *Fax:* +33 (1) 42 89 14 02
Contact: Jean-Philippe Teytaut

CABINET CUBAYNES ET PUJO
4 rue Mariotte, 66000 PERPIGNAN
Tel: +33 68 67 20 92 *Fax:* +33 68 67 32 62
Contact: Jean-Paul Cubaynes

ÉTUDES ET RÉALISATIONS JURIDIQUES ET FISCALES
23 rue Chauchat, 75009 PARIS
Tel: +33 (1) 48 24 94 02 *Fax:* +33 (1) 48 24 08 01
Contact: Gerald Hauff

EUROPÉENNE AUDIT SA
3 rue des Deux Boules, 75001 PARIS
Tel: +33 (1) 42 33 52 64 *Fax:* +33 (1) 42 33 26 73
Contact: Bich van Ngo

FIDUCIAIRE FINANCIÈRE DE PARIS (F.F.P.)
3 rue des Deux Boules, 75001 PARIS
Tel: +33 (1) 42 33 52 64 *Fax:* +33 (1) 42 33 26 73
Contact: Gerard Bienaime

JEAN SCHAAR SA, EUROPÉENE D'AUDIT ET DE CONSEIL
40 rue Mascart, 59300 VALENCIENNES
Tel: +33 27 45 01 91 *Fax:* +33 27 41 46 16
Contact: Jean Schaar

JEAN SCHAAR SA, EUROPÉENE D'AUDIT ET DE CONSEIL
39 rue de la Vallée, 59178 MILLONFOSSE
Tel: +33 27 48 91 02 *Fax:* +33 27 48 05 36

JEAN SCHAAR SA, EUROPÉENE D'AUDIT ET DE CONSEIL
48 avenue du Peuple Belge, 59000 LILLE
Tel: +33 20 63 23 23 *Fax:* +33 20 74 23 18

Total Number of Offices: 12

CONSEIL & EXPERTISE

21/23 boulevard Richard-Lenoir, 75011 PARIS
Tel: +33 (1) 43 38 10 57
Fax: +33 (1) 48 05 19 32

European Affiliation: IAG International

International Contact: Jean-Luc Boulot

OTHER OFFICES

CONSEIL & EXPERTISE
23 rue de la Maison Rouge, Marne La Vallée, 77200 LOGNES

CONSEIL & EXPERTISE
134 avenue de Palavas, 34000 MONTPELLIER

Total Number of Offices: 3

CABINET CONSTANTIN

66 rue de Caumartin, 75009 Paris
Tel: +33 (1) 42 85 71 10

International Contact: Laurent Dominique

CONSULTAUDIT SA

134 rue Legendre, 75017 PARIS
Tel: +33 (1) 46 27 60 60
Fax: +33 (1) 46 27 37 75

European Affiliation: SC International

International Contact: Frédéric Duthilleul

Total Number of Offices: 2

COOPERS & LYBRAND

56 rue de Ponthieu, 75008 PARIS
Tel: +33 (1) 44 20 80 00
Fax: +33 (1) 45 62 74 96
Mailing Address: B.P. 451-08, 75366 PARIS CEDEX 08

European Affiliation: Coopers & Lybrand Europe

International Contact: Michael S. Balfour

Partners: 126
Professional staff: 1,152
Non-professional staff: 317
Total Staff: 1,595

CONTACT INFORMATION

Chairman: Michael S. Balfour
Accountancy (General): Jean-Pierre Payrau
Audit: Gilles Gufflet
Corporate Finance: Mike K. Geary
Insolvency: Henri R. Paradis
Management Consultancy: Marie-Noëlle Gauthier
Administration: Charles Herry
Public Sector: Serge Villepelet
Tax (Corporate & International): Gerard Nicolaÿ
Marketing: Etienne Jaquemin
Corporate Communications: L. Pierre Schneider

CLIENT SERVICES

All Services, Executive Selection/Search, Health Care Consultancy

Industry Specialisations: Financial Services, Public Sector, Media, Construction, Pharmaceutical, Automotive, Chemical, Food & Drink

OTHER OFFICES

COOPERS & LYBRAND
4 rue de Segonzac, 16100 COGNAC
Tel: +33 45 82 52 00 *Fax:* +33 45 82 45 48

COOPERS & LYBRAND
Immeuble de l'Horloge, 2 allée des Mitaillères,
38240 GRENOBLE-MEYLAN
Tel: +33 76 90 11 98 *Fax:* +33 76 41 21 62

COOPERS & LYBRAND
37 rue du Vieux Faubourg, 59800 LILLE
Tel: +33 20 12 50 59 *Fax:* +33 20 51 34 56

COOPERS & LYBRAND
177 rue Garibaldi, 69328 LYON CEDEX 03
Tel: +33 78 62 32 53 *Fax:* +33 78 95 17 12

COOPERS & LYBRAND
141 avenue du Prado, 13008 MARSEILLE
Tel: +33 91 25 65 66 *Fax:* +33 91 25 66 67

COOPERS & LYBRAND
Parc-Club du Millénaire, Bâtiment 19, 1025 rue Henri-Becquerel,
34054 MONTPELLIER 1
Tel: +33 67 22 13 00 *Fax:* +33 67 22 13 01
Contact: Luc Deschamps

COOPERS & LYBRAND
Le Palmeira, 45 rue Saint-Philippe, 06000 NICE
Tel: +33 93 37 20 20 *Fax:* +33 93 37 20 00

COOPERS & LYBRAND
4 avenue Ile de France, 35000 RENNES
Tel: +33 99 33 85 11 *Fax:* +33 99 54 55 94

COOPERS & LYBRAND
18 avenue Jean-Jaurès, B.P. 15, 35401 SAINT-MALO CEDEX
Tel: +33 99 56 68 73 *Fax:* +33 99 56 01 44

COOPERS & LYBRAND
87 rue Pierre-Brossolette, 02100 SAINT-QUENTIN
Tel: +33 23 06 28 00 *Fax:* +33 23 67 15 75

COOPERS & LYBRAND
Terrasse du Centre Commercial, 24 place des Halles, 6700 STRASBOURG
Tel: +33 88 75 10 50 *Fax:* +33 88 22 20 61

COOPERS & LYBRAND
Immeuble Delphes - 2nd Floor, 30 boulevard du Maréchal-Leclerc,
31000 TOULOUSE
Tel: +33 62 27 08 09 *Fax:* +33 62 27 11 00

Total Number of Offices: 18

DELARUE-HEDIEU

63 boulevard Côte Blatin, 63000 CLERMONT FERRAND
Tel: +33 73 93 28 60
Fax: +33 73 35 48 01

European Affiliation: Eura-Audit International

International Contact: O. Delarue
D-A. Hedieu

OTHER OFFICES

DELARUE-HEDIEU
13 avenue Kennedy, 63500 ISSOIRE
Tel: +33 73 89 49 58
Contact: O. Delarue

Total Number of Offices: 2

DELOITTE ROSS TOMMATSU

185 avenue Charles-de-Gaulle, 92201 NEUILLY SUR SEINE, Paris
Tel: +33 (1) 40 88 28 00
Fax: +33 (1) 40 88 28 28
Mailing Address: B.P. 136, 92200 NEUILLY SUR SEINE CEDEX, Paris

European Affiliation: DRT International

International Contact: Jacques Manardo

Total Staff: 1,150

CLIENT SERVICES

All Services

MAJOR CLIENTS

Air France, Au Printemps, Banque Français du Commerce Extérieur, Beghin-Say, Bull, Compagnie Générale des Eaux, Crédit du Nord, Crédit National, Dassault, D.M.C., Euromarché, Hermes, Lafarge Coppée, Lesieur, Merlin Gerin, N.M.P.P., Paribas, Pechiney, Perrier, Renault

Total Number of Offices: 5

DFK FRANCE

33 rue Daru, 75008 PARIS
Tel: +33 (1) 47 66 76 10
Fax: +33 (1) 46 22 39 02

European Affiliation: DFK International

Total Staff: 360

FEE INCOME

Year End: 1990	%
Accountancy & Audit:	85.5
Tax:	2.0
Other:	12.5

CONTACT INFORMATION

Chairman: Christian Duverdier
Managing Partner: Olivier Bietrix

CLIENT SERVICES

Accountancy (General), Audit, Computer Installation, Corporate Finance Advice, Insolvency & Corporate Restructuring, Management & Business Advice, Mergers & Acquisitions, Taxation (Corporate), Taxation (International)

OTHER OFFICES

CABINET BAU ET ASSOCIÉS
49 rue Servient, 69005 LYON
Tel: +33 78 60 27 77 *Fax:* +33 78 62 33 45
Contact: Philippe Bau

CECA
37 bis, rue Maréchal-Joffre, 06000 NICE
Tel: +33 93 88 78 70 *Fax:* +33 93 16 08 46
Contact: Roger David

CONSEILS ASSOCIÉS SA
33 rue Daru, 75008 PARIS
Tel: +33 (1) 47 66 76 10 *Fax:* +33 (1) 46 22 39 02
Contact: Christian Duverdier

FHG - FIDUCIAIRE HERBERT GENGOUX
1 chemin du Vieux Chêne, 38241 ZIRST
Mailing Address: B.P. 27, 38241 MEYLAN CEDEX
Tel: +33 76 90 80 54 *Fax:* +33 76 90 74 53
Contact: Claude Gengoux

GORIOUX & ASSOCIÉS
2 E boulevard Moulin de Melguen, 2900 QUIMPER
Tel: +33 98 55 27 48 *Fax:* +33 98 55 06 15
Contact: Vincent Gorioux

MENARD ET ASSOCIÉS CONSEIL
46 rue des Canonniers, 59800 LILLE
Tel: +33 20 51 30 25 *Fax:* +33 20 51 31 55
Contact: Xavier Tailliez

CABINET OREGLIA
56 rue de Periole, 31500 TOULOUSE
Tel: +33 61 26 11 11 *Fax:* +33 61 61 23 07
Contact: Alexandre Oreglia

F.M. RICHARD ET ASSOCIÉS
7 avenue de Friedland, 75008 PARIS
Tel: +33 (1) 45 62 60 70 *Fax:* +33 (1) 45 63 88 34
Contact: Ginette Piquy

SECAL
10 avenue Molière, 67200 STRASBOURG
Tel: +33 88 26 27 28 *Fax:* +33 88 26 82 05
Contact: Jean-Paul Mohr

SNA EXPERTS
19 rue d'Anjou, 75008 PARIS
Tel: +33 (1) 47 42 35 97 *Fax:* +33 (1) 42 65 00 61
Contact: Norbert de Montety

SYREC
109 bis, rue Jean-Mermoz, 13272 MARSEILLE CEDEX 08
Tel: +33 91 77 69 20 *Fax:* +33 91 77 08 32
Contact: Roger-Louis Cazalet

Total Number of Offices: 23

D.G.R. CONSEIL

100 rue Martre, 92110 CLICHY, Paris
Tel: +33 (1) 42 70 12 93
Fax: +33 (1) 42 70 11 79

European Affiliation: Alliott Peirson International

International Contact: Francois Debrégeas
Patrice Gilbert

DMV - EUREXCO

57 rue de Gand, 59800 LILLE
Tel: +33 20 55 82 51
Fax: +33 20 06 38 89

European Affiliation: Eura-Audit International

International Contact: L. Delplace
A. Mortier
M. Vercruysse

OTHER OFFICES

DMV SA
Château Rouge, 282 avenue de la Marne, 59700 MARCQ EN BAROEUL
Tel: +33 20 72 01 60 *Fax:* +33 20 98 27 14
Contact: L. Deplace

DMV - SOVALEC
ZAE "Les Dix Muids", "Espace Mercure", avenue Henry-Barbusse, B.P. 85, 59583 MARLY CEDEX
Tel: +33 27 46 18 51 *Fax:* +33 27 42 14 92
Contact: L. Deplace

Total Number of Offices: 3

DSA

22 place du Général-Catroux, 75017 PARIS
Tel: +33 (1) 42 67 95 05
Fax: +33 (1) 43 80 07 33

European Affiliation: ATD International

International Contact: Pierre-Pascal Bruneau

Partners:	7
Professional staff:	50
Non-professional staff:	13
Total Staff:	**70**

CONTACT INFORMATION

Chairman: Jean-Luc Sfez
Managing Partner: Jean-Luc Zbirou
Accountancy (General): Jean-Luc Zbirou
Audit: Serge Gautier
Management Consultancy: Thierry Lansade
Corporate Finance & Insolvency: Jean-Luc Sfez
Administration & Public Sector: Thierry Lansade
Tax: Pierre-Pascal Bruneau
Financing: Jerôme Le Cesne
Mergers & Acquisitions: René-Paul Jacquesson

CLIENT SERVICES

Accountancy (General), Audit, Computer Installation, Corporate Finance Advice, Insolvency & Corporate Restructuring, Litigation/Legal Services, Management & Business Advice, Management Buy-outs, Mergers & Acquisitions, Taxation (Corporate), Taxation (International)

Industry Specialisations: Audio-Visual, Paper, Textiles, Clothing, Health & Medical, Banking & Finance

OTHER OFFICES

DSA
20 alleé Turcat Méry, 13008 MARSEILLE
Contact: Hélène Chastel

Total Number of Offices: 2

ERNST & YOUNG

Tour Manhattan, CEDEX 21, 6 place de l'Iris, 92095 PARIS LA DEFENSE 2
Tel: +33 (1) 46 93 60 00
Fax: +33 (1) 47 76 20 33

European Affiliation: Ernst & Young Europe

International Contact: Michel Poisson

OTHER OFFICES

ERNST & YOUNG
5 bis boulevard Foch, 49100 ANGERS
Tel: +33 41 20 91 91 *Fax:* +33 41 86 97 22
Contact: Jean-Paul Martin-Borret

ERNST & YOUNG
Technoparc, Les Bureaux du Lac, Immeuble T, rue Robert-Caumont, 33049 BORDEAUX CEDEX
Tel: +33 56 50 62 21 *Fax:* +33 56 43 27 92
Contact: Claude Hazard

▷

ERNST & YOUNG
35 avenue de la Narne, 59290 WASQUEHAL, Communauté Urbaine de Lille
Tel: + *33* 20 27 42 42 *Fax:* + *33* 20 27 78 42
Contact: Fabienne Degrave

ERNST & YOUNG
16 rue du Professeur-Depéret, 69160 TASSIN
Tel: + *33* 78 34 32 01 *Fax:* + *33* 78 34 89 76
Contact: Jacques Tassi

ERNST & YOUNG
485 avenue du Prado, 13008 MARSEILLE
Tel: + *33* 91 22 57 22 *Fax:* + *33* 91 22 51 30
Contact: Francis Gidoin

ERNST & YOUNG
10 rue du Président-Herriot, 44000 NANTES
Tel: + *33* 40 35 44 45 *Fax:* + *33* 40 89 55 09
Contact: Jean-Paul Martin-Borret

ERNST & YOUNG
"Le Sébastopol", 3 quai Kléber, 67055 STRASBOURG CEDEX
Tel: + *33* 88 22 26 00 *Fax:* + *33* 88 22 21 16
Contact: Gérard Holtzer

ERNST & YOUNG
22 rue du Cordier, 01000 BOURG-EN-BRESSE
Tel: + *33* 74 22 58 55 *Fax:* + *33* 74 22 35 57

ERNST & YOUNG
16 rue du Professeur Depéret, 69160 TASSIN LA DEMI-LUNE
Tel: + *33* 78 34 32 01 *Fax:* + *33* 78 34 89 76

ERNST & YOUNG
Le Compans, Immeuble B, 1 place Alfonse-Jourdain, 31000 TOULOUSE
Tel: + *33* 62 15 43 30 *Fax:* + *33* 61 22 86 00

Total Number of Offices: 11

EURA-AUDIT INTERNATIONAL SARL

8 rue de Turin, 75008 PARIS
Tel: + *33* (1) 42 93 82 13
Fax: + *33* (1) 43 87 91 49

European Affiliation: Eura-Audit International

International Contact: G. Michel
A. Dupré

ASSOCIATED FIRMS

AUDITEX
32 bis, avenue Félix-Faure, 69366 LYON CEDEX 07
Tel: + *33* 78 72 06 92 *Fax:* + *33* 72 73 47 14
Contact: F-M. Fleur

COMPTAGEX
Zone de La Basse Haie, B.P. 32, 35220 CHATEAUBOURG
Tel: + *33* 99 00 74 60 *Fax:* + *33* 99 00 90 46
Contact: G. Le Bohec

FIDALSEC
102 rue Vauban, B.P. 3208, 68064 MULHOUSE CEDEX
Tel: + *33* 89 45 26 73 *Fax:* + *33* 89 56 51 48
Contact: J.G. Cottin

INSTITUT FRANÇAIS DES AFFAIRES
1 place du Pont à Seille, 57000 METZ
Tel: + *33* 87 74 00 75
Contact: D. Lorrain

INSTITUT PIXEL FORMATION
allées des Sapins, B.P. 445, 44474 CARQUEFOU CEDEX
Tel: + *33* 40 68 20 30 *Fax:* + *33* 40 93 78 20
Contact: M. Delaporte

SOCIÉTÉ ALCO
4 quai Koch, 67000 STRASBOURG
Contact: M. Betzinger

SORHOGECO - SOCIÉTÉ RHODANIENNE DE GESTION ET DE COMPTABILITÉ
117 rue Garibaldi, 69006 LYON
Tel: + *33* 72 74 27 50
Contact: R. Blairon

Total Number of Offices: 8

EXCO FRANCE

6 square de l'Opera Louis-Jouvet, 75009 PARIS
Tel: + *33* (1) 47 42 69 23
Fax: + *33* (1) 42 66 29 93

European Affiliation: Grant Thornton International

International Contact: Philippe Auzas

Partners:	87
Professional staff:	639
Non-professional staff:	164
Total Staff:	**890**

FEE INCOME

Year End: 31.12.90	**FFr (000)**	**%**
Accountancy & Audit:	272,736,000	79.0
Consultancy:	17,262,000	5.0
Tax:	44,880,000	13.0
Other:	10,358,000	3.0
Total:	**345,236,000**	

CONTACT INFORMATION

Managing Partner: André Zagouri
Accountancy (General): F. Blanchot
Audit: S.P. Cordier
Corporate Finance: S.L.L. Carpentier
Management Consultancy: M. Darmon
Administration: B. Barret
Public Sector: S.L. Gaillac
Tax (International): Sylvian Quagliapolli

CLIENT SERVICES

Accountancy (General), Audit, Corporate Finance Advice, Litigation/ Legal Services, Management Buy-outs, Mergers & Acquisitions, Taxation (Corporate), Taxation (International), Management Consultancy

Industry Specialisations: Petroleum, Engineering, Transport, Appliances, Department Stores, Not for Profit Organisations

MAJOR CLIENTS

Babolat VS, Boehringer Mannheim France, CGI Informatique, Coflexip, Comexol, Delbard, Edition Hatier, Eternit, Fichet Bauche, Fininfo, Groupe Expansion, Krups, Labinal, Look, Moulinex, Primagaz, Primistere Reynoird, Samaritaine, Spot Image, Strafor Facom

OTHER OFFICES

EXCO - ALSACE ET DOME AUDIT INTERNATIONAL
Cité Parc Glück, 23 allée Glück, 68200 MULHOUSE
Tel: + *33* 89 59 12 79 *Fax:* + *33* 89 59 12 78

EXCO - ALSACE ET DOME AUDIT INTERNATIONAL
37 avenue de la Forêt Noire, B.P. 21/R1, 67001 STRASBOURG
Tel: + *33* 88 61 08 02 *Fax:* + *33* 88 60 67 10

EXCO - AQUITAINE
64 rue François-Marceau, B.P. 208, 33021 BORDEAUX CEDEX
Tel: + *33* 56 42 43 44 *Fax:* + *33* 56 42 43 80

EXCO - ATLANTIQUE
34 rue Russell, 44000 NANTES
Tel: + *33* 40 20 21 22 *Fax:* + *33* 40 08 04 30

EXCO - CHATELLERAULT
123 avenue du Maréchal Leclerc, B.P. 520, 864105 CHATELLERAULT
Tel: +*33* 49 21 06 61 *Fax:* +*33* 49 93 34 33

EXCO - CLERMONT-FERRAND
14 avenue Marx-Dormoy, 63000 CLERMONT-FERRAND
Tel: +*33* 73 35 32 70 *Fax:* +*33* 73 93 58 64

EXCO - FIDUCIAIRE DU SUD-OUEST
12 place du Maquis, 81000 ALBI
Tel: +*33* 63 54 63 57

EXCO - FIDUCIAIRE DU SUD-OUEST
44 avenue Foch, 64100 BAYONNE
Tel: +*33* 59 25 58 42

EXCO - FIDUCIAIRE DU SUD-OUEST
7 boulevard du Collège, 40104 DAX CEDEX
Tel: +*33* 58 74 74 41 *Fax:* +*33* 58 56 08 80

EXCO - FIDUCIAIRE DU SUD-OUEST
8 avenue Sadi Carnot, 40000 MONT DE MARSAN
Tel: +*33* 58 51 54 00

EXCO - FIDUCIAIRE DU SUD-OUEST
Résidence Les Arcades, 25 avenue du Général-Guillaut, 66101 PERPIGNAN CEDEX
Tel: +*33* 68 85 17 24 *Fax:* +*33* 68 85 17 31

EXCO - FIDUCIAIRE DU SUD-OUEST
Résidence "le Neuilly", 24 rue Georges-Magnoac, 65000 TARBES
Tel: +*33* 62 93 47 90 *Fax:* +*33* 62 93 31 54

EXCO - FIDUCIAIRE DU SUD-OUEST
2 rue des Feuillants, 31076 TOULOUSE CEDEX
Tel: +*33* 61 42 03 66 *Fax:* +*33* 61 59 20 08

EXCO - LORRAINE
Tour Montet Octroi, 9 square de Liège, B.P. 29, 54501 VANDOEUVRE-NANCY CEDEX
Tel: +*33* 83 56 05 66 *Fax:* +*33* 83 56 68 11

EXCO - MÉDITERRANÉE
99 boulevard Sakakini, B.P. 82, 13352 MARSEILLE CEDEX 05
Tel: +*33* 91 47 63 05 *Fax:* +*33* 91 42 48 72

EXCO - ORLÉANS
11 boulevard Jean-Jaurès, 45000 ORLÉANS
Tel: +*33* 38 62 44 61 *Fax:* +*33* 38 77 24 85

EXCO - PARIS
6 square de l'Opéra Louis-Jouvet, 75009 PARIS
Tel: +*33* (1) 47 42 69 23 *Fax:* +*33* (1) 42 66 29 93

EXCO - POITIERS
2 rue Louis-Renard, 86000 POITIERS
Tel: +*33* 49 88 02 99 *Fax:* +*33* 49 60 28 95

EXCO - RÉGION NORD
156 boulevard Delbecque, B.P. 99, 59502 DOUAI CEDEX
Tel: +*33* 27 87 28 36 *Fax:* +*33* 27 98 82 60

EXCO - SEVRES
18 rue du 24 Février, B.P. 224, 79007 NIORT CEDEX
Tel: +*33* 49 28 20 44 *Fax:* +*33* 49 28 14 43

EXCO - SUD-EST
Espace Européen d'Ecully, 7 allée Claude-Debussy, B.P. 102, 69136 ECULLY
Tel: +*33* 78 44 23 83 *Fax:* +*33* 78 87 12 91

NORD-AUDIT - EXCO
679 avenue de la République, 59800 LILLE
Tel: +*33* 21 51 81 15 *Fax:* +*33* 20 06 90 58

Total Number of Offices: 23

EXPERTS COMPTABLES ASSOCIÉS

138 avenue de Castres, 31500 TOULOUSE
Tel: +*33* 61 80 37 31
Fax: +*33* 61 80 77 47

European Affiliation: Eura-Audit International

International Contact: R. Vialar Combes
F. Molina
J-L. Le Manach
R. Boucher

EXPERTS FRANCE

10 rue de Laborde, 75008 PARIS
Tel: +*33* (1) 42 93 64 73
Fax: +*33* (1) 42 93 73 04

European Affiliation: Russell Bedford International

International Contact: Pierre Abitbol

FCC AUDIT ET CONSEIL

8 boulevard Berthier, 75838 PARIS
Tel: +*33* (1) 40 25 17 17
Fax: +*33* (1) 40 25 18 97

European Affiliation: GMN International

International Contact: André Cresteil

Partners:	12
Professional staff:	100
Non-professional staff:	8
Total Staff:	**120**

Total Number of Offices: 4

FIDAL

2 bis, rue de Villiers, 92309 LEVALLOIS-PERRET
Tel: +*33* (1) 46 39 46 46
Fax: +*33* (1) 47 58 81 21

European Affiliation: KPMG

International Contact: Jean-Louis Paul

Partners:	487
Professional staff:	582
Non-professional staff:	824
Total Staff:	**1,893**

FEE INCOME

Year End: 30.09.91	**FFr**	**%**
Tax:	346,000,000	39.0
Other:	542,000,000	61.0
Total:	**888,000,000**	

CONTACT INFORMATION
Chairman: Claude Colin
Managing Partner: Jacob Atlan
Tax (Corporate): Michel Noemie
Tax (International): Loic Steunou
Public Sector, Marketing & PR: Pierre Berger
Partner: Michel Janicaud
Partner: Paul Troussiere

CLIENT SERVICES
Insolvency & Corporate Restructuring, Litigation/Legal Services, Management Buy-outs, Mergers & Acquisitions, Taxation (Corporate), Taxation (International), Trust Settlement & Estates, EC Law, International Law, Labour Law, Local Government Law, Non-Profit Law

Industry Specialisations: High Tech, Food & Beverage, Non-Profit Organisations, Local Authorities

Total Number of Offices: 110

▷

GROUPE FIDETA

61 avenue Kléber, 75116 PARIS
Tel: +33 (1) 47 04 34 70
Fax: +33 (1) 47 55 49 30

European Affiliation: InterContinental Consultants (ICC)

International Contact: Edouard Jagodnik

ASSOCIATED FIRMS

AUDIT FIDETA MISSIONS/A.F.M.
B.P. 216, 77441 MARNE LA VALLÉE CEDEX 02
Tel: +33 (1) 60 17 00 89 *Fax:* +33 (1) 60 17 24 25
Contact: Michel Vantelot

C.F.E.- COMPTABILITÉ-FINANCE-ECONOMIE
Z.A.C. du Saut-Le-Cerf, avenue Leon-Blum, 88000 ÉPINAL
Tel: +33 29 34 31 27 *Fax:* +33 29 31 35 97
Contact: Alain Cadré

CABINET BAURIAUD
12-14 rue Cruveilher, 87000 LIMOGES
Tel: +33 55 79 54 60 *Fax:* +33 55 77 44 77
Contact: Raymond Bauriaud

COGEX
18 rue de Koufra, B.P. 906, 44025 NANTES CEDEX 03
Tel: +33 40 49 62 42 *Fax:* +33 40 93 18 11
Contact: Bernard Lemarié

COGEX
16 rue des Frères Lumière, Z.A. de Kerniol, 56000 VANNES
Tel: +33 97 40 32 70 *Fax:* +33 97 40 97 33
Contact: P. Roussin le Texier

CABINET J. DECUP
82 boulevard des Batignolles, 75017 PARIS
Tel: +33 (1) 43 87 55 97 *Fax:* +33 (1) 42 93 09 33
Contact: Jean Decup

J.M.C.C. DUVERNOIS
8 boulevard Berthier, 75738 PARIS CEDEX 17
Tel: +33 (1) 40 25 18 18 *Fax:* +33 (1) 40 25 18 96
Contact: Martine Joly

CABINET GEESE
61 avenue Kléber, 75116 PARIS
Tel: +33 (1) 47 04 42 52 *Fax:* +33 (1) 40 04 87 66
Contact: Wieland Geese

CABINET RÉCHARD
25 rue Baugier, 79000 NIORT
Tel: +33 49 79 39 39 *Fax:* +33 49 73 33 59
Contact: Louis Réchard

REVIGESTION
51 boulevard de Valmy, B.P. 129, 59653 VILLENEUVE-D'ASCQ CEDEX
Tel: +33 20 05 13 00 *Fax:* +33 20 47 04 24
Contact: Michel Goulois

S.A.D.E.C.L.A.
6 rue Auguste-Payant, 69007 LYON
Tel: +33 72 73 01 85 *Fax:* +33 72 72 97 10
Contact: Jean-Max Rode

SAREGE
172 avenue Marcel-Dassault, 6000 BEAUVAIS
Tel: +33 44 45 11 33 *Fax:* +33 44 45 11 85
Contact: Alain Doh

SAREGE
32 rue de Général-Leclerc, 02300 CHAUNY
Tel: +33 23 52 04 78 *Fax:* +33 23 52 37 40
Contact: Jules Sobesky

SAREGE
50 rue Franck-Hémon, B.P. 52, 77503 CHELLES CEDEX
Tel: +33 (1) 60 08 03 99 *Fax:* +33 (1) 60 08 57 49
Contact: Jacques Raynal

SAREGE
3 bis, rue de Lesseps, Zac de Mercières, 60200 COMPIÉGNE
Tel: +33 44 86 42 33 *Fax:* +33 44 86 20 65
Contact: Annie Ducet

SAREGE
rue du Clos-Barrois, Z.I. Nogent-sur-Oise, 60180 CREIL
Tel: +33 44 25 01 16 *Fax:* +33 44 55 29 32
Contact: Jules Sobesky

SAREGE
32 rue de Fortmahon, B.P. 76, 02004 LAON CEDEX
Tel: +33 23 23 47 49
Contact: Georges Lezin

SAREGE
31 Grande Allée du Février 1934, 77186 NOISIEL
Mailing Address: B.P. 216, 77441 MARNE LA VALLÉE 02
Tel: +33 (1) 60 17 00 89 *Fax:* +33 (1) 60 17 24 25
Contact: Michel Vantelot

SAREGE
12 chemin de la Blanquette, 76130 MONT-SAINT-AIGNAN
Tel: +33 35 74 95 15 *Fax:* +33 35 74 42 47
Contact: Marc Labrunye

SAREGE
55 avenue Réne-Firmin, 60410 VERBERIE
Tel: +33 44 40 55 55 *Fax:* +33 44 40 64 17
Contact: Jules Sobesky

SAREGE - GESTAUDIT
6 boulevard de Strasbourg, B.P. 204, 02205 SOISSONS CEDEX
Tel: +33 23 53 66 75 *Fax:* +33 23 59 39 02
Contact: Michel Piszczek

SEC MARCHE LIMOUSIN
30 avenue d'Auvergne, B.P. 161, 23000 GUÉRET
Tel: +33 55 52 41 96 *Fax:* +33 55 52 78 42
Contact: Alain Verrier

SOCIÉTÉ FIDUCIAIRE DE BORDEAUX ET DU SUD-OUEST AUDIAL
21 avenue Ariane, B.P. 23, 33702 BORDEAUX-MÉRIGNAC CEDEX
Tel: +33 56 34 60 00 *Fax:* +33 56 13 05 11
Contact: Michel Bouilly

SOPYREC
25 rue Capucins, 46000 CAHORS
Tel: +33 65 22 64 49 *Fax:* +33 65 22 17 89
Contact: Rita Botreau

SOPYREC
10 impasse René-Cauzinet, B.P. 5014, 31021 TOULOUSE CEDEX
Tel: +33 62 16 13 63 *Fax:* +33 62 16 13 62
Contact: Georges Consalés

Total Number of Offices: 26

SA FIDEURAF

8 rue de Turin, 75008 PARIS
Tel: +33 (1) 43 87 71 25
Fax: +33 (1) 42 93 47 40

European Affiliation: Eura-Audit International

International Contact: Y. Blaise

FIDUCIAIRE COMPTABLE DU NORD

90 avenue Ledru-Rollin, 75011 PARIS
Tel: +33 (1) 47 00 40 62

European Affiliation: Midsnell International

International Contact: Lysian Krol

▷

OTHER OFFICES

FIDUCIAIRE COMPTABLE DU NORD
2 rue Léger Bertin, 51200 ÉPERNAY
Tel: + *33* 26 54 14 44
Contact: Marc Fath

FIDUCIAIRE COMPTABLE DU NORD
45 rue des Moissons, B.P. 334, 51062 REIMS CEDEX
Tel: + *33* 26 47 60 17 ***Fax:*** + *33* 26 40 41 83
Contact: Daniel Mehaut

Total Number of Offices: 19

FIDUCIAIRE DE STRASBOURG

5 Rue du Dôme, 67000 STRASBOURG
Tel: + *33* 88 32 33 76
Fax: + *33* 88 32 33 78
Mailing Address: B.P. 155/R4, 67004 STRASBOURG CEDEX

European Affiliation: Moores Rowland International

International Contact: Bernard Harder

FIDUCIAIRE EXPERTISES CONSEILS (F.E.C.)

rue du Faubourg-Saint-Honoré 237, 75008 PARIS
Tel: + *33* (1) 45 63 81 50
Fax: + *33* (1) 42 89 25 29

European Affiliation: Pannell Kerr Forster Worldwide

International Contact: André Chabran
Michèle le Bozec

Total Number of Offices: 3

FIDUCIAIRE VIDOR SA

1 rue Damrémont, 75018 PARIS
Tel: + *33* (1) 42 23 42 22
Fax: + *33* (1) 42 62 96 88

European Affiliation: Midsnell International

International Contact: Gilles Guillet

FIDULOR

81 boulevard de Stalingrad, B.P. 1215, 69611 VILLEURBANNE-LYON
Tel: + *33* 78 93 42 16
Fax: + *33* 78 94 39 06

European Affiliation: Moores Rowland International

International Contact: Jean-Marie Vilmint

OTHER OFFICES

FIDULOR
81/83 rue Saint-Georges, 54000 NANCY
Tel: + *33* 83 35 48 82 ***Fax:*** + *33* 83 37 85 29
Contact: Michel Thoilliez

FIDULOR
1 rue du 11 Novembre, 14000 CAEN
Tel: + *33* 31 83 29 30 ***Fax:*** + *33* 31 34 74 14
Contact: Jean-Jacques Lemaitre

FIDULOR
6 rue Belle Ile en Mer, Le Braden, 29000 QUIMPER
Tel: + *33* 98 53 19 81 ***Fax:*** + *33* 98 52 21 33
Contact: Bernard Lachiver

FIDULOR
7 boulevard Maréchal-Foch, 51000 REIMS
Tel: + *33* 26 47 52 75 ***Fax:*** + *33* 26 88 23 85
Contact: Étienne Libert

FIDULOR
26 place Marnac, 31520 RAMONVILLE ST AGNÉ-TOULOUSE
Tel: + *33* 21 39 49 89 ***Fax:*** + *33* 21 93 50 63
Contact: Guy Taillandier

FIDULOR
8 rue Franz-Heller, B.P. 1808, 35018 RENNES
Tel: + *33* 99 63 55 55 ***Fax:*** + *33* 99 63 66 84
Contact: Bernard Meunier

FIDULOR
8 boulevard Ferdinand-de-Lesseps, 7600 ROUEN
Tel: + *33* 35 98 61 11 ***Fax:*** + *33* 35 98 70 82
Contact: Benoit Leclerc

FIDULOR
12 rue du Docteur-Herpin, 37000 TOURS
Tel: + *33* 47 47 15 91 ***Fax:*** + *33* 47 66 56 49
Contact: William Rapaud

FIDULOR
99 rue d'Arras, 62500 SAINT OMER
Tel: + *33* 21 39 49 89 ***Fax:*** + *33* 21 93 50 63
Contact: Jean-Paul Marvalin

FIDULOR
275 avenue du Prado, 13008 MARSEILLE
Tel: + *33* 91 25 69 44 ***Fax:*** + *33* 91 25 51 05
Contact: Michel Brun

FIDULOR
22 boulevard Gambetta, 87000 LIMOGES
Tel: + *33* 55 34 63 40 ***Fax:*** + *33* 55 34 70 57

FIDULOR
29 route d'Épinal, Valparc, 25048 BESANÇON
Tel: + *33* 81 88 39 87 ***Fax:*** + *33* 81 50 37 36
Contact: Philippe Abeille

FIDULOR
6 rue du Professeur-Lemière, Les Portes de Montreuil, 75020 PARIS
Tel: + *33* (1) 40 30 03 80 ***Fax:*** + *33* (1) 40 30 00 80
Contact: Guy Flochlay

FIDULOR
29 rue de l'École Normale, 33073 BORDEAUX
Tel: + *33* 56 02 67 22 ***Fax:*** + *33* 56 02 27 01
Contact: Gilles Passemard

FIDULOR
25 avenue Aristide-Briand, 34170 CASTELNEAU LE LEZ-MONTPELLIER
Tel: + *33* 67 72 02 22 ***Fax:*** + *33* 67 72 92 15
Contact: Jean-Charles Palies

FIDULOR
1 rue Dewet, B.P. 340, 71108 CHALON SUR SAONE
Tel: + *33* 85 48 19 09 ***Fax:*** + *33* 85 48 34 54
Contact: François Pons

FIDULOR
105-107 avenue de la République, 59110 LA MADELEINE LILLE
Tel: + *33* 20 55 42 13 ***Fax:*** + *33* 20 31 04 58
Contact: Philippe Truffier

FIDULOR
8 rue Deurbroucq, 44000 NANTES
Tel: + *33* 40 48 52 39 ***Fax:*** + *33* 40 35 36 95
Contact: Philippe Beurais

Total Number of Offices: 19

FRANCE EXPERTISE ASSOCIÉS (F.E.A.)

122 boulevard Malesherbes, 75017 PARIS

European Affiliation: Growth & Progress Challenge

International Contact: Jean Allimant

▷

GROUPE ECAF

333 boulevard Président-Wilson, 33200 BORDEAUX-CAUDERAN
Tel: +33 56 02 61 39
Fax: +33 56 08 19 14

European Affiliation: The International Group of Accounting Firms Ltd (IGAF)

International Contact: Pierre Goguet

GROUPE FRANCE AUDIT

138 boulevard Haussmann, 75008 PARIS
Tel: +33 (1) 43 55 79 18
Fax: +33 (1) 40 21 79 52

European Affiliation: HLB International

International Contact: Yves Hannoyer

Partners:	58
Professional staff:	375
Non-professional staff:	81
Total Staff:	**514**

CONTACT INFORMATION

Chairman: Fouad El Mghazli

CLIENT SERVICES

Accountancy (General), Audit, Computer Installation, Corporate Finance Advice, Management & Business Advice, Management Buy-outs, Mergers & Acquisitions, Taxation (Corporate), Taxation (International)

ASSOCIATED FIRMS

FIMECO
12 rue Elie-Vinet, 16300 BARBEZIEUX
Tel: +33 45 78 02 07

FIMECO
28 place de l'Hôtel de Ville, 16210 CHALAIS
Tel: +33 45 98 21 30

FIMECO
Bourg Nouveau, 17500 JONZAC
Tel: +33 46 48 04 94

FIMECO
2 ter avenue de la République, 16340 L'ISLE D'ESPAGNAC
Tel: +33 45 69 19 19

FIMECO
Les Reigniers, 17600 MEDIS
Tel: +33 46 06 70 04

FIMECO
3 rue des Pensées Les Romains, Trellisac, 24750 PERIGUEUX
Tel: +33 53 53 02 34

FIMECO
Z.I. du Graveau, 17412 SAINT JEAN D'ANGELY
Tel: +33 46 32 27 51

FIMECO
125 avenue Gambetta, 17103 SAINTES
Tel: +33 46 93 70 91 *Fax:* +33 46 92 12 69
Contact: Jean-Claude Ferron

FIDUCIAIRE GORI SA
6 rue du Maréchal-Ornano, 20000 AJACCIO
Tel: +33 95 21 43 04 *Fax:* +33 95 21 84 66
Contact: Alain Perret

FIDUCIAIRE GORI SA
U Centru, route de Bastia, 20137 PORTO VECCHIO
Tel: +33 95 70 28 64 *Fax:* +33 95 70 54 44

FIDUCIAIRE GORI SA
Immeuble Marina II, avenue Pandolfi, 20110 PROPRIANO
Tel: +33 95 76 09 89 *Fax:* +33 95 76 10 30

L.R. AUDIT
11 rue Henri-Dunant, 34500 BÉZIERS
Tel: +33 67 30 17 60

L.R. AUDIT
Parc club du Millénaire, Bât 10, 1025 rue Henri-Becquerel, 34036 MONTPELLIER
Tel: +33 67 22 00 92 *Fax:* +33 67 22 35 01
Contact: Alain Camoin

L.R. AUDIT
17 quai Vauban, Résidence Eros, 34200 SETE
Tel: +33 67 74 61 01 *Fax:* +33 67 74 13 88

CABINET OLLIVIER ET ASSOCIÉS
Casa Di i Mori, Casatoria, 20600 BASTIA, Haute Corse
Tel: +33 95 39 63 02

CABINET OLLIVIER ET ASSOCIÉS
2a boulevard de Louvain, 13008 MARSEILLE
Tel: +33 91 25 54 00 *Fax:* +33 91 80 37 88
Contact: Jean-François Coutant

ORPRACO
149 boulevard Stalingrad, 69100 LYON VILLEURBANNE
Tel: +33 78 94 39 17 *Fax:* +33 78 89 64 62
Contact: Olivier Brisac

CABINET QUEMOUN - CAVY GPA
29 & 35 rue Jacquemars Gielée, 59800 LILLE
Tel: +33 20 57 72 63 *Fax:* +33 20 30 00 43
Contact: Jean-Pierre Quemoun

SOGESCO SA
5 rue de la République, 90003 BELFORT
Mailing Address: B.P. 137, 90003 BELFORT CEDEX
Tel: +33 84 28 09 61 *Fax:* +33 84 55 06 06
Contact: Jean-François Orosco

CABINET VAINQUEUR
11 rue François-Villon, 75015 PARIS
Tel: +33 (1) 48 42 12 51 *Fax:* +33 (1) 30 54 30 75

Total Number of Offices: 39

GUÉRARD VIALA

125 rue de Montreuil, 75011 PARIS
Tel: +33 (1) 43 48 55 33
Fax: +33 (1) 43 48 98 63

European Affiliation: BKR International

International Contact: Didier Gabriel Sabatier

Partners:	51
Professional staff:	497
Non-professional staff:	52
Total Staff:	**600**

FEE INCOME

Year End: 30.09.90	**US$**	**%**
Accountancy & Audit:	50,754,560	90.0
Consultancy:	2,819,698	5.0
Tax:	2,819,697	5.0
Total:	**56,393,955**	

CONTACT INFORMATION

Chairman: Louis Viala
Managing Partner: Claude Guérard

CLIENT SERVICES

Accountancy (General), Audit, Computer Installation, Litigation/Legal Services, Management & Business Advice, Management Buy-outs, Mergers & Acquisitions, Taxation (Corporate), Taxation (International), Management Consultancy

Industry Specialisations: Banking, Insurance, Communications, Space Industry, Farm Products

MAJOR CLIENTS

Air Afrique, Arianespace, Banque Nationale de Paris (BNP), Bidermann, Champagnes Pommery & Lanson, Computerland, Dassault Aviation, Europe 1 Communication, Galleries Lafayette (subsidiaries), Générale Occidentale, Gervais Danone France, Groupe Express, Kenzo, Kronenbourg, Lazard Frères et Cie, Matra, Nouvelles Frontiéres, Pathé Cinema, Pirelli, Van Cleef & Arpels

OTHER OFFICES

GUÉRARD VIALA
7 rue Saint-François-de-Sales, 74000 ANNECY
Tel: + *33* 50 45 08 88 *Fax:* + *33* 50 45 83 02
Contact: Jean Cros

GUÉRARD VIALA
180 rue Judaïque, 33000 BORDEAUX
Tel: + *33* 56 24 46 29 *Fax:* + *33* 56 93 01 74
Contact: Erik Flamant

GUÉRARD VIALA
route de Chartres, Dreux-Vernouillet, 28500 VERNOUILLET
Tel: + *33* 37 42 00 30 *Fax:* + *33* 37 42 28 95
Contact: François Belin

GUÉRARD VIALA
11 rue Gastelier, 72000 LE MANS
Tel: + *33* 43 24 80 70 *Fax:* + *33* 43 24 98 34
Contact: Bruno Chenin

GUÉRARD VIALA
150 rue du 8 Mai 1945, 59650 VILLENEUVE D'ASCQ
Tel: + *33* 20 91 92 79 *Fax:* + *33* 20 91 93 73
Contact: Jean-Louis Zhâ

GUÉRARD VIALA
14 avenue Georges-Pompidou, 69212 LYON
Mailing Address: B.P. 3170, 69212 LYON CEDEX 30
Tel: + *33* 72 33 99 99 *Fax:* + *33* 78 53 18 65
Contact: Pierre Chevallier

GUÉRARD VIALA
14 boulevard du Commandeur, 13274 MARSEILLE
Mailing Address: B.P. 65, 13274 MARSEILLE CEDEX 09
Tel: + *33* 91 77 03 06 *Fax:* + *33* 91 77 03 60
Contact: Louis Pigeon

GUÉRARD VIALA
36 boulevard de la Paix, 51058 REIMS
Mailing Address: B.P. 1216, 51058 REIMS CEDEX
Tel: + *33* 26 88 48 51 *Fax:* + *33* 26 88 27 01
Contact: Alain Lecompte

GUÉRARD VIALA
CD 63, B.P. 4, 67116 REICHSTETT
Tel: + *33* 88 20 11 81 *Fax:* + *33* 88 20 24 66
Contact: Jean-Jacques Seybel

GUÉRARD VIALA
B.P. 1543, 1 rue Bernard Palissy, 25000 BESANÇON CEDEX
Tel: + *33* 81 53 28 55 *Fax:* + *33* 81 53 22 50
Contact: Claude Barthod

Total Number of Offices: 11

GUIBERT ET ASSOCIÉS

80 rue Blanche, 75009 PARIS
Tel: + *33* (1) 42 85 16 55
Fax: + *33* (1) 40 16 90 49
National Affiliation: Crane & Partners

International Contact: Lionel J. Guibert

Partners:	9
Professional staff:	50
Non-professional staff:	10
Total Staff:	**69**

FEE INCOME

Year End: 1990	**FFr**	**%**
Accountancy & Audit:	41,000,000	95.0
Tax:	2,000,000	5.0
Total:	**43,000,000**	

CONTACT INFORMATION

Managing Partner: Lionel J. Guibert
Partner (USA): Caroline de Ravel

CLIENT SERVICES

Accountancy (General), Audit, Corporate Finance Advice, Insolvency & Corporate Restructuring, Management & Business Advice, Management Buy-outs, Mergers & Acquisitions, Pensions Planning, Taxation (Corporate), Taxation (International), Trust Settlement & Estates, Financial Analysis & Simulations

Industry Specialisations: Real Estate (All types), Luxury Goods (Perfumes etc), Foreign-owned Companies

MAJOR CLIENTS

Caisse des Depôts, Cie Générale des Papiers, Courrèges, Crédit Fongier, Orlane

Total Number of Offices: 3

GUYOT, VARONA ET ASSOCIÉS

8 rue de Florence, 75008 PARIS
Tel: + *33* (1) 45 22 79 31
Fax: + *33* (1) 45 22 45 20

European Affiliation: Urbach Hacker Young International

International Contact: Gerard Varona

OTHER OFFICES

GUYOT, VARONA ET ASSOCIÉS
105 avenue Raymond-Poincaré, 75116 PARIS
Tel: + *33* (1) 45 00 76 00
Contact: F. Guyot

Total Number of Offices: 2

KPMG FIDUCIAIRE DE FRANCE

2 bis, rue de Villiers, 92309 LEVALLOIS-PERRET
Tel: + *33* (1) 46 39 46 39
Fax: + *33* (1) 47 58 81 21

European Affiliation: KPMG

Partners:	443
Professional staff:	2,914
Non-professional staff:	1,239
Total Staff:	**4,596**

▷

FEE INCOME

Year End: 30.09.91	FFr	%
Accountancy & Audit:	1,706,000,000	90.0
Consultancy:	190,000,000	10.0
Total:	**1,896,000,000**	

CONTACT INFORMATION
Chairman: Robert Piard
Managing Partner: Arnaud Bertrand
Audit: Claude Briolay
Corporate Finance: Bernard Bringuier
Management Consultancy: André Meary
Public Sector, Marketing & PR: Martial Thevenot
Partner: Jean-Paul Griziaux
General Secretary: Michel Janicaud

CLIENT SERVICES
Accountancy (General), Audit, Computer Installation, Corporate Finance Advice, Management & Business Advice, Value for Money Studies

Industry Specialisations: Banking, Insurance, Transport, High Tech, Media, Entertainment, Publishing, Food & Beverage

Total Number of Offices: 227

KPMG PEAT MARWICK SA

Tour Fiat, Cedex 16, 92084 PARIS/LA DÉFENSE
Tel: +*33* (1) 47 96 20 00
Fax: +*33* (1) 47 96 20 58

European Affiliation: KPMG

Partners:	10
Professional staff:	160
Non-professional staff:	65
Total Staff:	**235**

CONTACT INFORMATION
Chairman: Jean-Claude Petit
Partner: Jean Marc Baron
Partner: Jaques Cellard
Partner: Jean-Claude Cohadon
Partner: Jean-Louis Richard
Partner: Joel Templier

CLIENT SERVICES
Computer Installation, Management & Business Advice, Data Processing, Systems Implementation, Executive Search

Industry Specialisations: Electronics, Computers, Aerospace, Steel, Oil, Chemicals, Banking, Insurance, Transportation, Health

LECLERCQ ET ASSOCIÉS

92 rue Saint-Brice, B.P. 128, 28003 CHARTRES CEDEX
Tel: +*33* 37 30 04 22
Fax: +*33* 37 30 90 44

European Affiliation: Affiliated Conference of Practising Accountants International (ACPA)

International Contact: Michel Leclercq

Partners:	4
Professional staff:	16
Total Staff:	**20**

FEE INCOME

Year End: 1990	FFr	%
Accountancy & Audit:	3,000,000	50.0
Consultancy:	1,000,000	17.0
Tax:	2,000,000	33.0
Total:	**6,000,000**	

CONTACT INFORMATION
Chairman & Managing Partner: Michel Leclercq
Accountancy & Tax: Alain Romet
Administration: Michele Billaud

CLIENT SERVICES
Accountancy (General), Audit, Corporate Finance Advice, Management & Business Advice, Mergers & Acquisitions, Pensions Planning, Taxation (Corporate), Taxation (International), Management Consultancy

M.B.B.R.

208 rue Raymond-Losserand, 75014 PARIS
Tel: +*33* (1) 40 44 19 00
Fax: +*33* (1) 45 43 63 61

European Affiliation: Clark Kenneth Leventhal

International Contact: Emmanuel du Doüet de Graville

Partners:	9
Professional staff:	18
Non-professional staff:	10
Total Staff:	**37**

FEE INCOME

Year End: 1990	%
Tax:	100.0

CLIENT SERVICES
Taxation (Corporate), Taxation (International), Trust Settlement & Estates

NICE AUDIT GESTION CONSEIL

Transit Centre, 16 avenue Thiers, 06000 NICE
Tel: +*33* 93 88 30 70
Fax: +*33* 93 87 35 99

European Affiliation: Alliott Peirson International

International Contact: Denis Potier

ORCOM CENTRE

2 avenue de Paris, 45056 ORLEANS
Tel: +*33* 38 77 76 75
Fax: +*33* 38 77 76 83

European Affiliation: K.S. International

International Contact: Serge Aubailly

Partners:	10
Professional staff:	73
Non-professional staff:	7
Total Staff:	**90**

FEE INCOME

Year End: 1990	FFr
Total:	**43,000,000**

CONTACT INFORMATION
Chairman: Serge Aubailly
Audit: Benoit Desbois
Corporate Finance: Étienne Chaline
Insolvency: Philippe Parisot
Management Consultancy: Michel Martin
Public Sector: Patrick Imbert
Tax (Corporate): Joel Allezy
Banks Audit & Data Processing: Serge Aubailly
Mergers & Acquisitions: Michel Martin

CLIENT SERVICES
Accountancy (General), Audit, Computer Installation, Corporate Finance Advice, Insolvency & Corporate Restructuring, Litigation/Legal Services, ▷

France

Management & Business Advice, Management Buy-outs, Mergers & Acquisitions, Taxation (Corporate), Trust Settlement & Estates, Training

PRICE WATERHOUSE

98 rue de Courcelles, 75017 PARIS
Tel: +33 (1) 44 01 30 00
Fax: +33 (1) 42 27 33 84

European Affiliation: Price Waterhouse

International Contact: Pardeep Narain

Partners:	90
Professional staff:	808
Non-professional staff:	297
Total Staff:	**1,195**

FEE INCOME

Year End: 30.06.91	**FFr**	**%**
Accountancy & Audit:		85.0
Consultancy:		4.0
Tax:		11.0
Total:	**860,000,000**	

CONTACT INFORMATION

Chairman: Jean Raffegeau
Managing Partner: Gérard Petiteau
Managing Partner: Pierre Dufils
Accountancy (General): Antoine Reiss
Audit: Gérard Petiteau
Corporate Finance: Fernand Dubois
Management Consultancy: Peter Davis
Public Sector: Alain Paquier
Tax (Corporate): Philippe Moisand
Tax (International): Michel Boutin
Human Resources: Jean-Emmanuel Combes
Finance: Daniel Palavioux
Practice Development: Jean-Claude Viarnaud

CLIENT SERVICES

Accountancy (General), Audit, Computer Installation, Corporate Finance Advice, Litigation/Legal Services, Management & Business Advice, Management Buy-outs, Value for Money Studies, Taxation (Corporate), Taxation (International)

Industry Specialisations: Banking, Insurance

MAJOR CLIENTS

Axa-Midi, Bongrain, BSN, Darty, Essilor, FNAC, GAN, L'Oreal, Majorette, Michelin, Navigation Mixte, Pechiney, Perrier, Peugeot, Rhône-Poulenc, Saint-Gobain, Schneider, Suez, Thomson, Victoire

OTHER OFFICES

PRICE WATERHOUSE
parc de la Vatine, 30 rue Aron, 76130 MONT-SAINT-AIGNAN, Rouen
Tel: +33 35 59 00 85 *Fax:* +33 35 59 95 96

PRICE WATERHOUSE
74 F rue de Paris, 35069 RENNES CEDEX
Tel: +33 99 36 21 96 *Fax:* +33 99 38 95 80
Contact: Gerard Estival

PRICE WATERHOUSE
1 place Alfonse-Jourdain, 31000 TOULOUSE
Tel: +33 61 21 18 71 *Fax:* +33 61 21 03 60

PRICE WATERHOUSE
1 rue Daumier, 13008 MARSEILLE
Tel: +33 91 37 27 36 *Fax:* +33 91 81 21 55
Contact: Alain Gourlay

PRICE WATERHOUSE
1 rue de la République, 69001 LYON
Tel: +33 78 27 50 50 *Fax:* +33 78 27 50 99
Contact: Andre Pasqual

PRICE WATERHOUSE
Le Sebastopol, 3 quai Kleber, 67055 STRASBOURG CEDEX
Tel: +33 88 22 22 00 *Fax:* +33 88 75 64 01
Contact: Olivier Auscher

PRICE WATERHOUSE
11/13 rue Douet-Garnier, B.P. 471, 44015 NANTES CEDEX
Tel: +33 40 76 99 52 *Fax:* +33 40 94 42 85
Contact: Gerard Estival

PRICE WATERHOUSE
boulevard de Touraine, Z.I. Légère, B.P. 7, 49308 CHOLET CEDEX
Tel: +33 41 62 13 28 *Fax:* +33 41 62 81 89
Contact: Gerard Estival

Total Number of Offices: 9

PROGESTION

122 boulevard Malesherbes, 75017 PARIS
Tel: +33 (1) 47 66 16 50

European Affiliation: Growth & Progress Challenge

International Contact: Jacques Ryvol

CONSTANTIN RAPTI

53 avenue des Perdrix, 94210 LA VARENNE, Saint Hilaire
Tel: +33 (1) 48 85 86 89

European Affiliation: Growth & Progress Challenge

International Contact: Constantin Rapti

DIDIER REMY

29 rue Labbottière, 33000 BORDEAUX
Tel: +33 56 52 04 04
Fax: +33 56 51 69 00

European Affiliation: Eura-Audit International

International Contact: D. Remy

RÉVISION ET CONTROLE

88 avenue Niel, 75017 PARIS
Tel: +33 (1) 47 64 08 36
Fax: +33 (1) 42 27 43 93

European Affiliation: Jeffreys Henry International

International Contact: Phillippe Barbet-Massin

OTHER OFFICES

RÉVISION ET CONTROLE
269 ter avenue de la République, 59300 LILLE LA MADELEINE
Tel: +33 20 55 75 81 *Fax:* +33 20 31 99 43
Contact: Jean-Bernard Croenne

RÉVISION ET CONTROLE
4 avenue Georges-Clemenceau, 06000 NICE
Tel: +33 93 88 42 91 *Fax:* +33 93 82 03 48
Contact: Raymond Lelouche

Total Number of Offices: 3

S & W ASSOCIÉS

47 rue de Chaillot, 75116 PARIS
Tel: +33 (1) 47 23 00 63
Fax: +33 (1) 47 20 33 81

European Affiliation: S & W International

▷

Partners:	5
Professional staff:	30
Non-professional staff:	8
Total Staff:	**43**

CONTACT INFORMATION
Managing Partner: Rodolphe Ankaoua
Accountancy (General): Bertrand Bodet
Audit: David M.W. Dowse
Management Consultancy: John W. Moffatt
Tax (Corporate): Paul Grabli

CLIENT SERVICES
All Services

OTHER OFFICES
S & W ASSOCIÉS
6 rue Gautherin, RAMBOUILLET 78120
Tel: + *33* (1) 34 83 31 45 *Fax:* + *33* (1) 34 83 14 80
Contact: R. Ankaoua

Total Number of Offices: 2

SALUSTRO REYDEL
65 rue de Courcelles, 75008 PARIS
Tel: + *33* (1) 44 15 38 00
Fax: + *33* (1) 42 67 90 55

European Affiliation: DRM Internationally

International Contact: Antoine Guilland

Partners:	30
Professional staff:	362
Non-professional staff:	79
Total Staff:	**471**

FEE INCOME

Year End: 31.12.90	**FFr**	**%**
Accountancy & Audit:	200,000,000	80.0
Consultancy:	43,000,000	17.0
Other:	8,000,000	3.0
Total:	**251,000,000**	

CONTACT INFORMATION
Chairman: André Reydel
Managing Partner: Edouard Salustro
Managing Partner: Jean-Claude Reydel
Accountancy (General): Bernard Nicot
Management Consultancy: Jean-Luc Dumont
Administration: François Chevreux
Public Sector: Benoit Lebrun
Audit & Communication Industry: Dominique Ledouble
Construction Industry: Jacques Ponsart
Construction Industry: Ameziane Keloua
Corporate Finance & Finance Sector: Guy Stievenart

CLIENT SERVICES
Accountancy (General), Audit, Computer Installation, Corporate Finance Advice, Management & Business Advice, Management Buy-outs, Mergers & Acquisitions

Industry Specialisations: Communication, Energy, Finance, Distribution, Transport, Automotive, Information, Publishing, Services

MAJOR CLIENTS
Banco do Brasil, Paribas (Filiales), Matif, Bred, Banque Hervet, Sovac, Banco Bilbao Vizcaya, Caisse Centrale des Banques Populaires (CCBP), CGM, CGEA, TFE, Groupe Verney, Cie Générale des Eaux, Coface, Staf, Elis, Area, Citroen, Fiat France, Toyota, Valeo, EEM, Cochery, Sari, Saunier deVal (SDEL), SCIC, Esso, Mobile, Cogemo, Total (Filiales), Gaillimard/Denoel, Bayard Presse, CEP, Comareg, Havas, Canal Plus, TFI, Gaumont, TV Sports, IBM, Thomson CSF, Bricard, Sopad Nestlé, Intermarché, Conforma, Canon, Akai, Konica, LaRouse/Nathan, Science et Vies, Pretabail, Credit Lyonnaies (Filiales), SGE, SCREG, Fougerolle, CBC Campenon, Bernard, Sligos, CGI, GSI, Tonna Electronique, Laboratories UPSA, De Dietrich, Tunnel du Mont Blanc, Tunnel de Frejus

ASSOCIATED FIRMS
ADEFI
3 allée des Coquelicots, 78120 RAMBOUILLET
Tel: + *33* (1) 30 41 86 16 *Fax:* + *33* (1) 34 85 54 49

DMA
33 rue Nicholas-Bornier, 21000 DIJON
Tel: + *33* 80 66 68 00 *Fax:* + *33* 80 66 44 65

FIDUCIAIRE DE L'EST
48-50 place Mazelle, 57045 METZ CEDEX 01
Tel: + *33* 87 36 16 28 *Fax:* + *33* 87 36 53 60

GROUPE SECO
24 place du Général-Catroux, 75017 PARIS
Tel: + *33* (1) 42 67 20 80 *Fax:* + *33* (1) 42 27 03 11

GROUPE SECO
6 rue Saint-Lazare, 27201 VERNON CEDEX
Mailing Address: B.P. 142, 27201 VERNON CEDEX
Tel: + *33* 32 51 44 87 *Fax:* + *33* 32 51 15 69

HOCHE FISCALITÉ
31 rue Daru, 75008 PARIS
Tel: + *33* (1) 47 64 30 34 *Fax:* + *33* (1) 42 67 77 44

CABINET P. MASSONNAT
304 rue Garibaldi, 69007 LYON
Tel: + *33* 78 72 88 80 *Fax:* + *33* 78 69 86 94

PALMADE & ASSOCIÉS
37 rue de Turenne, 66000 PERPIGNAN
Tel: + *33* 68 50 14 26 *Fax:* + *33* 68 66 88 78

GABRIEL POIGNANT & ASSOCIÉS
13 avenue Hoche, 75008 PARIS
Tel: + *33* (1) 44 15 38 00 *Fax:* + *33* (1) 42 67 90 55

REVIREX
3 bis, rue Lucien-Servanty, 31500 TOULOUSE
Tel: + *33* 61 20 24 29 *Fax:* + *33* 61 80 44 64

RSA - SEEC
100 rue Lafayette, 75010 PARIS
Tel: + *33* (1) 42 46 82 30 *Fax:* + *33* (1) 42 46 86 57

CABINET SCORE
175 boulevard de la République, 92210 SAINT-CLOUD
Tel: + *33* (1) 49 11 06 47 *Fax:* + *33* (1) 46 02 19 30

SEC - PSA
1 rue de la Badouillere, B.P. 47, 42002 ST ÉTIENNE CEDEX 1
Tel: + *33* 77 33 12 81 *Fax:* + *33* 77 38 06 79

SECNO
Parc de la Vatine, 28 rue Alfred Kastler, 76137 MONT-SAINT-AIGNAN CEDEX
Mailing Address: B.P. 278, 76137 MONT-SAINT-AIGNAN CEDEX
Tel: + *33* 35 59 76 76 *Fax:* + *33* 35 59 11 55

STIRNWEISS FINCK & ASSOCIÉS
9 rue des Champs, B.P. 19, 67540 OSTWALD, Strasbourg
Tel: + *33* 88 30 12 21 *Fax:* + *33* 88 30 23 30

Total Number of Offices: 16

▷

France

CABINET SBC CIRON

108 bis, cours du Médoc, 33000 BORDEAUX
Tel: +*33* 56 39 25 41
Fax: +*33* 56 39 36 31

European Affiliation: Eura-Audit International

International Contact: J-L. Ciron
J.M. Descouens

SECFI

23 rue d'Anjou, 75008 PARIS
Tel: +*33* (1) 47 42 12 00
Fax: +*33* (1) 47 42 41 49

European Affiliation: Independent Accountants International

International Contact: Quentin Symington

SEECF/UNF

197 boulevard Malesherbes, 75017 PARIS
Tel: +*33* 47 66 04 72
Fax: +*33* 46 22 89 79

European Affiliation: The Channel International Association

International Contact: Patrick Aubart

SIGEX

27 avenue de la Constellation, 95800 CERGY ST CHRISTOPHE
Tel: +*33* 30 73 43 44
Fax: +*33* 30 73 40 34

International Contact: J.F. Lecue

SOCIÉTÉ CIVILE DHINAUN FAYSSE, PETIT

2 rue de la Claire, 69009 LYON
Tel: +*33* 78 47 86 66
Fax: +*33* 78 64 11 09

European Affiliation: Alliott Peirson International

International Contact: Pierre Petit

SOCIÉTÉ FIDUCIAIRE DE CONTROLE ET DE RÉVISION

32 bis, avenue Félix-Faure, 69007 LYONS
Tel: +*33* 78 72 06 92
Fax: +*33* 72 73 47 14

European Affiliation: Eura-Audit International

International Contact: G. Michel
P. Selignan
F-M. Fleur

OTHER OFFICES

SOCIÉTÉ FIDUCIAIRE DE CONTROLE ET DE RÉVISION
2 rue Dacquin, 73100 AIX LES BAINS
Tel: +*33* 79 35 05 59 *Fax:* +*33* 79 88 13 07
Contact: F-M. Fleur

Total Number of Offices: 2

SODAREX - SOCIÉTÉ D'ANALYSES, DE RÉVISION ET D'EXPERTISES COMPTABLES

cours Journu-Auber 50, 33300 BORDEAUX
Tel: +*33* 56 50 94 92
Fax: +*33* 56 50 87 07

European Affiliation: Russell Bedford International

International Contact: Frédéric Sellam

SOFICO FRANCE

Centre d'Affaires de Metz, 1 place du Pont à Seille, 57000 METZ
Tel: +*33* 87 36 16 66
Fax: +*33* 87 75 35 75

European Affiliation: Eura-Audit International

International Contact: J. Martin
D. Lorrain
A. Lefevre

OTHER OFFICES

SOFICO FRANCE
24 rue Raymond-Mondon, 57120 ROMBAS
Tel: +*33* 87 67 18 42 *Fax:* +*33* 87 67 18 83
Contact: M. Colleony

SOFICO FRANCE
43 avenue Poincaré, 54400 LONGWY
Tel: +*33* 82 24 90 91 *Fax:* +*33* 82 25 65 69
Contact: C. Michaux

SOFICO FRANCE
5 rue Fabert, 57600 FORBACH
Tel: +*33* 87 85 53 06 *Fax:* +*33* 87 84 12 64
Contact: L. Dietsch

SOFICO FRANCE
10 rue Joffre, 57100 THIONVILLE
Tel: +*33* 82 82 88 88 *Fax:* +*33* 82 82 70 13
Contact: G. Brun

SOFICO FRANCE
19 rue de Wengel, 57700 HAYANGE
Tel: +*33* 82 84 13 41 *Fax:* +*33* 82 84 20 42
Contact: P. Dieterling

Total Number of Offices: 6

SOREGOR

18 rue Bouche-Thomas, B.P. 244, 49002 ANGERS CEDEX
Tel: +*33* 41 68 68 10
Fax: +*33* 41 47 47 95

European Affiliation: The International Group of Accounting Firms Ltd (IGAF)

International Contact: G. Houdousse

CABINET SOREL

59 rue la Boetie, 75008 PARIS
Tel: +*33* (1) 45 63 09 09
Fax: +*33* (1) 45 63 36 19

European Affiliation: K.S. International

International Contact: Christophe Gansmandel

Partners:	8
Professional staff:	51
Non-professional staff:	13
Total Staff:	72

▷

FEE INCOME

Year End: 31.12.90	FFr	%
Accountancy & Audit:	28,000,000	85.0
Other:	5,000,000	15.0
Total:	**33,000,000**	

CONTACT INFORMATION
Chairman: Claude Audan

CLIENT SERVICES
Accountancy (General), Audit, Management & Business Advice, Taxation (Corporate)

Industry Specialisations: Real Estate, Catering, Clothing, Health, Distribution (Food)

SOVEC

Le Concorde, 48 boulevard Georges-Pompidou, 00500 GAP, Hautes Alpes
Tel: +*33* 92 51 33 69
Fax: +*33* 92 53 63 92

European Affiliation: The International Group of Accounting Firms Ltd (IGAF)

International Contact: John Elms

OTHER OFFICES

SOVEC
Immeuble La Clarée, avenue du Lautaret 22, B.P. 107, 05102 BRIANÇON, Hautes Alpes
Tel: +*33* 92 20 30 20 *Fax:* +*33* 92 20 43 70
Contact: Pierre Trinquier

SOVEC
20 rue Fernand-Pelloutier, 38431 ECHIROLLES CEDEX, GRENOBLE, Isère
Tel: +*33* 76 09 50 54 *Fax:* +*33* 76 40 79 93

SOVEC
Saint Baldoph, 42 route d'Apremont, 73190 CHALLES LES EAUX, Savoie
Tel: +*33* 79 33 10 63 *Fax:* +*33* 79 28 21 36
Contact: Guy Astruc

SOVEC
7 boulevard Wilson, 73100 AIX LES BAINS, Savoie
Tel: +*33* 79 35 09 98 *Fax:* +*33* 79 88 05 63
Contact: Gerard Pernet

Total Number of Offices: 5

CLAUDINE VERGNOLLE-CHARANSONNET

12 place des Victoires, 75002 PARIS
Tel: +*33* (1) 42 60 96 78
Fax: +*33* (1) 39 59 24 33

European Affiliation: Affiliated Conference of Practising Accountants International (ACPA)

International Contact: Claudine Vergnolle-Charansonnet

Germany

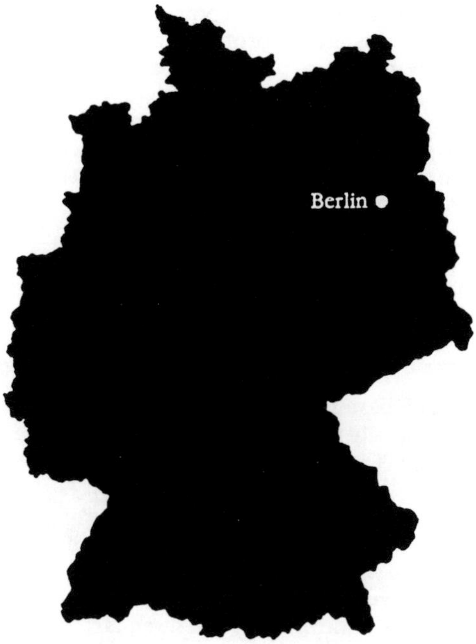

Area: 357,041 sq km (137,857 sq miles)
Population: 77,812,298 (1986/87 estimates)
Density: 217.9 per sq km
Capital: Berlin

GDP: DM2.65 trn, US$1.7 trn
GDP per head: US$21,500 (1991 forecast)
Inflation: 1990 - 2.8%
1991 - 3.8% (forecast)

Official and Spoken Languages: German. English spoken in cities. French also spoken in some areas.

Time: GMT + 1 (in Summer GMT + 2)
Telephone Dialling Code: +49 (West) +37 (East)

Currency: Deutsche Mark (DM) = 100 pfennigs
Banking Hours: 0830-1300 and 1430-1600 Monday-Friday Open till 1730 on Thursdays in main cities (West). 0800-1200 Monday-Friday plus 1430-1730 on Tuesday and Thursday
Professional accountancy body: Institut der wirtschaftsprufer in Deutschland (IDW)

Corporate Tax Data

Information supplied by Richard Citron, international tax partner of Stoy Hayward.

The tax year; nature and rates of tax

The tax year is the calendar year. Corporation tax (Koerperschaftsteuer) is levied at 50% on a company's undistributed income; the rate applied to distributed income is 36%. From 1 July 1991 to 30 June 1992, a surcharge on income and corporation tax of 7.5% (ie. 3.75% for 1991 and 1992) of the **tax** due will be levied.

Residence and territoriality

German resident companies are liable to corporation tax on their worldwide income. A company is treated as resident if it is incorporated or has its principal place of management in Germany.

The tax base

Method of computation. Taxable profits are computed by comparing the company's net worth at the beginning and end of the accounting period.

Disallowable items. The major disallowable items are gifts, 20% of business entertaining expenses, formation expenses, taxes on non-deductible expenses and other expenses incurred in connection with non-taxable income or gains.

Exempt income/special deductions. Deductions in assessing net worth include capital contributions, the share premium on shares issued in the period and certain investment grants, pension fund contributions, other taxes, charitable donations within the statutory limits and "stock relief".

Interest paid. Interest is deductible on an accruals basis. It is disallowed if incurred in connection with income and gains permanently exempt from German tax.

Stock. Stock and work in progress is valued at the lower of cost and market value. A form of stock relief is available for certain foreign source materials which are subject to price fluctuations. ▷

Depreciation. A variety of methods (straightline, reducing balance and others) is permitted and the rates vary over different types of asset (e.g. industrial buildings at a straightline rate of 2-4% and motor vehicles at a straightline rate of 20-25%).

Treatment of dividends

Dividends received from German companies. Dividends received from German companies are subject to corporation tax and the trade tax on the gross amount of the dividend (net dividend plus tax credit of 36/64ths). The tax credit may be set against the recipient company's own corporation tax liability. Exemption from the trade tax is granted if the recipient has a holding of at least 10% in the paying company. The net dividend is also subject to 25% withholding tax which is creditable against the recipient's corporation tax.

Dividends received from abroad. These dividends are subject to corporation tax and trade tax but most tax treaties will exempt them from German tax.

Dividends paid to German residents. Distributed profits are taxed at the lower rate (36%) of corporation tax. This corporation tax may be set against the income tax of the shareholder.

Dividends paid to non-residents. The same rules apply except that the foreign shareholder is not generally entitled to the 36% tax credit.

Anti-avoidance measures

There are no statutory thin capitalisation rules. Transfer pricing rules operate on transactions between a German company and a foreign related party. There are also complex controlled foreign company rules.

Treatment of losses

Current period. Trading and capital losses are automatically offset against profits of the same period by virtue of the net worth basis.

Past periods. Where a tax loss arises in any period, it is automatically set against non-distributed income and gains of the two preceding periods, up to a maximum of DM 10 million. There is no carry back.

Future periods. To the extent that an overall current tax loss has not been set off against prior periods, it is carried forward indefinitely.

Treatment of capital gains

Method of computation. Gains are computed by deducting the cost (or net book value, where appropriate) of an asset from the sale proceeds.

Treatment. Capital gains are treated as income.

Rollover. Gains may be rolled over where they arise from the disposal of real property, depreciable movable property with a minimum useful life of 25 years and shares, held for a minimum of six years.

Treatment of groups and branches

There is no general recognition of groups for tax purposes but "integrated companies" (Organschaften) may consolidate profits and losses of subsidiaries. The profits of a German resident branch of a non-resident company are computed according to the rules for a resident company but only German source profits are taxable. There is a special flat rate branch tax of 46%. Branches are also liable to the net worth tax and the trade tax and also the 7.5% surtax. There is no withholding tax on remittances of branch profit abroad.

Other taxes

A *two tier trade tax* (Gewerbesteuer) is payable as a local tax on a company's taxable income and capital.

(1) The base for the income element of the tax is basically the corporation tax profit. The basic rate is 5% multiplied by a factor of between 2 and 4.8, depending on the locality.
(2) The base for the capital element of the tax is the net worth tax base as adjusted. A deduction of DM 120,000 is available to reduce the adjusted base.The basic rate is 0.2% multiplied by the same factor.
(3) The trade tax is deductible in computing the tax itself.

Taxes on capital. In addition to the capital element of the trade tax, there is also a net worth tax (Vermoegensteuer) on the worldwide assets of resident companies with certain exemptions. The tax is charged in 1992 at a rate of 0.6% on 75% of the adjusted base in excess of DM 125,000 (DM 500,000 in future years). There is also a local property tax (Grundsteuer) on the assessed value of property.

Turnover taxes. There is a valued added tax (Mehrwertsteuer) on the supply of goods and services at a rate of 14% in 1992 (15% in future years). A reduced rate of 7% also applies.

Transaction taxes. There is a real property transfer tax of 2%.

Payroll taxes. Employers pay social security premiums which can in total amount to 36.3% of gross monthly salary (there is a ceiling). One half of the amount paid may be recovered from the employee.

Incentives. Investments in the territory of the former German Democratic Republic ("GDR") and West Berlin may qualify for an investment grant. The grant amounts to 12% for investments concluded before 1 July 1992. It is reduced to 8% for investments concluded after 30 June 1992 and before 1 January 1995 if the investment commences before 31 December 1992 Neither the net worth tax nor the trade tax on capital are to be levied in the territories of the former GDR until 1 January 1995. There are also special depreciation rates for investment in the former GDR. Lower corporate tax rates and VAT preferences apply to west Berlin enterprises until 1994 and 1993 respectively.

ADVISOR TREUHAND GmbH

Tulpenhofstrasse 18, 6050 OFFENBACH AM MAIN 1
Tel: + *49* (69) 81 70 27
Fax: + *49* (69) 88 18 86

European Affiliation: DRM Internationally

International Contact: Ernst Helmut Rehm

Partners:	5
Professional staff:	20
Non-professional staff:	5
Total Staff:	**30**

CONTACT INFORMATION

Managing Partner: Ernst Helmut Rehm

CLIENT SERVICES

Accountancy (General), Audit, Taxation (Corporate), Taxation (International), Legal

OTHER OFFICES

ADVISOR TREUHAND GmbH
Klosterweg 3, 6400 FULDA
Tel: + *49* (661) 7 20 48 *Fax:* + *49* (661) 7 43 63
Contact: Dr. Erich Muth

DR. MUTH & PARTNER
Langestrasse 3, 5020 ERFURT
Tel: + *37* (3763) 75 73 00
Contact: Josef Weiss

Total Number of Offices: 3

ALLREVISION GmbH

Widenmayerstrasse 5, 8000 MUNICH 22
Tel: + *49* (89) 2 35 09 60
Fax: + *49* (89) 23 50 96 39

European Affiliation: Summit International Associates Inc

International Contact: Dr. Hans Maerz

Partners:	3
Professional staff:	34
Non-professional staff:	6
Total Staff:	**43**

FEE INCOME

Year End: 1990	%
Accountancy & Audit:	50.0
Tax:	40.0
Other:	10.0

CONTACT INFORMATION

Managing Partner: Dr. Peter Ehrsam
Accountancy & Audit: Peter Haupt
Tax: Dr. Hans Maerz
Mergers & Acquisitions: Dr. Peter Ehrsam

CLIENT SERVICES

Accountancy (General), Audit, Management Buy-outs, Mergers & Acquisitions, Taxation (Corporate), Taxation (International)

OTHER OFFICES

ALLREVISION GmbH
Katharinenstrasse 17, 7010 LEIPZIG
Contact: Dr. Hans Maerz

ALLREVISION GmbH
Marienstrasse 5, 7000 STUTTGART 1
Contact: Dr. Hans Maerz

Total Number of Offices: 4

ALL-AUDIT REVISION UND TREUHAND GmbH

Grossherzog Friedrich Strasse 40, 6600 SAARBRÜCKEN
Tel: + *49* (681) 3 94 48
Fax: + *49* (681) 3 94 47

European Affiliation: Eura-Audit International

International Contact: O. Fess
H. Porn

ARTHUR ANDERSEN & CO

Friedrich-Ebert-Anlage 2-14, Postfach 11 01 12, 6000 FRANKFURT AM MAIN 11
Tel: + *49* (69) 7 57 10
Fax: + *49* (69) 74 80 96

European Affiliation: Arthur Andersen Worldwide

International Contact: Jürgen Schülzke

CLIENT SERVICES

Accountancy (General), Audit, Computer Installation, Corporate Finance Advice, Insolvency & Corporate Restructuring, Litigation/Legal Services, Management & Business Advice, Management Buy-outs, Mergers & Acquisitions, Pensions Planning, Value for Money Studies, Taxation (Corporate), Taxation (International)

OTHER OFFICES

ARTHUR ANDERSEN & CO
Tauentzienstrasse, Europa Center, 1000 BERLIN 30
Tel: + *49* (30) 25 47 10 *Fax:* + *49* (30) 2 62 94 63

ARTHUR ANDERSEN & CO
Obenmarspforten 21, 5000 COLOGNE 1
Tel: + *49* (221) 20 64 00 *Fax:* + *49* (221) 24 81 82

ARTHUR ANDERSEN & CO
Cecilienallee 6, Postfach 32 01 07, 4000 DUSSELDORF 30
Tel: + *49* (211) 4 95 80 *Fax:* + *49* (211) 4 95 81 20

ARTHUR ANDERSEN & CO
Bleichenbrücke 10, 2000 HAMBURG 36
Tel: + *49* (40) 35 60 70 *Fax:* + *49* (40) 35 60 72 22

ARTHUR ANDERSEN & CO
Sophienstrasse 5, 3000 HANNOVER 1
Tel: + *49* (511) 36 80 70 *Fax:* + *49* (511) 32 34 24

ARTHUR ANDERSEN & CO
Nymphenburger Strasse 1, 8000 MUNICH 2
Tel: + *49* (89) 5 51 47 01 *Fax:* + *49* (89) 55 14 72 25

ARTHUR ANDERSEN & CO
Augustenstrasse 7, 7000 STUTTGART 1
Tel: + *49* (711) 6 14 90 *Fax:* + *49* (711) 62 27 70

ARTHUR ANDERSEN & CO
Kanzlerstrasse 4, 9005 CHEMNITZ
Tel: + *37* (71) 3 81 44 *Fax:* + *37* (71) 3 81 43

ARTHUR ANDERSEN & CO
Lingnerallee 3, 8012 DRESDEN
Tel: + *37* (51) 4 87 57 33 *Fax:* + *37* (51) 4 87 38 23

▷

ARTHUR ANDERSEN & CO
Waagegasse 2, 5020 ERFURT
Tel: + *37* (61) 2 25 21 *Fax:* + *37* (61) 2 25 21

ARTHUR ANDERSEN & CO
Brühl 42-50, 7010 LEIPZIG
Tel: + *37* (41) 7 97 13 41 *Fax:* + *37* (41) 29 44 57

ARTHUR ANDERSEN & CO
Holbeinplatz 14, 2510 ROSTOCK 5
Tel: + *37* (81) 85 61 *Fax:* + *37* (81) 8 11 23 48

Total Number of Offices: 13

AWT AUDITRON WIRTSCHAFTS-TREUHAND GmbH

Willy-Lessing Strasse 12, 8600 BAMBERG
Tel: + *49* (951) 98 09 80
Fax: + *49* (951) 9 80 98 22

European Affiliation: DRM Internationally

International Contact: Herbert Brauner

Partners:	5
Professional staff:	20
Non-professional staff:	15
Total Staff:	**40**

FEE INCOME

Year End: 1990	%
Accountancy & Audit:	64.0
Tax:	28.0
Other:	8.0

CONTACT INFORMATION

Audit: Herbert Brauner
Audit: Fabio Casicci
Corporate Finance: Erwin Kiefer
Audit & Tax: Petra Sirsch
Tax & Administration: Hans F. Wolfinger
Audit & Tax: Franz Huber
Audit & Tax: Dietmar Hahn

CLIENT SERVICES

Accountancy (General), Audit, Computer Installation, Corporate Finance Advice, Management & Business Advice, Management Buy-outs, Mergers & Acquisitions, Taxation (Corporate), Taxation (International)

OTHER OFFICES

AWT AUDITRON WIRTSCHAFTS-TREUHAND GmbH
Moerikestrasse 34, 7000 STUTTGART 1
Tel: + *49* (711) 64 95 70 *Fax:* + *49* (711) 6 49 57 44
Contact: Erwin J. Kiefer

Total Number of Offices: 2

DR. KARL WALTER BACH

Maximilianstrasse 20, 8000 MUNICH 22
Tel: + *49* (89) 29 32 98
Fax: + *49* (89) 29 86 85

European Affiliation: InterContinental Consultants (ICC)

International Contact: Dr. Karl Walter Bach

BACHEM, FERVERS, JANSSEN & MEHRHOFF

Hohenzollernring 57-63, 5000 COLOGNE 1
Tel: + *49* (221) 20 64 30
Fax: + *49* (221) 2 06 43 10

European Affiliation: Clark Kenneth Leventhal

International Contact: Hellmuth Bachem

Partners:	7
Professional staff:	54
Non-professional staff:	19
Total Staff:	**80**

FEE INCOME

Year End: 1990	%
Accountancy & Audit:	49.0
Tax:	29.0
Other:	22.0

CLIENT SERVICES

Accountancy (General), Audit, Corporate Finance Advice, Insolvency & Corporate Restructuring, Management & Business Advice, Taxation (Corporate), Taxation (International)

OTHER OFFICES

BACHEM, FERVERS, JANSSEN & MEHRHOFF
Schlagbaumer Strasse 59A, 5650 SOLINGEN 1
Tel: + *49* (212) 5 20 41 *Fax:* + *49* (212) 5 66 70
Contact: The Cologne Office

Total Number of Offices: 2

BAYERN-REVISION GmbH

Agnes-Bernauer-Strasse 90, Postfach 21 05 29, 8000 MUNICH 21
Tel: + *49* (89) 5 89 85 05
Fax: + *49* (89) 5 89 85 57

European Affiliation: The International Group of Accounting Firms Ltd (IGAF)

International Contact: Guido Mohring

OTHER OFFICES

BAYERN-REVISION GmbH
Marienstrasse 8, Postfach 1441, 8500 NUREMBERG 1
Tel: + *49* (911) 2 45 77
Contact: Herbert Poller

Total Number of Offices: 2

BDO DEUTSCHE WARENTREUHAND AG

Ferdinandstrasse 59, 2000 HAMBURG 1
Tel: + *49* (40) 30 29 30
Fax: + *49* (40) 30 29 32 88

European Affiliation: BDO Binder

International Contact: Hans-Heinrich Otte

Partners:	869
Professional staff:	596
Non-professional staff:	273
Total Staff:	**1,738**

FEE INCOME

Year End: 31.12.90	**DM**	%
Accountancy & Audit:	94,560,000	75.0
Consultancy:	10,086,000	8.0
Tax:	20,174,000	16.0
Other:	1,200,000	1.0
Total:	**126,020,000**	

▷

CONTACT INFORMATION
Corporate Finance: Sven Tern
Management Consultancy: Uwe Hansen
Administration: Dr. Kurt Boysen
Public Sector: Gottfried Hohlfeldt
Accountancy & audit: Dr. Hans-Joachim Jacob
Tax: Dr. Richard Wellmann

CLIENT SERVICES
All Services

OTHER OFFICES
BDO DEUTSCHE WARENTREUHAND AG
Kurfürstendamm 182-183, 1000 BERLIN 15
Tel: + *49* (30) 88 20 71 *Fax:* + *49* (30) 8 83 82 99
Contact: Gottfried Hohlfeldt

BDO DEUTSCHE WARENTREUHAND AG
Josef-Wirmer-Strasse 1-3, 5300 BONN 1
Tel: + *49* (228) 52 00 70 *Fax:* + *49* (228) 61 42 10
Contact: Ulrich Pago

BDO DEUTSCHE WARENTREUHAND AG
Martinistrasse 57, 2800 BREMEN 1
Tel: + *49* (421) 17 06 38 *Fax:* + *49* (421) 17 10 18
Contact: Peter Dannenbaum

BDO DEUTSCHE WARENTREUHAND AG
Konrad-Adenauer-Ufer 79-81, 5000 COLOGNE 1
Tel: + *49* (221) 77 10 70 *Fax:* + *49* (221) 7 39 03 95
Contact: Dr. Peter Lauter

BDO DEUTSCHE WARENTREUHAND AG
Grünaer Strasse 2, 8010 DRESDEN
Tel: + *37* (51) 4 87 42 22 *Fax:* + *37* (51) 4 87 32 26
Contact: Gottfried Hohlfeldt

BDO DEUTSCHE WARENTREUHAND AG
Berliner Allee 59, 4000 DUSSELDORF 1
Mailing Address: Postfach 48 25, 4000 DUSSELDORF 1
Tel: + *49* (211) 1 37 10 *Fax:* + *49* (211) 1 37 11 20
Contact: Paul Stalschus

BDO DEUTSCHE WARENTREUHAND AG
Wilhelm-Wolff-Strasse 7, 5087 ERFURT
Tel: + *37* (61) 41 50 03
Contact: Klaus Neukirchen

BDO DEUTSCHE WARENTREUHAND AG
Zweigertstrasse 41, 4300 ESSEN 1
Mailing Address: Postfach 34 01 07, 4300 ESSEN 1
Tel: + *49* (201) 87 21 50 *Fax:* + *49* (201) 78 39 85
Contact: Dr. Dirk Rosenbaum

BDO DEUTSCHE WARENTREUHAND AG
Dr-Todsen-Strasse 7, 2390 FLENSBURG
Tel: + *49* (461) 1 75 88 *Fax:* + *49* (461) 1 26 03
Contact: Dieter Priess

BDO DEUTSCHE WARENTREUHAND AG
Neue Mainzer Strasse 57, 6000 FRANKURT 1
Tel: + *49* (69) 2 73 90 30 *Fax:* + *49* (69) 25 00 86
Contact: Dr. Hans-Joachim Jacob

BDO DEUTSCHE WARENTREUHAND AG
Uhlemeyerstrasse 9 & 11, 3000 HANNOVER 1
Tel: + *49* (511) 33 80 20 *Fax:* + *49* (511) 3 38 02 40
Contact: Heinz Pohlentz

BDO DEUTSCHE WARENTREUHAND AG
Dahlmannstrasse 1-3, 2300 KIEL 1
Tel: + *49* (431) 5 12 46 *Fax:* + *49* (431) 55 18 09
Contact: Gottfried Hohlfeldt

BDO DEUTSCHE WARENTREUHAND AG
Antonienstrasse 61, 7031 LEIPZIG
Tel: + *37* (41) 4 96 62 17
Contact: Dr. Johannes Ditges

BDO DEUTSCHE WARENTREUHAND AG
Alfstrasse 38, 2400 LÜBECK
Tel: + *49* (451) 7 18 89 *Fax:* + *49* (451) 7 25 05
Contact: Dr. Ulrich Krauss

BDO DEUTSCHE WARENTREUHAND AG
Agnetenstrasse 14, 3024 MAGDEBURG
Tel: + *37* (91) 59 52 75 *Fax:* + *37* (91) 59 54 83
Contact: Heinz Pohlentz

BDO DEUTSCHE WARENTREUHAND AG
Elisenstrasse 3, 8000 MUNICH 2
Tel: + *49* (89) 55 16 80 *Fax:* + *49* (89) 5 51 68 99
Contact: Wolf Goppelt

BDO DEUTSCHE WARENTREUHAND AG
Holbein-Platz 14, Haus der Hochseefischer, 2510 ROSTOCK 5
Tel: + *37* (81) 85 61 *Fax:* + *37* (81) 81 13 48
Contact: Dr. Ulrich Krauss

BDO DEUTSCHE WARENTREUHAND AG
Bahnhofstrasse 44-46, 6200 WIESBADEN 1
Mailing Address: Postfach 21 25, 6200 WIESBADEN 1
Tel: + *49* (611) 37 80 50 *Fax:* + *49* (611) 37 72 66
Contact: Hans G. Bungers

BDO DEUTSCHE WARENTREUHAND AG
Heidenheimer Strasse 6, 7250 LEONBERG
Mailing Address: Postfach 1364, 7250 LEONBERG
Tel: + *49* (7152) 4 80 68 *Fax:* + *49* (7152) 7 55 86
Contact: Knut Aye

ASSOCIATED FIRMS
BDO GRÜNEWÄLDER TREUHAND GmbH
Berliner Allee 59, 4000 DUSSELDORF
Mailing Address: Postfach 48 25, 4000 DUSSELDORF 1
Tel: + *49* (211) 1 37 10 *Fax:* + *49* (211) 1 37 11 60
Contact: Dr. Fritz Nehles

BDO SÜDWESTTREUHAND GmbH
Kaiser-Joseph-Strasse 274, 7800 FREIBURG
Tel: + *49* (761) 3 67 30 *Fax:* + *49* (761) 3 03 07
Contact: Hans Gerhard

DR. GERLING, KLÖCKER & PAGO
Josef-Wirmer-Strasse 1-3, 5300 BONN 1
Mailing Address: Postfach 16 01 29, 5300 BONN 1
Tel: + *49* (228) 52 00 70 *Fax:* + *49* (288) 61 42 10
Contact: Ulrich Pago

DR. H. KESSLER, VON RIEGEN & PARTNER GmbH
Martinistrasse 57, 2800 BREMEN 1
Tel: + *49* (421) 17 06 38
Contact: Peter Dannenbaum

DR. LAUTER & FISCHER GmbH
Konrad-Adenauer-Ufer 79-81, 5000 COLOGNE 1
Tel: + *49* (221) 77 10 70 *Fax:* + *49* (221) 7 39 03 95
Contact: Dr. Peter Lauter

LTG LEONBERGER TREUHAND DR. NEUBERT - DR. WENDEL GmbH
Heidenheimer Strasse 6, 7250 LEONBERG
Tel: + *49* (7152) 2 00 51 *Fax:* + *49* (7152) 4 78 72
Contact: Dr. Siegfried Wendel

MÖSCHKE & SCHEBEN TREUHANDGESELLSCHAFT mbH
Bahnhofstrasse 44-46, 6200 WIESBADEN 1
Mailing Address: Postfach 43 46, 6200 WIESBADEN 1
Tel: + *49* (611) 37 80 50
Contact: Hans G. Bungers

NWT NORDWESTDEUTSCHE TREUHAND GmbH
Dr. Todsen-Strasse 7, 2390 FLENSBURG
Tel: + *49* (461) 1 75 88 *Fax:* + *49* (461) 1 26 03
Contact: Dieter Priess

▷

DR. TH. RUNTE WIRTSCHAFTSPRÜFUNGS GmbH
Zweigertstrasse 41, 4300 ESSEN 1
Mailing Address: Postfach 34 01 07, 4300 ESSEN 1
Tel: + *49* (201) 79 00 51 *Fax:* + *49* (201) 78 39 85
Contact: Dr. Peter Goetze

TREUHANDGESELLSCHAFT DR. SALZMANN GmbH
Elisenstrasse 3, 8000 MUNICH 2
Tel: + *49* (89) 22 71 00 *Fax:* + *49* (89) 5 51 68 99
Contact: Wolf Goppelt

Total Number of Offices: 30

BEEH & HAPPICH

Praunheimer Landstrasse 32, 6000 FRANKFURT AM MAIN 90
Tel: + *49* (69) 9 76 51 50
Fax: + *49* (69) 97 65 15 11

European Affiliation: Russell Bedford International

International Contact: Dieter Beeh

BEISEL, HAFELE, VOLL, ZWEIFEL & PARTNER

Gartenstraße 46, 6000 FRANKFURT AM MAIN 70
Tel: + *49* (69) 6 09 00 90
Fax: + *49* (69) 69 62 22 35

European Affiliation: Morison International

International Contact: Manfred Paulat

Partners:	6
Professional staff:	15
Non-professional staff:	12
Total Staff:	**33**

FEE INCOME

Year End: 31.12.90	**DM**
Total:	**4,900,000**

CONTACT INFORMATION
Managing Partner: Michael Häfele
Managing Partner: Manfred Paulat
Accountancy (General): Hans Heilmann
Audit: Manfred Paulat
Corporate Finance: Achim Zweifel
VAT: Ramona Drechsler

CLIENT SERVICES
All Services

Industry Specialisations: Manufacturing, Engineering, Construction, Publishing, Breweries, Transportation, Foundry

DIPL-KFM KARL BERG GmbH

Rheinberger Strasse 2, 4000 DUSSELDORF 30
Tel: + *49* (211) 43 42 66
Fax: + *49* (211) 45 22 58

European Affiliation: S & W International

International Contact: Dr. Paul J. Heuser

DR. BREIDENBACH - DR. GÜLDENAGEL & PARTNER

Hofave 95, Postfach 13 23 64, 5600 WUPERTAL-ELBERFELD
Tel: + *49* (202) 49 37 40
Fax: + *49* (202) 44 48 92

European Affiliation: Moores Rowland International

International Contact: Hans Peter Arnold

BTR BERATUNG UND TREUHAND RING GmbH

BTR Secretariat, Hansa-Allee 201, 4000 DUSSELDORF 11
Tel: + *49* (211) 59 47 22
Fax: + *49* (211) 59 68 14

European Affiliation: Nexia International

International Contact: Burkhardt Müller
Eppo Horlings

Partners:	36
Professional staff:	197
Non-professional staff:	59
Total Staff:	**292**

FEE INCOME

Year End: 1990	**DM**	**%**
Accountancy & Audit:	20,000,000	50.0
Consultancy:	8,000,000	20.0
Tax:	12,000,000	30.0
Total:	**40,000,000**	

CONTACT INFORMATION
Chairman: Burkhardt Müller
Managing Partner: Juergen Ott
Corporate Finance: Juergen Ott
Insolvency: Georg von Hartmann
Management Consultancy: Wolfgang Amonat
Administration: Heinz Seeger
Public Sector: Burkhardt Mueller
Accountancy & Audit: Gerhard Nolze
Tax: Reinhard Scholz
Health Care: Karl F. Maierhofer

CLIENT SERVICES
Accountancy (General), Audit, Corporate Finance Advice, Insolvency & Corporate Restructuring, Litigation/Legal Services, Management & Business Advice, Management Buy-outs, Mergers & Acquisitions, Pensions Planning, Value for Money Studies, Taxation (Corporate), Taxation (International), Trust Settlement & Estates

Industry Specialisations: Health Care, Charitable Trusts, Sports & Leisure

OTHER OFFICES

BTR BERATUNG UND TREUHAND RING GmbH
Hufelandstrasse 32-34, 1055 BERLIN
Tel: + *37* (2) 4 37 18 01 *Fax:* + *37* (2) 4 36 80 36
Contact: George Holler

BTR BERATUNG UND TREUHAND RING GmbH
Hillmannplatz 13/15, 2800 BREMEN 1
Tel: + *49* (421) 30 20 51 *Fax:* + *49* (421) 30 20 57
Contact: Heinzgünter Daubert

BTR BERATUNG UND TREUHAND RING GmbH
Friedensstrasse 57, 5000 COLOGNE 90
Tel: + *49* (2203) 2 10 94 *Fax:* + *49* (2203) 2 67 16
Contact: Wolfgang Amonat

BTR BERATUNG UND TREUHAND RING GmbH
Huyssenallee 99-103, 4300 ESSEN 1
Mailing Address: Postfach 10 21 25, 4300 ESSEN 1
Tel: + *49* (201) 23 10 14 *Fax:* + *49* (201) 22 89 81
Contact: Hermann Krüger

BTR BERATUNG UND TREUHAND RING GmbH
Plaza Hamburger Allee 2-10, 6000 FRANKFURT 90
Tel: + *49* (69) 77 20 06 *Fax:* + *49* (69) 70 18 04
Contact: Jürgen Ott

BTR BERATUNG UND TREUHAND RING GmbH
Hildastrasse 25, 7800 FREIBURG
Tel: + *49* (761) 7 20 78 *Fax:* + *49* (761) 70 15 16
Contact: Hubert Welte

BTR BERATUNG UND TREUHAND RING GmbH
Hindenburgstrasse 4-8, 5270 GUMMERSBACH 1
Mailing Address: Postfach 10 07 61, 5270 GUMMERSBACH 1
Tel: + 49 (2261) 6 40 51 *Fax:* + 49 (2261) 2 66 90
Contact: Burkhardt Müller

BTR BERATUNG UND TREUHAND RING GmbH
Joliot-Curie-Platz 1, 4020 HALLE
Tel: + 37 (46) 3 61 87 *Fax:* + 37 (46) 3 61 87

BTR BERATUNG UND TREUHAND RING GmbH
Burchardstrasse 17, 2000 HAMBURG 1
Tel: + 49 (40) 3 39 71 10 *Fax:* + 49 (40) 32 64 85
Contact: Albrecht Müller von Blumencron

BTR BERATUNG UND TREUHAND RING GmbH
Hohenzollernstrasse 13, 3000 HANNOVER 1
Tel: + 49 (511) 3 40 40 *Fax:* + 49 (511) 3 40 41 40
Contact: Hartwig Scholz

BTR BERATUNG UND TREUHAND RING GmbH
Diezmannstrasse 20, 7064 LEIPZIG
Tel: + 37 (41) 4 96 22 30 *Fax:* + 37 (41) 4 96 22 30

BTR BERATUNG UND TREUHAND RING GmbH
Max-Joseph-Strasse 7b, 8000 MUNICH 2
Tel: + 49 (89) 5 51 70 80 *Fax:* + 49 (89) 55 17 08 10
Contact: Karl F. Maierhofer

BTR BERATUNG UND TREUHAND RING GmbH
Regerstrasse 19, 7000 STUTTGART 1
Tel: + 49 (711) 69 91 10 *Fax:* + 49 (711) 6 99 11 51
Contact: Horst Ott

Total Number of Offices: 17

BUSE, KOCH, GORSLER, NESSELHAUF, MOERCHEN

Abteistrasse 57, 2000 HAMBURG 13
Tel: + 49 (40) 41 29 81
Fax: + 49 (40) 4 44 82 23

European Affiliation: IAG International

International Contact: Bernd Koch
Ines Heydach

CLIENT SERVICES

Litigation/Legal Services, Taxation (Corporate), Taxation (International)

OTHER OFFICES

BUSE, KOCH, GORSLER, NESSELHAUF, MOERCHEN
Neue Ross-Strasse 11, 1020 BERLIN
Tel: + 37 (2) 2 79 17 60 *Fax:* + 37 (2) 2 79 17 60

Total Number of Offices: 2

DR. CLARENZ - DR ZACHARIAS

Kaiser-Wilhelm-Ring 24, 5000 COLOGNE 1
Tel: + 49 (221) 13 20 61
Fax: + 49 (221) 12 46 62

European Affiliation: Moores Rowland International

International Contact: Harald Weese

DR. H. CLAUSS - DR. E. PAAEL

Achtermannstrasse 11, 4400 MÜNSTER
Tel: + 49 (251) 51 10 98
Fax: + 49 (251) 5 81 46

European Affiliation: Summit International Associates Inc

International Contact: Helmut Clauss

CONFIDA AG

Rathausstrasse 12, 2000 HAMBURG 1
Tel: + 49 (40) 33 50 87
Fax: + 49 (40) 32 19 43

European Affiliation: Eura-Audit International

International Contact: Dr. H. Schmidt
Dr. A. Kosanke

COOPERS & LYBRAND/TREUHAND VEREINIGUNG AG

Wöhlerstrasse 6-10, 6000 FRANKFURT 1
Tel: + 49 (69) 7 11 00
Fax: + 49 (69) 7 11 00
Mailing Address: Postfach 17 05 52, 6000 FRANKFURT 1

European Affiliation: Coopers & Lybrand Europe

International Contact: Dr. Wolf Kroneberger

Total Staff: 3,500

CONTACT INFORMATION

Managing Partner: Dr. Wolf Kroneberger
Corporate Finance: Günther Betz
Management Consultancy: Herbert Sielhorst
Tax: Heinz-Peter Müller
Tax: Michael Bullinger
Actuarial & Benefits: Hans Georg Klein

CLIENT SERVICES

All Services

Industry Specialisations: Automotive, Banking, Chemicals, Communications, Engineering, Food &, Drink, Insurance, Pharmaceuticals

OTHER OFFICES

COOPERS & LYBRAND/TREUHAND-VEREINIGUNG AG
Kurfürstendamm 178, 1000 BERLIN 15
Mailing Address: Postfach 15 07 41, 1000 BERLIN 15
Tel: + 49 (30) 8 81 80 18 *Fax:* + 49 (30) 8 81 95 08
Contact: Hans-Jürgen Warlich

COOPERS & LYBRAND/TREUHAND-VEREINIGUNG AG
Wallstrasse 17-21, 1020 BERLIN-MITTE
Tel: + 49 (372) 2780 10
Contact: Björn Ahrenkiel

COOPERS & LYBRAND/TREUHAND-VEREINIGUNG AG
Welle 8, 4800 BIELEFELD 1
Tel: + 49 (521) 17 10 11 *Fax:* + 49 (521) 17 69 47
Contact: Hans-Helmut Kebschull

COOPERS & LYBRAND/TREUHAND-VEREINIGUNG AG
Brückenstrasse 12, 9001 CHEMNITZ
Tel: + 37 (71) 8 55 21 11
Contact: Christian Bergmann

COOPERS & LYBRAND/TREUHAND-VEREINIGUNG AG
Münzmeisterhaus, 8630 COBURG
Mailing Address: Postfach 15 44, 8630 COBURG
Tel: + 49 (9561) 9 50 91 *Fax:* + 49 (9561) 9 47 59
Contact: Jürgen Hahn

COOPERS & LYBRAND/TREUHAND-VEREINIGUNG AG
Hohenzollering 21-23, 5000 COLOGNE 1
Tel: + 49 (221) 2 08 40 *Fax:* + 49 (221) 25 23 35
Contact: Heinz-Peter Müller

COOPERS & LYBRAND/TREUHAND-VEREINIGUNG AG
Florianstrasse 3, 4600 DORTMUND 1
Tel: + 49 (231) 12 30 40 *Fax:* + 49 (231) 10 45 51
Contact: Manfred Wetzstein

COOPERS & LYBRAND/TREUHAND-VEREINIGUNG AG
Grunaer Strasse 2, 8012 DRESDEN
Tel: + *37* (51) 4 87 43 52
Contact: Joachim Werckenthin

COOPERS & LYBRAND/TREUHAND-VEREINIGUNG AG
Freiligrathstrasse 1, 4000 DUSSELDORF 30
Mailing Address: Postfach 78 26, 4000 DUSSELDORF 1
Tel: + *49* (211) 49 90 83 *Fax:* + *49* (211) 4 98 04 94
Contact: Johannes Stützel

COOPERS & LYBRAND/TREUHAND-VEREINIGUNG AG
Rüttenscheider Stern 5, 4300 ESSEN
Mailing Address: Postfach 10 19 42, 4300 ESSEN 1
Tel: + *49* (201) 7 29 00 *Fax:* + *49* (201) 77 58 13

COOPERS & LYBRAND/TREUHAND-VEREINIGUNG AG
Erbprinzenstrasse 2a, 7800 FREIBURG
Tel: + *49* (761) 3 10 63 *Fax:* + *49* (761) 3 10 64
Contact: Hans Peter Kerkermeier

COOPERS & LYBRAND/TREUHAND-VEREINIGUNG AG
Jungfernstieg 51, 2000 HAMBURG 36
Mailing Address: Postfach 30 54 26, 2000 HAMBURG 36
Tel: + *49* (40) 3 50 81 50 *Fax:* + *49* (40) 34 53 48
Contact: Ingeborg Köhler

COOPERS & LYBRAND/TREUHAND-VEREINIGUNG AG
Landschaftstrasse 6a, 3000 HANNOVER 1
Tel: + *49* (511) 32 63 41 *Fax:* + *49* (511) 32 92 24
Contact: Gerhard Wrede

COOPERS & LYBRAND/TREUHAND-VEREINIGUNG AG
Gartenstrasse 82-84, 7500 KARLSRUHE 1
Mailing Address: Postfach 63 29, 7500 KARLSRUHE 1
Tel: + *49* (721) 84 00 20 *Fax:* + *49* (721) 8 40 02 32
Contact: Klaus Kaiser

COOPERS & LYBRAND/TREUHAND-VEREINIGUNG AG
Opernstrasse 2, 3500 KASSEL
Tel: + *49* (561) 71 29 20 *Fax:* + *49* (561) 77 08 88
Contact: Rudolf Lieberum

COOPERS & LYBRAND/TREUHAND-VEREINIGUNG AG
Arno-Nitzsche-Strasse 43-45, 7030 LEIPZIG
Tel: + *37* (41) 8 84 10
Contact: Dr. Gerhard Haustein

COOPERS & LYBRAND/TREUHAND-VEREINIGUNG AG
Breite Strasse 95-97, 2400 LÜBECK 1
Tel: + *49* (451) 7 10 17 *Fax:* + *49* (451) 7 88 08
Contact: Manfred Golgert

COOPERS & LYBRAND/TREUHAND-VEREINIGUNG AG
Walter-Rathenau-Strasse 43, 3024 MAGDEBURG
Tel: + *37* (91) 5 82 71
Contact: Dr Leopold Horstmann

COOPERS & LYBRAND/TREUHAND-VEREINIGUNG AG
Prielmayerstrasse 3, 8000 MUNICH 2
Tel: + *49* (89) 51 40 10 *Fax:* + *49* (89) 5 14 01 49
Contact: Ludwig Glasel

COOPERS & LYBRAND/TREUHAND-VEREINIGUNG AG
Theodorstrasse 3, 8500 NUREMBERG 20
Tel: + *49* (911) 53 40 20 *Fax:* + *49* (911) 53 40 27
Contact: Dr. Winfried Morck

COOPERS & LYBRAND/TREUHAND-VEREINIGUNG AG
Simter Strasse 6, 6780 PIRMASENS
Tel: + *49* (6331) 7 30 15 *Fax:* + *49* (6331) 3 14 91
Contact: Werner Kaucher

COOPERS & LYBRAND/TREUHAND-VEREINIGUNG AG
Am Leuchtturm 15, 2350 ROSTOCK-WARNEMÜNDE
Tel: + *37* (81) 50 51 *Fax:* + *37* (81) 5 53 75
Contact: Dr. Günter Pubanz

COOPERS & LYBRAND/TREUHAND-VEREINIGUNG AG
Spandauer Strasse 18, 5900 SIEGEN
Tel: + *49* (271) 33 60 37 *Fax:* + *49* (271) 33 91 62
Contact: Jürgen Naskrent

COOPERS & LYBRAND/TREUHAND-VEREINIGUNG AG
Birkenwaldstrasse 163, 7000 STUTTGART 1
Tel: + *49* (711) 25 10 81 *Fax:* + *49* (711) 2 57 91 10
Contact: Jan Rogmans

Total Number of Offices: 25

TREUARBEIT AG

Bockenheimer Anlage 15, 6000 FRANKFURT 1
Tel: + *49* (69) 7 12 30
Fax: + *49* (69) 7 12 34 59
Mailing Address: Postfach 11 18 42, 6000 FRANKFURT 1

European Affiliation: Coopers & Lybrand Europe

International Contact: Prof. Dr. Karl-Heinz Forster

CONTACT INFORMATION

Managing Partner: Dr. Karl-Heinz Forster
Corporate Finance: Wolfgang Wagner
Tax: Heinz-Peter Muller
Actuarial & Benefits: Karl-Heinz Kilion

CLIENT SERVICES

All Services

Industry Specialisations: Automotive, Banking, Chemicals, Communications, Engineering, Food & Drink, Insurance

OTHER OFFICES

TREUARBEIT AG
Emser Strasse 40-41, 1000 BERLIN 15
Mailing Address: Postfach 120, 1000 BERLIN 15
Tel: + *49* (30) 88 84 20 20 *Fax:* + *49* (30) 88 42 02 57
Contact: Dr. Hugo-Manfred Kriebel

TREUARBEIT AG
Bundeskanzlerplatz, Bonn-Center HI-402, 5300 BONN 1
Tel: + *49* (228) 21 20 21 *Fax:* + *49* (228) 22 00 34
Contact: Georg Rabenstein

TREUARBEIT AG
Hanseatenhof 6 (Bremer Carrée), 2800 BREMEN 1
Tel: + *49* (421) 30 89 90 *Fax:* + *49* (421) 3 08 99 50
Contact: Gert-Michael Raabe

TREUARBEIT AG
Breischeidstrasse 80, 0845 DRESDEN
Tel: + *37* (51) 2 25 82 27
Contact: Friedrich Brune

TREUARBEIT AG
Auf'm Hennekamp 47, 4000 DUSSELDORF 1
Tel: + *49* (211) 3 39 41 *Fax:* + *49* (211) 3 39 42 60
Contact: Günter Siepe

TREUARBEIT UNTERNEHMENSBERATUNG GmbH
Kopstadtplatz 13, 4300 ESSEN 1
Tel: + *49* (201) 81 08 50 *Fax:* + *49* (201) 8 10 85 22
Contact: Rolf Bergmann

TREUARBEIT UNTERNEHMENSBERATUNG GmbH
Bockenheimer Anlage 15, 6000 FRANKFURT 1
Mailing Address: Postfach 11 18 42, 6000 FRANKFURT 1
Tel: + *49* (69) 7 12 35 24 *Fax:* + *49* (69) 7 12 34 59

TREUARBEIT AG
New-York Ring 13, 2000 HAMBURG 60
Tel: + *49* (40) 6 37 80 *Fax:* + *49* (40) 6 37 81 03
Contact: Dr. Günter Buschmann

TREUARBEIT UNTERNEHMENSBERATUNG GmbH
New-York-Ring 13, 2000 HAMBURG 60
Mailing Address: Postfach 60 27 20, 2000 HAMBURG 60
Tel: + *49* (40) 6 37 80 *Fax:* + *49* (40) 63 71 20
Contact: Klause Blöse

TREUARBEIT AG
Fuhrberger Strasse 5, 3000 HANNOVER 61
Tel: + *49* (511) 5 35 71 *Fax:* + *49* (511) 5 35 72 87
Contact: Hermann Eichner

TREUARBEIT AG
Untere Königsstrasse 79, 3500 KASSEL
Tel: + *49* (561) 1 41 07 *Fax:* + *49* (561) 77 83 38
Contact: Manfred Meyer

TREUARBEIT AG
Faulstrasse 18, 2300 KIEL 1
Tel: + *49* (431) 9 58 54 *Fax:* + *49* (431) 9 51 38
Contact: Harald von Hoch

TREUARBEIT AG
Georgiring 1-3, 7010 LEIPZIG
Tel: + *37* (41) 79 95 33 13 *Fax:* + *37* (41) 7 95 34 16
Contact: Dr. Georg Kämpfer

TREUARBEIT AG
Breiter Weg 193, 3024 MAGDEBURG
Tel: + *37* (91) 3 33 03
Contact: Dieter Thiemann

TREUARBEIT AG
Romanstrasse 35, 8000 MUNICH 19
Tel: + *49* (89) 1 79 00 40 *Fax:* + *49* (89) 17 90 04 49
Contact: Adolf Eiber

TREUARBEIT AG
Heinrich-Böcking-Strasse 1, 6600 SAARBRÜCKEN 3
Tel: + *49* (681) 68 79 40 *Fax:* + *49* (681) 6 87 94 54
Contact: Dr. Heinrich Voss

TREUARBEIT UNTERNEHMENSBERATUNG GmbH
Talstrasse 15, 6600 SAARBRÜCKEN
Tel: + *49* (681) 5 50 33 35 *Fax:* + *49* (681) 58 24 14
Contact: Ernst Jeanrond

TREUARBEIT AG
Rotebühlplatz 20a, 7000 STUTTGART 1
Tel: + *49* (711) 29 94 11 *Fax:* + *49* (711) 29 94 13
Contact: Hans Wagener

TREUARBEIT AG
Rimbachstrasse 30, 6000 SUHL
Tel: + *37* (66) 2 10 23
Contact: Hermann Eber-Huber

Total Number of Offices: 20

DFK GERMANY

Maria-Theresia Strasse 5, 8000 MUNICH 80
Tel: + *49* (89) 4 16 09 90
Fax: + *49* (89) 41 60 99 45

European Affiliation: DFK International

International Contact: Christopher Schönberger

ASSOCIATED FIRMS

NIETHAMMER, POSEWANG & PARTNER GmbH
Jessenstrasse 4, Postfach 50 11 25, 2000 HAMBURG 50
Tel: + *49* (40) 38 96 01 *Fax:* + *49* (40) 38 26 93
Contact: Wolfgang Krug

PETERS, SCHÖNBERGER & PARTNER
Maria-Theresia-Strasse 5, 8000 MUNICH 80
Tel: + *49* (89) 4 16 09 90 *Fax:* + *49* (89) 41 60 99 45
Contact: Christopher Schönberger

PETERS, SCHÖNBERGER & PARTNER
Rähnitzgasse 20 b, 8060 DRESDEN
Tel: + *37* (51) 5 38 49 *Fax:* + *37* (51) 5 38 49
Contact: Matthias Schreiber

RÖLFS, BUHLER, STÜMPGES, HAUCK & PARTNER
Neanderstrasse 34, Postfach 1265, 4006 ERKRATH 1, Dusseldorf
Tel: + *49* (211) 24 60 84 *Fax:* + *49* (211) 24 26 78
Contact: Joachim Rölfs

RÖLFS, BUHLER, STÜMPGES, HAUCK & PARTNER
Kaiserstrasse 22, 4600 DORTMUND 1
Tel: + *49* (231) 5 70 71 *Fax:* + *49* (231) 5 70 74
Contact: Michael Stümpges

RÖLFS, DR. RÖDL, SLOWINSKI & PARTNER GmbH
Holzhausenstrasse 44, 6000 FRANKFURT 1
Tel: + *49* (69) 55 02 73 *Fax:* + *49* (69) 59 86 26
Contact: Harald Lauber

Total Number of Offices: 7

DR. DORNBACH & PARTNER

Markenbildchenweg 20, 5400 KOBLENZ
Tel: + *49* (261) 13 90 70
Fax: + *49* (261) 1 39 07 65

European Affiliation: GMN International

International Contact: Dr. Eike Dornbach

Partners:	7
Professional staff:	108
Non-professional staff:	25
Total Staff:	**140**

OTHER OFFICES

DR. DORNBACH, DARSCHEID & PARTNER GmbH
Clara-Zetkin-Platz 3, 4500 DESSAU
Tel: + *37* (47) 72 95
Contact: Dr. Hans Gehrz

Total Number of Offices: 3

DORNHOF KLOSS UND PARTNER GmbH

Mönckebergstrasse 18, Domhof, 2000 HAMBURG 1
Tel: + *49* (40) 3 29 10 00
Fax: + *49* (40) 32 91 00 49
Mailing Address: Postfach 11 06 49, 2000 HAMBURG 11

European Affiliation: Summit International Associates Inc

International Contact: Heinrich Dornhof

Partners:	7
Professional staff:	39
Non-professional staff:	20
Total Staff:	**66**

FEE INCOME

Year End: 31.12.91	**DM**	**%**
Accountancy & Audit:	3,240,000	49.0
Insolvency:	352,000	5.0
Tax:	3,002,000	46.0
Total:	**6,594,000**	

CONTACT INFORMATION

Audit: J. Andreas Schnapauff
Audit: Verena V. Tresckow
Corporate Finance & Tax: Heinrich Dornhof
Management Consultancy: Juergen Stenwedel
Administration & Tax: Thomas Kloss
Administration: Juergen Stenwedel
Public Sector: Horst Mathes
Tax: Harald Johst

▷

Germany

CLIENT SERVICES
Accountancy (General), Audit, Corporate Finance Advice, Mergers & Acquisitions, Taxation (Corporate), Taxation (International), Trust Settlement & Estates

OTHER OFFICES

DORNHOF KLOSS UND PARTNER GmbH
Semperstrasse 2, 8020 DRESDEN
Tel: + *37* (51) 4 64 85 03 *Fax:* + *37* (51) 4 64 86 65
Contact: Dietmar Krueger

DORNHOF KLOSS UND PARTNER GmbH
Marienstrasse 5, 7000 STUTTGART 1
Tel: + *49* (711) 22 14 18 *Fax:* + *49* (711) 22 62 41
Contact: Harald Johst

DORNHOF KLOSS UND PARTNER GmbH
Am Packhof 6, 2758 SCHWERIN
Tel: + *37* (84) 86 35 88
Contact: Dr. Siegfried Friedrich

DORNHOF KLOSS UND PARTNER GmbH
Annaberger Strasse 73, 9010 CHEMNITZ
Tel: + *37* (71) 56 36 43 *Fax:* + *37* (71) 56 32 04
Contact: Renate Lang

Total Number of Offices: 6

DUSSELDORFER TREUHAND-GESELLSCHAFT ALTENBURG & TEWES AG

Am Wehrhahn/Worringer Strasse 2-4, 4000 DUSSELDORF 1
Tel: + *49* (211) 16 10 24
Fax: + *49* (211) 35 34 01

European Affiliation: Clark Kenneth Leventhal

International Contact: Jürgen Spielberg

Partners:	6
Professional staff:	65
Non-professional staff:	35
Total Staff:	**106**

FEE INCOME

Year End: 1990	%
Accountancy & Audit:	53.0
Tax:	19.0
Other:	28.0

CLIENT SERVICES
Accountancy (General), Audit, Corporate Finance Advice, Insolvency & Corporate Restructuring, Management & Business Advice, Taxation (Corporate), Taxation (International)

OTHER OFFICES

DTG ALTENBURG & TEWES AG
Juri-Gagarin-Ring 152, 5020 ERFURT
Tel: + *37* (61) 57 23 31
Contact: Dr Jens Pensel

DTG ALTENBURG & TEWES AG
Dr. Kurt-Fischer-Strasse 2, 7010 LEIPZIG
Tel: + *37* (41) 7 13 92 26
Contact: Dr. Paul J. Heuser

DTG ALTENBURG & TEWES AG
Heinrich-Rau-Allee 8, 1560 POTSDAM
Tel: + *37* (33) 2 30 05
Contact: Dr. Jens Pensel

DTG ALTENBURG & TEWES AG
Werth 91-93, 5600 WUPPERTAL 2
Tel: + *49* (202) 59 40 68 *Fax:* + *49* (202) 59 55 49
Contact: Jürgen Spielberg

Total Number of Offices: 5

DR. EBNER, DR. STOLZ UND PARTNER GmbH

Stiftstrasse 5, 7000 STUTTGART 1
Tel: + *49* (711) 2 04 90
Fax: + *49* (711) 2 04 93 33
Mailing Address: Postfach 10 12 53, 7000 STUTTGART 1

European Affiliation: SC International

International Contact: Gerhard Weigl

OTHER OFFICES

DR. EBNER, DR. STOLZ UND PARTNER GmbH
Steinstrasse 27, 4000 DUSSELDORF 1
Tel: + *49* (211) 8 07 77 *Fax:* + *49* (211) 32 84 59
Contact: Thomas Bula

DR. EBNER, DR. STOLZ UND PARTNER GmbH
Wolfgang-Heinze-Strasse 51, 7030 LEIPZIG
Mailing Address: Postfach 92, 7030 LEIPZIG
Tel: + *37* (41) 31 06 87 *Fax:* + *37* (41) 31 04 63
Contact: Beate Winkow

Total Number of Offices: 5

DR. HANS-UWE EHLERS

Brahmsallee 18, 2000 HAMBURG 13
Tel: + *49* (40) 44 15 51
Fax: + *49* (40) 45 59 57

European Affiliation: Independent Accountants International

International Contact: Dr. Hans-Uwe Ehlers

HANS ESCHER

Zeil 29-31, 6000 FRANKFURT AM MAIN 1
Tel: + *49* (69) 28 06 45
Fax: + *49* (69) 29 35 23

European Affiliation: TGI International

International Contact: Hans Escher

EVERS, POHL & REISCHER GmbH

Widenmayerstrasse 36, 8000 MUNICH 22
Tel: + *49* (89) 22 91 46
Fax: + *49* (89) 22 96 33

European Affiliation: The Channel International Association

International Contact: Clemens Pohl

FALK & CO GmbH

Slevogtstrasse 6, 6900 HEIDELBERG
Tel: + *49* (6221) 39 90
Fax: + *49* (6221) 37 40 69

European Affiliation: Moores Rowland International

International Contact: Dieter Stocker

OTHER OFFICES

FALK & CO GmbH
Beethovenstrasse 29, 6000 FRANKFURT
Tel: + *49* (69) 74 01 56 *Fax:* + *49* (69) 75 17 32
Contact: Armin Grothe

FALK & CO GmbH
Schwerdstrasse 5, 6720 SPEYER
Tel: + *49* (6232) 7 50 38 *Fax:* + *49* (6232) 2 66 69
Contact: Hans Peter Ertle

Total Number of Offices: 3

▷

"FIDES" TREUHANDGESELLSCHAFT REINFENRATH & CO

Contrescarpe 97, 2800 BREMEN 1
Tel: +49 (421) 3 01 30
Fax: +49 (421) 3 01 31 00
Mailing Address: Postfach 10 57 27, 2800 BREMEN 1

European Affiliation: Clark Kenneth Leventhal

International Contact: Günter von Bremen

Partners:	11
Professional staff:	115
Non-professional staff:	44
Total Staff:	**170**

FEE INCOME

Year End: 1990	%
Accountancy & Audit:	50.0
Tax:	50.0

CLIENT SERVICES

Accountancy (General), Audit, Taxation (Corporate), Taxation (International)

OTHER OFFICES

"FIDES" TREUHANDGESELLSCHAFT REINFENRATH & CO
Steinstrasse 27, VIII, 2000 HAMBURG 1
Tel: +49 (40) 33 75 67 *Fax:* +49 (40) 33 86 28
Contact: Horst Droemer

Total Number of Offices: 2

FISCHER + PARTNER KG

Flachsland 29-31, 2000 HAMBURG 76
Tel: +49 (40) 2 98 00 10
Fax: +49 (40) 29 80 01 30

European Affiliation: Morison International

International Contact: Hans Riesch

Partners:	7
Professional staff:	41
Non-professional staff:	18
Total Staff:	**66**

FEE INCOME

Year End: 31.12.90	**DM**
Accountancy & Audit:	2,800,000
Insolvency:	100,000
Consultancy:	500,000
Tax:	2,900,000
Total:	**6,300,000**

CONTACT INFORMATION

Managing Partner: Helmut Fischer
Accountancy (General): Gerhard Briese
Audit: Hans Riesch
Public Sector: Dr. Wilhelm Lienau
Accountancy & Tax: Bernhard Glier
Corporate Finance & Consultancy: Helmut Fischer
Insolvency & Tax: Hans-Christoph Seewald
Tax & Management Consultancy: Heinz Meyer

CLIENT SERVICES

Accountancy (General), Audit, Corporate Finance Advice, Insolvency & Corporate Restructuring, Management & Business Advice, Mergers & Acquisitions, Taxation (Corporate), Taxation (International)

OTHER OFFICES

FISCHER + PARTNER
Parkstrasse 2, 2850 BREMERHAVEN
Tel: +49 (471) 8 99 30 *Fax:* +49 (471) 89 93 75

FISCHER + PARTNER KG
Bürgermeister Schmidt Strasse 56, 2800 BREMEN
Tel: +49 (421) 3 08 96 01 *Fax:* +49 (421) 3 08 96 75
Contact: Hans-Christoph Seewald

Total Number of Offices: 4

FRANZ X. KIRSCHNER E-CONSULTING GmbH

Schlosspark Gern, 8330 EGGENFELDEN
Tel: +49 (87) 21 40 41
Fax: +49 (87) 21 75 24

European Affiliation: The International Group of Accounting Firms Ltd (IGAF)

International Contact: Franz Kirshner

FRÜCHTNICHT UND PARTNER

Amelungstrasse 5, 2000 HAMBURG 36
Tel: +49 (40) 35 15 91
Fax: +49 (40) 34 40 22

European Affiliation: TGI International

International Contact: Hans-Peter Franck

DR. GENAUST-BÖTTCHER-BÜCHL

Mittelweg 118, Ecke Alsterchaussee, 2000 HAMBURG 13
Tel: +49 (40) 44 74 44
Fax: +49 (40) 44 74 10

European Affiliation: Moores Rowland International

International Contact: Dr Paul Genaust

GOUTIER, KNOPF, TULLOCH & PARTNER

Holzhausenstrasse 25, 6000 FRANKFURT
Tel: +49 (69) 59 07 57
Fax: +49 (69) 55 41 05

European Affiliation: Clark Kenneth Leventhal

International Contact: Anthony D. Tulloch

Partners:	4
Professional staff:	2
Non-professional staff:	4
Total Staff:	**10**

FEE INCOME

Year End: 1990	%
Tax:	70.0
Other:	30.0

CLIENT SERVICES

Accountancy (General), Corporate Finance Advice, Management & Business Advice, Taxation (Corporate), Taxation (International)

OTHER OFFICES

GOUTIER, KNOPF, TULLOCH & PARTNER
Schutzallee 85, 1000 BERLIN 37
Tel: +49 (30) 8 11 73 00 *Fax:* +49 (30) 8 11 24 85
Contact: Dr. Thomas Kaligin

Total Number of Offices: 2

▷

GRANT THORNTON GmbH

Kastanienallee 9/11, 2900 OLDENBURG
Tel: +*49* (441) 9 71 00
Fax: +*49* (441) 9 71 02 30

European Affiliation: Grant Thornton International

International Contact: Dr. Martin Gutsche

Partners:	20
Professional staff:	219
Non-professional staff:	91
Total Staff:	**330**

FEE INCOME

Year End: 1990	**DM**
Total:	**26,219,000**

CONTACT INFORMATION

Managing Partner: Dr. Martin Gutsche

OTHER OFFICES

GRANT THORNTON GmbH
Bruno-Taut-Strasse 8, 1185 BERLIN
Tel: +*37* (30) 26 76 26 03 ***Fax:*** +*37* (30) 26 76 24 22

GRANT THORNTON GmbH
Gereonstrasse 16, 5000 COLOGNE 1
Tel: +*49* (221) 12 01 63 ***Fax:*** +*49* (221) 13 79 88

GRANT THORNTON GmbH
Lyoner Strasse 30, 6000 FRANKFURT 71
Tel: +*49* (69) 6 66 61 40 ***Fax:*** +*49* (69) 6 66 61 76

GRANT THORNTON GmbH
Mittelweg 180, 2000 HAMBURG 13
Tel: +*49* (40) 41 52 20 ***Fax:*** +*49* (40) 41 52 21 11

GRANT THORNTON GmbH
Erich-Weinert-Platz 3/4, 7010 LEIPZIG
Tel: +*37* (41) 7 18 24 68

GRANT THORNTON GmbH
Ungererstrasse 75, 8000 MUNICH 40
Tel: +*49* (89) 3 60 80 50 ***Fax:*** +*49* (89) 3 61 65 40

GRANT THORNTON GmbH
Am Fischkombinat I, 2510 ROSTOCK
Tel: +*37* (81) 8 11 22 54 ***Fax:*** +*37* (81) 8 11 24 59

GRANT THORNTON GmbH
Gablenberger Haupstrasse 77, 7000 STUTTGART 1
Tel: +*49* (711) 46 40 36 ***Fax:*** +*49* (711) 46 40 26

Total Number of Offices: 9

G.R.T. GESELLSCHAFT FÜR REVISION UND TREUHAND mbH

Brönerstrasse 11, 6000 FRANKFURT
Tel: +*49* (69) 28 32 84
Fax: +*49* (69) 28 78 11

European Affiliation: TEG (The European Group of Accounting & Auditing Firms)

International Contact: Willi Mecklenburg

OTHER OFFICES

G.R.T. GESELLSCHAFT FÜR REVISION UND TREUHAND mbH
Klosterstrasse 56/58, 4000 DUSSELDORF 1
Mailing Address: Postfach 24 01 42, 4000 DUSSELDORF 1
Tel: +*49* (211) 16 90 10 ***Fax:*** +*49* (211) 1 69 01 19

Total Number of Offices: 2

GTW - TREUHAND GmbH

Briennerstrasse 16, 8000 MUNICH 2
Tel: +*49* (89) 28 60 01
Fax: +*49* (89) 2 80 03 79

European Affiliation: Moores Rowland International

International Contact: Dr. Siegfried Zitzelsberger

HAAG, HAAG & PARTNERS

Max Beckmann Strasse 53, 6000 FRANKFURT AM MAIN 70
Tel: +*49* (69) 68 10 58
Fax: +*49* (69) 68 22 97

European Affiliation: Affiliated Conference of Practising Accountants International (ACPA)

HAARMANN, HEMMELRATH & PARTNER

Effnerstrasse 38, 8000 MUNICH 81
Tel: +*49* (89) 92 40 00
Fax: +*49* (89) 9 10 20 47

European Affiliation: DRM Internationally

International Contact: Dr. Wilhelm Haarmann

Partners:	10
Professional staff:	29
Non-professional staff:	19
Total Staff:	**58**

CONTACT INFORMATION

Audit: Bodo Richardt
Tax (International): Dr. Alexander Hemmelrath

CLIENT SERVICES

Audit, Taxation (International)

OTHER OFFICES

HAARMANN, HEMMELRATH & PARTNER
Heinrich-Heine-Allee 22, 4000 DUSSELDORF 1
Tel: +*49* (211) 1 64 50 ***Fax:*** +*49* (211) 1 64 51 33
Contact: Dr. Bernd Sagasser

HAARMANN, HEMMELRATH & PARTNER
Budapesterstrasse 40, 1000 BERLIN 30
Tel: +*37* (30) 26 47 30 ***Fax:*** +*37* (30) 26 47 31 33
Contact: Detlef Olufs

Total Number of Offices: 3

HANSABERATUNG GmbH

Wachtstrasse 17-24, Postfach 10 51 44, 2800 BREMEN 1
Tel: +*49* (421) 32 14 58
Fax: +*49* (421) 32 14 61

European Affiliation: Moores Rowland International

International Contact: Günter R. Meier

W. HARTMANN - W. BEERMANN

Matthiasstrasse 6, 4440 RHEINE 1
Tel: +*49* (5971) 5 51 51
Fax: +*49* (5971) 5 08 45

European Affiliation: Affiliated Conference of Practising Accountants International (ACPA)

International Contact: Wilfried Beermann

DR. HARZEM & PARTNER GmbH

Godesberger Allee 125-127, 5300 BONN 2
Tel: + *49* (228) 81 00 00
Fax: + *49* (228) 8 10 00 20

European Affiliation: Summit International Associates Inc

International Contact: Dr. Rolf Harzem

Partners:	9
Professional staff:	109
Non-professional staff:	41
Total Staff:	**159**

FEE INCOME

Year End: 31.12.91	**DM**	%
Accountancy & Audit:		25.0
Consultancy:		25.0
Tax:		25.0
Other:		25.0
Total:	**16,000,000**	

CONTACT INFORMATION
Managing Partner: Dr. Rolf Harzem

CLIENT SERVICES
All Services

Industry Specialisations: Automotive, Public Services, Hospitals

OTHER OFFICES

BIẞLING & PARTNER GmbH
Godesberger Allee 125-127, 5300 BONN 2
Tel: + *49* (228) 8 10 00 50 *Fax:* + *49* (228) 8 10 00 20

DR. BROCKHUAS, STAHLSCHMIDT, DR. HARZEM GmbH
Leverkusener Strasse 57, 5060 BERGISCH GLADBACH 2
Tel: + *49* (2202) 80 66 *Fax:* + *49* (2202) 80 68
Contact: Dr. Rolf Harzem

DR. HARZEM & PARTNER GmbH
Königstrasse 65, 5303 BORNHEIM 1
Tel: + *49* (2222) 10 33 *Fax:* + *49* (2222) 10 36
Contact: Dr. Rolf Harzem

DR. HARZEM & PARTNER GmbH
Carmanstrasse 48, 5350 EUSKIRCHEN
Tel: + *49* (2251) 5 60 55 *Fax:* + *49* (2251) 7 20 08
Contact: Dr. Rolf Harzem

DR. HARZEM & PARTNER GmbH
Düsseldorfer Strasse 13, 6236 ESCHBORN BEI FRANKFURT
Tel: + *49* (6196) 7 02 30 *Fax:* + *49* (6196) 70 23 30
Contact: Otto Leistner

KNABE, STAHLSCHMIDT, DR. HARZEM GmbH
Kaiserstrasse 35, 5270 GUMMERSBACH 1
Tel: + *49* (2261) 6 10 95 *Fax:* + *49* (2261) 6 65 17
Contact: Dr. Rolf Harzem

SEIBERT, STAHLSCHMIDT, DR. HARZEM GmbH
Walkurenalle 7, 5600 WUPPERTAL 1
Tel: + *49* (202) 74 00 15 *Fax:* + *49* (202) 74 00 17
Contact: Dr. Rolf Harzem

ZEH & PARTNER GmbH
Magdeburgstrasse 11, 6270 IDSTEIN
Tel: + *49* (6126) 59 40 *Fax:* + *49* (6126) 5 94 28

Total Number of Offices: 90

HEINZELMANN & PARTNERS

Babenhäuserstrasse 31, 6057 DIETZENBACH, Frankfurt
Tel: + *49* (6074) 4 34 67
Fax: + *49* (6074) 4 35 78
Mailing Address: Postfach 13 09, 6057 DIETZENBACH, Frankfurt

European Affiliation: Growth & Progress Challenge

International Contact: Siegfried Heinzelmann

Partners:	3
Professional staff:	12
Non-professional staff:	2
Total Staff:	**17**

FEE INCOME

Year End: 31.12.90	%
Accountancy & Audit:	40.0
Consultancy:	20.0
Tax:	40.0

CONTACT INFORMATION
Managing Partner: Siegfried Heinzelmann
Accountancy (General): Susanne Schmidt
Administration: Diana P. Heinzelmann
Tax (Corporate): Mr Gutacker
Partner: Siegfried Heinzelmann

CLIENT SERVICES
Accountancy (General), Audit, Insolvency & Corporate Restructuring, Litigation/Legal Services, Management & Business Advice, Management Buy-outs, Mergers & Acquisitions, Pensions Planning, Value for Money Studies, Taxation (Corporate), Taxation (International), Trust Settlement & Estates, Investment Grants & Subsidies, Foreign Investment in Germany, Treasury Fund Negotiations

ASSOCIATED FIRMS

IPG INDUSTRIEPRÜFUNGS GmbH
Bronnerstrasse 7, 4600 DORTMUND 1
Tel: + *49* (231) 57 90 11 *Fax:* + *49* (231) 57 90 10
Contact: Friedhelm Weber

KNM TREUHAND GmbH
Widenmayerstrasse 27, 8000 MUNICH 22
Tel: + *49* (89) 21 23 09 66 *Fax:* + *49* (89) 21 23 09 66
Contact: Thomas Kantenwein

MÜNDEL & SCAFER
Rheinstrasse 49, 7640 KEHL AM RHEIN
Tel: + *49* (7851) 40 58 *Fax:* + *49* (7851) 59 01
Contact: Mr Mündel

MICHAEL UNKELBACH
Königsallee 13, 4000 DUSSELDORF
Tel: + *49* (211) 13 25 66 *Fax:* + *49* (211) 13 25 66
Contact: Michael Unkelbach

Total Number of Offices: 5

HHG HORWATH & HORWATH GmbH

Alexanderstrasse 12, 7000 STUTTGART 10
Tel: + *49* (711) 2 10 58
Fax: + *49* (711) 23 23 74
Mailing Address: Postfach 10 30 23, 7000 STUTTGART 10

European Affiliation: Horwath International

International Contact: Dr. Werner Schulen

OTHER OFFICES

HORWATH & GELBERT GmbH
Ostbahnhofstrasse 13, 6000 FRANKFURT AM MAIN 1
Tel: + *49* (69) 44 60 51 *Fax:* + *49* (69) 4 99 07 56
Contact: Dr. Werner Schülen

MÖHRLE & PARTNER GmbH
Haferweg 11, 2000 HAMBURG 50
Mailing Address: Postfach 50 10 48, 2000 Hamburg 50
Tel: + *49* (40) 85 39 19 *Fax:* + *49* (40) 85 30 11 66
Contact: Dr. Sigwart Möhrle

▷

ASSOCIATED FIRMS

AWT ALLGEMEINE WIRTSCHAFTSTREUHAND GmbH
Würmtalstrasse 51/51a & 54, 8000 MUNICH 70
Tel: + *49* (89) 71 09 60 *Fax:49* (89) 7 10 96 44
Contact: Alfred Angermann

DRES. BRÖNNER TREUHAND-REVISION GmbH
Hohenzollerndamm 123, 1000 BERLIN 33
Tel: + *49* (30) 82 50 21 *Fax:* + *49* (30) 8 26 62 43
Contact: Dr. Herbert Brönner

HANSEATISCHE MERCATOR TREUHAND GmbH
Haferweg 11, Postfach 50 10 48, 2000 HAMBURG 50
Tel: + *49* (40) 85 30 10 *Fax:* + *49* (40) 85 30 11 66
Contact: Olaf Scharfenberg

Total Number of Offices: 6

HLB TREUHAND GmbH

Hofkamp 24, 5600 WUPPERTAL 1
Tel: + *49* (202) 45 96 00
Fax: + *49* (202) 4 59 60 60
Mailing Address: Postfach 13 01 12, 5600 WUPPERTAL 1

European Affiliation: HLB International

International Contact: Wolfgang Blecken

Partners:	34
Professional staff:	210
Non-professional staff:	73
Total Staff:	**317**

CONTACT INFORMATION

Chairman: Dieter L. Schmidt
Partner: Dr. Werner Linn
Partner: Dr. W. Edelfried Schneider
Partner: Dr. Hein Granobs
Partner: Dr. Bernhard Knagge
Partner: Ernst Kreymborg
Partner: Gisela Starke
Partner: Hans-Joachim Nettelbeck
Partner: Harro K. Ordemann
Partner: Joseph Riehl
Partner: Klaus H. Oppenberg
Partner: Klaus Schierloh
Partner: Wolfgang Blecken

CLIENT SERVICES

Accountancy (General), Audit, Litigation/Legal Services, Management & Business Advice, Taxation (Corporate)

ASSOCIATED FIRMS

COMMERZIAL TREUHAND GmbH/ORDEMANN, DR. KNAGGE & PARTNER
Bismarckstrasse 13, 2900 OLDENBURG
Tel: + *49* (441) 77 00 00 *Fax:* + *49* (441) 7 50 15
Contact: Harro K. Ordemann

COMMERZIAL TREUHAND GmbH/ORDEMANN, DR. KNAGGE & PARTNER
Fuchteler Strasse 37, 2848 VECHTA
Tel: + *49* (4441) 40 31 *Fax:* + *49* (4441) 8 29 34
Contact: C.O. Ordemann

CT COMMERZIAL TREUHAND KG
Bahnhofstrasse 32, 2800 BREMEN 1
Tel: + *49* (421) 17 08 48 *Fax:* + *49* (421) 1 51 23
Contact: Dr. Bernhard Knagge

CT COMMERZIAL TREUHAND KG
Bgm. Martin-Donandt-Platz 1, 2850 BREMERHAVEN
Tel: + *49* (471) 4 40 44 *Fax:* + *49* (471) 41 49 92
Contact: Joseph Riehl

DR. DIENST & PARTNER
Rheinstrasse 2a, 5400 KOBLENZ
Tel: + *49* (261) 1 23 41 *Fax:* + *49* (261) 1 23 49
Contact: Dr. W. Edelfried Schneider

DR. GRANOBS & PARTNER GmbH
Kurfurstendamm 46, 1000 BERLIN 15
Tel: + *49* (30) 8 82 72 59 *Fax:* + *49* (30) 8 81 71 61
Contact: Dr. H. Granobs

DR. KLEESE UND PARTNER
Westendplatz 34, 6000 FRANKFURT 1
Tel: + *49* (69) 71 90 10 *Fax:* + *49* (69) 7 19 01 31
Contact: G. Starke

HAMBURGER TREUHAND GESELLSCHAFT KOCH & NETTELBECK
Ferdinandstrasse 47, 2000 HAMBURG 1
Mailing Address: Postfach 10 27 06, 2000 HAMBURG 1
Tel: + *49* (40) 3 23 34 30 *Fax:* + *49* (40) 33 54 54
Contact: Hans-Joachim Nettelbeck

TREUMERKUR DR. SCHMIDT UND PARTNER KG
Fashion House 1, Danziger Strasse 101, 4000 DUSSELDORF 30
Tel: + *49* (211) 4 54 15 02 *Fax:* + *49* (202) 4 59 60 60
Contact: Dieter L. Schmidt

TREUMERKUR DR. SCHMIDT UND PARTNER
Postfach 13 01 12, 5600 WUPPERTAL 1
Tel: + *49* (202) 45 96 00 *Fax:* + *49* (202) 4 59 60 60
Contact: Wolfgang Blecken

TREUMERKUR DR. SCHMIDT UND PARTNER KG
c/o Societat RAE Gaudig, Geyr & Dr. Koll-Mollenhoff, Brabanter Strasse 37-39, 5000 COLOGNE 1
Tel: + *49* (221) 52 10 32 *Fax:* + *49* (221) 52 92 66
Contact: Wolfgang Blecken

DR. SCHUMACHER UND PARTNER GmbH
Piusallee 121, 4400 MUNSTER
Mailing Address: Postfach 74 69, 4400 MÜNSTER
Tel: + *49* (251) 23 06 31 *Fax:* + *49* (251) 2 30 17 95
Contact: Ernst Kreymborg

SEIFRIED, LINN & PARTNER
Barellistrasse 9a, 8000 MUNICH 19
Tel: + *49* (89) 1 79 09 30 *Fax:* + *49* (89) 17 90 93 80
Contact: Dr. W. Linn

Total Number of Offices: 14

DR. HUPPERTZ, WALTER, WIRTZ GmbH

Josefstrasse 53, 4054 NETTETAL 1
Tel: + *49* (2153) 7 20 61
Fax: + *49* (2153) 7 07 12
Mailing Address: Postfach 31 63, 4054 NETTETAL 1

European Affiliation: Midsnell International

International Contact: Peter Walter

Partners:	4
Professional staff:	25
Non-professional staff:	3
Total Staff:	**32**

CONTACT INFORMATION

Managing Partner: Heinz-Peter Wirtz

CLIENT SERVICES

Accountancy (General), Audit, Corporate Finance Advice, Insolvency & Corporate Restructuring, Litigation/Legal Services, Management & Business Advice, Management Buy-outs, Mergers & Acquisitions, Taxation (Corporate), Taxation (International), Trust Settlement & Estates

▷

INTRACONSULT TREUHAND GmbH

Windmühlstrasse 2, 6000 FRANKFURT
Tel: + 49 (69) 2 42 52 20
Fax: + 49 (69) 23 62 10

European Affiliation: Eura-Audit International

International Contact: J. Bamberger

JÄGER

Konigstrasse 62, 6000 STUTTGART 1
Tel: + 49 (711) 29 94 69
Fax: + 49 (711) 2 26 19 07

European Affiliation: Eura-Audit International

International Contact: K.H. Jäger
W. Maier

JESSEN & PARTNER

Geffckenstrasse 21, 2000 HAMBURG 20
Tel: + 49 (40) 47 50 93
Fax: + 49 (40) 46 42 15

European Affiliation: Russell Bedford International

International Contact: Peter Jessen

Total Number of Offices: 3

KIEFFER STUBBEN

Morsenbroicher Weg 200, 4000 DUSSELDORF 30
Tel: + 49 (211) 28 20 28
Fax: + 49 (211) 28 81 96

European Affiliation: The Channel International Association

International Contact: W. Kieffer
D. Stubben

DR. KLEINERTZ UND PARTNER GmbH

Benrather Schlossallee 49-53, 4000 DUSSELDORF 13 (Benrath)
Tel: + 49 (211) 9 96 10
Fax: + 49 (211) 71 46 68

European Affiliation: Moores Rowland International

International Contact: Dr. Arnold Kleinertz

OTHER OFFICES

DR. KLEINERTZ UND PARTNER GmbH
Ruttenscheider Strasse 106, 4300 ESSEN 1
Tel: + 49 (201) 77 40 35 *Fax:* + 49 (201) 77 40 38
Contact: Dr. Dieter Stuckwisch

Total Number of Offices: 2

KPMG

KPMG DEUTSCHE TREUHAND GRUPPE

Beethovenstrasse 8-10, 6000 FRANKFURT 1
Tel: + 49 (69) 7 57 30
Fax: + 49 (69) 74 90 17
Mailing Address: Postfach 11 05 61, 6000 FRANKFURT 1

European Affiliation: KPMG

Partners: 326

Total Staff: 4,500 approx

FEE INCOME

Year End: 31.12.90	DM	%
Accountancy & Audit:	390,000,000	61.3
Consultancy:	60,000,000	9.4
Tax:	110,000,000	17.3
Other:	56,000,000	12.0
Total:	**616,000,000**	

CLIENT SERVICES

Accountancy (General), Audit, Computer Installation, Corporate Finance Advice, Insolvency & Corporate Restructuring, Litigation/Legal Services, Management & Business Advice, Management Buy-outs, Mergers & Acquisitions, Pensions Planning, Value for Money Studies, Taxation (Corporate), Taxation (International), Trust Settlement & Estates, Executive Search, Human Resources, Actuarial Reports, Training & Education

Industry Specialisations: Automotive, Banking & Finance, Insurance, High Tech, Trade, Steel, Machinery

OTHER OFFICES

KPMG DEUTSCHE TREUHAND GESELLSCHAFT
Kurfürstendamm 56, 1000 BERLIN 15
Tel: + 49 (30) 32 90 90 *Fax:* + 49 (30) 3 24 28 32

KPMG DEUTSCHE TREUHAND GESELLSCHAFT
Ritterstrasse 19, 4800 BIELEFELD
Tel: + 49 (521) 17 11 66 *Fax:* + 49 (521) 17 10 33

KPMG DEUTSCHE TREUHAND GESELLSCHAFT
Am-Alten-Stadtpark 35, 4630 BOCHUM
Tel: + 49 (234) 5 85 41 *Fax:* + 49 (234) 5 85 41

KPMG DEUTSCHE TREUHAND GESELLSCHAFT
Güldenstrasse 21, 3300 BRAUNSCHWEIG
Tel: + 49 (531) 1 30 61 *Fax:* + 49 (531) 4 55 31

KPMG DEUTSCHE TREUHAND GESELLSCHAFT
Domshof 18-20, 2800 BREMEN 1
Tel: + 49 (421) 33 55 70 *Fax:* + 49 (421) 3 35 57 55

KPMG DEUTSCHE TREUHAND GESELLSCHAFT
Strasse-der-Nationen 12, 9010 CHEMNITZ
Tel: + 37 (71) 65 12 44 13

KPMG DEUTSCHE TREUHAND GESELLSCHAFT
Hardefustrasse 1, 5000 COLOGNE
Tel: + 49 (221) 3 38 80 *Fax:* + 49 (221) 32 49 10

KPMG DEUTSCHE TREUHAND GESELLSCHAFT
Südwall 15, 4600 DORTMUND 1
Tel: + 49 (231) 57 90 64 *Fax:* + 49 (231) 52 10 83

KPMG DEUTSCHE TREUHAND GESELLSCHAFT
Franklinstrasse 20-22, 8020 DRESDEN
Tel: + 37 (51) 4 71 59 09 *Fax:* + 37 (51) 4 71 99 60

KPMG DEUTSCHE TREUHAND GESELLSCHAFT
Am Bonneshof 5, 4000 DUSSELDORF 30
Tel: + 49 (211) 4 57 70 *Fax:* + 49 (211) 4 54 19 87

KPMG DEUTSCHE TREUHAND GESELLSCHAFT
Dalbergsweg 4, 5020 ERFURT
Tel: + 37 (61) 5 15 31 *Fax:* + 37 (61) 2 41 94

KPMG DEUTSCHE TREUHAND GESELLSCHAFT
Hans-Böcker-Allee 5, 3000 HANNOVER 1
Tel: + 49 (40) 32 01 52 33 *Fax:* + 49 (40) 32 01 52 51

KPMG DEUTSCHE TREUHAND GESELLSCHAFT
Arndstrasse 14b, 7030 LEIPZIG
Tel: + 37 (41) 3 98 71 *Fax:* + 37 (41) 3 98 75 00

KPMG DEUTSCHE TREUHAND GESELLSCHAFT
Moislinger Allee 7, 2400 LÜBECK
Tel: + 49 (451) 86 52 53 *Fax:* + 49 (451) 86 15 02

KPMG DEUTSCHE TREUHAND GESELLSCHAFT
Uferstrasse 27, 6500 MAINZ
Tel: + 49 (6131) 23 39 27 *Fax:* + 49 (6131) 22 44 37

▷

KPMG DEUTSCHE TREUHAND GESELLSCHAFT
Mollstrasse 42, 6800 MANNHEIM 1
Tel: + *49* (621) 4 26 70 ***Fax:*** + *49* (621) 4 26 72 00

KPMG DEUTSCHE TREUHAND GESELLSCHAFT
Friedrich-Ebert-Strasse 2, 4330 MÜLHEIM
Tel: + *49* (208) 30 00 50 ***Fax:*** + *49* (208) 3 50 11

KPMG DEUTSCHE TREUHAND GESELLSCHAFT
Uhlandstrasse 8, 8000 MUNICH 2
Tel: + *49* (89) 5 15 91 ***Fax:*** + *49* (89) 53 31 46

KPMG DEUTSCHE TREUHAND GESELLSCHAFT
Stengelstrasse 5, 6600 SAARBRÜCKEN 1
Tel: + *49* (681) 5 40 14 ***Fax:*** + *49* (681) 58 33 86

KPMG DEUTSCHE TREUHAND GESELLSCHAFT
Werkstrasse 2, 2781 SCHWERIN
Tel: + *37* (84) 39 21 82 ***Fax:*** + *37* (84) 39 21 43

KPMG DEUTSCHE TREUHAND GESELLSCHAFT
Tübinger Strasse 8-10, 7000 STUTTGART
Tel: + *49* (711) 22 99 40 ***Fax:*** + *49* (711) 29 89 06

Total Number of Offices: 35

LAUER & DILLER

Maximilianplatz 12, 8000 MUNICH 2
Tel: + *49* (89) 22 55 05
Fax: + *49* (89) 2 91 34 56

European Affiliation: Urbach Hacker Young International

Partners:	2
Professional staff:	16
Non-professional staff:	5
Total Staff:	**23**

FEE INCOME

Year End: 31.12.90	**DM**	**%**
Accountancy & Audit:	1,500,000	71.0
Consultancy:	200,000	10.0
Tax:	400,000	19.0
Total:	**2,100,000**	

CONTACT INFORMATION

Managing Partner: Reinhold Lauer
Accountancy & Audit: Herbert Diller
Tax: Reinhold Lauer

CLIENT SERVICES

Accountancy (General), Audit, Management Buy-outs, Mergers & Acquisitions, Taxation (Corporate), Taxation (International)

Industry Specialisations: Hotel & Restaurant, Film, Building

OTHER OFFICES

LAUER & DILLER
Zimmerstrasse 86-91, 1080 BERLIN
Tel: + *37* (30) 3 91 43 17 ***Fax:*** + *37* (30) 3 91 44 34
Contact: Jürgen Mahle

Total Number of Offices: 2

DR. LEFEVRE & SCHMIDT

Eulenkrugpfad 2, 2000 HAMBURG 67
Tel: + *49* (40) 6 03 12 21
Fax: + *49* (40) 6 03 13 50

European Affiliation: Urbach Hacker Young International

Partners:	2
Non-professional staff:	15
Total Staff:	**17**

FEE INCOME

Year End: 1990	**%**
Accountancy & Audit:	40.0
Consultancy:	10.0
Tax:	40.0
Other:	10.0

CONTACT INFORMATION

Managing Partner: Dr. Bernhard Lefèvre
Managing Partner: Rudolf Schmidt
Tax (International): Uwe Siebert

CLIENT SERVICES

Accountancy (General), Audit, Litigation/Legal Services, Management & Business Advice, Management Buy-outs, Mergers & Acquisitions, Taxation (Corporate), Taxation (International)

Industry Specialisations: Real Estate

DR. LEYH & DR. KOSSOW

Weidenweg 9, 5060 BERGISCH GLADBACH, Cologne
Tel: + *49* (2204) 2 00 90
Fax: + *49* (2204) 20 09 21
Mailing Address: Postfach 30 20 40, 5060 BERGISCH GLADBACH, Cologne

European Affiliation: Urbach Hacker Young International

Partners: 4

FEE INCOME

Year End: 1990	**%**
Accountancy & Audit:	40.0
Insolvency:	10.0
Consultancy:	20.0
Tax:	30.0

CONTACT INFORMATION

Managing Partner: Dr. Bernd H. Kossow
Managing Partner: Dr. Horst Leyh
Accountancy (General): Michael Kettner
Audit: Mr Schröder
Insolvency: Jörg Müller
Administration: Andrea Faulhaber
Tax (Corporate): Dr. Hans Ott
Tax (International): Dr. Bernd H. Kossow
Corporate Finance & Consultancy: Franz B. Daum

OTHER OFFICES

DAUM, DR. KOSSOW, DR. LEYH, DR. OTT STEUERBERATER
Gottleubaer Strasse 5, 8021 DRESDEN
Tel: + *37* (51) 3 46 26 03

DAUM, DR. KOSSOW, DR. LEYH, DR. OTT STEUERBERATER
Gartenstrasse 14, 8300 PIRNA
Tel: + *37* (56) 35 04 ***Fax:*** + *37* (56) 35 04

DR. LEYH & DR. KOSSOW
Berghauser Strasse 62, 5630 REMSCHEID

DR. LEYH, DR. KOSSOW, MÜLLER STEUERBERATUNGSGESELLSCHAFT mbH
Moltkestrasse 12, 5270 GUMMERSBACH
Mailing Address: Postfach 21 02 19, 5270 GUMMERSBACH
Tel: + *49* (2261) 6 63 69 ***Fax:*** + *49* (2261) 6 63 79

SPINDLER, DR. LEYH & DR. KOSSOW STEUERBERATUNGSGESELLSCHAFT
Zollstockgürtel 7, 5000 COLOGNE 51
Tel: + *49* (221) 36 90 55 ***Fax:*** + *49* (221) 36 46 81

Total Number of Offices: 6

▷

DR. HERBERT LINK

Im Birkets 15, 6942 MÖRLENBACH-WEIHER
Tel: + *49* (62) 09 18 80
Fax: + *49* (62) 09 18 81

European Affiliation: TGI International

International Contact: Herbert Link

DRS. R. MATZENBACH & W. THIER

Corneliusstrasse 4, 6000 FRANKFURT 1
Tel: + *49* (69) 74 79 84
Fax: + *49* (69) 74 53 44

European Affiliation: Independent Accountants International

International Contact: Rolf Matzenbach

M.B.B.R. (ET ASSOCIÉS)

Plank Strasse 7, 3010 MAGDEBURG
Tel: + *37* (91) 3 25 39
Fax: + *37* (91) 3 25 39

European Affiliation: Clark Kenneth Leventhal

International Contact: Mathias Bloch

MERCATORPRUFUNG GmbH

Am Buchenbaum 28, 4100 DUISBERG 1
Tel: + *49* (203) 2 55 56
Fax: + *49* (203) 28 73 40
Mailing Address: Postfach 10 09 63, 4100 DUISBERG 1

European Affiliation: Midsnell International

International Contact: D. Eckhard

MEYER-SIEVERS, OPITZ, KILIAN

Petersweg 1a, 2100 HAMBURG 90
Tel: + *49* (40) 77 62 52
Fax: + *49* (40) 7 65 12 35

European Affiliation: IAG International

MS BERATUNGS-UND-TREUHAND-UNION GmbH

Hildesheimer Strasse 9, 3000 HANNOVER 1
Tel: + *49* (511) 28 20 61
Fax: + *49* (511) 28 20 64

European Affiliation: Moore Stephens

International Contact: Wolfgang Gebler

ASSOCIATED FIRMS

DR. BUCHHOLZ, DR. VINKEN, DR. HERKER
Kuhlenwall 8, 4100 DUISBURG 1
Tel: + *49* (203) 2 02 75
Contact: Dr. Rolf Buchholz

DR. FREI, BLUMENAUER & PARTNER
Koenigsteiner Strasse 6a, 6232 BAD SODEN
Tel: + *49* (6196) 2 90 91 *Fax:* + *49* (6196) 2 84 91
Contact: Dr. Juergen Frei

FRIEBE-RISSE-PRINZ & PARTNER
Staberger Strasse 5, 5880 LÜDENSCHEID
Tel: + *49* (2351) 1 53 30 *Fax:* + *49* (2351) 15 33 80
Contact: Dr. Gunter Friebe

HECHT-SCHUBERT-GERHARDT
Knesebeckstrasse 68/69, 1000 BERLIN 12
Tel: + *49* (30) 8 81 40 31 *Fax:* + *49* (30) 8 81 40 34
Contact: Manfred Hecht

ICR INTERCONSULT UND REVISION GmbH
Rotebuehlstrasse 102, 7000 STUTTGART
Tel: + *49* (711) 61 60 83 *Fax:* + *49* (711) 61 01 99
Contact: Hans-Georg Koehler

LOEBA TREUHAND GmbH
Haagener Strasse 25, 7850 LÖRRACH
Tel: + *49* (7621) 40 98 50 *Fax:* + *49* (7621) 40 98 98
Contact: Dr. Manfred Hauser

RING-TREUHAND GmbH
Adalbertstrasse 110, 8000 MUNICH 40
Tel: + *49* (89) 2 71 65 65 *Fax:* + *49* (89) 2 73 08 02
Contact: Elisabeth Puerzer

RINKE TREUHAND GmbH
Wall 39, 5600 WUPPERTAL 1
Tel: + *49* (202) 49 39 10 *Fax:* + *49* (202) 4 93 91 19
Contact: Dr. Jochen Leonhardt

SCHEIDLE & PARTNERS
Grottenau 6, 8900 AUGSBURG
Tel: + *49* (821) 15 60 81 *Fax:* + *49* (821) 51 43 09
Contact: Dr. Gunther Scheidle

SOCIETÄTS-TREUHAND GmbH
Hildesheimer Strasse 9, 3000 HANNOVER 1
Tel: + *49* (511) 2 82 06 13 *Fax:* + *49* (511) 28 20 64
Contact: Dr. Wolfgang Gebler

SOCIETÄTS-TREUHAND GmbH
Niedersachenstrasse 14, 4500 OSNABRÜCK
Mailing Address: Postfach 27 67, 4500 OSNABRÜCK
Tel: + *49* (541) 3 20 01 *Fax:* + *49* (541) 2 15 35
Contact: Reinhard Wenk

SOCIETÄTS-TREUHAND GmbH
Schweriner Strasse 48, 8010 DRESDEN
Tel: + *37* (51) 4 95 30 31 *Fax:* + *37* (51) 4 95 30 29
Contact: Dr. Jurgen Hesse

TURNBULL & IRRGANG GmbH
Grosse Strasse 21, 2070 AHRENSBURG
Tel: + *49* (4102) 5 15 00 *Fax:* + *49* (4102) 51 50 45
Contact: Peter E. Turnbull

TURNBULL & IRRGANG GmbH
Bleichenbrücke 9, 2000 HAMBURG 36
Tel: + *49* (40) 3 56 00 40 *Fax:* + *49* (40) 35 60 04 45
Contact: Peter E. Turnbull

TURNBULL & IRRGANG GmbH
Lindenstrasse 3a, 2757 SCHWERIN
Tel: + *49* (84) 86 49 00 *Fax:* + *49* (84) 86 44 47
Contact: Peter E. Turnbull

UWP & UNTERA GESELLSCHAFT FUR UNTERNEHMENSBERATUNG mbH
Calvinstrasse 21, 5600 WUPPERTAL 1
Tel: + *49* (202) 4 93 91 59 *Fax:* + *49* (202) 4 93 91 19
Contact: Horst-Dieter Wolf

WESTFALEN-REVISION GmbH
Märkische Strasse 212-218, 4600 DORTMUND 1
Tel: + *49* (231) 41 90 40 *Fax:* + *49* (231) 4 19 04 49
Contact: Dr. Fred Schaefermeyer

Total Number of Offices: 18

▷

OBERBAYERISCHE TREUHAND UND REVISIONS GmbH

Landsberger Strasse 478, 8000 MUNICH 60
Tel: + *49* (89) 8 34 80 17
Fax: + *49* (89) 8 34 02 40

European Affiliation: Alliott Peirson International

International Contact: Karl-Heinz Maier

OTHER OFFICES

OBERBAYERISCHE TREUHAND UND REVISIONS-GESELLSCHAFT GmbH
Von-Brug-Strasse 2, 8100 GARMISCH-PARTENKIRCHEN
Tel: + *49* (8821) 5 80 47 *Fax:* + *49* (8821) 7 46 34
Contact: Claus Dopfer

OBERBAYERISCHE TREUHAND UND REVISIONS-GESELLSCHAFT GmbH
Hainstrasse 19, 7010 LEIPZIG
Contact: Karl-Heinz Maier

Total Number of Offices: 3

PANNELL KERR FORSTER GmbH

Jungfernstieg 7, 2000 HAMBURG 36
Tel: + *49* (40) 35 21 34
Fax: + *49* (40) 35 31 86
Mailing Address: Postfach 30 49 23, 2000 HAMBURG 36

European Affiliation: Pannell Kerr Forster Worldwide

International Contact: Gerd Heymann

OTHER OFFICES

HELLINGER, HAHEMANN, SCHULTE-GROSS & PARTNER
Parlerstrasse 16, 7000 STUTTGART 1
Tel: + *49* (7) 11 25 20 81 *Fax:* + *49* (7) 112 57 93 71
Contact: Dr. Horst Schulte-Gross

PANNELL KERR FORSTER GmbH
Seelenbinderstrasse 124, 1170 BERLIN
Tel: + *37* (2) 650 92 09 *Fax:* + *37* (2) 656 56 79

PANNELL KERR FORSTER GmbH
Viktoriastrasse 18-20, 4800 BIELEFELD 1
Mailing Address: Postfach 35 04, 4800 BIELEFELD 1
Tel: + *49* (521) 6 90 41 *Fax:* + *49* (521) 6 90 43
Contact: Peter Giese

PANNELL KERR FORSTER GmbH
Walther-Rathenau-Strasse 24, 4400 BITTERFELD
Tel: + *37* (44) 32 60
Contact: Dr. Otto Rensing

PANNELL KERR FORSTER GmbH
Gereonstrasse 34-36, 5000 COLOGNE 1
Tel: + *49* (221) 1 64 31 19 *Fax:* + *49* (221) 1 64 31 12
Contact: H. Reiner Hower

PANNELL KERR FORSTER GmbH
Zellescher Weg 24, 8020 DRESDEN
Tel: + *37* (51) 4 66 22 05 *Fax:* + *37* (51) 4 66 22 06

PANNELL KERR FORSTER GmbH
Keetmanstrasse 3-7, 4100 DUISBURG 1
Mailing Address: Postfach 10 04 62, 4100 DUISBURG 1
Tel: + *49* (203) 30 00 10 *Fax:* + *49* (203) 3 00 01 67
Contact: Dr. Jürgen Kleine-Cosack

PANNELL KERR FORSTER GmbH
Feuerbachstrasse 8, 6000 FRANKFURT
Tel: + *49* (69) 1 70 00 00 *Fax:* + *49* (69) 17 00 00 99
Contact: Wolfgang Hofmann

PANNELL KERR FORSTER GmbH
Strasse Republik 5, 4070 HALLE
Tel: + *37* (46) 4 47 44
Contact: Ingo Richter

PANNELL KERR FORSTER GmbH
Maximilianstrasse 27, 8000 MUNICH 22
Tel: + *49* (89) 29 63 64 *Fax:* + *49* (89) 29 94 16
Contact: Dr. Eugen Herrmann

PANNELL KERR FORSTER GmbH
Rankestrasse 56, 8500 NUREMBERG 40
Tel: + *49* (911) 47 43 35 *Fax:* + *49* (911) 47 43 33
Contact: Dr. Helmut Fischer

PANNELL KERR FORSTER GmbH
Schildern 17-19, 4790 PADERBORN
Tel: + *49* (525) 2 64 84 *Fax:* + *49* (525) 2 42 60

PANNELL KERR FORSTER GmbH
Doberaner Strasse 44-47, 2500 ROSTOCK 1
Tel: + *37* (81) 367 34 63

PANNELL KERR FORSTER GmbH
Magdeburger Strasse 20, 2751 SCHWERIN
Tel: + *37* (84) 35 52 09 *Fax:* + *37* (84) 35 52 09

Total Number of Offices: 15

PLATZ & VON OERTZEN GmbH

Grafenberger Allee 32, 4000 DUSSELDORF
Tel: + *49* (211) 67 50 43
Fax: + *49* (211) 67 89 21

European Affiliation: Affiliated Conference of Practising Accountants International (ACPA)

International Contact: Christoph Platz

Partners:	3
Professional staff:	14
Non-professional staff:	2
Total Staff:	**19**

FEE INCOME

Year End: 31.12.90	**DM**
Accountancy & Audit:	550,000
Consultancy:	100,000
Tax:	650,000
Total:	**1,300,000**

CONTACT INFORMATION

Managing Partner: Christoph Platz
Accountancy (General): Ulrich Von Oertzen
Audit: Christoph Platz
Management Consultancy: Andrea Knappe
Tax (Corporate): Ulrich Von Oertzen

CLIENT SERVICES

Accountancy (General), Audit, Computer Installation, Corporate Finance Advice, Management & Business Advice, Taxation (Corporate), Taxation (International)

OTHER OFFICES

PLATZ & VON OERTZEN GmbH
Strasse der Einheit 8, 9300 ANNABERG-BUCHHOLZ
Tel: + *37* (765) 41 26 *Fax:* + *37* (765) 41 26

PLATZ & VON OERTZEN GmbH
Mendelejew Strasse 12, 9033 CHEMNITZ
Tel: + *37* (71) 85 35 36 *Fax:* + *37* (71) 85 35 36
Contact: Andrea Knappe

Total Number of Offices: 3

TREUHANDPARTNER PLENKER JÄGER, FINKEN, WELLING GmbH

Eichendorffstrasse 46, 4150 KREFELD
Tel: + *49* (2151) 50 90
Fax: + *49* (2151) 50 92 00

European Affiliation: Moores Rowland International

International Contact: Jürgen Finken

PROF. DR. ERWIN POUGIN GmbH

Hohenstaugenring 62, 5000 COLOGNE 1
Tel: + *49* (221) 20 30 50
Fax: + *49* (221) 24 29 46

European Affiliation: Alliott Peirson International

International Contact: Irmgard Alefelder

PRICE WATERHOUSE GmbH

Gervinusstrasse 17, 6000 FRANKFURT
Tel: + *49* (69) 15 20 40
Fax: + *49* (69) 15 20 41 07
Mailing Address: Postfach 17 04 64, 6000 FRANKFURT 17

European Affiliation: Price Waterhouse

International Contact: Jermyn Brooks

Partners:	72
Professional staff:	760
Non-professional staff:	240
Total Staff:	**1,072**

FEE INCOME

Year End: 30.06.91	**DM**
Accountancy & Audit:	60,800,000
Consultancy:	25,500,000
Tax:	44,400,000
Other:	9,800,000
Total:	**140,500,000**

CONTACT INFORMATION

Managing Partner: Jermyn Brooks
Accountancy (General): Willi Mecklenburg
Audit: Michel D.J. Dressler
Corporate Finance: Phillip Wright
Insolvency: Ulrich Hochstetter
Management Consultancy: John A. Laycock
Administration: Götz Heuser
Public Sector: Burkhard Klein
Tax: Wolfgang Krause

CLIENT SERVICES

Accountancy (General), Audit, Computer Installation, Corporate Finance Advice, Insolvency & Corporate Restructuring, Management & Business Advice, Management Buy-outs, Mergers & Acquisitions, Pensions Planning, Value for Money Studies, Taxation (Corporate), Taxation (International), Taxation (Personal), Company Valuations, Management Consultancy

Industry Specialisations: Financial Services, Retailing, Petroleum, Pharmaceuticals

MAJOR CLIENTS

Allied Signal Inc, Amadeus, Barclays Bank International, Baxter Travenol Laboratories Inc, Beecham Group Ltd, Borden Inc., Bristol-Myers Company, Eastman Kodak Company, Exxon Corporation, Goodyear Tyre & Rubber Company, Grace & Co, IBM Corporation, Rathenower Optische Werke GmbH, Redland plc, Royal Dutch Shell Group, Seagram Company Ltd, Sony Corporation, Stora Group, TI Group plc, Treuhandanstalt, Berlin

OTHER OFFICES

FMP GESELLSCHAFT FÜR REVISION UND TREUHAND mbH
Klosterstrasse 56-58, 4000 DUSSELDORF 1
Tel: + *49* (211) 16 90 10 *Fax:* + *49* (211) 1 69 01 19
Contact: Willi Mecklenburg

DR. KÖCKE & PARTNER GmbH
Grafenberger Allee 277, 4000 DUSSELDORF 1
Tel: + *49* (211) 6 88 10 *Fax:* + *49* (211) 6 88 13 50
Contact: Dr. Dieter Hammer

PRICE WATERHOUSE GmbH
Max-Joseph-Strasse 7, 8000 MUNICH 2
Tel: + *49* (89) 55 14 80 *Fax:* + *49* (89) 59 58 53
Contact: Hans L. Steskal

PRICE WATERHOUSE GmbH
Theodor-Heuss-Strasse 11, 7000 STUTTGART 10
Tel: + *49* (711) 2 07 30 *Fax:* + *49* (711) 29 06 22
Contact: Jochen Pape

PRICE WATERHOUSE GmbH
Martin-Luther-Strasse 1, 1000 BERLIN 30
Tel: + *49* (30) 21 09 40 *Fax:* + *49* (30) 2 10 94 99
Contact: Robert C. Megaw

PRICE WATERHOUSE GmbH
Ostra-Allee 25, 8012 DRESDEN
Tel: + *37* (51) 4 86 02 60 *Fax:* + *37* (51) 4 86 02 45
Contact: Dieter Sackmann

PRICE WATERHOUSE GmbH
Elisabethstrasse 22, 4000 DUSSELDORF 1
Tel: + *49* (211) 38 70 40 *Fax:* + *49* (211) 3 87 04 65
Contact: Malcolm Heath

PRICE WATERHOUSE GmbH
Warburgstrasse 28, 2000 HAMBURG 36
Tel: + *49* (40) 4 14 00 30 *Fax:* + *49* (40) 41 40 03 67
Contact: Jürgen Wagner

PRICE WATERHOUSE GmbH
Brühl 76, 7010 LEIPZIG
Tel: + *37* (41) 7 95 42 13 *Fax:* + *37* (41) 7 95 42 48
Contact: Christopher Smith

Total Number of Offices: 10

PROFUNDA TREUHAND GmbH

Reimersbrucke 5, 2000 HAMBURG 11
Tel: + *49* (40) 36 68 68
Fax: + *49* (40) 36 71 39

International Contact: Michael Tille
Werne von Salzen

FRANZ REISSNER TREUHANDGESELLSCHAFT mbH

Prinz-Georg-Strasse 15, 4000 DUSSELDORF 30
Tel: + *49* (211) 48 70 05
Fax: + *49* (211) 44 16 25

European Affiliation: TGI International

International Contact: Gerhard Kaiser

▷

RHEINREVISION GmbH

Wilhelm-Strausse-Strasse 45-47, 4050 MÖNCHENGLADBACH 2, Dusseldorf
Tel: + *49* (2166) 97 10
Fax: + *49* (2166) 97 11 23
Mailing Address: Postfach 20 10 51, 4050 MÖNCHENGLADBACH 2, Dusseldorf

European Affiliation: BKR International
International Contact: Peter Walter

Partners:	4
Professional staff:	55
Non-professional staff:	15
Total Staff:	74

FEE INCOME

Year End: 1990	%
Accountancy & Audit:	40.0
Consultancy:	20.0
Tax:	20.0

CONTACT INFORMATION
Chairman: Heinz-Peter Wirtz
Management Consultancy: Heinz-Peter Wirtz
Tax: Peter Walter

CLIENT SERVICES
Accountancy (General), Audit, Corporate Finance Advice, Insolvency & Corporate Restructuring, Litigation/Legal Services, Management & Business Advice, Management Buy-outs, Mergers & Acquisitions, Taxation (Corporate), Taxation (International)

OTHER OFFICES

WBT TREUHAND GmbH
Wilhelm-Strausse-Strasse 45-47, 4050 MÖNCHENGLADBACH 2
Mailing Address: Postfach 20 14 51, 4050 MÖNCHENGLADBACH 2
Tel: + *49* (2166) 97 10 *Fax:* + *49* (2166) 97 11 23
Contact: Herman-Josef Schmitz

Total Number of Offices: 3

BERND RODL & PARTNER

Erlenstegenstrasse 10, 8500 NUREMBERG 20
Tel: + *49* (911) 5 97 60
Fax: + *49* (911) 5 97 86

European Affiliation: CPA Associates Inc

International Contact: Dr. Nikolaus Weber

ROOLF & PARTNER GmbH

Kennedyallee 55, 6000 FRANKFURT AM MAIN 70
Tel: + *49* (69) 63 50 91
Fax: + *49* (69) 63 40 74

European Affiliation: TGI International

International Contact: Hans H. Roolf

OTHER OFFICES

ROOLF & PARTNER GmbH
Dotzheimer Strasse 164, 6200 WIESBADEN
Tel: + *49* (611) 98 90 00 *Fax:* + *49* (611) 80 57 54
Contact: Uwe Stengert

Total Number of Offices: 2

RÖVER & PARTNER

Douglasstrasse 18, 1000 BERLIN 33
Tel: + *49* (30) 8 29 90 20
Fax: + *49* (30) 82 99 02 79

European Affiliation: Moores Rowland International

International Contact: Ruprecht Röver

RTS REVISION, TREUHAND GmbH

Faktoreistrasse 4, 6600 SAARBRÜCKEN
Tel: + *49* (681) 4 10 11 01
Fax: + *49* (681) 4 10 11 00

European Affiliation: Moores Rowland International

International Contact: Wolfgang Rau

R.& K. TREUHANDGESELLSCHAFT mbH

Hessenring 99b, 6380 BAD HOMBURG
Tel: + *49* (6172) 12 90 04

European Affiliation: A.E.E. International

International Contact: G. Kaufmann

SCHITAG SCHWÄBISCHE TREUHAND AG

Jägerstrasse 26, 7000 STUTTGART 10
Tel: + *49* (711) 2 03 50
Fax: + *49* (711) 2 03 52 28

European Affiliation: Ernst & Young Europe

International Contact: Hubert Graf von Treuberg
Total Staff: **2000**

FEE INCOME

Year End: 31.12.90	**DM**	%
Accountancy & Audit:		49.0
Consultancy:		12.0
Tax:		28.0
Other:		11.0
Total:	**307,000,000**	

CLIENT SERVICES
All Services

OTHER OFFICES

DR. DIEZ-DR. PFLEIDERER GmbH
Regerstrasse 19, 7000 STUTTGART 10
Tel: + *49* (711) 69 40 51 *Fax:* + *49* (711) 69 14 20

E & W ERNST & WHINNEY
Gewerbezentrum Gasstrasse 18, 2000 HAMBURG 50
Tel: + *49* (40) 89 08 17 02 *Fax:* + *49* (40) 890 26 03

ERNST & YOUNG GmbH
Am Wehrhahn 50, 4000 DÜSSELDORF 1
Tel: + *49* (211) 493 12 71 *Fax:* + *49* (211) 4 98 03 80
Contact: Karl G. Reifert

ERNST & YOUNG GmbH
Corneliusstrasse 18, 6000 FRANKFURT 1
Tel: + *49* (69) 7 56 10 40 *Fax:* + *49* (69) 75 61 04 20
Contact: Gerd Duell

ERNST & YOUNG GmbH
Eschersheimer Landstrasse 14, 6000 FRANKFURT 1
Tel: + *49* (69) 1 52 08 01 *Fax:* + *49* (69) 15 20 82 84
Contact: Helmut Becker

▷

ERNST & YOUNG GmbH
Herrengraben 3, 2000 HAMBURG 11
Tel: + *49* (40) 36 13 20 *Fax:* + *49* (40) 3 74 33 48

ERNST & YOUNG GmbH
Elisenstrasse 3a, 8000 MUNICH 2
Tel: + *49* (89) 55 98 50 *Fax:* + *49* (89) 59 83 66
Contact: Herbert Kögl

ERNST & YOUNG GmbH
Zweinaundorfer Strasse 59, 7050 LEIPZIG
Tel: + *37* (41) 6 82 15 89

ERNST & YOUNG GmbH
Hauptstätter Strasse 112, 7000 STUTTGART 10
Tel: + *49* (711) 60 30 11 *Fax:* + *49* (711) 6 40 89 29

HEILBRONNER TREUHAND GmbH
Uhlandstrasse 39, 8010 DRESDEN
Tel: + *37* (51) 4 66 02 55 *Fax:* + *49* (51) 4 66 02 84

SCHITAG SCHWÄBISCHE TREUHAND AG
M 2 4-5, 6800 MANNHEIM 1
Tel: + *49* (621) 1 26 06 21 *Fax:* + *49* (621) 1 26 06 12

SCHITAG SCHWÄBISCHE TREUHAND AG
Uhlandstrasse 39, 8010 DRESDEN
Tel: + *37* (51) 4 66 02 29 *Fax:* + *37* (51) 4 66 02 84

SCHITAG SCHWÄBISCHE TREUHAND AG
Hardenbergstrasse 4-5, 1000 BERLIN 12
Tel: + *49* (30) 31 90 40 *Fax:* + *49* (30) 3 19 04 53

SCHITAG SCHWÄBISCHE TREUHAND AG
Rosastrasse 17, 7800 FREIBURG I. BR.
Tel: + *49* (761) 3 19 11 40 *Fax:* + *49* (761) 3 19 11 78
Contact: Dr. Max-Burkhard Zwosta

SCHITAG SCHWÄBISCHE TREUHAND AG
Karolinenstrasse 44, 8500 NÜRNBERG
Tel: + *49* (911) 20 85 26 *Fax:* + *49* (911) 22 67 03
Contact: Gerhard Sussbauer

SCHITAG SCHWÄBISCHE TREUHAND-AG
Am Wehrhahn 50, 4000 DÜSSELDORF 1
Tel: + *49* (211) 9 35 20 *Fax:* + *49* (211) 49 91 66

Total Number of Offices: 32

DIPL.-KFM. DR. H.-J. SCHMIDT-WILKE

Am Holzgraben, 3000 HANNOVER 1
Tel: + *49* (511) 34 83 00
Fax: + *49* (511) 3 48 30 24

European Affiliation: Midsnell International

International Contact: Dr. Hans-Jurgen Schmidt-Wilke

HANS LUDWIG SCHMITZ

Tivolistrasse 46, 5160 DUREN
Tel: + *49* (2421) 4 30 03

European Affiliation: Growth & Progress Challenge

International Contact: Dr Hans Ludwig Schmitz

DIPL-KFM CLAUS SECURS

Achenbachstrasse 8, 4000 DUSSELDORF 1
Tel: + *49* (211) 66 61 77
Fax: + *49* (211) 66 56 17

European Affiliation: Russell Bedford International

International Contact: Claus Securs

RODERICH CORNELIUS SIEGERT

Dingolfinger Strasse 2, 8000 MUNICH 80
Tel: + *49* (89) 41 86 96 0
Fax: + *49* (89) 41 86 96 98

European Affiliation: Growth & Progress Challenge

International Contact: Roderich Siegert

DIPL-KFM GERHARD SLAMAL

Franz-Vaahsen-Weg 5a, 4000 DUSSELDORF 31
Tel: + *49* (211) 4 06 26
Fax: + *49* (211) 4 08 04 36

European Affiliation: Independent Accountants International

International Contact: Gerhard Slamal

Partners:	1
Professional staff:	4
Non-professional staff:	2
Total Staff:	7

FEE INCOME

Year End: 31.12.90	**DM**	**%**
Accountancy & Audit:	400,000	53.0
Consultancy:	100,000	13.0
Tax:	120,000	16.0
Other:	130,000	18.0
Total:	**750,000**	

CONTACT INFORMATION
Partner: Gerhard Slamal

CLIENT SERVICES
Accountancy (General), Audit, Computer Installation, Corporate Finance Advice, Litigation/Legal Services, Management & Business Advice, Taxation (Corporate), Taxation (International), Trust Settlement & Estates

Industry Specialisations: Construction/Real Estate, Copper Casting & Wire Industry, Food

DR. KARL-RÜDIGER STEEB

Ismaninger Strasse 106, 8000 MUNICH 80
Tel: + *49* (89) 98 71 43
Fax: + *49* (89) 98 19 54

European Affiliation: Affiliated Conference of Practising Accountants International (ACPA)

International Contact: Dr. Karl-Rüdiger Steeb

CONTACT INFORMATION
Managing Partner: Dr. Karl-Rüdiger Steeb

TREUHAND UNION FINK & PARTNER GmbH

Burgermeister-Smidt Strasse 59/61, 2800 BREMEN 1
Tel: + *49* (421) 17 06 53
Fax: + *49* (421) 1 80 17

European Affiliation: BKR International

TREUHAND-GESELLSCHAFT "HANSA" mbH

Kajen 6, 2000 HAMBURG 11
Tel: + *49* (40) 36 13 06
Fax: + *49* (40) 36 67 77

▷

European Affiliation: BKR International

International Contact: Klaus Linne

Total Number of Offices: 2

TREUPLAN GmbH

Gleueler Strasse 303-313, 5000 COLOGNE 41 (Deckstein)
Tel: + *49* (221) 46 67 96
Fax: + *49* (221) 43 19 20

European Affiliation: InterContinental Consultants (ICC)

International Contact: Günter Alder

G. ULRICHS

Hohe Bleichen 5, 2000 HAMBURG 36
Tel: + *49* (40) 35 29 66
Fax: + *49* (40) 34 23 91

European Affiliation: A.E.E. International

International Contact: G. Ulrichs

CLIENT SERVICES

All Services

UWP UNITREU GmbH

Arndtstrasse 39, 6000 FRANKFURT/MAIN
Tel: + *49* (69) 74 09 66
Fax: + *49* (69) 75 27 48

European Affiliation: INPACT - International Network of Professional Accountants

International Contact: Peter Goldsche
Wolfgang Schimm

Partners:	4
Professional staff:	38
Non-professional staff:	6
Total Staff:	**48**

FEE INCOME

Year End: 1990	%
Accountancy & Audit:	40.0
Consultancy:	20.0
Tax:	40.0

CONTACT INFORMATION

Partner: Horst Gehr
Partner: Helmut Schmelzetsen
GDP: Gerhard Muser
GDP: Martin Spieger

CLIENT SERVICES

All Services, Internal Audits

Industry Specialisations: Banks, All Sectors excluding Insurance

ASSOCIATED FIRMS

GEHR & PARTNER
Arndtstrasse 39, 6000 FRANKFURT 1
Tel: + *49* (69) 74 09 66 *Fax:* + *49* (69) 75 27 48
Contact: Peter Goldsche

INCOTAX GmbH
Oranienstrasse 23, 6200 FRANKFURT
Tel: + *49* (611) 37 94 15 *Fax:* + *49* (611) 37 95 97

SAMES & PARTNER GmbH
Karl-Bene-Strasse 11-13, 6300 GIESSEN
Tel: + *49* (641) 6 30 71 *Fax:* + *49* (641) 6 72 29

SAMES & PARTNER GmbH ERFURT
Schloesserstrasse 7, 5020 ERFURT
Tel: + *49* (611) 37 94 15 *Fax:* + *49* (611) 37 95 97

Total Number of Offices: 5

VERHULSDONK & PARTNER GmbH

Elisabethstrasse 16, 4000 DUSSELDORF 1
Tel: + *49* (211) 38 95 01
Fax: + *49* (211) 37 06 44

European Affiliation: Moores Rowland International

International Contact: Dr. Michael Kunz

OTHER OFFICES

VERHÜLSDONK & PARTNER GmbH
Friesenplatz 17, 5000 COLOGNE
Tel: + *49* (221) 20 70 00 *Fax:* + *49* (221) 2 07 00 22
Contact: Alois Pagenstedt

VERHÜLSDONK & PARTNER GmbH
Viktoriastrasse 4, Postfach 426, 5400 KOBLENZ
Tel: + *49* (261) 31 04 46 *Fax:* + *49* (261) 3 26 07
Contact: Heribert Brixius

VERHÜLSDONK & PARTNER GmbH
Rheinbahnstrasse 28, 4050 MÖNCHENGLADBACH 1
Tel: + *49* (2161) 18 10 69 *Fax:* + *49* (2161) 20 86 51
Contact: Claus Christmann

Total Number of Offices: 4

DR. VONDERRECK UND SCHULTE

Marktstrasse 61-63, 4200 OBERHAUSEN 1
Tel: + *49* (208) 85 98 80
Fax: + *49* (208) 8 59 88 26

European Affiliation: InterContinental Consultants (ICC)

International Contact: Bernhard Schulte

DR. WAHL & PARTNER GmbH

Prinzregentenstrasse 54, 8000 MUNICH 22
Tel: + *49* (89) 22 73 61
Fax: + *49* (89) 29 40 88

European Affiliation: TGI International

International Contact: Dr. Adalbert Wahl

DR. BOHN WEGNER & PARTNER

Beethovenstrasse 8, 8000 MUNICH 2
Tel: + *49* (89) 53 03 85
Fax: + *49* (89) 53 52 95

European Affiliation: Clark Kenneth Leventhal

International Contact: Eckard Wegner

Partners:	3
Professional staff:	6
Non-professional staff:	3
Total Staff:	**12**

▷

FEE INCOME

Year End: 1990	%
Accountancy & Audit:	56.0
Tax:	42.0
Other:	2.0

CLIENT SERVICES

Accountancy (General), Audit, Corporate Finance Advice, Insolvency & Corporate Restructuring, Management & Business Advice, Taxation (Corporate), Taxation (International)

WEHNER-ZIMMER & PARTNER GmbH

Benesisstrasse 8-12, 5000 COLOGNE 1
Tel: + *49* (221) 20 20 60
Fax: + *49* (221) 23 32 68

European Affiliation: TGI International

International Contact: Hans-Peter Wehner

WESTDEUTSCHE REVISIONS + TREUHAND GmbH

Schottweg 3, 2000 HAMBURG 76
Tel: + *49* (40) 22 70 07 02
Fax: + *49* (40) 22 70 07 25

European Affiliation: Jeffreys Henry International

International Contact: H.P. Walker

Partners:	15
Professional staff:	260
Non-professional staff:	55
Total Staff:	**330**

FEE INCOME

Year End: 31.12.90	**DM**	%
Accountancy & Audit:	25,700,000	60.0
Consultancy:	2,100,000	5.0
Tax:	12,900,000	30.0
Other:	2,200,000	5.0
Total:	**42,900,000**	

CONTACT INFORMATION

Chairman: Klaus Juergensen
Managing Partner: Eberhard Gutberlet
Accountancy (General): Bernd Hartmann
Audit: Carl A. Petzoldt
Corporate Finance: Dr. Juergen Hutzel
Administration: Konrad Roski
Public Sector: Dr. Hermann Wundt
Tax (Corporate): Klaus Juergensen
Tax & Management Consultancy: Dr. Bruno Germscheid

CLIENT SERVICES

Accountancy (General), Audit, Corporate Finance Advice, Management & Business Advice, Mergers & Acquisitions, Pensions Planning, Value for Money Studies, Taxation (Corporate), Taxation (International), Trust Settlement & Estates

OTHER OFFICES

WESTDEUTSCHE REVISIONS + TREUHAND GmbH
Schleussner Strasse 26, 6380 BAD HOMBURG
Tel: + *49* (6172) 1 80 90 *Fax:* + *49* (6172) 18 09 40
Contact: Eberhard Gutberlet

WESTDEUTSCHE REVISIONS + TREUHAND GmbH
Schadow Platz 11, 4000 DUSSELDORF
Tel: + *49* (211) 32 90 18 *Fax:* + *49* (211) 32 47 41

WESTDEUTSCHE REVISIONS + TREUHAND GmbH
Brienner Strasse 16, 8000 MUNICH 2
Tel: + *49* (89) 28 60 01 *Fax:* + *49* (89) 2 80 03 79
Contact: Dr. Siegfried Zitzelsberger

WESTDEUTSCHE REVISIONS + TREUHAND GmbH
Charlottenstrasse 45-51, 7410 REUTLINGEN
Tel: + *49* (7121) 48 90 *Fax:* + *49* (7121) 48 93 33
Contact: Heinz Peter Wacker

Total Number of Offices: 5

WIDMANN UND PARTNER

Kriegstrasse 81, 7500 KARLSRUHE
Tel: + *49* (721) 85 30 01
Fax: + *49* (721) 85 30 07
Mailing Address: Postfach 66 40, 7500 KARLSRUHE

European Affiliation: ATD International

International Contact: Benno Stratmann

Dipl-Kfm H. WILLMS GmbH

Hansaallee 201, 4000 DUSSELDORF
Tel: + *49* (211) 59 60 05
Fax: + *49* (211) 59 39 08

European Affiliation: K.S. International

International Contact: Hubert Willms

CLIENT SERVICES

Accountancy (General), Mergers & Acquisitions, Tax Planning, Lease Structuring, Sale of Companies

Industry Specialisations: Real Estate, Non-Profit Making Organisations

WIRTSCHAFTSTREUHAND GmbH

Herdweg 18, 7000 STUTTGART 1
Tel: + *49* (711) 22 77 40
Fax: + *49* (711) 2 27 74 60

European Affiliation: Clark Kenneth Leventhal
National Affiliation: WIRSCHAFTSTREUHAND GROUP

International Contact: Hans Eisenmann

Partners:	10
Professional staff:	77
Non-professional staff:	17
Total Staff:	**104**

CLIENT SERVICES

Accountancy (General), Audit, Corporate Finance Advice, Insolvency & Corporate Restructuring, Management & Business Advice, Taxation (Corporate), Taxation (International)

ASSOCIATED FIRMS

COMMERZ-UND-INDUSTRIE-TREUHAND GmbH
Kiehnlestr 8a, 7530 PFORZHEIM
Tel: + *49* (7231) 3 20 81 *Fax:* + *49* (7231) 1 36 32
Contact: Hans Eisenmann

PROF. FISCHER & PARTNER
Rehhaldenweg 58-60, 7060 SCHORNDORF
Tel: + *49* (7181) 6 30 86 *Fax:* + *49* (7181) 6 51 14
Contact: Hans Eisenmann

Total Number of Offices: 3

WOLLERT-ELMENDORFF DEUTSCHE INDUSTRIE-TREUHAND GmbH

Bahnstrasse 16, 4000 DUSSELDORF 1
Tel: + 49 (211) 87 72 01
Fax: + 49 (211) 8 77 22 77
Mailing Address: Postfach 87 29, 4000 DUSSELDORF 1

European Affiliation: DRT International

International Contact: Horst Thoennes

Total Staff: **1,150**

CLIENT SERVICES
All Services

MAJOR CLIENTS
Adam, Opel, BASF, Bayernwerk, Joh Benckiser, Deutsche Bundesbank, FAG Kugelfisher Georg Schaeffer, Hypobank, MAN (Nutzfahrzeuge/ Roland), Victoria-Gruppe, Volkswagen, Wuestenrot-Gruppe

Total Number of Offices: 14

DR. WOLTER & PARTNER mbH

Postfach 6066, Luisenstrasse 4, 3000 HANNOVER 1
Tel: + 49 (511) 36 38 82
Fax: + 49 (511) 32 30 05

European Affiliation: TGI International

International Contact: Jochen Herrmann

Area: 131,957 sq km (50,949 sq miles)
Population: 9,990,000 (1987 estimate)
Density: 75.7 per sq km
Capital: Athens

GDP: Dr12.8 trn, US$75 bn (1991 forecast)
GDP per head: US$7,450 (1991 forecast)
Inflation: 1990 - 23%
1991 - 17% (forecast)

Official and Spoken Languages: Greek. Those connected with tourism will speak some English, French, Italian or German

Time: GMT + 2 (in Summer GMT + 3)
Telephone Dialling Code: + 30

Currency: Drachma (Dr)
Banking Hours: 0800-1400 Monday-Friday. Many banks in larger centres are open in afternoons/evenings for currency exchange.
Professional accountancy bodies: Institute of Certified Public Accountants of Greece (SDL)
Association of Certified Accountants & Auditors (SELE)

Corporate Tax Data

Information supplied by Richard Citron, international tax partner of Stoy Hayward.

The tax year; nature and rates of tax

The tax year is the calendar year.

The corporation tax is levied at a standard rate of 46% on the income of an anonymos etairea, or AE (equivalent to a French SA). A limited liability company (etairea periosmenis efthinis), or EPE, is not subject to corporation tax and its income is imputed to its partners, although the company pays a 15% withholding tax, which is credited against their liability. The comments below apply to the AE (a "company"). Lower rates apply to certain manufacturing and mining companies incorporated in Greece. Only undistributed income is liable to corporation tax.

Special regime for Greek holding companies. Holding companies, investment holding companies and mutual trusts are exempt from all major direct taxes on capital and income.

Residence and territoriality

Greek resident companies are taxable on their worldwide income. A company is resident in Greece if it is incorporated there or has its central place of management in Greece.

The tax base

Method of computation. Taxable profits are based on the profit reported in the accounts.

Disallowable items. In general, expenses must be related to the business to be deductible. The major disallowable items include the corporation tax itself (most other taxes are deductible), certain gifts exceeding Dr 80,000, compulsory payments to the statutory reserve (5% of profits must generally be set ▷

aside each year) and payments to the (optional) extraordinary reserve.

Exempt income/special deductions. Exempt income includes interest from deposits with Greek banks and profits from property sales. Deductions are allowed for bad debt provisions for debts written off and charitable donations.

Interest paid. Interest is deductible on an accruals basis. Interest payments to resident companies must be made under deduction of 25% withholding tax.

Stock. Stock is valued at the lower of cost and market value on a consistent basis.

Depreciation. Depreciation is on the straight line basis on cost, according to fixed rates for different types of asset, eg buildings 5%-8%, plant and machinery 10%-15%. Land is not depreciable. In certain instances accelerated depreciation is available as is an investment allowance of between 40% and 70% of the amount invested (limited to Dr 1,600 million) which may be set against a percentage (varying from 60% to 90%) of taxable profits. Both the investment allowance and accelerated depreciation are to be withdrawn after 31 December 1992. Various other investment incentives exist.

Treatment of dividends

Dividends received from Greek companies. Dividends received from other Greek companies are exempt from corporation tax. However, they are paid under deduction of withholding tax at rates of between 42% and 50%. This withholding tax is not repayable but may be set against the withholding tax for which the recipient company must account.

Dividends received from abroad. These may be taxed in Greece if the treaty with the source country so provides. In the absence of a treaty, the dividends will usually not be taxable in Greece where the Greek company has a permanent establishment in the source country. A foreign tax credit is available.

Dividends paid. Dividend distributions to both residents and non-residents are deductible in computing profits for corporation tax. The paying company must deduct withholding tax (at between 42% and 50%).

Anti-avoidance measures

The only significant anti-avoidance legislation in Greece concerns transfer pricing. Transactions between two or more related companies must be made at arm's length.

Treatment of losses

Current period. Losses (including capital losses) may be set off against profits of the same period (there is no carry-back).

Future periods. Any losses unrelieved in the current period may be carried forward for a maximum of five years. Capital losses may not be carried forward.

Treatment of capital gains

Treatment. Most capital gains are taxed as income at normal corporation tax rates, but gains from certain types of asset are taxed separately.

(1) Gains from the disposal of immovable property and ships (unless these assets are stock in trade) are exempt.
(2) Gains from the disposal of other fixed assets may be deferred.
(3) Gains from the assignment of trade marks, patents etc are taxed at 30%.
(4) Gains from the disposal of an entire business (including intangible assets) or its shares (if registered and issued) are taxed at 20%.

Computation. Gains are computed by deducting cost from sale proceeds.

Rollover. Gains in category (2) are taxed as ordinary income but may be deferred if credited to a special reserve to be used for the acquisition of replacement assets within two years of the disposal.

Special treatment of shares. Gains from the disposal of shares can be deferred by being transferred to a reserve account for set off against future losses from the disposal of securities.

Treatment of groups and branches

There is no concept of grouping in Greek law. In general, the Greek branch of a non-resident company is subject to tax in the same manner as a Greek resident company. A special deduction of 2% of profits can be made to represent head office expenses. There is no withholding tax on remittances of profits from the branch.

Other taxes

Taxes on capital. Greek companies are subject to an annual tax on the value of immovable property as reduced by any outstanding charges against the property or loans taken out for its acquisition or improvement. The first Dr 50,000,000 is free of tax and the remainder is taxed at 1.5%.

Turnover taxes. There is a value added tax. The standard rate is 18%, with reduced rates of 4% and 8% and a luxury rate of 36%.

Transaction taxes. There is a tax on the transfer of immovable property, generally at 11% of the value. There is also a capital duty of 1% on the capital subscribed to a company and on further issues.

Payroll taxes. Employers are obliged to pay social security contributions. The rate is generally 22.35% for office and white collar workers and can rise to 26.75% for others. There is an additional 3% tax rate on directors fees.

ALEXANDER, YOUNG & CO

5-7 Filellinon Street, 185 36 PIRAEUS
Tel: +30 (1) 453 2277
Fax: +30 (1) 418 3849

European Affiliation: Horwath International

International Contact: Spiros Logothetis

Partners:	2
Professional staff:	16
Non-professional staff:	4
Total Staff:	**22**

CONTACT INFORMATION
Managing Partner: Spiros Logothetis
Computer Services & Software: Fragiskos Molinas

CLIENT SERVICES
Accountancy (General), Audit, Computer Installation, Management & Business Advice, Taxation (Corporate), Software Development, Company Computer Organisation

Industry Specialisations: Shipping

I. J. ANDRONIS

28 Kapodistrou Street, 106 82 ATHENS
Tel: +30 (1) 363 0512
Fax: +30 (1) 363 4584

European Affiliation: DFK International

International Contact: I.J. Andronis

ARTHUR ANDERSEN & CO

Syngrou Avenue 377, 175 64 ATHENS
Tel: +30 (1) 942 5661
Fax: +30 (1) 942 5681

European Affiliation: Arthur Andersen Worldwide

International Contact: Stefanos Pantzopoulos

CONTACT INFORMATION
Audit: Stefanos Pantzopoulos
Tax (Corporate): Timoleon N. Lizardos

CLIENT SERVICES
Accountancy (General), Audit, Computer Installation, Corporate Finance Advice, Insolvency & Corporate Restructuring, Litigation/Legal Services, Management & Business Advice, Management Buy-outs, Mergers & Acquisitions, Pensions Planning, Value for Money Studies, Taxation (Corporate), Taxation (International)

COOPERS & LYBRAND

Abacus House, 9 Semitelou Street, 115 28 ATHENS
Tel: +30 (1) 771 0112
Fax: +30 (1) 777 7390

European Affiliation: Coopers & Lybrand Europe

International Contact: Vassos Ioannou

Partners:	6
Professional staff:	39
Non-professional staff:	13
Total Staff:	**58**

CONTACT INFORMATION
Managing Partner: Vassos Ioannou
Management Consultancy: Andreas Acavalas
Tax (Corporate): George Samothrakis

CLIENT SERVICES
Audit, Corporate Finance Advice, Management & Business Advice, Mergers & Acquisitions, Taxation (Corporate)

Industry Specialisations: Banking, Insurance, Pharmaceuticals, Food & Drink, Automotive, Communications

OTHER OFFICES

COOPERS & LYBRAND
3 Aghiou Nicolaou Street, 185 37 PIRAEUS
Tel: +30 (1) 451 5841 *Fax:* +30 (1) 418 3760
Contact: Dimitris Potamitis

COOPERS & LYBRAND
47 Vas Eraklìou Street, 546 23 THESSALONIKI
Tel: +30 (31) 268 898
Contact: Costas Kouvelas

Total Number of Offices: 3

COSTOURIS, MICHAELIDES & CO

64 Kifisias Avenue, 2nd Floor, 151 25 MAROUSI, Athens
Tel: +30 (1) 685 0670
Fax: +30 (1) 685 2075

European Affiliation: Grant Thornton International

International Contact: Michalakis Costouris

Partners:	14
Professional staff:	70
Non-professional staff:	19
Total Staff:	**103**

FEE INCOME

Year End: 31.12.90	**Dr**
Total:	**722,667,000**

CONTACT INFORMATION
Managing Partner: Michalakis Costouris

CLIENT SERVICES
Accountancy (General), Audit, Computer Installation, Corporate Finance Advice, Management & Business Advice, Mergers & Acquisitions, Taxation (Corporate), Taxation (International)

Industry Specialisations: Construction, Hotels, Food & Beverages

DELOITTE & TOUCHE

P.O. Box 75195, Kallithea, 176 10 ATHENS
Tel: +30 (1) 956 6655
Fax: +30 (1) 956 9736
Mailing Address: 180 Syngrou Avenue, Kallithea, 176 71 ATHENS

European Affiliation: DRT International

International Contact: Michael Hadjipavlou

Total Staff: **60**

CLIENT SERVICES
All Services

MAJOR CLIENTS
Alcatez Chandris Cables, Aspis Bank, Frank E. Baeil Inc, Benckiser, Boehringer Ingelheim, Ciments Lafarge, Greek Progress Fund, Interamerican Insurance, Laskarides Shipping, Linette Hellas, National Bank of Greece, Olympiaki Victoria Insurance, SATO, Soya Hellas, Sun Alliance, Transmed Shipping, Wagon Lits

Total Number of Offices: 3

▷

Greece

ELEKTIKI-LOGISTIKI-FOROTECHNIKI LTD

19 Akadimias Street, 106 71 ATHENS
Tel: +*30* (1) 363 6913
#12Fax: + *30* (1) 361 1017

European Affiliation: HLB International

International Contact: Joula Maravelea

Partners:	2
Professional staff:	3
Non-professional staff:	3
Total Staff:	**8**

CONTACT INFORMATION
Managing Partner: Joula Maravelea
Partner: Jannis Antonakopoulos

CLIENT SERVICES
All Services

E.P.Y. LTD

66 Piraeus, 183 46 MOSKATO
Tel: +*30* (1) 481 8492
Fax: + *30* (1) 322 3866

Partners:	2
Professional staff:	3
Non-professional staff:	5
Total Staff:	**10**

CONTACT INFORMATION
Chairman: Byron Catsaros
Accountancy (General): Aphrodite Aktyri

CLIENT SERVICES
Accountancy (General), Computer Installation, Management & Business Advice, Management Consultancy

MAJOR CLIENTS
Catsaros Automation SA, Pyra Ltd, Tilemikaniki SA, Xenon SA

ERNST & YOUNG

Athens Tower, 23rd Floor, 2 Messogion Street, 115 27 ATHENS
Tel: +*30* (1) 775 9780
Fax: + *30* (1) 775 9790

European Affiliation: Ernst & Young Europe

Partners:	6
Professional staff:	65
Non-professional staff:	13
Total Staff:	**84**

CONTACT INFORMATION
Managing Partner: Angelos Nicolaou
Corporate Finance: Christos Glavanis
Management Consultancy: Yannis Methodios
Accountancy & Audit: John Christodoulides
Accountancy & Audit: Christos Glavanis
Accountancy & Audit: David Gould
Tax: Themis Lianopoulos

CLIENT SERVICES
Accountancy (General), Audit, Corporate Finance Advice, Management & Business Advice, Taxation (Corporate), Taxation (International)

Industry Specialisations: Banking, Oil, Manufacturing, Music

E. HELLINAKIS & CO

95 Timotheou Street, 16231 ATHENS
Tel: +*30* (1) 722 7990
Fax: + *30* (1) 724 6907

European Affiliation: Summit International Associates Inc

International Contact: Eftychios Hellinakis

Partners:	3
Professional staff:	1
Non-professional staff:	1
Total Staff:	**5**

CONTACT INFORMATION
Managing Partner: Eftychios Hellinakis
Audit: Martha Barris Karantzalis
Audit: Eftychios Hellinakis
Management Consultancy: Jim Katiforis

CLIENT SERVICES
Audit, Management Consultancy Only

KOLOKOTRONIS - PAPAKYRIACOU & CO

Veritas House, 27-31 Hatzikyriacou Avenue, 185 38 PIRAEUS
Tel: +*30* (1) 452 3212
Fax: + *30* (1) 453 9755

European Affiliation: Nexia International

International Contact: Loizos E. Kolokotronis

Partners:	2
Professional staff:	13
Non-professional staff:	2
Total Staff:	**17**

CONTACT INFORMATION
Partner: Loizos E. Kolokotronis
Partner: George Papakyriacou

CLIENT SERVICES
Accountancy (General), Audit, Corporate Finance Advice, Insolvency & Corporate Restructuring, Management & Business Advice, Management Buy-outs, Mergers & Acquisitions, Taxation (Corporate), Taxation (International)

Industry Specialisations: Breweries, Motor Car, Oil, Shipping, Hotels, Cement, Construction

KPMG

KPMG PEAT MARWICK KYRIACOU

15 Mesoghion Avenue, Ambelokipi, 115 26 ATHENS
Tel: +*30* (1) 775 2001
Fax: + *30* (1) 770 4182
Mailing Address: P.O. Box 14111, 115 10 ATHENS

European Affiliation: KPMG

International Contact: Marios T. Kyriacou

Partners:	3
Professional staff:	60
Non-professional staff:	11
Total Staff:	**74**

FEE INCOME

Year End: 30.06.90	**%**
Accountancy & Audit:	60.0
Consultancy:	12.0
Tax:	28.0

CONTACT INFORMATION
Managing Partner: M.T. Kyriacou
Audit: C.P. Panayiotides
Management Consultancy: Y. Charalambous

CLIENT SERVICES
All Services

Industry Specialisations: Financial, High Tech, Transport, Non-Profit Institutions, Pharmaceuticals, Manufacturing

KYPRIS AND COMPANY

293 Kifissia Avenue, Kifissia, 145 61 ATHENS
Tel: +*30* (1) 801 6310
Fax: +*30* (1) 808 6465
Mailing Address: P.O. Box 51 190, Kifissia, 145 10 ATHENS

European Affiliation: Independent Accountants International

International Contact: Phidias Kypris

Partners:	2
Professional staff:	2
Non-professional staff:	4
Total Staff:	**8**

CONTACT INFORMATION
Managing Partner: Phidias Kypris
Accountancy & Audit: Costas Kypris
Legal Services: Anastassia Palazi
Computer Installation: Elisabeth Marinou

CLIENT SERVICES
All Services

Industry Specialisations: Shipping

MOORE STEPHENS

93 Akti Miaouli, 185 38 PIRAEUS
Tel: +*30* (1) 452 9111
Fax: +*30* (1) 418 1150
Mailing Address: P.O. Box 80-132, 185 10 PIRAEUS

European Affiliation: Moore Stephens

International Contact: Damianos Constantinou

OTHER OFFICES

MOORE STEPHENS
Academias Street, 106 71 ATHENS
Tel: +*30* (1) 363 0526 *Fax:* +*30* (1) 418 1150
Contact: Damianos Constantinou

Total Number of Offices: 2

PRICE WATERHOUSE

Tower of Athens, 16th Floor, 2 Messogion Avenue, 115 27 ATHENS
Tel: +*30* (1) 770 6201
Fax: +*30* (1) 775 7259
Mailing Address: P.O. Box 14018, 115 10 ATHENS

European Affiliation: Price Waterhouse

International Contact: Richard Caseley

OTHER OFFICES

PRICE WATERHOUSE
5-7 Kanari Street, 185 37 PIRAEUS
Tel: +*30* (1) 451 3554 *Fax:* +*30* (1) 451 8589
Contact: Christo Andreadis

Total Number of Offices: 2

CONSTANTIN SIGALAS DIPL. KAUFMANN

Syngrou Avenue 76, 117 42 ATHENS
Tel: +*30* (1) 922 6864
Fax: +*30* (1) 922 6866

European Affiliation: Moores Rowland International

International Contact: Constantin Sigalas

ATHOS STYLIANOU ASSOCIATES EPE

Ethnikis Antistaseos 84, 152 31 ATHENS
Tel: +*30* (1) 647 7819
Fax: +*30* (1) 672 6099

European Affiliation: DRM Internationally

Partners:	2
Non-professional staff:	1
Total Staff:	**3**

CONTACT INFORMATION
Managing Partner: Athos Stylianou
Tax: P. Mantzouranis

CLIENT SERVICES
Accountancy (General), Audit, Computer Installation, Management & Business Advice, Mergers & Acquisitions, Taxation (Corporate), Taxation (International)

Industry Specialisations: Construction, Shipping, Insurance

MAJOR CLIENTS
Fortress (UK) Ltd, Magna Holdings, The Paint Navigating Co Ltd

C.D. TZAVELLAS & CO

192b Alexandras Avenue, 115 21 ATHENS
Tel: +*30* (1) 646 5652
Fax: +*30* (1) 646 2477
Mailing Address: P.O. Box 14316, 115 10 ATHENS

European Affiliation: Urbach Hacker Young International

YANNES G. YAMARELLOS SA

Agiou Konstantinou Street 4, 104 31 ATHENS
Tel: +*30* (1) 522 1880
Fax: +*30* (1) 523 1102

European Affiliation: BDO Binder

International Contact: Pantelis Yamarellos

Partners:	3
Professional staff:	8
Non-professional staff:	6
Total Staff:	**17**

▷

Greece

FEE INCOME

Year End: 31.12.90	**US$**	**%**
Accountancy & Audit:	46,000	10.0
Consultancy:	46,000	10.0
Tax:	300,000	65.0
Other:	68,000	15.0
Total:	**460,000**	

CONTACT INFORMATION

Chairman: Yannis Yamarellos
Managing Partner: Yorgos Yamarellos
Accountancy & Audit: E. Vakiris
Accountancy, Corporate Finance & Tax: Yanis Yamarellos
Audit: Pantelis Yamarellos
Value Added Tax: Yorgos Krekoukias
Litigation: Helen Stamouli
Income Tax & Corporate Finance: Konstantin Kotzageorgis
Public Sector & Administration: Yorgos Yamarellos
Management Consultancy: Yannis Yamarellos

CLIENT SERVICES

Accountancy (General), Audit, Litigation/Legal Services, Management & Business Advice, Mergers & Acquisitions, Taxation (Corporate), Taxation (International), Trust Settlement & Estates

MAJOR CLIENTS

AEG Hellas SA, Beiersdorf Hellas SA, Diapharm SA, Elias SA, Elvak - I Schroeder SA, Helvetia Insurances SA, International Research, Ioannidis - Demag SA, Lever Hellas SA, Lintas Advertising Ltd, Milupa Hellas SA, Mouriadis SA, Nur Toyristic GmbH, Reemtsma Hellas SA, Schering Hellas SA, J.W. Thompson Adv SA, Toyota Hellas SA, Unilever NV, United Distilleries Boutaris SA

Ireland (Republic of)

Area: 68,895 sq km (27,136 sq miles)
Population: 3,538,000 (1988 official estimate)
Density: 50.3 per sq km
Capital: Dublin

GDP: IR£27.1 bn, US$46 bn
GDP per head: US$13,070
Inflation: 1990 - 3.3%
1991 - 3.7%

Official and Spoken Language: English. Irish (Gaelic) is spoken

Time: GMT (in Summer GMT + 1)
Telephone Dialling Code: +353

Currency: Irish Punt (IR£) = 100 pennies
Banking Hours: 1000-1230 and 1330-1500 Monday-Friday. Late opening one night per week (Dublin – Thursday, elsewhere – varies)
Professional accountancy body: Institute of Chartered Accountants in Ireland

Corporate Tax Data

Information supplied by Richard Citron, international tax partner of Stoy Hayward.

The tax year; nature and rates of tax

The financial year is the calendar year but corporation tax rates are set for years ending on 31 March.

The corporation tax is levied at a rate of 40% on distributed and undistributed income. A special rate of 10% applies to companies manufacturing in Ireland until 31 December 2010 and to companies providing certain financial services.

Residence and territoriality

Irish resident companies are liable to corporation tax on their worldwide income and gains. A company is resident in Ireland if its central management and control is exercised there.

The tax base

Method of computation. Taxable profits are based on the profit reported in the accounts.

Disallowable items. The major disallowable items are expenditure not incurred wholly and exclusively for the purposes of the trade, non-staff entertaining, capital expenditure and depreciation.

Exempt income/special deductions. Capital allowances are deductible in computing profits. Income from Irish registered patents is exempt if the work leading to the patent was carried out in Ireland. A special deduction of up to IR600,000 over three years is available for investment in Irish resident film production companies.

Interest paid. Interest paid is normally deductible on an accruals basis. Where interest is paid other than to a bank, the company must deduct a withholding tax of 29% which is regularly reduced to zero under the terms of a tax treaty. Where interest is paid by an Irish resident company to an overseas parent with a participation of 75% or over, or is profit related, it is non-deductible and treated similarly to a dividend payment. ▷

Stock. Stock and work in progress is valued at the lower of cost and market value.

Depreciation. There is a system of capital allowances for specified classes of assets.

(1) Plant and machinery (other than motor vehicles) are entitled to an accelerated allowance of 25% in the first year and an annual allowance in the first and subsequent years of 10%, 12.5% or 25% on a reducing balance basis.
(2) Motor vehicles attract an annual allowance of 20% per annum (limited to IR£1400 for private vehicles) on a reducing balance basis.
(3) Industrial buildings attract an accelerated allowance of 25% in the first year and an annual allowance of 4% on a straight line basis.
(4) Urban renewal allowances of up to 100% are available on construction expenditure in certain areas.

Accelerated allowances will be completely phased out by 1 April 1992.

The treatment of dividends

Dividends received from Irish companies. Dividends received from Irish resident companies are exempt from corporation tax. The tax credit attaching to them may be used to reduce the advance corporation tax payable by the company on its own dividends.

Dividends received from abroad. Where the recipient company's holding is 10% or more, dividends received from abroad are liable to corporation tax on their gross amount. A foreign tax credit is available amounting to the withholding tax and the underlying tax.

Dividends paid to Irish residents. Advance corporation tax (ACT) is payable at a rate of 25/75 of the net dividend and an equivalent tax credit is available to the recipient. ACT may be used (as reduced by the tax credit on incoming dividends) to reduce the company's corporation tax liability on its income.

Dividends paid to non-residents. The company must still pay ACT but non-residents are not entitled to the tax credit represented by the ACT. However, dividends paid by 75% subsidiaries to a parent resident in a treaty country are free of ACT.

Anti-avoidance measures

There are measures designed to prevent the accumulation of profits in "close" (primarily family owned) companies. Transfer pricing legislation exists. There are also wide ranging measures to prevent avoidance by transfer of income abroad, and a general anti-avoidance power allowing the tax authorities to counteract transactions carried out primarily to create an artificial tax benefit.

Treatment of losses

Current period. Trading losses may be set off against all income and gains of the same period, except gains from development land.

Past periods. A trading loss may be carried back and set against all income and gains of the preceding period, except gains from development land.

Future periods. To the extent that they remain unrelieved in the current or preceding periods, trading losses may be carried forward indefinitely against profits from the same trade.

Treatment of capital gains

Treatment. A company's capital gains are assessable to corporation tax. Gains on assets held for three years or less are taxed at 50%, gains on assets held for more than three years but not more than six are taxed at 35%, and gains on assets held for more than six years at 30%.

Computation. Capital gains are computed by deducting the adjusted cost from sale proceeds. The cost of acquisition is adjusted for inflation.

Rollover. Deferral of a gain by rolling it over against the cost of replacement assets is often possible.

Treatment of groups

Group treatment is available for various tax free transactions between members of a 75% or more owned group of Irish resident companies. Tax losses of the current period may be transferred to other companies in the group and assets may be transferred between group companies free of capital gains tax. Dividends and interest may be paid free of ACT or income (withholding) tax and surplus ACT may be surrendered within a group.

Treatment of branches

The profits and gains of an Irish branch of a non-resident company are computed in the same way as those of an Irish resident company but tax is charged on Irish source income only. There is no withholding tax and no ACT on remittances of profits.

Other taxes

A *local authority rate* is levied on the annual (rental) value on the occupier of property.

Turnover taxes. A value added tax is charged. There is a standard rate of 21% and lower rates of 12.5% and 10%. Exports are zero rated.

Transaction taxes. There is a capital duty of 1% on share issues and stamp duties on the transfer of shares and other property.

Payroll taxes. Social security contributions are payable by employers at 12.2% on salaries of up to IR£19,300 per annum.

ARTHUR ANDERSEN & CO

Andersen House, International Financial Servs Ctr, DUBLIN 1
Tel: +353 (1) 6701000
Fax: +353 (1) 6701010

European Affiliation: Arthur Andersen Worldwide

International Contact: Adrian A. Burke

CONTACT INFORMATION
Audit: Breffni J. Byrne
Tax (Corporate): Roderick P. Ryan

CLIENT SERVICES
Accountancy (General), Audit, Computer Installation, Corporate Finance Advice, Insolvency & Corporate Restructuring, Litigation/Legal Services, Management & Business Advice, Management Buy-outs, Mergers & Acquisitions, Pensions Planning, Value for Money Studies, Taxation (Corporate), Taxation (International)

BASTOW CHARLETON

Marine House, Clanwilliam Court, DUBLIN 2
Tel: +353 (1) 760951
Fax: +353 (1) 609108

European Affiliation: The Channel International Association

International Contact: Justin Baily
Colm Deignan

BDO BINDER

Setanta Centre, Nassau Street, DUBLIN 2
Tel: +353 (1) 6797500
Fax: +353 (1) 6797520

European Affiliation: BDO Binder

International Contact: John Conran

Partners:	7
Professional staff:	54
Non-professional staff:	11
Total Staff:	**72**

FEE INCOME

Year End: 30.04.91	**IR£**	**%**
Accountancy & Audit:	1,034,000	47.0
Insolvency:	176,000	8.0
Consultancy:	220,000	10.0
Tax:	484,000	22.0
Other:	286,000	13.0
Total:	**2,200,000**	

CONTACT INFORMATION
Managing Partner: John Conran
Accountancy (General): Charles Russell
Audit: Tom Mason
Corporate Finance: Liam Dowdall
Insolvency: David Fleetwood
Tax (Corporate): Bill Ledwidge

CLIENT SERVICES
Accountancy (General), Audit, Computer Installation, Corporate Finance Advice, Insolvency & Corporate Restructuring, Life & Risk Assurance, Litigation/Legal Services, Management & Business Advice, Management Buy-outs, Mergers & Acquisitions, Pensions Planning, Value for Money Studies, Taxation (Corporate), Taxation (International), Trust Settlement & Estates

BUTLER, FITZPATRICK, CAVANAGH, DONNELLY

90 Ranelagh Road, DUBLIN 6
Tel: +353 (1) 970935
Fax: +353 (1) 960061

European Affiliation: Morison International

International Contact: Michael Donnelly

Partners:	5
Professional staff:	15
Non-professional staff:	3
Total Staff:	**23**

FEE INCOME

Year End: 31.12.90	**IR£**
Total:	**700,000**

CONTACT INFORMATION
Chairman: Richard Butler
Managing Partner: Frank Cavanagh
Accountancy (General): Dan Collins
Audit: William Fitzpatrick
Corporate Finance: Michael Donnelly
Insolvency: Richard Butler
Management Consultancy: Frank Cavanagh
Tax & Litigation Support: Victor Smith
Computer Systems: Frank Cavanagh
Grants: William Fitzpatrick

CLIENT SERVICES
All Services

Industry Specialisations: Retail, Construction, Manufacturing, Professional Services, Agricultural

CAPLIN MEHAN

Adelaide House, 19/20 Adelaide Road, DUBLIN 2
Tel: +353 (1) 784833
Fax: +353 (1) 784391

European Affiliation: Independent Accountants International

International Contact: Julian Caplin

CHAPMAN FLOOD & CO

Mount Herbert Court, 34 Upper Mount Street, DUBLIN 2
Tel: +353 (1) 761116
Fax: +353 (1) 766640

European Affiliation: Summit International Associates Inc

International Contact: David L. Chapman

Partners:	4
Professional staff:	26
Non-professional staff:	7
Total Staff:	**37**

CONTACT INFORMATION
Managing Partner: David L. Chapman
Management Consultancy: Simon Coyle
Public Sector: David L. Chapman
Corporate Finance & Insolvency: Simon Coyle
Administration, Accountancy & Audit: David Flood
Tax (Corporate & International): Peter O'Neill
Mergers & Acquisitions: David L. Chapman

CLIENT SERVICES
Accountancy (General), Audit, Computer Installation, Corporate Finance Advice, Insolvency & Corporate Restructuring, Litigation/Legal Services, Management & Business Advice, Management Buy-outs, Mergers & ▷

Acquisitions, Taxation (Corporate), Taxation (International), Trust Settlement & Estates

Industry Specialisations: Food, Print & Packaging, Property

COOPERS & LYBRAND

Fitzwilliam House, Wilton Place, DUBLIN 2
Tel: + *353* (1) 610333
Fax: + *353* (1) 601782
Mailing Address: P.O. Box 1283, DUBLIN 2

European Affiliation: Coopers & Lybrand Europe

International Contact: E. Richard Lane

Partners:	38
Professional staff:	409
Non-professional staff:	90
Total Staff:	**537**

CONTACT INFORMATION

Corporate Finance: Dr. Michael McGrail
Insolvency: Desmond Guilfoyle
Administration: Peter Fitzpatrick
Accountancy & Audit: William Cunningham
Consultancy & Public Sector: Thomas McCarthy
Tax (Corporate & International): Patrick Wall
Pensions: Gearoid Griffin

CLIENT SERVICES

Accountancy (General), Audit, Corporate Finance Advice, Insolvency & Corporate Restructuring, Litigation/Legal Services, Management & Business Advice, Management Buy-outs, Mergers & Acquisitions, Pensions Planning, Taxation (Corporate), Taxation (International), Company Secretarial, Financial Advice - Inward Investors

Industry Specialisations: Agriculture, Pharmaceuctical, Banking, Food & Drink, Automotive, Insurance, Communications

OTHER OFFICES

COOPERS & LYBRAND
26 South Mall, CORK
Tel: + *353* (21) 277883 *Fax:* + *353* (21) 277009
Contact: James Mangan

COOPERS & LYBRAND
20 Patrick Street, KILKENNY
Tel: + *353* (56) 21998 *Fax:* + *353* (56) 65962
Contact: Martin Hanrahan

COOPERS & LYBRAND
88 O'Connell Street, LIMERICK
Tel: + *353* (61) 314622 *Fax:* + *353* (61) 317691
Contact: Patrick Roche

COOPERS & LYBRAND
Ballycar House, Newton, WATERFORD
Tel: + *353* (51) 74858 *Fax:* + *353* (51) 72312
Contact: Frank Kelly

COOPERS & LYBRAND
Cornmarket, WEXFORD
Tel: + *353* (53) 24822 *Fax:* + *353* (53) 23616
Contact: Paul Hennessy

Total Number of Offices: 6

COPSEY, MURRAY & CO

Charter House, 5 Pembroke Row, DUBLIN 2
Tel: + *353* (1) 610144
Fax: + *353* (1) 606203

European Affiliation: Midsnell International

Partners:	3
Professional staff:	5
Non-professional staff:	10
Total Staff:	**18**

CONTACT INFORMATION

Managing Partner: Roger Copsey
Accountancy (General): Anthony Kenny
Insolvency: Gerard Murray
Tax (Corporate): Roger Copsey

CLIENT SERVICES

All Services

KIERAN CORRIGAN & CO

41 Fitzwilliam Place, DUBLIN 2
Tel: + *353* (1) 764460
Fax: + *353* (1) 764368

European Affiliation: DRM Internationally

International Contact: Kieran Corrigan

Partners:	3
Professional staff:	18
Non-professional staff:	6
Total Staff:	**27**

FEE INCOME

Year End: 31.08.91	%
Accountancy & Audit:	25.0
Insolvency:	2.0
Consultancy:	8.0
Tax:	55.0
Other:	10.0

CONTACT INFORMATION

Managing Partner: Kieran Corrigan
Tax (International): Anne Corrigan
Administration, Public Sector & Tax: Patrick Cleary
Accountancy & Consultancy: Kieran Corrigan

CLIENT SERVICES

All Services

Industry Specialisations: International Financial Services, Property, Leisure & Entertainment

---

CREMIN, MCCARTHY & CO

28 Harcourt Street, DUBLIN 2
Tel: + *353* (1) 542766
Fax: + *353* (1) 783331

European Affiliation: S & W International

International Contact: Paul Phillips

DELOITTE & TOUCHE

Deloitte & Touche House, Earlsfort Centre, Earlsfort Terrace, DUBLIN 2
Tel: + *353* (1) 618311
Fax: + *353* (1) 618622

European Affiliation: DRT International

International Contact: John Donnelly

Total Staff: **550**

CLIENT SERVICES
Accountancy (General), Audit, Computer Installation, Corporate Finance Advice, Insolvency & Corporate Restructuring, Litigation/Legal Services, Management & Business Advice, Management Consultancy, Management Buy outs, Mergers & Acquisitions, Pensions Planning, Value for Money Studies, Taxation (Corporate), Taxation (International), Trust Settlement & Estates

MAJOR CLIENTS
BASF, Dunnes Stores, General Motors, Irish Ferries, Kerry Group plc, Northern Telecom, Power Corporation, Procter & Gamble, Sandoz, Toyota Ireland

Total Number of Offices: 3

DONNELLY & CO
Taney Hall, Eglinton Terrace, Dundrum, DUBLIN 14
Tel: +353 (1) 987911
Fax: +353 (1) 985162

European Affiliation: Alliott Peirson International

International Contact: Tony Donnelly

DUIGNAN & CO/KIDSONS IMPEY
84 Northumberland Road, Ballsbridge, DUBLIN 4
Tel: +353 (1) 683266
Fax: +353 (1) 600501

European Affiliation: HLB International

International Contact: Brian Fitzpatrick

Partners:	4
Professional staff:	22
Non-professional staff:	4
Total Staff:	**30**

CONTACT INFORMATION
Chairman: Noel Rennick
Managing Partner: Vincent Duignan
Audit: Joseph Duff
Insolvency: Vincent Duignan
Management Consultancy: Michael Doody
Administration: Noel Rennick
Accountancy & Audit: Michael Doody
Tax: Brian Fitzpatrick
Company Secretarial: Michele Walsh

CLIENT SERVICES
All Services

Industry Specialisations: Agri-Business, Agricultural & Dairy Co-Operatives, Bloodstock, Electronics

EATON DOWD
First Floor, McConnell House, DUBLIN 2
Tel: +353 (1) 783666
Fax: +353 (1) 782748

International Contact: George Eaton

ERNST & YOUNG
Stephen Court, 18/21 St Stephens Green, DUBLIN 2
Tel: +353 (1) 760151
Fax: +353 (1) 616971

European Affiliation: Ernst & Young Europe

International Contact: John Hogan

OTHER OFFICES

ERNST & YOUNG
Stapleton House, 89 South Mall, CORK
Tel: +353 (21) 277116 *Fax:* +353 (21) 273849

ERNST & YOUNG
Marine House, Clanwilliam Place, DUBLIN 2
Tel: +353 (1) 609433 *Fax:* +353 (1) 761740

ERNST & YOUNG
Kiltartan House, Forster Street, GALWAY
Tel: +353 (91) 61184 *Fax:* +353 (91) 65242

ERNST & YOUNG
Barrington House, Barrington Street, LIMERICK
Tel: +353 (61) 319988 *Fax:* +353 (61) 319865

ERNST & YOUNG
Annaville House, Newtown, WATERFORD
Tel: +353 (51) 72094 *Fax:* +353 (51) 72392

Total Number of Offices: 6

FARRELL, GRANT, SPARKS & CO
Molyneux House, 67/69 Bride Street, DUBLIN 8
Tel: +353 (1) 758137
Fax: +353 (1) 752044

European Affiliation: INPACT - International Network of Professional Accountants

International Contact: Pearse Farrell

CONTACT INFORMATION
Tax: John O'Callaghan
Partner: Gregory Sparks
Partner: Pearse Farrell

FAULKNER ORR
1 Adelaide Court, Adelaide Road, DUBLIN 2
Tel: +353 (1) 753100
Fax: +353 (1) 753341

European Affiliation: K.S. International

International Contact: David Orr

Partners:	2
Total Staff:	**19**

CLIENT SERVICES
Accountancy (General), Audit, Corporate Finance Advice, Management & Business Advice, Mergers & Acquisitions, Taxation (Corporate), Taxation (Personal), Training

FITZGERALD & ASSOCIATES
11 Anglesea Street, DUBLIN 2
Tel: +353 (1) 771200
Fax: +353 (1) 771284

European Affiliation: InterContinental Consultants (ICC)

International Contact: John Fitzgerald

OTHER OFFICES

FITZGERALD & ASSOCIATES
6 Sullivans Quay, CORK
Tel: +353 (21) 963877 *Fax:* +353 (21) 310272
Contact: John Fitzgerald

Total Number of Offices: 2

OLIVER FREANEY & COMPANY

45 Northumberland Road, DUBLIN 4
Tel: +353 (1) 688644
Fax: +353 (1) 689755

European Affiliation: Nexia International

International Contact: Paul G. Wyse

Partners:	9
Professional staff:	75
Non-professional staff:	22
Total Staff:	**106**

FEE INCOME

Year End: 31.10.90	**IR£**	**%**
Accountancy & Audit:		47.0
Insolvency:		7.5
Consultancy:		20.0
Tax:		17.5
Other:		8.0
Total:	**34,000,000**	

CONTACT INFORMATION
Chairman: Noel Fox
Managing Partner: Paul G. Wyse
Accountancy (General): Frank Byrne
Audit: Pat O'Dono
Management Consultancy: Noel Fox
Tax: John McCarthy
Personal Financial Planning: Patrick Walsh

CLIENT SERVICES
All Services, Company Secretarial Services, European Information Services

Industry Specialisations: Health Care, Retail, Manufacturing, Leisure & Tourism, Motor Distributors

GILROY GANNON

Stephen Street, SLIGO
Tel: +353 (71) 61747
Fax: +353 (71) 43283

Partners:	6
Professional staff:	35
Non-professional staff:	10
Total Staff:	**51**

CONTACT INFORMATION
Managing Partner: Alan Palmer
Audit: Calhail O'Donnell
Corporate Finance: Paul Horan
Insolvency: Joe Gannon
Administration: Declan Gilroy
Public Sector: Brian Kilfeather
Accountancy & Consultancy: Alan Palmer
Tax: Ken McMoreland

CLIENT SERVICES
All Services

Industry Specialisations: Agri-business, Clothing, Plastics

MAJOR CLIENTS
Hanson Ltd, North Connacht Farmers Co-Op, North Western Health Board, Shannonside Co-Op

GORMAN & ASSOCIATES

66 Lower Baggott Street, DUBLIN 2
Tel: +353 (1) 789266
Fax: +353 (1) 612632

European Affiliation: ATD International

International Contact: W.J. Gorman

Partners:	1
Professional staff:	6
Non-professional staff:	3
Total Staff:	**10**

CONTACT INFORMATION
Managing Partner: W.J. Gorman
Corporate Finance & Adminstration: I.G. Burns
Tax: J. Curtin

CLIENT SERVICES
Accountancy (General), Audit, Corporate Finance Advice, Insolvency & Corporate Restructuring, Management & Business Advice, Management Buy-outs, Mergers & Acquisitions, Taxation (Corporate), Taxation (International), Trust Settlement & Estates

GRANT THORNTON

Kinnear Court, Cumberland Street South, DUBLIN 2
Tel: +353 (1) 714677
Fax: +353 (1) 717209

European Affiliation: Grant Thornton International

International Contact: Sean Murray

Partners:	14
Professional staff:	65
Non-professional staff:	16
Total Staff:	**95**

FEE INCOME

Year End: 31.07.90	**IR£**
Total:	**2,750,545**

CONTACT INFORMATION
Managing Partner: Sean Murray

CLIENT SERVICES
Accountancy (General), Audit, Computer Installation, Corporate Finance Advice, Insolvency & Corporate Restructuring, Management & Business Advice, Management Buy-outs, Mergers & Acquisitions, Pensions Planning, Taxation (Corporate), Taxation (International), Computer Consultancy/Training

OTHER OFFICES
GRANT THORNTON
Dublin Road, MULLINGAR, Co Westmeath
Tel: +353 (44) 41421 *Fax:* +353 (44) 41427

Total Number of Offices: 2

HAYDEN BROWN

Grafton Buildings, 34 Grafton Street, DUBLIN 2
Tel: +353 (1) 771951
Fax: +353 (1) 771308

European Affiliation: SC International

International Contact: Val O'Connor

JOY McNABOLA MURRAY

17 Earlsfort Terrace, DUBLIN 2
Tel: +353 (1) 766066
Fax: +353 (1) 761340

European Affiliation: The International Group of Accounting Firms Ltd (IGAF)

International Contact: J.P. McNabola

KPMG

KPMG STOKES KENNEDY CROWLEY

1 Stokes Place, St Stephen's Green, DUBLIN 2
Tel: +353 (1) 7081000
Fax: +353 (1) 7081122

European Affiliation: KPMG

Partners:	46
Professional staff:	728
Non-professional staff:	151
Total Staff:	**925**

FEE INCOME

Year End: 30.04.91	**IR£**
Accountancy & Audit:	17,900,000
Insolvency:	4,200,000
Consultancy:	3,800,000
Tax:	7,800,000
Total:	**33,700,000**

CONTACT INFORMATION
Managing Partner: Ronald Bolger
Corporate Finance: Gerard Flood
Insolvency: Ray Jackson
Management Consultancy: Michael Spellman
Administration: Ron Harris
Public Sector: Noel Cooke
Accountancy & Audit: Chris Cullen
Tax: Gerry McEvoy

CLIENT SERVICES
All Services

Industry Specialisations: Financial Institutions, Banks, Thrifts, Food & Agri-Business, Manufacturing

MAJOR CLIENTS
Aer Rianta plc, B & I Line plc, Barlo Group plc, Cambridge Group plc, Elan Corporation plc, Electricity Supply Board, Food Industries plc, Fyffes plc, GPA Group Ltd, Green Property plc, IRG plc, Irish National Petroleum Corporation Ltd, Irish Permanent Building Society, The Jones Group plc, National Irish Bank Ltd, Norish plc, Northern Bank Ltd, United Drug plc, Waterford Foods plc, Woodchester Investments plc

OTHER OFFICES

KPMG STOKES KENNEDY CROWLEY
Ninety South Mall, CORK
Tel: +353 (21) 270372 *Fax:* +353 (21) 273230
Contact: Jerome Kennedy

KPMG STOKES KENNEDY CROWLEY
Odeon House, Eyre Square, GALWAY
Tel: +353 (91) 63064 *Fax:* +353 (91) 65567
Contact: Ben Bradish

Total Number of Offices: 5

McGRATH & CO

Kildress House, Pembroke Row, Lower Baggot Street, DUBLIN 2
Tel: +353 (1) 616766
Fax: +353 (1) 615526

European Affiliation: Affiliated Conference of Practising Accountants International (ACPA)

International Contact: Tom Kavanagh

McQUILLANS - DFK

Drury Court, 56-58 Drury Street, DUBLIN 2
Tel: +353 (1) 6797663
Fax: +353 (1) 6797761

European Affiliation: DFK International

International Contact: Kenneth McQuillan

OTHER OFFICES

McQUILLANS - DFK
7 Park Street, DUNDALK, Co Louth
Tel: +353 (42) 34086 *Fax:* +353 (42) 34086

Total Number of Offices: 2

MERRY, MULLEN & CO

6 Gardiner Place, DUBLIN 1
Tel: +353 (1) 742 177
Fax: +353 (1) 721 357

European Affiliation: GMN International

International Contact: Brian Merry

MOORE STEPHENS

6 Fitzwilliam Place, DUBLIN 2
Tel: +353 (1) 612272
Fax: +353 (1) 682679

European Affiliation: Moore Stephens

International Contact: Nicholas O'Conor

Partners:	4
Professional staff:	12
Non-professional staff:	2
Total Staff:	**18**

CLIENT SERVICES
All Services

V.F. NATHAN & CO

Christchurch Square, DUBLIN 8
Tel: +353 (1) 544333
Fax: +353 (1) 544690

European Affiliation: Clark Kenneth Leventhal

International Contact: Vivian Nathan

Partners:	4
Professional staff:	34
Non-professional staff:	17
Total Staff:	**55**

FEE INCOME

Year End: 1990	%
Accountancy & Audit:	40.0
Tax:	30.0
Other:	30.0

CLIENT SERVICES
Accountancy (General), Audit, Corporate Finance Advice, Insolvency & Corporate Restructuring, Management & Business Advice, Taxation (Corporate), Taxation (International)

OTHER OFFICES

V.F. NATHAN & CO
Lavitts Quay, CORK
Tel: +353 (21) 275176 *Fax:* +353 (21) 277305
Contact: Michael J. Mullins

Total Number of Offices: 2

Ireland (Republic of)

ORPEN FRANKS

28-30 Burlington Road, DUBLIN 4
Tel: +*353* (1) 689622
Fax: +*353* (1) 689004

European Affiliation: A.E.E. International

O'CONNOR, LEDDY & HOLMES

Century House, Harold's Cross Road, DUBLIN 6
Tel: +*353* (1) 961444
Fax: +*353* (1) 961637

European Affiliation: Urbach Hacker Young International

International Contact: David Holmes

Partners:	7
Professional staff:	36
Non-professional staff:	6
Total Staff:	**49**

FEE INCOME

Year End: 31.05.91	**IR£**	**%**
Accountancy & Audit:		57.0
Insolvency:		10.0
Tax:		20.0
Other:		13.0
Total:	**1,390,000**	

CONTACT INFORMATION
Accountancy (General): John Leddy
Accountancy (General): Paul Stevens
Audit: John Hamilton
Corporate Finance: David Holmes
Insolvency: Barry Forrest
Administration: Mark Tully
Tax (Corporate): Denis O'Connor
Tax Consultancy: Kieran O'Byrne
Financial Services: Frank Nugent
Property Management: Vincent Ceillier

CLIENT SERVICES
All Services, Property Management Services

O'SULLIVAN KEOGH

OSK House, 29 Lower Baggot Street, DUBLIN 2
Tel: +*353* (1) 619256
Fax: +*353* (1) 614233

European Affiliation: CPA Associates Inc

International Contact: David Keogh

Partners:	2
Professional staff:	11
Non-professional staff:	2
Total Staff:	**15**

FEE INCOME

Year End: 31.05.91	**IR£**	**%**
Accountancy & Audit:	200,000	50.0
Consultancy:	100,000	25.0
Tax:	100,000	25.0
Total:	**400,000**	

CONTACT INFORMATION
Managing Partner: David Keogh
Accountancy & Audit: Tadhg O'Sullivan
Corporate Finance & Consultancy: David Keogh
Tax: Paula Oliver
Tax (Personal): Terry Oliver

CLIENT SERVICES
All Services

Industry Specialisations: Printing, Music, Tour Operators/Travel Agents, Manufacturing, Retail

PANNELL KERR FORSTER

17 Percy Place, DUBLIN 4
Tel: +*353* (1) 606444
Fax: +*353* (1) 682007

European Affiliation: Pannell Kerr Forster Worldwide

CONTACT INFORMATION
Managing Partner: C.J. Blackwell

POWER & HUNTER

48 Fitzwilliam Square, DUBLIN 2
Tel: +*353* (1) 764120
Fax: +*353* (1) 618143

European Affiliation: Jeffreys Henry International

International Contact: Ian Hunter

PRICE WATERHOUSE

Gardner House, Wilton Place, DUBLIN 2
Tel: +*353* (1) 605199
Fax: +*353* (1) 607638

European Affiliation: Price Waterhouse

International Contact: William McCann

Partners:	46
Professional staff:	520
Non-professional staff:	75
Total Staff:	**641**

CONTACT INFORMATION
Managing Partner: William McCann
Accountancy (General): John B. Dillon
Corporate Finance: Bryan Evans
Insolvency: Tom Grace
Management Consultancy: Roy Hanan
Administration: Andrew Craig
Public Sector: David Devlin
Tax: Tadhg O'Donoghue
Secretarial/Registration Services: Thomas Meehan

CLIENT SERVICES
All Services

OTHER OFFICES

PRICE WATERHOUSE
Gardner House, 1 South Mall, CORK
Tel: +*353* (21) 276631 *Fax:* +*353* (21) 276630
Contact: Michael Long

PRICE WATERHOUSE
Sarsfield House, Francis Street, LIMERICK
Tel: +*353* (61) 416644 *Fax:* +*353* (61) 416331
Contact: Boland P. Gerry

Total Number of Offices: 3

▷

RYAN GLENNON & CO.

Trinity House, Charleston Road, Ranelagh, DUBLIN 6
Tel: +353 (1) 965388
Fax: +353 (1) 965880

European Affiliation: TGI International

International Contact: Liam Ryan

SIMPSON XAVIER

20 Merchants Quay, DUBLIN 8
Tel: +353 (1) 6790022
Fax: +353 (1) 6790111

European Affiliation: Horwath International

Partners:	14
Professional staff:	82
Non-professional staff:	24
Total Staff:	**120**

FEE INCOME

Year End: 31.05.91	**IR£**	**%**
Accountancy & Audit:	1,520,000	43.3
Insolvency:	365,000	10.4
Consultancy:	300,000	8.5
Tax:	600,000	17.1
Other:	725,000	20.7
Total:	**3,510,000**	

CONTACT INFORMATION

Managing Partner: Anthuan Xavier
Accountancy (General): David Simpson
Audit: Colm Nagle
Corporate Finance: Anthuan Xavier
Insolvency: Patrick McSwiney
Management Consultancy: Ronan King
Administration: Jim Donnely
Public Sector: Ronan King
Tax (Corporate): James Skehan
Tax (International): Frank Sheedy
Family Businesses: Philip Smyth

CLIENT SERVICES

Accountancy (General), Audit, Computer Installation, Corporate Finance Advice, Insolvency & Corporate Restructuring, Life & Risk Assurance, Litigation/Legal Services, Management & Business Advice, Management Buy-outs, Mergers & Acquisitions, Pensions Planning, Taxation (Corporate), Taxation (International), Family Business Consultancy

Industry Specialisations: Leisure, Tourism, Franchising, Retail, Printing & Packaging

OTHER OFFICES

SIMPSON XAVIER
4 Michael Street, LIMERICK
Tel: +353 (61) 44455 *Fax:* +353 (61) 44172

Total Number of Offices: 2

TYNON DILLON & CO

57 Amiens Street, DUBLIN 1
Tel: +353 (1) 749058
Fax: +353 (1) 364565

International Contact: Barry J. Dillon

JOHN WOODS & CO

Woods House, BLACKROCK, Co Dublin
Tel: +353 (42) 886851
Fax: +353 (42) 888208

European Affiliation: Moores Rowland International

International Contact: Barry Butterly

Area: 301,279 sq km (116,324 sq miles)
Population: 57,399,108 (1987 estimate)
Density: 190.5 per sq km
Capital: Rome

GDP: L1,320 trn, US$1.18 trn
GDP per head: US$20,450
Inflation: 1990 - 6.3%
1991 - 7.0% (forecast)

Official and Spoken Languages: Italian. German widely spoken in the area bordering Austria, French spoken in French and Swiss border areas. Slovenian spoken in provinces adjacent to Yugoslavia. English, French and German spoken in large cities.

Time: GMT + 1 (in Summer GMT + 2)
Telephone Dialling Code: + 39

Currency: Italian Lira (L)
Banking Hours: Generally 0830-1330 and 1530-1630 Monday-Friday, but varies from city to city.
Professional accountancy bodies: Consiglio Nazionale dei Dottori Commercialisti (CNDC) Consiglio Nazionale dei Ragionieri e Periti Commerciali (CNR)

Corporate Tax Data

Information supplied by Richard Citron, international tax partner of Stoy Hayward.

The tax year; the nature and rates of tax

The tax year is the calendar year.

Italian companies are liable to both national income tax (imposta sul reddito delle persone giuridiche or IRPEG) and local income tax (imposta locale sui redditi or ILOR). IRPEG is charged at a single rate of 36% and ILOR is charged at 16.2%. New industrial undertakings setting up in the Mezzogiorno (the south of Italy) receive a ten year exemption from IRPEG.

Residence and territoriality

Companies resident in Italy are liable to IRPEG on their world wide income and gains. ILOR is levied on Italian source income and gains only. A company is resident in Italy if it is incorporated there, if its legal or administrative headquarters is in Italy or if its principal business is carried on there.

The tax base

Method of calculation. Taxable profits for IRPEG and ILOR are based on the profit reported in the accounts.

Disallowable items. The major disallowable items are expenses incurred in relation to non-taxable income, two thirds of entertaining expenses and pension contributions.

Exempt income/special deductions. A maximum of 0.5% of trade debtors may be deducted until the total provision is equal to 5% of trade debtors. The ILOR liability is deductible in computing liability to IRPEG (although limited to 75% of the ILOR payable).

Interest paid. Interest is deductible on an accruals basis. A withholding tax of 12.5% or 30% (treated as an advance payment of IRPEG) must be deducted on interest payments to residents. ▷

Stock. Stock is valued at the lower of cost and market value.

Depreciation. Depreciation is on the straightline basis at rates prescribed by the tax authorities (ie. industrial buildings 3-7% and motor vehicles 25%) although companies may choose to restate their assets at open market value. Accelerated depreciation is available for tangible assets in the first three years of use.The excess of sale proceeds over net book value of assets disposed of is included in taxable income, as are any losses arising. Expenditure on assets costing less than L1,000,000 may be written off in the year it is incurred.

Treatment of dividends

Dividends received from Italian companies. These are subject to IRPEG only. For IRPEG purposes, the dividend is grossed up for withholding tax and a tax credit of 9/16 (56.25%). Both the withholding tax and tax credit can be set off against the resulting IRPEG liability. The result is that the dividend is effectively tax free.

Dividends received from abroad. Dividends received from foreign companies are liable to IRPEG in Italy. The foreign tax paid on the dividend can be used as a credit against IRPEG. Where the Italian company has a participation of 10% or more in the paying company (or 5% where the paying company is quoted), 60% of the dividends received are exempt from IRPEG.

Dividends paid to Italian residents. A withholding tax of 10% must be deducted from dividends payable to residents of Italy. In addition, if the paying company distributes more than 64% of its income liable to IRPEG or distributions are made from income that has not suffered the full rate of IRPEG, the paying company must pay an equalisation tax (imposta di conguaglio) by way of additional IRPEG at 56.25% on the excess.

Dividends paid to non-residents. Withholding tax of 32.4% (reduced under the terms of most treaties) must be deducted from dividends paid to non-residents.

Anti-avoidance measures

Transfer pricing provisions operate to adjust transactions between Italian companies and foreign affiliates to arm's length values.

Treatment of losses

Current period. Trading and capital losses may be set off against other income and gains of the same period (there is no carry-back).

Future periods. For IRPEG purposes only, losses may also be carried forward against income and gains for a maximum of five years.

Treatment of capital gains

Treatment. Capital gains are treated as taxable income.

Computation. Gains are generally computed by deducting the cost of the asset (or, for depreciable assets, their net book value) from sale proceeds.

Rollover. Where the disposal proceeds are reinvested in replacement assets, the gain realised may be spread over a maximum of five years.

Treatment of groups

Italian tax law does not recognise the group concept.

Treatment of branches

The profits and gains of the Italian branch of a non-resident company are computed in the same way as those of a resident company. The branch will be liable to IRPEG and ILOR on its Italian source income and gains. There is no withholding tax on remittances of profit from the branch.

Other taxes.

Unlike ILOR, the local property tax INVIM (imposta comunale sull'incremento divalore degli immobili) varies locally. It is both a transaction tax, chargeable on the vendor of real property and a decennial capital tax on property, levied on the increase in value of real property. The rate also varies according to the period of ownership and, on the occasion of a disposal, to the proportion the gain bears to the cost. INVIM is a deductible expense in calculating the capital gain on disposal of real property and in computing liability to IRPEG and ILOR. Rates vary between 5% and 30%.

Turnover taxes. Value added tax (imposta sul valore aggiunto) is charged on the supply of goods and services. The standard rate is 19%; there are lower rates of 4%and 9% and a luxury rate of 38%. Exports are zero rated.

Transaction taxes. There are various transfer taxes. A 10% registration tax is payable by the purchaser of real property; a 1% capital duty is charged on the issue of shares and a 0.14% transfer tax is payable on share transfers. When a business is transferred as a going concern, a 3% registration tax is payable.

Payroll taxes. Employers' social security contributions amount to between 35% and 45% of gross payroll.

A substitute tax applies (at 16% or 20%) on an asset revaluation in a SRL (Società responsibilita limitata or limited liability company).

A corporate Franchise Tax ("Tassa di Concessione Governativa") is based on the share capital of companies and varies from a minimum of L3.5 million to L12 million.

ARTHUR ANDERSEN & CO

Via Campania 47, 00187 ROME
Tel: +39 (6) 482971
Fax: +39 (6) 4823684

European Affiliation: Arthur Andersen Worldwide

International Contact: Maurizio Milanesi

CLIENT SERVICES

Accountancy (General), Audit, Computer Installation, Corporate Finance Advice, Insolvency & Corporate Restructuring, Litigation/Legal Services, Management & Business Advice, Management Buy-outs, Mergers & Acquisitions, Pensions Planning, Value for Money Studies, Taxation (Corporate), Taxation (International)

OTHER OFFICES

ARTHUR ANDERSEN & CO
Piazza Malpighi 42, 40123 BOLOGNA
Tel: +39 (51) 238133 *Fax:* +39 (51) 230874

ARTHUR ANDERSEN & CO
Piazza della Vittoria 8, 25121 BRESCIA
Tel: +39 (30) 2400550 *Fax:* +39 (30) 2400531

ARTHUR ANDERSEN & CO
Viale Matteotti 25, 50121 FLORENCE
Tel: +39 (55) 582743 *Fax:* +39 (55) 574439

ARTHUR ANDERSEN & CO
Piazza della Vittoria 15/35, 16121 GENOA
Tel: +39 (10) 564364 *Fax:* +39 (10) 585130

ARTHUR ANDERSEN & CO
Via Della Moscova 3, 20121 MILAN
Tel: +39 (2) 623412 *Fax:* +39 (2) 6572876

ARTHUR ANDERSEN & CO
Riviera di Chiaia 180, 80122 NAPLES
Tel: +39 (81) 7611933 *Fax:* +39 (81) 7614173

ARTHUR ANDERSEN & CO
Via degli Scrovengni 29, 35100 PADUA
Tel: +39 (49) 8754399 *Fax:* +39 (49) 8754525

ARTHUR ANDERSEN & CO
Piazzale della Macina 3, 43100 PARMA
Tel: +39 (251) 236580

ARTHUR ANDERSEN & CO
Piazza San Vito 37, 31100 TREVISO
Tel: +39 (422) 58752 *Fax:* +39 (422) 579471

ARTHUR ANDERSEN & CO
Galleria San Frederico 54, 10121 TURIN
Tel: +39 (11) 5597 *Fax:* +39 (11) 544756

ARTHUR ANDERSEN & CO
Via Albere 19, 37138 VERONA
Tel: +39 (45) 567844 *Fax:* +39 (45) 577583

Total Number of Offices: 12

STUDIO ASSOCIATO DI CONSULENZA BERNELLI MASSOLO E SCHIESARI

Via C. Colombo 1, 10128 TURIN
Tel: +39 (11) 500220
Fax: +39 (11) 505030

European Affiliation: INPACT - International Network of Professional Accountants

International Contact: Roberto Schiesari
Dr. Francesco Massolo

STUDIO BERNONI

Piazza Filippo Meda 3, 20121 MILAN
Tel: +39 (2) 783351
Fax: +39 (2) 781879

European Affiliation: Jeffreys Henry International

International Contact: Guiseppe Bernoni

BOMPANI AUDIT SAS

Viale Monte Rosa 3, 20149 MILAN
Tel: +39 (2) 4697440
Fax: +39 (2) 4818143

European Affiliation: Moores Rowland International

International Contact: Mario Fantechi

OTHER OFFICES

BOMPANI AUDIT SAS
Piazza D'Azeglio 39, 50121 FLORENCE
Tel: +39 (55) 2477851 *Fax:* +39 (55) 214933
Contact: Dr. Bruno Dei

BOMPANI AUDIT SAS
Via Nazionale 172, 00184 ROME
Tel: +39 (6) 6783437 *Fax:* +39 (6) 6791675
Contact: Remo Simonetti

Total Number of Offices: 3

GUISEPPE BROGI

Via Landino 5, FLORENCE
Tel: +39 (55) 496404
Fax: +39 (55) 472755

European Affiliation: The International Group of Accounting Firms Ltd (IGAF)

International Contact: Guiseppe Brogi

STUDIO TRIBUTARIO VINCENZO CAFIERO

Via G. Carducci 4, 00187 ROME
Tel: +39 (6) 4746941
Fax: +39 (6) 4818530

European Affiliation: DRM Internationally

International Contact: Vincenzo Cafiero

Partners:	1
Professional staff:	3
Non-professional staff:	2
Total Staff:	6

CONTACT INFORMATION

Tax: Vincenzo Cafiero
Tax: Stefano Tonti
Tax: Marco Ciccozzi

CLIENT SERVICES

Accountancy (General), Insolvency & Corporate Restructuring, Life & Risk Assurance, Mergers & Acquisitions, Taxation (Corporate), Taxation (International)

DR. CORRADO CASSINIS

Via Mascheroni 29, 20145 MILAN
Tel: +*39* (2) 48193670
Fax: +*39* (2) 48193591

European Affiliation: S & W International

International Contact: Dr. Corrado Cassinis

DR. GOFFREDO CAVERNI

Via 2 Settembre 14, 56100 PISA
Tel: +*39* (50) 533076
Fax: +*39* (50) 533076

European Affiliation: Midsnell International

International Contact: Dr. Goffredo Caverni

CHARTERED SAS

Via Ugo Foscolo 4, 20121 MILAN
Tel: +*39* (2) 863216
Fax: +*39* (2) 72001322

European Affiliation: TGI International

International Contact: Roberto Ferrari

STUDIO CHILODI

Via B. Bosco 57-9, 16121 GENOA
Tel: +*39* (10) 565894
Fax: +*39* (10) 543485

European Affiliation: The International Group of Accounting Firms Ltd (IGAF)

International Contact: Marco Odaglia

Partners:	3
Professional staff:	2
Non-professional staff:	3
Total Staff:	**8**

FEE INCOME

Year End: 31.12.90	**US$**	**%**
Accountancy & Audit:	50,000	10.0
Consultancy:	100,000	20.0
Tax:	200,000	40.0
Other:	150,000	30.0
Total:	**500,000**	

CONTACT INFORMATION

Chairman: Sergio Chiodi
Managing Partner: Mario Passavanti
Accountancy & Audit: Marco Odaglia
Management Consultancy: Sergio Chiodi
Administration: Mario Passavanti
Tax: Sergio Chiodi
Accountancy: Serenella Pestarino
Tax Returns: Saina Chiodi

CLIENT SERVICES

Accountancy (General), Audit, Management & Business Advice, Management Buy-outs, Mergers & Acquisitions, Taxation (Corporate), Taxation (International)

Industry Specialisations: Taxation (Corporate) Valuation, Mergers & Acquisitions

MAJOR CLIENTS

Acquedotto de Ferrari Galliera SPA, Acquedotto Nicolay SPA, Belotti Service SPA, Belotti SPA, Biamino & Figli SPA, Complesso Europa Appartotel SPA, Connei SPA, de Barbieri SPA, Fidite SPA, Francesco Panarello SPA, Giglio Bagnara SPA, Gi. Bi. SPA, Isi Impianti SPA, Italiana Prpdptto Minerali SRL, Mecox SPA, Nord Terminal SRL, Parodi & De-Rege SPA, Plastica Entella SPA, Rinaldo Rinaldi SPA, Termoplastici Ind. Ligur SPA

OTHER OFFICES

STUDIO DOTTORI COMMERCIALISTI ASSOCIATI
Via Manara 15, 20122 MILAN
Tel: +*39* (2) 5450070 *Fax:* +*39* (2) 55012459
Contact: Pietro Pongiglione

Total Number of Offices: 2

STUDIO RENATO CINELLI

Via Colona 12, 33170 PORDENONE
Tel: +*39* (434) 28571
Fax: +*39* (434) 28572

European Affiliation: Growth & Progress Challenge

International Contact: Renato Cinelli

CONCORDE EUROFIDUCIARIA SRL

Via Cosimo del Fante 16, 20122 MILAN
Tel: +*39* (2) 58310284
Fax: +*39* (2) 58310285

European Affiliation: Moore Stephens

International Contact: Giuseppe Barranco

OTHER OFFICES

CONCORDE EUROFIDUCIARIA SRL
Viale Regina Margherita 15, 00198 ROME
Tel: +*39* (6) 8848176
Contact: Dr. Sergio Camabuci

Total Number of Offices: 4

CONSULAUDIT SAS

3 Via XX Settembre, 10121 TURIN
Tel: +*39* (11) 5612722
Fax: +*39* (11) 553286

European Affiliation: Nexia International

International Contact: Attilio Arietti

CONTACT INFORMATION

Partner: Enrico Arietti
Partner: Massimo Milan
Partner: Bruno Piazza

OTHER OFFICES

CONSULAUDIT SAS
Via Paolo da Cannobio 11, 20122 MILAN
Tel: +*39* (2) 870141 *Fax:* +*39* (2) 72021578
Contact: Attilio Arietti

CONSULAUDIT SAS
Via Novara 53, 00198 ROME
Tel: +*39* (6) 8543605 *Fax:* +*39* (6) 8842194
Contact: Roberto Bianco

CONSULAUDIT SAS
Corso Porta Nuova 99, 37122 VERONA
Tel: +*39* (45) 8005183 *Fax:* +*39* (45) 8001019
Contact: Francesco Lentini

CONSULAUDIT SAS
3/30 Via Fieschi, 16121 GENOA
Tel: +*39* (10) 585432
Contact: Renato Rovida

Total Number of Offices: 5

COOPERS & LYBRAND SAS

Via Vittor Pisani 20, 20124 MILAN
Tel: +39 (2) 67831
Fax: +39 (2) 66981433

European Affiliation: Coopers & Lybrand Europe

International Contact: Giuseppe Nistri

Partners:	27
Professional staff:	398
Non-professional staff:	93
Total Staff:	**518**

CONTACT INFORMATION

Chairman: Roberto Robotti
Managing Partner: Angelo Pighini
Managing Partner: Michele Rondelli
Accountancy (General): Angelo Pighini
Audit: Roberto Robotti
Marketing: Albino Pedrazzini
EDP Audit: Mariano Arcelloni

CLIENT SERVICES

Audit

Industry Specialisations: All Sectors

OTHER OFFICES

COOPERS & LYBRAND SAS
Piazza Umberto 49, 70121 BARI
Tel: +39 (80) 5237241 *Fax:* +39 (80) 232980
Contact: Antonio Pennisi

COOPERS & LYBRAND SAS
Via Santo Stefano 97, 40125 BOLOGNA
Tel: +39 (51) 345762 *Fax:* +39 (51) 345781
Contact: Gianni Fanizza

COOPERS & LYBRAND SAS
Via Aldo Moro 10, 25124 BRESCIA
Tel: +39 (30) 2420292 *Fax:* +39 (20) 2422408
Contact: Roberto Pirola

COOPERS & LYBRAND SAS
Viale Matteotti 25, 50121 FLORENCE
Tel: +39 (55) 580747 *Fax:* +39 (55) 587163
Contact: Valerio Capoferri

COOPERS & LYBRAND SAS
Via Roccatagliata Ceccardi 4, 16121 GENOA
Tel: +39 (10) 5702030 *Fax:* +39 (10) 5702052
Contact: Onofrio Contu

COOPERS & LYBRAND SAS
Via Santa Brigida 51, 80133 NAPLES
Tel: +39 (81) 5526700 *Fax:* +39 (81) 5529110
Contact: Carmine Casalini

COOPERS & LYBRAND SAS
Largo Europa 16, 35137 PADUA
Tel: +39 (49) 662177 *Fax:* +39 (49) 662182
Contact: Antonio Taverna

COOPERS & LYBRAND SAS
Via delle Quattro Fontane 15, 00184 ROME
Tel: +39 (6) 4818565 *Fax:* +39 (6) 4814636
Contact: Robert Ware

COOPERS & LYBRAND SAS
Corso Vittorio Emanuele 97, 10128 TURIN
Tel: +39 (11) 5570131 *Fax:* +39 (11) 534993
Contact: Giuseppe Nistri

COOPERS & LYBRAND SAS
Via Malenza 2, 37121 VERONA
Tel: +39 (45) 8002561 *Fax:* +39 (45) 8003820
Contact: Alberto Carcano

Total Number of Offices: 12

COREVI LOMBARDIA SAS

Viale Campania 46, 20133 MILAN
Tel: +39 (2) 7381936
Fax: +39 (2) 70001877

European Affiliation: K.S. International

International Contact: Dr. Alberto Crosti

Partners:	13
Professional staff:	6
Non-professional staff:	35
Total Staff:	**54**

FEE INCOME

Year End: 1990	L	%
Accountancy & Audit:	72,024,000	80.0
Consultancy:	18,006,000	20.0
Total:	**90,030,000**	

CONTACT INFORMATION

Chairman: Alberto Crosti
Accountancy & Audit: Alberto Crosti
Partner: Antonio Ortolani

CLIENT SERVICES

Accountancy (General), Audit, Corporate Finance Advice, Insolvency & Corporate Restructuring, Management & Business Advice, Mergers & Acquisitions, Taxation (Corporate), Business Start Ups, Company Sales, Taxation (Partnership), Taxation (Personal)

OTHER OFFICES

COREVI
Via XX Settembre 10/9, 16121 GENOA
Contact: Dr. Ettore Cano

COREVI BOLZANO
Corso Liberta 50, 39100 BOLZANO
Tel: +39 (471) 287115 *Fax:* +39 (471) 272473
Contact: Dr. Nesler Andrea

COREVI POGUA SNC
Viale J.F. Kennedy 50, 70124 BARI
Tel: +39 (80) 420076
Contact: Dr. Antonio Campangua

COREVI SNC
Via Pietro Micca 10, 20122 TURIN
Tel: +39 (11) 539980
Contact: Dr. Zanonimario

Total Number of Offices: 5

STUDIO COMMERCIALISTA CORTELLAZZO & SOATTO

Via Porciglia 14, PADUA
Tel: +39 (49) 661877
Fax: +39 (49) 8754640

European Affiliation: INPACT - International Network of Professional Accountants

International Contact: Antonio Cortellazzo
Enzo Nalli

COSTAGUTA & SALMONI

Via C.R. Ceccardi 4/42, 16121 GENOA
Tel: +39 (10) 582202
Fax: +39 (10) 589576

▷

European Affiliation: INPACT - International Network of Professional Accountants

International Contact: Roberto R. Costaguta

Partners:	5
Non-professional staff:	8
Total Staff:	**13**

FEE INCOME

Year End: 31.12.90	**L (000)**	**%**
Accountancy & Audit:	220,000	19.0
Insolvency:	130,000	11.0
Consultancy:	360,000	
Tax:	200,000	17.0
Other:	260,000	22.0
Total:	**1,170,000**	

CONTACT INFORMATION
Managing Partner: Vittorio Salmoni
Accountancy (General): Ilda Romano
Insolvency: Simona Dellepiane
Tax (Corporate): Alessandro Miglio
Corporate Finance & Tax: Roberto Costaguta
Consultancy & Administration: Vittorio Salmoni

CLIENT SERVICES
Accountancy (General), Corporate Finance Advice, Insolvency & Corporate Restructuring, Litigation/Legal Services, Management & Business Advice, Management Buy-outs, Mergers & Acquisitions, Taxation (Corporate), Taxation (International), Trust Settlement & Estates

MAJOR CLIENTS
Cofaco Group (Portugal), Marina Yachting SPA (Italy), Mazola SPA (Italy), Zerbone Catering SRL (Italy)

STUDIO ASSOCIATI DAL MAS

Via Papa Giovanni XXIII 9, 22055 MERATE
Tel: +*39* (39) 9903487
Fax: +*39* (39) 9900651

International Contact: Pier G. Dal Mas

Partners:	3
Professional staff:	1
Non-professional staff:	4
Total Staff:	**8**

FEE INCOME

Year End: 31.12.91	**%**
Accountancy & Audit:	40.0
Consultancy:	30.0
Tax:	30.0

CONTACT INFORMATION
Managing Partner: Pier G. Dal Mas
Management Consultancy: Maurizio Dal Mas
Tax (Corporate): Francesco Dal Mas

CLIENT SERVICES
Accountancy (General), Management & Business Advice, Taxation (Corporate)

STUDIO DE LEONE

Via Ampère 47, 20122 MILAN
Tel: +*39* (2) 2664201
Fax: +*39* (2) 2361511

European Affiliation: Midsnell International

International Contact: Antonio de Leone

PROF. GIROLAMO DELL'OLIO & ASSOCIATI

Argiro 29, 70122 BARI
Tel: +*39* (80) 5218668
Fax: +*39* (80) 5594130

European Affiliation: The International Group of Accounting Firms Ltd (IGAF)

International Contact: Gioacchino Dell'Olio

DELOITTE & TOUCHE

Via Monte di Pieta 24, 20121 MILAN
Tel: +*39* (2) 8801
Fax: +*39* (2) 870868

European Affiliation: DRT International

International Contact: Hamish Clifton-Brown

Total Staff: **300**

CLIENT SERVICES
Audit only

MAJOR CLIENTS
Banco di Sardegna, Cariplo, Cassa di Risparmio di Torino, Cassa di Risparmio di Venezia, Consorzio Yenezia Nuova, Edison, Finarte Group, Fiscambi, Genny Group, Gogefar-Impresit, ILVA Group, INA, Luxottica Group, Manuli Group, Marangoni Group, RIV-SKF, Sicilcassa, SME Group, SOPAF Group, Trussardi

Total Number of Offices: 12

DELTA ERRE SPA

Galleria Trieste 5, 35100 PADUA
Tel: +*39* (49) 650322
Fax: +*39* (49) 8751306

Partners:	3
Non-professional staff:	4
Total Staff:	**7**

FEE INCOME

Year End: 1990	**%**
Accountancy & Audit:	25.0
Other:	75.0

CONTACT INFORMATION
Managing Partner: Dr. Carla Sanero

CLIENT SERVICES
Audit, Trust Settlement & Estates, Corporate Valuation (Net Worth)

DFK ITALIA SNC

Via Visconti di Modrone 38, 20122 MILAN
Tel: +*39* (2) 76021514
Fax: +*39* (2) 780513

European Affiliation: DFK International

International Contact: Aldo Camagni

Partners:	5
Professional staff:	15
Non-professional staff:	14
Total Staff:	**34**

CONTACT INFORMATION
Chairman: Dr. Enrico Nicolini
Audit: Antonio Fontana
Tax (Corporate): Lino de Vecchi

CLIENT SERVICES
All Services

STUDIO OSCAR DIOZZI & PARTNERS

Via Fontana 26, 21019 SOMMA LOMBARDO (VA)
Tel: +*39* (331) 255769
Fax: +*39* (331) 254620

Partners:	4
Professional staff:	3
Non-professional staff:	4
Total Staff:	**11**

FEE INCOME

Year End: 31.12.90	%
Accountancy & Audit:	34.0
Insolvency:	1.0
Consultancy:	25.0
Tax:	40.0

CONTACT INFORMATION
Chairman: Oscar Diozzi
Audit: Renato Zanichelli
Insolvency: Piero Cesare Iametti
Management Consultancy: Oscar Diozzi
Tax (Corporate): Gilberto Salatti

CLIENT SERVICES
Accountancy (General), Audit, Insolvency & Corporate Restructuring, Life & Risk Assurance, Litigation/Legal Services, Management & Business Advice, Mergers & Acquisitions, Taxation (Corporate)

FIDALTA

Piazza della Repubblica 9, 20121 MILAN
Tel: +*39* (2) 29000610
Fax: +*39* (2) 29000387

European Affiliation: Urbach Hacker Young International

Partners:	4
Professional staff:	8
Non-professional staff:	2
Total Staff:	**14**

FEE INCOME

Year End: 31.12.90	L	%
Accountancy & Audit:	719,000,000	78.0
Consultancy:	96,000,000	10.0
Tax:	54,000,000	6.0
Other:	52,000,000	6.0
Total:	**921,000,000**	

CONTACT INFORMATION
Chairman: Dr. Antonio Fiore
Managing Partner: Ivo Costa
Accountancy (General): Luigi Stefanini
Audit: Ivo Costa
Management Consultancy: Dr. Antonio Fiore
Tax (Corporate): Dr. Giorgio Ghizzoni

CLIENT SERVICES
Accountancy (General), Audit, Management & Business Advice, Taxation (Corporate)

Industry Specialisations: Leasing, Building, Freight Forwarders

MAJOR CLIENTS
ABB Group, Alfa Romeo, Bolla International Wine, Edilcapriano, Eurovetrocap, G.B. Braun Italia, JAS - Jet Air Service, Locafit, Pittway Group

OTHER OFFICES

NIELSEN
Via S. Quintino 28, 10143 TURIN
Tel: +*39* (11) 515421 *Fax:* +*39* (11) 518612
Contact: Giorgio Querelante

Total Number of Offices: 2

FIDERCONSULT/AUDIREVI

Via Birmania 81, 00144 ROME
Tel: +*39* (6) 5917469
Fax: +*39* (6) 5913582

European Affiliation: Alliott Peirson International

International Contact: Paolo Lenzi

FIDIREVISA ITALIA SRL

Via Senato 12, 20121 MILAN
Tel: +*39* (2) 796061
Fax: +*39* (2) 782598

European Affiliation: TEG (The European Group of Accounting & Auditing Firms)

Partners:	2
Professional staff:	9
Non-professional staff:	4
Total Staff:	**15**

FEE INCOME

Year End: 1990	L	%
Accountancy & Audit:	600,000,000	55.0
Consultancy:	100,000,000	9.0
Other:	400,000,000	36.0
Total:	**1,100,000,000**	

CONTACT INFORMATION
Managing Partner: Dr. Giorgio Antonini
Tax (International): Dr. Giorgio Antonini
Audit & Management Consultancy: Michael Golding

CLIENT SERVICES
Accountancy (General), Audit, Corporate Finance Advice, Management & Business Advice, Taxation (International), Company Valuation, Fiduciary Services, International Business Consultancy

Industry Specialisations: Airport Consultancy, Royalty Audits

OTHER OFFICES

FIDIREVISA ITALIA SRL
Via Denza 20, 00197 ROME
Tel: +*39* (6) 8076659 *Fax:* +*39* (6) 8083283
Contact: Michael Golding

Total Number of Offices: 2

STUDIO FIRMA

Via Palladio 29/a, 37136 VERONA
Tel: +*39* (45) 575222
Fax: +*39* (45) 575548

European Affiliation: INPACT - International Network of Professional Accountants

International Contact: Dr. Marco Bronzato

STUDIO GIANNONE PROFESSIONISTI E ASSOCIATI

Corso Garibaldi 148, 84100 SALERNO
Tel: +*39* (89) 237388
Fax: +*39* (89) 251105

European Affiliation: INPACT - International Network of Professional Accountants

International Contact: Domenico de Luca
Dr. Ernesto Giannone

▷

STUDIO MAURIZIO GORDOL

Cia Senato 20, MILAN
Tel: + *39* (2) 76004057
Fax: + *39* (2) 784585

European Affiliation: SC International

HODGSON LANDAU BRANDS SAS

Piazza Velasca 5, 20122 MILAN
Tel: + *39* (2) 867643
Fax: + *39* (2) 864033

European Affiliation: HLB International

International Contact: R.L. Calogero

Partners:	8
Professional staff:	35
Non-professional staff:	13
Total Staff:	**56**

CONTACT INFORMATION

Chairman: R.L. Calogero
Managing Partner: Lorenzo Penca
Accountancy (General): M. Crescenzio
Accountancy (General): A. Airoldi
Accountancy (General): G. Beretta
Accountancy (General): G. Croci
Accountancy (General): Licio Duca
Audit: Dino Mangiarotti
Management Consultancy: Lorenzo Penca
Administration: M. Crescenzio
Tax (International): R.L. Calogero

CLIENT SERVICES

Accountancy (General), Audit, Management & Business Advice, Management Buy-outs, Mergers & Acquisitions, Taxation (International), Management Consultancy

Industry Specialisations: Food, Insurance, Long-term Contractors, Mechanical & Textile Industries

OTHER OFFICES

HODGSON LANDAU BRANDS SAS
Via Nizza 53, 00198 ROME
Tel: + *39* (6) 8840901 *Fax:* + *39* (6) 8557469
Contact: Licio Ducla

HODGSON LANDAU BRANDS SAS
Via San Tommaso 70, 10121 TURIN
Tel: + *39* (11) 5611185 *Fax:* + *39* (11) 5611185
Contact: Lorenzo Penca

HODGSON LANDAU BRANDS SAS
Via Verdi 33, 30172 MESTRE (Venice)
Tel: + *39* (41) 961235
Contact: Dino Mangiarotti

HODGSON LANDAU BRANDS SAS
Via Verdi 22, 35139 PADUA
Tel: + *39* (49) 652835 *Fax:* + *39* (49) 650586
Contact: Dino Mangiarotti

Total Number of Offices: 5

HORWATH & HORWATH ITALIA SAS

Via Calabrian 7, 00187 ROME
Tel: + *39* (6) 4746053
Fax: + *39* (6) 4741989

European Affiliation: Horwath International

International Contact: Marco Bongiovanni

Partners:	12
Professional staff:	51
Non-professional staff:	10
Total Staff:	**73**

FEE INCOME

Year End: 31.12.90	**US$**	**%**
Accountancy & Audit:	3,676,460	72.0
Consultancy:	663,806	13.0
Tax:	765,929	15.0
Total:	**5,106,195**	

CONTACT INFORMATION

Managing Partner: Aldo Sanchini
Accountancy (General): Fabio Porfiri
Audit: Massiro de Rosa
Insolvency: Giuseppe Righi
Management Consultancy: Francesco Follina
Administration: Cesare Fabbri
Tax (Corporate): Vittorio Silvestri
Tax (International): Maria Sarno
Tax Litigation: Giovanni Trasarti

CLIENT SERVICES

All Services

Industry Specialisations: Construction, Finance, Publishing, Hospitality, Tourism

MAJOR CLIENTS

Adriatica Navigazione, Cassa Rispartio Vignola, Gruppo di Penta Costruzioni, Iris Ceramiche, Pacchetti, Rusconi Editore, Selecta Travel Agency, Sheraton Hotels, Tirrenia Navigazione, Todini Costruzioni Generali, Traforo Monte Bianco

OTHER OFFICES

FIDREV - FIDUCIARIA E DI REVISIONE
Piazza della Liberta 10, 00 ROME
Tel: + *39* (6) 6867841 *Fax:* + *39* (6) 6896075
Contact: Maria Sarno

HORWATH & HORWATH ITALIA
Via Mauro Macchi 65, 20124 MILAN
Tel: + *39* (2) 6709313 *Fax:* + *39* (2) 6705142
Contact: Fausto Vittucci

HORWATH & HORWATH ITALIA
Piazza Matteotti 13, 41100 MODENA
Tel: + *39* (59) 214453 *Fax:* + *39* (59) 217982
Contact: Marco Bongiovanni

PALANDRI HORWATH
Piazza Navona 49, 00186 ROME
Tel: + *39* (6) 6867841 *Fax:* + *39* (6) 6896075
Contact: Aldo Sanchini

Total Number of Offices: 5

HUMPHREYS AND GATES

Piazza Velasca 5, 20122 MILAN
Tel: + *39* (2) 8058637
Fax: + *39* (2) 864033

International Contact: John F. Gates

ITALAUDIT SPA

Via Durini 18, 20122 MILAN
Tel: + *39* (2) 783041
Fax: + *39* (2) 781396

European Affiliation: Grant Thornton International

International Contact: Dr. Claudio Muollo

Partners:	6
Professional staff:	46
Non-professional staff:	9
Total Staff:	**61**

FEE INCOME

Year End: 31.12.89	**L (million)**
Total:	**5,666,952**

CONTACT INFORMATION
Managing Partner: Dr. Claudio Muollo

CLIENT SERVICES
Accountancy (General), Audit, Corporate Finance Advice, Mergers & Acquisitions, Taxation (Corporate), Taxation (International)

Industry Specialisations: Banking, Publishers, Home Building, Textiles

MAJOR CLIENTS
Banca Antoniana, Banca Popolare Brescia, Banca Popolare Venetal, Bo Frost, Class Editori, Co Fi Mo, Fagioli Transport, Ferrovie Torino Nord, Impresa Castelli, Istituto Farmacologico Serono, Leykam, Locafit, Moulinex Italy, Sacma, Schickedane, Universita' L. Bocconi

OTHER OFFICES

GRANT THORNTON
Corso di Porta Nuova 22, 37122 VERONA
Tel: + *39* (45) 597984 *Fax:* + *39* (45) 596236

ITALAUDIT SPA
Via Donizetti 7, 00198 ROME
Tel: + *39* (6) 8442371 *Fax:* + *39* (6) 8543265

ITALAUDIT SPA
Via Parigi 13, 40121 BOLOGNA
Tel: + *39* (51) 263857 *Fax:* + *39* (51) 239617

ITALAUDIT SPA
Via Santa Brigida 51, 80133 NAPLES
Tel: + *39* (81) 5529052 *Fax:* + *39* (81) 5519055

ITALAUDIT SPA
Via Sparano 115, 70121 BARI
Tel: + *39* (80) 5219946 *Fax:* + *39* (80) 5214688

Total Number of Offices: 6

KPMG FIDES FIDUCIARIA SPA

Via Vittor Pisani 25, 20124 MILAN
Tel: + *39* (2) 67641
Fax: + *39* (2) 67645833

European Affiliation: KPMG

Partners:	2
Professional staff:	72
Non-professional staff:	39
Total Staff:	**113**

FEE INCOME

Year End: 30.09.90	**L**
Total:	**5,500,000,000**

CONTACT INFORMATION
Managing Partner: Carlo Pecoraro

CLIENT SERVICES
Accountancy (General), Management & Business Advice, Taxation (Corporate), Trust Settlement & Estates, Company Foundation, Payroll Administration

OTHER OFFICES

KPMG FIDES FIDUCIARIA SPA
Corte Lambruschini, Torre A - Piano 11º, 16129 GENOA
Tel: + *39* (10) 564992 *Fax:* + *39* (10) 5535159
Contact: Carlo Pecoraro

KPMG FIDES FIDUCIARIA SPA
Via Sicilia 66, 00187 ROME
Tel: + *39* (6) 4740541 *Fax:* + *39* (6) 4940734
Contact: Carlo Pecoraro

Total Number of Offices: 3

KPMG PEAT MARWICK FIDES SNC

Via Vittor Pisani 25, 20124 MILAN
Tel: + *39* (2) 67631
Fax: + *39* (2) 67632445

European Affiliation: KPMG

International Contact: Giorgio Loli

Partners:	32
Professional staff:	482
Non-professional staff:	84
Total Staff:	**598**

FEE INCOME

Year End: 30.09.90	**L (000)**	**%**
Accountancy & Audit:	56,000,000	100.0
Total:	**56,000,000**	

CONTACT INFORMATION
Managing Partner: Giuseppe Angiolini

CLIENT SERVICES
Accountancy (General), Audit

Industry Specialisations: Banks, Insurance, Food, Textile, Construction, High Technology

MAJOR CLIENTS
Agip, Assitalia, Banca Commerciale Italiana, Cogefar, Credito Italiano, Fisac, Girola, Italfarmaco, Mantero, Mondadori, Pirelli, Recchi, Selenia, SME, Snam, SNIA, Versage

OTHER OFFICES

KPMG PEAT MARWICK FIDES
Piazza Repubblica 15, 60121 ANCONA
Tel: + *39* (71) 2070374

KPMG PEAT MARWICK FIDES
Via Calefati 6, 70121 BARI
Tel: + *39* (80) 5243203 *Fax:* + *39* (80) 237535
Contact: S. Sanna

KPMG PEAT MARWICK FIDES
Piazzale Repubblica 2, 24100 BERGAMO
Tel: + *39* (35) 240218 *Fax:* + *39* (35) 240220
Contact: R. Guerini

KPMG PEAT MARWICK FIDES
Viale Aldo Moro 64, 40127 BOLOGNA
Tel: + *39* (51) 6460046 *Fax:* + *39* (51) 6460073
Contact: F. Garilli

KPMG PEAT MARWICK FIDES
Castel Roncolo 14, 39100 BOLZANO
Tel: + *39* (71) 973121 *Fax:* + *39* (71) 978811
Contact: Bruno Borgia

KPMG PEAT MARWICK FIDES
Via Garibaldi 69, 22100 COMO
Tel: + *39* (31) 301977 *Fax:* + *39* (31) 301979
Contact: P.G. Valle

KPMG PEAT MARWICK FIDES
Via della Fortezza 6, 50129 FLORENCE
Tel: + *39* (55) 470912 *Fax:* + *39* (55) 470913
Contact: S. Capuano

KPMG PEAT MARWICK FIDES
Corte Lambruschini, Torre A, Piano 11º, 9, 16129 GENOA
Tel: + *39* (10) 564922 *Fax:* + *39* (10) 5535159
Contact: D. Grasgano

KPMG PEAT MARWICK FIDES
Piazza F. Meda 3, 20121 MILAN
Tel: + *39* (2) 67631 *Fax:* + *39* (2) 76004865

KPMG PEAT MARWICK FIDES
Via Vittor Pissani 22, 20124 MILAN
Tel: + *39* (2) 67631 *Fax:* + *39* (2) 6693424

KPMG PEAT MARWICK FIDES
Via dei Mille 16, 80121 NAPLES
Tel: + *39* (81) 402597 *Fax:* + *39* (81) 421289
Contact: B. Mastrangelo

KPMG PEAT MARWICK FIDES
Galleria Trieste 6, 35121 PADUA
Tel: + *39* (49) 650555 *Fax:* + *39* (49) 650632
Contact: M. Galanti

KPMG PEAT MARWICK FIDES
Piazza Castelnuovo 12, 90141 PALERMO
Tel: + *39* (91) 6111445 *Fax:* + *39* (91) 6111442
Contact: O. Scarpellini

KPMG PEAT MARWICK FIDES
Via Sardegna 40, 00187 ROME
Tel: + *39* (6) 485718 *Fax:* + *39* (6) 4958341
Contact: F. Iannoni

KPMG PEAT MARWICK FIDES
Corso Vittorio Emanuele II, 18, 10123 TURIN
Tel: + *39* (11) 88395144 *Fax:* + *39* (11) 871651
Contact: G.P. Ghigo

KPMG PEAT MARWICK FIDES
Via Giovanni de Udine 25, 33100 UDINE
Tel: + *39* (432) 293256
Contact: P. Pascot

KPMG PEAT MARWICK FIDES
Corso Cavour 39, 37121 VERONA
Tel: + *39* (45) 8005031 *Fax:* + *39* (45) 591843
Contact: Bruno Borgia

Total Number of Offices: 18

KPMG PEAT MARWICK SNC

Via Vittor Pisani 25, 20124 MILAN
Tel: + *39* (2) 676431
Fax: + *39* (2) 67643603

European Affiliation: KPMG

Partners:	7
Professional staff:	86
Non-professional staff:	14
Total Staff:	**107**

CONTACT INFORMATION
Chairman: Vincenzo Gagliardi

CLIENT SERVICES
Computer Installation, Corporate Finance Advice, Management & Business Advice, Management Buy-outs, Mergers & Acquisitions, Pensions Planning

OTHER OFFICES

KPMG PEAT MARWICK SNC
Abate Gimma 30, 70121 BARI
Tel: + *39* (80) 5243203 *Fax:* + *39* (80) 5243425
Contact: Massimo Schiavo

KPMG PEAT MARWICK SNC
Viale Aldo Moro 64, 40127 BOLOGNA
Tel: + *39* (51) 6330076 *Fax:* + *39* (51) 6330073
Contact: Antonio Bigatti

KPMG PEAT MARWICK SNC
Via Dei Mille 16, 80121 NAPLES
Tel: + *39* (81) 402597 *Fax:* + *39* (81) 421289
Contact: Alessandro Campana

KPMG PEAT MARWICK SNC
Piazza Castelnuovo 12, 90141 PALERMO
Tel: + *39* (91) 6111622 *Fax:* + *39* (91) 6111442
Contact: Massimo Schiavo

KPMG PEAT MARWICK SNC
Via Sardegna 40, 00187 ROME
Tel: + *39* (6) 4826251 *Fax:* + *39* (6) 4871280
Contact: Franco Masera

KPMG PEAT MARWICK SNC
Via Carlo Alberto 65, 10123 TURIN
Tel: + *39* (11) 836036 *Fax:* + *39* (11) 871651
Contact: Antonio Bigatti

KPMG PEAT MARWICK SNC
Corso Cavour 39, 37121 VERONA
Tel: + *39* (45) 8005031 *Fax:* + *39* (45) 591843
Contact: Franco Papa

Total Number of Offices: 8

STUDIO LAURI ED ASSOCIATI

Viale dell'Esperanto 10, 00144 ROME
Tel: + *39* (6) 5917053
Fax: + *39* (6) 5924060

European Affiliation: Russell Bedford International

International Contact: Maurizio Lauri

METODO

Foro Buonaparte 69, 20121 MILAN
Tel: + *39* (2) 6702543
Fax: + *39* (2) 8690528

European Affiliation: ATD International

MOORE STEPHENS & CO SAS

Via Cosimo del Fante 16, 20122 MILAN
Tel: + *39* (2) 58310527
Fax: + *39* (2) 58310285

European Affiliation: Moore Stephens

International Contact: Giancarlo Rossi

OTHER OFFICES

MOORE STEPHENS & CO SAS
Piazza Corvetto 1, 16122 GENOA
Tel: + *39* (10) 885621
Contact: Giancarlo Rossi

Total Number of Offices: 4

STUDIO GAETANO NAPOLITANO

Via delle Coppelle 35, 00186 ROME
Tel: +*39* (6) 6879950
Fax: +*39* (6) 6869571

European Affiliation: INPACT - International Network of Professional Accountants

International Contact: Dr. Gaetano Napolitano
Dr. Stefano Pasquali

GIANCARLO PAGLIARINI SOCI SAS

Via G.B. Morgagni 11, 20129 MILAN
Tel: +*39* (2) 29518820
Fax: +*39* (2) 29404971

European Affiliation: Independent Accountants International

International Contact: Dario Colombo

Partners:	8
Professional staff:	4
Non-professional staff:	2
Total Staff:	**14**

FEE INCOME

Year End: 31.12.90	**L (million)**
Total:	**665**

CONTACT INFORMATION

Managing Partner: Giancarlo Pagliarini
Accountancy (General): Giancarlo Pagliarini
Audit: Dario Colombo
Tax (Corporate): Antonio Cigala
Constructions: Elena Cavallo

CLIENT SERVICES

Audit

Industry Specialisations: Construction

MAJOR CLIENTS

Arsonsisi SPA, Aurel SPA, Bancolini SPA, Beleggings Maatschappij Maasdisk, Biosystems Italia SPA, Cifo SPA, Cotonificio Oltolina SPA, Depurimpianti SPA, Dyaguar SPA, Fingest SPA, F.lli Costanzo, Globtrade SPA, Immobiliare Prati, Impresa Costruzioni Magri Geom. Anselmo SPA, Interpump SPA, Junghanns SPA, Nuove Smalterie Lombarde SPA, Trafilerie di Valmadrera SPA, Veneta Leasing SPA, Vignale Finanziaria

Total Number of Offices: 2

STUDIO PASCUCCI

Via F. Caracciolois, 80122 NAPLES
Tel: +*39* (81) 7614290
Fax: +*39* (81) 7611250

European Affiliation: The International Group of Accounting Firms Ltd (IGAF)

International Contact: Roberto Pascucci

STUDIO PICCINELLI

Via Pontida 3, 25121 BRESCIA
Tel: +*39* (30) 3772472
Fax: +*39* (30) 41276

European Affiliation: InterContinental Consultants (ICC)

International Contact: Guido Piccinelli
Franco Piccinelli

PRICE WATERHOUSE

Corso Europa 2, 20122 MILAN
Tel: +*39* (2) 77851
Fax: +*39* (2) 7785240

European Affiliation: Price Waterhouse

International Contact: A. Gargiulo

Partners:	35
Professional staff:	390
Non-professional staff:	97
Total Staff:	**522**

FEE INCOME

Year End: 30.06.91	**L (billion)**	**%**
Accountancy & Audit:	59.9	100.0
Total:	**59.9**	

CLIENT SERVICES

Audit

MAJOR CLIENTS

Agip, Alitalia, Autogerma, Banca Popolare di Novara, Banco di Napoli, Banco di Sicilia, Barilla, CIGA Hotels, Enichem, Esso Italiana, Ferruzzi, Fiat, Gemina, IBM Italia, Industria Italiana Petroli, Istituto Mobiliare Italiano, Italstat, Montedison, Rai, Standa

OTHER OFFICES

PRICE WATERHOUSE
Via Corridoni 2, 60123 ANCONA
Tel: +*39* (71) 36881 *Fax:* +*39* (71) 36623
Contact: R.M. Dunatov

PRICE WATERHOUSE
Via Vallescura 2, 40136 BOLOGNA
Tel: +*39* (51) 334893 *Fax:* +*39* (51) 330756
Contact: R.M. Dunatov

PRICE WATERHOUSE
Via S. Lucifero 97, 09100 CAGLIARI
Tel: +*39* (70) 666253 *Fax:* +*39* (70) 663393
Contact: V. Santarcangelo

PRICE WATERHOUSE
Via Fieschi 3/14, 16121 GENOA
Tel: +*39* (10) 530061 *Fax:* +*39* (10) 593996
Contact: G. Galli

PRICE WATERHOUSE
Via Del Rione Sirignano 7, 80121 NAPLES
Tel: +*39* (81) 7614100 *Fax:* +*39* (81) 667802
Contact: A. Dell'Isola

PRICE WATERHOUSE
Via Carlo Cassan 34, 35100 PADUA
Tel: +*39* (49) 655222 *Fax:* +*39* (49) 657814
Contact: A. von Gebsattel

PRICE WATERHOUSE
Viale Tanara 20/A, 43100 PARMA
Tel: +*39* (521) 242848 *Fax:* +*39* (521) 71844
Contact: F. Facchini

PRICE WATERHOUSE
Via Aniene 30, 00198 ROME
Tel: +*39* (6) 8440151 *Fax:* +*39* (6) 8414649
Contact: E. Palma

PRICE WATERHOUSE
Via S. Francesco 8, 38100 TRENTO
Tel: +*39* (461) 237004 *Fax:* +*39* (461) 239077
Contact: M.T. Bernelli

PRICE WATERHOUSE
Via Bogino 23, 10123 TURIN
Tel: +*39* (11) 8395421 *Fax:* +*39* (11) 8395613
Contact: S. Duca

▷

PRICE WATERHOUSE
Largo Augusto 1/3, 20122 MILAN
Tel: + *39* (2) 77851 *Fax:* + *39* (2) 7785240

PRICE WATERHOUSE
Via Bonifacio Lupi 11, 50129 FLORENCE
Tel: + *39* (55) 471747 *Fax:* + *39* (55) 470779
Contact: R.M. Dunatov

PRICE WATERHOUSE
Via Leonardo da Vinci 12, 39100 BOLZANO
Tel: + *39* (471) 976303
Contact: A. von Gebsattel

Total Number of Offices: 14

PROREVI, SOCIETA PROFESSIONALE DI REVISIONE E CERTIFICAZIONE

Via C. Battisti 8, 20122 MILAN
Tel: + *39* (2) 5512918
Fax: + *39* (2) 792046

European Affiliation: A.E.E. International

International Contact: G. Verna

CLIENT SERVICES
All Services

STUDIO PROTO

Via Regina Margherita 28, 88074 CROTONE
Tel: + *39* (962) 22897
Fax: + *39* (962) 902243

European Affiliation: INPACT - International Network of Professional Accountants

International Contact: Dr. Michele Proto

STUDIO RAMONDELLI

Via Lucrezio Caro 7A, 00193 ROME
Tel: + *39* (6) 3213042
Fax: + *39* (6) 3210892

European Affiliation: Jeffreys Henry International

International Contact: Dr. Aldo Ramondelli

RECONTA ERNST & YOUNG

Via Torino 68, 20123 MILAN
Tel: + *39* (2) 722121
Fax: + *39* (2) 72212037

European Affiliation: Ernst & Young Europe

International Contact: Bruno Gimpel

OTHER OFFICES

RECONTA ERNST & YOUNG
Via Amendola 12, 10121 TURIN
Tel: + *39* (11) 544471 *Fax:* + *39* (11) 547042
Contact: Mario Lamprati

RECONTA ERNST & YOUNG
Via Agusto Murri 9, 40137 BOLOGNA
Tel: + *39* (51) 342000 *Fax:* + *39* (51) 347066

RECONTA ERNST & YOUNG
Corso Magenta 29, 25121 BRESCIA
Tel: + *39* (30) 40627 *Fax:* + *39* (30) 295437
Contact: Egidio Tempini

RECONTA ERNST & YOUNG
Piazza della Repubblica 50, 95131 CATANIA
Tel: + *39* (95) 317785 *Fax:* + *39* (95) 317663
Contact: Gianfranco Consorti

RECONTA ERNST & YOUNG
Via Lorenzo il Magnifico 10, 50129 FLORENCE
Tel: + *39* (55) 476295 *Fax:* + *39* (55) 496794
Contact: Carlo Cassamagnaghi

RECONTA ERNST & YOUNG
Salita di Santa Caterina 6/2, 16123 GENOA
Tel: + *39* (10) 5535184 *Fax:* + *39* (10) 5535186
Contact: Mario Lamprati

RECONTA ERNST & YOUNG
Via Carlo Sigonio 50, 41100 MODENA
Tel: + *39* (59) 218121 *Fax:* + *39* (59) 220673
Contact: Anthony C. Kavanaugh

RECONTA ERNST & YOUNG
Via F. Crispi 74, 80121 NAPLES
Tel: + *39* (81) 7611909 *Fax:* + *39* (81) 7611992
Contact: Gianfranco Consorti

RECONTA ERNST & YOUNG
Via N. Tommaseo 60, 35131 PADUA
Tel: + *39* (49) 661733 *Fax:* + *39* (49) 662832
Contact: Demetrio Tomba

RECONTA ERNST & YOUNG
Via F.lli Cairoll 10, 65122 PESCARA
Tel: + *39* (85) 4224178 *Fax:* + *39* (85) 4216436

RECONTA ERNST & YOUNG
Via Abruzzi 25, 00187 ROME
Tel: + *39* (6) 48121 *Fax:* + *39* (6) 487 3353
Contact: Riccardo Bottigelli

RECONTA ERNST & YOUNG
Via Cavour, 1, 10123 TURIN
Tel: + *39* (11) 543570 *Fax:* + *39* (11) 537438
Contact: Antonio Faraudo

RECONTA ERNST & YOUNG
Via Mantica 12, 33100 UDINE
Tel: + *39* (432) 506352 *Fax:* + *39* (432) 510854
Contact: Mauro Castelli

RECONTA ERNST & YOUNG
Via D. Manin 6, 37122 VERONA
Tel: + *39* (45) 8007630 *Fax:* + *39* (45) 8003993
Contact: Giovanni Aspes

Total Number of Offices: 32

REVITALIA SRL

Via Nerino 8, 20123 MILAN
Tel: + *39* (2) 72021052
Fax: + *39* (2) 72021056

International Contact: Vincenzo Lamberti

Partners:	11
Professional staff:	20
Non-professional staff:	8
Total Staff:	**39**

FEE INCOME

Year End: 31.12.90	**L**	**%**
Accountancy & Audit:	1,250,557,000	47.0
Consultancy:	193,809,000	7.0
Tax:	100,423,000	4.0
Other:	1,124,469,000	42.0
Total:	**2,669,258,000**	

CONTACT INFORMATION
Chairman: Angelo Bassi
Managing Partner: Renato Bolongaro
Accountancy (General): Maria Silvani
Audit: Vincenzo Lamberti
Corporate Finance: Nino Clerici
Insolvency: Enrico Monti
Management Consultancy: Sigfrido Lazzari
Tax (International): Walter Granillo
Audit & Administration: Marco Jouvenal
Audit & Public Sector: Leonardo Milani
Audit & Tax (Corporate): Carlo Lamberti

CLIENT SERVICES
Accountancy (General), Audit, Management & Business Advice, Mergers & Acquisitions, Value for Money Studies, Taxation (Corporate), Taxation (International), Trustee Business

SALA SCELSI FARINA BDO

Piazza del Liberty 4, 20121 MILAN
Tel: +39 (2) 784563
Fax: +39 (2) 784567

European Affiliation: BDO Binder

International Contact: Giorgio Farina

Partners:	6
Professional staff:	30
Non-professional staff:	6
Total Staff:	**42**

FEE INCOME

Year End: 31.12.90	%
Accountancy & Audit:	100.0

CONTACT INFORMATION
Managing Partner: Giorgio Farina
Managing Partner: Paolo Scelsi
Accountancy (General): Paolo Scelsi
Audit: Giorgio Farina

CLIENT SERVICES
Audit

Industry Specialisations: Insurance

OTHER OFFICES
SALA SCELSI FARINA BDO
Viale G. Mazzini 113, 00195 ROME
Tel: +39 (6) 3701660 *Fax:* +39 (6) 3722063
Contact: Giorgio Farina

Total Number of Offices: 2

STUDIO SEMERIA DOTTORI ANTONIO

Via Gioberti 29, 18038 SAN REMO
Tel: +39 (184) 570000
Fax: +39 (184) 658209

European Affiliation: INPACT - International Network of Professional Accountants

International Contact: Dr. Antonio Semeria

S.E.R.C.A.

Via XX Settembre 19, 25121 BRESCIA
Tel: +39 (30) 46332
Fax: +39 (30) 51513

European Affiliation: Clark Kenneth Leventhal

International Contact: Giovanni Brondi

Partners:	3
Professional staff:	17
Non-professional staff:	1
Total Staff:	**21**

FEE INCOME

Year End: 1990	%
Accountancy & Audit:	86.0
Other:	14.0

CLIENT SERVICES
Accountancy (General), Audit, Corporate Finance Advice, Insolvency & Corporate Restructuring, Management & Business Advice, Taxation (Corporate), Taxation (International)

OTHER OFFICES
S.E.R.C.A.
Corso di Porta Nuova 34, 20122 MILAN
Tel: +39 (2) 6590319
Contact: Giovanni Brondi
S.E.R.C.A.
Via Divisione Julia 7, 24100 BERGAMO
Tel: +39 (35) 221531
Contact: Giovanni Brondi

Total Number of Offices: 3

SINTEA SAS

Corso Buenos Aires 23, 20124 MILAN
Tel: +39 (2) 228032
Fax: +39 (2) 29510646

European Affiliation: Pannell Kerr Forster Worldwide

International Contact: Salvatore Del Vecchio

OTHER OFFICES
SINTEA SAS
Via Flaminia 217, 00196 ROME
Tel: +39 (6) 3200426 *Fax:* +39 (6) 3613447
Contact: Gianluca Venturi

Total Number of Offices: 2

SOCIETA GENERALE DI REVISIONE E CERTIFICAZIONE

Via XX Settembre 1, 00187 ROME
Tel: +39 (6) 4885909
Fax: +39 (6) 4880568

European Affiliation: DRM Internationally

International Contact: Mario A. Barranco

Partners:	3
Professional staff:	12
Non-professional staff:	3
Total Staff:	**18**

FEE INCOME

Year End: 31.12.90	L
Total:	**1,600,000,000**

CONTACT INFORMATION
Managing Partner: Mario A. Barranco
Administration: Cesia Filippi
Public Sector & Consultancy: Mario A. Barranco
Accountancy & Audit: Maurizio Luciani Cantalupo
Tax (Corporate & International): Vincenzo Cafiero

CLIENT SERVICES
All Services

OTHER OFFICES

SOCIETA GENERALE DI REVISIONE E CERTIFICAZIONE SAS
Via Andegari 18, 20122 MILAN

Total Number of Offices: 2

SOFIRESA
Via dei Bossi 7, 20122 MILAN
Tel: +39 (2) 878760
Fax: +39 (2) 805 6069

European Affiliation: Alliott Peirson International

International Contact: Vittorio Salvi

DI LUIGI STAFFICO & CO
Corso Venezia 16, 20121 MILAN
Tel: +39 (2) 76001970
Fax: +39 (2) 76005520

European Affiliation: InterContinental Consultants (ICC)

International Contact: Luigi Staffico
Guido Cavalli

STUDIO ASSOCIATO TARGA-DI PACO-PAGANI-VICHI
Via Vittor Pisani 27, 20124 MILAN
Tel: +39 (2) 67644741
Fax: +39 (2) 67644758

European Affiliation: KPMG

Partners:	7
Professional staff:	81
Non-professional staff:	25
Total Staff:	**113**

FEE INCOME

Year End: 30.09.90	**L (000)**	**%**
Tax:	11,300,000	100.0
Total:	**11,300,000**	

CONTACT INFORMATION
Managing Partner: Giorgio Targa

CLIENT SERVICES
Litigation/Legal Services, Taxation (Corporate), Taxation (International)

OTHER OFFICES

STUDIO ASSOCIATO TARGA-DI PACO-PAGANI-VICHI
Via Abate Gimma 30, 70121 BARI
Tel: +39 (80) 5243320 *Fax:* +39 (80) 5243425

STUDIO ASSOCIATO TARGA-DI PACO-PAGANI-VICHI
Viale Aldo Moro 64, 40127 BOLOGNA
Tel: +39 (51) 6460074 *Fax:* +39 (51) 6460073
Contact: Francesco Guidi

STUDIO ASSOCIATO TARGA-DI PACO-PAGANI-VICHI
Piazza G. Mazzini 3, 73100 LECCE
Tel: +39 (832) 592728 *Fax:* +39 (832) 57871

STUDIO ASSOCIATO TARGA-DI PACO-PAGANI-VICHI
Via Sicilia 66, 00187 ROME
Tel: +39 (6) 4740541 *Fax:* +39 (6) 4940734

STUDIO ASSOCIATO TARGA-DI PACO-PAGANI-VICHI
Corso Cavour 39, 37121 VERONA
Tel: +39 (45) 8012300 *Fax:* +39 (45) 8012292

Total Number of Offices: 6

STUDIO TRAVIA
Via Gesu 13, 20121 MILAN
Tel: +39 (2) 781520
Fax: +39 (2) 783128

European Affiliation: The Channel International Association

International Contact: Giovanni Travia

STUDIO VECCHIETTI MASSACCI
Viale Carducci 19, 40125 BOLOGNA
Tel: +39 (51) 342728
Fax: +39 (51) 347924

European Affiliation: Affiliated Conference of Practising Accountants International (ACPA)

International Contact: Nicola Vecchietti Massacci

STUDIO VERNA
Via Cesare Battisti 21, 20122 MILAN
Tel: +39 (2) 55187551
Fax: +39 (2) 55187584

European Affiliation: INPACT - International Network of Professional Accountants

International Contact: Giuseppe Verna

Partners:	4
Professional staff:	3
Non-professional staff:	7
Total Staff:	**14**

FEE INCOME

Year End: 1990	**%**
Accountancy & Audit:	15.0
Insolvency:	25.0
Consultancy:	20.0
Tax:	25.0
Other:	15.0

CONTACT INFORMATION
Accountancy (General): Franco Spreafico
Management Consultancy: M. Balestrazz
Tax (Corporate): Alessandro Milia
Audit & Insolvency: Giuseppe Verna

CLIENT SERVICES
Accountancy (General), Audit, Insolvency & Corporate Restructuring, Management & Business Advice, Taxation (Corporate), Taxation (International)

Luxembourg

Area: 2,586 sq km (999 sq miles)
Population: 378,400 (1990 official estimate)
Density: 143.9 per sq km
Capital: Luxembourg-Ville

GDP: LFr288 bn, US$8.8 bn (1990)
GDP per head: US$23,533
Inflation: 1990 - 3.7%
1991 - 3.1%
1992 - 3.5% (forecast)

Official and Spoken Languages: French. The commercial language, and that of the press, however, is German. Luxembourgeois, the national language of mixed German and French, is spoken by most

Time: GMT + 1 (in Summer GMT + 2)
Telephone Dialling Code: +352

Currency: Luxembourg Franc (LFr) = 100 centimes (on par with Belgian Franc)
Banking Hours: 0900-1200 and 1330-1630 Monday-Friday
Professional accountancy body: Ordre des Experts Comptables Luxembourgeois
Institut des Reviseurs d'Entreprises

Corporate Tax Data

Information supplied by Richard Citron, international tax partner of Stoy Hayward.

The tax year; nature and rates of tax

The tax year is the calendar year.

Companies are liable to corporate income tax (impôt sur le revenu des collectivités) at a standard rate of 33% (plus a supplementary levy of 1% of the tax itself) on distributed and undistributed income. Taxable profits of below LF 1,312,000 benefit from lower rates. For Luxembourg holding companies, see below. A communal business tax is also payable on income (see below).

Special regimes. Luxembourg has special taxation regimes as follows:

(1) Coordination centres. Broadly similar to Belgium's, these must be Luxembourg companies providing administrative services to members of a multinational group. Inter alia, the group must have members in at least two other countries and the ultimate parent must be resident outside Luxembourg. Qualifying coordination centres pay corporate income tax on 5% of relevant expenses, with a minimum tax for this purpose of LF 75,000.

(2) Luxembourg holding companies. These generally require a minimum share capital and have prescribed activities (eg holding and trading in shares of other companies both Luxembourgeois and foreign, currency holding, financing subsidiaries, holding licences and patents). Qualifying companies are completely exempt from most taxes. Their only tax liability is to capital duty and the annual capital tax (at a special rate of 0.2%).

(3) Certain finance companies also enjoy special tax status. ▷

Luxembourg

Residence and territoriality

Luxembourg resident companies are liable to corporate income tax on their worldwide income and capital gains (with the exception of holding companies). A company is treated as resident in Luxembourg if its registered office or principal place of business is in Luxembourg.

The tax base

Method of calculation. Taxable profits are derived by comparing the net worth of the company at the beginning and end of the accounting period.

Disallowable items. Contributions to capital and dividends paid during the accounting period must be deducted when computing taxable profits. The major disallowable expense items are excess expenses paid to related parties, general provisions for bad debts, expenses incurred in relation to non-taxable income, other taxes (except the communal business tax), fees to directors and others for supervisory services and excessive gifts.

Exempt income/special deductions. Pension provisions are deductible within certain limits, as are specific bad debt provisions and provisions for certain, but unquantified, losses. Unrealised exchange losses are deductible.

Interest paid. Interest paid is generally deductible on an accruals basis. Interest paid to related parties is deductible only to the extent of arm's length rates.

Stock. Stock is valued at the lower of cost or market value.

Depreciation. Either the straightline or reducing balance methods may be used. The annual rates used may be individually agreed with the tax authorities, although there is a spread of rates in general use for particular types of asset (ie. for buildings a straight-line rate of 2-4% and for motor vehicles a straight-line rate of 16-25%). Accelerated depreciation is available for certain types of asset; certain small items may be written off in full immediately. Tax credits are available in addition for many types of asset including on the acquisition of assets with a useful life of over four years.

Treatment of dividends

Dividends received from Luxembourg companies. Dividends are received after a deduction of 15% withholding tax. The withholding tax is credited against the company's corporate income tax liability. However, dividends from "substantial participations" (ie. LF 50m or a direct holding of 10% or more) can be exempt from withholding tax and corporate income tax in the recipient company's hands.

Dividends received from abroad. Unless the dividends stem from a substantial participation (in which case the same rules as above apply as long as the foreign paying company is subject to corporate income tax corresponding to that in Luxembourg), they are subject to corporate income tax; any foreign tax paid is allowed as a tax credit.

Dividends paid to Luxembourg residents. A 15% withholding tax must be deducted from dividends paid, unless the recipient has a substantial participation, in which case the dividend is paid gross.

Dividends paid to non-residents. The rate of withholding tax will often be reduced under the terms of a treaty. Dividends paid to shareholder companies incorporated in the EC having a qualifying "participation" (it will inter alia need to hold 10% of the shares) are exempt from Luxembourg withholding tax.

Anti-avoidance measures

Transfer pricing rules are operated to adjust all transactions with affiliates to arm's length values. There are no other significant anti-avoidance measures.

Treatment of losses

Current period. Trading and capital losses of the same period are automatically set against each other by virtue of the net worth basis of computation (there is no carryback).

Future periods. A loss (representing a decrease in net worth, as adjusted) may be carried forward indefinitely.

Treatment of capital gains

Treatment. Capital gains are taxed as income.

Computation. Gains are computed by deducting book value from sale proceeds. Gains and losses are automatically netted with other income by virtue of the net worth computation for the corporate and communal business tax.

Rollover. Gains on assets held for a minimum of five years can either be rolled over into the cost of replacement assets or frozen until the company as a whole is sold.

Special treatment for shares. Only Luxembourg holding companies do not pay tax on gains.

Treatment of groups

It is possible to consolidate the profits of a parent company with its 99% subsidiaries. All companies must be Luxembourg resident. Intra-group dividends are free of withholding tax.

Treatment of branches

The taxable profits of a Luxembourg branch of a non-resident company are computed on the same basis as those of a resident company although the branch's tax base is its assets situated in Luxembourg. The branch will be liable to communal business tax and national net worth tax. There is no withholding tax on remittance of branch profits.

Other taxes

Communal business tax (impôt commercial) has two components – one based on profits and one on net worth.

(1) The income element is levied on the corporate income tax base, as adjusted for, inter alia: salaries and fees payable to major shareholders, 60% of the interest on long term debts and all payroll costs, 10% of the assessed value of business real property, losses of the preceding five years, income from a substantial participation and foreign branch profits. An across-the-board allowance of LF 700,000 is made to all companies. The basic rate is 4%, multiplied by a factor varying between communes; 2.5 is a common factor.

(2) The net worth element uses the net worth tax base, adjusted for inter alia: 60% of long term debts, the assessed value of business real property, the net assets of a foreign branch and participations of a minimum 10% in resident companies (deducted). An across-the-board allowance of LF1,800,000 is made to all companies. The basic rate is 0.2%, multiplied by a factor varying between communes.

The communal business tax is deductible in computing the corporate income tax liability.

Taxes on capital. There is an annual 0.5% net worth tax (impôt sur la fortune) levied on the value of a company's worldwide assets (Luxembourg assets in the case of a branch). In addition to the net worth tax, there is a communal property tax levied on 5%-10% of the market value of property at a rate fixed by the commune. An annual subscription tax also applies on the average value of shares and other securities issued by Luxembourg holding companies at the rate of 0.2% (minimum LF2,500 pa).

Turnover taxes. A value added tax (taxe sur la valeur ajoutée) is charged on the supply of goods and services. The standard rate is 15%, with lower rates of 3% and 6%. Exports are zero rated.

Transaction taxes. A capital duty (droit d'apport) of 1% is payable on the initial capital subscriptions to a company and on subsequent capital increases. There is also a transfer tax on the transfer of real property at a rate of 6% or 9% on the sale price, and a mortgage "charge" of 1%.

Payroll taxes. Social security premiums for employers are set at 12.85% of salary for office etc staff and at 14.75% for manual workers.

Luxembourg

ARTHUR ANDERSEN & CO

672 rue de Neudorf, 2220 LUXEMBOURG
Tel: +*352* 437039
Fax: +*352* 437076

European Affiliation: Arthur Andersen Worldwide

International Contact: Norbert R. Becker

CONTACT INFORMATION
Audit: Douglas F. Sutherland
Tax (Corporate): Alex Sulkowski

CLIENT SERVICES
Accountancy (General), Audit, Computer Installation, Corporate Finance Advice, Insolvency & Corporate Restructuring, Litigation/Legal Services, Management & Business Advice, Management Buy-outs, Mergers & Acquisitions, Pensions Planning, Value for Money Studies, Taxation (Corporate), Taxation (International)

BDO BINDER (LUXEMBOURG) SARL

17 rue des Pommiers, 2343 LUXEMBOURG
Tel: +*352* 423042
Fax: +*352* 423040

European Affiliation: BDO Binder

International Contact: Georg Peter Rockel

Partners:	2
Professional staff:	8
Non-professional staff:	4
Total Staff:	**14**

CONTACT INFORMATION
Tax (Corporate): Jean Rhein

CLIENT SERVICES
Audit, Corporate Finance Advice, Management & Business Advice, Management Buy-outs, Mergers & Acquisitions, Pensions Planning, Taxation (Corporate), Taxation (International)

FIDUCIAIRE LEX BENOY

13 rue Bertholet, B.P. 618, 2016 LUXEMBOURG
Tel: +*352* 454363
Fax: +*352* 455754

European Affiliation: Affiliated Conference of Practising Accountants International (ACPA)

International Contact: Alex Benoy

Partners:	2
Professional staff:	6
Non-professional staff:	13
Total Staff:	**21**

FEE INCOME

Year End: 31.12.90	%
Accountancy & Audit:	15.0
Insolvency:	5.0
Consultancy:	20.0
Tax:	60.0

CONTACT INFORMATION
Chairman: Alex Benoy
Managing Partner: Guy Waltener
Administration: Astrid Marck
Accountancy & Tax: Alex Benoy
Audit, Corporate Finance & Tax: Guy Waltener
Insolvency & Consultancy: Lex Benoy
Computer: Nicole Hack

CLIENT SERVICES
Accountancy (General), Audit, Corporate Finance Advice, Insolvency & Corporate Restructuring, Management & Business Advice, Management Buy-outs, Mergers & Acquisitions, Taxation (Corporate), Taxation (International), Trust Settlement & Estates

Industry Specialisations: Media, Maritime

CALLENS PIRENNE

boulevard d'Avranches 12-14, 1012 LUXEMBOURG
Tel: +*352* 406134
Fax: +*352* 490038
Mailing Address: B.P. 1233, 1012 LUXEMBOURG

European Affiliation: BKR International

International Contact: Baudoin Callens

FIDUCIAIRE CENTRALE DU LUXEMBOURG

4 rue Henri Schnadt, 2530 LUXEMBOURG
Tel: +*352* 403727
Fax: +*352* 403723

European Affiliation: Moores Rowland International

International Contact: Francois Peusch
Jean B. Zeimet

COOPERS & LYBRAND

16 Rue Eugène Ruppert, 2453 LUXEMBOURG
Tel: +*352* 497491
Fax: +*352* 49749 400
Mailing Address: B.P. 1446, 1014 LUXEMBOURG

European Affiliation: Coopers & Lybrand Europe

International Contact: Marie-Jeanne Chèvremont
D. Mouget

Partners:	3
Professional staff:	197
Non-professional staff:	15
Total Staff:	**115**

CONTACT INFORMATION
Managing Partner: Marie-Jeanne Chevremont

CLIENT SERVICES
All Services

Industry Specialisations: Investment Funds, (Re)Insurance, Banking Holdings

ERNST & YOUNG

6 avenue Emile Reuter, B.P. 351, 2013 LUXEMBOURG
Tel: +*352* 468111
Fax: +*352* 46811 201

European Affiliation: Ernst & Young Europe

International Contact: Jean-Jacques Soisson

FIDUCIAIRE FERNAND FABER

15 boulevard Roosevelt, 2450 LUXEMBOURG
Tel: +*352* 225626
Fax: +*352* 462019
Mailing Address: B.P. 814, 2018 LUXEMBOURG

European Affiliation: Nexia International

International Contact: Claude Faber

Partners:	2
Professional staff:	25
Non-professional staff:	5
Total Staff:	**32**

CLIENT SERVICES
All Services

FIDUCIAIRE CONTINENTALE

allée Marconi 16, 2012 LUXEMBOURG
Tel: +352 453145
Fax: +352 453147
Mailing Address: B.P. 260, 2012 LUXEMBOURG

European Affiliation: Summit International Associates Inc

International Contact: Paul Lutgen

Partners:	1
Professional staff:	9
Non-professional staff:	2
Total Staff:	**12**

FEE INCOME

Year End: 31.12.90	**US$**	%
Accountancy & Audit:		30.0
Tax:		20.0
Other:		50.0
Total:	**1,100,000**	

CONTACT INFORMATION
Managing Partner: Emile Kraemer

CLIENT SERVICES
Accountancy (General), Audit, Corporate Finance Advice, Taxation (Corporate), Taxation (International), Trust Settlement & Estates

FIDUCIAIRE GÉNÉRALE DE LUXEMBOURG

3 route d'Arlon, 8009 STRASSEN
Tel: +352 451451
Fax: +352 45145 404

European Affiliation: DRT International

International Contact: Arno Schleich
Total Staff: **225**

CLIENT SERVICES
All Services
Total Number of Offices: 2

FIDUCIAIRE ALBERT HUBERTY

49 boulevard Royal, 2449 LUXEMBOURG
Tel: +352 24595
Fax: +352 21637

European Affiliation: INPACT - International Network of Professional Accountants

International Contact: Joseph Treis

INTERFIDUCIAIRE & INTERAUDIT

121 avenue de la Faïencerie, 1511 LUXEMBOURG
Tel: +352 4768472
Fax: +352 465235

European Affiliation: Clark Kenneth Leventhal

International Contact: Carlo Damgé

Partners:	4
Professional staff:	24
Non-professional staff:	3
Total Staff:	**31**

FEE INCOME

Year End: 1990	%
Accountancy & Audit:	58.0
Tax:	30.0
Other:	22.0

CLIENT SERVICES
Accountancy (General), Audit, Corporate Finance Advice, Insolvency & Corporate Restructuring, Management & Business Advice, Taxation (Corporate), Taxation (International)

KPMG

KPMG PEAT MARWICK INTER-REVISION

283 route d'Arlon, 1150 LUXEMBOURG
Tel: +352 4555111
Fax: +352 446627

European Affiliation: KPMG

International Contact: John Li

Partners:	8
Professional staff:	85
Non-professional staff:	28
Total Staff:	**121**

CONTACT INFORMATION
Chairman: A.D. Hayward
Audit: A.D. Hayward
Management Consultancy: Colin Holland
Tax: Guy Lange

CLIENT SERVICES
Audit, Computer Installation, Management & Business Advice, Taxation (Corporate), Taxation (International)

Industry Specialisations: Banking

MAJOR CLIENTS
Arbed, Banque et Caisse d'Epargne de L'Etat, Cedel

PRICE WATERHOUSE

24 avenue de la Liberté, 1930 LUXEMBOURG
Tel: +352 4024551
Fax: +352 402455 600
Mailing Address: B.P. 1443, 1014 LUXEMBOURG

European Affiliation: Price Waterhouse

Partners:	6
Professional staff:	65
Non-professional staff:	20
Total Staff:	**91**

FEE INCOME

Year End: 1990	%
Accountancy & Audit:	67.0
Tax:	33.0

CONTACT INFORMATION
Managing Partner: Christian Billon
Audit: Christian Billon
Management Consultancy: Alan Johnson
Tax: Alain Steichen
Banking: J. Robert Lentz

CLIENT SERVICES
Accountancy (General), Audit, Management & Business Advice, Taxation (Corporate), Taxation (International)

Industry Specialisations: Investment Funds

REVILUX SARL
15 boulevard Roosevelt, 2450 LUXEMBOURG
Tel: *+352* 25626
Fax: *+352* 462019
Mailing Address: B.P. 814, 2018 LUXEMBOURG

European Affiliation: DRM Internationally

Partners:	2
Professional staff:	25
Non-professional staff:	5
Total Staff:	**32**

CLIENT SERVICES
All Services

Industry Specialisations: Corporate Finance

REVISION ET CONSEILS ASSOCIÉS
33 bld Grand Duchesse Charlotte, 1331 LUXEMBOURG
Tel: *+352* 459164
Fax: *+352* 452203

European Affiliation: Grant Thornton International

International Contact: Jeffrey Davies

CONTACT INFORMATION
Partner: Martin Rutledge
Partner: Jeffrey Davies

CLIENT SERVICES
Audit

FIDUCIAIRE RUTLEDGE & WILSON SA
7 rue Pierre d'Aspelt, 1142 LUXEMBOURG
Tel: *+352* 450450
Fax: *+352* 452531

European Affiliation: Grant Thornton International

International Contact: Martin A. Rutledge

CLIENT SERVICES
Accountancy (General)

UNIVERSALIA (FIDUCIAIRE) SA
3b boulevard de Prince Henri, 1724 LUXEMBOURG
Tel: *+352* 471615
Fax: *+352* 474585
Mailing Address: B.P. 860, 1724 LUXEMBOURG

European Affiliation: Jeffreys Henry International

International Contact: Yves Wallers

The Netherlands

Area: 33,937 sq km (13,103 sq miles)
Population: 14,757,848 (1988 estimate)
Density: 434.9 per sq km
Capital: Amsterdam

GDP: NGu526 bn, US$294 bn
GDP per head: US$19,710
Inflation: 1990 - 2.3%
1991 - 3.1%

Official and Spoken Languages: Dutch. English very widely spoken, German and French also spoken

Time: GMT + 1 (in Summer GMT + 2)
Telephone Dialling Code: + 31

Currency: Guilder (NGu) = 100 cents
Banking Hours: 0900-1600 Monday-Friday
Professional accountancy body: Nederlands Instituut van Registeraccountants (NIVRA)

Corporate Tax Data

Information supplied by Richard Citron, international tax partner of Stoy Hayward.

The tax year; nature and rates of tax

The tax year is the calendar year.

Dutch companies are liable to corporation tax (vennootschapsbelasting) at a combination of two rates: at 40% on the first DFl 250,000 and at 35% on the remainder.

Residence and territoriality

Netherlands resident companies are liable to corporation tax on their worldwide income. A company is resident in the Netherlands if it is incorporated under Netherlands law or its actual management is located there.

The tax base

Method of calculation. Taxable profits are based on the comparison of net worth at the beginning and end of the accounting period and also by reference to the company's net worth over its entire existence. Contributions and withdrawals of capital are left out of calculation as are distributions of profit.

Disallowable items. In general, expenses are allowable as long as they relate directly or closely to the conduct of the business. Payments made to related parties are restricted to arm's length values. Withdrawals of capital and dividend payments must be added back.

Exempt income/special deductions. Capital contributions must be deducted from net worth. A general bad debt provision is allowable if justifiable. A tax deductible reserve to cover variable future expenditure may be set up.

Interest paid. Interest is generally deductible on an accruals basis for interest related to the cost of ▷

funding a subsidiary that produces non-taxable income.

Stock. The preferred method of valuation is at the lower of cost and market value.

Depreciation. Depreciation is usually provided on a straightline basis (although the reducing balance basis is permissible) according to the estimated useful life of the asset. Generally, both depreciation periods and rates are at the option of the taxpayer provided not unreasonable. Land is not depreciable. A special investment deduction (of between 2% and 18%) for investment in assets of between DFl 3,100 and Dfl 471,000 annually is also available.

Treatment of dividends

Dividends received from Netherlands companies. These are generally taxable although dividends qualifying for the "participation exemption" are paid gross and are exempt from tax in the hands of the recipient company. To qualify for a participation exemption, a holding must be at least 5% of the issued share capital of the investee company. The investing company must be resident in the Netherlands (or be the Netherlands branch of a non-resident company) neither company can be a special purpose investment company (subject to review) and the holding should not be held as inventory.

Dividends received from abroad. Shareholdings in foreign companies may qualify for the participation exemption as above, but the investee company must be subject to a corporate income tax (levied on profits) in its country of residence and the shareholding must not be a portfolio or passive investment. The tax authorities may insist when giving their advance ruling on participation exemption status that the investor company report a profit of at least 25% of the costs of managing the foreign shareholding per annum and that it finance the purchase of a qualifying subsidiary with a minimum of 15% shareholders' equity. Where participation exemption is not available, the dividend is subject to corporation tax. Foreign tax paid is credited against the Netherlands corporation tax liability and unused foreign tax credits may be carried forward.

Dividends paid to Netherlands residents. Withholding tax of 25% must be deducted from dividend payments to resident individuals.

Dividends paid to non-residents. Withholding tax of 25% must be deducted although reducible under a double tax treaty.

Anti-avoidance measures

There are no formal thin capitalisation rules but debt may in certain circumstances be treated as equity. Transfer pricing provisions exist in relation to transactions with affiliates.

Treatment of losses

Current period. Losses of whatever description are automatically netted off against income of the same period by virtue of the net worth basis.

Past periods. Losses may be carried back against profits of the past three years.

Future periods. Net losses may be carried forward for a maximum of eight years. Losses incurred during a company's first six years may be carried forward indefinitely.

Treatment of capital gains

Treatment. Capital gains are treated as income for tax purposes.

Computation. Gains are computed by deducting cost or net book value (depreciated) from sale proceeds.

Rollover. Gains on the sale of tangible or intangible assets may be rolled over against the cost of similar replacement assets acquired within four years.

Special treatment of shares. Gains arising from a holding qualifying for the participation exemption are exempt from corporation tax.

Treatment of groups

A Netherlands holding company and its 100% Netherlands resident subsidiaries may form a single fiscal unit (tax group). Profits and losses are pooled for tax purposes and assets may be transferred free of capital gains, VAT and stamp duty. Dividends paid intra-group are exempt from tax.

Treatment of branches

The profits of the Netherlands branch of a non-resident company are computed in the same way as those of a resident company on the basis of its assets in the Netherlands. There is no withholding tax on remittances of profit.

Other taxes

Taxes on capital. There is a local property tax based on the economic value or size of the property.

Turnover taxes. A value added tax (belasting over de toegevoegde waarde) is charged. There is a standard rate of 18.5% and a lower rate of 6%. Exports are zero rated.

Transaction taxes. There is a capital duty of 1% on the value of capital contributions in cash or in kind for shares by a company and a 6% transfer tax payable by the purchaser on property transfers or on the sale of shares in a company 70% or more of whose assets consist of Netherlands real property.

Payroll taxes. Employers and employees must pay social security premiums.

ARENTHALS CHAUDRON

Buitenveldertselaan 158, 1081 AB AMSTERDAM
Tel: +*31* (20) 6426554
Fax: +*31* (20) 6445553
Mailing Address: P.O. Box 71003, 1008 BA AMSTERDAM

European Affiliation: Grant Thornton International

International Contact: Ludo Gribling

Partners:	18
Professional staff:	118
Non-professional staff:	46
Total Staff:	**182**

FEE INCOME

Year End: 31.12.90	**Gu (million)**
Total:	**20,583**

CONTACT INFORMATION
Chairman: Henk Moesbergen
Managing Partner: Peter Prein
Tax (International): Elias Chaudron

CLIENT SERVICES
Accountancy (General), Audit, Litigation/Legal Services, Taxation (Corporate), Taxation (International), Trust Settlement & Estates, Computer Consultancy

OTHER OFFICES

ARENTHALS CHAUDRON
Halvervege 3, 2402 NK ALPHEN A/D RIJN
Mailing Address: P.O. Box 330, 2400 AH ALPHEN A/D RIJN
Tel: +*31* (1720) 30774 *Fax:* +*31* (1720) 34342

ARENTHALS CHAUDRON
Bleulandweg 1b, 2803 HG GOUDA
Tel: +*31* (1820) 31922 *Fax:* +*31* (1820) 30878

Total Number of Offices: 9

ARTHUR ANDERSEN & CO

Zwaansvliet 20, 1081 AP AMSTERDAM
Tel: +*31* (20) 5414414
Fax: +*31* (20) 6612914

European Affiliation: Arthur Andersen Worldwide

International Contact: Pieter Maaskant

CONTACT INFORMATION
Audit: Pieter Maaskant
Tax (Corporate): Marinus J. van Dieren

CLIENT SERVICES
Accountancy (General), Audit, Computer Installation, Corporate Finance Advice, Insolvency & Corporate Restructuring, Litigation/Legal Services, Management & Business Advice, Management Buy-outs, Mergers & Acquisitions, Pensions Planning, Value for Money Studies, Taxation (Corporate), Taxation (International)

OTHER OFFICES

ARTHUR ANDERSEN & CO
Pastoor Petersstraat 162, 5612 LV EINDHOVEN
Tel: +*31* (40) 458300 *Fax:* +*31* (40) 447958

ARTHUR ANDERSEN & CO
Coolsingel 139, 3012 AG ROTTERDAM
Tel: +*31* (10) 4035403 *Fax:* +*31* (10) 4111044

Total Number of Offices: 4

BARNVELD SCHEVERS

P.O. Box 409, Rietgors 10, 3430 NIEUWEGEIN
Tel: +*31* (3402) 37334
Fax: +*31* (3402) 35409

European Affiliation: TEG (The European Group of Accounting & Auditing Firms)

International Contact: Kees van Rhee

BDO CAMPSOBERSGROEP

Central Services, Fellenoord 240, 5611 ZC EINDHOVEN
Tel: +*31* (40) 433914
Fax: +*31* (40) 436314
Mailing Address: P.O. Box 182, 5600 AD EINDHOVEN

European Affiliation: BDO Binder

Partners:	50
Professional staff:	628
Non-professional staff:	162
Total Staff:	**840**

FEE INCOME

Year End: 1990	**US$**	**%**
Accountancy & Audit:	40,686,000	72.0
Consultancy:	3,291,000	6.0
Tax:	12,767,000	22.0
Total:	**56,744,000**	

CONTACT INFORMATION
Chairman: Jacques W.M. van Erven
Accountancy (General): A. Korving
Management Consultancy: T.J.C. Langerwerf
Administration: Johan A.M. van Gils
Tax (Corporate): P.W.E. Geraads
EDP-Audit: J.M. Suerink

CLIENT SERVICES
Accountancy (General), Audit, Corporate Finance Advice, Management & Business Advice, Mergers & Acquisitions, Taxation (Corporate), Taxation (International)

OTHER OFFICES

BDO CAMPSOBERSGROEP
Raadhuisstraat 102, 2406 AH ALPHEN A/D RIJN
Mailing Address: P.O. Box 223, 2400 AE ALPHEN A/D RIJN
Tel: +*31* (1720) 72641 *Fax:* +*31* (1720) 75890
Contact: Ton de Waardt

BDO CAMPSOBERSGROEP
Paasheuvelweg 8, 1105 BH AMSTERDAM ZUID-OOST
Mailing Address: P.O. Box 12176, 1100 AD AMSTERDAM ZUID-OOST
Tel: +*31* (20) 6910211 *Fax:* +*31* (20) 6912781
Contact: Sibe Hoekstra

BDO CAMPSOBERSGROEP
"De Brinkhof", Nieuwstraat 7f, 7311 HX APELDOORN
Tel: +*31* (55) 218888 *Fax:* +*31* (55) 212597
Contact: Loek de Jong

BDO CAMPSOBERSGROEP
Jansbuitensingel 20, 6811 AD ARNHEM
Mailing Address: P.O. Box 1062, 6801 BB ARNHEM
Tel: +*31* (85) 424742 *Fax:* +*31* (85) 427592
Contact: Martin van Roekel

BDO CAMPSOBERSGROEP
Heerbaan 250, 4817 NL BREDA
Tel: +*31* (76) 714900 *Fax:* +*31* (76) 714833
Contact: Harry J.M. Berden

▷

The Netherlands

BDO CAMPSOBERSGROEP
Hoge Bakstraat 44, 3311 WJ DORDRECHT
Mailing Address: P.O. Box 795, 3300 AT DORDRECHT
Tel: + *31* (78) 140666 *Fax:* + *31* (78) 140941
Contact: Rob Glimmerveen

BDO CAMPSOBERSGROEP
Fellenoord 240, 5611 ZC EINDHOVEN
Mailing Address: P.O. Box 229, 5600 AE EINDHOVEN
Tel: + *31* (40) 433914 *Fax:* + *31* (40) 460825
Contact: Jos F.M. Beenker

BDO CAMPSOBERSGROEP
Geleenbeeklaan 80, 6166 GR GELEEN
Mailing Address: P.O. Box 1, 6160 AA GELEEN
Tel: + *31* (46) 785252 *Fax:* + *31* (46) 740410
Contact: Jos P.C. Verspaget

BDO CAMPSOBERSGROEP
Gevers Deynootweg 130, 2586 HM THE HAGUE
Mailing Address: P.O. Box 17408, 2502 CK THE HAGUE
Tel: + *31* (70) 3514711 *Fax:* + *31* (70) 3555300
Contact: Gerard M.M. Ellenbroek

BDO CAMPSOBERSGROEP
Aarle Rixtelseweg 76, 5707 GM HELMOND
Mailing Address: P.O. Box 427, 5700 AK HELMOND
Tel: + *31* (4920) 38478 *Fax:* + *31* (4920) 49975
Contact: Cees H. Laan

BDO CAMPSOBERSGROEP
Bruistensingel 300, 5232 AE 's-HERTOGENBOSCH
Mailing Address: P.O. Box 3191, 5203 DD 's-HERTOGENBOSCH
Tel: + *31* (73) 405705 *Fax:* + *31* (73) 427730
Contact: Rob P.A. Bröcheler

BDO CAMPSOBERSGROEP
Stokdijkkade 19, 2671 GX NAALDWIJK
Mailing Address: P.O. Box 197, 2670 AD NAALDWIJK
Tel: + *31* (1740) 25801 *Fax:* + *31* (1740) 21930
Contact: Juub Poldervaart

BDO CAMPSOBERSGROEP
Kerkenbos 1023, 6546 BB NIJMEGEN
Mailing Address: P.O. Box 40025, 6504 AA NIJMEGEN
Tel: + *31* (80) 782745 *Fax:* + *31* (80) 782395
Contact: Paul J. Leeuwerik

BDO CAMPSOBERSGROEP
Laan van Brabant 72, 4701 BL ROOSENDAAL
Mailing Address: P.O. Box 1415, 4700 BK ROOSENDAAL
Tel: + *31* (1650) 35650 *Fax:* + *31* (1650) 33994
Contact: Johan A.M. van Gils

BDO CAMPSOBERSGROEP
K.P. van der Mandelelaan 60, 3062 MB ROTTERDAM
Tel: + *31* (10) 4529925 *Fax:* + *31* (10) 4530102
Contact: Cees Alblas

BDO CAMPSOBERSGROEP
Parklaan 9, 6131 KE SITTARD
Mailing Address: P.O. Box 383, 6130 AJ SITTARD
Tel: + *31* (4490) 510651 *Fax:* + *31* (4490) 527236
Contact: Jacq L.P.M. Visser

BDO CAMPSOBERSGROEP
Dr. Hub. van Doorneweg 91, 5026 RB TILBURG
Mailing Address: P.O. Box 757, 5000 AT TILBURG
Tel: + *31* (13) 686951 *Fax:* + *31* (13) 670207
Contact: Jacques W.M. van Erven

BDO CAMPSOBERSGROEP
't Goylaan 13, 3525 AA UTRECHT
Mailing Address: P.O. Box 4053, 3502 HB UTRECHT
Tel: + *31* (30) 884077 *Fax:* + *31* (30) 897554
Contact: Piet Feyt

Total Number of Offices: 19

BLÖMER & CO

Krÿtwal 1-3, 3430 AA NIEUWEGEIN
Tel: + *31* (3402) 58511
Fax: + *31* (3402) 45526
Mailing Address: P.O. Box 5, 3430 AA NIEUWEGEIN

European Affiliation: Independent Accountants International

International Contact: Peter Spierenburg

Partners:	5
Professional staff:	40
Non-professional staff:	5
Total Staff:	**50**

FEE INCOME

Year End: 31.12.90	**Gu**
Total:	**6,000,000**

CONTACT INFORMATION
Chairman: Frans van Lent
Managing Partner: Peter Spierenburg
Accountancy (General): Hans Odyk
Insolvency: Gert Dykstra
Audit & Public Sector: Dick Kamsteeg
Tax: Frans Van Lent

CLIENT SERVICES
Accountancy (General), Audit, Insolvency & Corporate Restructuring, Management & Business Advice, Management Buy-outs, Mergers & Acquisitions, Taxation (Corporate), Taxation (International)

BORRIE & CO

P.O. Box 8565, 3009 AN ROTTERDAM
Tel: + *31* (10) 4470499
Fax: + *31* (10) 4472036

European Affiliation: Alliott Peirson International

International Contact: Wim Borrie

OTHER OFFICES

BORRIE & CO
Koninginneweg 32, 1217 LA HILVERSUM
Tel: + *31* (35) 48752 *Fax:* + *31* (35) 215257
Contact: Gijs J. Brand

BORRIE & CO
Guido Gezellestraat 1, 4532 EA TERNEUZEN
Tel: + *31* (1150) 12864 *Fax:* + *31* (1150) 20240
Contact: Wim Borrie

Total Number of Offices: 3

COOPERS & LYBRAND DIJKER VAN DIEN

Prins Bernhardplein 200, 1097 JB AMSTERDAM
Tel: + *31* (20) 5686666
Fax: + *31* (20) 5686888
Mailing Address: P.O. Box 4200, 1009 AE AMSTERDAM

European Affiliation: Coopers & Lybrand Europe

Partners:	255
Professional staff:	2,824
Non-professional staff:	840
Total Staff:	**3,919**

CONTACT INFORMATION
Chairman: Cees van Luijk
Vice Chairman: Gilles Izebould

CLIENT SERVICES

Accountancy (General), Audit, Corporate Finance Advice, Insolvency & Corporate Restructuring, Management & Business Advice, Management Buy-outs, Mergers & Acquisitions, Pensions Planning, Value for Money Studies, Taxation (Corporate), Taxation (International), Computer Audit, Information Systems Security, Interim Management

Industry Specialisations: Insurance, Banking, Pharmaceutical, Leisure, Real Estate, Communication, Non-Profit, Government, Automotive

OTHER OFFICES

COOPERS & LYBRAND DIJKER VAN DIEN
Wognumsebuurt 1, 1817 BH ALKMAAR
Mailing Address: P.O. Box 379, 1800 AJ ALKMAAR
Tel: + *31* (72) 190800 *Fax:* + *31* (72) 150582
Contact: Art C. Smaal

COOPERS & LYBRAND DIJKER VAN DIEN
Spoordreef 22, 1315 GP ALMERE
Mailing Address: P.O. Box 10016, 1301 AA ALMERE
Tel: + *31* (3240) 33104 *Fax:* + *31* (3240) 36968
Contact: Erik O.H.C. Härtenhoff

COOPERS & LYBRAND DIJKER VAN DIEN
Amersfoortsestraat 123, 3769 AJ SOESTERBERG
Mailing Address: P.O. Box 809, 3800 AV AMERSFOORT
Tel: + *31* (33) 671811 *Fax:* + *31* (33) 650701
Contact: Jan Los

COOPERS & LYBRAND DIJKER VAN DIEN
Velperweg 35, 6824 BE ARNHEM
Mailing Address: P.O. Box 5381, 6802 EJ ARNHEM
Tel: + *31* (85) 712500 *Fax:* + *31* (85) 712590
Contact: Marjo J.L. van Ool

COOPERS & LYBRAND DIJKER VAN DIEN
Peter Vineloolaan 50, 4611 AN BERGEN OP ZOOM
Mailing Address: P.O. Box 524, 4600 AM BERGEN OP ZOOM
Tel: + *31* (1640) 53888 *Fax:* + *31* (1640) 66733
Contact: Paul B. Eilander

COOPERS & LYBRAND DIJKER VAN DIEN
Langendijk 34-36, 4819 EW BREDA
Mailing Address: P.O. Box 1042, 4801 BA BREDA
Tel: + *31* (76) 240500 *Fax:* + *31* (76) 210462
Contact: Hans C.M. Waser

COOPERS & LYBRAND DIJKER VAN DIEN
Martinus Nijhofflaan 2, 2624 ES DELFT
Mailing Address: P.O. Box 425, 2600 AK DELFT
Tel: + *31* (15) 625667 *Fax:* + *31* (15) 625451

COOPERS & LYBRAND DIJKER VAN DIEN
Beukenlaan 77, 5616 VC EINDHOVEN
Mailing Address: P.O. Box 6365, 5600 HJ EINDHOVEN
Tel: + *31* (40) 500600 *Fax:* + *31* (40) 500605
Contact: Peter Heere

COOPERS & LYBRAND DIJKER VAN DIEN
Hooggoorns, 7812 AM EMMEN
Mailing Address: P.O. Box 317, 7800 AH EMMEN
Tel: + *31* (5910) 17777 *Fax:* + *31* (5910) 41611
Contact: Teun J. Boersma

COOPERS & LYBRAND DIJKER VAN DIEN
Stationsplein 3, 2801 AK GOUDA
Mailing Address: P.O. Box 383, 2800 AJ GOUDA
Tel: + *31* (1820) 21177 *Fax:* + *31* (1820) 10103
Contact: A.G. Rob Cornelis

COOPERS & LYBRAND DIJKER VAN DIEN
Lange Vijverberg 11, 2513 AC THE HAGUE
Mailing Address: P.O. Box 30715, 2500 GS THE HAGUE
Tel: + *31* (70) 3426111 *Fax:* + *31* (70) 3426400
Contact: Ruud Dekkers

COOPERS & LYBRAND DIJKER VAN DIEN
Rooseveltplantsoen 4, 2517 KR THE HAGUE
Mailing Address: P.O. Box 29716, 2502 LS THE HAGUE
Tel: + *31* (70) 3525252 *Fax:* + *31* (70) 3525300
Contact: Bob van Boven

COOPERS & LYBRAND DIJKER VAN DIEN
Van Swietenlaan 25, 9728 NX GRONINGEN
Mailing Address: P.O. Box 8060, 9702 KB GRONINGEN
Tel: + *31* (50) 264826 *Fax:* + *31* (50) 262025

COOPERS & LYBRAND DIJKER VAN DIEN
Schipholpoort 66, 2034 MB HAARLEM
Mailing Address: P.O. Box 266, 2100 AG HEEMSTEDE
Tel: + *31* (23) 430130 *Fax:* + *31* (23) 400014
Contact: Wim H. Oudheusden

COOPERS & LYBRAND DIJKER VAN DIEN
Diamantstraat 2, 7554 TA HENGELO
Mailing Address: P.O. Box 65, 7550 AB HENGELO
Tel: + *31* (74) 439055 *Fax:* + *31* (74) 428387
Contact: Herman C.A. Bruins Slot

COOPERS & LYBRAND DIJKER VAN DIEN
Pettelaarpark 100, 5216 PR 's-HERTOGENBOSCH
Mailing Address: P.O. Box 70050, 5201 DZ 's-HERTOGENBOSCH
Tel: + *31* (73) 877777 *Fax:* + *31* (73) 138075
Contact: Philip J.M. van Eekeren

COOPERS & LYBRAND DIJKER VAN DIEN
Peerlkamplaan 7, 1217 RT HILVERSUM
Mailing Address: P.O. Box 1701, 1200 BS HILVERSUM
Tel: + *31* (35) 233948 *Fax:* + *31* (35) 211846

COOPERS & LYBRAND DIJKER VAN DIEN
Crerarstraat 10b, 7901 AE HOOGEVEEN
Mailing Address: P.O. Box 375, 7900 AJ HOOGEVEEN
Tel: + *31* (5280) 66455 *Fax:* + *31* (5280) 73719
Contact: Teun J. Boersma

COOPERS & LYBRAND DIJKER VAN DIEN
Badweg 2, 8934 AA LEEUWARDEN
Mailing Address: P.O. Box 321, 8901 BC LEEUWARDEN
Tel: + *31* (58) 862100 *Fax:* + *31* (58) 890616
Contact: Ton J.E. Jansman

COOPERS & LYBRAND DIJKER VAN DIEN
St Pieterskade 26, 6212 AD MAASTRICHT
Mailing Address: P.O. Box 1314, 6201 BH MAASTRICHT
Tel: + *31* (43) 254858 *Fax:* + *31* (43) 253585
Contact: Jaap F. van Wijck

COOPERS & LYBRAND DIJKER VAN DIEN
Roozenburglaan 10, 4337 JH MIDDELBURG
Mailing Address: P.O. Box 7055, 4330 GB MIDDELBURG
Tel: + *31* (1180) 36551 *Fax:* + *31* (1180) 38931
Contact: Willem Verhage

COOPERS & LYBRAND DIJKER VAN DIEN
Oranjesingel 58, 6511 NX NIJMEGEN
Mailing Address: P.O. Box 1161, 6501 BD NIJMEGEN
Tel: + *31* (80) 230847 *Fax:* + *31* (80) 239553
Contact: Louis J. Dercks

COOPERS & LYBRAND DIJKER VAN DIEN
Roerderweg 35, 6041 NR ROERMOND
Mailing Address: P.O. Box 77, 6040 AB ROERMOND
Tel: + *31* (4750) 15851 *Fax:* + *31* (4750) 11590
Contact: Harry C.M. van Baarle

COOPERS & LYBRAND DIJKER VAN DIEN
Marten Meesweg 25, 3068 AV ROTTERDAM
Mailing Address: P.O. Box 8800, 3009 AV ROTTERDAM
Tel: + *31* (10) 4075500 *Fax:* + *31* (10) 4564333
Contact: Gerard A. Bergers

▷

COOPERS & LYBRAND DIJKER VAN DIEN
Weena 151-161, 3013 CK ROTTERDAM
Mailing Address: P.O. Box 2755, 3000 CT ROTTERDAM
Tel: + *31* (10) 4000400 *Fax:* + *31* (10) 4331401
Contact: Jan Willem Broekhuysen

COOPERS & LYBRAND DIJKER VAN DIEN
dr. Hub van Doorneweg 81, 5026 RB TILBURG
Mailing Address: P.O. Box 222, 5000 AE TILBURG
Tel: + *31* (13) 684981 *Fax:* + *31* (13) 632428
Contact: Wil E. Melchior

COOPERS & LYBRAND DIJKER VAN DIEN
Archimedeslaan 21, 3584 BA UTRECHT
Mailing Address: P.O. Box 85096, 3508 AB UTRECHT
Tel: + *31* (30) 562256 *Fax:* + *31* (30) 562222
Contact: Pieter de Lange

COOPERS & LYBRAND DIJKER VAN DIEN
Churchillaan 11, 3527 GV UTRECHT
Tel: + *31* (30) 928892 *Fax:* + *31* (30) 964222
Contact: Geert R.A. de Jong

COOPERS & LYBRAND DIJKER VAN DIEN
Ebbehout 1, 1507 EA ZAANDAM
Mailing Address: P.O. Box 1248, 1500 EA ZAANDAM
Tel: + *31* (75) 172354 *Fax:* + *31* (75) 178598
Contact: Tom Bijl

COOPERS & LYBRAND DIJKER VAN DIEN
Burg. van Royensingel 2, 8011 CS ZWOLLE
Mailing Address: P.O. Box 513, 8000 AM ZWOLLE
Tel: + *31* (38) 218046 *Fax:* + *31* (38) 213668
Contact: Pem H. van Heek

Total Number of Offices: 31

CROP, DE KLEUVER & CO

Johan van Oldenbarneveltlaan 34, 3818 HB AMERSFOORT
Tel: + *31* (33) 635727
Fax: + *31* (33) 635480

European Affiliation: The International Group of Accounting Firms Ltd (IGAF)

International Contact: Adriaan van den Brink

CLIENT SERVICES

Audit, Taxation (Corporate), Taxation (International)

OTHER OFFICES

CROP, DE KLEUVER & COMPANY
Jansbuitensingel 29, 6811 AD ARNHEM
Tel: + *31* (85) 510228 *Fax:* + *31* (85) 510228
Contact: H. Snetselaar

CROP, DE KLEUVER & COMPANY
Hoofdweg-Oostzijde 622, 2132 MJ HOOFDDORP
Tel: + *31* (2503) 26248 *Fax:* + *31* (2503) 26308
Contact: G.L. Telling

CROP, DE KLEUVER & COMPANY
Speelkamb 28, 3831 PE LEUSDEN
Tel: + *31* (33) 952500 *Fax:* + *31* (33) 952626
Contact: Adriaan van den Brink

CROP, DE KLEUVER & COMPANY
Krijtwal 25, 3432 ZT NIEUWIGEIN
Tel: + *31* (3402) 40035 *Fax:* + *31* (3402) 26308

CROP, DE KLEUVER & COMPANY
Rubensstraat 169, 6717 VE EDE
Tel: + *31* (8380) 23799 *Fax:* + *31* (8380) 38399
Contact: Adriaan van den Brink

Total Number of Offices: 6

DE ROO & VAN DER VEEN GROEP

Noordsingel 208-210, 3032 BM ROTTERDAM
Tel: + *31* (10) 4657044
Fax: + *31* (10) 4657670

European Affiliation: Clark Kenneth Leventhal

International Contact: Hans Joziasse

Partners:	12
Professional staff:	108
Non-professional staff:	29
Total Staff:	**149**

FEE INCOME

Year End: 1990	%
Accountancy & Audit:	65.0
Tax:	20.0
Other:	15.0

CLIENT SERVICES

Accountancy (General), Audit, Corporate Finance Advice, Insolvency & Corporate Restructuring, Management & Business Advice, Taxation (Corporate), Taxation (International)

OTHER OFFICES

DE ROO & VAN DER VEEN GROEP
Seissingel 100, 4330 AH MIDDLEBURG
Tel: + *31* (1180) 34000 *Fax:* + *31* (1180) 25417

DE ROO & VAN DER VEEN GROEP
Oranjestraat 1, 3361 HN SLIEDRECHT
Tel: + *31* (1840) 14766 *Fax:* + *31* (1840) 19421

Total Number of Offices: 3

DE ZEEUW & DE KEIZER REGISTERACCOUNTANTS

Jacob Obrechtstraat 56, 1071 KN AMSTERDAM
Tel: + *31* (20) 6640031
Fax: + *31* (20) 6750157

European Affiliation: Russell Bedford International

International Contact: Louis Baars

OTHER OFFICES

DE ZEEUW & DE KEIZER REGISTERACCOUNTANTS
Kerkenbos 10-25, P.O. Box 451, 6500 HL NIJMEGEN
Tel: + *31* (80) 778100 *Fax:* + *31* (80) 790099

DE ZEEUW & DE KEIZER REGISTERACCOUNTANTS
's Gravenweg 310, 3006 AH ROTTERDAM
Mailing Address: P.O. Box 4308, 3006 AH ROTTERDAM
Tel: + *31* (10) 4529111 *Fax:* + *31* (10) 4527400

Total Number of Offices: 4

EBBEN SLAATS DE JONGE

Bovendonk 9, 4707 ZH ROOSENDAAL
Tel: + *31* (1650) 80200
Fax: + *31* (1650) 60395
Mailing Address: P.O. Box 1388, 4700 BJ ROOSENDAAL

European Affiliation: International Association of Practising Accountants (IAPA)

International Contact: Jan de Jonge

Partners:	5
Professional staff:	60
Non-professional staff:	5
Total Staff:	**70**

FEE INCOME

Year End: 31.12.90	**Gu**	
Total:	**10,000,000**	

CONTACT INFORMATION

Chairman: Albert Ebben
Managing Partner: Jos Slaats
Audit: Jack Coppens
Management Consultancy: Albert Ebben
Accountancy, Corporate Finance: Jan de Jonge
Tax (Corporate & International): Jos Slaats

CLIENT SERVICES

Accountancy (General), Audit, Corporate Finance Advice, Insolvency & Corporate Restructuring, Management & Business Advice, Management Buy-outs, Mergers & Acquisitions, Taxation (Corporate), Taxation (International)

OTHER OFFICES

EBBEN SLAATS DE JONGE
Heuvel 21, 4901 KB OOSTERHOUT
Tel: + *31* (1620) 57000 *Fax:* + *31* (1620) 26557
Contact: Koos de Geus

Total Number of Offices: 2

ESHUIS GROEP

Twentelaan 5, 7600 RE ALMELO
Tel: + *31* (54) 9011361
Fax: + *31* (54) 9010611
Mailing Address: Postbus 206, 7600 AE ALMELO

European Affiliation: Affiliated Conference of Practising Accountants International (ACPA)

FERNHOUT, STRUIJK & VAN DER VEKEN ACCOUNTANTS BV

Korte Steigerstraat 6, 5301 CE ZALTBOMMEL
Tel: + *31* (4180) 15080
Fax: + *31* (4180) 12920
Mailing Address: P.O. Box 128, 5300 AC ZALTBOMMEL

European Affiliation: S & W International

International Contact: A. Fernhout

Partners:	4
Professional staff:	40
Total Staff:	**44**

FEE INCOME

Year End: 31.12.90	**Gu**	**%**
Accountancy & Audit:	1,000,000	62.5
Tax:	400,000	25.0
Other:	200,000	12.5
Total:	**1,600,000**	

CONTACT INFORMATION

Chairman: W. Leyte
Accountancy (General): A. Fernhout
Audit: L. Struijk
Management Consultancy: D. van der Veken
Tax (Corporate): W. Leyte
Tax (International): Dr. J. Campagne
Legal affairs: M. van Kessel

CLIENT SERVICES

All Services

OTHER OFFICES

FERNHOUT, STRUIJK & VAN DER VEKEN ACCOUNTANTS BV
Zandstraat 58, 4101 ED CULEMBORG
Tel: + *31* (3450) 17058 *Fax:* + *31* (3450) 19164
Contact: D. van der Veken

FERNHOUT, STRUIJK & VAN DER VEKEN ACCOUNTANTS BV
Buitenhaven 12, 5211 TP 's-HERTOGENBOSCH
Tel: + *31* (73) 135558 *Fax:* + *31* (73) 130340
Contact: W. Leijte

FERNHOUT, STRUIJK & VAN DER VEKEN ACCOUNTANTS BV
Msr van der Boerpark 2-2a, 5342 CD OSS
Tel: + *31* (4120) 45578 *Fax:* + *31* (4120) 45469
Contact: W. Brands

Total Number of Offices: 4

FOEDERER GROEP ACCOUNTANTS NV

Zernikestraat 10, 5612 HZ EINDHOVEN
Tel: + *31* (40) 433980
Fax: + *31* (40) 433976

European Affiliation: DFK International

International Contact: J.A.N. Foederer

Partners:	5
Professional staff:	152
Total Staff:	**157**

FEE INCOME

Year End: 1990	**%**
Accountancy & Audit:	60.0
Consultancy:	15.0
Tax:	15.0
Other:	10.0

CLIENT SERVICES

Accountancy (General), Audit, Computer Installation, Management & Business Advice, Taxation (Corporate), Taxation (International), Management Consultancy

OTHER OFFICES

A.C.A. BV
Parklaan 42-A, 5613 BG EINDHOVEN
Tel: + *31* (40) 457445 *Fax:* + *31* (40) 448975
Contact: J.A.N. Foederer

ACCOUNTANTSKANTOOR FOEDERER BV
Raphaelstraat 20, 1077 PV AMSTERDAM
Tel: + *31* (20) 6717752 *Fax:* + *31* (20) 6710580
Contact: M. Ketelaar

ACCOUNTANTSKANTOOR FOEDERER BV
Dr Nassaulaan 3, 9401 HJ ASSEN
Tel: + *31* (5920) 17288 *Fax:* + *31* (5920) 17295
Contact: M. Ketelaar

ACCOUNTANTSKANTOOR FOEDERER BV
Mierloseweg 1-C, 5707 AA HELMOND
Tel: + *31* (4920) 40330 *Fax:* + *31* (4920) 50356
Contact: Drs. J.H.M. van den Reek

ACCOUNTANTSKANTOOR FOEDERER BV
De Botter 11-07, 8232 JN LELYSTAD
Tel: + *31* (3200) 50444 *Fax:* + *31* (3200) 55034
Contact: M. Ketelaar

ACCOUNTANTSKANTOOR FOEDERER BV
Oranjesingel 6, 6511 NT NIJMEGEN
Tel: + *31* (80) 236614 *Fax:* + *31* (80) 602219
Contact: M.A.J. van Beers

ACCOUNTANTSKANTOOR FOEDERER BV
Kerkbuurt 27-29, 1511 BB OOSTZAAN
Tel: + *31* (2984) 1327 *Fax:* + *31* (2984) 1300
Contact: M. Ketelaar

▷

ACCOUNTANTSKANTOOR FOEDERER BV
Kapellerlaan 19, 6041 JB ROERMOND
Tel: + *31* (4750) 19141 *Fax:* + *31* (4750) 31106
Contact: P.A.J.M. Sniekers

ACCOUNTANTSKANTOOR FOEDERER BV
Margrietstraat 7, 5401 CH UDEN
Tel: + *31* (4132) 68585 *Fax:* + *31* (4132) 60128
Contact: Drs. M.J.J.M. van Grootel

ACCOUNTANTSKANTOOR FOEDERER BV
Emmasingel 48-50, 6001 BD WEERT
Tel: + *31* (4950) 30555 *Fax:* + *31* (4950) 24215
Contact: J.W. Govers

COSAM BV
De Veste 10-02, 8231 JA LELYSTAD
Tel: + *31* (3200) 45064 *Fax:* + *31* (3200) 26770
Contact: J.A.N. Foederer

FOEDERER GROEP ACCOUNTANTS NV
Herkenrodesingel 23, Bus 3, 3500 HASSELT
Tel: + *31* (32) 11255312 *Fax:* + *31* (32) 11255366
Contact: J.A.N. Foederer

Total Number of Offices: 13

GOVERS ACCOUNTANTS/ CONSULTANTS

Geldropseweg 26, 5611 SJ EINDHOVEN
Tel: + *31* (40) 116355
Fax: + *31* (40) 110956
Mailing Address: P.O. Box 657, 5600 AR EINDHOVEN

European Affiliation: Urbach Hacker Young International

International Contact: Dick Boers

Partners:	6
Professional staff:	84
Total Staff:	**90**

CONTACT INFORMATION

Chairman: Jef Boemaars
Managing Partner: Dick Boers
Partner: M.P.B. Berben
Partner: Jef Boemaars
Partner: P.M. Dubbers
Partner: A.J. Follon
Partner: H.N.M. van den Heuvel

CLIENT SERVICES

All Services

Industry Specialisations: All Sectors of Industry

OTHER OFFICES

ADMINISTRATIE-EN ADVIESBUREAU NOORD-BRABANT BV
Geldropseweg 28, 5611 SJ EINDHOVEN
Mailing Address: P.O. Box 7619, 5601 JP EINDHOVEN
Tel: + *31* (40) 116161 *Fax:* + *31* (40) 113005
Contact: Jan Lubse

C.I.C. INTERIM CONSULT BV
Geldropseweg 26, 5611 SJ EINDHOVEN
Mailing Address: P.O. Box 657, 5600 AR EINDHOVEN
Tel: + *31* (40) 116155 *Fax:* + *31* (40) 110956
Contact: Peter Hartgers

GOVERS WEERT BV
Wilhelminasingel 245, 6001 GS WEERT
Mailing Address: P.O. Box 598, 6000 AN WEERT
Tel: + *31* (4950) 21730 *Fax:* + *31* (4950) 41717
Contact: Henk Smits

Total Number of Offices: 4

HAAGSE ACCOUNTANTS GROEP

Lange Voorhout 14, 2514 ED 's-GRAVENHAGE
Tel: + *31* (70) 3615969
Fax: + *31* (70) 3652185

European Affiliation: IAG International

International Contact: André van Wasbeek
H. Th. Rietbergen

HAMELINK VAN GILS

Westerkade 2b, 3016 CL ROTTERDAM
Tel: + *31* (10) 4365888
Fax: + *31* (10) 4363327

International Contact: Ben C.J. van Gils

HLB NEDERLAND ACCOUNTANTS & CONSULTANTS

Cronenburg 73, 1081 GM AMSTERDAM
Tel: + *31* (20) 6464011
Fax: + *31* (20) 6463251

European Affiliation: HLB International

International Contact: Alex H. Otten

Partners:	17
Professional staff:	130
Non-professional staff:	40
Total Staff:	**187**

CONTACT INFORMATION

Chairman: Alex H. Otten

CLIENT SERVICES

Accountancy (General), Audit, Computer Installation, Corporate Finance Advice, Insolvency & Corporate Restructuring, Litigation/Legal Services, Management & Business Advice, Management Buy-outs, Mergers & Acquisitions, Taxation (Corporate)

Industry Specialisations: Wholesale, Agriculture, Construction, Real Estate, Computer Services

OTHER OFFICES

DEN HARTOG REGISTERACCOUNTANTS
Grindweg 90-96, 3055 VD ROTTERDAM
Tel: + *31* (10) 4223588 *Fax:* + *31* (10) 4223175

NANNEN & CO
van Schaikweg 11, 7800 AG EMMEN
Mailing Address: P.O. Box 251, 7800 AG EMMEN
Tel: + *31* (5910) 15321 *Fax:* + *31* (5910) 43288
Contact: Alex H. Otten

NANNEN & CO
Vachtstraat 31-1, 9700 AP GRONINGEN
Mailing Address: P.O. Box 615, 9700 AP GRONINGEN
Tel: + *31* (50) 266533 *Fax:* + *31* (50) 256374

NANNEN & CO
Midwolderweg 1-3, 9350 AC LEEK
Mailing Address: P.O. Box 129, 9350 AC LEEK
Tel: + *31* (5945) 12175 *Fax:* + *31* (5945) 18123

SCHIPPERS & CO ACCOUNTANTS
Cornelius Pronklaan 44, 1816 NP ALKMAAR
Tel: + *31* (72) 122142 *Fax:* + *31* (72) 123081

SCHIPPERS & CO ACCOUNTANTS
Henry Dunantstraat 36, 3822 XE AMERSFOORT
Tel: + *31* (33) 559400 *Fax:* + *31* (33) 559815

SCHIPPERS & CO ACCOUNTANTS
Cronenburg 73, 1081 GM AMSTERDAM
Tel: + *31* (20) 6464011 *Fax:* + *31* (20) 6463251

SCHIPPERS & CO ACCOUNTANTS
Linieweg 6, 1783 BA DEN HELDER
Tel: + *31* (2230) 28284 *Fax:* + *31* (2230) 25334

VAN DAAL & PARTNERS
Mr. van Coothstraat 7, 5140 AL WAALWIJK
Mailing Address: P.O. Box 460, 5140 AL WAALWIJK
Tel: + *31* (4160) 30505 *Fax:* + *31* (4160) 38384
Contact: Alex H. Otten

VAN DAAL & PARTNERS
Karbeel 20, 5420 AB GEMERT
Mailing Address: P.O. Box 92, 5420 AB GEMERT
Tel: + *31* (4923) 61248 *Fax:* + *31* (4923) 63855

VAN DAAL & PARTNERS
St Josephstraat 76, 5100 AG DONGEN
Mailing Address: P.O. Box 250, 5100 AG DONGEN
Tel: + *31* (1623) 22000 *Fax:* + *31* (1623) 17717

VAN DAAL & PARTNERS
Grotestraat 282, 5150 AD DRUNEN
Mailing Address: P.O. Box 179, 5150 AD DRUNEN
Tel: + *31* (4163) 75500 *Fax:* + *31* (4163) 78123

Total Number of Offices: 13

HOEGEN DIJKHOF & VAN BRAKEL

Wilhelminapark 24, 3581 NE UTRECHT
Tel: + *31* (30) 520 220
Fax: + *31* (30) 516 885

European Affiliation: IAG International

International Contact: Hans J. Hoegen Dijkhof

OTHER OFFICES

HOEGEN DIJKHOF & VAN BRAKEL
Emmastraat 40, 1075 HW AMSTERDAM
Tel: + *31* (20) 791 801 *Fax:* + *31* (20) 769 081

Total Number of Offices: 2

HORLINGS, BROUWER & HORLINGS

Koningslaan 30, 1075 AD AMSTERDAM
Tel: + *31* (20) 6769955
Fax: + *31* (20) 6764478

European Affiliation: Nexia International

International Contact: Eppo Horlings

Partners:	15
Professional staff:	85
Non-professional staff:	3
Total Staff:	**103**

FEE INCOME

Year End: 31.12.90	**Gu**	**%**
Accountancy & Audit:	13,000,000	87.0
Insolvency:	200,000	1.0
Consultancy:	500,000	3.0
Tax:	1,300,000	9.0
Total:	**15,000,000**	

CONTACT INFORMATION

Chairman: Eppo Horlings
Accountancy (General): Robert Brouwer
Audit: Willem Smeets
Insolvency: Dick Hibma
Administration: Jan Miner
Public Sector: Matthieu van Winsen
Tax (Corporate): Fred Bootsma
Tax (International): John Graham
Corporate Finance & Consultancy: Eppo Horlings
EDP Audit: Constant Scholten

CLIENT SERVICES

All Services

Industry Specialisations: Transport

OTHER OFFICES

GRAHAM & HORLINGS
Koningslaan 30, 1075 AD AMSTERDAM
Tel: + *31* (20) 6752121 *Fax:* + *31* (20) 6753628
Contact: John H. Graham

Total Number of Offices: 2

JOANKNECHT & VAN ZELST

Dr. Berlagelaan 22, 5622 HD EINDHOVEN
Tel: + *31* (40) 444220
Fax: + *31* (40) 433647
Mailing Address: P.O. Box 263, 5600 AG EINDHOVEN

European Affiliation: TGI International

Partners:	12
Professional staff:	74
Non-professional staff:	12
Total Staff:	**98**

FEE INCOME

Year End: 31.12.90	**Gu**	**%**
Accountancy & Audit:	7,250,000	50.0
Consultancy:	2,175,000	15.0
Tax:	4,350,000	30.0
Other:	725,000	5.0
Total:	**14,500,000**	

CONTACT INFORMATION

Accountancy (General): P.C.A. Aben
Accountancy (General): W.A.C. Bourgonje
Accountancy (General): D.L.M. Driessen
Accountancy (General): M.T. Eggermont
Accountancy (General): J.E.I. van Hout
Accountancy (General): W.H.L.M. Prüst
Accountancy (General): P.A.S. van der Putten
Accountancy (General): Th. A. Rövekamp
Accountancy (General): J.A.M. van Zelst
Management Consultancy: J.E.I. van Hout
Tax (Corporate): F.H.G.M. van den Berg
Tax (Corporate): B.M.H.S. Cranssen
Tax Advisor: E. Saoud-Stienstra
Tax Advisor: A.E.J. Verkuilen
Tax Advisor: P.A.G. Loomans

CLIENT SERVICES

Accountancy (General), Audit, Computer Installation, Corporate Finance Advice, Insolvency & Corporate Restructuring, Litigation/Legal Services, Management & Business Advice, Management Buy-outs, Mergers & Acquisitions, Pensions Planning, Value for Money Studies, Taxation (Corporate), Taxation (International), Trust Settlement & Estates

JOORE (REGISTERACCOUNTANTS)

Ringbaan Noord 179, 5046 AA TILBURG
Tel: + *31* (13) 359800
Fax: + *31* (13) 362090

European Affiliation: Affiliated Conference of Practising Accountants International (ACPA)

International Contact: G.A.P. Joore

▷

CONTACT INFORMATION
Managing Partner: G.A.P. Joore

OTHER OFFICES
JOORE (REGISTERACCOUNTANTS)
Kuiperberweg 50, 11101 AV AMSTERDAM
Tel: + *31* (20) 978021 *Fax:* + *31* (20) 977961
Contact: J.B. Jonker

Total Number of Offices: 2

KOOIJ & PARTNERS
Maliesingel 26, 3581 BH UTRECHT
Tel: + *31* (30) 317344
Fax: + *31* (30) 313249

European Affiliation: BKR International

International Contact: Thomas A. Kooÿ

Partners:	4
Professional staff:	31
Non-professional staff:	5
Total Staff:	**40**

FEE INCOME
Year End: 31.12.90	%
Accountancy & Audit:	44.0
Insolvency:	5.0
Consultancy:	22.0
Tax:	25.0
Other:	4.0

CONTACT INFORMATION
Managing Partner: W.P.I. Boschman
Accountancy (General): W.P.I. Boschman
Audit: A.A. van Nieuwenhuizen
Management Consultancy: W.P.I. Boschman
Corporate Finance & Insolvency: Thomas A. Kooÿ
Tax: G. de Wildt

CLIENT SERVICES
Accountancy (General), Audit, Computer Installation, Corporate Finance Advice, Insolvency & Corporate Restructuring, Management & Business Advice, Management Buy-outs, Mergers & Acquisitions, Pensions Planning, Value for Money Studies, Taxation (Corporate), Taxation (International), Trust Settlement & Estates

Industry Specialisations: Building Industry, Architects, Hotel & Catering, Estate Agency, Automation, Insurance, Professions

KPMG

KPMG KLYNVELD
Burgemeester Rijnderslaan 10-20, KPMG Building,
1185 MC AMSTELVEEN
Tel: + *31* (20) 6567890
Fax: + *31* (20) 6567700
Mailing Address: P.O. Box 7137, 1007 JC AMSTERDAM

European Affiliation: KPMG

International Contact: M.A. Lewis

Partners:	293
Professional staff:	2,318
Non-professional staff:	797
Total Staff:	**3,408**

FEE INCOME
Year End: 31.12.90	**Gu**	**%**
Accountancy & Audit:	372,000,000	64.4
Consultancy:	95,000,000	16.4
Tax:	111,000,000	19.2
Total:	**578,000,000**	

CONTACT INFORMATION
Chairman: Johan Steenmeijer
Accountancy (General): R.J.J. Koedijk
Audit: J. Klaassen
Corporate Finance: J.A.W.M. van Rooijen
Management Consultancy: J. Wessel Ganzevoort
Administration: B. Nab
Public Sector: R.L. van Marion
Tax (Corporate): Gerard Telkamp
Tax (International): R.D. Kramer

CLIENT SERVICES
All Services

Industry Specialisations: Entertainment, Media, Publishing, Education, Banks, Insurance, Health Organisations, Utilities

MAJOR CLIENTS
AKZO, AMEV, Avero Centraal Beheer Group, Campina Melkunie, Dutch Government, Fokker, Furness, HCS Technology, Heineken, Hoogovens, Internatio Muller, KLM, Koninklijke Wessanen, Kon. Bijenkorf Beheer (KBB), NBM Amstelland, Nedlloyd, NMB Postbank, Pakhoed, Philips, Royal Dutch Shell

OTHER OFFICES
BYWATER NEDERLAND
Euclideslaan 1, 3584 BL UTRECHT
Tel: + *31* (30) 525211
Contact: H.J. Hagenberg

KPMG DATAM
Picassolaan 201, 1816 MT ALKMAAR
Tel: + *31* (72) 118780
Contact: T.M. Steltenpool

KPMG DATAM
Twenthe Centrum, Twenthelein 3-9, 7607 GZ ALMELO
Tel: + *31* (5490) 30321
Contact: J.M. Brinkhof

KPMG DATAM
Grote Markt 38-40, 1315 JG ALMERE-STAD
Tel: + *31* (3240) 30919
Contact: M. Sibbel

KPMG DATAM
Prins Frederiklaan 4, 3818 KC AMERSFOORT
Tel: + *31* (33) 610541
Contact: H. van de Groep

KPMG DATAM
Burgemeester Rijnderslaan 10-20, 1185 MC AMSTELVEEN
Tel: + *31* (20) 6568656
Contact: E. Loos

KPMG DATAM
Prins Willem-Alexanderlaan 380, 7311 SZ APELDOORN
Tel: + *31* (55) 220849
Contact: B. Nab

KPMG DATAM
Burgemeester Matsersingel 200, 6843 NZ ARNHEM
Tel: + *31* (85) 815595
Contact: W.B.J. Boerkamp

KPMG DATAM
Noordsingel 214-216, 4611 SM BERGEN OP ZOOM
Tel: + *31* (1640) 37754
Contact: H.A.A. Meijer

KPMG DATAM
Burg de Manlaan 2, 4837 BN BREDA
Tel: + *31* (76) 611551
Contact: T.W.L. Meertens

KPMG DATAM
Keulenstraat 19, 7418 ET DEVENTER
Tel: + *31* (5700) 20512
Contact: A.M. van Beest

KPMG DATAM
Hofstraat 22, 7001 CD DOETINCHEM
Tel: + *31* (8340) 44260
Contact: A.H. Lindenschot

KPMG DATAM
Berglaan 56A, 9203 EJ DRACHTEN
Tel: + *31* (5120) 32505
Contact: A. Rooks

KPMG DATAM
Croy 5, 5653 LC EINDHOVEN
Tel: + *31* (40) 526825
Contact: H.M. Gijsbers

KPMG DATAM
Wilhelminastraat 102, 7811 JN EMMEN
Tel: + *31* (5910) 14920
Contact: M.R. Reitsema

KPMG DATAM
Meidenmarkt 2, 1601 HL ENKHUIZEN
Tel: + *31* (2280) 13635
Contact: W.C.L. van Kalleveen

KPMG DATAM
Burg. van Reenensingel 101, 2803 PA GOUDA
Tel: + *31* (1820) 31055
Contact: B. Houdé

KPMG DATAM
Van Ketwich Verschuurlaan 98, 9721 SW GRONINGEN
Tel: + *31* (50) 266687
Contact: A. Rooks

KPMG DATAM
Van Eedenstraat 9, 2012 EL HAARLEM
Tel: + *31* (23) 319189
Contact: T.M. Steltenpool

KPMG DATAM
Churchillplein 6, 2517 JW THE HAGUE
Tel: + *31* (70) 3382444
Contact: B. Houdé

KPMG DATAM
Vlotstraat 10, 6417 CB HEERLEN
Tel: + *31* (45) 717887
Contact: W.A. Bemelmans

KPMG DATAM
Drienerparkweg 16, 7552 EB HENGELO
Tel: + *31* (74) 437155
Contact: A. Nijhuis

KPMG DATAM
Pettelaarpark 30-34, 5216 PD 's-HERTOGENBOSCH
Tel: + *31* (73) 130462
Contact: J.M.M. Meulenbroek

KPMG DATAM
Minister Hartsenlaan 7, 1217 LR HILVERSUM
Tel: + *31* (35) 232502
Contact: R.R. de Groot

KPMG DATAM
Stationsweg 4, 2131 XG HOOFDDORP
Tel: + *31* (2503) 21924
Contact: A. Enter

KPMG DATAM
Nieuwe Steen 10, 1625 HV HOORN
Tel: + *31* (2290) 33144
Contact: W.C.L. van Kalleveen

KPMG DATAM
Meentweg 14, 8224 BP LELYSTAD
Tel: + *31* (3200) 49113
Contact: W.P. Hötzel

KPMG DATAM
Molenwater 63, 4331 SE MIDDELBURG
Tel: + *31* (1180) 35732
Contact: J.J.J. van Tongeren

KPMG DATAM
Schoolstraat 23, 2151 AA NIEUW-VENNEP
Tel: + *31* (2526) 87141
Contact: A. Enter

KPMG DATAM
Kronenburgersingel 211, 6511 AR NIJMEGEN
Tel: + *31* (80) 236863
Contact: P.J.J. Hendriks

KPMG DATAM
Almelosestraat 40a, 8102 HD RAALTE
Tel: + *31* (5720) 57190
Contact: B.J.A. van Duuren

KPMG DATAM
Brainpark, K.P. van der Mandelelaan 41, 3062 MB ROTTERDAM
Tel: + *31* (10) 4534555
Contact: J.C. Los

KPMG DATAM
Wilhelminapark 31, 5041 EC TILBURG
Tel: + *31* (13) 353350
Contact: H.M. Gijsbers

KPMG DATAM
Beneluxlaan 43, 3526 KK UTRECHT
Tel: + *31* (30) 810280
Contact: L.J.A. Godvliet

KPMG DATAM
Van Beresteijnstraat 20, 9641 AB VEENDAM
Tel: + *31* (5987) 14090
Contact: A. Hoorn

KPMG DATAM
Vendelier 23, 3905 PB VEENENDAAL
Tel: + *31* (8385) 10930
Contact: L. Zaal

KPMG DATAM
Bergweg 25A, 3701 JJ ZEIST
Tel: + *31* (3404) 16114
Contact: H.R. de Groot

KPMG DATAM
De Zwolse Poort, Burgemeester Roelenweg 11, 8021 EV ZWOLLE
Tel: + *31* (38) 227441
Contact: J. Harink

KPMG GEBOUW
Burgemeester Rijnderslaan 10-20, 1185 MC AMSTELVEEN

KPMG KLYNVELD
Gebouw De Hoefstede, Picassolaan 201, 1816 MT ALKMAAR
Tel: + *31* (72) 122135 *Fax:* + *31* (72) 152761
Contact: Herman A.J. Wolzak

KPMG KLYNVELD
Grote Markt 38-40, 1315 JG ALMERE-STAD
Tel: + *31* (3240) 36468
Contact: Henk Lafèbre

▷

The Netherlands

KPMG KLYNVELD
Prins Frederiklaan 4, 3818 KC AMERSFOORT
Tel: + *31* (33) 621144
Contact: Henk E.G. Buter

KPMG KLYNVELD
Burgemeester Rijnderslaan 10-20, 1185 MC AMSTELVEEN
Tel: + *31* (20) 6567020
Contact: J.L.M. Pulles

KPMG KLYNVELD
Prins Willem-Alexanderlaan 380, 7311 SZ APELDOORN
Tel: + *31* (55) 219855
Contact: David W. Voetelink

KPMG KLYNVELD
Wassenaarweg 30, 6843 NW ARNHEM
Tel: + *31* (85) 814242
Contact: J. Boer

KPMG KLYNVELD
Burg de Manlaan 2, 4837 BN BREDA
Tel: + *31* (76) 613551
Contact: G.C.J. van Loon

KPMG KLYNVELD
Keulenstraat 19, 7418 ET DEVENTER
Tel: + *31* (5700) 20555
Contact: Jan Schermerhorn

KPMG KLYNVELD
Hofstraat 22, 7001 CD DOETINCHEM
Tel: + *31* (8340) 43218
Contact: W. Stoer

KPMG KLYNVELD
Berglaan 56A, 9203 EJ DRACHTEN
Tel: + *31* (5120) 18218
Contact: J.A. Kruijer

KPMG KLYNVELD
Singel 271, 3311 KS DORDRECHT
Tel: + *31* (78) 134544
Contact: C.J. van den Berg

KPMG KLYNVELD
Croy 5, 5653 LC EINDHOVEN
Tel: + *31* (40) 527775
Contact: J.L.C. Jansen

KPMG KLYNVELD
Piet Heinstraat 8, 7511 JE ENSCHEDE
Tel: + *31* (53) 308555
Contact: H.W. van de Weijer

KPMG KLYNVELD
Burg. van Reenensingel 101, 2803 PA GOUDA
Tel: + *31* (1820) 31055
Contact: L.P.B. van der Werf

KPMG KLYNVELD
Van Ketwich Verschuurlaan 98, 9721 SW GRONINGEN
Tel: + *31* (50) 266826
Contact: J.B. Boekhold

KPMG KLYNVELD
Van Eedenstraat 16, 2012 EM HAARLEM
Tel: + *31* (23) 152215
Contact: Herman A.J. Wolzak

KPMG KLYNVELD
Churchillplein 6, 2517 JW THE HAGUE
Tel: + *31* (70) 3382222
Contact: P. Boer

KPMG KLYNVELD
Vlotstraat 10, 6417 CB HEERLEN
Tel: + *31* (45) 7169305
Contact: M.M.W. Frankort

KPMG KLYNVELD
Drienerparkweg 16, 7552 EB HENGELO
Tel: + *31* (74) 918861
Contact: A. de Jong

KPMG KLYNVELD
Pettelaarpark 30-34, 5216 PD 's-HERTOGENBOSCH
Tel: + *31* (73) 125499
Contact: Gerrit-Jan H. Moonen

KPMG KLYNVELD
Minister Hartsenlaan 7, 1217 LR HILVERSUM
Tel: + *31* (35) 236335
Contact: J.A.L. van Diejie

KPMG KLYNVELD
Stationsweg 4, 2131 XG HOOFDDORP
Tel: + *31* (2503) 22304
Contact: P. van Wijngaarden

KPMG KLYNVELD
Nieuwe Steen 2, 1625 HV HOORN
Tel: + *31* (2290) 30744
Contact: Theo Boomsma

KPMG KLYNVELD
Schrans 48, 8932 NG LEEUWARDEN
Tel: + *31* (58) 151545
Contact: J.A. Kruijer

KPMG KLYNVELD
Bourgognestraat 2, 6221 BX MAASTRICHT
Tel: + *31* (43) 217443
Contact: E.J.C. van Velzen

KPMG KLYNVELD
Molenwater 63, 4331 SE MIDDELBURG
Tel: + *31* (1180) 35220
Contact: Joost Boter

KPMG KLYNVELD
Kronenburgersingel 211, 6511 AR NIJMEGEN
Tel: + *31* (80) 228322
Contact: A.H.T.J. Seesing

KPMG KLYNVELD
Brainpark, K.P. van der Mandelelaan 41, 3062 MB ROTTERDAM
Tel: + *31* (10) 4534111
Contact: A. Vermaas

KPMG KLYNVELD
Wilhelminapark 31, 5041 EC TILBURG
Tel: + *31* (13) 366500
Contact: G.J. Loof

KPMG KLYNVELD
Beneluxlaan 43, 3526 KK UTRECHT
Tel: + *31* (30) 810210
Contact: A. Douglas

KPMG KLYNVELD
De Zwolse Poort, Burgemeester Roelenweg 11, 8021 EV ZWOLLE
Tel: + *31* (38) 217958
Contact: Coen H.A. Grafhorst

KPMG TEGELER & CO
Prinsestraat 1, 7513 AM ENSCHEDE
Tel: + *31* (53) 353765
Contact: W.J.M. Beckers

MEIJBURG & CO
Gebouw De Hoefstede, Picassolaan 201, 1816 MT ALKMAAR
Tel: + *31* (72) 111297
Contact: A. Wattèl

MEIJBURG & CO
Prins Frederiklaan 4, 3818 KC AMERSFOORT
Tel: + *31* (33) 621144
Contact: D. Fraterman

MEIJBURG & CO
Burgemeester Rijnderslaan 10-20, 1185 MS AMSTELVEEN
Tel: + *31* (20) 6561656
Contact: G. Telkamp

MEIJBURG & CO
Prins Willem-Alexanderlaan 380, 7311 SZ APELDOORN
Tel: + *31* (55) 219410
Contact: J. Snoeken

MEIJBURG & CO
Wassenaarweg 30, 6842 NW ARNHEM
Tel: + *31* (85) 862911
Contact: W. Timmer

MEIJBURG & CO
Burg. de Manlaan 2, 4837 BN BREDA
Tel: + *31* (76) 614857
Contact: C.M. Dubbelman

MEIJBURG & CO
Keulenstraat 19, 7418 ET DEVENTER
Tel: + *31* (5700) 29833
Contact: E.J. Huizingh

MEIJBURG & CO
Hofstraat 22, 7001 CD DOETINCHEM
Tel: + *31* (8340) 44544
Contact: Mickey J.M.W. Vuylsteke

MEIJBURG & CO
Singel 271, 3311 KS DORDRECHT
Tel: + *31* (78) 148666
Contact: J.D. de Kruif

MEIJBURG & CO
Croy 5, 5653 LC EINDHOVEN
Tel: + *31* (40) 526355
Contact: Clemens M. Bolhaar

MEIJBURG & CO
Prinsestraat 1, 7513 AM ENSCHEDE
Tel: + *31* (53) 308272
Contact: Gerard van Ginkel

MEIJBURG & CO
Burg. van Reenensingel 101, 2803 PA GOUDA
Tel: + *31* (1820) 70377
Contact: T.J.J. Bouwman

MEIJBURG & CO
Van Ketwich Verschuurlaan 98, 9721 SW GRONINGEN
Tel: + *31* (50) 262662
Contact: A.C. van Leijenhorst

MEIJBURG & CO
Van Eedenstraat 16, 2012 EM HAARLEM
Tel: + *31* (23) 152250
Contact: Drs. J.H.W. Schipper

MEIJBURG & CO
Churchillplein 6, 2517 JW THE HAGUE
Tel: + *31* (70) 3382682
Contact: Toby J.J. Bouman

MEIJBURG & CO
Vlotstraat 10, 6417 CB HEERLEN
Tel: + *31* (45) 719990
Contact: Paul I.H. Wintgens

MEIJBURG & CO
Drienerparkweg 16, 7552 EB HENGELO
Tel: + *31* (74) 426755
Contact: M.A. van Brussel

MEIJBURG & CO
Pettelaarpark 30-34, 5216 PD 's-HERTOGENBOSCH
Tel: + *31* (73) 130667
Contact: Jan C.F. Swinkels

MEIJBURG & CO
Minister Hartsenlaan 7, 1217 LR HILVERSUM
Tel: + *31* (35) 235335
Contact: Drs. Jac Korpershoek

MEIJBURG & CO
Stationsweg 4, 2131 XG HOOFDDORP
Tel: + *31* (2503) 22304
Contact: R.J.M. van Moorsel

MEIJBURG & CO
Nieuwe Steen 2, 1625 HV HOORN
Tel: + *31* (2290) 42442
Contact: A. Wattèl

MEIJBURG & CO
Schrans 48, 8932 NG LEEUWARDEN
Tel: + *31* (58) 151585
Contact: H. Bakker

MEIJBURG & CO
Bourgognestraat 2, 6221 BX MAASTRICHT
Tel: + *31* (43) 216565
Contact: P.I.H. Wintgens

MEIJBURG & CO
Kronenburgersingel 211, 6511 AR NIJMEGEN
Tel: + *31* (80) 233152
Contact: G.J.M. van Gastel

MEIJBURG & CO
"Brainpark", K.P. van der Mandelelaan 41, 3062 MB ROTTERDAM
Tel: + *31* (10) 4536888
Contact: Th.J.F. Zeegers

MEIJBURG & CO
Wilhelminapark 31, 5041 EC TILBURG
Tel: + *31* (13) 366500
Contact: Leo Th.J.M. Geertman

MEIJBURG & CO
Beneluxlaan 43, 3526 KK UTRECHT
Tel: + *31* (30) 893534
Contact: Frans J. Burger

MEIJBURG & CO
"De Zwolse Poort", Burgemeester Roelenweg 11, 8021 EV ZWOLLE
Tel: + *31* (38) 219644
Contact: Gert E.A. Neppelenbroek

NOLAN, NORTON & CO
Euclideslaan 1, 3584 BL UTRECHT
Tel: + *31* (30) 525211
Contact: A.H.J.B. Schotgerrits

Total Number of Offices: 101

KROESE WEVERS & CO

Auke Vleerstraat 5, 7521 PE ENSCHEDE
Tel: + *31* (53) 334475
Fax: + *31* (51) 337041

European Affiliation: Summit International Associates Inc

International Contact: Ben W.G. Wevers

OTHER OFFICES

KROESE WEVERS & CO
Hyacinthstraat 80, 7572 BD OLDENZAAL
Tel: + *31* (5410) 12439 *Fax:* + *31* (5410) 20609
Contact: Ben W. G. Wevers

Total Number of Offices: 7

The Netherlands

LUITEN BRAET

Meent 24, 4141 AC LEERDAM
Tel: + *31* (3451) 18344
Fax: + *31* (3451) 18054
Mailing Address: P.O. Box 89, 4140 AB LEERDAM

European Affiliation: GMN International

International Contact: Cees Luiten

Partners:	2
Professional staff:	27
Non-professional staff:	3
Total Staff:	**32**

FEE INCOME

Year End: 1990	%
Accountancy & Audit:	60.0
Consultancy:	30.0
Tax:	10.0

CONTACT INFORMATION

Chairman: Cees Luiten
Managing Partner: Cees Luiten
Accountancy (General): Henk Braet
Audit: Piet Bons
Management Consultancy: Eric van den Adel
Administration: Cees Luiten
Tax: Menno Venstra
Corporate Law: Jan de Hoog

CLIENT SERVICES

Accountancy (General), Audit, Corporate Finance Advice, Litigation/Legal Services, Management & Business Advice, Management Buy-outs, Pensions Planning, Taxation (Corporate), Taxation (International)

OTHER OFFICES

LUITEN BRAET
Avelingen West 5, 4202 MS GORINCHEM
Mailing Address: P.O. Box 487, 4200 AL GORINCHEM
Tel: + *31* (1830) 31055 *Fax:* + *31* (1830) 35993
Contact: Erik van den Adel

LUITEN BRAET
Westeringer 92, 3015 LC ROTTERDAM

LUITEN BRAET
Taxandriaweg 12, 5142 PA WAALWIJK
Tel: + *31* (4160) 44500 *Fax:* + *31* (4160) 44350
Contact: Henk Braet

Total Number of Offices: 4

MASMAN BOSMAN & CO

Laan Copes van Cattenburch 92, 2585 GE 's GRAVENHAGE, The Hague
Tel: + *31* (70) 3523461
Fax: + *31* (70) 3521301

European Affiliation: ATD International

International Contact: G.C. Bosman

Partners:	3
Professional staff:	20
Non-professional staff:	2
Total Staff:	**25**

CONTACT INFORMATION

Managing Partner: Eric Smits
Administration: Hans Lensen

CLIENT SERVICES

Accountancy (General), Audit, Computer Installation, Corporate Finance Advice, Insolvency & Corporate Restructuring, Management & Business Advice, Management Buy-outs, Mergers & Acquisitions, Taxation (Corporate), Taxation (International), Trust Settlement & Estates

OTHER OFFICES

MASMAN BOSMAN & CO
Haringbuisweg 35-37, 3133 KP VLAARDINGEN
Tel: + *31* (10) 4353535 *Fax:* + *31* (10) 4351138
Contact: Hans Lensen

Total Number of Offices: 2

MOORE STEPHENS NETHERLANDS

Noordhollandstraat 71, 1081 AS AMSTERDAM
Tel: + *31* (20) 442168
Fax: + *31* (20) 444347

European Affiliation: Moore Stephens

International Contact: Cees Mulckhuijse

OTHER OFFICES

MOORE STEPHENS
Bozenhoven 76, 3641 AH MIJDRECHT
Tel: + *31* (2979) 81705 *Fax:* + *31* (2979) 83987
Contact: J.C.K. van Loo

MOORE STEPHENS
Aalsmeerderweg 600-602, 1437 EJ ROZENBURG
Tel: + *31* (2977) 22606 *Fax:* + *31* (2977) 29708
Contact: C. Lievaart

Total Number of Offices: 3

MORET ERNST & YOUNG

MORET ERNST & YOUNG

G.H. Betzweg 1, 3068 AZ ROTTERDAM
Tel: + *31* (10) 4074444
Fax: + *31* (10) 4556850
Mailing Address: P.O. Box 488, 3000 AL ROTTERDAM

European Affiliation: Ernst & Young Europe

International Contact: B. Goossens

Partners:	337
Professional staff:	3,620
Non-professional staff:	842
Total Staff:	**4,799**

FEE INCOME

Year End: 31.12.90	**Gu**	%
Accountancy & Audit:	455,000,000	70.0
Consultancy:	63,000,000	10.0
Tax:	132,000,000	20.0
Total:	**650,000,000**	

CONTACT INFORMATION

Chairman: P.A. Wortel
Managing Partner: J.F. Oudejans
Management Consultancy: C.H.A. Mutsaers
Administration: P. Verhoeven
Accountancy & Audit: P.A. Wortel
Tax: K.C. Kunen
Educational Inst/Municipalities: P.A.J. Houdijk
Insurance: K.C. van den Hoven
Banking: J.G.I.M. Reijrink
Health Care: K. Starreveld
Central Government: R. Toppen
Computer Audit: B. van den Berg

Mergers & Acquisitions: B. Terra
Tax (Personal): W. Pierik

CLIENT SERVICES

Accountancy (General), Audit, Corporate Finance Advice, Insolvency & Corporate Restructuring, Litigation/Legal Services, Management & Business Advice, Management Buy-outs, Mergers & Acquisitions, Value for Money Studies, Taxation (Corporate), Taxation (International), Trust Settlement & Estates, Subsidies & Grants, Privatisation, Recruitment, Marketing, Quality Policy & Quality Control

Industry Specialisations: Banking, Co-op Associations, Customs, Education, Extraction, Government, Health Care, Insurance

MAJOR CLIENTS

ABN AMRO Bank, Aegon NV, BP Nederland Holdings BV, Bührmann-Tetterode NV, Cebeco Handelsraad BA, DAF NV, DSM NV, Hollandsche Beton Groep NV, International Nederlanden Groep, Koninklijke Borsumij Wehry NV, Koninklijke Emballage Industrie van Leer BV, Koninklijke Gist Brocades NV, Koninklijke Nederlandse Papierfabrieken NV, Koninklijke Van Ommeren Ceteco NV, Koninklijke Volker Stevin NV, Nederlandse Spoorwegen NV, Rabobank, Verenigd Bezit VNU NV, Ver. Coop Melkindustrie Coberco BA, Volvo Car BV

OTHER OFFICES

MORET ERNST & YOUNG
G.H. Betzweg 1, 3068 AZ ROTTERDAM
Mailing Address: P.O. Box 488, 3000 AL ROTTERDAM
Tel: + *31* (10) 4074444 *Fax:* + *31* (10) 4556440

MORET ERNST & YOUNG
Rubenslaan 2, 1816 MB ALKMAAR
Mailing Address: P.O. Box 344, 1800 AH ALKMAAR
Tel: + *31* (72) 154004 *Fax:* + *31* (72) 154436

MORET ERNST & YOUNG
Wierdensestraat 22a, 7607 GJ ALMELO
Mailing Address: P.O. Box 328, 7600 AH ALMELO
Tel: + *31* (5490) 24545 *Fax:* + *31* (5490) 29265

MORET ERNST & YOUNG
Blekerssingel 5, 3816 VV AMERSFOORT
Mailing Address: P.O. Box 412, 3800 AK AMERSFOORT
Tel: + *31* (33) 614348 *Fax:* + *31* (33) 616943

MORET ERNST & YOUNG
Drentestraat 20, 1083 HK AMSTERDAM
Mailing Address: P.O. Box 7883, 1008 AB AMSTERDAM
Tel: + *31* (20) 5497222 *Fax:* + *31* (20) 6462553

MORET ERNST & YOUNG
P.W. Alexanderlaan 1419, 7312 GA APELDOORN
Mailing Address: P.O. Box 652, 7300 AR APELDOORN
Tel: + *31* (55) 291400 *Fax:* + *31* (55) 556157

MORET ERNST & YOUNG
Velperweg 157, 6824 MB ARNHEM
Mailing Address: P.O. Box 2008, 6802 CA ARNHEM
Tel: + *31* (85) 640800 *Fax:* + *31* (85) 641926

MORET ERNST & YOUNG
Noorderstaete 40, 9402 XB ASSEN
Mailing Address: P.O. Box 900, 9400 AX ASSEN
Tel: + *31* (5920) 44466 *Fax:* + *31* (5920) 44205

MORET ERNST & YOUNG
Zijde 41, 2771 EK BOSKOOP
Tel: + *31* (1727) 15340 *Fax:* + *31* (1727) 13561

MORET ERNST & YOUNG
Bijster 26, 4817 HX BREDA
Mailing Address: P.O. Box 2049, 4800 CA BREDA
Tel: + *31* (76) 225500 *Fax:* + *31* (76) 147075

MORET ERNST & YOUNG
Oude Terborgseweg 202, 7004 KA DOETINCHEM
Mailing Address: P.O. Box 600, 7000 AP DOETINCHEM
Tel: + *31* (8340) 70311 *Fax:* + *31* (8340) 24561

MORET ERNST & YOUNG
Burg. de Raadtsingel. g3, 3311 JG DORDRECHT
Mailing Address: P.O. Box 290, 3300 AG DORDRECHT
Tel: + *31* (78) 135066 *Fax:* + *31* (78) 136561

MORET ERNST & YOUNG
Achterdoelen 32, 6711 AV EDE
Mailing Address: P.O. Box 8143, 6710 AC EDE
Tel: + *31* (8380) 19162 *Fax:* + *31* (8380) 12990

MORET ERNST & YOUNG
Prof. Dr. Dorgelolaan 12, 5613 AM EINDHOVEN
Mailing Address: P.O. Box 455, 5600 AL EINDHOVEN
Tel: + *31* (40) 602206 *Fax:* + *31* (40) 602299

MORET ERNST & YOUNG
Vreding 2-4, 7811 AZ EMMEN
Mailing Address: P.O. Box 470, 7800 AL EMMEN
Tel: + *31* (5910) 10544 *Fax:* + *31* (5910) 18007

MORET ERNST & YOUNG
M.H. Tromplaan 8, 7511 JK ENSCHEDE
Mailing Address: P.O. Box 1073, 7500 BB ENSCHEDE
Tel: + *31* (53) 320005 *Fax:* + *31* (53) 304065

MORET ERNST & YOUNG
M.H. Tromplaan 5-9, 7511 JJ ENSCHEDE
Mailing Address: P.O. Box 132, 7500 AC ENSCHEDE
Tel: + *31* (53) 314449 *Fax:* + *31* (53) 310089

MORET ERNST & YOUNG
Hanzeweg 14, 2803 MC GOUDA
Mailing Address: P.O. Box 29, 2800 AA GOUDA
Tel: + *31* (1820) 70188 *Fax:* + *31* (1820) 36311

MORET ERNST & YOUNG
Chopinlaan 12, 9722 KE GRONINGEN
Mailing Address: P.O. Box 997, 9700 AZ GRONINGEN
Tel: + *31* (50) 201200 *Fax:* + *31* (50) 270852

MORET ERNST & YOUNG
Westerkade 15-3, 9718 AS GRONINGEN
Mailing Address: P.O. Box 1259, 9701 BG GRONINGEN
Tel: + *31* (50) 185030 *Fax:* + *31* (50) 122630

MORET ERNST & YOUNG
Dreef 48, 2012 HS HAARLEM
Mailing Address: P.O. Box 1119, 2001 BC HAARLEM
Tel: + *31* (23) 159393 *Fax:* + *31* (23) 328769

MORET ERNST & YOUNG
Wassenaarseweg 80, 2596 CZ THE HAGUE
Mailing Address: P.O. Box 90636, 2509 LP THE HAGUE
Tel: + *31* (70) 3286666 *Fax:* + *31* (70) 3244003

MORET ERNST & YOUNG
Johanniterlaan 5, 3841 DS HARDERWIJK
Mailing Address: P.O. Box 126, 3840 AC HARDERWIJK
Tel: + *31* (3410) 13707 *Fax:* + *31* (3410) 15705

MORET ERNST & YOUNG
Haskeruitgang 1, 8447 CK HEERENVEEN
Mailing Address: P.O. Box 182, 8440 AD HEERENVEEN
Tel: + *31* (5130) 27425 *Fax:* + *31* (5130) 27286

MORET ERNST & YOUNG
Bekkerweg 1, 6411 EG HEERLEN
Mailing Address: P.O. Box 216, 6400 AE HEERLEN
Tel: + *31* (45) 714408 *Fax:* + *31* (45) 718058

MORET ERNST & YOUNG
Bekkerweg 29/31, 6411 EG HEERLEN
Tel: + *31* (45) 719980 *Fax:* + *31* (45) 740551

MORET ERNST & YOUNG
St. Teunislaan 3, 5231 BS 's-HERTOGENBOSCH
Mailing Address: P.O. Box 3180, 5203 DD 's-HERTOGENBOSCH
Tel: + *31* (73) 404211 *Fax:* + *31* (73) 417645

▷

MORET ERNST & YOUNG
Laapersveld 27, 1213 VB HILVERSUM
Mailing Address: P.O. Box 766, 1200 AT HILVERSUM
Tel: + *31* (35) 216954 *Fax:* + *31* (35) 43792

MORET ERNST & YOUNG
Dykweg 66, 2675 AE HONSELERSDŸK
Mailing Address: P.O. Box 517, 2675 ZT HONSELERSDŸK
Tel: + *31* (1740) 26511

MORET ERNST & YOUNG
Het Haagje 141, 7902 LE HOOGEVEEN
Mailing Address: P.O. Box 177, 7900 AD HOOGEVEEN
Tel: + *31* (5280) 67051 *Fax:* + *31* (5280) 77291

MORET ERNST & YOUNG
Westersingel 52, 8913 CL LEEUWARDEN
Mailing Address: P.O. Box 727, 8901 BM LEEUWARDEN
Tel: + *31* (58) 981234 *Fax:* + *31* (58) 132488

MORET ERNST & YOUNG
Schipholweg 87, 2316 ZL LEIDEN
Mailing Address: P.O. Box 117, 2300 AC LEIDEN
Tel: + *31* (71) 241414 *Fax:* + *31* (71) 215800

MORET ERNST & YOUNG
Oranjeplein 10, 6224 KD MAASTRICHT
Mailing Address: P.O. Box 100, 6200 AC MAASTRICHT
Tel: + *31* (43) 636636 *Fax:* + *31* (43) 634663

MORET ERNST & YOUNG
Damplein 33, 4331 GC MIDDELBURG
Mailing Address: P.O. Box 201, 4330 AE MIDDELBURG
Tel: + *31* (1180) 15951 *Fax:* + *31* (1180) 33089

MORET ERNST & YOUNG
Tiendweg 32, 2671 SB NAALDWIJK
Mailing Address: P.O. Box 136, 2670 AC NAALDWIJK
Tel: + *31* (1740) 21001 *Fax:* + *31* (1740) 22347

MORET ERNST & YOUNG
Nassausingel 2, 6511 EV NIJMEGEN
Mailing Address: P.O. Box 473, 6500 AL NIJMEGEN
Tel: + *31* (80) 224762 *Fax:* + *31* (80) 241924

MORET ERNST & YOUNG
Mgr.v.d. Boerpark 6, 5342 CD OSS
Tel: + *31* (4120) 34906 *Fax:* + *31* (4120) 30305

MORET ERNST & YOUNG
Mensingheweg 1, 9301 KA RODEN
Tel: + *31* (5908) 16800 *Fax:* + *31* (5908) 13689

MORET ERNST & YOUNG
Olympialaan 1, 6042 JZ ROERMOND
Mailing Address: P.O. Box 1228, 6040 KE ROERMOND
Tel: + *31* (4750) 40022 *Fax:* + *31* (4750) 15145

MORET ERNST & YOUNG
Marten Meesweg 51, 3068 AV ROTTERDAM
Mailing Address: P.O. Box 2295, 3000 CG ROTTERDAM
Tel: + *31* (10) 4072222 *Fax:* + *31* (10) 4552737

MORET ERNST & YOUNG
Marten Meesweg 115, 3068 AV ROTTERDAM
Mailing Address: P.O. Box 1448, 3000 BK ROTTERDAM
Tel: + *31* (10) 4072444 *Fax:* + *31* (10) 4565130

MORET ERNST & YOUNG
Beursplein 37, 3011 AA ROTTERDAM
Mailing Address: P.O. Box 30114, 3001 DC ROTTERDAM
Tel: + *31* (10) 4052525 *Fax:* + *31* (10) 4052528

MORET ERNST & YOUNG
Herengracht 7, 4531 GM TERNEUZEN
Mailing Address: P.O. Box 113, 4530 AC TERNEUZEN
Tel: + *31* (1150) 97151 *Fax:* + *31* (1150) 30488

MORET ERNST & YOUNG
Laan van Westroyen 2, 4003 AZ TIEL
Mailing Address: P.O. Box 6114, 4000 HC TIEL
Tel: + *31* (3440) 13545 *Fax:* + *31* (3440) 15244

MORET ERNST & YOUNG
Tivolistraat 1, 5017 HM TILBURG
Mailing Address: P.O. Box 10069, 5000 JB TILBURG
Tel: + *31* (13) 435015 *Fax:* + *31* (13) 930103

MORET ERNST & YOUNG
Europalaan 450, 3526 KS UTRECHT
Mailing Address: P.O. Box 3101, 3502 GC UTRECHT
Tel: + *31* (30) 811811 *Fax:* + *31* (30) 899133

MORET ERNST & YOUNG
Lomanlaan 55, 3526 XC UTRECHT
Mailing Address: P.O. Box 3053, 3502 GB UTRECHT
Tel: + *31* (30) 824911 *Fax:* + *31* (30) 898260

MORET ERNST & YOUNG
Veestraat 5, 5914 RJ VENLO
Mailing Address: P.O. Box 391, 5900 AJ VENLO
Tel: + *31* (77) 540800 *Fax:* + *31* (77) 545317

MORET ERNST & YOUNG
Taxandriaweg 8a, 5141 PA WAALWIJK
Mailing Address: P.O. Box 579, 5140 AN WAALWIJK
Tel: + *31* (4160) 32914 *Fax:* + *31* (4160) 33638

MORET ERNST & YOUNG
Vissersdijk 19, 9671 EG WINSCHOTEN
Mailing Address: P.O. Box 78, 9670 AB WINSCHOTEN
Tel: + *31* (5970) 13213 *Fax:* + *31* (5970) 20173

MORET ERNST & YOUNG
Dokter Stolteweg 25, 8025 AV ZWOLLE
Mailing Address: P.O. Box 634, 8000 AP ZWOLLE
Tel: + *31* (38) 542433 *Fax:* + *31* (38) 544307

Total Number of Offices: 52

OVERGAAUW & VAN DER SPEK BV

Bongerd 2, 2900 AS CAPELLE A/D IJSSEL
Tel: + *31* (10) 4517444
Fax: + *31* (10) 4581362
Mailing Address: P.O. Box 734, 2900 AS CAPELLE A/D IJSSEL

European Affiliation: SC International

International Contact: Arie Vonk

P & H GROEP

Calandstraat 41, 3016 CA ROTTERDAM
Tel: + *31* (10) 4364944
Fax: + *31* (10) 4360466
Mailing Address: P.O. Box 23123, 3001 KC ROTTERDAM

European Affiliation: Moores Rowland International

International Contact: H. Slob

Partners: 64

FEE INCOME

Year End: 31.12.90	**Gu**
Total:	**75,000,000**

CONTACT INFORMATION
Chairman: A.J.Th. van Eijndhoven
Managing Partner: J.M.A. van Huut
Accountancy (General): A.J.Th. van Eijndhoven
Corporate Finance: H. Slob
Insolvency: H.Th.F. Magielse
Management Consultancy: J.P. Kostense
Public Sector: C.A.A. Ringeling

Tax (Corporate): C.W. van Hemert
Tax (International): H. Bosman

CLIENT SERVICES
Accountancy (General), Audit, Computer Installation, Corporate Finance Advice, Insolvency & Corporate Restructuring, Management & Business Advice, Management Buy-outs, Mergers & Acquisitions, Taxation (Corporate), Taxation (International)

OTHER OFFICES
PAARDEKOOPER & HOFFMAN
Amsteldijk 194, 1079 LK AMSTERDAM
Tel: + *31* (20) 465051 *Fax:* + *31* (20) 448051
Contact: Harry Bosman

PAARDEKOOPER & HOFFMAN
Deventerstraat 184, 7321 CG APELDOORN
Tel: + *31* (55) 660655 *Fax:* + *31* (55) 667531
Contact: Hans Peperkamp

PAARDEKOOPER & HOFFMAN
Lucernaflat, St Josephstraat 65, 4611 MK BERGEN OP ZOOM
Tel: + *31* (1640) 59753 *Fax:* + *31* (1640) 35909
Contact: Jacques Tempelaars

PAARDEKOOPER & HOFFMAN
Druivenstraat 1, 4816 KB BREDA
Tel: + *31* (76) 712171 *Fax:* + *31* (76) 712123
Contact: Jacques Maas

PAARDEKOOPER & HOFFMAN
Fellenoord 47, 5612 AA EINDHOVEN
Tel: + *31* (40) 458331 *Fax:* + *31* (40) 454412
Contact: Wim van Leeuwen

PAARDEKOOPER & HOFFMAN
Kerkstraat 21, 7471 AE GOOR
Tel: + *31* (5470) 75855 *Fax:* + *31* (5470) 73188

PAARDEKOOPER & HOFFMAN
Burg van Reenensingel 101, 2803 PA GOUDA
Tel: + *32* (1820) 33566 *Fax:* + *31* (1820) 39920

PAARDEKOOPER & HOFFMAN
Nieuwe Gracht 53, 2011 ND HAARLEM
Tel: + *31* (23) 326355 *Fax:* + *31* (23) 328039
Contact: Joop Smit

PAARDEKOOPER & HOFFMAN
Babylon Building A, Kon Julianaplein 30-10, 2595 AA THE HAGUE
Tel: + *31* (70) 3824594 *Fax:* + *31* (70) 3852536
Contact: Jos van Huut

PAARDEKOOPER & HOFFMAN
Akerstraat 138b, 6417 BR HEERLEN
Tel: + *31* (45) 713171 *Fax:* + *31* (45) 714326

PAARDEKOOPER & HOFFMAN
Pettelaarpark 20, 5216 PD 's-HERTOGENBOSCH
Tel: + *31* (73) 122777 *Fax:* + *31* (73) 122860

PAARDEKOOPER & HOFFMAN
Blankenstein 102, 7943 PE MEPPEL
Tel: + *31* (5220) 52963 *Fax:* + *31* (5220) 61774

PAARDEKOOPER & HOFFMAN
Mr Risseeuwstraat 2, 4501 CW OOSTBURG
Tel: + *31* (1170) 53452 *Fax:* + *31* (1170) 53349

PAARDEKOOPER & HOFFMAN
Reggesingel 30, 7461 AK RIJSSEN
Tel: + *31* (5480) 19555 *Fax:* + *31* (5480) 17587
Contact: Hans Peperkamp

PAARDEKOOPER & HOFFMAN
Jan van Eijkplein 10, 4703 GV ROOSENDAAL
Tel: + *31* (1650) 67700 *Fax:* + *31* (1650) 61199

PAARDEKOOPER & HOFFMAN
Calandstraat 41, 3016 CA ROTTERDAM
Tel: + *31* (10) 4364944 *Fax:* + *31* (10) 4360466
Contact: Ton van Eijndhoven

PAARDEKOOPER & HOFFMAN
Schuttershof Building, Schuttershofweg 1, 4538 AA TERNEUZEN
Tel: + *31* (1150) 95251 *Fax:* + *31* (1150) 30337
Contact: Marc van de Vijver

PAARDEKOOPER & HOFFMAN
Australiëlaan 9, 3526 AB UTRECHT
Tel: + *31* (30) 896512 *Fax:* + *31* (30) 880799
Contact: Cor Kroes

PAARDEKOOPER & HOFFMAN
Westzijde 346, 1506 GK ZAANDAM
Tel: + *31* (75) 350571 *Fax:* + *31* (75) 700836
Contact: Theo Bien

Total Number of Offices: 21

PRICE WATERHOUSE
Hofplein 19, 3032 AC ROTTERDAM
Tel: + *31* (10) 4008600
Fax: + *31* (10) 4008670
Mailing Address: P.O. Box 881, 3000 AW ROTTERDAM

European Affiliation: Price Waterhouse

Partners:	30
Professional staff:	376
Non-professional staff:	130
Total Staff:	**536**

FEE INCOME
Year End: 1990/91	**Gu**	**%**
Accountancy & Audit:	32,600,000	41.0
Consultancy:	5,200,000	6.0
Tax:	42,600,000	53.0
Total:	**80,400,000**	

CONTACT INFORMATION
Managing Partner: W. Hogeweg
Insolvency: Piet Kraan
Corporate Finance & Consultancy: J. Charles van Leeuwen
Accountancy & Audit: Alan Kelly
Tax: Jan Savelbergh
EDP Audit & Banking: Fred Gertsen

CLIENT SERVICES
All Services

OTHER OFFICES
PRICE WATERHOUSE
Strawinskylaan 3127, 1077 ZX AMSTERDAM
Mailing Address: P.O. Box 7067, 1007 JB AMSTERDAM
Tel: + *31* (20) 5498200 *Fax:* + *31* (20) 5498250
Contact: David J. Fairhead

PRICE WATERHOUSE
Hanzeweg 70, 7418 AT DEVENTER
Mailing Address: P.O. Box 447, 7400 AK DEVENTER
Tel: + *31* (5700) 87700 *Fax:* + *31* (5700) 87777
Contact: Piet Kraan

PRICE WATERHOUSE
Koninginnegracht 8, 2514 AA THE HAGUE
Mailing Address: P.O. Box 30439, 2500 GK THE HAGUE
Tel: + *31* (70) 3108308 *Fax:* + *31* (70) 3108305
Contact: Emile J.F.A. de Haas

Total Number of Offices: 4

REYN, DE BLAEY ROTTERDAM

Marten Meesweg 119, 3068 AV ROTTERDAM
Tel: + *31* (10) 4552955
Fax: + *31* (10) 4204481
Mailing Address: P.O. Box 84003, 3009 CA ROTTERDAM

International Contact: Egbert Modderaar

Partners:	7
Professional staff:	60
Non-professional staff:	10
Total Staff:	**77**

FEE INCOME

Year End: 1990	**%**
Accountancy & Audit:	50.0
Consultancy:	25.0
Tax:	25.0

CONTACT INFORMATION

Chairman: Jos Hoogendijk
Managing Partner: Herman Vooys
Accountancy (General): Sijt de Boom
Accountancy (General): Hein Lems
Accountancy (General): Ton de Nijs
Management Consultancy: Rob Scheepbouwer
Tax Advisory: Lijneke van Reeven

CLIENT SERVICES

All Services

Industry Specialisations: Quoted, Medium and Small Companies, Professions, Government Bodies, Non-profit Organisations

---

SCHADĖ HARKEMA & PARTNERS

Reimersbeek 2, 1082 AG AMSTERDAM
Tel: + *31* (20) 6610234
Fax: + *31* (20) 429998
Mailing Address: P.O. Box 87081, 1080 JB AMSTERDAM

European Affiliation: DRM Internationally

International Contact: Peter Prÿs

Partners:	6
Professional staff:	81
Non-professional staff:	18
Total Staff:	**105**

CONTACT INFORMATION

Chairman: Rienk Harkema
Managing Partner: Rienk Harkema
Managing Partner: Meine Harkema
Accountancy (General): Gert Niehorster
Tax (International): René Bemt
Corporate Finance & Insolvency: Peter Prÿs
Tax (Corporate & International): Lex Weisscher
Tax Consultant: Loes Wolffgramm

CLIENT SERVICES

All Services

OTHER OFFICES

SCHADÉ HARKEMA & PARTNERS
91 De Molen, 3990 GC HOUTEN
Tel: + *31* (3403) 73014 *Fax:* + *31* (3403) 79274
Contact: Gert Niehorster

SCHADÉ HARKEMA & PARTNERS
112 Haagweg, 2282 AG RIJSWIJK
Tel: + *31* (70) 3192555 *Fax:* + *31* (70) 3995441
Contact: Hans van Minde

SCHADÉ HARKEMA & PARTNERS
Bredaseweg 412, 5037 LH TILBURG
Tel: + *31* (13) 633345 *Fax:* + *31* (13) 680513

Total Number of Offices: 4

SPRINGELING AND VERSTEGEN REGISTERACCOUNTANTS

Koningin Emmaplein 10, 3016 AB ROTTERDAM
Tel: + *31* (10) 4362211
Fax: + *31* (10) 4362158
Mailing Address: P.O. Box 23090, 3106 AB ROTTERDAM

European Affiliation: Midsnell International

International Contact: Leo A.J. Veth

OTHER OFFICES

SPRINGELING AND VERSTEGEN REGISTERACCOUNTANTS
Noordendijk 203, 3300 AN DORDRECHT
Mailing Address: P.O. Box 574, 3300 AN DORDRECHT
Tel: + *31* (78) 147022 *Fax:* + *31* (78) 313126
Contact: Wim B. van der Hoek

Total Number of Offices: 2

STEENS & PARTNERS

Thomas Mannplaats 311, 3009 GD ROTTERDAM
Tel: + *31* (10) 4564677
Fax: + *31* (10) 4568141
Mailing Address: P.O. Box 81167, 3069 NJ ROTTERDAM

European Affiliation: Jeffreys Henry International

International Contact: Theo Bakker

TRN GROEP

Admiraliteitskade 50, 3063 ED ROTTERDAM
Tel: + *31* (10) 4988222
Fax: + *31* (10) 4529000
Mailing Address: P.O. Box 2031, 3000 CA ROTTERDAM

European Affiliation: DRT International

International Contact: Piet Hoogendoorn

Total Staff: **3,203**

CLIENT SERVICES

All Services

MAJOR CLIENTS

ASM International, Bavaria, Cement Bouw Beheer, Cerestar, Dow Benelux, Holdingmij de Telegraaf, Koninklijke Begemann Groep, Kononklijke Bunge, Mitsui & Co International (Europe), Nissan Europe, Schuitema, Sodufa, Univend Group, Wilma International, (Koninklijke) Ahold

Total Number of Offices: 60

VAN DEN REEK & ASSOCIATES

President Rooseveltlaan 4a, 5707 GD HELMOND
Tel: +*31* (4920) 50775
Fax: +*31* (4920) 51425
Mailing Address: P.O. Box 221, 5700 AE HELMOND

European Affiliation: INPACT - International Network of Professional Accountants

International Contact: W.A.J. van den Reek

Partners:	4
Professional staff:	14
Total Staff:	**18**

FEE INCOME

Year End: 1990	**%**
Accountancy & Audit:	75.0
Tax:	25.0

CONTACT INFORMATION
Administration: L. van den Reek
Tax (Corporate): H. Spoormakers
Accountancy & Audit: W.A.J. van den Reek
Wages Administration: F. van Wel

CLIENT SERVICES
Accountancy (General), Audit, Corporate Finance Advice, Management & Business Advice, Value for Money Studies, Taxation (Corporate), Taxation (International)

VAN DER HOEK EN BLOK

Rosestraat 1033, 3008 AD ROTTERDAM
Tel: +*31* (10) 4961400
Fax: +*31* (10) 4855923
Mailing Address: P.O. Box 5172, 3008 AD ROTTERDAM

European Affiliation: Morison International

International Contact: René de Vries

Partners:	8
Professional staff:	128
Non-professional staff:	21
Total Staff:	**161**

FEE INCOME

Year End: 31.12.90	**Gu**
Total:	**16,000,000**

CONTACT INFORMATION
Managing Partner: Piet Blok
Managing Partner: René de Vries
Managing Partner: Leon Hermans
Accountancy (General): Piet Blok
Audit: Leon Hermans
Corporate Finance: Jan de Jong
Litigation Support: William Lie
Tax: René de Vries
Legal Services: Peter Verheijden
Computer Systems: Peter Krooswijk
Grants: John Jansen
Mergers & Acquistions: Edgar de Jong

CLIENT SERVICES
All Services

OTHER OFFICES

VAN DER HOEK EN BLOK
Sportlaan 11, 3223 EV HELLEVOETSLUIS
Tel: +*31* (1883) 16333 *Fax:* +*31* (1883) 23177
Contact: Henk de Bruijn

VAN DER HOEK EN BLOK
Vlierbaan 20, 2908 LR CAPELLE A/D IJSSEL
Tel: +*31* (10) 4423600 *Fax:* +*31* (10) 4583039
Contact: Jan de Jong

VAN DER HOEK EN BLOK
Uitstraat 10, 3201 EN SPIJKENISSE
Tel: +*31* (1880) 22111 *Fax:* +*31* (1880) 26527
Contact: Willem Batenburg

VAN DER HOEK EN BLOK
Rijnstraat 321, 3363 EJ SLIEDRECHT
Tel: +*31* (1840) 13333 *Fax:* +*31* (1840) 21343
Contact: Wim Stuij

VAN DER HOEK EN BLOK
Raadhuislaan 6, 3271 BT MIJNSHEERENLAND
Tel: +*31* (1862) 3222 *Fax:* +*31* (1862) 2513
Contact: Leon Hermans

Total Number of Offices: 6

VAN DER HOEK EN LENGTON BV

Singel 197, 3311 KR DORDRECHT
Tel: +*31* (78) 137088
Fax: +*31* (78) 134027
Mailing Address: P.O. Box 865, 3300 AW DORDRECHT

European Affiliation: InterContinental Consultants (ICC)

International Contact: Leendert C. van der Hoek

OTHER OFFICES

VAN DER HOEK EN LENGTON BV
Lange Noordstraat 37, 4331 CB MIDDELBURG
Mailing Address: P.O. Box 215, 4330 AE MIDDLEBURG
Tel: +*31* (1180) 36453 *Fax:* +*31* (1180) 27360
Contact: Willem J. Lengton

Total Number of Offices: 2

VB ACCOUNTANTS

Nassaulaan 12, 2593 GK THE HAGUE
Tel: +*31* (70) 3738486
Fax: +*31* (70) 3652954
Mailing Address: P.O. Box 19331, 2500 CH THE HAGUE

International Contact: F. Renssen

Partners:	45
Professional staff:	1,150
Non-professional staff:	130
Total Staff:	**1,325**

CONTACT INFORMATION
Chairman: A.G.V. Vergeer
Managing Partner: B. van Nes
Accountancy (General): P.J.A. Emans
Audit: S. van der Schaaf
Management Consultancy: A. Michael
Public Sector: A.O. Bac
Tax (Corporate): J.C. Dijkman
Training Centre: J. de Vries
Environmental Consultancy: A.S. de Vreeze

CLIENT SERVICES
Accountancy (General), Audit, Computer Installation, Management & Business Advice, Value for Money Studies, Taxation (Corporate), Environmental Consultancy

Industry Specialisations: Government, Non-profit organisations

Total Number of Offices: 30

▷

VEKEMANS & BERK

Maliebaan 74, 3581 CV UTRECHT
Tel: +*31* (30) 315812
Fax: +*31* (30) 333599
Mailing Address: P.O. Box 85007, 3508 AA UTRECHT

European Affiliation: Summit International Associates Inc

International Contact: Jan Pelt

Partners:	22
Professional staff:	393
Non-professional staff:	38
Total Staff:	**453**

FEE INCOME

Year End: 31.12.90	**US$**	**%**
Accountancy & Audit:	13,160,000	40.0
Consultancy:	4,935,000	15.0
Tax:	8,225,000	25.0
Other:	6,580,000	20.0
Total:	**32,900,000**	

CONTACT INFORMATION

Managing Partner: Jan Pelt
Corporate Finance: Jan Pelt
Management Consultancy: Jan Pelt
Administration: Peter van de Geer
Tax (Corporate): Guurt Berghoef
Tax (International): Joost de Beer
Accountancy & Audit: Jan Pelt

CLIENT SERVICES

Accountancy (General), Audit, Computer Installation, Corporate Finance Advice, Litigation/Legal Services, Management & Business Advice, Management Buy-outs, Mergers & Acquisitions, Pensions Planning, Taxation (Corporate), Taxation (International)

Industry Specialisations: Building, Textiles, Computer Services, Engineering, Service Business

OTHER OFFICES

VEKEMANS & BERK
Adastraat 7, 7607 HA ALMELO
Tel: +*31* (5490) 27000 *Fax:* +*31* (5490) 18766
Contact: Dr. Bienze Wijbenga

VEKEMANS & BERK
Wamberg 35, 1083 CW AMSTERDAM
Mailing Address: P.O. Box 7893, 1008 AB AMSTERDAM
Tel: +*31* (20) 6442840 *Fax:* +*31* (20) 6463507
Contact: Dr. Jan J.P. Matze

VEKEMANS & BERK
Stavorenweg 4, 2803 PT GOUDA
Mailing Address: P.O. Box 200, 2800 AE GOUDA
Tel: +*31* (1820) 70677 *Fax:* +*31* (1820) 71113
Contact: Albert A.J. Wiegerink

VEKEMANS & BERK
Laapersveld 68, 1213 VB HILVERSUM
Mailing Address: P.O. Box 514, 1200 AM HILVERSUM
Tel: +*31* (35) 238355 *Fax:* +*31* (35) 282214
Contact: Wim L.J. Veldhuizen

VEKEMANS & BERK
Schuttersveld 26, 2316 ZD LEIDEN
Mailing Address: P.O. Box 504, 2300 EB LEIDEN
Tel: +*31* (71) 214725 *Fax:* +*31* (71) 214373
Contact: Wim van Wouwe

VEKEMANS & BERK
Kerkenbos 10-27, 6546 BB NIJMEGEN
Mailing Address: P.O. Box 10525, 6500 MB NIJMEGEN
Tel: +*31* (80) 228115 *Fax:* +*31* (80) 600651
Contact: Tom de Lange

VEKEMANS & BERK
Michelangelostraat 2, 3066 NM ROTTERDAM
Mailing Address: P.O. Box 8290, 3009 AG ROTTERDAM
Tel: +*31* (10) 4551988 *Fax:* +*31* (10) 4567543
Contact: Pim W. van der Marel

VEKEMANS & BERK
Laan Copes van Cattenburch 71, 2585 EW 's-GRAVENHAGE
Mailing Address: P.O. Box 85745, 2508 CK 's-GRAVENHAGE
Tel: +*31* (70) 3617007 *Fax:* +*31* (70) 3617188
Contact: Wim van Wouwe

VEKEMANS & BERK
Pettelaarpark 62, 5216 PP 's-HERTOGENBOSCH
Mailing Address: P.O. Box 1120, 5200 BD 's-HERTOGENBOSCH
Tel: +*31* (73) 131686 *Fax:* +*31* (73) 145290
Contact: Mart T. van Ginkel

VEKEMANS & BERK
Bloemendalstraat 18, 8011 PJ ZWOLLE
Mailing Address: P.O. Box 508, 8000 AM ZWOLLE
Tel: +*31* (38) 212166 *Fax:* +*31* (38) 225807
Contact: Ton H. van Kesteren

Total Number of Offices: 11

WALGEMOED GROEP

Weerdestein 117, 1083 GH AMSTERDAM
Tel: +*31* (20) 6462746
Fax: +*31* (20) 6461248
Mailing Address: P.O. Box 71730, 1008 DE AMSTERDAM

European Affiliation: Horwath International

International Contact: Stan Ackermans

Partners:	26
Professional staff:	565
Non-professional staff:	30
Total Staff:	**621**

FEE INCOME

Year End: 1990	**Gu**	**%**
Accountancy & Audit:	45,000,000	69.0
Consultancy:	9,900,000	15.0
Tax:	7,600,000	11.0
Other:	2,900,000	5.0
Total:	**65,400,000**	

CONTACT INFORMATION

Managing Partner: Stan Ackermans
Tax (Corporate): A. Harlaar

CLIENT SERVICES

Accountancy (General), Audit, Computer Installation, Corporate Finance Advice, Insolvency & Corporate Restructuring, Management & Business Advice, Management Buy-outs, Mergers & Acquisitions, Pensions Planning, Value for Money Studies, Taxation (Corporate), Taxation (International)

OTHER OFFICES

HARLAAR & CO (TAX ADVISORS)
Nieuwe Steen 8, 1625 HV HOORN NH
Tel: +*31* (2290) 41689 *Fax:* +*31* (2290) 39934
Contact: Auke Harlaar

HARLAAR & CO (TAX ADVISORS)
Koningslaan 60, 3583 GN UTRECHT
Mailing Address: P.O. Box 14148, 3508 SE UTRECHT
Tel: +*31* (30) 518988 *Fax:* +*31* (30) 522018
Contact: Auke Harlaar

WALGEMOED
Voltastraat 1, 1817 DD ALKMAER
Tel: +*31* (72) 110164 *Fax:* +*31* (72) 151580
Contact: Gerard Dorenbos

WALGEMOED
Parkstraat 47, 3743 AD BAARN
Mailing Address: P.O. Box 299, 3740 AG BAARN
Tel: + 31 (2154) 11645 *Fax: + 31* (2135) 10076
Contact: E. Jan Wijers

WALGEMOED
Arnhemstraat 17, 6971 AN BRUMMEN
Mailing Address: P.O. Box 102, 6970 AC BRUMMEN
Tel: + 31 (5756) 2393 *Fax: + 31* (5756) 4410
Contact: Jan Minks

WALGEMOED
Plansoenstraat 93, 7001 AB DOETINCHEM
Mailing Address: P.O. Box 538, 7000 AM DOETINCHEM
Tel: + 31 (8340) 34153 *Fax: + 31* (8340) 24948
Contact: Jan Minks

WALGEMOED
Zuidendijk 35B, 3314 CP DORDRECHT
Tel: + 31 (78) 312466 *Fax: + 31* (78) 310372
Contact: E. Jan Wijers

WALGEMOED
Klinkenbergerweg 30-A, 6711 MK EDE
Mailing Address: P.O. Box 8178, 6710 AD EDE
Tel: + 31 (8380) 52060 *Fax: + 31* (8380) 50166
Contact: Simon J. Vermeulen

WALGEMOED
Benoordenhoutseweg 43, 2596 BC 's-GRAVENHAGE
Tel: + 31 (70) 3245304 *Fax: + 31* (70) 3242938
Contact: Gys G. van Roalten

WALGEMOED
Fonteinlaan 9, 2012 JG HAARLEM
Tel: + 31 (23) 319364 *Fax: + 31* (23) 311128
Contact: Jan van Ginkel

WALGEMOED
M. van Heemskerckstraat 21, 1961 EB HEEMSKERK
Mailing Address: P.O. Box 74, 1960 AB HEEMSKERK
Tel: + 31 (2510) 42414 *Fax: + 31* (2510) 37846
Contact: Gerard B.M. de Groot

WALGEMOED
Brinkstraat 53, 7902 AC HOOGEVEEN
Tel: + 31 (5280) 67252 *Fax: + 31* (5280) 72581
Contact: Tsijse Hotsma

WALGEMOED
Nieuwe Steen 8, 1625 HV HOORN NH
Tel: + 31 (2290) 36264 *Fax: + 31* (2290) 39934
Contact: Fok W. de Boer

WALGEMOED
Kennemerplein 23, 1971 EW IJMUIDEN
Mailing Address: P.O. Box 117, 1970 AC IJMUIDEN
Tel: + 31 (2550) 19105 *Fax: + 31* (2550) 13337
Contact: Peter J. Peppelenbos

WALGEMOED
Rijnsburgerweg 91-93, 2334 BJ LEIDEN
Tel: + 31 (71) 177441 *Fax: + 31* (71) 177181
Contact: Gijs G. van Raalten

WALGEMOED
Waterlandlaan 96, 1441 RS PURMEREND
Mailing Address: P.O. Box 213, 1440 AE PURMEREND
Tel: + 31 (2990) 22485 *Fax: + 31* (2990) 22300
Contact: Gerrit Blorn

WALGEMOED
Koningslaan 60, 3583 GN UTRECHT
Mailing Address: P.O. Box 14148, 3508 SE UTRECHT
Tel: + 31 (30) 518988 *Fax: + 31* (30) 522018
Contact: E. Jan Wijers

WALGEMOED
Peperstraat 92, 1502 AK ZAANDAM
Tel: + 31 (75) 169259 *Fax: + 31* (75) 162045
Contact: Ton A.B. Noords

WALGEMOED
Marspoortstraat 2, 7201 JB ZUTPHEN
Mailing Address: P.O. Box 130, 7200 AC ZUTPHEN
Tel: + 31 (5750) 18515 *Fax: + 31* (5750) 10966
Contact: Ton A.F. Mantel

Total Number of Offices: 20

WALLAST & STAM

Karrepad 2, 2623 AP DELFT
Tel: + 31 (15) 613121
Fax: + 31 (15) 615382
Mailing Address: P.O. Box 332, 2600 AH DELFT

European Affiliation: Pannell Kerr Forster Worldwide

International Contact: Ton Wallast

Partners:	13
Professional staff:	118
Non-professional staff:	16
Total Staff:	**147**

FEE INCOME

Year End: 31.12.90		**Gu**
Total:	**15,700,000**	

CONTACT INFORMATION
Chairman: Ton Wallast

CLIENT SERVICES
Accountancy (General), Audit, Corporate Finance Advice, Litigation/Legal Services, Management & Business Advice, Management Buy-outs, Mergers & Acquisitions, Pensions Planning, Taxation (Corporate), Taxation (International)

OTHER OFFICES

WALLAST & STAM
P.O. Box 297, 2670 AH NAALDWYK
Tel: + 31 (1740) 24801 *Fax: + 31* (1740) 22176
Contact: Bram Breecterveld

WALLAST & STAM
Mathenesserlaan 342, 3021 HZ ROTTERDAM
Tel: + 31 (10) 4774455 *Fax: + 31* (10) 4257410
Contact: Fred Spanjaard

WALLAST & STAM
Kanaalweg 17, 3581 CH UTRECHT
Tel: + 31 (30) 871088 *Fax: + 31* (30) 898989
Contact: Hans van Hamersveld

WALLAST & STAM
Wipmolenlaan 1, 3447 GJ WOERDEN
Tel: + 31 (3480) 16262 *Fax: + 31* (3480) 14280
Contact: Jack Visser

Total Number of Offices: 5

WITLOX ADVIES

Kempenlandstraat 1, 5262 CA VUGHT
Tel: + 31 (73) 579116
Fax: + 31 (73) 560945
Mailing Address: P.O. Box 2031, 5260 CA VUGHT

European Affiliation: Morison International

International Contact: Henry Jan van Dun

Partners:	7
Professional staff:	75
Non-professional staff:	15
Total Staff:	**97**

▷

FEE INCOME

Year End: 31.12.90	**Gu**	**%**
Accountancy & Audit:	4,800,000	60.0
Tax:	3,200,000	40.0
Total:	**8,000,000**	

CONTACT INFORMATION

Chairman: Jan van Rijt
Managing Partner: Frans van Empel
Accountancy (General): Frans van Empel
Audit: Arie Verbakel
Administration: Ardy van der Ham
Tax (International): Henry Jan van Dun
Tax (International): Jan van Rijt
Accountancy & Public Sector: Peter Poirters
Corporate Finance & Insolvency: Ad van Strijdhoven
Management Consultancy & Tax: John Samuels

CLIENT SERVICES

All Services

OTHER OFFICES

WITLOX VCX
P.O. Box 3341, 4800 DH BREDA
Tel: + *31* (76) 225330 *Fax:* + *31* (76) 149889
Contact: Arie Verbakel

Total Number of Offices: 2

Area: 323,878 sq km (125,050 sq miles)
Population: 4,091,132 (1988 estimate)
Density: 13.0 per sq km
Capital: Oslo

GDP: NKr719 bn, US$118 bn
GDP per head: US$27,830
Inflation: 1990 - 4.7%
1991 - 4.5% (forecast)

Official and Spoken Languages: Norwegian (Bokmal and Nynorsk). English widely spoken

Time: GMT + 1 (in Summer GMT + 2)
Telephone Dialling Code: + 47

Currency: Krone (Kr) = 100 ore
Banking Hours: 0815-1530 Monday-Friday except Thursdays, 0815-1700. Summer: 0815-1500 Monday-Friday except Thursdays 0815-1700
Professional accountancy body: Norges Statsautoriserte Revisorers

Corporate Tax Data

Information supplied by Richard Citron, international tax partner of Stoy Hayward.

The tax year; nature and rates of tax

The tax year is the calendar year.

Trading profits and other income are liable to a single national rate of corporate income tax of 28%.

Residence and territoriality

Norwegian resident companies are liable to corporate tax on their worldwide income and gains. A company is resident in Norway only if it is incorporated in Norway.

The tax base

Method of computation. Taxable profits are based on the profit reported in the accounts but adjusted for certain items. Capital contributions and withdrawals are usually ignored.

Disallowable items. The general rule is that expenses must be wholly and exclusively incurred for the purposes of the trade to be deductible. Specifically, entertaining expenses are disallowable, as are most gifts (except to scientific and educational institutes to a limited extent) and charitable donations. Most taxes are not deductible with the exception of the local property tax.

Exempt income/special deductions. All special incentives etc were removed with effect from 1 January 1992.

Interest paid. Interest is generally deductible.

Stock. Stock is valued at the lower of cost and market value.

Depreciation. Depreciation is charged for different types of asset on a reducing balance basis at prescribed rates as follows: (1) industrial buildings, hotels and restaurants: 5% to 10%; (2) offices and shops: 2% to 4%; (3) plant and machinery ▷

(excluding cars): maximum of 30%; (4) cars: 20%; (5) ships: 20%; (6) aircraft and oil rigs: 12%. Certain small items may be written off to revenue. Special rules apply to intangible assets.

Treatment of dividends

Dividends received from Norwegian companies. There is no withholding tax on dividends from Norwegian companies. In the hands of the recipient company dividends are liable to the corporate income tax but a credit is available for the 28% tax paid by the distributing company so that the net tax is zero.

Dividends received from abroad. Dividends from foreign companies are liable to corporate income tax. Where the source of the dividend is a treaty country, the foreign tax paid may be relieved by way of credit. Otherwise the foreign tax is generally treated as an expense.

Dividends paid to Norwegian residents. Dividends are not deductible in calculating the company's corporate income tax liability.

Dividends paid to non-residents. A withholding tax of 25% (subject to treaty) applies to dividends paid to non-residents.

Anti-avoidance measures

Transfer pricing rules are applied to all transactions between affiliates.

Treatment of losses

Current period. The net worth basis of computation grants relief for losses against profits of the same period automatically (there is no carry back except on liquidation).

Future periods. Losses may be carried forward for a maximum of ten years.

Treatment of capital gains

Treatment. Capital gains are treated as income.

Computation. Gains are computed by deducting cost from sale proceeds.

Rollover. From 1 January 1992, it is only possible to defer tax on capital gains on an involuntary (ie. forced) disposal. Gains on the sale of shares are treated as income.

Special treatment for shares. The special treatment existing in previous years was abolished with effect from 1 January 1992.

Treatment of groups

A Norwegian resident parent company and any of its 91% Norwegian resident subsidiaries may form a tax group where profits and losses are consolidated and gains rolled over utilised by the group as a whole.

Treatment of branches

The taxable profits of a Norwegian branch of a non-resident company are computed on the same basis as those of a resident company but the base for the tax is limited to Norwegian source profits and gains and assets located in Norway. There is no withholding tax on remittances of profit.

Other taxes

Taxes on income. In addition to the county and national income tax, there is a petroleum revenue tax of 35% imposed on income from oil exploitation activities.

Capital taxes. There is a national net worth tax (formueskatt til staten) at a rate of 0.3% on the assessed value of worldwide net assets and local net worth taxes but these will not apply to companies limited by shares. There is also a local property tax at a rate ranging from 0.2% to 1%. This tax is deductible for corporate income tax purposes.

Turnover taxes. A value added tax (merverdiavgift) is charged on the supply of goods and services, at a single rate of 20%. An investment tax of 7% is charged on some goods purchased by a company that can claim a VAT deduction for the purchase. Exports are zero rated.

Payroll taxes. Payroll taxes amount to 16.7% of payroll, with reduced rates applying to employees resident in development areas.

ARTHUR ANDERSEN & CO

Drammensveien 134, 0212 OSLO 2
Tel: + 47 (2) 462800
Fax: + 47 (2) 468714
Mailing Address: Postboks 228 Skøyen, 0212 OSLO 2

European Affiliation: Arthur Andersen Worldwide

International Contact: Finn Berg Jacobsen

CONTACT INFORMATION
Audit: Henning Strøm
Tax (Corporate): Finn Berg Jacobsen

CLIENT SERVICES
Accountancy (General), Audit, Computer Installation, Corporate Finance Advice, Insolvency & Corporate Restructuring, Litigation/Legal Services, Management & Business Advice, Management Buy-outs, Mergers & Acquisitions, Pensions Planning, Value for Money Studies, Taxation (Corporate), Taxation (International)

OTHER OFFICES
ARTHUR ANDERSEN & CO
Bradbenken 1, 5023 BERGEN
Mailing Address: Postboks 4092 Dreggen, 5023 BERGEN
Tel: + 47 (5) 323880 *Fax:* + 47 (5) 323932
ARTHUR ANDERSEN & CO
Jernbaneveien 5, 4005 STAVANGER
Tel: + 47 (4) 534550 *Fax:* + 47 (4) 536995
ARTHUR ANDERSEN & CO
Jomfrugt. 18, 7010 TRONDHEIM
Tel: + 47 (7) 511844 *Fax:* + 47 (7) 523994

Total Number of Offices: 4

AUDINOR A/S

Postboks 1363, 1401 SKI
Tel: + 47 (9) 874066
Fax: + 47 (9) 875757

European Affiliation: Alliott Peirson International

International Contact: Finn Thv Utne

OTHER OFFICES
AUDINOR A/S
Postboks 1784 Vika, 0122 OSLO 1
Tel: + 47 (2) 838623 *Fax:* + 47 (2) 838071
Contact: Finn Thv Utne

Total Number of Offices: 2

BAKKE & HJELMAASLARSEN

Billingstadsletta 19a, Postboks 66, 1312 SLEPENDEN
Tel: + 47 (2) 846255
Fax: + 47 (2) 980570

European Affiliation: Moore Stephens

International Contact: Helge A. Ostvold

BDO LORANGE OG BRÆNDE & CO

Rådhusgt. 17, 0158 OSLO 1
Tel: + 47 (2) 204400
Fax: + 47 (2) 419987

European Affiliation: BDO Binder

International Contact: Tore Setsaas

Partners:	6
Professional staff:	22
Non-professional staff:	5
Total Staff:	**33**

FEE INCOME

Year End: 31.12.90	**US$**	**%**
Accountancy & Audit:	2,946,000	90.0
Consultancy:	164,000	5.0
Tax:	164,000	5.0
Total:	**3,274,000**	

CONTACT INFORMATION
Managing Partner: Olai Lorange
Administration: Odd Eide-Fredriksen
Tax (Corporate & International): Olav Mjånes

CLIENT SERVICES
Audit, Management & Business Advice, Mergers & Acquisitions, Taxation (Corporate), Trust Settlement & Estates

BIRKELAND OG UVHOLTS REVISJONSBYRÅ

Schwensenagt. 7, 0170 OSLO 1
Tel: + 47 (2) 463860
Fax: + 47 (2) 460084

European Affiliation: Clark Kenneth Leventhal

International Contact: Lars Uvholt

Partners:	5
Professional staff:	11
Non-professional staff:	2
Total Staff:	**18**

FEE INCOME

Year End: 1990	**%**
Accountancy & Audit:	70.0
Tax:	30.0

CLIENT SERVICES
Accountancy (General), Audit, Taxation (Corporate), Taxation (International)

COOPERS & LYBRAND A/S

Havnelageret, 0150 OSLO 1
Tel: + 47 (2) 400000
Fax: + 47 (2) 425091

European Affiliation: Coopers & Lybrand Europe

International Contact: Anders Grini

Partners:	63
Professional staff:	425
Non-professional staff:	42
Total Staff:	**530**

CONTACT INFORMATION
Chairman: Tom Møller
Managing Partner: Anders Grini
Corporate Finance: Esben Fiane
Insolvency: Kjell Melhus
Management Consultancy: Kristoffer Grude
Administration: Anders Grini
Public Sector: Jan Overaasen
Tax (Corporate): Han-Olav Rostviet
Tax (International): Rolf Nicolaissen
Accountancy & Audit: Anders Grini

CLIENT SERVICES
All Services

Total Number of Offices: 20

▷

Norway

DYBWAD REVISION A/S
Bygdøy Allé 23, 0262 OSLO
Tel: + 47 (2) 442280
Fax: + 47 (2) 430089

European Affiliation: DRM Internationally

International Contact: Edvard Tvedt

Partners:	8
Professional staff:	16
Non-professional staff:	4
Total Staff:	**28**

FEE INCOME

Year End: 31.12.90	**£**	**%**
Accountancy & Audit:	1,200,000	80.0
Consultancy:	75,000	5.0
Tax:	225,000	15.0
Total:	**1,500,000**	

CONTACT INFORMATION
Chairman: Håkon Toften
Managing Partner: Erik Enger

CLIENT SERVICES
Accountancy (General), Audit, Management & Business Advice, Mergers & Acquisitions, Taxation (Corporate), Taxation (International)

Industry Specialisations: Food Retailers

ELIASSEN & ALMVANG ANS
Tollbugaten 28, 0157 OSLO
Tel: + 47 (2) 414190
Fax: + 47 (2) 336903

European Affiliation: The International Group of Accounting Firms Ltd (IGAF)

International Contact: Jill Almvang

Partners:	3
Professional staff:	4
Non-professional staff:	1
Total Staff:	**8**

CONTACT INFORMATION
Partner: Trond Ryland
Partner: Jill Almvang

CLIENT SERVICES
All Services

ERNST & YOUNG
Stenersgt. 10, 0184 OSLO 1
Tel: + 47 (2) 171800
Fax: + 47 (2) 170577

European Affiliation: Ernst & Young Europe

International Contact: Erik Gudbrandsen

Partners:	70
Professional staff:	408
Non-professional staff:	85
Total Staff:	**563**

FEE INCOME

Year End: 31.12.90	**Kr**	**%**
Accountancy & Audit:	274,000,000	90.6
Consultancy:	17,000,000	5.7
Tax:	11,000,000	3.7
Total:	**302,000,000**	

CONTACT INFORMATION
Chairman: Ernst Alsaker
Managing Partner: Torstein Hokholt
Management Consultancy: Erik Gudbrandsen
Administration: Torstein Hokholt
Public Sector: Helge Bettmo
Accountancy & Audit: Helge Bettmo
Tax: Ivar V. Amundsen
Tax: Einar Brask
Oil & Gas: Jostein Johannessen

CLIENT SERVICES
Accountancy (General), Audit, Corporate Finance Advice, Management & Business Advice, Mergers & Acquisitions, Taxation (Corporate), Taxation (International)

Industry Specialisations: Oil, Transportation, Saving Banks

MAJOR CLIENTS
Amerada Hess Norge A/S, BP Norway Limited, Braathens SAFE, Elf Aquitaine Norge A/S, Falconbridge Nikkelverk A/S, Far Shipping A/S, Ikea A/S, Isola-group, KEFAS A/S, Midland Montagu A/S, Mobil Oil A/S Norge, Moller-group, Samvirke Skadeforsikring, Skibs A/S Storli, Statoil, Total Marine Norsk A/S, Ugland-group, Vestenfjeldske Bykredittforening, Wideroe Flyveselskap A/S

OTHER OFFICES

ERNST & YOUNG
Grimmergt. 4, 6002 ÅLESUND
Tel: + 47 (71) 24213 *Fax:* + 47 (71) 20051

ERNST & YOUNG
Kittelsbuktveien 1, Postboks 299, 4801 ARENDAL
Tel: + 47 (41) 24560 *Fax:* + 47 (41) 23991

ERNST & YOUNG
Lars Hillesgt. 20B, Postboks 4284, Nygårdstangen, 5028 BERGEN
Tel: + 47 (5) 314670 *Fax:* + 47 (5) 310695

ERNST & YOUNG
Sjøtun - Rønvikveien 9, Postboks 594, 8001 BODØ
Tel: + 47 (81) 26560 *Fax:* + 47 (81) 23092

ERNST & YOUNG
Nedre Storgt. 46, Postboks 560, Brakerøya, 3002 DRAMMEN
Tel: + 47 (3) 838890 *Fax:* + 47 (3) 838625

ERNST & YOUNG
Torvgåden, Postboks 108, 4371 EGERSUND
Tel: + 47 (4) 490399 *Fax:* + 47 (4) 493703

ERNST & YOUNG
Råadhusveien 1, Postboks 302, 9031 FINNSNES
Tel: + 47 (89) 41600 *Fax:* + 47 (89) 41217

ERNST & YOUNG
Havnegt. 7, Postboks 43, 3081 HOLMESTRAND
Tel: + 47 (33) 52288 *Fax:* + 47 (33) 53234
Contact: Øivind Haugen

ERNST & YOUNG
Torvet 5, 3190 HORTEN
Tel: + 47 (33) 46520 *Fax:* + 47 (33) 43132

ERNST & YOUNG
Kirketorget 5, 3600 KONGSBERG
Tel: + 47 (3) 732622 *Fax:* + 47 (3) 736477

ERNST & YOUNG
Kirkegt. 9, Postboks 230, 3771 KRAGERØ
Tel: + 47 (3) 983555 *Fax:* + 47 (3) 983540

ERNST & YOUNG
Vestre Strandgt. 24 A, Postboks 184, 4601 KRISTIANSAND
Tel: + 47 (42) 22540 *Fax:* + 47 (42) 22615

ERNST & YOUNG
Brannvaksgt. 5, Postboks 183, 3251 LARVIK
Tel: + 47 (34) 81163 *Fax:* + 47 (34) 82633

ERNST & YOUNG
Storgt. 132, Postboks 396, 2601 LILLEHAMMER
Tel: + 47 (62) 53124 *Fax:* + 47 (62) 51049

ERNST & YOUNG
Prinsensgt. 6, 1500 MOSS
Tel: + 47 (9) 253008 *Fax:* + 47 (9) 255778

ERNST & YOUNG
Dronningensgt. 49, Postboks 379, 8501 NARVIK
Tel: + 47 (82) 46091 *Fax:* + 47 (82) 42160

ERNST & YOUNG
Storgt. 54, 3670 NOTODDEN
Tel: + 47 (36) 10800 *Fax:* + 47 (36) 11565

ERNST & YOUNG
Fred Olsens Gt. 6, 0512 OSLO 1
Tel: + 47 (2) 862700 *Fax:* + 47 (2) 333413

ERNST & YOUNG
Stenersgt. 10, 0184 OSLO 1
Tel: + 47 (2) 862700 *Fax:* + 47 (2) 170577
Contact: Ernst Alsaker

ERNST & YOUNG
Olavsgt. 26, Postboks 64, 3901 PORSGRUNN
Tel: + 47 (3) 552090 *Fax:* + 47 (3) 559688

ERNST & YOUNG
Storgt. 27, Postboks 2057, 3201 SANDEFJORD
Tel: + 47 (34) 67701 *Fax:* + 47 (34) 68219

ERNST & YOUNG
Strandgt. 31, Postboks 286, 8401 SORTLAND
Tel: + 47 (88) 23322 *Fax:* + 47 (88) 23395

ERNST & YOUNG
Fridtjof Nansens Vei 48, 4019 STAVANGER
Tel: + 47 (4) 589060 *Fax:* + 47 (4) 883388

ERNST & YOUNG
Hellantunet, Postboks 123, 3800 BØ I TELEMARK
Tel: + 47 (3) 952000 *Fax:* + 47 (3) 951950
Contact: Johannes Forberg

ERNST & YOUNG
Kirkeveien 6, 3100 TØNSBERG
Tel: + 47 (33) 20603 *Fax:* + 47 (33) 21603
Contact: Per Jacobsen

ERNST & YOUNG
Bankgt. 7, Postboks 529, 9001 TROMSØ
Tel: + 47 (83) 89620 *Fax:* + 47 (83) 84370

ERNST & YOUNG
Prinsens Gt. 348, 7011 TRONDHEIM
Tel: + 47 (7) 526703 *Fax:* + 47 (7) 509190

ERNST & YOUNG
Hovdeveien 9, Postboks 49, 3371 VIKERSUND
Tel: + 47 (3) 787299 *Fax:* + 47 (3) 787796

Total Number of Offices: 29

FORUM TOUCHE ROSS

Pilestredet 75C, OSLO 3
Tel: + 47 (2) 464770
Fax: + 47 (2) 698904

European Affiliation: DRT International

International Contact: Henrik Aass

Total Staff: **440**

CLIENT SERVICES
All Services

MAJOR CLIENTS
DNL/Scandinavian Airline Systems (SAS), Dyno Industrier, Elopak/Tiedemanns, Fearnley Group, Forenede-Gruppe, Joh Johansson, Kommunal Landspensjonskasse, Norsk Hydro, Norwegian Red Cross, Rasmussen-Gruppen, Star Shipping, Sundal Gollier Montagu, Torvald Klaveness, Vesta-Gruppen, Vital

Total Number of Offices: 9

GRANT THORNTON NORGE A/S

Wesselsgate 8, 0165 OSLO
Tel: + 47 (2) 200400
Fax: + 47 (2) 200410

European Affiliation: Grant Thornton International

International Contact: Paul Bellamy

Partners:	4
Professional staff:	8
Non-professional staff:	1
Total Staff:	**13**

FEE INCOME

Year End: 31.12.89	**Kr (million)**
Total:	**5,745**

CONTACT INFORMATION
Accountancy (General): Hans C. Axelsen
Audit & Administration: Odd Ekholt
Corporate Finance: Hans C. Axelsen
Insolvency & Tax: Frede Baumann
Public Sector & Consultancy: Paul Bellamy
Operational Audit Manager: Anne M. Hagasaet

CLIENT SERVICES
All Services, Operational Audit

Industry Specialisations: Banking, Shipping, Publishing

GRIMSRUD & CO

Drammensveien 21, 0255 OSLO 2
Tel: + 47 (2) 551821
Fax: + 47 (2) 434063

European Affiliation: Summit International Associates Inc

Partners:	2
Professional staff:	12
Non-professional staff:	2
Total Staff:	**16**

FEE INCOME

Year End: 31.12.90	**US$**
Total:	**1,300,000**

CONTACT INFORMATION
Managing Partner: Kåre Uppstrøm
Managing Partner: Jan Olaf Poulsen

CLIENT SERVICES
Accountancy (General), Audit, Insolvency & Corporate Restructuring, Litigation/Legal Services, Management & Business Advice, Management Buy-outs, Mergers & Acquisitions, Taxation (Corporate)

HUBERT & CO

Holbergsgt. 19, 0166 OSLO 1
Tel: + 47 (2) 426910
Fax: + 47 (2) 112564

▷

European Affiliation: Affiliated Conference of Practising Accountants International (ACPA)

International Contact: Per Hubert

KPMG

KPMG PEAT MARWICK A/S

Brynsveien 12, 0611 OSLO
Tel: + 47 (2) 721570
Fax: + 47 (2) 729282
Mailing Address: Postboks 150, Bryn, 0611 OSLO

European Affiliation: KPMG

International Contact: Bjørn Rist

Partners:	53
Professional staff:	233
Non-professional staff:	54
Total Staff:	**340**

FEE INCOME

Year End: 30.09.90	**Kr**	**%**
Accountancy & Audit:	169,000,000	95.0
Consultancy:	5,000,000	2.8
Tax:	4,000,000	2.2
Total:	**178,000,000**	

CONTACT INFORMATION
Chairman: Kaare Eimhjellen
Managing Partner: Ole Klette
Audit: Arne Giertsen
Corporate Finance: Bjørn Rist
Insolvency: Lars P. Ose
Management Consultancy: Bjørn Rist
Administration: Thor R. Andersen
Public Sector: Ole Klette
Tax: John Killengreen
International Contacts: Morten Pieker

CLIENT SERVICES
Audit, Corporate Finance Advice, Management & Business Advice, Management Buy-outs, Mergers & Acquisitions, Taxation (Corporate), Taxation (International)

MAJOR CLIENTS
Block Watne, Ekornes, Fina, Forma, Frank Mohn, Fred Olsen & Co, Freia Marabou, Frionor, Jebsen Group, Jotun, Kverneland, NPC, Rieber & Son, Saga Petroleum, Smedvig Group, Uni Storebrand

OTHER OFFICES

KPMG PEAT MARWICK A/S
Apotekergt. 9B, 6001 ÅLESUND
Mailing Address: Postboks 295, 6001 ÅLESUND
Tel: + 47 (71) 21470 *Fax:* + 47 (71) 28030
Contact: Gerd Leira

KPMG PEAT MARWICK A/S
Iuellsklev. 4, 4801 ARENDAL
Mailing Address: Postboks 103, 4801 ARENDAL
Tel: + 47 (41) 24648 *Fax:* + 47 (41) 23818
Contact: Terje H. Holst

KPMG PEAT MARWICK A/S
Sandviksboder 5, 5035 BERGEN-SANDVIKEN
Tel: + 47 (5) 310510 *Fax:* + 47 (5) 321166
Contact: Sverre Grimstad

KPMG PEAT MARWICK A/S
Trysilvn 6, 2401 ELVERUM
Mailing Address: Postboks 58, 2401 ELVERUM
Tel: + 47 (64) 10500 *Fax:* + 47 (64) 14720
Contact: Ole Peder Lomo

KPMG PEAT MARWICK A/S
Petroleumsveien 6, 4033 FORUS
Mailing Address: Postboks 57, 4033 FORUS
Tel: + 47 (4) 570233 *Fax:* + 47 (4) 571229
Contact: Jan W. Grytten

KPMG PEAT MARWICK A/S
Vestre Strandgt. 42, 4612 KRISTIANSAND
Tel: + 47 (42) 71140 *Fax:* + 47 (42) 71144

KPMG PEAT MARWICK A/S
Julsundveien 47, 6401 MOLDE
Mailing Address: Postboks 130, 6401 MOLDE
Tel: + 47 (72) 54477 *Fax:* + 47 (72) 51180

KPMG PEAT MARWICK A/S
Peter Grønsgt 4, 3201 SANDEFJORD
Mailing Address: Postboks 150, 3201 SANDEFJORD
Tel: + 47 (34) 65770 *Fax:* + 47 (34) 62697

KPMG PEAT MARWICK A/S
Industriveien 2, 1301 SANDVIKA
Mailing Address: Postboks 503, 1301 SANDVIKA
Tel: + 47 (2) 514060 *Fax:* + 47 (2) 514210
Contact: Ragnar Hedenstad

KPMG PEAT MARWICK A/S
Heiane Kontorsenter, 5400 STORD
Mailing Address: Postboks 1236, 5400 STORD
Tel: + 47 (54) 14344 *Fax:* + 47 (54) 15370
Contact: Sverre Grimstad

KPMG PEAT MARWICK A/S
Ramdalveien 6, 3101 TØNSBERG
Mailing Address: Postboks 269, 3101 TØNSBERG
Tel: + 47 (33) 20601 *Fax:* + 47 (33) 20201

KPMG PEAT MARWICK A/S
Vestregt. 42, 9001 TROMSØ
Mailing Address: Postboks 845, 9001 TROMSØ
Tel: + 47 (83) 56200 *Fax:* + 47 (83) 57807
Contact: Finn Heggdal

KPMG PEAT MARWICK A/S
Kjopmannsgt. 61, 7011 TRONDHEIM
Tel: + 47 (7) 517055 *Fax:* + 47 (7) 517615

Total Number of Offices: 14

OTTERSTADS REVISJONSKONTOR A/S

Henrik Ibsensgt. 7, 0179 OSLO 1
Tel: + 47 (2) 112484
Fax: + 47 (2) 203718

European Affiliation: S & W International

International Contact: Terje Kromwoll

PRICE WATERHOUSE A/S

Stensberggt. 26, 0110 OSLO 1
Tel: + 47 (2) 363440
Fax: + 47 (2) 363455
Mailing Address: Postboks 1205 - VIKA, 0170 OSLO 1

European Affiliation: Price Waterhouse

Partners:	10
Professional staff:	108
Non-professional staff:	26
Total Staff:	**144**

FEE INCOME

Year End: 30.06.91	Kr	%
Accountancy & Audit:	59,500,000	67.9
Insolvency:	2,600,000	3.0
Consultancy:	13,800,000	15.8
Tax:	11,700,000	13.3
Total:	**87,600,000**	

CONTACT INFORMATION
Managing Partner: Jan Egil Haga
Audit: John Wheatley
Management Consultancy: Sigurd Ellingsen
Corporate Finance & Insolvency: Jan Egil Haga
Tax: Pål Hasner

CLIENT SERVICES
Audit, Corporate Finance Advice, Insolvency & Corporate Restructuring, Management & Business Advice, Mergers & Acquisitions, Value for Money Studies, Taxation (Corporate), Taxation (International)

Industry Specialisations: Banking & Financial Services, Insurance, Oil & Gas

OTHER OFFICES

PRICE WATERHOUSE A/S
C. Sundtsgt. 39, 5004 BERGEN
Mailing Address: Postboks 1807 - Nordnes, 5024 BERGEN
Tel: + 47 (5) 312925 *Fax:* + 47 (5) 232682
Contact: Thorbjørn Grindhaug

PRICE WATERHOUSE A/S
Harald Haarfagresgt. 8, 4014 STAVANGER
Tel: + 47 (4) 563311 *Fax:* + 47 (4) 527750
Contact: Alan McIntyre

Total Number of Offices: 3

REVICO SANDVIKA A/S

Hamangskogen 60, 1300 SANDVIKA
Tel: + 47 (2) 549560
Fax: + 47 (2) 549184
Mailing Address: Postboks 455, 1301 SANDVIKA

European Affiliation: HLB International

International Contact: Helge Eide-Fredriksen

Partners:	14
Professional staff:	36
Non-professional staff:	6
Total Staff:	**56**

CONTACT INFORMATION
Chairman: Harald Eide-Fredriksen
Managing Partner: Petter Greaker
Audit: Tor Andersen
Accountancy & Administration: Petter Greaker
Spanish Language: Jo Fundingsrud

CLIENT SERVICES
All Services

Industry Specialisations: Shipbuilding

ASSOCIATED FIRMS

ANDERSEN & SVENKESEN A/S
Nedre Hjellegt. 1, 3701 SKIEN
Mailing Address: Postboks 818, 3701 SKIEN
Tel: + 47 (35) 23005 *Fax:* + 47 (35) 30332

EKKEREN REVISJONSBYRÅ A/S
Jonas Lies Gt. 15, 2201 KONESVINGER
Mailing Address: Postboks 57, 2201 KONESVINGER
Tel: + 47 (66) 13101 *Fax:* + 47 (66) 18580

HAUGESUND REVISJONSINSTITUTT A/S
Strandgt. 92, 5501 HAUGESUND
Mailing Address: Postboks 478, 5501 HAUSGESUND
Tel: + 47 (4) 722299 *Fax:* + 47 (4) 725616

REVICO HALLINGDAL A/S
Forretningsgarden, 3550 GOL
Tel: + 47 (67) 75510 *Fax:* + 47 (67) 75585
Contact: Helge Eide-Fredriksen

REVICO SKEDSMO
Hvamstubben 17, 2013 SKJETTEN
Tel: + 47 (6) 844770 *Fax:* + 47 (6) 845255

Total Number of Offices: 6

REVINOR A/S

Storgaten 37, 0182 OSLO
Tel: + 47 (2) 423950
Fax: + 47 (2) 202891

European Affiliation: DFK International

International Contact: Ola Krohn-Nydal

ASSOCIATED FIRMS

HAGESTUEN & VAARDAL
Kalfarveien 57 A, 5018 BERGEN
Tel: + 47 (5) 318580 *Fax:* + 47 (5) 320108
Contact: Ivar Hagestuen

NILS HAUGE ABRAHAMSEN
Hegdehaugsveien 24, Postboks 7154 Homansbyen, 0307 OSLO 3
Tel: + 47 (2) 602390 *Fax:* + 47 (2) 568834
Contact: Tom Thomassen

KJELL KARLSEN
Josefines Gate 26, Postboks 7204 Homansbyen, 0307 OSLO 3
Tel: + 47 (2) 608100
Contact: Kjell Karlsen

OLA KROHN-NYDAL
Storgaten 37, 0182 OSLO 1
Tel: + 47 (2) 423950 *Fax:* + 47 (2) 202891
Contact: Ola Krohn-Nydal

LANGSETH & MANGRUD A/S
Stroket, Postboks 205, 2381 BRUMMUNDDAL
Tel: + 47 (65) 41360
Contact: Arild Langseth

SIGMUND LOKKEN & CO ANS
Kronprinsengate 5, 0251 OSLO 2
Tel: + 47 (2) 831190 *Fax:* + 47 (2) 831669
Contact: Robert Henriksen

THOR H. MARTHINSEN
Hegdehaugsveien 24, Postboks 7154 Homansbyen, 0307 OSLO 3
Tel: + 47 (2) 602390 *Fax:* + 47 (2) 568834
Contact: Thor H. Marthinsen

SIGURD MJAALAND
V Strandgate 16, Postboks 240, 4601 KRISTIANSAND S
Tel: + 47 (42) 29860 *Fax:* + 47 (42) 29069
Contact: Sigurd Mjaaland

REGNSKAPS REVISJON A/S
Storhamargaten 34, 2300 HAMAR
Tel: + 47 (65) 25095 *Fax:* + 47 (65) 27874
Contact: Knut Mengshoel

REVISJONSSELSKAPET FLADSTAD, MJELVE OG ØSTBO ANS
Hegdehaugsveien 24, Postboks 7154, Homansbyen, 0307 OSLO 3
Tel: + 47 (2) 602390 *Fax:* + 47 (2) 568834
Contact: Leif Leø Østbo

Total Number of Offices: 12

▷

Norway

REVISIONSFIRMÆT ÅSVANG & CO A/S

Storgaten 13, P.O. Box 334, 3101 TØNSBERG
Tel: + 47 (33) 12540
Fax: + 47 (33) 11536

European Affiliation: TGI International

International Contact: Sven Rich Åsvang

REVISJONSFIRMAET KETIL ELLEFSEN

Tollbugt. 21, Postboks 2063, 3003 DRAMMEN, Oslo
Tel: + 47 (3) 832038
Fax: + 47 (3) 832411

European Affiliation: INPACT - International Network of Professional Accountants

International Contact: Ketil Ellefsen

REVISOR-GRUPPEN NORGE A/S

Holtegt. 22, 0355 OSLO 3
Tel: + 47 (2) 692060
Fax: + 47 (2) 602801

European Affiliation: Moores Rowland International

International Contact: Kjell Kr. Olsen

ASSOCIATED FIRMS

BERGENS MERKANTILE BUREAU A/S
Lars Hillesgt. 21, 5009 BERGEN
Tel: + 47 (5) 328150 *Fax:* + 47 (5) 327557
Contact: Knut Hagelien

JOSTEIN BØYUM
Uttrågt. 35, Postboks 136, 5700 VOSS
Tel: + 47 (5) 512440 *Fax:* + 47 (5) 512440
Contact: Jostein Bøyum

OTTAR HAUGEN A/S
Kongegt. 31, Postboks 61, 3251 LARVIK
Tel: + 47 (34) 87390 *Fax:* + 47 (34) 85685
Contact: Ottar Haugen

NORPARTNER REVISJON
Holtegt. 22, 0355 OSLO 3
Tel: + 47 (2) 692060 *Fax:* + 47 (2) 602801
Contact: Kjell Kr. Olsen

REVISOR-GRUPPEN STAVANGER A/S
Fabrikkveien 5, Postboks 96, 4033 FORUS, Stavanger
Tel: + 47 (4) 800690 *Fax:* + 47 (4) 800697
Contact: Øla Hausberg

OVE RISANGER
Strandgt. 54, Postboks 566, 5501 HAGESUND
Tel: + 47 (4) 721244 *Fax:* + 47 (4) 721603
Contact: Ove Risanger

VESTREVISJON
Lars Hillsegt. 21, 5008 BERGEN
Tel: + 47 (5) 323800 *Fax:* + 47 (5) 327120
Contact: Bjørn Rasmussen

Total Number of Offices: 8

REVISOR-KONTORET A/S

Sandakervn 35b, Torshov, 0402 OSLO 4
Tel: + 47 (2) 222200
Fax: + 47 (2) 222333
Mailing Address: Postboks 4319, Torshov, 0402 OSLO 4

European Affiliation: Horwath International

SAMARBEIDENDE REVISORER A/S

Strandgt. 17, 2801 GJØVIK
Tel: + 47 (61) 75320
Fax: + 47 (61) 74450
Mailing Address: Postboks 398, 2801 GJØVIK

European Affiliation: Pannell Kerr Forster Worldwide

International Contact: Steinar Farstad

OTHER OFFICES

SAMARBEIDENDE REVISORER A/S
Smietorget, Postboks 79, 2750 GRAN
Tel: + 47 (63) 31688

SAMARBEIDENDE REVISORER A/S
Bogstadveien 50, 0366 OSLO 3
Tel: + 47 (2) 690010 *Fax:* + 47 (2) 690764

Total Number of Offices: 4

REVISJONSFIRMÆT VEEL, KARLSEN & CO

Fr. Nansens Plass 9, 0160 OSLO
Tel: + 47 (2) 422650
Fax: + 47 (2) 413097

European Affiliation: ATD International

International Contact: Richard Karlsen

Partners:	3
Professional staff:	5
Non-professional staff:	1
Total Staff:	**9**

CONTACT INFORMATION

Audit: Kåre Kjøllesdal
Tax (Corporate): Erik Veel

CLIENT SERVICES

Accountancy (General), Audit, Corporate Finance Advice, Management & Business Advice, Management Buy-outs, Mergers & Acquisitions, Taxation (Corporate)

Area: 92,072 sq km (33,549 sq miles)
Population: 10,350,000 (1987 estimate)
Density: 112.4 per sq km
Capital: Lisbon

GDP: Esc9.5 trn, US$63 bn
GDP per head: US$6,020
Inflation: 1990 - 12.8%
1991 - 11.0% (forecast)

Official and Spoken Language: Portuguese

Time: GMT (in Summer GMT + 1)
Telephone Dialling Code: +351

Currency: Escudo (Esc) = 100 centavos
Banking Hours: Generally 0830-1500 Monday-Friday. Some banks in Lisbon open 1600-2300 Monday-Friday
Professional accountancy body: Camara dos Revisores Officiais de Contas (CROS)

Corporate Tax Data

Information supplied by Richard Citron, international tax partner of Stoy Hayward.

The tax year; nature and rates of tax

The tax year is the calendar year.

Portuguese companies are generally liable to corporate income tax (imposto sobre orendimento das pessoas colectivas) of 36%, but there may also be a local surcharge of approximately 10% on the tax. Companies in Madeira and the Azores are exempt.

Residence and territoriality

Portuguese resident companies are liable to corporate income tax on their worldwide income. A company is treated as resident in Portugal if its head office or effective place of management is there.

The tax base

Method of computation. Taxable profits are based on a comparison of the net worth of the company at the beginning and end of the accounting period.

Disallowable items. All properly substantiated business expenses are deductible.Contributions to certain reserves are not allowable.

Exempt income/special deductions. Income from a branch in Macau is exempt. A provision for doubtful debts, at fixed percentages, is tax deductible. The 5% withheld on dividend and interest payments on account of the substitute inheritance and gift tax is deductible. Non-resident companies may set up tax-free operations in Madeira or the Azores.

Interest paid. Interest payable for business purposes is deductible. Interest paid to related parties is deductible only to the extent of arm's length rates.

Stock. Stock must be valued consistently according to sound commercial practice by the historic cost method. Where the market value of stock is lower ▷

than the cost, the difference may be transferred to a devaluation reserve. This transfer is deductible in computing taxable profits.

Depreciation. Tax depreciation is on the straight-line balance basis at the following rates: (1) electronic equipment 20%; (2) office buildings 2%; (3) machine tools 20%; (4) motor vehicles 14.28% - 25%. Where extraordinary wear and tear can be demonstrated, these rates can be increased by up to 50%. A reducing balance basis may be used at the taxpayer's option for tangible fixed assets.

Treatment of dividends

Dividends received from Portuguese companies. Dividends are received net of withholding tax and are taxable.

(1) Only 80% (60% proposed for 1992) of dividends on shares quoted in Portugal are liable to corporate income tax.
(2) Only 60% of dividends from newly privatised companies are liable for the first five years.
(3) A tax credit of 20% of the underlying corporate income tax paid by the distributing company is allowed against the recipient company's income tax liability.
(4) Under the affiliation privilege, 95% of dividends received from companies where the recipient company has held at least 25% of the share capital for a minimum of two years are exempt.
(5) All domestic dividend income is subject to the 5% substitute inheritance and gift tax.

Dividends received from abroad. Dividends received from abroad are liable to corporate income tax and the affiliation privilege does not apply. Where there is a treaty with the source country relief for foreign tax paid will be granted according to the terms of that treaty (normally by credit). Otherwise it will be treated as an expense.

Dividends paid to residents. Withholding tax (at rates of 15% to 25%) is deductible on dividends paid to domestic shareholders. In addition, the substitute inheritance and gift tax must be withheld at source.

Dividends paid to non-residents. The same rates of withholding tax, including the 5% substitute inheritance and gift tax (not reducible by treaty, non-creditable and non-deductible), are applicable to distributions to non-resident shareholders.

Anti-avoidance measures

Transfer pricing rules operate under which the tax authorities may adjust transactions between related parties to arm's length values.

Treatment of losses

Current period. Losses are automatically netted off against profits of the same period by virtue of the net worth basis (there is no carry back).

Future periods. Any aggregate unabsorbed loss may be carried forward for a maximum of five years.

Treatment of capital gains

Treatment. Capital gains are generally taxable as income.

Computation. Gains are computed by deducting cost from sale proceeds. Where the gain arises from the disposal of fixed assets held for more than two years, the cost is adjusted for inflation.

Rollover. Deferral of tax on capital gains on tangible fixed assets is available by rollover of the disposal proceeds against the cost of replacement tangible fixed assets acquired within two years. Rollover is also available for financial fixed assets (including shares). Gains realised directly by non-resident companies on the disposal of shares are exempt.

Treatment of groups

A holding company and its 91% subsidiaries (all of which must be resident in Portugal) can form a tax group, with permission from the tax authorities. Within a group, profits and losses may be pooled and dividends and interest may be paid free of withholding tax (but not of the 5% substitute inheritance tax deduction). Intra-group asset transfers are exempt from tax on capital gains.

Treatment of branches

The Portuguese branch of a non-resident company is taxed on the same basis as a resident company. Its taxable base is its profits derived from operations in Portugal, measured with respect to its Portuguese assets. Tax is paid at the general rate. There is no withholding tax on remittances of profit.

Other taxes

Taxes on income. Companies are liable to a local municipal tax of up to 10% of the corporate income tax liability in certain municipalities. A further tax on particular income (inter alia, dividends and interest) is the substitute inheritance and gift tax (5%).

Turnover taxes. There is a value added tax (imposto sobre o valor acrescentado). The standard rate is 17% (16% proposed for 1992); there is a reduced rate of 8% (5% proposed for 1992) and a luxury rate of 30%. Exports and basic foodstuffs are zero rated.

Payroll taxes. Employers social security contributions are payable at a rate of 24.5% on gross salary.

Property taxes. There is a property transfer tax, the rate of which is 10% for buildings and land for construction. Any other commercial property transfer is subject to a 8% rate.

Stamp duty. Charged on certain acts and documents at various rates.

ANTONIO ALMEIDA, BERNARDO E MURALHA

Rua Tomas Ribeiro 41, 3º dtº, 1000 LISBON
Tel: +*351* (1) 571635

European Affiliation: Midsnell International

International Contact: Antônio de Almeida

Partners:	3
Professional staff:	4
Non-professional staff:	2
Total Staff:	**9**

FEE INCOME

Year End: 31.12.90	**Esc**
Total:	**33,694,544**

CONTACT INFORMATION

Audit: Josê Muralha
Audit: Antônio Bernardo
Audit: Artemiu Vaz
Audit: Raul Almeida Alves
Audit: Rogerio Funseca
Administration: Antônio de Almeida

CLIENT SERVICES

Audit, Legal Functions, Management Control, Legal Certification of Accounts

Industry Specialisations: Construction, Electronic Industries, Food Products

MAJOR CLIENTS

BBV - Real Estate Group SA, Construcoes Têchicas SA, Pfizer Lab SA, Rank Xerox Ltd, Vitrohm Port Ltd

ALVES, COSTA & ASSOCIADOS SROC

Avenida da Repûblica 48, 1000 LISBON
Tel: +*351* (1) 793 8460
Fax: +*351* (1) 793 7074

European Affiliation: Moores Rowland International

Partners:	3
Professional staff:	19
Non-professional staff:	4
Total Staff:	**26**

FEE INCOME

Year End: 31.12.90	**Esc**	**%**
Accountancy & Audit:	56,000,000	70.0
Consultancy:	16,000,000	20.0
Tax:	4,000,000	5.0
Other:	4,000,000	5.0
Total:	**80,000,000**	

CONTACT INFORMATION

Managing Partner: Carlos Baptista da Costa
Managing Partner: Leopoldo Alves
Audit: Carlos Baptista da Costa
Management Consultancy: Leopoldo Alves

CLIENT SERVICES

Accountancy (General), Audit, Corporate Finance Advice, Management & Business Advice, Taxation (Corporate), Management Consultancy

Industry Specialisations: Construction, Distribution, Hotels, Forwarding, Manufacturing, Travel, Maritime Agencies, Stevedores

ARTHUR ANDERSEN & CO

Amoreiras Torre 1, 15, 1000 LISBON
Tel: +*351* (1) 387 0991
Fax: +*351* (1) 656446

European Affiliation: Arthur Andersen Worldwide

International Contact: T. David Sargison

CONTACT INFORMATION

Audit: T. David Sargison
Tax (Corporate): William T. Cunningham

CLIENT SERVICES

Accountancy (General), Audit, Computer Installation, Corporate Finance Advice, Insolvency & Corporate Restructuring, Litigation/Legal Services, Management & Business Advice, Management Buy-outs, Mergers & Acquisitions, Pensions Planning, Value for Money Studies, Taxation (Corporate), Taxation (International)

OTHER OFFICES

ARTHUR ANDERSEN & CO
Edificio Aviz, Avenida da Boavista 3523, 1, 4100 OPORTO
Tel: +*351* (2) 610 1179 *Fax:* +*351* (2) 610 1204

Total Number of Offices: 2

AUDITE - AUDITORIAS CONTABILISTICAS METÅDOS E ORGANIZACAO LDA

Rua Tomas Ribeiro 41, 4º Esq, 1000 LISBON
Tel: +*351* (1) 546245
Fax: +*351* (1) 352 6316

European Affiliation: Alliott Peirson International

Partners:	4
Professional staff:	13
Non-professional staff:	2
Total Staff:	**19**

FEE INCOME

Year End: 1990	**Esc (000)**	**%**
Accountancy & Audit:	41,600	92.2
Consultancy:	1,500	3.3
Tax:	2,000	4.4
Total:	**45,100**	

CONTACT INFORMATION

Accountancy (General): Josê Muralha
Insolvency & Tax: Dr. Jacques Almeida
Management Consultancy: Dr. Júlio Ferrolho
Accountancy & Audit: Dr. Júlio Ferrolho
Public Sector & Administration: Dr. Júlio Ferrolho

CLIENT SERVICES

Accountancy (General), Audit, Corporate Finance Advice, Insolvency & Corporate Restructuring, Litigation/Legal Services, Management & Business Advice, Management Buy-outs, Mergers & Acquisitions, Value for Money Studies, Taxation (Corporate), Taxation (International), Trust Settlement & Estates

MAJOR CLIENTS

Axergie Lda, Barros & Barros Lda, Capsulas Corao SA, Cavan SA, Cidadela SA, Colegio Principe Carlos Lda, Esquadria - Transf Madeiras Mucifal SA, Hidrowatt SA, Hispormedica - Mat, Cirurgia e Midcina Lda, Hotel de Turismo de Abrantes, Inst Nacional Cardiologia Preventiva, LPE - Lisboa, Publicidade Espectaculos Lda, Ministry of Employment/Social European Fund Dept, Pinto de Almedia Engenharia Lda, Plano X - Arquitectura e Engenharia Lda, Regit Lda, Sema Electronicas SA, Soberana SA, Texaco Portugal SA, Turama - Viagens e Turismo Lda ▷

Portugal

BARROSO, DA SILVA, DIAS, CASAVAO & ASOCIADOS

Avenida da República 50, 10th Floor, 1000 LISBON
Tel: +*351* (1) 793 5565
Fax: +*351* (1) 797 4433

European Affiliation: BDO Binder

International Contact: José Soares Barroso

Partners:	6
Professional staff:	62
Non-professional staff:	9
Total Staff:	77

FEE INCOME

Year End: 31.12.90	%
Accountancy & Audit:	84.0
Insolvency:	1.0
Consultancy:	12.0
Tax:	2.0
Other:	1.0

CONTACT INFORMATION
Chairman: Ernesto Ferreira da Silva
Managing Partner: Ernesto Ferreira da Silva
Management Consultancy: Ernesto Ferreira da Silva
Public Sector: Carlos Fontão de Carvalho
Accountancy & Audit: Manuel Rui Caseirão
Corporate Finance & Insolvency: Pedro Aleixo Dias
Tax (Corporate & International): José Soares Barroso
Audit: Paulo Sousa Ferreira

CLIENT SERVICES
Accountancy (General), Audit, Corporate Finance Advice, Insolvency & Corporate Restructuring, Litigation/Legal Services, Management & Business Advice, Management Buy-outs, Mergers & Acquisitions, Value for Money Studies, Taxation (Corporate), Taxation (International)

Industry Specialisations: Banking, Insurance, Broadcasting, European Community Financial Funds, Credit & Financial Institutions

MAJOR CLIENTS
AEG Portuguesa SA, Banco de Cabo Verde, Banco de Fomento E Exterior SA, Beirsdorf Portuguesa SA, Companhia de Seguros Império SA, CPR - Comp. Portuguesa Resseguro SA, Emptel SA (Siemens Group), Fabricas Triunfo SA, Grupo Centrel, Grupo Fnac, Iapmei, IPE - Investimentos E Par. Empres., Ministério Da Industria, Ministério Do Trabalho, Promindustria - Soc. Port. Cap. Risco SA, RTC - Radiotelevisao Comercial LDA, RTP - Radiotelevisao Portuguesa SA, Schering Portuguesa SA, Sopol SA, Soponata SA

OTHER OFFICES
BARROSO, DA SILVA, DIAS, CASAVAO & ASOCIADOS
Largo Eng. Antônio de Almeida 70, 1st Floor Sala 358, 4100 OPORTO
Tel: +*351* (2) 600 6135 *Fax:* +*351* (2) 600 1787
Contact: Dr. Ernesto Ferreira da Silva

Total Number of Offices: 2

BECKETT & CO

Largo Alves Rocadas, 8400 LAGOA
Tel: +*351* (82) 53195
Fax: +*351* (82) 53422

Partners:	2
Professional staff:	10
Non-professional staff:	3
Total Staff:	**15**

CONTACT INFORMATION
Managing Partner: Brian C.J. Beckett
Accountancy (General): Brian C.J. Beckett
Tax (Corporate): Dr. Joao Cascao

CLIENT SERVICES
Accountancy (General), Audit, Computer Installation, Management & Business Advice, Taxation (Corporate), Taxation (International), Trust Settlement & Estates, Technical Translations (Financial, Reports) - English/Portugese

OTHER OFFICES
BECKETT & CO
Avenida da Liberdade 192, 9º, 1200 LISBON
Tel: +*351* (1) 452 5008 *Fax:* +*351* (1) 546551
Contact: Duncan MacGregor

Total Number of Offices: 2

EUGÉNIO BRANCO - GESTAO E SERVIÇOS SA

Praça Francisco Sã Carneiro 293, 1º, 4200 PORTO
Tel: +*351* (2) 490276
Fax: +*351* (2) 496477

European Affiliation: Independent Accountants International

International Contact: Eugénio Branco

Partners:	6
Professional staff:	55
Non-professional staff:	10
Total Staff:	71

FEE INCOME

Year End: 31.12.90	**US$**	%
Accountancy & Audit:	520,000	26.0
Consultancy:	340,000	17.0
Tax:	800,000	40.0
Other:	340,000	17.0
Total:	**2,000,000**	

CONTACT INFORMATION
Chairman: Eugénio Branco
Managing Partner: Eugénio Branco
Accountancy (General): Ana Maria Pinto
Audit: Mário Eduardo Sousa
Management Consultancy: Joao Paulo Moreira
Tax (Corporate): Helder Borges
Tax & Administration: Eugénio Branco
Human Resources/Training: Virginia Vieira
Data Processing: Isabel Sousa

CLIENT SERVICES
Accountancy (General), Audit, Computer Installation, Corporate Finance Advice, Litigation/Legal Services, Management & Business Advice, Mergers & Acquisitions, Taxation (Corporate), Taxation (International)

Total Number of Offices: 2

CACHUDO NUNES & ASSOCIADOS CONSULTORES DE GESTAO E INVESTIMENTO LDA

Rua Sampaio e Pina 58, 2º dto, 1000 LISBON
Tel: +*351* (1) 387 1736
Fax: +*351* (1) 686273

European Affiliation: Summit International Associates Inc

International Contact: Luís Cachudo Nunes

Partners:	2
Professional staff:	10
Non-professional staff:	3
Total Staff:	**15**

FEE INCOME

Year End: 31.12.90	US$
Total:	650,000

CONTACT INFORMATION
Chairman: Luís Cachudo Nunes
Managing Partner: Luís Cachudo Nunes
Accountancy (General): Manuel Correia Amaro
Audit: Duncan MacGregor
Corporate Finance: António Medeiros
Tax (Corporate): Caetano Augusto
Consultancy & Administration: Joao Vicente

CLIENT SERVICES
Accountancy (General), Audit, Corporate Finance Advice, Insolvency & Corporate Restructuring, Litigation/Legal Services, Management & Business Advice, Management Buy-outs, Mergers & Acquisitions, Taxation (Corporate)

Industry Specialisations: Construction, Public Works, Oil, Chemical, Ceramics, Tourism, Marble, Merchant Banking, Plastics

MAJOR CLIENTS
Constroibem - Soc. Ind. Const. Turismo SA, Elf - Lubrificantes de Portugal Lda, Empetrol Portugal - Combustiveis p/Navios Lda, ETC - Terminais Marítimos SA, Guia - Soc. Const. e Turismo SA, Oxinorte - Oxigénio do Norte SA, Soc. Portugesa do Ar Líquido SA

OTHER OFFICES
CACHUDO NUNES & ASSOCIADOS
Rua da Sabrosa 91, 1º D, 4300 OPORTO
Tel: + *351* (2) 510 2004 *Fax:* + *351* (2) 510 2003
Contact: Manuel Correia Amaro

Total Number of Offices: 2

A.M. CALADO CORTES
Third Floor, Rua de Crucifixo 28, 1100 LISBON
Tel: + *351* (1) 327902
Fax: + *351* (1) 371477

European Affiliation: INPACT - International Network of Professional Accountants

International Contact: A.M. Calado Cortes

CCA - CAIANO PEREIRA, CONSULTORES ASSOCIADOS LDA
Rua David de Sousa 10, r/c Esq, 1000 LISBON
Tel: + *351* (1) 793 5091
Fax: + *351* (1) 793 5188

European Affiliation: Urbach Hacker Young International

International Contact: Carlos Lisboa Nunes

Partners:	4
Professional staff:	25
Non-professional staff:	5
Total Staff:	**34**

FEE INCOME

Year End: 1990	US$	%
Accountancy & Audit:	605,000	55.0
Insolvency:	5,000	5.0
Consultancy:	390,000	30.0
Other:	100,000	10.0
Total:	**1,100,000**	

CONTACT INFORMATION
Managing Partner: Carlos Caiano Pereira
Corporate Finance: Carlos Lisboa Nunes
Insolvency: Alvaro Vistas Oliveira
Accountancy, Audit & Tax: Carlos Lisboa Nunes
Administration & Public Sector: Carlos Caiano Pereira
Audit: José Bragança
Consultancy: Anabela Reis
Organization: Clara Rebelo

CLIENT SERVICES
Accountancy (General), Audit, Corporate Finance Advice, Insolvency & Corporate Restructuring, Management & Business Advice, Management Buy-outs, Mergers & Acquisitions, Taxation (Corporate), Taxation (International)

Industry Specialisations: Ceramic, Alcohol, Transport

MAJOR CLIENTS
APC, CA Capris de Ferro, Ceres, Cinca, Coonapor, CTT, Docapesca, Ricardo Gallo, ICEP, IEFP, Ine, Interpress, Metropolitano de Lisboa, Ministerio Transportes da Guine, Poceram, Portucel, Setenave, Sistel, Sociedade A'gua do Luso, Vista Alegre SA

CIC CENTRO DE INFORMATICA E CONTABILIDADE LDA
Rua Conde de Sabugosa 15, 2º-A, 1700 LISBON
Tel: + *351* (1) 804014
Fax: + *351* (1) 803291

European Affiliation: DFK International

International Contact: Fernando Mendes

CONSULTEAM/INTERAUDIT
Rua Tomás Ribeiro 50, 1º, 1000 LISBON
Tel: + *351* (1) 543770
Fax: + *351* (1) 535324

European Affiliation: Nexia International

International Contact: H. Lisboa Afonso

Partners:	5
Professional staff:	16
Non-professional staff:	4
Total Staff:	**25**

FEE INCOME

Year End: 31.12.90	Esc	%
Accountancy & Audit:	59,000	43.0
Consultancy:	75,000	54.0
Tax:	4,000	3.0
Total:	**138,000**	

CONTACT INFORMATION
Managing Partner: Francisco Brites
Managing Partner: Jose Paiva Novo
Accountancy (General): Carlos Pinto Silva
Audit: H. Lisboa Afonso
Insolvency: Francisco Brites
Management Consultancy: Jose Paiva Novo
Tax (Corporate): Joaquim Ribeiro Almeida

CLIENT SERVICES
Accountancy (General), Audit, Insolvency & Corporate Restructuring, Management & Business Advice, Mergers & Acquisitions, Taxation (Corporate)

OTHER OFFICES
CONSULTEAM/INTERAUDIT
Pr. Alexandre Herculano 22, 48A, 8000 FARO
Tel: + *351* (89) 21589
Contact: J.A. Paiva Novo

Total Number of Offices: 2

COOPERS & LYBRAND LDA

Av Antonio Josẽ D'Almeida SF 2c, 1000 LISBON
Tel: +351 (1) 793 0023
Fax: +351 (1) 767998
Mailing Address: P.O. Box 1910, 1004 LISBON CODEX

European Affiliation: Coopers & Lybrand Europe

International Contact: William H. Woolston

Partners:	10
Professional staff:	200
Non-professional staff:	40
Total Staff:	**250**

CONTACT INFORMATION
Chairman: William H. Woolston
Tax (Corporate): J.S. Jorge
Accountancy, Audit & Tax: C.M. Bernardes
Corporate Finance & Consultancy: J.P. Esteves
Administration & Public Sector: J.B. Nunes
Manufacturing & Logistics: I. Bahar
Human Resources: J. Russinho
Information Technology: P. Harowick

CLIENT SERVICES
Accountancy (General), Audit, Computer Installation, Corporate Finance Advice, Management & Business Advice, Mergers & Acquisitions, Taxation (Corporate), Taxation (International), Management Consultancy

Industry Specialisations: Tourism & Leisure, Banking, Pharmaceutical, Insurance, Automotive, Communications

OTHER OFFICES
COOPERS & LYBRAND LDA
Rua Oliveira Monteiro 168, 4000 PORTO
Tel: +351 (2) 699497 *Fax:* +351 (2) 692892
Contact: M.H. Sismeiro

Total Number of Offices: 2

JOHN DE LAROQUE

Vivenda do Alto da Bonita, Rua do Alto da Bonita, Ranholas, 2710 SINTRA
Tel: +351 (1) 923 0448
Fax: +351 (1) 827676

European Affiliation: Moores Rowland International

Partners:	1
Professional staff:	2
Non-professional staff:	4
Total Staff:	7

CONTACT INFORMATION
Managing Partner: John de Laroque

CLIENT SERVICES
All Services

DELOITTE ROSS TOHMATSU

Avenida das Descobertas, Galerias Alto da Barra, Piso 3, 2780 OEIRAS
Tel: +351 (1) 441 1134
Fax: +351 (1) 441 1750

European Affiliation: DRT International

International Contact: Stewart Siewert

Partners:	10
Professional staff:	125
Non-professional staff:	26
Total Staff:	**161**

CLIENT SERVICES
Accountancy (General), Audit, Computer Installation, Corporate Finance Advice, Insolvency & Corporate Restructuring, Life & Risk Assurance, Litigation/Legal Services, Management & Business Advice, Management Buy-outs, Mergers & Acquisitions, Pensions Planning, Value for Money Studies, Taxation (Corporate), Taxation (International), Trust Settlement & Estates, EEC Consultancy

MAJOR CLIENTS
Banco Pinto & Sotto Mayor, BASF, Carris, Centraicer, Cia de Seguros Bonança, Construções Tecnicas, ESA - Euro Services Alimontares, Mabor, Neste, Prazol

Total Number of Offices: 3

ERNST & YOUNG & CIA

Avda. Antonio Augusto de Aguiar 21, 3º E, 1000 LISBON
Tel: +351 (1) 352 8889
Fax: +351 (1) 352 8271
Mailing Address: Apartado 1137, 1003 LISBON CODEX

European Affiliation: Ernst & Young Europe

International Contact: William South

Partners:	18
Professional staff:	303
Non-professional staff:	62
Total Staff:	**383**

FEE INCOME

Year End: 30.06.91	**Esc**	**%**
Accountancy & Audit:	1,300,000,000	63.0
Consultancy:	400,000,000	19.0
Tax:	250,000,000	12.0
Other:	125,000,000	6.0
Total:	**2,075,000,000**	

CONTACT INFORMATION
Managing Partner: Spencer Hart
Corporate Finance: William South
Management Consultancy: Teresa Cochito
Administration: Lucilia Estevão
Tax (Corporate): Fernando Bras
Tax (International): Albino Jacinto
Insurance: Jose Placido
Accountancy & Audit: Manuel Lima
Banking: William South

CLIENT SERVICES
Accountancy (General), Audit, Corporate Finance Advice, Life & Risk Assurance, Management & Business Advice, Mergers & Acquisitions, Taxation (Corporate), Taxation (International), Information Services

OTHER OFFICES
ERNST & YOUNG & CIA
Rua Dr. Fernao de Ornelas 35, 3ºD, 9000 FUNCHAL (Madeira)
Tel: +351 (91) 21492 *Fax:* +351 (91) 33228

ERNST & YOUNG & CIA
Rua do Melo 44, 2º, 9500 PONTA DELGADA (Azores)
Tel: +351 (96) 22113 *Fax:* +351 (96) 22113

ERNST & YOUNG & CIA
Rua Júlio Dinis 891, 3º, 4000 PORTO
Tel: +351 (2) 600 2015 *Fax:* +351 (2) 600 0004

Total Number of Offices: 4

GRANT THORNTON & KENNARD LDA

Avenue Miguel Bombarda 21, 3º esq, 1000 LISBON
Tel: +351 (1) 352 6329
Fax: +351 (1) 541559

European Affiliation: Grant Thornton International

International Contact: John Kennard

Partners:	1
Professional staff:	5
Non-professional staff:	2
Total Staff:	**8**

FEE INCOME

Year End: 31.12.90	**US$**	**%**
Accountancy & Audit:	97,000	71.7
Consultancy:	29,000	21.7
Tax:	6,000	4.3
Other:	3,000	2.3
Total:	**135,000**	

CONTACT INFORMATION

Managing Partner: John Kennard
Management Consultancy: Edward Godfrey

CLIENT SERVICES

Accountancy (General), Audit, Management & Business Advice, Mergers & Acquisitions, Taxation (Corporate), Taxation (International)

HORWATH CONSULTING (TURISMO) LDA

Rua Joao da Silva, Lote 33, 1900 LISBON
Tel: *+351* (1) 847 2703
Fax: *+351* (1) 847 2718

European Affiliation: Horwath International

International Contact: Humberto Leal

Partners:	2
Professional staff:	16
Non-professional staff:	6
Total Staff:	**24**

FEE INCOME

Year End: 1990	**Esc**	**%**
Accountancy & Audit:	42,000,000	10.0
Consultancy:	306,200,000	73.0
Tax:	16,800,000	4.0
Other:	55,000,000	13.0
Total:	**420,000,000**	

CONTACT INFORMATION

Chairman: Humberto Leal
Managing Partner: José Curvelo
Management Consultancy: Humberto Leal
Public Sector: José Curvelo
Real Estate: Américo Duque
Tourism: Marc Finney
Golf: Gregg Rockett

CLIENT SERVICES

Audit, Management & Business Advice, Mergers & Acquisitions, Taxation (Corporate), Appraisal of Tourism Facilities, Market & Feasibility Studies, Marketing Plans & Trend Analysis

Industry Specialisations: Tourism, Golf, Hotels, Real Estate

MAJOR CLIENTS

BANIF - Banco Internacional do Funchal, Blandy Brothers, Buckingham Portugal S.G.P.S. Lda, Camara Municipal de Castelo Branco, Comissao Regional de Turismo Costa Azul, Direcçao Geral do Turismo, ESSI - Espirito Santo Soc. de Investimentos, Fundo de Turismo, Lusotur, Soc. Financeira de Turismo, Multinvest-Invest. Imobiliarios Lds, M-N Invest. Hoteleiros e Turisticos SA, NOGA - Hotel de Lisboa, NOKIA - Electronica de Consumo, Novotel, Orion SA, SODIM, SOPETE, Tomen Corporation, Total Finance, United Investments (Portugal)

KPMG PEAT MARWICK

Avenida da República 24, 1000 LISBON
Tel: *+351* (1) 352 2377
Fax: *+351* (1) 315 3036

European Affiliation: KPMG

Partners:	5
Professional staff:	148
Non-professional staff:	37
Total Staff:	**190**

FEE INCOME

Year End: 30.09.90	**Esc**	**%**
Accountancy & Audit:	657,478,000	69.0
Consultancy:	153,646,000	16.0
Tax:	119,420,000	13.0
Other:	15,662,000	2.0
Total:	**946,206,000**	

CONTACT INFORMATION

Managing Partner: Neil Durie
Accountancy (General): Clive Brooks
Audit & Administration: Neil Durie
Corporate Finance & Insolvency: Philip Arnold
Public Sector & Privatisations: Antonio P. Catalao
Tax: Antonio Proença

CLIENT SERVICES

Accountancy (General), Audit, Computer Installation, Corporate Finance Advice, Insolvency & Corporate Restructuring, Management & Business Advice, Mergers & Acquisitions, Value for Money Studies, Taxation (Corporate), Taxation (International)

Industry Specialisations: Banking & Finance, Leisure & Tourism, Pharmaceuticals

MAJOR CLIENTS

Allied Lyons, Banco Bilbao-Vizcaya, Banco Comercial Português, Banco Pinto & Sotto Mayor, Banque Nationale de Paris, Buckingham PLC, Calouste Gulbenkian Foundation, Daimler-Benz, Deutsche Bank, Empresa de Electricidade da Madeira, Grand Metropolitan, Grundig, ICI, Nedlloyd, Philips, Reader's Digest, SAPEC, Siemens, TAP - Air Portugal, Valmet

OTHER OFFICES

KPMG PEAT MARWICK
Rue 5 de Outubro 61, 1º D, 8500 PORTIMAO
Tel: *+351* (1) 352 2377 *Fax:* *+351* (1) 315 3036

KPMG PEAT MARWICK
Avenida da Boavista 3477 - 3521, 1st Floor, 4100 PORTO
Tel: *+351* (2) 617 6167 *Fax:* *+351* (2) 617 7821

Total Number of Offices: 3

DUNCAN MacGREGOR & COMPANY

Rua Projectada, Escola Secundaria da Parede, Lote 7, 1º esq, 2775 PAREDE
Tel: *+351* (1) 452 5008
Fax: *+351* (1) 546551

Partners:	1
Professional staff:	2
Non-professional staff:	1
Total Staff:	**4**

▷

Portugal

FEE INCOME

Year End: 31.12.90	%
Accountancy & Audit:	35.0
Consultancy:	20.0
Tax:	20.0
Other:	25.0

CONTACT INFORMATION

Managing Partner: Duncan MacGregor

CLIENT SERVICES

All Services

MOORE STEPHENS

Av Freimiguel Contreiras 54, 10º, 1700 LISBON
Tel: +*351* (1) 734839
Fax: +*351* (1) 771148

European Affiliation: Moore Stephens

International Contact: Antonio Gonçalves Monterio

Total Number of Offices: 2

PATRICIO, MIMOSO E MENDES JORGE

Rua Nogueira e Sousa 8, 1º, 1100 LISBON
Tel: +*351* (1) 355 4459
Fax: +*351* (1) 356 1952

European Affiliation: DRM Internationally

International Contact: Joaquim Patrício da Silva

Partners:	3
Professional staff:	21
Non-professional staff:	9
Total Staff:	**33**

FEE INCOME

Year End: 31.12.91	**Esc**	%
Accountancy & Audit:	34,692,000	44.0
Insolvency:	790,000	1.0
Consultancy:	3,940,000	5.0
Tax:	2,400,000	3.0
Other:	36,952,000	47.0
Total:	**78,774,000**	

CONTACT INFORMATION

Chairman: Joaquim Patrício da Silva
Managing Partner: Joaquim Patrício da Silva
Insolvency: Joaquim Patrício da Silva
Management Consultancy: Joao F. Mendes Jorge
Management Consultancy: Alberto Arnauth Ribeiro
Administration: Augusto Brites Mimoso
Public Sector: Rui Neto Isidoro

CLIENT SERVICES

Accountancy (General), Audit, Computer Installation, Corporate Finance Advice, Insolvency & Corporate Restructuring, Life & Risk Assurance, Litigation/Legal Services, Management & Business Advice, Management Buy-outs, Mergers & Acquisitions, Pensions Planning, Value for Money Studies, Taxation (Corporate), Taxation (International), Trust Settlement & Estates, Feasibility Studies, Management Consultancy

Industry Specialisations: Maritime, Rail, Road, Shipbuilding, Engineering, Chemicals, Textiles, Banking, Insurance, Mining, Hotels

MAJOR CLIENTS

APEC - Agro SA, Banco Espirito Santo e Comercial de Lisboa, Banco Manufacturers Hanover (Portugal) SA, COSEC - Companhia de Seguros de Creditos, Laprovar SA (Pepsico), Lisnave - Estaleiros Navais de Lisboa, Mercedes-Benz Portugal SA, Occidental Holding SGPS SA (Insurance), Sacor Maritima SA, Somincor - Sociedade Mineira SA

OTHER OFFICES

AUDIOCONSULTE LDA
Rua Nogueira E Sousa 8, 1º, 1100 LISBON
Tel: +*351* (1) 355 4459 *Fax:* +*351* (1) 356 1952
Contact: Joaquim Patrício da Silva

Total Number of Offices: 2

PRICE WATERHOUSE

Avenida Eng. Duarte Pacheco 19, 8º, 1000 LISBON
Tel: +*351* (1) 387 8540
Fax: +*351* (1) 387 8651

European Affiliation: Price Waterhouse

Partners:	12
Professional staff:	202
Non-professional staff:	42
Total Staff:	**256**

FEE INCOME

Year End: 30.06.90	**Esc**	%
Accountancy & Audit:	720,000,000	48.0
Consultancy:	575,000,000	39.0
Tax:	195,000,000	13.0
Total:	**1,490,000,000**	

CONTACT INFORMATION

Managing Partner: José M. Pena
Audit: Paul C.Q. Mallett
Management Consultancy: Peter N. Mollet
Tax (Corporate): John P. Duggan
Tax (Corporate & Legal): Belarmino Martins

CLIENT SERVICES

Accountancy (General), Audit, Computer Installation, Corporate Finance Advice, Insolvency & Corporate Restructuring, Litigation/Legal Services, Management & Business Advice, Management Buy-outs, Mergers & Acquisitions, Value for Money Studies, Taxation (Corporate), Taxation (International), Management Consultancy

OTHER OFFICES

PRICE WATERHOUSE
Rua Marquês de Subserra 10, 1000 LISBON
Tel: +*351* (1) 655451 *Fax:* +*351* (1) 655411
Contact: Antônio Nunes

PRICE WATERHOUSE
Parque Itália, Rua Júlio Dinis 728, 9º D, 4000 PORTO
Tel: +*351* (2) 600 2684 *Fax:* +*351* (2) 600 4336

PRICE WATERHOUSE
Rua Gonçalo Cristóvao 217, 13º, 4000 PORTO
Tel: +*351* (2) 312614 *Fax:* +*351* (2) 319985
Contact: Eugénio Ferreira

Total Number of Offices: 4

TECHNOPLANO

Avenida Joa Crisostomo 66, 4 E, 1000 LISBON
Tel: +*351* (1) 570994
Fax: +*351* (1) 563734

European Affiliation: A.E.E. International

International Contact: N. Montes

Area: 504,782 sq km (194,896 sq miles)
Population: 39,209,765 (1988 estimate)
Density: 77.7 per sq km
Capital: Madrid

GDP: Pta34.5 trn, US$532 bn
GDP per head: US$13,450
Inflation: 1990 - 7.0%
1991 - 7.0% (forecast)

Official and Spoken Languages: Spanish (Castilian), Catalan, Galician, Basque

Time: GMT + 1 (in Summer GMT + 2). The Canaries GMT (in Summer GMT + 1)
Telephone Dialling Code: + 34

Currency: Peseta (Pta)
Banking Hours: 0900-1400 Monday-Friday. 0900-1300 Saturday
Professional accountancy body: Instituto de Censores Jurados de Cuentas de Espana (ICJCE)

Corporate Tax Data

Information supplied by Richard Citron, international tax partner of Stoy Hayward.

The tax year; nature and rates of tax

The tax year is the calendar year.

Corporation tax (impuesto sobre sociedades) is levied at a flat rate of 35% on both distributed and undistributed income. Special tax regimes operate in Navarre, the Basque country, Ceuta and Melilla. Special tax rates apply to investment fund companies (1%) and those involved in hydrocarbon exploration (40%).

Residence and territoriality

Spanish resident companies are taxed on their worldwide income and gains. All companies incorporated in Spain are treated as resident there, as are foreign incorporated companies having their registered office or effective centre of management and administration in Spain.

The tax base

Method of calculation. Taxable profits are based on the profit as reported in the accounts. Taxable income includes dividends, capital gains and non-trading income. The revenue authorities retain the option to assess a company on the increase in its net worth.

Disallowable items. The major disallowable items are some bonuses etc to shareholders and board members and non-charitable gifts. There are special rules for bad and doubtful debts.

Exempt income and special deductions. For dividends from substantial participations, see below. Provisions for a fall in value of investments and pensions are generally allowable.

Interest paid. Interest is deductible on an accruals basis. Interest payable to foreign lenders must obtain government approval to be tax deductible. ▷

Stock. Stock is valued at the lower of cost and market value.

Depreciation. There are three recognised methods of depreciation: (i) a straightline basis at rates published in official tables (eg. machinery at 10%, industrial buildings at 3%); (ii) a reducing balance basis for new tangible assets with a life of more than three years; (iii) on an individual basis proposed by the company and approved by the authorities. An investment credit of 5% is additionally available on the purchase of new assets. The sum of all investment credits is limited to 20% of the company's corporation tax liability.

Treatment of dividends

Dividends received from Spanish companies. These form part of taxable income and are subject to 25% withholding tax, which serves as a tax credit for the recipient company. However, where the recipient company has had a holding of more than 25% throughout the previous year, or is a portfolio investment company, the dividends are wholly exempt. Where the holding is 25% or less, there is a 50% exemption.

Dividends received from abroad. These form part of taxable income and credit is obtained for foreign taxes directly payable on the dividend (ie withholding only).

Dividends paid. The company must withhold tax at 25% from dividends to residents and non-residents alike.

Anti-avoidance

The profits of some companies can be imputed directly to their shareholders: the companies involved are essentially holding companies and portfolio investment companies controlled by a single family group or by ten or fewer persons and companies serving as vehicles for carrying on a profession.

Treatment of losses

Current period. Trading losses may be set off against income (but not capital gains) of the current period (there is no carry back). Capital losses may be set off against capital gains only.

Future periods. Trading losses may be carried forward for a maximum of five years. Capital losses may be carried forward for set off against capital gains.

Treatment of capital gains

Treatment. Capital gains are taxed as income.

Computation. The gain is computed by deducting the net book (depreciated) value from the sale proceeds. Costs of sale are also deductible.

Rollover. Rollover is available for tangible business assets if reinvested in assets of a similar type within two (sometimes four) years.

Treatment of groups

The results of a group of companies may be consolidated for tax purposes, if permitted by the tax authorities. Such a group must be headed by a Spanish resident company and consist of 91% subsidiaries, which have been owned for a minimum of two years. There is no withholding tax on dividends or interest paid within a tax group.

Treatment of branches

Spanish branches are essentially treated in the same way as Spanish resident companies and are liable on assets located in Spain. Remittances of profits are generally free of withholding tax.

Other taxes

A surcharge of 1.5% of the corporation tax is payable to the local chamber of commerce. The surcharge is deductible for corporation tax purposes.

Taxes on capital. There is a tax of 1% on capital contributions to Spanish companies and branches.

Turnover taxes. Value added tax (impuesto sobre el valor anadido) is payable on the supply of goods and services. There is a standard rate of 12%, a reduced rate of 6% and a luxury rate of 33%. Exports are zero rated.

Payroll taxes. Social security premiums are payable. The general charge is 24%.

There is a wide variety of local taxes, such as a business licence tax, an opening licence tax, a construction licence tax and a property tax (contribucion). There is a planned major revision of the local tax system with effect from 1 January 1992.

A.E.A. AUDITORES DE EMPRESAS ASOCIADOS SA

Alfonso XII 18, 20, 28014 MADRID
Tel: + *34* (1) 5219671
Fax: + *34* (1) 5216524

European Affiliation: INPACT - International Network of Professional Accountants

International Contact: Luis Felipe Suarez-Olea Martinez

CONTACT INFORMATION
Audit: Luis Felipe Suarez-Olea Martinez
Management Consultancy: Fernando Magnet
Tax (Corporate): Manuel Ibarra

CLIENT SERVICES
All Services

ALBERT & ASOCIADOS, ABOGADOS GESCONTROL AUDITORES SA

Espalter 13, 2º izqda, 28014 MADRID
Tel: + *34* (1) 4203319
Fax: + *34* (1) 4203411

European Affiliation: Alliott Peirson International

International Contact: Juan C. Albert Gómez

ALCAIN Y RIBA AUDITORES SA

Plaza Francesc Macia 3, 2-1, 08021 BARCELONA
Tel: + *34* (3) 4146390
Fax: + *34* (3) 4143854

European Affiliation: INPACT - International Network of Professional Accountants

International Contact: Jorge de Riba Solderila

ALVAREZ, MOLINERO & CIA

C/Ferraz 28, 3 izqda, 28008 MADRID
Tel: + *34* (1) 5417084
Fax: + *34* (1) 5421719

European Affiliation: Morison International

International Contact: Pascual G. Diaz

Partners:	5
Professional staff:	5
Non-professional staff:	4
Total Staff:	**14**

CONTACT INFORMATION
Managing Partner: Abdón Fernandez Cabrero
Accountancy & Systems/Computers: Arsenio Gómez Otero
Audit & Legal Services: Pascual G. Diaz
Corporate Finance & Marketing: Luis Alvarez Garcia de Uribarri
Tax: Abdón Fernandez Cabrero

CLIENT SERVICES
All Services

Industry Specialisations: Mining, Shipping, Airlines, State Enterprises, Fishing, Transport

---

ARTHUR ANDERSEN & CO

Raimundo Fernández Villaverde 65, Edificio Windsor, 28003 MADRID
Tel: + *34* (1) 5970000
Fax: + *34* (1) 5566469

European Affiliation: Arthur Andersen Worldwide

International Contact: Enrique Alvarez

CONTACT INFORMATION
Audit: Enrique Alvarez
Tax (Corporate): Alberto Terol Esteban

CLIENT SERVICES
Accountancy (General), Audit, Computer Installation, Corporate Finance Advice, Insolvency & Corporate Restructuring, Litigation/Legal Services, Management & Business Advice, Management Buy-outs, Mergers & Acquisitions, Pensions Planning, Value for Money Studies, Taxation (Corporate), Taxation (International)

OTHER OFFICES

ARTHUR ANDERSEN & CO
Avenida Maissonave 28-bis, planta 3ª, 03003 ALICANTE
Tel: + *34* (65) 111770 *Fax:* + *34* (65) 228967

ARTHUR ANDERSEN & CO
Avenida Diagonal 654, 08034 BARCELONA
Tel: + *34* (3) 2051012 *Fax:* + *34* (3) 2051250

ARTHUR ANDERSEN & CO
Rodriguez Arias 15, 4 y 5, 48008 BILBAO
Tel: + *34* (4) 4447000 *Fax:* + *34* (4) 4447430i

ARTHUR ANDERSEN & CO
Santa Catalina 11, 2, Edificio Las Nieves, 15003 LA CORUÑA
Tel: + *34* (81) 220916 *Fax:* + *34* (81) 227116

ARTHUR ANDERSEN & CO
Avenida de la Constitucion 22a, 18012 GRANADA
Tel: + *34* (58) 288967 *Fax:* + *34* (58) 289704

ARTHUR ANDERSEN & CO
Hilera 8, II 2D, 29007 MALAGA
Tel: + *34* (52) 276454 *Fax:* + *34* (52) 277740

ARTHUR ANDERSEN & CO
Gil de Jaz 3, 33004 OVIEDO
Tel: + *34* (85) 253400 *Fax:* + *34* (85) 244511

ARTHUR ANDERSEN & CO
Barón de Pinopar 22, 5, 07012 PALMA DE MALLORCA
Tel: + *34* (71) 719929 *Fax:* + *34* (71) 710098

ARTHUR ANDERSEN & CO
Avenida Pio XXII 4, 1, 31008 PAMPLONA
Tel: + *34* (48) 170086 *Fax:* + *34* (48) 172791

ARTHUR ANDERSEN & CO
Avenida Infanta Cristina 11, 20008 SAN SEBASTIAN
Tel: + *34* (43) 217033 *Fax:* + *34* (43) 218479

ARTHUR ANDERSEN & CO
Avenida de Blas Infante 8, 41011 SEVILLE
Tel: + *34* (5) 4456811 *Fax:* + *34* (5) 4459975

ARTHUR ANDERSEN & CO
Pascual y Genis 1, 46002 VALENCIA
Tel: + *34* (6) 3529125 *Fax:* + *34* (6) 3519884

ARTHUR ANDERSEN & CO
Zúñiga 2, 47001 VALLADOLID
Tel: + *34* (83) 350866 *Fax:* + *34* (83) 372328

ARTHUR ANDERSEN & CO
Policarpo Sanz 3, 6, 36202 VIGO
Tel: + *34* (86) 433766 *Fax:* + *34* (86) 430316

ARTHUR ANDERSEN & CO
Plaza de Aragon 10, 50004 ZARAGOZA
Tel: + *34* (76) 214675 *Fax:* + *34* (76) 235540

Total Number of Offices: 16

▷

Spain

A.T.D. AUDITORES SA

C/Claudio Coello 20, 2ºD, 28001 MADRID
Tel: +*34* (1) 5780739
Fax: +*34* (1) 5775228

European Affiliation: Affiliated Conference of Practising Accountants International (ACPA)

International Contact: José Manuel Gredilla Bastos

Partners:	4
Professional staff:	10
Non-professional staff:	2
Total Staff:	**16**

CONTACT INFORMATION

Accountancy & Public Sector: Justo Varona Rojo
Audit & Corporate Finance: José Manuel Gredilla Bastos
Consultancy & Administration: José Maria Gredilla Bastos
Tax: Tomas Pedreno Bey

CLIENT SERVICES

Accountancy (General), Audit, Corporate Finance Advice, Management & Business Advice, Mergers & Acquisitions, Taxation (Corporate), Taxation (International), Management Consultancy

OTHER OFFICES

A.T.D. AUDITORES SA
Cecilio Metelo 7, 07003 PALMA
Tel: +*34* (71) 721377 *Fax:* +*34* (71) 727902

Total Number of Offices: 2

AUDIGRUP AUDITORS ASSOCIATS SCR

Dr. Carulla 34b, 08017 BARCELONA
Tel: +*34* (3) 2125566
Fax: +*34* (3) 4340536

International Contact: Manuel Ventura

Partners:	4
Professional staff:	9
Non-professional staff:	7
Total Staff:	**20**

FEE INCOME

Year End: 1990	%
Accountancy & Audit:	55.0
Consultancy:	15.0
Tax:	20.0
Other:	10.0

CONTACT INFORMATION

Accountancy (General): Manuel Ventura
Audit: Anna Calvet
Management Consultancy: Jordi Arrau
Tax (Corporate): Pere Cuyas
Human Resources Consulting: Ivette Noguera

CLIENT SERVICES

Accountancy (General), Audit, Computer Installation, Corporate Finance Advice, Life & Risk Assurance, Litigation/Legal Services, Mergers & Acquisitions, Taxation (Corporate), Management Consultancy

OTHER OFFICES

CENTRO ADIMINISTRATIVO DE EMPRESAS SL
Major 34, 2º, 08221 TERRASSA
Tel: +*34* (3) 7891585 *Fax:* +*34* (3) 7889208
Contact: Jordi Arrau

Total Number of Offices: 2

AUDIHISPANA

Avenida Pau Casals 13-15, 08021 BARCELONA
Tel: +*34* (3) 4144776
Fax: +*34* (3) 2021723

European Affiliation: Nexia International

International Contact: Alberto Ribas

Partners:	23
Professional staff:	285
Non-professional staff:	90
Total Staff:	**398**

FEE INCOME

Year End: 31.12.90	**Pta**	%
Accountancy & Audit:	555,000,000	18.0
Insolvency:	650,000,000	21.0
Consultancy:	475,000,000	16.0
Tax:	1,350,000,000	45.0
Total:	**3,030,000,000**	

CONTACT INFORMATION

Managing Partner: Alberto Ribas
Accountancy (General): Donato Moreno
Audit: Alejandro Martinez
Insolvency: Javier Castrodeza
Management Consultancy: Oscar Pierre
Tax (Corporate): Rafael Fontana
Tax (International): Enrique Picatol

CLIENT SERVICES

Accountancy (General), Audit, Computer Installation, Corporate Finance Advice, Insolvency & Corporate Restructuring, Life & Risk Assurance, Litigation/Legal Services, Management & Business Advice, Management Buy-outs, Mergers & Acquisitions, Pensions Planning, Value for Money Studies, Taxation (Corporate), Taxation (International), Trust Settlement & Estates, International Cash Management

OTHER OFFICES

AUDIHISPANA
Colon de Larreategui 30, 48009 BILBAO
Tel: +*34* (4) 4237492 *Fax:* +*34* (4) 4242341

AUDIHISPANA SUR
Plaza San Severiano 1, 1ºK (nucleo 3), 11007 CADIZ
Tel: +*34* (56) 278317 *Fax:* +*34* (56) 278403
Contact: Antonio Rosado

AUDIHISPANA
San Agustin 3, 3º, 28014 MADRID
Tel: +*34* (1) 4296662 *Fax:* +*34* (1) 4202441
Contact: Francisco Lajusticia

AUDIHISPANA - MALAGA
Armengual de la Mota 1, 2C, Edificio Torre Alameda, 29007 MALAGA
Tel: +*34* (52) 708762 *Fax:* +*34* (52) 304401
Contact: Manuel Jiménez Ballesteros

AUDIHISPANA
Avenida Puerta del Mar 5, 29600 MARBELLA (Malaga)
Tel: +*34* (52) 773212 *Fax:* +*34* (52) 861849
Contact: José Urbano Pomares

AUDIHISPANA - NAVARRA
Castillo de Maya 21, 31004 PAMPLONA (Navarra)
Tel: +*34* (48) 241010 *Fax:* +*34* (48) 231583
Contact: Jesus Brun Barcos

AUDIHISPANA - CASTILLA
Pozo Hilera 32-36, 4ºB, 37002 SALAMANCA
Tel: +*34* (23) 260174 *Fax:* +*34* (23) 211809
Contact: Paco Lajusticia

AUDIHISPANA - COSTA DEL SOL
Marqués del Duero 84, 5 B, 29670 SAN PEDOR DE ALCANTARA (Malaga)
Tel: + *34* (52) 783139 *Fax:* + *34* (52) 785644
Contact: Juan Carlos Ronco Corsi

AUDIHISPANA - GALACIA
Uruguay 8, 5º, 36201 VIGO (Pontevedra)
Tel: + *34* (86) 226452 *Fax:* + *34* (86) 220360

Total Number of Offices: 10

AUDIT SA

Calle Josep Tarradellas 147, 2º 1a, 08029 BARCELONA
Tel: + *34* (3) 4192545
Fax: + *34* (3) 4193818

European Affiliation: BKR International

International Contact: Emilio Gironello

OTHER OFFICES

AUDIT SA
Passeig de Pere III 24, 5º 3a, Manresa, 08240 BARCELONA
Tel: + *34* (3) 8720311

AUDIT SA
Calle Ancha 23, 1º izqda, 11001 CADIZ
Tel: + *34* (56) 228909 *Fax:* + *34* (56) 228908

AUDIT SA
Calle Tutor 43, 1º B, 28008 MADRID
Tel: + *34* (1) 5418036 *Fax:* + *34* (1) 5418115

AUDIT SA
Avenida de Andalucía 11, 1º, 29002 MALAGA
Tel: + *34* (52) 327450 *Fax:* + *34* (52) 327454

AUDIT SA
Jacinto Benavente 3, 1º 9, 29600 MARBELLA (Malaga)
Tel: + *34* (52) 863911 *Fax:* + *34* (52) 861938

AUDIT SA
Avenida del Canal s/n 2º, 25230 MOLLERUSA (Lérida)
Tel: + *34* (73) 600142

AUDIT SA
Calle Jesús 1, 2º 3a, 46007 VALENCIA
Tel: + *34* (6) 3528847 *Fax:* + *34* (6) 3523460

AUDIT SA
Calle Santiago 2, 4º D, 47001 VALLADOLID
Tel: + *34* (83) 343666

Total Number of Offices: 9

AUDIT NETWORK SA

Paseo San Juan 140, pral 1ª, 08037 BARCELONA
Tel: + *34* (3) 4592570
Fax: + *34* (3) 2076617

European Affiliation: International Association of Practising Accountants (IAPA)

International Contact: Jose Mª Serena

Partners:	14
Professional staff:	128
Total Staff:	**142**

FEE INCOME

Year End: 31.12.90	**Pta**	**%**
Accountancy & Audit:	210,000,000	60.0
Consultancy:	42,000,000	15.0
Tax:	42,000,000	15.0
Other:	35,000,000	10.0
Total:	**329,000,000**	

CONTACT INFORMATION

Chairman: Jose Serena
Insolvency: Alberto Reines
Management Consultancy: Antonio Torres
Administration: Ignacio Martorell
Public Sector: Luis Fornes
Tax (International): Manuel Cordon
Tax (International): Jose Mª Serena
Accountancy, Audit & Public Sector: Jose Serena
Marketing: Andres Jurkievich
Legal: Luis Roca

CLIENT SERVICES

Accountancy (General), Audit, Computer Installation, Corporate Finance Advice, Litigation/Legal Services, Management & Business Advice, Management Buy-outs, Mergers & Acquisitions, Taxation (Corporate), Taxation (International), Start-ups for Foreign Companies

MAJOR CLIENTS

Pelege Group, Scapa

OTHER OFFICES

AUDIT NETWORK SA
Edificio Albia I, planta 7ª deptº 7 y 8, C San Vicente 8, 48001 BILBAO
Tel: + *34* (4) 4233552 *Fax:* + *34* (4) 4244418
Contact: Manuel Gimeno

AUDIT NETWORK SA
Apartado Correos 231, 12002 CASTELLON
Mailing Address: Navarra 89, Bajo Entlo, 12002 CASTELLON
Tel: + *34* (64) 209649 *Fax:* + *34* (64) 200373
Contact: A. Jesús Ramos Estall

AUDIT NETWORK SA
C/Huesca 66, Edificio Presidente, bajos, 22520 FRAGA
Tel: + *34* (74) 471572 *Fax:* + *34* (74) 473147
Contact: Joaquín Salo

AUDIT NETWORK SA
C/Buensuceso 9, 1ª planta oficina 2, 18002 GRANADA
Tel: + *34* (58) 263741 *Fax:* + *34* (58) 253397
Contact: Roman Arranz

AUDIT NETWORK SA
Avenida España 24, bajos, 07080 IBIZA
Tel: + *34* (71) 300404 *Fax:* + *34* (71) 300408
Contact: D. Felix Balbas

AUDIT NETWORK SA
Avenida Rafael Cabrera 6, oficina D, Edificio Colombia, 35002 LAS PALMAS (Gran Canaria)
Tel: + *34* (28) 360188 *Fax:* + *34* (28) 360388
Contact: J. Jose Cabrera

AUDIT NETWORK SA
C/Monte Esquinza 37, 3º, MADRID
Tel: + *34* (1) 3085084 *Fax:* + *34* (1) 3085113
Contact: Alberto Gonzalez Atanes

AUDIT NETWORK SA
Pje Sta Catalina de Siena, 2 Edificio España, 4ª planta pta B, 07002 PALMA DE MALLORCA
Tel: + *34* (71) 725663 *Fax:* + *34* (71) 723519
Contact: Antonio Balaguer Llabres

AUDIT NETWORK SA
Arrieta 3, 31002 PAMPLONA
Tel: + *34* (48) 229098 *Fax:* + *34* (48) 229893
Contact: José Luis Sanchez Casas

AUDIT NETWORK SA
Urzaiz 38, 4º C, 36201 VIGO
Tel: + *34* (86) 435454 *Fax:* + *34* (86) 435454
Contact: Pedro P. Rey Vera

▷

Spain

AUDIT NETWORK SA
San Vicente Martir 23, esc 1ª 10º izqda, 50008 ZARAGOZA
Tel: + *34* (61) 225098

Total Number of Offices: 12

AUDITORIA Y CONSULTA SA

Paeso de las Delicias 3, 4º izqda, 41001 SEVILLE
Tel: + *34* (5) 4222247
Fax: + *34* (5) 4210694

European Affiliation: INPACT - International Network of Professional Accountants

International Contact: José Ma Pagola Serra
Jesus Bustamante Leon

BDO BINDER SA

Serrano 85, 28006 MADRID
Tel: + *34* (1) 5636773
Fax: + *34* (1) 5631820

European Affiliation: BDO Binder

International Contact: Peter Houdelet

Partners:	5
Professional staff:	80
Non-professional staff:	10
Total Staff:	**95**

FEE INCOME

Year End: 31.12.90	**Pta**
Accountancy & Audit:	300,000,000
Tax:	30,000,000
Other:	20,000,000
Total:	**350,000,000**

CONTACT INFORMATION
Managing Partner: Peter Houdelet
Accountancy (General): Mario Herrero
Audit: Antonio Peidro
Tax (Corporate & International): David Morgan
EDP Systems: Claudio Schutz

CLIENT SERVICES
All Services

OTHER OFFICES
BDO BINDER SA
San Elias 29, 35, 08006 BARCELONA
Tel: + *34* (3) 2003233 *Fax:* + *34* (3) 2018238
Contact: Agustin Checa

Total Number of Offices: 2

BLACKSTONE FRANKS plc

Daoiz y Velarde 6, Edificio Beneco 2a y 3a, Apartado de Correos 159, 29640 FUENGIROLA (Malaga)
Tel: + *34* (52) 479400
Fax: + *34* (52) 476246

European Affiliation: IAG International

International Contact: John McCann

BOVE MONTERO Y CIA

Mariano Cubi 7 & 9, atico 2ª, 08006 BARCELONA
Tel: + *34* (3) 2180708
Fax: + *34* (3) 2382175

European Affiliation: HLB International

International Contact: Jose M. Bove

Partners:	6
Professional staff:	30
Non-professional staff:	4
Total Staff:	**40**

CONTACT INFORMATION
Accountancy (General): Josep Serra
Management Consultancy: Cundy Urcera
Tax (Corporate): Jose A. Rodríguez
Tax (International): Enrique de la Orden

CLIENT SERVICES
Accountancy (General), Audit, Computer Installation, Management & Business Advice, Mergers & Acquisitions, Taxation (Corporate), Taxation (International)

OTHER OFFICES
BOVE MONTERO & CIA
Avenida Menéndez Pelayo 2, 3º derecha, 28009 MADRID
Tel: + *34* (1) 4319215 *Fax:* + *34* (1) 5783151

Total Number of Offices: 2

BUFETE DIAZ ARIAS

Plaza de las Cortes 4-10, 28014 MADRID
Tel: + *34* (1) 4294517
Fax: + *34* (1) 4294505

European Affiliation: ATD International

RAIMON CASANELLAS SL

C/Valencia 362, ent 1ª, 08009 BARCELONA
Tel: + *34* (3) 2076300
Fax: + *34* (3) 2577152

European Affiliation: A.E.E. International

International Contact: Raimon Casanellas

Partners:	1
Professional staff:	2
Non-professional staff:	5
Total Staff:	**8**

FEE INCOME

Year End: 31.12.90	**%**
Accountancy & Audit:	25.0
Insolvency:	5.0
Consultancy:	30.0
Tax:	25.0
Other:	15.0

CONTACT INFORMATION
Chairman: Raimon Casanellas

CLIENT SERVICES
Accountancy (General), Audit, Corporate Finance Advice, Insolvency & Corporate Restructuring, Management & Business Advice, Management Buy-outs, Mergers & Acquisitions, Value for Money Studies, Taxation (Corporate), Taxation (International)

CLEMARES Y CIA SRC

Sagasta 16, 4º deha, 28004 MADRID
Tel: + *34* (1) 4454154
Fax: + *34* (1) 4463706

European Affiliation: SC International

International Contact: Javier Vinader

Total Number of Offices: 4

COC SERVICIOS

Paseo de Gracia 120, 08008 BARCELONA
Tel: +*34* (3) 4150600
Fax: +*34* (3) 2187883

European Affiliation: The Channel International Association

International Contact: M. Bertin

CONSULTOR SA

Ronda General Mitre 160, 3º, 08006 BARCELONA
Tel: +*34* (3) 4171375
Fax: +*34* (3) 4178324

European Affiliation: Urbach Hacker Young International

Partners:	21
Professional staff:	62
Non-professional staff:	20
Total Staff:	**103**

FEE INCOME

Year End: 1990	%
Accountancy & Audit:	45.0
Insolvency:	5.0
Consultancy:	5.0
Tax:	25.0

CONTACT INFORMATION

Managing Partner: Francesc Campos I. Flores
Accountancy (General): José Carlos de Alos Martin
Audit: Jordi Artigas Pomes
Corporate Finance: Julian Rebato Alemany
Insolvency: Oscar Lugo Montforte
Management Consultancy: Juan Marce Sanahuja
Administration: Enric Soler Font
Public Sector: Josep Ferre Sempere
Tax (Corporate): Guillem Pedra Inglesias
Tax (International): Antonio Cores Carles

CLIENT SERVICES

Accountancy (General), Audit, Computer Installation, Corporate Finance Advice, Insolvency & Corporate Restructuring, Litigation/Legal Services, Management & Business Advice, Mergers & Acquisitions, Taxation (Corporate), Taxation (International)

Industry Specialisations: Public Sector, Health Care

ASSOCIATED FIRMS

AUDITORES ASOCIADOS DE CANARIAS SL
C/J.R. Hamilton, edificio Daida, Portal A 203,
38001 SANTA CRUZ (Tenerife)
Contact: Lorenzo Hernandez Perez

AUDITORES ASOCIADOS DE CANARIAS SL
Graciliano Afonso 7, bajos, 35005 LAS PALMAS (Gran Canaria)
Tel: +*34* (28) 232477 *Fax:* +*34* (28) 240062
Contact: José Carlos Orama Manrique

AUDITORES ASOCIADOS DE GALICIA SA
Avenida Finisterre 2, 2ºC, 15004 LA CORUÑA
Tel: +*34* (81) 268608 *Fax:* +*34* (81) 251707
Contact: José Ramon Perez Sante

AUDITORES ASOCIADOS DE GALICIA SA
Rúa Neuva 28, 1ª, 15702 SANTIAGO DE COMPOSTELA
Tel: +*34* (81) 562880 *Fax:* +*34* (81) 581561
Contact: Juan Salle Barreiro

ECONOMISTAS CONSULTORES ASOCIADOS SA
Avenida César Augusto 3, 6º D, 50004 ZARAGOZA
Tel: +*34* (76) 440999 *Fax:* +*34* (76) 441013
Contact: Juan Olivares Alfonso

GREGORIO MARTINEZ EZCARAY
C/ Navas de Tolosa 27, 31002 PAMPLONA
Tel: +*34* (48) 331427
Contact: Gregorio Martinez Ezcaray

GABINETE FISCAL Y CONTABLE SA
Goya 21, 1º dcha, 28001 MADRID
Tel: +*34* (1) 5772716 *Fax:* +*34* (1) 5779463
Contact: Joaquin Santamaria Lopez

GABINETE FISCAL Y GESTION EMPRESARIAL SL
Gran Via 26, A 1º B, 26002 LOGROÑO
Contact: Nicholas Larrauri Soria

GATEFI SA
Ronda General Mitre 160, 3º, 08006 BARCELONA
Tel: +*34* (3) 3210900 *Fax:* +*34* (3) 4195818
Contact: José Carlos de Alos Martin

Total Number of Offices: 10

COOPERS & LYBRAND SA

Rosario Pino 14-16, planta 16, 28020 MADRID
Tel: +*34* (1) 5720233
Fax: +*34* (1) 5700042
Mailing Address: Apartado de Correos 36, 191, 28080 MADRID

European Affiliation: Coopers & Lybrand Europe

International Contact: Angel Luis Linares

CONTACT INFORMATION

Managing Partner: Angel Luis Linares
Corporate Finance: Colin Blessly
Management Consultancy: José Ramón Magarzo
Tax: Antonio-Luis Bañón

CLIENT SERVICES

All Services

Industry Specialisations: Automotive, Banking, Communications, Food & Drink, Insurance, Pharmaceuticals

OTHER OFFICES

COOPERS & LYBRAND SA
Edificio Heron, Avenida Diagonal 601, 10a plant, 08028 BARCELONA
Tel: +*34* (3) 3220114 *Fax:* +*34* (3) 4394068
Contact: Anselmo Constans

COOPERS & LYBRAND SA
Edificio San Joseren, Avenida Zugazarte 52, 48930 LAS ARENAS (Vizcaya)
Tel: +*34* (4) 4645644 *Fax:* +*34* (4) 4645200
Contact: José F. Elorriaga

COOPERS & LYBRAND SA
Perdomo 1, 2º, 35002 LAS PALMAS (Gran Canaria)
Tel: +*34* (28) 380184 *Fax:* +*34* (28) 367901
Contact: Ronald J. MacKay

COOPERS & LYBRAND SA
General Vara de Rey 21, 23 3D, 26002 LOGROÑO
Tel: +*34* (41) 252344 *Fax:* +*34* (41) 259084
Contact: Javier Bonet

COOPERS & LYBRAND SA
Alameda de Colón 9, 29001 MALAGA
Tel: +*34* (52) 210510 *Fax:* +*34* (52) 225346
Contact: George P. Lumby

COOPERS & LYBRAND SA
Sancho el Fuerte 77, 2E, 31008 PAMPLONA
Tel: +*34* (43) 175843 *Fax:* +*34* (43) 175862
Contact: José Luis Goñi

COOPERS & LYBRAND SA
Paseo de Colón 2, 1 dcha, 20002 SAN SEBASTIAN
Tel: +*34* (43) 283977 *Fax:* +*34* (43) 288177
Contact: Carlos Bellver

▷

COOPERS & LYBRAND SA
Eduardo Benot 5, 3 B y C, 39003 SANTANDER
Tel: + 34 (42) 313862 *Fax:* + 34 (42) 221441
Contact: César Camblor

COOPERS & LYBRAND SA
Ramón de Carranza 22, 41011 SEVILLE
Tel: + 34 (5) 4458122
Contact: Jorge Moya

COOPERS & LYBRAND SA
Correos 1, planta 4ª, 46002 VALENCIA
Tel: + 34 (6) 3518194 *Fax:* + 34 (6) 3514225
Contact: Jorge Molina

COOPERS & LYBRAND SA
Urzáiz 68, 7ª planta, 36204 VIGO
Tel: + 34 (86) 421711 *Fax:* + 34 (86) 416747
Contact: Bernard de Speville

COOPERS & LYBRAND SA
San Prudencio 8, A 3, 1005 VITORIA
Tel: + 34 (45) 231144 *Fax:* + 34 (45) 130198

Total Number of Offices: 15

CORTES Y CIA

Rosellon 255, 5º, 08008 BARCELONA
Tel: + 34 (3) 2182919
Fax: + 34 (3) 2182666

European Affiliation: Jeffreys Henry International

International Contact: Juan Cortés Gustems

Partners:	3
Professional staff:	18
Non-professional staff:	2
Total Staff:	**23**

FEE INCOME

Year End: 1990	%
Accountancy & Audit:	95.0
Other:	5.0

CONTACT INFORMATION

International Correspondence: Michael Meulbroek

CLIENT SERVICES

Audit

Total Number of Offices: 3

CORTÉS, PERÉZ Y CIA AUDITORES

Gutenberg 3-13, 5º A, 08224 TERRASSA (Barcelona)
Tel: + 34 (3) 7881662
Fax: + 34 (3) 7890428

European Affiliation: CPA Associates Inc

International Contact: Joel Cortés Casals
José Pérez Copons

OTHER OFFICES

CORTÉS, PERÉZ Y CIA AUDITORES
Casanovas 27, 6º 4ª, BARCELONA
Tel: + 34 (3) 4510553 *Fax:* + 34 (3) 4512745

Total Number of Offices: 2

DELOITTE & TOUCHE

Torre Picasso, planta 38, 28020 MADRID
Tel: + 34 (1) 5550252
Fax: + 34 (1) 5567430

European Affiliation: DRT International

International Contact: Thomas Presby

Partners:	25
Professional staff:	350
Non-professional staff:	75
Total Staff:	**450**

CLIENT SERVICES

Accountancy (General), Audit, Computer Installation, Litigation/Legal Services, Management & Business Advice, Mergers & Acquisitions, Taxation (Corporate), Taxation (International), Asset Valuation, Computer Security, Strategic Planning, Enironmental Auditing

MAJOR CLIENTS

Asland (Lafarge Coppee Group), Asturiana de Zinc SA, BASF, Bull Iberica SA, Cereol Iberica SA (Groups), Cinzano SA, Dow Chemical Iberica SA, Firestone Hispania SA, General Motors Espana SA, Kiope SA (Beshin Say-Ferruzi Groups), MAN, Procter & Gamble Espana SA, Racal SA, Volvo Concesionarios SA

Total Number of Offices: 13

DFK ESPAÑA SA

Rambla de Catalunya 135, pral, 08008 BARCELONA
Tel: + 34 (3) 4150522
Fax: + 34 (3) 4154461

European Affiliation: DFK International

International Contact: Xavier Mercadé

ASSOCIATED FIRMS

FABREGAS, MERCADÉ & CO
Rambla de Catalunya 135, pral., 08008 BARCELONA
Tel: + 34 (3) 4150422 *Fax:* + 34 (3) 4154461
International Contact: Xavier Mercadé

FABREGAS, MERCADÉ & CO
Plaza de Espana 18, 15º num 4, Edificio Torre de Madrid, 28008 MADRID
Tel: + 34 (1) 2478202 *Fax:* + 34 (1) 5591867
Contact: Fernando Lesmes

ALONSO HERNANDEZ ASOCIADOS
Bravo Murillo 26, 35003 LAS PALMAS (Gran Canaria)
Tel: + 34 (28) 368005 *Fax:* + 34 (28) 380418
Contact: Alonso Hernandez

MONCLUS & NIVELA ASOCIADOS
Zurita 10, entb 129, 50001 ZARAGOZA
Tel: + 34 (76) 239865 *Fax:* + 34 (76) 223566
Contact: Emilio Monclus

Total Number of Offices: 4

ECHEVERRIA, SEGURA ILLA Y CIA

Roger de Lluria 36, atico, 08009 BARCELONA
Tel: + 34 (3) 3185144
Fax: + 34 (3) 3024744

European Affiliation: SC International

International Contact: Emilio Echeverria Quintana

ECU AUDITORES Y CONSULTORES SA

Paseo de la Castellana 170, 8º izqda, 28046 MADRID
Tel: + 34 (1) 3459103
Fax: + 34 (1) 3459191

International Contact: Mario Alonso

Partners:	9
Professional staff:	21
Non-professional staff:	6
Total Staff:	**36**

FEE INCOME

Year End: 1990	Pta	%
Accountancy & Audit:	87,000,000	57.0
Consultancy:	6,000,000	4.0
Tax:	45,000,000	29.0
Other:	15,000,000	10.0
Total:	**153,000,000**	

CONTACT INFORMATION

Chairman: Mario Alonso
Corporate Finance: Francisco Cayuela
Management Consultancy: Angel Gonzalez
Tax (Corporate): Eduardo Luque
Accountancy & Audit: Mario Alonso
Computers: Regino Huentas

CLIENT SERVICES

All Services

ERNST & YOUNG

Alberto Alcocer 24, 28036 MADRID
Tel: + *34* (1) 2502800
Fax: + *34* (1) 4578917

European Affiliation: Ernst & Young Europe

International Contact: José Luis Díez García

OTHER OFFICES

ERNST & YOUNG
Audit/Consulting Departments, Balmes 89, 08008 BARCELONA
Tel: + *34* (3) 3232877 *Fax:* + *34* (3) 3233824
Contact: Carlos Soria Sendra

ERNST & YOUNG
Tax/Legal Departments, Avenida Diagonal 618, 08021 BARCELONA
Tel: + *34* (3) 2011888 *Fax:* + *34* (3) 2099703
Contact: Carlos Soria Sendra

ERNST & YOUNG
Colón de Larreátegui 26, 48009 BILBAO
Tel: + *34* (4) 4243777 *Fax:* + *34* (4) 4242745
Contact: Eduardo Diez Santamaria

ERNST & YOUNG
Audit Department, Triana 120, 35002 LAS PALMAS (Gran Canaria)
Tel: + *34* (28) 364199 *Fax:* + *34* (28) 370249
Contact: Raymond Pringle

ERNST & YOUNG
Tax/Consulting Departments, Rafael Cabrera, 15 bajo, Edificio Masiega, 35002 LAS PALMAS (Gran Canaria)
Tel: + *34* (28) 381666 *Fax:* + *34* (28) 380098
Contact: Raymond Pringle

ERNST & YOUNG
Hermanos Moroy 8, 26001 LOGROÑO
Tel: + *34* (41) 248274
Contact: Jesús Pajares Azpiroz

ERNST & YOUNG
Audit Department, Orense 4, 28020 MADRID
Tel: + *34* (1) 5971142 *Fax:* + *34* (1) 5550662

ERNST & YOUNG
Edificio Valería, Paseo de la Farola 5, 29016 MALAGA
Tel: + *34* (52) 228506 *Fax:* + *34* (52) 226616

ERNST & YOUNG
Edificio Minaco, Avenida Alejandro Roselló 15, 07002 PALMA DE MALLORCA
Tel: + *34* (71) 722576 *Fax:* + *34* (71) 714681
Contact: Antonio Salas Santandreu

ERNST & YOUNG
Avenida Baja Navarra 1, 31002 PAMPLONA
Tel: + *34* (48) 228872 *Fax:* + *34* (48) 224999
Contact: Jesús Pajares Azpiroz

ERNST & YOUNG
Avenida de Anaga 9, 38001 SANTA CRUZ (Tenerife)
Tel: + *34* (22) 243086 *Fax:* + *34* (22) 243087
Contact: Douglas Dunlop

ERNST & YOUNG
Avenida San Francisco Javier 21, 3, 41005 SEVILLE
Tel: + *34* (5) 4662012 *Fax:* + *34* (5) 4662259
Contact: Robert Gibb

ERNST & YOUNG
Colón 1, 46004 VALENCIA
Tel: + *34* (6) 3940622 *Fax:* + *34* (6) 3523318
Contact: Francisco Aranda Llauradó

ERNST & YOUNG
Santiago 16, 4º, 47001 VALLADOLID
Tel: + *34* (83) 371625 *Fax:* + *34* (83) 371571

ERNST & YOUNG
Uruguay 8, Edificio "El Dorado", 36201 VIGO
Tel: + *34* (86) 431399 *Fax:* + *34* (86) 430021
Contact: Antonio Ramirez Izquierdo

ERNST & YOUNG
Paseo de la Constitución 6, 50008 ZARAGOZA
Tel: + *34* (76) 230910 *Fax:* + *34* (76) 212353

Total Number of Offices: 17

ESPAUDIT - GABINETE DE AUDITORIA SA

Serrano 78, piso 6 dcha, 28006 MADRID
Tel: + *34* (1) 5766806
Fax: + *34* (1) 4355474

European Affiliation: GMN International

International Contact: Juan Oliveros

Partners:	4
Professional staff:	21
Non-professional staff:	4
Total Staff:	**29**

CONTACT INFORMATION

Chairman: Juan Oliveros
Accountancy (General): Hermann Hengstenberg
Audit: Juan Oliveros
Tax (Corporate): Antonio Sempere

CLIENT SERVICES

Accountancy (General), Audit, Management & Business Advice, Mergers & Acquisitions, Taxation (Corporate)

MAJOR CLIENTS

Auto Herramientas, Carnicas Vaquero, Cereales de la Mancha, Cimisa, Construcciones Danton, Cremades, Fierro, Groupe Sidergie (España), Impresos y Revistas, Industrias Duero, Industrias Gareta, Lariga, Lumac, Ondyne, Vda J. Ortega, Peraile, Seguros Cordoba, Soft/Star, Solan de Cabras, Trialsa

OTHER OFFICES

ESPAUDIT - GABINETE DE AUDITORIA SA
Marques de Molins 7, 02001 ALBACETE
Tel: + *34* (67) 215247 *Fax:* + *34* (67) 215247
Contact: Antonio Sempere

Total Number of Offices: 4

▷

FAURA-CASAS SL AUDITORS-CONSULTORS

C/Casp 31, 2º 1ª, 08010 BARCELONA
Tel: +*34* (3) 3011400
Fax: +*34* (3) 3026596

European Affiliation: Affiliated Conference of Practising Accountants International (ACPA)

International Contact: Daniel Faura

Partners:	5
Professional staff:	22
Non-professional staff:	8
Total Staff:	**35**

FEE INCOME

Year End: 31.12.90	**US$**	**%**
Accountancy & Audit:	110,000,000	61.0
Consultancy:	20,000,000	11.0
Tax:	20,000,000	11.0
Other:	30,000,000	17.0
Total:	**180,000,000**	

CONTACT INFORMATION

Managing Partner: Daniel Faura
Managing Partner: Joan B. Casas
Management Consultancy: Joan B. Casas
Accountancy & Audit: Ignasi Llorens
Corporate Finance & Insolvency: Joan B. Casas
Tax & Administration: Jordi Casals
Public Sector & Tax: Daniel Faura
Human Resources: José A. Lavado
Litigation: Ramon Vallbé

CLIENT SERVICES

Accountancy (General), Audit, Corporate Finance Advice, Litigation/ Legal Services, Management & Business Advice, Management Buy-outs, Mergers & Acquisitions, Taxation (Corporate), Taxation (International), Human Resources

Industry Specialisations: Hospitals, Public Sector, Hotels, Metallurgic Industry, Food & Beverages

OTHER OFFICES

FAURA-CASAS SL AUDITORS-CONSULTORS
Passeig Pere III 56, 3er. 1ª, 08240 MANRESA (Barcelona)
Tel: +*34* (3) 8726299
Contact: Pere Ruiz

FAURA-CASAS SL AUDITORS-CONSULTORS
C/Alfonso XIII 42, 3ª, 08202 SABADELL (Barcelona)
Tel: +*34* (3) 7259999 *Fax:* +*34* (3) 7274748
Contact: Ramon Vallbé

Total Number of Offices: 3

FIDEM AUDITORS SA

Mallorca 260, atica, 08008 BARCELONA
Tel: +*34* (3) 2155989
Fax: +*34* (3) 4872876

European Affiliation: Alliott Peirson International

FULCHI DE PASCUAL ASOCIADOS

c/o Corcega 302-304, 3º 2ª, 08010 BARCELONA
Tel: +*34* (3) 2177312
Fax: +*34* (3) 2185950

International Contact: Plinio Coll

GASSO Y CIA AUDITORES

Ronda General Mitre 126, 6º 2º, 08021 BARCELONA
Tel: +*34* (3) 4184747
Fax: +*34* (3) 2111166

European Affiliation: Horwath International

International Contact: José Ma Gassó Vilafranca

OTHER OFFICES

GASSO Y CIA AUDITORES
Marqués del Puerto 4, 3º izda, 48009 BILBAO
Tel: +*34* (4) 4243992 *Fax:* +*34* (4) 4235430
Contact: Javier Corral Madariaga

GASSO Y CIA AUDITORES
Rambla Ferran 2, 6º A, 25007 LÉRIDA
Tel: +*34* (73) 243444 *Fax:* +*34* (73) 242513

GASSO Y CIA AUDITORES
Abad Ruiz del Arbol y Asoc. SA, Fernández de la Hoz 64, bajo drcha, 28010 MADRID
Tel: +*34* (1) 4423022 *Fax:* +*34* (1) 4422477
Contact: Roberto Pérez Reclusa

GASSO Y CIA AUDITORES
Parelladas 12, 1º, 07003 PALMA DE MALLORCA
Tel: +*34* (71) 727349 *Fax:* +*34* (71) 723513

GASSO Y CIA AUDITORES
Avenida Carlos III 11, 31002 PAMPLONA
Tel: +*34* (48) 226306 *Fax:* +*34* (48) 226305
Contact: Javier del Coso Lampreabe

GASSO Y CIA AUDITORES
San Pablo 1, casa F, 4º G, 41001 SEVILLE
Tel: +*34* (54) 228633
Contact: José M. Bravo Ferrer

GASSO Y CIA AUDITORES
Pare Palau 10, 2º D, 43001 TARRAGONA
Tel: +*34* (77) 220772 *Fax:* +*34* (77) 217562
Contact: Rodolfo Marsal Cavallé

GASSO Y CIA AUDITORES
Gabinete Vicente Urios, Cirilo Amoros 66, 4º, 46004 VALENCIA
Tel: +*34* (6) 3516676 *Fax:* +*34* (6) 3516894

GASSO Y CIA AUDITORES
MAG A.M. Consultores SA, Muro 3, 1º, 47004 VALLADOLID
Tel: +*34* (83) 306711 *Fax:* +*34* (83) 306722
Contact: Alejandro Marigómez Marugán

Total Number of Offices: 10

HERREROS Y DE LA FUENTE

Calvo Sotelo 11, SANTANDER 39002
Tel: +*34* (42) 310962
Fax: +*34* (42) 214607

European Affiliation: S & W International

International Contact: Carlos Herreros

Partners:	4
Professional staff:	15
Non-professional staff:	2
Total Staff:	**21**

CONTACT INFORMATION

Chairman: Manuel de la Fuente
Managing Partner: Ramon Cifrian
Accountancy (General): Gad de la Fuente
Audit: Ramon Cifrian
Insolvency, Tax & Consultancy: Manuel de la Fuente
Tax & Management Consultancy: Carlos Herreros

CLIENT SERVICES

Accountancy (General), Audit, Computer Installation, Corporate Finance Advice, Insolvency & Corporate Restructuring, Management & Business Advice, Taxation (Corporate), Taxation (International)

Total Number of Offices: 2

INTERSER-INTERMEDIACION Y SERVICIOS INTERNACIONALES SA

Gurtubay 6, 28001 MADRID
Tel: +34 (1) 4350169
Fax: +34 (1) 5760648

European Affiliation: InterContinental Consultants (ICC)

Partners:	1
Professional staff:	4
Non-professional staff:	6
Total Staff:	**11**

FEE INCOME

Year End: 1990	%
Accountancy & Audit:	40.0
Tax:	40.0
Other:	20.0

CONTACT INFORMATION

Chairman: Pedro Pascual
Accountancy (General): Emiliano Penas
Administration: Francisco Bueno
Public Sector: Carmen Pascual
Tax (Corporate): Juan Calderon

CLIENT SERVICES

Accountancy (General), Management & Business Advice, Taxation (Corporate), Taxation (International), Company Administration

OTHER OFFICES

INTERSER - INTERMEDIACION Y SERVICIOS INTERNACIONALES SA
Gran Via 662, pral 2ª, 08010 BARCELONA
Tel: +34 (3) 3175236 *Fax:* +34 (3) 4123561

INTERSER - INTERMEDIACION Y SERVICIOS INTERNACIONALES SA
Avenida Jesus Santos Rein 4, 4ºB, 29640 FUENGIROLA (Malaga)
Tel: +34 (52) 462193 *Fax:* +34 (52) 465931
Contact: Fabiola Lozano

Total Number of Offices: 3

L. IRANZO PRADA Y CIA

Plaza de la Independencia 5, 28001 MADRID
Tel: +34 (1) 5781641
Fax: +34 (1) 5768119

International Contact: Alejandro Canal Lopez

Partners:	3
Professional staff:	20
Non-professional staff:	2
Total Staff:	**25**

FEE INCOME

Year End: 31.12.90	%
Accountancy & Audit:	80.0
Insolvency:	10.0
Tax:	10.0

CONTACT INFORMATION

Insolvency: Francisco Prada Gayoso
Tax (Corporate): Fernando Lopez Iranzo
Accountancy & Audit: Alejandro Canal Lopez

CLIENT SERVICES

Accountancy (General), Audit, Insolvency & Corporate Restructuring, Mergers & Acquisitions, Taxation (Corporate)

IVC AUDITORES SA

Felix Boix 14, entreplanta dcha, 28036 MADRID
Tel: +34 (1) 2501983
Fax: +34 (1) 4572645

European Affiliation: Independent Accountants International

International Contact: G. Stevens

Partners:	7
Professional staff:	35
Non-professional staff:	12
Total Staff:	**54**

FEE INCOME

Year End: 1990	%
Accountancy & Audit:	10.0
Insolvency:	5.0
Consultancy:	35.0
Tax:	10.0
Other:	40.0

CONTACT INFORMATION

Chairman: R. Chapatte
Managing Partner: E. Kavelaars
Corporate Finance: R. Chapatte
Tax (Corporate): M.A. Rubio
Tax (International): J.A. Cerutti
Accountancy & Audit: G. Stevens
Insolvency & Consultancy: E. Kavelaars
Mergers & Acquisitions: J. Corcuera

CLIENT SERVICES

Accountancy (General), Audit, Corporate Finance Advice, Insolvency & Corporate Restructuring, Litigation/Legal Services, Management & Business Advice, Mergers & Acquisitions, Taxation (Corporate), Taxation (International), Market Studies, Translation Service, Personnel Recruitment, Executive Search

Industry Specialisations: Medium-sized Foreign Firms

MAJOR CLIENTS

Ahlers, Banco Real, Campina - Melcunie, Cosigsa, Crystal Fashions Ltd, International Müller Group, Kömmerung, Löwenbrau, James Martin Associates, Oldenbourg GmbH, J. Ortiz SA, Peri SA, Rabo Bank, Rittmeyer, Walter Schlewer, Tennant International, Transuft AG, Unmgro, VIB BV, Ziehlemb

Total Number of Offices: 3

KPMG

KPMG PEAT MARWICK Y CIA

Edificio Torre Europa, Paseo de la Castellana 95, 28046 MADRID
Tel: +34 (1) 5555363
Fax: +34 (1) 5550132

European Affiliation: KPMG

International Contact: Jesus Peregrina

Partners:	35
Professional staff:	540
Non-professional staff:	180
Total Staff:	**755**

FEE INCOME

Year End: 30.06.90	**Pta**	%
Accountancy & Audit:	3,700,000,000	57.8
Consultancy:	1,442,000,000	22.5
Tax:	1,121,000,000	17.5
Other:	140,000,000	2.2
Total:	**6,403,000,000**	

CONTACT INFORMATION

Chairman: Jesus Peregrina

▷

Corporate Finance: Gloria Alonso
Public Sector: Miguel Ibañez
Tax (Corporate): Vicente Muñoz
Tax (International): Mercedes de Rosas
Banking, Accountancy & Audit: Jose L. Saenz de Miera
Professional Practices: Angel Aranda
Real Estate: José L. Perez
Consultancy & Administration: Jesus Peregrina

CLIENT SERVICES
All Services

Industry Specialisations: Banking, Insurance, Construction, Real Estate, Food & Beverage, Oil & Gas, Transportation

OTHER OFFICES

KPMG PEAT MARWICK Y CIA
Edificio Masters 9-11, Pedro i Pons, 08034 BARCELONA
Tel: + *34* (3) 2800304 *Fax:* + *34* (3) 2804916
Contact: Luis Walter

KPMG PEAT MARWICK Y CIA
Edificio Aurora Polar, Iparraguirr 29, 2º planta, 48011 BILBAO
Tel: + *34* (4) 4162100 *Fax:* + *34* (4) 4152967
Contact: Pedro Larrea

KPMG PEAT MARWICK Y CIA
Grober 6, 17001 GERONA
Tel: + *34* (72) 220120 *Fax:* + *34* (72) 222245
Contact: Juan Lagen

KPMG PEAT MARWICK Y CIA
Edificio Iruña Park 1, 3º, Arcadio M. Larraona, 31008 PAMPLONA
Tel: + *34* (48) 171408 *Fax:* + *34* (48) 173531
Contact: Jesus Rodríguez

KPMG PEAT MARWICK Y CIA
Edificio Condes de Bunol 8, Isabel la Catolica, 46004 VALENCIA
Tel: + *34* (6) 3526819 *Fax:* + *34* (6) 3512729
Contact: Juan F. Latorre

KPMG PEAT MARWICK Y CIA
Uruguay 8, 36201 VIGO
Tel: + *34* (86) 228505 *Fax:* + *34* (86) 438565
Contact: Julian Martin

KPMG PEAT MARWICK Y CIA
Avenida Luis de morales 32, 32 Edificio Forum, 41018 SEVILLE
Tel: + *34* (5) 4532801 *Fax:* + *34* (5) 4539343
Contact: Julian Martin

KPMG PEAT MARWICK Y CIA
Santiago 19, 47001 VALLADOLID
Tel: + *34* (83) 372375 *Fax:* + *34* (83) 372519
Contact: Valeriano Perez

KPMG PEAT MARWICK Y CIA
Parelladas 12, 1º, 07003 PALMA DE MALLORCA
Tel: + *34* (71) 721601 *Fax:* + *34* (71) 725809
Contact: Miguel Ferrer

KPMG PEAT MARWICK Y CIA
Avda Maisonave 26, Edificio Oficentro, 03003 ALICANTE
Tel: + *34* (6) 5920722 *Fax:* + *34* (6) 5227500
Contact: José Luis Perez

KPMG PEAT MARWICK Y CIA
Miracruz 10, B, 20001 SAN SEBASTIAN
Tel: + *34* (43) 279933 *Fax:* + *34* (43) 277711
Contact: Julio Mir

Total Number of Offices: 12

MACUA & CIA ASESORES SA

Dr. Achúcarro 7, 1ª planta, 48011 BILBAO
Tel: + *34* (4) 4153477
Fax: + *34* (4) 4150572

Partners:	9
Professional staff:	19
Non-professional staff:	13
Total Staff:	**41**

FEE INCOME

Year End: 31.12.90	**Pta**
Total:	**240,000,000**

CONTACT INFORMATION
Managing Partner: Jose Mª Macua
Accountancy (General): Beatriz Macua
Audit: Jose I. Garcia
Administration: Juana Gomez
Tax (Corporate): Miren Aurtenetxe

CLIENT SERVICES
Accountancy (General), Audit, Computer Installation, Litigation/Legal Services, Taxation (Corporate)

OTHER OFFICES

MACUA OFICINA TECNICA DE TRIBUTACION Y CONTABILIDAD SL
Dr. Achucarro 7-1º, 48011 BILBAO
Tel: + *34* (4) 4153477 *Fax:* + *34* (4) 4150572
Contact: Miren Aurtenetxe

MACUA S. Y CIA CENSORES JURADOS DE CUENTAS SRC
Maximo Aguirre 22, dpto 11, 48930 GUECHO
Tel: + *34* (4) 4638777 *Fax:* + *34* (4) 4648708
Contact: Jose I. Garcia

N.S.I. SA
Maximo Aguirre 22, dpto 11, 48930 GUECHO
Tel: + *34* (4) 4638777 *Fax:* + *34* (4) 4648708
Contact: Jon Zulueta

Total Number of Offices: 4

MOORE STEPHENS & SANTACANA GRUP SA

Avenida Diagonal 476, 4º 2ª, 08006 BARCELONA
Tel: + *34* (3) 4161511
Fax: + *34* (3) 4161131

European Affiliation: Moore Stephens

International Contact: D. José Santacana

Partners:	33
Professional staff:	255
Non-professional staff:	77
Total Staff:	**365**

CLIENT SERVICES
All Services

ASSOCIATED FIRMS

CJC AUDITORES SL
Colón 4, 6ºA, 46004 VALENCIA
Tel: + *34* (6) 3515023 *Fax:* + *34* (6) 3942940
Contact: Eduardo Rallo

EPG AUDITORES SA
Avenida Portugal 2, 3º izqda, 26001 LOGROÑO
Tel: + *34* (41) 220300
Contact: Francisco Espinosa

EPG AUDITORES SA
Rodriguez Arias 23, 2, 48011 BILBAO
Tel: + *34* (4) 4446600 *Fax:* + *34* (4) 4449546
Contact: Francisco Espinosa Lopez

SANATACANA & YGLESIAS SL
Plaza de España 13, 1º B, 37003 SALAMANCA
Tel: + *34* (23) 266312 *Fax:* + *34* (23) 266141
Contact: José Santacana Jubillar

SANTACANA GRUP SA
Velazques 26, 3ºA, 28001 MADRID
Tel: + *34* (1) 5766942 *Fax:* + *34* (1) 5782283
Contact: José Santacana

SANTACANA & GONZALES SL
Barbecho 29, 47014 VALLADOLID
Tel: + *34* (83) 354911 *Fax:* + *34* (83) 359985
Contact: José Santacana

VELASCO Y PEDREGAL AUDITORES SL
Melquiades Alvarez 6, 1ºD, Apartado 1240, 33002 OVIEDO
Tel: + *34* (85) 227515 *Fax:* + *34* (85) 220081

Total Number of Offices: 8

MTR Y ASOCIADOS

Plaza Francesc Macia 5, 1º 1ª, 08021 BARCELONA (Cataluna)
Tel: + *34* (3) 2097600
Fax: + *34* (3) 2095984

European Affiliation: Russell Bedford International

International Contact: José Marin

PANNELL KERR FORSTER

Travessera de Gracia Forster 29, 08021 BARCELONA
Tel: + *34* (3) 2093411
Fax: + *34* (3) 2005338

European Affiliation: Pannell Kerr Forster Worldwide

International Contact: Ferran Faus

OTHER OFFICES

PANNELL KERR FORSTER
Serrano 120, 3º ocha, 28006 MADRID
Tel: + *34* (1) 5644593 *Fax:* + *34* (1) 5644766
Contact: Peter D. Cook

PANNELL KERR FORSTER
General Garcia de la Herranz, s/n, Edificio Giraldi 7 A, 41013 SEVILLE
Tel: + *34* (54) 156526
Contact: José Alvea

Total Number of Offices: 3

P.B. AUDITORES SL

Avenida Diagonal 598, 08021 BARCELONA
Tel: + *34* (3) 2000933
Fax: + *34* (3) 2022907

European Affiliation: DRM Internationally

International Contact: Carlos Sahuquillo
David Radley-Searle

Partners:	6
Professional staff:	24
Non-professional staff:	14
Total Staff:	**44**

FEE INCOME

Year End: 31.12.90	%
Accountancy & Audit:	15.0
Insolvency:	10.0
Consultancy:	7.0
Tax:	20.0
Other:	48.0

CONTACT INFORMATION

Chairman: Pedro Brosa
Managing Partner: Pedro Brosa
Administration: Jan Reus
Audit & Public Sector: Ramon Catalan
Partner: Gines Torres
Corporate Finance, Tax & Law: Carlos Sahuquillo
Corporate Law: Ricardo Rebate

CLIENT SERVICES

Accountancy (General), Audit, Corporate Finance Advice, Insolvency & Corporate Restructuring, Litigation/Legal Services, Management & Business Advice, Management Buy-outs, Mergers & Acquisitions, Taxation (Corporate), Taxation (International), Trust Settlement & Estates

OTHER OFFICES

P.B. AUDITORES SL
Alfonso XII 18, 28014 MADRID
Tel: + *34* (1) 5228202 *Fax:* + *34* (1) 5223989
Contact: Ricardo Rebate

Total Number of Offices: 2

EDIFICIO PRICE WATERHOUSE

Paseo de la Castellana 43, 28046 MADRID
Tel: + *34* (1) 3083500
Fax: + *34* (1) 3083566

European Affiliation: Price Waterhouse

Partners:	67
Professional staff:	1,077
Non-professional staff:	330
Total Staff:	**1,474**

FEE INCOME

Year End: 30.06.91	**Pta**
Accountancy & Audit:	4,146,068,000
Consultancy:	4,334,275,000
Tax:	1,403,751,000
Other:	104,880,000
Total:	**9,988,974,000**

CONTACT INFORMATION

Chairman: Miguel Fernandez de Pinedo
Audit: Sergio Goycoolea
Corporate Finance: Mariano Gomez Agüero
Insolvency: Patrick Everard
Management Consultancy: Hugo Hanna
Administration: José Luis Fernãndez Baños
Public Sector: Antonio Tejerina
Tax (Corporate): Cesar Rodriquez
Tax (International): Patrick Everard

CLIENT SERVICES

Audit, Computer Installation, Corporate Finance Advice, Insolvency & Corporate Restructuring, Litigation/Legal Services, Management & Business Advice, Mergers & Acquisitions, Value for Money Studies, Taxation (Corporate), Taxation (International)

Industry Specialisations: Banking & Finance, Food, Oil & Gas, Chemical, Pharmaceutical, Steel, Energy, Electronics, Media ▷

OTHER OFFICES

PRICE WATERHOUSE
Oscar Esplá 30, entlo, 03003 ALICANTE
Tel: + *34* (6) 5923411 *Fax:* + *34* (6) 5222457
Contact: Rogelio Samper

PRICE WATERHOUSE
Torre Catalunya, Avenida de Roma 2 y 4, 08014 BARCELONA
Tel: + *34* (3) 4231581 *Fax:* + *34* (3) 4243801
Contact: Augustin Abello

PRICE WATERHOUSE TREUARBEIT AUDITORES SA
Torre Catalunya, Avenida de Roma 2 y 4, 08014 BARCELONA
Tel: + *34* (3) 4231581 *Fax:* + *34* (3) 4243801
Contact: Ulrich Roth

PRICE WATERHOUSE
Avenida de Zugazarte 8, Las Arenas (Vizcaya), BILBAO
Tel: + *34* (4) 4640022 *Fax:* + *34* (4) 4640931
Contact: Juan de Bias

PRICE WATERHOUSE
Medico Rodriquez 12-14, 1º izqda, 15004 LA CORUÑA
Tel: + *34* (81) 252014 *Fax:* + *34* (81) 267564
Contact: B. Francisco Amo

PRICE WATERHOUSE
Pilarillo Seco 8, 4ºC, Edificio Banco Vitalicio,
35002 LAS PALMAS (Gran Canaria)
Tel: + *34* (28) 360166 *Fax:* + *34* (28) 372607
Contact: Javier Puga

PRICE WATERHOUSE
Cister 5, 4º A-1, 29015 MALAGA
Tel: + *34* (52) 217555 *Fax:* + *34* (52) 219802
Contact: A. Enrique Munoz

PRICE WATERHOUSE
Navas de Tolosa 19, 2º, 31002 PAMPLONA
Tel: + *34* (48) 225870 *Fax:* + *34* (48) 228606
Contact: Fermin Gembero

PRICE WATERHOUSE
Plaza Sant Roc 21, 08201 SABADELL (Barcelona)
Tel: + *34* (3) 7258788
Contact: Xavier Brossa

PRICE WATERHOUSE
Calle Camino 7, 20004 SAN SEBASTIAN
Tel: + *34* (43) 424451 *Fax:* + *34* (43) 426917
Contact: José Luis Madariaga

PRICE WATERHOUSE
C/Robayna 6, 1 dcha, 36003 SANTA CRUZ (Tenerife)
Tel: + *34* (22) 246051 *Fax:* + *34* (22) 246052
Contact: Luis Polaino

PRICE WATERHOUSE
Av de la Républica Argentina 13, AC, 41011 SEVILLE
Tel: + *34* (5) 4275400 *Fax:* + *34* (5) 4276488
Contact: Baltasar Lobato

PRICE WATERHOUSE
Edificio Gran Via, Gran Via Marques del Turia 49, 46005 VALENCIA
Tel: + *34* (6) 3527017 *Fax:* + *34* (6) 3518657
Contact: Ignacio Escrivá

PRICE WATERHOUSE
Santiago 13, 1ºA, 47001 VALLADOLID
Tel: + *34* (83) 333477 *Fax:* + *34* (83) 371637
Contact: José Manuel Hernandez

PRICE WATERHOUSE
Plaza de Compostela 17, 2, 36201 VIGO
Tel: + *34* (86) 439177 *Fax:* + *36* (86) 226513
Contact: B. Francisco Armo

PRICE WATERHOUSE
Plaza de Aragón 10, 50004 ZARAGOZA
Tel: + *34* (76) 230080 *Fax:* + *34* (76) 212355
Contact: José Bosch

Total Number of Offices: 17

S & W AUDIT GROUP

Bailen 188, 08037 BARCELONA
Tel: + *34* (3) 2070700
Fax: + *34* (3) 2572374

European Affiliation: S & W International

International Contact: Luis Velasco

SANCHEZ ANDRES Y CIA

C/Diputación 4, bis 2º, 48009 BILBAO
Tel: + *34* (4) 4247807
Fax: + *34* (4) 4234729

European Affiliation: SC International

International Contact: Francisco José Sánchez Andrés

OTHER OFFICES

SANCHEZ ANDRES Y CIA
Edificio c-1/11, PUERTO DE SOTOGRANDE
Tel: + *34* (56) 970291 *Fax:* + *34* (56) 970382
Contact: Andriana Sánchez Andrés

Total Number of Offices: 2

ELISARDO SANCHEZ Y ASESORES ASOCIADOS SA

Alameda de Colono 28, 29001 MALAGA

European Affiliation: Growth & Progress Challenge

International Contact: Elisandro Sanchez

AUDISERVICIOS SATORRA Y PLANAS SRC

Muntaner 261, 4º 2ª, 08021 BARCELONA
Tel: + *34* (3) 2090467
Fax: + *34* (3) 2023078

European Affiliation: Clark Kenneth Leventhal

International Contact: Manuel Satorra

Partners:	2
Professional staff:	9
Non-professional staff:	5
Total Staff:	**16**

FEE INCOME

Year End: 1990	%
Accountancy & Audit:	60.0
Tax:	10.0
Other:	30.0

CLIENT SERVICES

Accountancy (General), Audit, Corporate Finance Advice, Insolvency & Corporate Restructuring, Management & Business Advice, Taxation (Corporate), Taxation (International)

OTHER OFFICES

AUDISERVICIOS SATORRA Y PLANAS
Plaza de España 18, 15º 4, Edificio Torre de Madrid, 28008 MADRID
Tel: + *34* (1) 2478201 *Fax:* + *34* (1) 5591867
Contact: Juan Planas

Total Number of Offices: 2

SERAUDIT AUDITORES ALDOMA PARELLA Y CIA SRC

C/ Mallorca 183-185, 5º 4ª, 08036 BARCELONA
Tel: + *34* (3) 4515156
Fax: + *34* (3) 4516362

International Contact: German Parella

Partners:	5
Professional staff:	21
Non-professional staff:	20
Total Staff:	**46**

CONTACT INFORMATION

Chairman: Francisco Palau
Managing Partner: Juan Aldoma
Accountancy (General): Francisco Palau
Audit: Juan Aldoma
Corporate Finance: Juan Antonio de Agustin
Management Consultancy: Emilio Garcia
Tax: German Parella

CLIENT SERVICES

Accountancy (General), Audit, Corporate Finance Advice, Insolvency & Corporate Restructuring, Litigation/Legal Services, Management & Business Advice, Management Buy-outs, Mergers & Acquisitions, Taxation (Corporate), Taxation (International), Management Consultancy

OTHER OFFICES

SERAUDIT
Apolonio Morales 10, despacho A-403, 28036 MADRID
Tel: + *34* (1) 2598193 *Fax:* + *34* (1) 2504692
Contact: Juan Antonio de Agustin

SERAUDIT AUDITORES ALDOMA PARELLA Y CIA
Unio 2, 2º, 08221 TERRASSA
Tel: + *34* (3) 7885400 *Fax:* + *34* (3) 7891044
Contact: Francisco Palau

Total Number of Offices: 3

SOCIEDAD FIDUCIARIA ESPAÑOLA

Diputacion 239, 08007 BARCELONA
Tel: + *34* (3) 4880167
Fax: + *34* (3) 4893562

European Affiliation: DRM Internationally

International Contact: Fernando Sanchez-Bosch

Partners:	4
Professional staff:	7
Non-professional staff:	2
Total Staff:	**13**

FEE INCOME

Year End: 1990	%
Accountancy & Audit:	80.0
Consultancy:	20.0
Tax:	20.0

CONTACT INFORMATION

Chairman: Liberto Cuatrecasas Membrado
Managing Partner: Liberto Cuatrecasas Contijoch
Accountancy & Tax: Marino Garcia Imbernon
Audit: Fernando Sanchez-Bosch

CLIENT SERVICES

Accountancy (General), Audit, Management & Business Advice, Taxation (Corporate)

SOLER, SAIZ, HOPEWELL SCP

Paseo de la Habana 54, 5th Floor, 28036 MADRID
Tel: + *34* (1) 5639476
Fax: + *34* (1) 5634964

European Affiliation: Summit International Associates Inc

International Contact: Lionel C. Hopewell

OTHER OFFICES

SOLER, SAIZ, HOPEWELL SCP
Mallorca 286, pral, 08037 BARCELONA
Tel: + *34* (1) 5639476 *Fax:* + *34* (1) 5634964

Total Number of Offices: 2

SOLER, SAIZ, HOPEWELL SCP

Paseo de la Habana No. 54, 5º Dcha, 28036 MADRID
Tel: + *34* (1) 5639476
Fax: + *34* (1) 5634964

European Affiliation: TGI International

International Contact: Lionel C. Hopewell

OTHER OFFICES

SOLER, SAIZ, HOPEWELL SCPS
Mallorca 286, Pral, 08037 BARCELONA
Tel: + *34* (3) 2074762 *Fax:* + *34* (3) 2584107
Contact: Lionel Hopewell

Total Number of Offices: 2

UNIAUDIT SA

Edificio Barcino, Tuset 20-24, 08006 BARCELONA
Tel: + *34* (3) 2173600
Fax: + *34* (3) 2182193

European Affiliation: Grant Thornton International

International Contact: Pedro Estefanell Coca

Partners:	25
Professional staff:	100
Non-professional staff:	50
Total Staff:	**175**

FEE INCOME

Year End: 1990	**Pta (million)**
Total:	**963,742**

CONTACT INFORMATION

Managing Partner: Juan Ros Petit

CLIENT SERVICES

Accountancy (General), Audit, Litigation/Legal Services, Management & Business Advice, Taxation (Corporate), Taxation (International), Computer Consultancy

OTHER OFFICES

AUDILAN - UNIAUDIT
Plaza Larrin 1, 2 piso, 25550 ARETXABALETA (Guipuzcoa)
Mailing Address: P.O. Box 24, 25500 MONDRAGON (Guipuzcoa)
Tel: + *34* (43) 793733 *Fax:* + *34* (43) 771038

GRANT THORNTON ESPAÑA SA
Pintor Cabrera 22, 4º b, 03003 ALICANTE
Tel: + *34* (65) 226253 *Fax:* + *34* (65) 227634

GRANT THORNTON ESPAÑA SA
Enmedia 67, 3º, 12001 CASTELLON DE LA PLANA
Tel: + *34* (64) 211115

GRANT THORNTON ESPAÑA SA
Centro Colon, Margués de la Ensenada 16, 28004 MADRID
Tel: + *34* (1) 3198300 *Fax:* + *34* (1) 3191562

GRANT THORNTON ESPAÑA SA
Plaza Santa Gertrudis 1, entlo B-C, 38001 MURCIA
Tel: + *34* (68) 220333 *Fax:* + *34* (68) 211727

GRANT THORNTON ESPAÑA SA
H. Rodriquez Lopez 4, 1º, 38005 SANTA CRUZ (Tenerife)
Tel: + *34* (22) 229296 *Fax:* + *34* (22) 203253

GRANT THORNTON ESPAÑA SA
Cronista Carreres 3, entlo 2º, 46003 VALENCIA
Tel: + *34* (6) 3524034 *Fax:* + *34* (6) 3528134

GRANT THORNTON ESPAÑA SA
Juan Ortuño 2, entlo B, 30510 YECIA
Tel: + *34* (68) 791209 *Fax:* + *34* (68) 704602

UNIAUDIT SA
Paseo Tomas Moralees 65, esq Obispo Encina,
35004 LAS PALMAS (Gran Canaria)
Tel: + *34* (28) 293120 *Fax:* + *34* (28) 290572

Total Number of Offices: 10

VELASCO, GAY Y CIA AUDITORES

Balmes 150, 08008 BARCELONA
Tel: + *34* (93) 2182124

International Contact: Carlos Velasco Gonzalez

OTHER OFFICES

VELASCO, GAY Y CIA AUDITORES
Paseo de la Habana 54, 5D, 28036 MADRID
Tel: + *34* (1) 5638398 *Fax:* + *34* (1) 5634964
Contact: Carlos Hopewell

Total Number of Offices: 2

Sweden

Area: 449,964 sq km (173,731 sq miles)
Population: 8,358,000 (1985 estimate)
Density: 18.57 per sq km
Capital: Stockholm

GDP: SKr1.47 trn, US$250 bn
GDP per head: US$29,530
Inflation: 1990 - 9.5%
1991 - 7.5% (forecast)

Official and Spoken Languages: Swedish, Finnish, English, German and Lapp

Time: GMT + 1 (in Summer GMT + 2)
Telephone Dialling Code: +46

*Currency:*Swedish Krona (SKr) = 100 ore
Banking Hours: Generally 0930-1500 Monday-Friday. In large cities, banks close at 1800
Professional accountancy bodies: Foreningen Aukteriserade Revisorer (FAR)
Association of Authorised Public Accountants

Corporate Tax Data

Information supplied by Richard Citron, international tax partner of Stoy Hayward.

The tax year; nature and rates of tax
The tax year is the calendar year.

Income tax (inkomstskatt) is levied at 30% on distributed and undistributed income of companies.

Residence and territoriality
A Swedish resident company is taxable on its worldwide income. Companies registered in Sweden are treated as resident there as are companies mainly holding or trading in securities that are effectively managed in Sweden and whose shares are mainly held by Swedish resident individuals.

The tax base
Method of calculation. Taxable profit is based on the profit reported by the accounts.

Disallowable items. The major disallowable items are mostly gifts, capital expenditure not related to the company's trade and some entertaining expenses.

Exempt income/special deductions. Certain dividends received are exempt and certain dividend payments are deductible - see below. There is a special tax deductible equalisation reserve (SURV); it is limited to a total of 30% of the company's equity capital and is based on the tax accounting values of certain assets less liabilities. Companies with a small equity capital, especially in the service sector, can base their SURV on a maximum 15% of payroll.

Interest paid. Normally deductible on an accruals basis. To the extent that interest between affiliated companies exceeds arm's length rates, it may be treated as a dividend.

▷

Stock. Stock is valued on a FIFO basis at the lower of cost and market value. Where valuation is based on cost, a further deduction of 3% is generally allowed.

Depreciation. The method of depreciation depends on the asset involved.

(1) For plant and machinery and intangible assets, two methods are recognised. One is to take a straight 25% of the depreciated (net book) value of the pool of assets. The other is computed by taking the higher of a figure based on 30% of the opening net book value of the pool (increased by acquisitions and decreased by disposals in the year) and 20% straightline depreciation on cost, categorising assets by year of acquisition.
(2) Buildings are depreciated on a straightline basis at fixed rates.

Treatment of dividends

Dividends received from Swedish companies. These form part of taxable income. However, where the recipient company holds 25% or more of the paying company, the dividend is exempt. The exemption is restricted in the case of holding companies. In order to qualify for the exemption, they must either redistribute the dividend or perform services for their subsidiaries (ie not act merely as a pure holding company).

Dividends received from abroad. Dividends from foreign companies are often exempt under a double tax treaty.

Dividends paid. Dividends paid to non-resident shareholders are subject to a 30% withholding tax. Companies carrying on a trade or engaged in agriculture or forestry may deduct certain dividends paid in calculating taxable income.

Anti-avoidance rules

There are rules designed to prevent accumulation of profits in companies holding primarily shares or real property. Transfer pricing rules operate to adjust all transactions with foreign affiliates to arm's length values. Controlled foreign company rules apply to attribute profits earned by investment companies resident in low tax jurisdictions and controlled by Swedish residents to those residents holding at least 10% of the foreign company's share capital.

Treatment of losses

Current period. Trading losses may be set off against income and gains in the current period (there is no carry-back).

Future periods. To the extent that they remain unrelieved in the current period, trading losses may be carried forward indefinitely.

Treatment of capital gains

Treatment. Capital gains are in principle taxed as income. Sale proceeds of plant, machinery and intangibles are reduced not by the cost but by the net book value of those assets, effectively increasing the taxable gain by the amount of tax deductible depreciation previously given.

Computation. Gains on the disposal of immovable property are computed by deducting the adjusted cost from the sale proceeds.

Rollover. There are no special rollover rules.

Treatment of shares. The gain on the disposal of securities is computed by deducting the cost from the sale proceeds. Intra-group sales may be tax free.

Treatment of groups

Profits may be adjusted within a group of companies by means of contribution payments, which are tax-deductible to the paying company and taxable in the hands of the payee company. Profit shifting by means of inter-company pricing is also recognised. A group of companies consists of a holding company and its 91% subsidiaries. The companies must be trading companies or engaged in real estate or agriculture. The holding company must perform services for its subsidiaries. All members of the group must be registered in Sweden.

Treatment of branches

The Swedish branch of a non-resident company is treated in much the same way as a Swedish resident company. Branches are also liable, unless exempted by treaty, to net worth tax on the value of assets located in Sweden. There is no withholding tax on remittance of branch profits.

Other taxes

Taxes on capital. A national net worth tax (statlig formogenhetsskatt) of between 1.5% and 3% is payable by non-resident companies on assets situated in Sweden. Treaties often provide exemption from this tax.

Turnover taxes. A value added tax (mervardeskatt) is payable on the supply of goods and services. There is a standard rate of 20% payable on the net price plus VAT.

Transaction taxes. Stamp duty is payable at 2% on share issues and at between 1.5% and 3% on the transfer of immovable property. The transfer of shares and debentures is subject to a tax of 0.5% of the sale price.

Social security. Payroll taxes amounting to 38.9% of payroll are payable by employers, in addition to a further tax of 8.9% on staff salaries and 6.1% on the salaries of other employees. A special payroll tax of 22.2% was levied in 1991.

A & C REVISIONSBYRÅ HB
Holmgatan 4, 211 45 MALMÖ
Tel: + *46* (40) 715 25
Fax: + *46* (40) 30 25 85

European Affiliation: Jeffreys Henry International

International Contact: Morris Adler

ARTHUR ANDERSEN & CO
Sveavägen 155, Box 23501, 104 35 STOCKHOLM
Tel: + *46* (8) 610 58 00
Fax: + *46* (8) 31 59 05

European Affiliation: Arthur Andersen Worldwide

International Contact: Paul Hoeve

CONTACT INFORMATION
Audit: Björn Sundkvist
Tax (Corporate): Conny T. Otteland

CLIENT SERVICES
Accountancy (General), Audit, Computer Installation, Corporate Finance Advice, Insolvency & Corporate Restructuring, Litigation/Legal Services, Management & Business Advice, Management Buy-outs, Mergers & Acquisitions, Pensions Planning, Value for Money Studies, Taxation (Corporate), Taxation (International)

OTHER OFFICES
ARTHUR ANDERSEN & CO
Södra Hamngatan 53, 411 06 GOTHENBURG
Tel: + *46* (31) 80 53 35 *Fax:* + *46* (31) 15 87 58

ARTHUR ANDERSEN & CO
Kungsgatan 2, 252 21 HELSINGBORG
Tel: + *46* (42) 11 12 88 *Fax:* + *46* (42) 11 36 63

ARTHUR ANDERSEN & CO
Lilla Fiskaregatan 4, 222 22 LUND
Tel: + *46* (46) 13 53 75 *Fax:* + *46* (46) 15 87 32

ARTHUR ANDERSEN & CO
Stortorget 31, 211 34 MALMÖ
Tel: + *46* (40) 10 34 45 *Fax:* + *46* (40) 12 74 70

ARTHUR ANDERSEN & CO
Odens Tvärgränd 3, Box 177, 231 23 TRELLEBORG
Tel: + *46* (410) 175 00 *Fax:* + *46* (410) 400 20

Total Number of Offices: 6

BDO REVISION AB
Klarabergsviadukten 70, 107 24 STOCKHOLM
Tel: + *46* (8) 78 00 57 00
Fax: + *46* (8) 24 06 15
Mailing Address: Box 70390, 107 24 STOCKHOLM

European Affiliation: BDO Binder

Partners:	46
Professional staff:	165
Non-professional staff:	33
Total Staff:	**244**

FEE INCOME

Year End: 31.12.90	**US$**	%
Accountancy & Audit:		62.0
Tax:		20.0
Other:		18.0
Total:	**21,500,000**	

CONTACT INFORMATION
Chairman: Gert Frej
International Liason: Leif Lundqvist

CLIENT SERVICES
All Services

OTHER OFFICES
BDO REVISION AB
Storgatan 21 C, 671 00 ARVIKA
Tel: + *46* (570) 199 15 *Fax:* + *46* (570) 805 13
Contact: Jan Jonsson

BDO REVISION AB
Fabriksgatan 11, 501 03 BORÅS
Mailing Address: Box 116, 501 03 BORÅS
Tel: + *46* (33) 10 47 40 *Fax:* + *46* (33) 10 47 48
Contact: Peter Lindberg

BDO REVISION AB
Västmannav 19, 737 47 FAGERSTA
Tel: + *46* (223) 166 01
Contact: Lennart Andrén

BDO REVISION AB
Kungsportsavenyn 2, 400 14 GOTHENBURG
Mailing Address: Box 53100, 400 14 GOTHENBURG
Tel: + *46* (31) 17 64 60 *Fax:* + *46* (31) 11 17 65
Contact: Gert Frej

BDO REVISION AB
Tränggatan 5, 281 50 HÄSSLEHOLM
Tel: + *46* (451) 892 90 *Fax:* + *46* (451) 892 93
Contact: Leif Reinhold

BDO REVISION AB
Drottninggatan 17, 252 21 HELSINGBORG
Tel: + *46* (42) 12 60 50 *Fax:* + *46* (42) 12 81 25
Contact: Christer Bronning

BDO REVISION AB
Christopher Schrödersgatan 8, 374 36 KARLSHAMN
Tel: + *46* (454) 143 15 *Fax:* + *46* (454) 137 41
Contact: Mats Jönsson

BDO REVISION AB
Bergsmansgatan 2, 691 31 KARLSKOGA
Tel: + *46* (586) 328 20 *Fax:* + *46* (586) 550 37
Contact: Eva-Britta Andersson

BDO REVISION AB
Krister Hornsgatan 2, 371 36 KARLSKRONA
Tel: + *46* (455) 844 50 *Fax:* + *46* (455) 137 68
Contact: Leif Höe

BDO REVISION AB
Köpmannagatan 2, 652 26 KARLSTAD
Tel: + *46* (54) 14 43 00 *Fax:* + *46* (54) 18 62 81
Contact: Jan Hedbern

BDO REVISION AB
Skaraborgsvägen 4, 681 00 KRISTINEHAMN
Tel: + *46* (550) 831 30 *Fax:* + *46* (550) 162 24
Contact: Eivind Larsen

BDO REVISION AB
Energigatan 10 A, 434 22 KUNGSBACKA
Mailing Address: Box 10147, 434 22 KUNGSBACKA
Tel: + *46* (300) 7 00 40 *Fax:* + *46* (300) 19 99 63
Contact: Leif Reinhold

BDO REVISION AB
Roxviksgatan 5, 581 02 LINKÖPING
Mailing Address: Box 60, 581 02 LINKÖPING
Tel: + *46* (13) 11 13 50 *Fax:* + *46* (13) 12 27 10
Contact: Lennart Carlsson

BDO REVISION AB
Bergsgatan 36, 214 22 MALMÖ
Tel: + *46* (40) 19 22 50 *Fax:* + *46* (40) 96 02 35
Contact: Bertil Raue

▷

BDO REVISION AB
Bredgatan 33, 293 00 OLOFSTRÖM
Tel: + *46* (454) 406 80 *Fax:* + *46* (454) 403 24
Contact: Mats Jönsson

BDO REVISION AB
Västra Torggatan 5, 372 37 RONNEBY
Tel: + *46* (457) 170 75 *Fax:* + *46* (457) 137 45
Contact: Kurt Andersson

BDO REVISION AB
Norra Nissastigen 11, 333 00 SMÅLANDSSTENAR
Mailing Address: Box 164, 333 00 SMÅLANDSSTENAR
Tel: + *46* (371) 325 10 *Fax:* + *46* (371) 329 80
Contact: Staffan Nevby

BDO REVISION AB
Industrivägen 2, 191 62 SOLLENTUNA
Tel: + *46* (8) 700 57 00 *Fax:* + *46* (8) 35 20 66
Contact: Bertil Oppenheimer

BDO REVISION AB
Östra Storgatan 5, 294 00 SÖLVESBORG
Tel: + *46* (456) 158 05 *Fax:* + *46* (456) 117 24
Contact: Mats Jönsson

BDO REVISION AB
Östra Köpmansgatan 20 A, 444 22 STENUNGSUND
Mailing Address: Box 179, 444 22 STENUNGSUND
Tel: + *46* (303) 849 70 *Fax:* + *46* (303) 844 30
Contact: Eivind Larsen

BDO REVISION AB
Köpmangatan 24, 2tr, 852 31 SUNDSVALL
Tel: + *46* (60) 11 52 00 *Fax:* + *46* (60) 17 54 70
Contact: Tommy Eriksson

BDO REVISION AB
Torsby Herrgård, 685 00 TORSBY
Mailing Address: Box 150, 685 00 TORSBY
Tel: + *46* (560) 126 85 *Fax:* + *46* (560) 139 64
Contact: Jan Jonsson

BDO REVISION AB
Sankt Persgatan 39c, 750 03 UPPSALA
Mailing Address: Box 3053, 750 03 UPPSALA
Tel: + *46* (18) 15 56 10 *Fax:* + *46* (18) 12 17 43
Contact: Hans-Gösta Warngren

BDO REVISION AB
Slånbärsgatan 12, 722 23 VÄSTERÅS
Tel: + *46* (21) 12 82 50 *Fax:* + *46* (21) 11 54 58
Contact: Kjell Wennerstrand

Total Number of Offices: 26

LARS BOCK & CO REVISIONSBYRÅ AB

Sergels Torg 12, 12th Floor, 111 57 STOCKHOLM
Tel: + *46* (8) 14 01 00
Fax: + *46* (8) 23 43 53
Mailing Address: Box 7438, 103 91 STOCKHOLM

European Affiliation: Moore Stephens

International Contact: Lars Bock

Partners:	5
Professional staff:	25
Non-professional staff:	3
Total Staff:	**33**

FEE INCOME

Year End: 30.06.91	%
Accountancy & Audit:	90.0
Consultancy:	5.0
Tax:	5.0

CLIENT SERVICES

Audit, Corporate Finance Advice, Insolvency & Corporate Restructuring, Management & Business Advice, Mergers & Acquisitions, Taxation (Corporate)

OTHER OFFICES

LARS BOCK & CO REVISIONSBYRÅ AB
Esplanaden 14, 852 32 SUNDSVALL
Tel: + *46* (60) 11 87 70 *Fax:* + *46* (60) 11 21 02
Contact: Christer Söderman

MOORE STEPHENS SWEDEN AB
Stortorget 29, 211 34 MALMÖ
Tel: + *46* (40) 10 33 65 *Fax:* + *46* (40) 23 25 38
Contact: Olle Hansson

Total Number of Offices: 4

DAHLSTRÖM & HOLMBERG REVISIONSBYRÅ AB

Birger Jarlsgatan 26, 1tr, 114 34 STOCKHOLM
Tel: + *46* (8) 679 85 35
Fax: + *46* (8) 611 32 99

European Affiliation: ATD International

International Contact: Peter Olofson
Bengt Beergrehn

Partners:	4
Professional staff:	4
Non-professional staff:	3
Total Staff:	**11**

CONTACT INFORMATION

Partner: Bengt Beergrehn
Partner: Göran Holmberg
Partner: Göran Dahlström
Partner: Peter Olofson

CLIENT SERVICES

Audit, Corporate Finance Advice, Taxation (Corporate)

EKONOMIGRUPPEN AB

Hälsingegatan 47, 100 31 STOCKHOLM
Tel: + *46* (8) 736 00 00
Fax: + *46* (8) 30 94 23
Mailing Address: Box 21044, 100 31 STOCKHOLM

European Affiliation: INPACT - International Network of Professional Accountants

International Contact: Kurt Kalmelid

Partners:	5
Professional staff:	18
Non-professional staff:	3
Total Staff:	**26**

FEE INCOME

Year End: 30.04.91	**SKr**	%
Accountancy & Audit:	9,300,000	65.0
Tax:	3,000,000	20.0
Other:	2,000,000	15.0
Total:	**14,300,000**	

CONTACT INFORMATION

Managing Partner: Göran Nygren
Managing Partner: Björn Lagerlöf
Accountancy (General): Bibbi Wallin
Audit: Kurt Kalmelid
Public Sector: Eva Blank
Tax (Corporate): Eva-Britt Nilsson
Computer Installation: Björn Lagerlöf

CLIENT SERVICES
Accountancy (General), Audit, Computer Installation, Insolvency & Corporate Restructuring, Management & Business Advice, Management Buy-outs, Pensions Planning, Taxation (Corporate)

ERNST & YOUNG

Adolf Fredriks Kyrkogata 2, 103 62 STOCKHOLM
Tel: + *46* (8) 613 90 00
Fax: + *46* (8) 10 57 38
Mailing Address: Box 3143, 103 62 STOCKHOLM

European Affiliation: Ernst & Young Europe

Partners:	155
Professional staff:	1,650
Non-professional staff:	300
Total Staff:	**2,105**

FEE INCOME

Year End: 30.04.91	%
Accountancy & Audit:	80.0
Consultancy:	10.0
Tax:	10.0

CONTACT INFORMATION
Chairman: Stig Nilsson
Managing Partner: Ulf Spång
Management Consultancy: Lars-Åke Lann
Accountancy & Audit: Torbjöm Hanson
Tax Consulting: Jan Kleerup

CLIENT SERVICES
Accountancy (General), Audit, Corporate Finance Advice, Management & Business Advice, Mergers & Acquisitions, Value for Money Studies, Taxation (Corporate), International Reporting, VAT, Stock Exchange Introductions, Information Technology

Industry Specialisations: Public Sector Audit

MAJOR CLIENTS
Aritmos, Asea, Asea Brown Boveri, BP, Cardo, Eken, Eldon, Electrolux, ESAB, Esselte, Euroc, FFV, Fläkt, Forsheda, Gambro, H&M Hennes & Mauritz, IKEA, Incentive, MODO, Perstorp

OTHER OFFICES

ERNST & YOUNG
Oxtorget, 343 24 ÄLMHULT
Mailing Address: Box 605, 343 24 ÄLMHULT
Tel: + *46* (476) 122 80 *Fax:* + *46* (476) 127 13
Contact: Jan Johnsson

ERNST & YOUNG
Storgatan 7, 262 32 ÄNGELHOLM
Tel: + *46* (431) 135 25 *Fax:* + *46* (431) 835 40
Contact: Bengt Jönsson

ERNST & YOUNG
Skolgatan 25, 671 23 ARVIKA
Mailing Address: Box 130, 671 23 ARVIKA
Tel: + *46* (570) 180 20 *Fax:* + *46* (570) 113 67
Contact: Sven Bertil Ryman

ERNST & YOUNG
Telegatan 12E, 774 24 AVESTA
Mailing Address: Box 174, 774 24 AVESTA
Tel: + *46* (226) 560 20 *Fax:* + *46* (226) 502 31
Contact: Vilmos Szabo

ERNST & YOUNG
Skaraborgsvägen 6, 502 34 BORÅS
Tel: + *46* (33) 10 00 30 *Fax:* + *46* (33) 14 01 97
Contact: Karl-Erik Wängnerud

ERNST & YOUNG
Eriksgatan 23, 745 35 ENKÖPING
Tel: + *46* (171) 278 15 *Fax:* + *46* (171) 278 25
Contact: Kurt Häggborn

ERNST & YOUNG
Energigatan 12, 434 37 KUNGSBACKA
Tel: + *46* (300) 707 90 *Fax:* + *46* (300) 707 80
Contact: Gösta Dahlström

ERNST & YOUNG
Kunsgatan 18, 632 21 ESKILSTUNA
Tel: + *46* (16) 14 73 10 *Fax:* + *46* (16) 14 79 30
Contact: Lars Erik Anderson

ERNST & YOUNG
Engelbrektsgatan 16, 791 26 FALUN
Mailing Address: Box 285, 791 26 FALUN
Tel: + *46* (23) 631 10 *Fax:* + *46* (23) 197 46
Contact: Björn Aspling

ERNST & YOUNG
Kalkugnsvägen 1, 612 23 FINSPÅNG
Mailing Address: Box 121, 612 23 FINSPÅNG
Tel: + *46* (122) 150 10 *Fax:* + *46* (122) 111 94
Contact: Lars Rydwall

ERNST & YOUNG
Södra Kungsgatan 7A, 642 00 FLEN
Mailing Address: Box 29, 642 00 FLEN
Tel: + *46* (157) 124 50 *Fax:* + *46* (157) 136 55
Contact: Ingrid Andersson

ERNST & YOUNG
Hantverkargatan 33, 801 35 GÄVLE
Mailing Address: Box 1110, 801 35 GÄVLE
Tel: + *46* (26) 18 47 20 *Fax:* + *46* (26) 14 19 09
Contact: Karl-Gustav Lindblom

ERNST & YOUNG
Köpmangatan 5, 332 21 GISLAVED
Mailing Address: Box 13, 332 21 GISLAVED
Tel: + *46* (371) 120 80 *Fax:* + *46* (371) 137 81
Contact: Mats Norin

ERNST & YOUNG
Odinsgatan 13, 401 82 GOTHENBURG
Mailing Address: Box 2171, 401 82 GOTHENBURG
Tel: + *46* (31) 63 77 00 *Fax:* + *46* (31) 15 40 50
Contact: Bertel Enlund

ERNST & YOUNG
Köpmansgatan 23, 302 42 HALMSTAD
Tel: + *46* (35) 11 89 00 *Fax:* + *46* (35) 11 11 48
Contact: Bo Persson

ERNST & YOUNG
Röingegatan 38, 281 38 HÄSSLEHOLM
Tel: + *46* (451) 846 15 *Fax:* + *46* (451) 859 69
Contact: Jerker Thorvaldsson

ERNST & YOUNG
Järnvägsgatan 14, 251 07 HELSINGBORG
Mailing Address: Box 780, 251 07 HELSINGBORG
Tel: + *46* (42) 17 78 00 *Fax:* + *46* (42) 17 78 90
Contact: Stig Nilsson

ERNST & YOUNG
Östra Storgatan 17, 550 02 JÖNKÖPING
Mailing Address: Box 2224, 550 02 JÖNKÖPING
Tel: + *46* (36) 30 10 00 *Fax:* + *46* (36) 30 10 80
Contact: Rolf Engdahl

ERNST & YOUNG
Skeppsbron 5, 391 27 KALMAR
Mailing Address: Box 753, 391 27 KALMAR
Tel: + *46* (480) 882 70 *Fax:* + *46* (480) 127 63
Contact: Carl-Axel I. Kullman

▷

Sweden

ERNST & YOUNG
Erik Dahlbergsvägen 24, 374 23 KARLSHAMN
Mailing Address: Box 151, 374 23 KARLSHAMN
Tel: + *46* (454) 195 60 *Fax:* + *46* (454) 149 16
Contact: Hans Ivarsson

ERNST & YOUNG
Kungsgatan 16, 651 11 KARLSTAD
Mailing Address: Box 477, 651 11 KARLSTAD
Tel: + *46* (54) 14 24 00 *Fax:* + *46* (54) 18 05 55
Contact: Olle Andersson

ERNST & YOUNG
Drottninggatan 11, 641 23 KATRINEHOLM
Mailing Address: Box 388, 641 23 KATRINEHOLM
Tel: + *46* (150) 164 30 *Fax:* + *46* (150) 150 80
Contact: Owe Svedberg

ERNST & YOUNG
Åsgränd 2, 731 22 KÖPING
Mailing Address: Box 95, 731 22 KÖPING
Tel: + *46* (221) 158 10 *Fax:* + *46* (221) 150 45
Contact: Sven-Erik Andersson

ERNST & YOUNG
Åsenvägen 2, 443 23 LERUM
Mailing Address: Box 153, 443 23 LERUM
Tel: + *44* (302) 116 70 *Fax:* + *46* (302) 171 52
Contact: Bo-Anders Arvidsson

ERNST & YOUNG
Repslagaregatan 21, 581 05 LINKÖPING
Mailing Address: Box 450, 581 05 LINKÖPING
Tel: + *46* (13) 11 59 70 *Fax:* + *46* (13) 13 75 07
Contact: Lars-Inge Johansson

ERNST & YOUNG
Kvartersmästargatan 16, 951 53 LULEÅ
Tel: + *46* (920) 940 55 *Fax:* + *46* (920) 949 64
Contact: Torbjörn Köhler

ERNST & YOUNG
Bredgatan 10, 222 21 LUND
Tel: + *46* (46) 15 01 05 *Fax:* + *46* (46) 12 66 10
Contact: Göran Carlsson

ERNST & YOUNG
Torggatan 2, 211 40 MALMÖ
Tel: + *46* (40) 24 95 00 *Fax:* + *46* (40) 23 70 91
Contact: Lennart Sjölin

ERNST & YOUNG
Drottninggatan 14, 285 21 MARKARYD
Mailing Address: Box 27, 285 21 MARKARYD
Tel: + *46* (433) 160 10 *Fax:* + *46* (433) 165 49
Contact: Owe Svensson

ERNST & YOUNG
Bispmotalagatan 11A, 591 24 MOTALA
Mailing Address: Box 384, 591 24 MOTALA
Tel: + *46* (141) 520 90 *Fax:* + *46* (141) 552 95
Contact: Torsten Johansson

ERNST & YOUNG
Drottninggatan 6, 600 40 NORRKÖPING
Mailing Address: Box 1050, 600 40 NORRKÖPING
Tel: + *46* (11) 10 67 30 *Fax:* + *46* (11) 16 09 11
Contact: Olof Bröte

ERNST & YOUNG
Stora Brogatan 2, 761 21 NORRTÄLJE
Mailing Address: Box 68, 761 21 NORRTÄLJE
Tel: + *46* (176) 241 20 *Fax:* + *46* (176) 238 78
Contact: Jan Erik Löfgren

ERNST & YOUNG
Sankt Annegatan 2, 611 34 NYKÖPING
Tel: + *46* (155) 670 80 *Fax:* + *46* (155) 823 18
Contact: Peter Söderström

ERNST & YOUNG
Oskarsparken 1, 702 12 ÖREBRO
Tel: + *46* (19) 10 48 20 *Fax:* + *46* (19) 13 49 85
Contact: Kurt Gezelius

ERNST & YOUNG
Viktoriaesplanaden 1C, 891 24 ÖRNSKÖLDSVIK
Mailing Address: Box 163, 891 24 ÖRNSKÖLDSVIK
Tel: + *46* (660) 856 90 *Fax:* + *46* (660) 144 02
Contact: Bengt Söderström

ERNST & YOUNG
Verkstadsgatan 13, 572 35 OSKARSHAMN
Tel: + *46* (491) 810 90 *Fax:* + *46* (491) 831 60
Contact: Göran Tyréus

ERNST & YOUNG
Kyrkgatan 84, 831 34 ÖSTERSUND
Tel: + *46* (63) 13 27 70 *Fax:* + *46* (63) 13 27 44
Contact: Ingegärd Henriksson

ERNST & YOUNG
Lillbrogatan 8, 941 32 PITEÅ
Tel: + *46* (911) 910 35 *Fax:* + *46* (911) 913 33
Contact: Björn Lundkvist

ERNST & YOUNG
Kyrkogatan 4, 661 00 SÄFFLE
Mailing Address: Box 140, 661 00 SÄFFLE
Tel: + *46* (533) 172 80 *Fax:* + *46* (533) 156 57
Contact: Stefan Persson

ERNST & YOUNG
Bråstagatan 1, 733 21 SALA
Mailing Address: Box 42, 733 21 SALA
Tel: + *46* (224) 130 15 *Fax:* + *46* (224) 162 47
Contact: Hans Johansson

ERNST & YOUNG
Nygatan 59, 931 31 SKELLEFTEÅ
Tel: + *46* (910) 538 90 *Fax:* + *46* (910) 138 32
Contact: Claes Rundquist

ERNST & YOUNG
Högskolevägen 6, 541 28 SKÖVDE
Mailing Address: Box 393, 541 28 SKÖVDE
Tel: + *46* (500) 105 90 *Fax:* + *46* (500) 887 38
Contact: Owe Hjalmarsson

ERNST & YOUNG
Källgatan 4, 645 22 STRÄNGNÄS
Tel: + *46* (152) 190 00 *Fax:* + *46* (152) 191 03

ERNST & YOUNG
Nytorpsvägen 34, 183 53 TÄBY
Tel: + *46* (8) 758 02 40 *Fax:* + *46* (8) 768 29 50

ERNST & YOUNG
Storgatan 31, 573 22 TRANÅS
Mailing Address: Box 198, 573 22 TRANÅS
Tel: + *46* (140) 171 30 *Fax:* + *46* (140) 158 69
Contact: Olle Hanning

ERNST & YOUNG
Kungsgatan 49A, 461 27 TROLLHÄTTAN
Mailing Address: Box 323, 461 27 TROLLHÄTTAN
Tel: + *46* (520) 182 05 *Fax:* + *46* (520) 110 06
Contact: Dan Brännström

ERNST & YOUNG
Långhagsgatan, 451 50 UDDEVALLA
Tel: + *46* (522) 980 90 *Fax:* + *46* (522) 104 20
Contact: Per Schwartzman

ERNST & YOUNG
Domarevägen 5, 904 02 UMEÅ
Mailing Address: Box 4017, 904 02 UMEÅ
Tel: + *46* (90) 13 48 15 *Fax:* + *46* (90) 12 69 85
Contact: Åke Ahlman

ERNST & YOUNG
Portalgatan 2B, 750 23 UPPSALA
Mailing Address: Box 23036, 750 23 UPPSALA
Tel: + *46* (18) 24 33 00 *Fax:* + *46* (18) 24 33 50
Contact: Ingemar Rindstig

ERNST & YOUNG
Västra Vallgatan 13, 432 40 VARBERG
Tel: + *46* (340) 890 20 *Fax:* + *46* (340) 808 97
Contact: Hans B. Diding

ERNST & YOUNG
Storgatan 26, 331 24 VÄRNAMO
Mailing Address: Box 447, 331 24 VÄRNAMO
Tel: + *46* (370) 186 00 *Fax:* + *46* (370) 174 60
Contact: Bo-Göran Vivhult

ERNST & YOUNG
Iggebygatan 12, 720 04 VÄSTERÅS
Mailing Address: Box 4023, 720 04 VÄSTERÅS
Tel: + *46* (21) 12 82 90 *Fax:* + *46* (21) 12 82 36
Contact: Lars-Henrik Andersson

ERNST & YOUNG
Fiskaretorget 1, 593 22 VÄSTERVIK
Mailing Address: Box 111, 593 22 VÄSTERVIK
Tel: + *46* (490) 168 70 *Fax:* + *46* (490) 136 85
Contact: Mats Hasselguist

ERNST & YOUNG
Värendsgatan 6, 352 34 VÄXJÖ
Tel: + *46* (470) 451 55 *Fax:* + *46* (470) 467 54
Contact: Bertil Pettersson

ERNST & YOUNG
Klostergatan 8, 352 30 VÄXJÖ
Tel: + *46* (470) 134 15 *Fax:* + *46* (470) 263 82
Contact: Peter Bjureberg

ERNST & YOUNG
Kvarnängsgatan 3, 598 00 VIMMERBY
Mailing Address: Box 63, 598 00 VIMMERBY
Tel: + *46* (492) 120 90 *Fax:* + *46* (492) 151 93
Contact: Ulf Saxholm

Total Number of Offices: 63

FÖRENADE REVISORER I ALINGSÅS AB

Tomasgårdsvägen 19, 441 39 ALINGSÅS
Tel: + *46* (322) 190 10
Fax: + *46* (322) 347 80

European Affiliation: Alliott Peirson International

International Contact: Sven-Erik Nilsson

FÖRENADE REVISORER I GÖTEBORG AB

Viktoriagatan 3, 411 25 GOTHENBURG
Tel: + *46* (31) 17 06 70
Fax: + *46* (31) 11 13 56

European Affiliation: Alliott Peirson International

GÖTEBORGS FORETAGS REVISION AB

Prinsgatan 12, 413 05 GOTHENBURG
Tel: + *46* (31) 14 52 00
Fax: + *46* (31) 12 01 25

European Affiliation: The International Group of Accounting Firms Ltd (IGAF)

International Contact: Ronny Erikson

IDEKO REVISIONSBYRÅ AB

Västra Hamngatan 12, 411 17 GOTHENBURG
Tel: + *46* (31) 17 58 00
Fax: + *46* (31) 11 93 20

European Affiliation: Urbach Hacker Young International

International Contact: Anders Agermark

SVEN JOSEFSONS REVISIONSBYRÅ AB

Huvudstagatan 1, 17 158 SOLNA, Stockholm
Tel: + *46* (8) 27 34 00
Fax: + *46* (8) 82 34 00

European Affiliation: Clark Kenneth Leventhal

International Contact: Arne Wallberg

Partners:	3
Professional staff:	11
Non-professional staff:	2
Total Staff:	**16**

FEE INCOME

Year End: 1990	**%**
Accountancy & Audit:	60.0
Tax:	15.0
Other:	25.0

CLIENT SERVICES
Accountancy (General), Audit, Corporate Finance Advice, Insolvency & Corporate Restructuring, Management & Business Advice, Taxation (Corporate), Taxation (International)

KPMG

KPMG BOHLINS REVISIONSBYRÅ AB

Tegelbacken 4, 103 23 STOCKHOLM
Tel: + *46* (8) 723 91 00
Fax: + *46* (8) 10 52 58
Mailing Address: Box 16106, 103 23 STOCKHOLM

European Affiliation: KPMG

International Contact: Owe Eurenius

Partners:	161
Professional staff:	1,736
Non-professional staff:	293
Total Staff:	**2,190**

FEE INCOME

Year End: 30.04.91	**SKr**
Total:	**983,000,000**

CONTACT INFORMATION
Chairman: Bo Fridman
Managing Partner: Karl-G. Giertz
Accountancy (General): Torulf Jönsson
Audit: Åke Näsman
Corporate Finance: Thomas Rynell
Insolvency: Arne Gunnarsson
Management Consultancy: Håkan Friberg
Administration: Bengt Holmström
Tax (Corporate): Clas Silfverhielm
Tax (International): Anders Köhlmark
Banking: Ole Claesson
Insurance: Peter Zell

▷

Sweden

CLIENT SERVICES
Accountancy (General), Audit, Corporate Finance Advice, Insolvency & Corporate Restructuring, Management & Business Advice, Management Buy-outs, Mergers & Acquisitions, Taxation (Corporate), Taxation (International)

MAJOR CLIENTS
AGA, Atlas Copco, Avesta, BPA, Handelsbanken, Marabou, NCC, Nordbanken, Postverket, Procordia, Ratos, Saab Scania, Sandvik, SAS, Skanska, Staora, S-E-Banken, Trelleborg, Trygg Hansa, Volvo

OTHER OFFICES

KPMG BOHLINS REVISIONSBYRÅ AB
Ramdemacherg 38, 632 20 ESKILSTUNA
Tel: + *46* (16) 16 77 00 *Fax:* + *46* (16) 13 95 35
Contact: Yngve Gustalsson

KPMG BOHLINS REVISIONSBYRÅ AB
Kristinegatan 28, 791 21 FALUN
Mailing Address: Box 7, 791 21 FALUN
Tel: + *46* (23) 217 20 *Fax:* + *46* (23) 229 74
Contact: Rolf Lekander

KPMG BOHLINS REVISIONSBYRÅ AB
Ruddammsgatan 30, 803 20 GÄVLE
Tel: + *46* (26) 15 06 00 *Fax:* + *46* (26) 15 06 99
Contact: Ola Dackell

KPMG BOHLIN & JACOBSSON AB
Norra Hamng 22, 404 39 GOTHENBURG
Mailing Address: Box 11908, 404 39 GOTHENBURG
Tel: + *46* (31) 61 48 00 *Fax:* + *46* (31) 15 26 55
Contact: Harry Ahlman

KPMG BOHLINS REVISIONSBYRÅ AB
Torsgatan 1, 302 36 HALMSTAD
Tel: + *46* (35) 15 43 00 *Fax:* + *46* (35) 11 29 21
Contact: Peter Zell

KPMG BOHLINS REVISIONSBYRÅ AB
Drottninggatan 14, 251 21 HELSINGBORG
Tel: + *46* (42) 19 59 00 *Fax:* + *46* (42) 19 59 99
Contact: Göran Nilsson

KPMG BOHLINS REVISIONSBYRÅ AB
Trädgårdsgatan 37, 551 14 JÖNKÖPING
Mailing Address: Box 214, 551 14 JÖNKÖPING
Tel: + *46* (36) 11 90 25 *Fax:* + *46* (36) 11 35 70
Contact: Lars Peterson

KPMG BOHLINS REVISIONSBYRÅ AB
Skeppsbrogatan 49, 392 31 KALMAR
Tel: + *46* (480) 881 60 *Fax:* + *46* (480) 289 79
Contact: Hasse Svensson

KPMG BOHLINS REVISIONSBYRÅ AB
Drottninggatan 21, 651 02 KARLSTAD
Mailing Address: Box 7, 651 02 KARLSTAD
Tel: + *46* (54) 11 62 65 *Fax:* + *46* (54) 11 38 05
Contact: Guidon Berggren

KPMG BOHLINS REVISIONSBYRÅ AB
Björkhemsvägen 15, 291 54 KRISTIANSTAD
Tel: + *46* (44) 18 35 00 *Fax:* + *46* (44) 11 48 60
Contact: Gert Enoksson

KPMG BOHLINS REVISIONSBYRÅ AB
Nygatan 18, 581 02 LINKÖPING
Mailing Address: Box 291, 581 02 LINKÖPING
Tel: + *46* (13) 28 98 00 *Fax:* + *46* (13) 13 14 34 30
Contact: Stig Byström

KPMG BOHLINS REVISIONSBYRÅ AB
Smadjegatan 14, 951 22 LULEÅ
Mailing Address: Box 139, 951 22 LULEÅ
Tel: + *46* (920) 941 10 *Fax:* + *46* (920) 148 30
Contact: Anders Åström

KPMG BOHLINS REVISIONSBYRÅ AB
Östra Mårtensgatan 15, 220 02 LUND
Mailing Address: Box 2025, 220 02 LUND
Tel: + *46* (46) 11 74 50 *Fax:* + *46* (46) 13 92 28
Contact: Kent Lindén

KPMG BOHLINS REVISIONSBYRÅ AB
Kaptensgatan 1, 203 14 MALMÖ
Mailing Address: Box 4288, 203 14 MALMÖ
Tel: + *46* (40) 35 62 00 *Fax:* + *46* (40) 12 70 47
Contact: Alf Svensson

KPMG BOHLINS REVISIONSBYRÅ AB
Hantverksgatan 7, 571 21 NÄSSJÖ
Mailing Address: Box 85, 571 21 NÄSSJÖ
Tel: + *46* (380) 740 40 *Fax:* + *46* (380) 102 92
Contact: Allan Pettersson

KPMG BOHLINS REVISIONSBYRÅ AB
Olai Kyrkogata 50, 600 02 NORRKÖPING
Mailing Address: Box 2223, 600 02 NORRKÖPING
Tel: + *46* (11) 21 54 00 *Fax:* + *46* (11) 13 22 31
Contact: Hans Åkervall

KPMG BOHLINS REVISIONSBYRÅ AB
Västra Kvarngatan 14, 611 31 NYKÖPING
Tel: + *46* (155) 174 90 *Fax:* + *46* (155) 896 69
Contact: Bengt Abrahamsson

KPMG BOHLINS REVISIONSBYRÅ AB
Slottsgatan 10, 701 43 ÖREBRO
Mailing Address: Box 174, 701 43 ÖREBRO
Tel: + *46* (19) 12 42 50 *Fax:* + *46* (19) 12 86 51
Contact: Jörgen Askengren

KPMG BOHLINS REVISIONSBYRÅ AB
Viktoriaesplanaden 8, 891 33 ÖRNSKÖLDSVIK
Tel: + *46* (660) 835 00 *Fax:* + *46* (660) 814 56
Contact: Tommy Nordman

KPMG BOHLINS REVISIONSBYRÅ AB
Trädgårdsgatan 8, 931 31 SKELLEFTEÅ
Tel: + *46* (910) 381 55 *Fax:* + *46* (910) 792 83
Contact: Tommy Israelsson

KPMG BOHLINS REVISIONSBYRÅ AB
Kolvägen 15, 852 29 SUNDSVALL
Tel: + *46* (60) 15 56 90 *Fax:* + *46* (60) 11 32 89
Contact: Stig Mellander

KPMG BOHLINS REVISIONSBYRÅ AB
Rådhusesplanaden 3 B, 901 06 UMEÅ
Mailing Address: Box 260, 901 06 UMEÅ
Tel: + *46* (90) 18 07 00 *Fax:* + *46* (90) 12 75 14
Contact: Lars Valfridsson

KPMG BOHLINS REVISIONSBYRÅ AB
Bangårdsgatan 13, 751 49 UPPSALA
Mailing Address: Box 1918, 751 49 UPPSALA
Tel: + *46* (18) 15 67 20 *Fax:* + *46* (18) 69 67 81
Contact: Lennart Jakobsson

KPMG BOHLINS REVISIONSBYRÅ AB
Kopparbergsvägen 14, Aros Centre 241, 722 10 VÄSTERÅS
Tel: + *46* (21) 10 62 00 *Fax:* + *46* (21) 14 42 44
Contact: Per-Oluf Hansen

KPMG BOHLINS REVISIONSBYRÅ AB
Västergatan 1, 352 30 VÄXJÖ
Tel: + *46* (470) 280 35 *Fax:* + *46* (470) 126 30
Contact: Håkan Lindström

Total Number of Offices: 100

LANDINS REVISIONSBYRÅ AB

Box 1236, 171 24 SOLNA
Tel: + *46* (8) 29 59 30
Fax: + *46* (8) 28 12 81

European Affiliation: The International Group of Accounting Firms Ltd (IGAF)

International Contact: Olle Landin

LINDEBERGS REVISIONSBYRÅ AB

Sveavägen 34, Box 3061, 103 61 STOCKHOLM
Tel: + *46* (8) 787 70 00
Fax: + *46* (8) 10 10 27

European Affiliation: Grant Thornton International

International Contact: Hans Franzen

Partners:	54
Professional staff:	214
Non-professional staff:	60
Total Staff:	**328**

FEE INCOME

Year End: 1990	**SKr (million)**
Total:	**30,791**

CONTACT INFORMATION

Managing Partner: Anders Östberg

CLIENT SERVICES

Accountancy (General), Audit, Insolvency & Corporate Restructuring, Management & Business Advice, Taxation (Corporate), Taxation (International), Computer Consultancy

OTHER OFFICES

LINDEBERGS REVISIONSBYRÅ AB
Lilla Brogatan 17, Box 126, 501 03 BORÅS
Tel: + *46* (33) 11 76 75 *Fax:* + *46* (33) 10 00 06

LINDEBERGS REVISIONSBYRÅ AB
Kungsgatan 10, 632 21 ESKILSTUNA
Tel: + *46* (16) 11 01 20 *Fax:* + *46* (16) 11 60 75

LINDEBERGS REVISIONSBYRÅ AB
Korsgatan 3, 1tr, 411 16 GOTHENBURG
Tel: + *46* (31) 11 76 05 *Fax:* + *46* (31) 11 27 65

LINDEBERGS REVISIONSBYRÅ AB
Järnvägsgaten 25, 252 24 HELSINGBORG
Tel: + *46* (42) 24 00 80 *Fax:* + *46* (42) 24 05 31

LINDEBERGS REVISIONSBYRÅ AB
Norra Klaragatan 4, Box 85, 651 03 KARLSTAD
Tel: + *46* (54) 10 25 60 *Fax:* + *46* (54) 10 00 55

LINDEBERGS REVISIONSBYRÅ AB
Allengaten 6, 291 59 KRISTIANSTAD
Tel: + *46* (44) 10 00 50 *Fax:* + *46* (44) 10 11 50

LINDEBERGS REVISIONSBYRÅ AB
Kungsgatan 41, 711 20 LINDESBERG
Tel: + *46* (581) 170 70 *Fax:* + *46* (581) 170 77

LINDEBERGS REVISIONSBYRÅ AB
Ågatan 31, 582 22 LINKÖPING
Tel: + *46* (13) 13 04 30 *Fax:* + *46* (13) 11 08 42

LINDEBERGS REVISIONSBYRÅ AB
Varvsgatan 47, Box 953, 951 29 LULEÅ
Tel: + *46* (920) 870 80 *Fax:* + *46* (920) 276 06

LINDEBERGS REVISIONSBYRÅ AB
Kaptensgaten 1, Box 4295, 203 14 MALMÖ
Tel: + *46* (40) 12 40 40 *Fax:* + *46* (40) 12 40 50

LINDEBERGS REVISIONSBYRÅ AB
Sankt Persgatan 95, Box 2323, 600 02 NORRKÖPING
Tel: + *46* (11) 10 88 00 *Fax:* + *46* (11) 10 88 10

LINDEBERGS REVISIONSBYRÅ AB
Folkungavägen 1, 611 34 NYKÖPING
Tel: + *46* (155) 894 00 *Fax:* + *46* (155) 824 90

LINDEBERGS REVISIONSBYRÅ AB
Järntorgsgatan 1, Box 504, 701 50 ÖREBRO
Tel: + *46* (19) 17 09 10 *Fax:* + *46* (19) 17 09 19

LINDEBERGS REVISIONSBYRÅ AB
Storgatan 26, Box 634, 831 27 ÖSTERSUND
Tel: + *46* (63) 12 70 90 *Fax:* + *46* (63) 11 29 10

LINDEBERGS REVISIONSBYRÅ AB
Storgatan 31, 852 30 SUNDSVALL
Tel: + *46* (60) 17 46 70 *Fax:* + *46* (60) 12 67 60

LINDEBERGS REVISIONSBYRÅ AB
Norra Ringvägen 36, 722 15 VÄSTERÅS
Tel: + *46* (21) 14 00 45 *Fax:* + *46* (21) 14 00 37

LINDEBERGS REVISIONSBYRÅ AB
Aulingatan 22, Box 93, 271 22 YSTAD
Tel: + *46* (411) 736 90 *Fax:* + *46* (411) 730 65

Total Number of Offices: 18

LRF REVISION AB

Karlbergsvägen 77-81, 100 31 STOCKHOLM
Tel: + *46* (8) 37 25 00
Fax: + *46* (8) 32 25 61

European Affiliation: Moores Rowland International

International Contact: Rolf Meyer

OTHER OFFICES

LRF REVISION AB
Allegatan 39, 501 07 BORÅS
Tel: + *46* (33) 11 92 50 *Fax:* + *46* (33) 11 26 54
Contact: Ingemar Cederlund

LRF REVISION AB
Hedåsgatan 3, 412 53 GOTHENBURG
Tel: + *46* (31) 81 05 75 *Fax:* + *46* (31) 20 24 17
Contact: Sune Apelqvist

LRF REVISION AB
Stabbgårdsgatan 3, 620 12 HEMSE
Tel: + *46* (497) 805 40 *Fax:* + *46* (497) 843 46
Contact: Anders Andersson

LRF REVISION AB
Box 2173, 550 02 JÖNKÖPING
Tel: + *46* (36) 16 00 35 *Fax:* + *46* (36) 16 02 13
Contact: Göran Arthursson

LRF REVISION AB
Box 565, 201 25 MALMÖ
Tel: + *46* (40) 724 35 *Fax:* + *46* (40) 30 30 79
Contact: Jens Kronblad

LRF REVISION AB
Nygatan 93, 602 34 NORRKÖPING
Tel: + *46* (11) 23 71 10 *Fax:* + *46* (11) 23 76 60
Contact: Rolf Meyer

LRF REVISION AB
Hertig Karls Allé 18, Box 372, 701 47 ÖREBRO
Tel: + *46* (19) 10 32 32 *Fax:* + *46* (19) 11 65 61
Contact: Peter Blomgren

LRF REVISION AB
Box 707, 941 28 PITEÅ
Tel: + *46* (911) 170 40 *Fax:* + *46* (911) 194 15
Contact: Thommy Isacsson

▷

LRF REVISION AB
Drottninggatan 17, 432 41 VARBERG
Tel: + *46* (340) 180 60 *Fax:* + *46* (340) 877 17
Contact: Daniel Carlsson

LRF REVISION AB
Box 1046, 621 21 VISBY
Tel: + *46* (498) 138 65 *Fax:* + *46* (498) 787 66
Contact: Tore Karlström

LRF SKATTEBYRÅN
Von Troilsvägen 1, 213 01 MALMÖ
Tel: + *46* (70) 22 50 50 *Fax:* + *46* (70) 21 32 37
Contact: Urban Rydin

Total Number of Offices: 12

REVISIONSBYRÅN LUNDBERG & CO AB

Aniaraplatsen 2, 191 23 SOLLENTUNA
Tel: + *46* (8) 35 91 20
Fax: + *46* (8) 96 51 08
Mailing Address: Box 179, 191 23 SOLLENTUNA

European Affiliation: Midsnell International

International Contact: Hannu Harju

Partners:	4
Professional staff:	7
Non-professional staff:	2
Total Staff:	**13**

FEE INCOME

Year End: 30.06.91	**Skr**	%
Accountancy & Audit:	2,500,000	76.0
Insolvency:	200,000	6.0
Consultancy:	300,000	9.0
Tax:	100,000	3.0
Other:	200,000	6.0
Total:	**3,300,000**	

CONTACT INFORMATION

Chairman: Lars Lundberg
Audit: Inger Stockhammar

CLIENT SERVICES

Accountancy (General), Audit, Corporate Finance Advice, Insolvency & Corporate Restructuring, Management & Business Advice, Management Buy-outs, Mergers & Acquisitions, Taxation (Corporate), Taxation (International), Trust Settlement & Estates

OTHER OFFICES

REVISIONSBYRÅN LUNDBERG & CO AB
Nybrogatan 14, 114 39 STOCKHOLM
Tel: + *46* (8) 24 38 70 *Fax:* + *46* (8) 661 16 64
Contact: Lars Lundberg

Total Number of Offices: 2

LARS NORBERG & CO AB

Södra Förstadsgatan 13, 200 10 MALMÖ
Tel: + *46* (40) 791 25
Fax: + *46* (40) 97 76 60
Mailing Address: Box 17084, 200 10 MALMÖ

European Affiliation: Urbach Hacker Young International

International Contact: Lars Norberg

Partners:	1
Professional staff:	7
Non-professional staff:	2
Total Staff:	**10**

FEE INCOME

Year End: 30.07.91	%
Accountancy & Audit:	80.0
Consultancy:	20.0

CONTACT INFORMATION

Audit & Tax: Lars Norberg
Audit & Administration: Anders Svensson

CLIENT SERVICES

Accountancy (General), Audit, Management & Business Advice, Management Buy-outs, Mergers & Acquisitions, Pensions Planning, Taxation (Corporate), Taxation (International)

ÖHRLINGS REVEKO AB

Tegeluddsvägen 31, 115 41 STOCKHOLM
Tel: + *46* (8) 666 80 00
Fax: + *46* (8) 662 19 83
Mailing Address: Box 27318, 102 54 STOCKHOLM

European Affiliation: Coopers & Lybrand Europe

International Contact: Robert Barnden

Total Staff: 2,330

CONTACT INFORMATION

Chairman: Bertil Edlund
Managing Partner: Ingvar Pramhäll
Corporate Finance: Göran Tidström
Management Consultancy: Olof Agervald
Administration: Ingvar Pramhäll
Public Sector: Lars Ryberg
Tax (Corporate): Lars W. Hemmingsson
Tax (International): Greger Olsson

CLIENT SERVICES

All Services

Industry Specialisations: Banking, Motor, Forestry, Insurance, Food & Drink, Pharmaceuticals, Communications

Total Number of Offices: 100

OSBORNE JOHNSONS REVISIONSBYRÅ AB

Kammakargatan 7, 11140 STOCKHOLM
Tel: + *46* (8) 23 87 50
Fax: + *46* (8) 11 03 02

European Affiliation: TGI International

International Contact: Kurt Hammarström

OTHER OFFICES

OSBORNE JOHNSONS REVISIONSBYRÅ AB
Västra Esplanaden 1, 352 30 VÄXJÖ
Tel: + *46* (470) 1 74 75 *Fax:* + *46* (470) 4 49 32

OSBORNE JOHNSONS REVISIONSBYRÅ AB
Bagersgatan 2, 211 25 MALMÖ
Tel: + *46* (40) 7 39 25 *Fax:* + *46* (40) 30 29 11

Total Number of Offices: 3

OSSERS REVISIONSBYRÅ AB

Drivhjulsvägen 28, 126 30 HÄGERSTEN, Stockholm
Tel: + *46* (8) 645 26 65
Fax: + *46* (8) 18 91 43

European Affiliation: S & W International

International Contact: Leif Osser

Partners:	3
Professional staff:	4
Non-professional staff:	1
Total Staff:	**8**

FEE INCOME

Year End: 30.04.91	**SKr**	**%**
Accountancy & Audit:		70.0
Insolvency:		5.0
Consultancy:		10.0
Tax:		5.0
Other:		10.0
Total:	**3,500,000**	

CONTACT INFORMATION

Managing Partner: Leif Osser
Administration: Magda Osser
Accountancy & Administration: Magda Osser
Corporate Finance & Insolvency: Leif Osser
Tax & Management Consultancy: Leif Osser

CLIENT SERVICES

Accountancy (General), Audit, Corporate Finance Advice, Insolvency & Corporate Restructuring, Management & Business Advice, Management Buy-outs, Mergers & Acquisitions, Pensions Planning, Taxation (Corporate), Taxation (International), Management Consultancy

Industry Specialisations: Engineering, Finance, Retail, Non-profit Organisations

ASSOCIATED FIRMS

RESAM AB
Västergatan 21, 201 24 MALMÖ
Mailing Address: Box 432, 201 24 MALMÖ
Tel: + *46* (40) 10 40 70 *Fax:* + *46* (40) 12 11 17

Total Number of Offices: 3

PREVISOR REVISIONSBURÅ AB

Karlbergsvägen 16, 113 27 STOCKHOLM
Tel: + *46* (8) 32 90 60
Fax: + *46* (8) 34 55 19

European Affiliation: GMN International

International Contact: Per-Anders Molin

Total Number of Offices: 2

PRICE WATERHOUSE

Regeringsgatan 66, 111 87 STOCKHOLM
Tel: + *46* (8) 723 98 00
Fax: + *46* (8) 20 06 45
Mailing Address: Box 1702, 111 87 STOCKHOLM

European Affiliation: Price Waterhouse

International Contact: Stephan Tolstoy

OTHER OFFICES

PRICE WATERHOUSE
Södra Hamngatan 53, 404 21 GOTHENBURG
Mailing Address: Box 11003, 404 21 GOTHENBURG
Tel: + *46* (31) 80 54 70 *Fax:* + *46* (31) 15 76 37

PRICE WATERHOUSE
Södra Allégatan 8, 402 35 GOTHENBURG
Mailing Address: Box 7274, 402 35 GOTHENBURG
Tel: + *46* (31) 17 94 25 *Fax:* + *46* (31) 11 43 17
Contact: Lars G. Eklund

PRICE WATERHOUSE
Billeplatsen 2, 252 23 HELSINGBORG
Mailing Address: Box 1061, 251 10 HELSINGBORG
Tel: + *46* (42) 18 51 40 *Fax:* + *46* (42) 12 18 70
Contact: Björn Fajersson

PRICE WATERHOUSE
Rökerigatan 5, 121 05 JOHANNESHOV, Stockholm
Mailing Address: Box 5026, 121 05 JOHANNESHOV, Stockholm
Tel: + *46* (8) 600 23 90 *Fax:* + *46* (8) 600 31 11

PRICE WATERHOUSE
Kyrkogatan 19, 292 00 KARLSHAMN
Mailing Address: Box 21, 292 00 KARLSHAMN
Tel: + *46* (454) 190 20 *Fax:* + *46* (454) 892 02

PRICE WATERHOUSE
Västra Torggatan 11, 652 25 KARLSTAD
Tel: + *46* (54) 10 25 20 *Fax:* + *46* (54) 18 21 58

PRICE WATERHOUSE
Finlandsgatan 56, 164 75 KISTA
Mailing Address: Box 6101, 164 06 KISTA
Tel: + *46* (8) 703 94 50 *Fax:* + *46* (8) 703 94 94
Contact: Jan E. Treffner

PRICE WATERHOUSE
Döbelnsgatan 6, Lilla Torg, 291 31 KRISTIANSTAD
Tel: + *46* (44) 10 36 30 *Fax:* + *46* (44) 12 78 99
Contact: Lars A. Helgesen

PRICE WATERHOUSE
Nya Stadens Torg 1a, 531 31 LINKÖPING
Tel: + *46* (510) 602 80 *Fax:* + *46* (510) 672 45

PRICE WATERHOUSE
Engelbrektsgatan 15, 211 33 MALMÖ
Tel: + *46* (40) 710 15 *Fax:* + *46* (40) 23 06 79
Contact: Olof A. Karlsson

PRICE WATERHOUSE
Hamngatan 12B, 271 34 YSTAD
Tel: + *46* (411) 725 70 *Fax:* + *46* (411) 140 01
Contact: Lars A. Helgesen

Total Number of Offices: 12

REVISIONSBYRAN PRÖÖM WESTMANN ÖSTERBERG AG

Fleminggatan 62b, 100 28 STOCKHOLM
Tel: + *46* (8) 54 19 05
Fax: + *46* (8) 50 56 35
Mailing Address: Box 49041, 100 28 STOCKHOLM

European Affiliation: Jeffreys Henry International

International Contact: Urmas Prööm

RANBY ODHAM REVISORER AB

Första Långgatan 30, 400 32 GOTHENBURG
Tel: + *46* (31) 42 00 45
Fax: + *46* (31) 24 64 65
Mailing Address: Box 31028, 400 32 GOTHENBURG

European Affiliation: DRM Internationally

International Contact: Sven-Inge Karlsson

Partners:	4
Professional staff:	6
Non-professional staff:	21
Total Staff:	**31**

▷

Sweden

FEE INCOME

Year End: 30.04.91	Skr	%
Accountancy & Audit:		50.0
Insolvency:		10.0
Consultancy:		10.0
Tax:		25.0
Other:		5.0
Total:	**22,000,000**	

CONTACT INFORMATION

Management Consultancy: Ove Hallberg
Accountancy & Audit: Sven-Inge Karlsson
Corporate Finance & Insolvency: Ove Hallberg
Administration & Public Sector: Bengt-Ake Gellerstedt
Tax: Hans Zahlander

CLIENT SERVICES

Accountancy (General), Audit, Corporate Finance Advice, Insolvency & Corporate Restructuring, Management & Business Advice, Management Buy-outs, Mergers & Acquisitions, Taxation (Corporate), Taxation (International)

OTHER OFFICES

RANBY REVISORER AB
Storgatan 28, 582 23 LINKÖPING
Tel: + *46* (13) 11 56 80 *Fax:* + *46* (13) 11 22 33
Contact: Ove Hallberg

RANBY REVISORER AB
Brovägen 9, 182 76 STOCKHOLM
Tel: + *46* (8) 85 01 10 *Fax:* + *46* (8) 85 93 90
Contact: Hans Zahlander

RANBY ODHAM REVISORER AB
Box 162, 442 22 KUNGÄLV
Tel: + *46* (303) 109 00 *Fax:* + *46* (303) 188 78
Contact: Jan-Erik Johansson

RANBY ODHAM REVISORER AB
Box 192, 444 23 STENUNGSUND
Tel: + *46* (303) 840 30 *Fax:* + *46* (303) 821 03
Contact: Annika Andersson

Total Number of Offices: 5

REVIDENTIA HB

Sibyllegatan 43-45, 114 42 STOCKHOLM
Tel: + *46* (8) 663 97 05
Fax: + *46* (8) 662 03 33

European Affiliation: SC International

International Contact: Petrus Olde

REVISIONSKOMPANIET REKO AB

Engelbrektsgatan 7, 203 13 MALMÖ
Tel: + *46* (40) 722 40
Fax: + *46* (40) 12 92 65
Mailing Address: Box 4176, 203 13 MALMÖ

European Affiliation: Alliott Peirson International

International Contact: Nils Albertsen

OTHER OFFICES

REVISIONSKOMPANIET REKO AB
Upplandsgatan 38, 4tr, 113 28 STOCKHOLM
Tel: + *46* (8) 30 00 70 *Fax:* + *46* (8) 32 23 80
Contact: Anders Roos

Total Number of Offices: 2

REVISORSRINGEN SVERIGE AB

Karlsbergsvägen 77-81, 100 31 STOCKHOLM
Tel: + *46* (8) 34 25 00
Fax: + *46* (8) 32 25 61
Mailing Address: Box 21064, 100 31 STOCKHOLM

European Affiliation: Russell Bedford International

International Contact: Herbert Arvidsson

OTHER OFFICES

REVISORSRINGEN SVERIGE AB
Distansgatan 2, 421 37 VÄSTRA FRÖLUNDA, Gothenburg
Tel: + *46* (31) 49 61 60 *Fax:* + *46* (31) 45 60 26

REVISORSRINGEN SVERIGE AB
Norra Vägen 34, 302 31 HALMSTAD
Tel: + *46* (35) 11 88 50 *Fax:* + *46* (35) 10 55 88

REVISORSRINGEN SVERIGE AB
Längebrogatan 111, 291 59 KRISTIANSTAD
Tel: + *46* (44) 11 51 50 *Fax:* + *46* (44) 11 35 51

Total Number of Offices: 15

REVISUM REVISIONSBYRÅ HB

Rehnsgatan 5, 113 57 STOCKHOLM
Tel: + *46* (8) 673 11 00
Fax: + *46* (8) 673 11 01

European Affiliation: Alliott Peirson International

International Contact: Peter Winblad

Partners:	2
Professional staff:	7
Non-professional staff:	1
Total Staff:	**10**

FEE INCOME

Year End: 30.04.91	%
Accountancy & Audit:	60.0
Insolvency:	5.0
Consultancy:	5.0
Tax:	30.0

CONTACT INFORMATION

Managing Partner: Lars Andersson
Managing Partner: Peter Winblad

CLIENT SERVICES

Audit, Corporate Finance Advice, Insolvency & Corporate Restructuring, Management & Business Advice, Management Buy-outs, Mergers & Acquisitions, Pensions Planning, Taxation (Corporate), Taxation (International), Trust Settlement & Estates

SET-SVENSSON, ERIKSON & TJUS REVISIONSBYRÅ HB

Kungsgatan 6, 211 49 MALMÖ
Tel: + *46* (40) 10 40 30
Fax: + *46* (40) 11 94 50

European Affiliation: Pannell Kerr Forster Worldwide

International Contact: Gunilla Malmsten

Partners:	25
Professional staff:	146
Non-professional staff:	25
Total Staff:	**196**

FEE INCOME

Year End: 31.08.91	**SKr**	**%**
Accountancy & Audit:	96,000,000	80.0
Insolvency:	6,000,000	5.0
Tax:	6,000,000	5.0
Other:	12,000,000	10.0
Total:	**120,000,000**	

CONTACT INFORMATION
Chairman: Gilbert Larsson
Managing Partner: Lars Engerup
Insolvency: Willard Möller
Management Consultancy: Steen Alex-Petersen
Administration: Kristina Lindestam
Public Sector: Eva Haage
Tax (Corporate): Tomas Persson
Audit & Tax: Lars-Ola Andersson

CLIENT SERVICES
Audit, Insolvency & Corporate Restructuring, Taxation (Corporate), Taxation (International)

Industry Specialisations: Building, Real Estate

OTHER OFFICES

SET - SVENSSON, ERIKSON & TJUS REVISIONSBYRÅ HB
Norra Hamngatan 36, 411 06 GOTHENBURG
Tel: + *46* (31) 80 62 00 *Fax:* + *46* (31) 15 84 66
Contact: Hasse Lundin

SET - SVENSSON, ERIKSON & TJUS REVISIONSBYRÅ HB
Järnvägsgatan 7, 252 24 HELSINGBORG
Tel: + *46* (42) 14 93 80 *Fax:* + *46* (42) 24 15 79
Contact: Lars Engerup

SET - SVENSSON, ERIKSON & TJUS REVISIONSBYRÅ HB
Östra Mårtensgatan 15, 220 02 LUND
Mailing Address: Box 2055, 220 02 LUND
Tel: + *46* (46) 14 01 85 *Fax:* + *46* (46) 14 10 88
Contact: Håkan Rylander

SET - SVENSSON, ERIKSON & TJUS REVISIONSBYRÅ HB
Parkgatan 2, 261 31 LANDSKRONA
Tel: + *46* (418) 280 30 *Fax:* + *46* (418) 285 15
Contact: Peter Pankko

SET - SVENSSON, ERIKSON & TJUS REVISIONSBYRÅ HB
Kungsgatan 36, 111 83 STOCKHOLM
Tel: + *46* (8) 796 37 00 *Fax:* + *46* (8) 20 96 96
Contact: Roy Eide

Total Number of Offices: 8

PER STRANDINS REVISIONSBYRÅ

Svämpvagen 7, 191 51 SOLLENTUNA
Tel: + *46* (8) 96 72 73
Fax: + *46* (8) 623 06 95

European Affiliation: Affiliated Conference of Practising Accountants International (ACPA)

International Contact: Per Strandin

CONTACT INFORMATION
Managing Partner: Per Strandin

SVEREV - DFK INTERNATIONAL (SWEDEN)

Sveavägen 13-15 VII, 111 57 STOCKHOLM
Tel: + *46* (8) 24 81 80
Fax: + *46* (8) 791 75 23

European Affiliation: DFK International

Partners:	26
Professional staff:	130
Non-professional staff:	24
Total Staff:	**180**

FEE INCOME

Year End: 31.12.90	**%**
Accountancy & Audit:	60.0
Consultancy:	10.0
Tax:	20.0
Other:	10.0

CONTACT INFORMATION
Chairman: Erik Rydström

CLIENT SERVICES
Accountancy (General), Audit, Management & Business Advice, Taxation (Corporate), Taxation (International)

ASSOCIATED FIRMS

TOMMY CARLSSONS, REVISIONSBYRÅ AB
Skolgatan 33, Box 19, 601 02 NORRKÖPING
Tel: + *46* (11) 10 68 30 *Fax:* + *46* (11) 19 97 97
Contact: Tommy Carlsson

CEDERBLADS REVISIONSBYRÅ AB
Österlanggatan 13a, 291 33 KRISTIANSTAD
Tel: + *46* (44) 12 63 75 *Fax:* + *46* (44) 10 97 94
Contact: Christer Cederblad

ENSKILDA REVISIONSBYRÅN AB & ASSOCIATES
Sveavägen 13-15 VII, 111 57 STOCKHOLM
Tel: + *46* (8) 24 81 80 *Fax:* + *46* (8) 791 75 23
Contact: Erik Rydström

KBB HÖGLUNDS REUISIONSBYRÅ
Druveforsvägen 29, 5-502 56 BORÅS
Tel: + *46* (33) 10 28 40 *Fax:* + *46* (33) 12 13 95

GERDTMANS REVISIONSBYRÅ AB
Slottsgatan 33, 722 11 VÄSTERÅS
Tel: + *46* (21) 18 53 35 *Fax:* + *46* (21) 11 82 07
Contact: Rolf Gerdtmann

LEVANDER REVISORER I UDDEVALLA AB
Karl Gustavsgatan 4A, 451 50 UDDEVALLA
Tel: + *46* (522) 135 60 *Fax:* + *46* (522) 382 25
Contact: Urban Forsberg

NANKLERS REVISIONSBYRÅ KB
Box 8476, 402 79 GOTHENBURG
Tel: + *46* (31) 79 09 20 *Fax:* + *46* (31) 79 09 50
Contact: Ulf Nankler

ÅKE PERSSONS REVISIONSBYRÅ AB
Södra Tullgatan 4A, 211 40 MALMÖ
Tel: + *46* (40) 10 04 10 *Fax:* + *46* (40) 12 01 78
Contact: Åke Persson

REVINORR
Lulsundsgatan 26, 951 36 LULEÅ
Tel: + *46* (920) 87800

STRÖMSTAD & BOKFÖRING REVISIONSBYRÅ KB
Box 41, 452 01 STRÖMSTAD
Tel: + *46* (526) 144 10 *Fax:* + *46* (526) 100 16
Contact: Ulf Nankler

WILKMARS REVISIONSBYRÅ AB
Torggatan 17, Box 223, 541 25 SKÖVDE
Tel: + *46* (500) 107 50 *Fax:* + *46* (500) 890 34

Total Number of Offices: 12

Sweden

GUNNAR THORENS REVISIONSBYRÅ AB

Sveavägen 155, 113 46 STOCKHOLM
Tel: + 46 (8) 31 10 45
Fax: + 46 (8) 32 37 48
European Affiliation: Affiliated Conference of Practising Accountants International (ACPA)
International Contact: Christer Frojd

CONTACT INFORMATION
Managing Partner: Carl Nordenskiold

TÖNNERVIK HORWATH AB

Tingsgatan 9, 372 37 RONNEBY
Tel: + 46 (457) 127 10
Fax: + 46 (457) 111 44
Mailing Address: Box 49046, 100 28 STOCKHOLM
European Affiliation: Horwath International
International Contact: Robert Uddmark

Partners: 49

OTHER OFFICES

TÖNNERVIKS
Knutsgatan 7, 343 00 ÅLMHULT
Contact: Christer Asplund

TÖNNERVIKS
Förskargatan 3, 781 27 BORLÄNGE
Tel: + 46 (243) 734 06 *Fax:* + 46 (243) 734 02
Contact: Björn Barle

TÖNNERVIKS
Stigaregatan 7, 791 73 FALUN
Tel: + 46 (23) 193 80 *Fax:* + 46 (23) 130 80
Contact: Björn Barle

TÖNNERVIKS
Centralgatan 13, 813 00 HOFORS
Tel: + 46 (290) 273 74
Contact: Björn Barle

TÖNNERVIKS
Box 48, 930 55 JÖRN
Tel: + 46 (916) 100 60
Contact: Ann-Mari Sandberg

TÖNNERVIKS
Regeringsgatan 56, 374 35 KARLSHAMN
Tel: + 46 (454) 890 20 *Fax:* + 46 (454) 132 25
Contact: Ulf Jangborn

TÖNNERVIKS
Ronnebygatan 16, 371 32 KARLSKRONA
Tel: + 46 (455) 150 00 *Fax:* + 46 (455) 112 24
Contact: Mats Carlström

TÖNNERVIKS
Drottningatan 7A, Box 325, 651 08 KARLSTAD
Tel: + 46 (54) 10 08 50 *Fax:* + 46 (54) 10 00 99
Contact: Christer Karlsson

TÖNNERVIKS
Föreningsgatan 11, 981 31 KIRUNA
Tel: + 46 (980) 800 11 *Fax:* + 46 (980) 822 11
Contact: Karl-Åke Larsson

TÖNNERVIKS
Smedjegatan 1, 341 30 LJUNGBY
Tel: + 46 (372) 810 60 *Fax:* + 46 (372) 817 28
Contact: Lars Engström

TÖNNERVIKS
Kungsgatan 5, 951 84 LULEÅ
Tel: + 46 (920) 943 25 *Fax:* + 46 (920) 895 62
Contact: Karl-Åke Larsson

TÖNNERVIKS
Storgatan 36, 921 00 LYCKSELE
Tel: + 46 (950) 388 70
Contact: Ann-Mari Sandberg

TÖNNERVIKS
Storgatan 27, 930 70 MALÅ
Contact: Ann-Mari Sandberg

TÖNNERVIKS
Box 5252, 200 72 MALMÖ
Tel: + 46 (40) 91 64 60 *Fax:* + 46 (40) 98 00 13
Contact: Lars Engström

TÖNNERVIKS
Drottningatan 1, Box 191, 591 22 MOTALA
Tel: + 46 (141) 530 60 *Fax:* + 46 (141) 506 08
Contact: Håkan Martinsson

TÖNNERVIKS
Box 2027, 935 00 NORSJÖ
Contact: Ann-Mari Sandberg

TÖNNERVIKS
Östra Storg 29 A, 293 34 OLOFSTRÖM
Tel: + 46 (454) 992 80
Contact: Robert Uddmark

TÖNNERVIKS
Furumäsvägen 102A, Box 772, 941 28 PITEÅ
Tel: + 46 (911) 680 15 *Fax:* + 46 (911) 370 32
Contact: Boo Ceder

TÖNNERVIKS
Hampnäsvägen 21, 890 23 SJÄLEVAD
Contact: Ann-Mari Sandberg

TÖNNERVIKS
Södra Järnvägsgatan 52B, Box 391, 931 24 SKELLEFTEÅ
Tel: + 46 (910) 771 50 *Fax:* + 46 (910) 756 05
Contact: Anna-Karin Norberg

TÖNNERVIKS
Bondevägen 4, Box 74, 923 00 STORUMAN
Tel: + 46 (951) 113 40 *Fax:* + 46 (951) 103 68
Contact: Ann-Mari Sandberg

TÖNNERVIKS
Bergastigen 2, 920 64 TÄRNABY
Tel: + 46 (954) 110 86 *Fax:* + 46 (954) 106 31
Contact: Ann-Mari Sandberg

TÖNNERVIKS
Formvägen 16, 902 61 UMEÅ
Tel: + 46 (90) 18 06 66 *Fax:* + 46 (90) 18 03 79
Contact: Ann-Mari Sandberg

TÖNNERVIKS
Box 121, 912 00 VILHELMINA
Tel: + 46 (940) 132 50 *Fax:* + 46 (940) 107 74
Contact: Svante Anderback

Total Number of Offices: 25

TRG REVISION AB

Arenavägen 55, 121 26 STOCKHOLM-GLOBEN
Tel: + 46 (8) 725 36 00
Fax: + 46 (8) 600 36 00
Mailing Address: Box 10152, 121 26 STOCKHOLM-GLOBEN
European Affiliation: DRT International
International Contact: Leif Lundfors
Total Staff: 825

CLIENT SERVICES
All Services

MAJOR CLIENTS
AB Scansped, ASG, Astra, Bonnierföretagen, Lansforsakringsbolagens, Nordbanken, Penninglotteriet, SAAB - Automobile AB, SAS - Scandinavian Airlines Systems, Skandia Group, Sparbankernas Bank, Statens Bostadsfinanserings AB, Stockholm Energi AB, Tipstja AB, VBB Viak, Vingresor

Total Number of Offices: 55

VERNER & PARTNERS
Birger Jarlsgatan 33, V, 111 45 STOCKHOLM
Tel: + *46* (8) 611 28 00
Fax: + *46* (8) 611 40 08

European Affiliation: BKR International

LEIF R. WAHLBERG REVISION AB
Herserudsvägen 3, 181 23 LIDINGÖ
Tel: + *46* (8) 731 27 00
Fax: + *46* (8) 731 71 51
Mailing Address: Box 1159, 181 23 LIDINGÖ

European Affiliation: Urbach Hacker Young International

International Contact: Leif Wahlberg

Partners:	2
Professional staff:	13
Non-professional staff:	2
Total Staff:	**17**

FEE INCOME
Year End: 31.12.90	**SKr**
Accountancy & Audit:	10,000,000
Total:	**10,000,000**

CONTACT INFORMATION
Chairman: Leif Wahlberg
Management Consultancy: Leif Wahlberg
Accountancy & Audit: Ewa Wahlberg

CLIENT SERVICES
All Services

WAHLBERGS REVISIONSBYRÅ AB
Kungsgatan 8, Fourth Floor, 111 43 STOCKHOLM
Tel: + *46* (8) 14 58 00
Fax: + *46* (8) 20 42 24

European Affiliation: Summit International Associates Inc

International Contact: Lars Berglund

Partners:	11
Professional staff:	61
Non-professional staff:	10
Total Staff:	**82**

FEE INCOME
Year End: 31.08.91	**SKr**
Total:	**40,000,000**

CONTACT INFORMATION
Chairman: Lars Berglund
Accountancy (General): Rune Persson
Audit: Lars Berglund
Corporate Finance: Ulf Ryderberg
Insolvency: Per Nilsson
Management Consultancy: Johan Bucht
Administration: Rune Persson
Public Sector: Lars Berglund
Tax (Corporate): Lars Furenius
Tax (International): Ulf Ryderberg

CLIENT SERVICES
Accountancy (General), Audit, Computer Installation, Corporate Finance Advice, Insolvency & Corporate Restructuring, Management & Business Advice, Mergers & Acquisitions, Taxation (Corporate)

OTHER OFFICES
WAHLBERGS REVISIONSBYRÅ I MALMÖ AB
Östergatan 26-28, Box 5310, 200 72 MALMÖ
Tel: + *46* (40) 719 10
Contact: Kenneth Larsson

WAHLBERGS REVISIONSBYRÅ I ÖSTERSUND AB
Tjalmargatan 8, 831 45 ÖSTERSUND
Tel: + *46* (63) 13 20 80 *Fax:* + *46* (63) 13 26 85
Contact: Kjell Björk

Total Number of Offices: 3

Switzerland

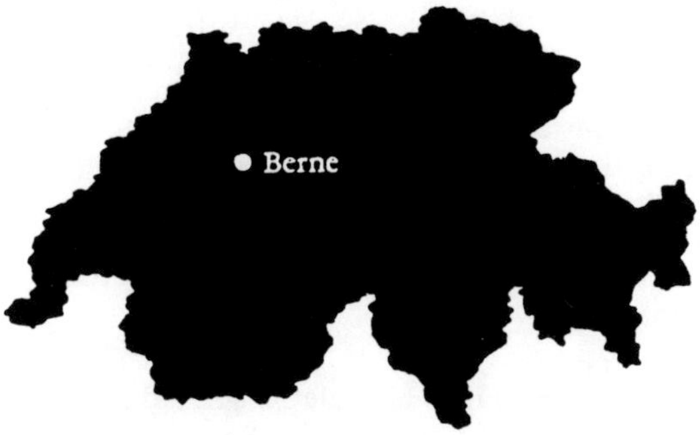

Area: 41,293 sq km (15,953 sq miles)
Population: 6,566,799 (1987 estimate)
Density: 159 per sq km
Capital: Berne

GDP: SFr327 bn, US$242 bn
GDP per head: US$35,820
Inflation: 1990 - 4.5%
1991 - 3.3%

Official and Spoken Languages: Swiss-German in the centre, north and east. French in the south and west. Italian in Ticino Canton. English is spoken by many

Time: GMT + 1 (in Summer GMT + 2)
Telephone Dialling Code: + 41

Currency: Swiss Franc (SFr) = 100 rappen or centimes
Banking Hours: 0830-1200 and 1400-1630 Monday-Thursday, 0830-1730 Friday
Professional accountancy bodies: Schweizerische Treuhand und Revisionskammer/Chambre Suisse des Sociétés Fiduciaires et des Experts-Comptables (Swiss Chamber of Fiduciaries & Auditors)
Vereinigung Eidgenossischer Diplomierter Buchhalter (Union of Federally Certified Book-keepers)

Corporate Tax Data

Information supplied by Richard Citron, international tax partner of Stoy Hayward.

The tax year; nature and rates of tax

The tax year is the calendar year.

Swiss companies are subject to income tax at three successive levels: communal, cantonal and federal. The federal income tax is charged on the average taxable profits of the two preceding years and is levied at progressive rates on a percentage of taxable profits determined according to the proportion profits bear to the total of capital and reserves (net worth). The minimum rate is 3.63% of taxable profits and the absolute ceiling is equivalent to 9.8% of profits. Cantonal and communal income taxes are levied on the same basis, at rates between 17% and 35%.

Special regime for holding companies. Many cantons exempt holding companies entirely from cantonal and municipal income tax and levy cantonal net worth tax (see below) at reduced rates. Federal income tax however still applies.

Residence and territoriality

Swiss resident companies are liable to federal, cantonal and communal income tax on their world-wide income, both distributed and undistributed. Companies incorporated in Switzerland are treated as resident there, as are companies whose effective management is carried out in Switzerland.

The tax base

Method of calculation. Taxable profits are based on the profits reported in the accounts.

Disallowable items. Any expenditure that is not commercially justifiable (eg most charitable donations) is non-deductible. ▷

Exempt income/special deductions. For dividends, see below. Deductions are available for write-downs of share and loan investments and contributions to pension reserves. Taxes paid in the period are deductible for federal income tax and in some cantons for cantonal income tax also.

Interest paid. Interest is deductible on an accruals basis.

Stock. Stock is valued at the lower of cost and market value. A deduction of up to 33.3% of stock value to cover obsolescence is nearly always available.

Depreciation. Either the straightline or reducing balance method may be used at specified rates (buildings 2% and motor vehicles 40% both on a reducing balance basis).

Treatment of dividends

Dividends received from Swiss and foreign companies. Complete exemption from federal (and usually cantonal and communal) income tax is available in respect of dividends (although included in net worth in order to compute the company's federal income tax rate on its other income) from Swiss and foreign companies in which the recipient company holds at least 20% or SFr 2,000,000 in value. The exemption will not apply to reduce the company's federal net worth tax base but individual cantons may allow it to reduce the cantonal net worth tax.

Dividends paid. Dividend payments to residents and non-residents are subject to 35% federal withholding tax.

Anti-avoidance

Thin capitalisation rules apply. Transfer pricing rules exist to adjust payments to and from foreign affiliates to arm's length values.

Treatment of losses

Current period. Trading and capital losses may be set off against income and gains of the current accounting period (there is no carry back).

Future periods. Losses may be carried forward against future profits for a maximum of seven years (federal income tax) and two to five years (cantonal income tax). Some cantons do not allow carry forward.

Treatment of capital gains

Treatment. Capital gains are treated as income and subject to federal and cantonal income tax (at rates differing from canton to canton). Gains on real property are subject to special treatment in some cantons.

Computation. Gains are computed by deducting cost from sale proceeds. Cost is substituted by net book (depreciated) value where depreciation has been claimed.

Rollover. There are no rollover or deferral provisions.

Treatment of groups

There is no tax consolidation for groups of companies.

Treatment of branches

A Swiss branch is treated for most purposes like a Swiss resident company. Branches pay federal, cantonal and communal income tax on profits arising in Switzerland but the rate depends on the ratio of their worldwide profits and net worth. There is no withholding tax on remittances of profits.

Other taxes

A 3% federal tax is payable on some discounts and rebates granted to customers. Some cantons levy a similar tax.

Taxes on capital. A net worth tax is levied at a rate of 0.825% at the federal level and at rates between 0.3% and 1% by the cantons. Branches are liable to this tax in respect of their Swiss net assets. A property tax is levied in some cantons.

Turnover taxes. A sales turnover tax is charged on the supply of goods within Switzerland and on imports. Rates are 6.2% (retailers) and 9.3% (wholesalers and importers).

Transaction taxes. Federal tax is payable on share issues (at 3%) and on certain share transfers.

Payroll taxes. Social security contributions are levied on employers and employees (the maximum premium is likely to be 19% of which the employer must pay at least 50%).

Other taxes. Most cantons levy a church tax and in certain cantons immovable property taxes are levied on the transfer of property.

ANCA FIDUCIAIRE SA

Rue de Lausanne 43, 1211 GENEVA 2
Tel: + *41* (22) 738 68 48
Fax: + *41* (22) 738 68 75
Mailing Address: Case postale 2051, 1211 GENEVA 2 Depot

European Affiliation: Affiliated Conference of Practising Accountants International (ACPA)

International Contact: André F. Cattin

Partners:	1
Professional staff:	4
Non-professional staff:	1
Total Staff:	**6**

CONTACT INFORMATION

Managing Partner: André F. Cattin
Accountancy (General): Irena Brysz
Audit: Paul Bagnara
Tax: Denise Perren

CLIENT SERVICES

Accountancy (General), Audit, Corporate Finance Advice, Life & Risk Assurance, Management & Business Advice, Mergers & Acquisitions, Value for Money Studies, Taxation (Corporate), Taxation (International), Trust Settlement & Estates, Internal Audit

Industry Specialisations: Banking & Financial Services, Hotels

ANSBACHER (SWITZERLAND) LTD

Mühlebachstrasse 32, 8032 ZURICH
Tel: + *41* (1) 252 11 55
Fax: + *41* (1) 251 45 81

European Affiliation: InterContinental Consultants (ICC)

Partners:	4
Professional staff:	10
Total Staff:	**14**

CONTACT INFORMATION

Chairman: John M. Button
Managing Partner: Urs Specker
Audit: Beat Lerch
Corporate Finance & Consultancy: Urs Specker
Accountancy, Insolvency & Tax: Zeno A. Meier
Common Law Trusts & Management: Peter Wirth
Director: Erich Zaehner
Director: Lindsay Leggat Smith
Director: Hans Rudolf Wegmueller

CLIENT SERVICES

Accountancy (General), Audit, Corporate Finance Advice, Management & Business Advice, Taxation (Corporate), Taxation (International), Trust Settlement & Estates, Company Formation & Administration, Real Estate, Participation, Invoicing, Trusts & Anstalts

Industry Specialisations: Shipping

ARTHUR ANDERSEN & CO

Lavaterstrasse 93, Postfach 71, 8027 ZURICH
Tel: + *41* (1) 208 11 11
Fax: + *41* (1) 201 01 63

European Affiliation: Arthur Andersen Worldwide

International Contact: Paul Hoeve

CONTACT INFORMATION

Audit: Paul Hoeve
Tax (Corporate): Adelaide B. Passos

CLIENT SERVICES

Accountancy (General), Audit, Computer Installation, Corporate Finance Advice, Insolvency & Corporate Restructuring, Litigation/Legal Services, Management & Business Advice, Management Buy-outs, Mergers & Acquisitions, Pensions Planning, Value for Money Studies, Taxation (Corporate), Taxation (International)

OTHER OFFICES

ARTHUR ANDERSEN & CO
53 Route de Malagnou, Case postale 275, 1211 GENEVA 17
Tel: + *41* (22) 786 42 42 *Fax:* + *41* (22) 736 45 40

ARTHUR ANDERSEN & CO
Via Monte Ceneri 1, 6901 LUGANO 1
Tel: + *41* (91) 23 77 77 *Fax:* + *41* (91) 23 78 08

ARTHUR ANDERSEN & CO
Monbijoustrasse 31, 3001 BERN
Tel: + *41* (31) 26 19 11 *Fax:* + *41* (31) 26 19 59

ARTHUR ANDERSEN & CO
Place Bel-Air 1, 1003 LAUSANNE
Tel: + *41* (21) 311 15 55 *Fax:* + *41* (21) 311 15 65

Total Number of Offices: 5

ATAG ERNST & YOUNG

Bleicherweg 21, 8002 ZURICH
Tel: + *41* (1) 286 31 11
Fax: + *41* (1) 286 30 04
Mailing Address: Postfach 5272, 8022 ZURICH

European Affiliation: Ernst & Young Europe

Partners:	137
Professional staff:	1,450
Non-professional staff:	470
Total Staff:	**2,057**

FEE INCOME

Year End: 31.12.90	**SFr**	**%**
Accountancy & Audit:	90,000,000	28.0
Consultancy:	125,000,000	38.0
Other:	110,000,000	34.0
Total:	**325,000,000**	

CONTACT INFORMATION

Chairman: Dr. Peider Mengiardi (Basel)
Managing Partner: Dr. Urs Widmer
Insolvency: Dr. Mathias Widmer
Management Consultancy: Dr. Markus Schär
Management Consultancy: Dr. Carlo Imboden
Information Technology: Jürg W. Dangel
Real Estate Consulting: Anton Schorer
Bookkeeping: Arthur Müller
Insurance Consulting: Hermann Arquint
Marketing: Karl Müller
Accountancy & Audit: Andreas Müller
Legal Consultancy/Insolvency: Yves Meili
Mergers & Acquisitions: Dr. Rudolf Lanz
Tax Consulting: Peter Spori

CLIENT SERVICES

All Services, Market & Opinion Research

Industry Specialisations: Banking

MAJOR CLIENTS

Banca della Svizzera Italiana, Banque Paribas, Bobst, BP Switzerland, Bühler, Calanda Haldengut, Careal Holding, Cementia Holding, Coca-Cola, Danzas, Feldschlösschen, Kühne & Nagel, Leica, Metro International, Oerlikon Bührle, Pelikan, Renault Finance, Ringier, SBB, Union Bank of Switzerland ▷

OTHER OFFICES

ATAG ERNST & YOUNG
Schauplatzgasse 21, 3001 BERN
Mailing Address: Postfach 5032, 3001 BERN
Tel: + *41* (31) 21 61 11 *Fax:* + *41* (31) 21 04 95

ATAG ERNST & YOUNG
Rue d'Italie 6, 1211 GENEVA 3
Mailing Address: Case postale 326, 1211 GENEVA 3
Tel: + *41* (22) 318 06 18 *Fax:* + *41* (22) 312 01 70

ATAG ERNST & YOUNG
Place St François 12-bis, 1002 LAUSANNE
Mailing Address: Case postale 3180, 1002 LAUSANNE
Tel: + *41* (21) 20 66 61 *Fax:* + *41* (21) 20 66 60

ATAG ERNST & YOUNG AG
Aeschengraben 9, 4002 BASLE
Mailing Address: Postfach 2149, 4002 BASLE
Tel: + *41* (61) 286 86 86 *Fax:* + *41* (61) 272 40 60

Total Number of Offices: 24

BALMER-ETIENNE TREUHAND AG

Kauffmannweg 4, 6003 LUCERNE
Tel: + *41* (41) 24 22 22
Fax: + *41* (41) 23 70 91

European Affiliation: Urbach Hacker Young International

International Contact: Dr. H.P. Balmer
M. Winkler

Partners:	6
Total Staff:	**6**

FEE INCOME

Year End: 31.12.90	**SFr**	**%**
Accountancy & Audit:	3,000,000	39.0
Consultancy:	1,600,000	21.0
Tax:	1,400,000	17.0
Other:	1,800,000	23.0
Total:	**7,800,000**	

CONTACT INFORMATION

Partner: F.P. Bissig
Partner: H. Costa
Partner: M. Schnüriger

CLIENT SERVICES

Accountancy (General), Audit, Computer Installation, Corporate Finance Advice, Insolvency & Corporate Restructuring, Litigation/Legal Services, Management & Business Advice, Mergers & Acquisitions, Taxation (Corporate), Taxation (International), Trust Settlement & Estates

Total Number of Offices: 2

ROBERTO BASSI & PARTNERS

Piazza Monte Ceneri 13, 6901 LUGANO
Tel: + *41* (91) 23 88 12
Fax: + *41* (91) 23 73 57
Mailing Address: Case postale 2899, 6901 LUGANO

European Affiliation: The International Group of Accounting Firms Ltd (IGAF)

International Contact: Roberto Bassi

ANDREAS BAUMANN & CO

Zürichstrasse 27 B, 8134 ADLISWIL
Tel: + *41* (1) 709 00 30
Fax: + *41* (1) 709 00 64

European Affiliation: S & W International

International Contact: Andreas Baumann

Partners:	2
Professional staff:	10
Non-professional staff:	6
Total Staff:	**18**

FEE INCOME

Year End: 30.09.90	**SFr**	**%**
Accountancy & Audit:		60.0
Insolvency:		5.0
Consultancy:		10.0
Tax:		20.0
Other:		5.0
Total:	**1,800,000**	

CONTACT INFORMATION

Chairman: Andreas Baumann
Managing Partner: Jeanette Frank
Audit: Arthur Exer
Corporate Finance & Insolvency: Andreas Baumann
Public Sector & Tax: Andreas Baumann
Accountancy & Administration: Jeanette Frank

CLIENT SERVICES

Accountancy (General), Audit, Computer Installation, Corporate Finance Advice, Insolvency & Corporate Restructuring, Litigation/Legal Services, Management & Business Advice, Management Buy-outs, Mergers & Acquisitions, Pensions Planning, Taxation (Corporate), Taxation (International), Trust Settlement & Estates

OTHER OFFICES

ABACOR AUDITING COMPANY
Eschfeldstrasse 2, 6312 STEINHAUSEN
Tel: + *41* (42) 41 58 41 *Fax:* + *41* (42) 41 58 35
Contact: Arthur Exer

ANDREAS BAUMANN FINANZ AG
Riedstrasse 9, 6300 CHAM
Tel: + *41* (1) 709 00 35 *Fax:* + *41* (1) 709 00 64
Contact: Andreas Baumann

ANDREAS BAUMANN & CO
Eschfeldstrasse 2, 6312 STEINHAUSEN
Tel: + *41* (42) 41 58 41 *Fax:* + *41* (42) 41 58 35
Contact: Jeanette Frank

Total Number of Offices: 4

BUDLIGER TREUHAND AG

Postfach 8059, Waffenplatzstrasse 64, 8002 ZURICH
Tel: + *41* (1) 202 10 40
Fax: + *41* (1) 201 62 06

European Affiliation: Midsnell International

International Contact: Bruno Wirth

Partners:	7
Professional staff:	26
Non-professional staff:	11
Total Staff:	**44**

FEE INCOME

Year End: 31.12.90	**%**
Accountancy & Audit:	60.0
Consultancy:	10.0
Tax:	30.0

CONTACT INFORMATION

Chairman: Louis Kaelin
Partner: Hans Meier
Partner: Louis Kaelin
Partner: Bruno Wirth
Partner: Edgar Bannwart
Partner: Hans Scherrer

Partner: Urs Karrer
Partner: Hans Haag

CLIENT SERVICES
Accountancy (General), Audit, Corporate Finance Advice, Insolvency & Corporate Restructuring, Management & Business Advice, Management Buy-outs, Mergers & Acquisitions, Taxation (Corporate), Taxation (International), Trust Settlement & Estates

Industry Specialisations: Motor, Wholesale & Retail, Hotels, Construction, Precision Apparatus, Print, Transport, Insurance, Wood

E.N. BURKE

Schaffhauserstrasse 351, 8050 ZURICH
Tel: + *41* (1) 312 38 58
Fax: + *41* (1) 312 42 72
Mailing Address: Postfach 8268, 8050 ZURICH

European Affiliation: A.E.E. International

International Contact: Edmond N. Burke

Partners:	1
Professional staff:	2
Non-professional staff:	1
Total Staff:	**4**

CONTACT INFORMATION
Managing Partner: Edmond N. Burke

CLIENT SERVICES
Accountancy (General), Audit, Computer Installation, Taxation (Corporate), Taxation (International), Trust Settlement & Estates

Industry Specialisations: Trust Services

CAMINADA TREUHAND AG ZUG

Baarerstrasse 112, 6300 ZUG
Tel: + *41* (42) 31 55 44
Fax: + *41* (42) 31 50 77

European Affiliation: INPACT - International Network of Professional Accountants

International Contact: Heinz Huber

Partners:	4
Professional staff:	6
Non-professional staff:	2
Total Staff:	**12**

FEE INCOME

Year End: 31.12.90	**SFr**	**%**
Accountancy & Audit:	741,190	47.0
Consultancy:	362,710	23.0
Tax:	315,400	20.0
Other:	157,700	10.0
Total:	**1,577,000**	

CONTACT INFORMATION
Chairman: Heinz Huber
Managing Partner: Walter Pfäffli
Audit: Holger Wanke
Management Consultancy: Heinz Huber
Accountancy & Administration: Heinz Klauz
Corporate Finance & Public Sector: Heinz Huber
Tax: Walter Pfäffli

CLIENT SERVICES
Accountancy (General), Audit, Corporate Finance Advice, Management & Business Advice, Management Buy-outs, Mergers & Acquisitions, Taxation (Corporate), Taxation (International), Trust Settlement & Estates

Industry Specialisations: Trading, Textiles, Steel

CAMINADA TREUHAND AG ZURICH

Zollikerstrasse 27, 8032 ZURICH
Tel: + *41* (1) 382 22 00
Fax: + *41* (1) 382 19 70

European Affiliation: INPACT - International Network of Professional Accountants

International Contact: Urs Muller

Partners:	3
Professional staff:	5
Non-professional staff:	10
Total Staff:	**18**

FEE INCOME

Year End: 31.12.90	**%**
Accountancy & Audit:	55.0
Consultancy:	15.0
Tax:	25.0
Other:	5.0

CONTACT INFORMATION
Chairman: Hans Boesch
Managing Partner: Bernhard Lehmann
Audit: Werner Mueller
Accountancy & Consultancy: Bernhard Lehmann
Tax: Urs Muller

CLIENT SERVICES
Accountancy (General), Audit, Corporate Finance Advice, Management & Business Advice, Taxation (Corporate), Taxation (International)

COMINS SARL

7 Avenue Pictet de Rochemont, 1207 GENEVA
Tel: + *41* (227) 36 57 60
Fax: + *41* (227) 36 89 43
Mailing Address: Case postale 111, 1211 GENEVA 6

European Affiliation: InterContinental Consultants (ICC)

International Contact: Myles T. Stott

COOPERS & LYBRAND AG

St. Jakobs-Strasse 25, 4052 BASEL
Tel: + *41* (61) 277 55 00
Fax: + *41* (61) 277 55 88
Mailing Address: Postfach 4152, 4002 BASEL

European Affiliation: Coopers & Lybrand Europe

Total Staff: **1130**

CONTACT INFORMATION
Managing Partner: Prof. Dr. Carl Helbling
Managing Partner: Stephan Bachmann
Corporate Finance: Kurt Hausheer
Management Consultancy: Anton Haas
Tax: Marcus Flubacher

CLIENT SERVICES
All Services

Industry Specialisations: Automotive, Banking, Chemicals, Communications, Engineering, Food &, Drink, Insurance, Pharmaceuticals

OTHER OFFICES

COOPERS & LYBRAND AG
Bleichemattstrasse 43, 5000 AARAU
Tel: + *41* (64) 27 77 27 *Fax:* + *41* (64) 27 77 55

▷

COOPERS & LYBRAND AG
Spitalgasse 2, 3011 BERNE
Tel: + *41* (31) 22 73 64 *Fax:* + *41* (31) 21 19 28

COOPERS & LYBRAND AG
Gartenstrasse 3, 7000 CHUR
Tel: + *41* (81) 24 50 50 *Fax:* + *41* (81) 24 19 49

COOPERS & LYBRAND AG
Route de Bale 25, 2800 DELEMONT
Tel: + *41* (66) 22 88 81 *Fax:* + *41* (66) 22 95 25

COOPERS & LYBRAND AG
Route de la Glane 107, 1752 Villars sur Glane, FRIBOURG
Tel: + *41* (37) 82 12 81 *Fax:* + *41* (37) 24 98 96

COOPERS & LYBRAND AG
50 Avenue Giuseppe-Motta, 1202 GENEVA
Mailing Address: Case Postale 417, 1211 GENEVA 16
Tel: + *41* (22) 734 81 50 *Fax:* + *41* (22) 733 11 77
Contact: Stephan A.J. Bachmann

COOPERS & LYBRAND AG
Hirschmattstrasse 36, 6003 LUCERNE
Tel: + *41* (41) 23 74 47 *Fax:* + *41* (41) 23 94 34

COOPERS & LYBRAND AG
Via C Frasca 3, 6900 LUGANO
Tel: + *41* (91) 23 81 12 *Fax:* + *41* (91) 23 70 97

COOPERS & LYBRAND AG
Rue du Seyon 1, 2000 NEUCHATEL
Tel: + *41* (38) 24 59 00 *Fax:* + *41* (38) 24 73 94

COOPERS & LYBRAND AG
45 Avenue CF Ramuz, 1009 PULLY/LAUSANNE
Tel: + *41* (21) 28 37 50 *Fax:* + *41* (21) 28 75 26

COOPERS & LYBRAND AG
Place du Midi 40, 1950 SION
Tel: + *41* (27) 22 06 91 *Fax:* + *41* (27) 22 09 15

COOPERS & LYBRAND AG
Florastrasse 3, 4500 SOLOTHURN
Tel: + *41* (65) 23 35 01 *Fax:* + *41* (65) 22 63 19

COOPERS & LYBRAND AG
St. Leonard-strasse 7, 9000 ST. GALL
Tel: + *41* (71) 22 49 86 *Fax:* + *41* (71) 23 61 77

COOPERS & LYBRAND AG
Romerstrasse 25, 8400 WINTERTHUR
Tel: + *41* (52) 27 34 62 *Fax:* + *41* (52) 27 95 68

COOPERS & LYBRAND AG
Stampfenbachstrasse 73, 8006 ZURICH
Mailing Address: Postfach 213, 8035 ZURICH
Tel: + *41* (1) 365 83 65 *Fax:* + *41* (1) 365 82 82

Total Number of Offices: 16

CURATOR & HORWATH

Freigutstrasse 27, 8039 ZURICH
Tel: + *41* (1) 201 38 40
Fax: + *41* (1) 201 08 37

European Affiliation: Horwath International

International Contact: Ruedi F. Fleischmann

Partners:	11
Professional staff:	80
Non-professional staff:	6
Total Staff:	**97**

FEE INCOME

Year End: 31.12.90	**SFr**	**%**
Accountancy & Audit:	8,300,000	58.0
Tax:	5,900,000	42.0
Total:	**14,200,000**	

CONTACT INFORMATION
Chairman: Dr. Giancarlo Cappello
Managing Partner: Dr. Giancarlo Cappello

CLIENT SERVICES
All Services, Marketing

OTHER OFFICES

ALFA TREUHAND & REVISIONS AG
Teufenerstrasse 12, 9000 ST GALLEN
Mailing Address: Postfach 6, 9001 ST GALLEN
Tel: + *41* (71) 22 24 94 *Fax:* + *41* (71) 22 57 27
Contact: Jean-Claude Diener

CURATOR & HORWATH
Laurenzenvorstadt 57, 5000 AARAU
Mailing Address: Postfach, 5000 AARAU
Tel: + *41* (64) 21 13 04 *Fax:* + *41* (64) 24 61 34

CURATOR & HORWATH
Via S. Balestra 27, 6900 LUGANO
Tel: + *41* (91) 23 98 16 *Fax:* + *41* (91) 23 30 64

CURATOR & HORWATH
Industriestrasse 7, 6301 ZUG
Mailing Address: Postfach 6301, ZUG
Tel: + *41* (42) 21 13 04

HORWATH FIDUCIAIRE & REVISION SA
Rue du Jeu-de-L'Arc 15, 1211 GENEVA
Mailing Address: Case postale 321, 1211 GENEVA 6
Tel: + *41* (22) 735 37 08 *Fax:* + *41* (22) 735 61 13
Contact: Robert Fehlmann

Total Number of Offices: 6

DELOITTE & TOUCHE

Zollikerstrasse 228, 8008 ZURICH
Tel: + *41* (1) 55 42 40
Fax: + *41* (1) 55 86 36

European Affiliation: DRT International

International Contact: David Wilson

Total Staff: **150**

CLIENT SERVICES
All Services

MAJOR CLIENTS
Aero Leasing, BAT (Suisse), Brother, Cinzano, I.A.T.A., Juvena, Montres Ebel, R.J. Reynolds, Marc Rich & Co, Sprecher Energie

Total Number of Offices: 2

DFK (SUISSE) SA GENEVE

Route de Frontenex 62, 1211 GENEVA 6
Tel: + *41* (22) 735 42 05
Fax: + *41* (22) 735 55 16
Mailing Address: Case postale 274, 1211 GENEVA 6

European Affiliation: DFK International

International Contact: Victor Fischer

Total Number of Offices: 7

EGLOFF FIDUCIARIA E REVISIONI SA

Via Motta 1, 6900 LUGANO
Tel: + *41* (91) 23 26 71
Fax: + *41* (91) 22 69 91

European Affiliation: Alliott Peirson International

International Contact: Peter Egloff

EXPERTA GROUP
Am Schanzengraden 23, 8002 ZURICH
Tel: + *41* (1) 201 71 71
Fax: + *41* (1) 201 14 71
Mailing Address: Postfach 970, 8039 ZURICH

European Affiliation: Nexia International

International Contact: Gerhard Ammann

Partners:	57
Professional staff:	276
Non-professional staff:	69
Total Staff:	**402**

FEE INCOME
Year End: 31.12.90 **SFr**
Total: 53,913,000

CONTACT INFORMATION
Chairman: Pierre N. Rossier
Audit & Tax: Gerhard Ammann
Insolvency: Dr. André Cuendet
Management Consultancy: Guido Suter
Administration: Pierre N. Rossier

CLIENT SERVICES
Accountancy (General), Audit, Computer Installation, Corporate Finance Advice, Insolvency & Corporate Restructuring, Litigation/Legal Services, Management & Business Advice, Management Buy-outs, Mergers & Acquisitions, Pensions Planning, Value for Money Studies, Taxation (Corporate), Taxation (International), Trust Settlement & Estates, Portfolio Management, Consultancy, Informatic Technology, Book-keeping, Executive Search, Trustee Functions

Industry Specialisations: OMB Field

OTHER OFFICES

EXPERTA GROUP
Steinengraben 22, 4002 BASLE
Tel: + *41* (61) 285 12 12 *Fax:* + *41* (61) 285 13 13

EXPERTA GROUP
Waisenhausplatz 28, 3011 BERN
Tel: + *41* (31) 21 51 11 *Fax:* + *41* (31) 21 34 61

EXPERTA GROUP
Rue Versonnex 7, 1207 GENEVA
Tel: + *41* (22) 786 18 61 *Fax:* + *41* (22) 786 55 42

EXPERTA GROUP
Avenue de la Gare 10, 1003 LAUSANNE
Tel: + *41* (21) 20 81 04 *Fax:* + *41* (21) 23 78 91

EXPERTA GROUP
Via Luigi Canonica 7, 6900 LUGANO
Tel: + *41* (91) 22 00 64 *Fax:* + *41* (91) 23 71 67

EXPERTA GROUP
Baarerstrasse 12, 6301 ZUG
Tel: + *41* (42) 21 15 77 *Fax:* + *41* (42) 22 14 15

Total Number of Offices: 8

FIDUCIAIRE OFOR SA
1 Place Saint-Gervais, 1211 GENEVA 1
Tel: + *41* (22) 731 70 50
Fax: + *41* (22) 732 20 48
Mailing Address: Case postale 1832, 1211 GENEVA 1

European Affiliation: Pannell Kerr Forster Worldwide

International Contact: Luc Jacquiér

FIDUCIAIRE VERIFID SA
Rue du Rhône 100, Case Postale 908, 1211 GENEVA 3
Tel: + *41* (22) 311 14 31
Fax: + *41* (22) 781 00 24

European Affiliation: Eura-Audit International

International Contact: J-B. Buchs
M. Vez

FIDUCIAIRE VIDOR SA
Boulevard de Grancy 7, 1006 LAUSANNE
Tel: + *41* (21) 617 62 79
Fax: + *41* (21) 617 58 07
Mailing Address: Case postale 645, 1001 LAUSANNE

European Affiliation: Midsnell International

International Contact: Bernard Knobl

Professional staff:	8
Non-professional staff:	3

CONTACT INFORMATION
Managing Partner: Bernard Knobl
Accountancy (General): Enrique Ardito
Audit: Michel Prodromides
Management Consultancy: Bernard Knobl
Tax & Administration: Lise Favre

CLIENT SERVICES
Accountancy (General), Audit, Management & Business Advice, Taxation (Corporate), Taxation (International), Trust Settlement & Estates

Industry Specialisations: Agro-Industry, Trading

OTHER OFFICES

FIDUCIAIRE VIDOR SA
Rue de la Servette 91, GENEVA 7
Mailing Address: Case postale 4, 1211 GENEVA
Tel: + *41* (22) 734 49 60 *Fax:* + *41* (22) 733 68 19
Contact: Michel Talec

Total Number of Offices: 3

FIREL & MANDACO SA
9 rue Charles-Humbert, 1205 GENEVA
Tel: + *41* (22) 28 16 44
Fax: + *41* (22) 781 22 59

European Affiliation: HLB International

International Contact: Raymond A. Felix

Partners:	5
Professional staff:	13
Non-professional staff:	7
Total Staff:	**25**

CONTACT INFORMATION
Chairman: Pierre Chessex
Managing Partner: Raymond A. Felix
Accountancy & Tax: Raymond A. Felix
Audit & Management Consultancy: Philippe Veillard

CLIENT SERVICES
Accountancy (General), Audit, Litigation/Legal Services, Management & Business Advice, Taxation (Corporate), Taxation (International), Trust Settlement & Estates

OTHER OFFICES

FIREL & MANDACO SA
Chemin du Devin 51, 1012 LAUSANNE
Tel: + *41* (21) 652 97 61 *Fax:* + *41* (21) 652 97 93
Contact: Mario Pasquini

▷

FIREL & MANDACO SA
Avenue General Guisan 15, 3960 SIERRE
Tel: + *41* (27) 56 16 56 *Fax:* + *41* (27) 56 16 58
Contact: Pierre-Alain Massy

Total Number of Offices: 3

GRANT THORNTON SA

26 Rue de la Corraterie, Case postale 45, 1211 GENEVA 11
Tel: + *41* (22) 21 30 42
Fax: + *41* (22) 21 45 88

European Affiliation: Grant Thornton International

International Contact: Gérard Béran

Partners:	38
Professional staff:	76
Non-professional staff:	45
Total Staff:	**159**

FEE INCOME

Year End: 30.04.90	**SFr (million)**
Total:	**20,146**

CONTACT INFORMATION

Managing Partner: Gérard Béran

OTHER OFFICES

GRANT THORNTON SA
Boulevard de Pérolles 55, Case postale 144, 1700 FRIBOURG 5
Tel: + *41* (37) 24 20 88 *Fax:* + *41* (37) 24 31 50

GRANT THORNTON SA
Rue du Petit-Chêne 38, Case gare 610, 1001 LAUSANNE
Tel: + *41* (21) 23 29 11 *Fax:* + *41* (21) 20 66 87

GRANT THORNTON SA
Place de Rome, Case postale 439, 1920 MARTIGNY
Tel: + *41* (26) 22 10 89 *Fax:* + *41* (26) 22 90 72

GRANT THORNTON SA
Case Postale 356, 3962 MONTANA
Tel: + *41* (27) 41 76 66 *Fax:* + *41* (27) 41 93 75

GRANT THORNTON SA
Rue de Puits-Godet 22, Case postale 125, 2005 NEUCHATEL 5
Tel: + *41* (38) 24 15 67 *Fax:* + *41* (38) 25 13 51

GRANT THORNTON SA
Rue du Vieux Canal, Case postale 358, 1951 SION
Tel: + *41* (27) 22 08 22 *Fax:* + *41* (27) 22 95 42

GRANT THORNTON SA
Amriswiler Strasse 155, 8570 WEINFELDEN
Tel: + *41* (72) 22 44 84 *Fax:* + *41* (72) 22 62 14

GRANT THORNTON SA
Dorfstrasse 67, 8302 ZURICH-KLOTEN
Tel: + *41* (1) 813 38 34 *Fax:* + *41* (1) 814 15 66

Total Number of Offices: 10

INTERCONSULTA, ACCOUNTANTS AND TRUSTEES

Nordstrasse 190, Postfach 801, 8037 ZURICH
Tel: + *41* (1) 363 90 20
Fax: + *41* (1) 363 90 47

European Affiliation: The International Group of Accounting Firms Ltd (IGAF)

International Contact: Peter Hubler

OTHER OFFICES

INTERCONSULTA, ACCOUNTANTS AND TRUSTEES
Poststrasse 9, 6300 ZUG
Tel: + *41* (42) 21 70 70

Total Number of Offices: 2

INTERNATIONALE TREUHAND AG

Hirzbodenweg 103, 4020 BASLE
Tel: + *41* (61) 312 99 20
Fax: + *41* (61) 312 66 02
Mailing Address: Postfach 317, 4020 BASLE

European Affiliation: SC International

International Contact: Konrad Annasohn

OTHER OFFICES

LA FIDUCIAIRE INTERNATIONALE SA
1 Place de Saint-Gervais, 1201 GENEVA
Tel: + *41* (22) 731 93 20
Contact: Konrad Annasohn

INTERNATIONALE TREUHAND AG
Kreuzbühlstrasse 8, 8008 ZURICH
Tel: + *41* (1) 261 93 41 *Fax:* + *41* (1) 251 64 88
Contact: Konrad Annasohn

Total Number of Offices: 3

KPMG

KPMG FIDES PEAT

Pflanzschulstrasse 2, 8026 ZURICH
Tel: + *41* (1) 249 31 31
Fax: + *41* (1) 249 33 50
Mailing Address: Postfach 766, 8026 ZURICH

European Affiliation: KPMG

International Contact: Dan Rees

Total Staff: **1,943**

FEE INCOME

Year End: 31.12.90	**SFr**	**%**
Accountancy & Audit:	65,000,000	18.2
Consultancy:	49,000,000	13.8
Tax:	14,000,000	4.0
Other:	228,000,000	64.0
Total:	**356,000,000**	

CONTACT INFORMATION

Chairman: Henry Glogg
Managing Partner: Günther Schultz

CLIENT SERVICES

All Services

MAJOR CLIENTS

ABB Asea Brown Boveri, Alusuisse, Bank Bär, Credit Suisse-First Boston, Crossair, Elektrowatt, Helvetia-Group, Jelmoli-Group, Jet Aviation, Landis & Gyr, Mettler-Toledo, Mövenpick, Reisebüro Kuoni, Rothschild-Bank, Vaudoise-Vie, Vita Life Insurance, Wander, Winterthur Insurance, + GF +

OTHER OFFICES

KPMG FIDES PEAT
Zelglistrasse 15, 5001 AARAU
Mailing Address: Postfach 3525, 5001 AARAU
Tel: + *41* (64) 43 40 44 *Fax:* + *41* (64) 43 78 65

KPMG FIDES PEAT
Innere Margarethenstrasse 5, 4002 BASEL
Tel: + *41* (61) 286 91 91 *Fax:* + *41* (61) 286 94 01

KPMG FIDES PEAT
Laupenstrasse 10, 3001 BERN
Mailing Address: Postfach 6135, 3001 BERN
Tel: + *41* (31) 50 76 00 *Fax:* + *41* (31) 25 35 52
Contact: Rolf Fischer

KPMG FIDES PEAT
Rue Hans-Hugi 3, 2502 BIENNE
Mailing Address: Case postale 1156, 2501 BIENNE
Tel: + *41* (32) 23 77 11 *Fax:* + *41* (32) 22 14 55
Contact: Konrad Althaus

KPMG FIDES PEAT
Route des Daillettes 21, 1701 FRIBOURG
Mailing Address: Case Postale 324, 1701 FRIBOURG
Tel: + *41* (37) 24 27 13 *Fax:* + *41* (37) 24 08 91
Contact: Jean-Pierre Gutknecht

KPMG FIDES PEAT
Chemin De-Normandie 14, 1211 GENEVA 25
Mailing Address: Case postale 361, 1211 GENEVA 25
Tel: + *41* (22) 47 82 00 *Fax:* + *41* (22) 47 73 13
Contact: Gion Clopath

KPMG FIDES PEAT
Avenue de Rumine 37, 1002 LAUSANNE
Mailing Address: Case postale 2800, 1002 LAUSANNE
Tel: + *41* (21) 20 13 45 *Fax:* + *41* (21) 20 53 07
Contact: Charles-Daniel Pache

KPMG FIDES PEAT
Via alla Ramogna 14, 6600 LOCARNO
Mailing Address: Casella postale 447, 6600 LOCARNO
Tel: + *41* (93) 31 40 13 *Fax:* + *41* (93) 31 98 91

KPMG FIDES PEAT
Buobenmatt 2, 6002 LUCERNE
Mailing Address: Postfach 2859, 6002 LUCERNE
Tel: + *41* (41) 49 37 37 *Fax:* + *41* (41) 23 64 62
Contact: Hubert Achermann

KPMG FIDES PEAT
Via Cantonale 19, 6901 LUGANO
Mailing Address: Casella postale 2913, 6901 LUGANO
Tel: + *41* (91) 23 38 16 *Fax:* + *41* (91) 22 99 32
Contact: Gianni Donati

KPMG FIDES PEAT
Avenue de la Gare 50, 1920 MARTIGNY
Mailing Address: Case postale 471, 1920 MARTIGNY
Tel: + *41* (26) 22 47 57 *Fax:* + *41* (26) 22 71 54

KPMG FIDES PEAT
Rue Saint-Maurice 10, 2001 NEUCHATEL
Mailing Address: Case postale 484, 2001 NEUCHATEL
Tel: + *41* (38) 24 32 24 *Fax:* + *41* (38) 24 29 49
Contact: Claude-Pascal Ruedin

KPMG FIDES PEAT
Rue des Tanneurs 5, 2900 PORRENTRUY 1
Mailing Address: Case postale 161, 2900 PORRENTRUY 1
Tel: + *41* (66) 66 48 49 *Fax:* + *41* (66) 66 50 77

KPMG FIDES PEAT
Avenue de France 6, 1951 SION
Mailing Address: Case postale 362, 1951 SION
Tel: + *41* (27) 22 09 30 *Fax:* + *41* (27) 22 09 33

KPMG FIDES PEAT
Unterer Graben 21, 9001 ST GALLEN
Mailing Address: Postfach 238, 9001 ST GALLEN
Tel: + *41* (71) 23 61 67 *Fax:* + *41* (71) 22 85 20
Contact: Hans Schnurrenberger

KPMG FIDES PEAT
Frutigenstrasse 2A, 3601 THUN
Mailing Address: Postfach 1120, 3601 THUN
Tel: + *41* (33) 22 98 66 *Fax:* + *41* (33) 22 41 39

KPMG FIDES PEAT
Poststrasse 4, 6301 ZUG
Mailing Address: Postfach 358, 6301 ZUG
Tel: + *41* (42) 22 22 33 *Fax:* + *41* (42) 22 10 20
Contact: Josef Bühler

Total Number of Offices: 18

MAAG, MÜLLI, SCHÖB & PARTNER AG

Bellerivestrasse 59, 8034 ZURICH
Tel: + *41* (1) 383 19 60
Fax: + *41* (1) 383 46 19

European Affiliation: Affiliated Conference of Practising Accountants International (ACPA)

International Contact: Urs Maag

Partners:	4
Professional staff:	8
Non-professional staff:	3
Total Staff:	**15**

FEE INCOME

Year End: 30.09.90	%
Accountancy & Audit:	32.0
Consultancy:	36.0
Tax:	26.0
Other:	6.0

CONTACT INFORMATION

Chairman: Kurt Schöb
Managing Partner: Dolf Mülli
Managing Partner: Christian Bigler
Accountancy (General): Kurt Schöb
Audit: Christian Bigler
Tax (Corporate): Urs Maag

CLIENT SERVICES

Accountancy (General), Audit, Corporate Finance Advice, Management & Business Advice, Taxation (Corporate), Taxation (International), Trust Settlement & Estates

MAYO ASSOCIATES SA

Avenue Pictet de Rochemont 7, 1207 GENEVA
Tel: + *41* (22) 736 57 60
Fax: + *41* (22) 736 89 43

European Affiliation: KPMG

International Contact: Myles T. Stott

MEGA FIDUCIARIA SA

Corso San Gottardo 32, 6830 CHIASSO
Tel: + *41* (91) 44 41 14
Fax: + *41* (91) 44 43 70
Mailing Address: Casella postale 34, 6830 CHIASSO

European Affiliation: Clark Kenneth Leventhal

International Contact: Dr. Geo Camponovo

▷

Partners:	8
Professional staff:	12
Non-professional staff:	22
Total Staff:	**42**

CLIENT SERVICES

Litigation/Legal Services, Taxation (Corporate), Taxation (International), Trust Settlement & Estates

OTHER OFFICES

MEGA FIDUCIARIA SA
Vicolo Nassetta 2, 6901 LUGANO
Tel: + *41* (91) 23 13 22 *Fax:* + *41* (91) 22 71 67
Contact: Geo Camponovo

Total Number of Offices: 2

METROPOLITAN FIDUCIAIRE SA

100 Rue du Rhône, 1211 GENEVA 3
Tel: + *41* (22) 21 60 44
Fax: + *41* (22) 21 94 47
Mailing Address: Case postale 518, 1211 GENEVA 3

European Affiliation: DRM Internationally

International Contact: David Steel

Partners:	1
Professional staff:	4
Non-professional staff:	2
Total Staff:	7

FEE INCOME

Year End: 1990	%
Accountancy & Audit:	75.0
Tax:	1.0
Other:	24.0

CLIENT SERVICES

Accountancy (General), Audit, Taxation (Corporate), Taxation (International), Company & Trust Administration

---

MOORE STEPHENS AG

Kanal Strasse 9, 8152 GLATTBRUGG, Zurich
Tel: + *41* (1) 47 23 13
Fax: + *41* (1) 252 65 92

European Affiliation: Moore Stephens

International Contact: André W. Cornu

OTHER OFFICES

MOORE STEPHENS AG
Schanz 4, 6300 ZUG
Tel: + *41* (42) 22 11 72 *Fax:* + *41* (42) 22 11 39
Contact: Anton Müller

MOORE STEPHENS SA
Air Center, Vernier, 16 Chemin des Coquelicots, 1215 GENEVA 15 Airport
Mailing Address: Case postale 464, 1215 GENEVA 15
Tel: + *41* (22) 41 23 57 *Fax:* + *41* (22) 41 23 54
Contact: Josef Blochlinger

Total Number of Offices: 3

MOORES & ROWLAND AG

Seefeldstrasse 45, Postfach 335, 8034 ZURICH
Tel: + *41* (1) 251 42 76
Fax: + *41* (1) 252 43 80

European Affiliation: Moores Rowland International

International Contact: Alex K. Haussmann

MULTIFIDUCIARE SA

Rue Faucigny 5, 1700 FRIBOURG
Tel: + *41* (37) 24 70 77

European Affiliation: S & W International

International Contact: Daniel Baudin
Marcel Schmid

OTHER OFFICES

MULTIFIDUCIARE SA
8 Karl Jasper-Allée, 4052 BASLE
Tel: + *41* (61) 42 96 62
Contact: Charles Huber

MULTIFIDUCIARE SA
Carrefour de Rive, Case postale 439, 1211 GENEVA 3
Tel: + *41* (22) 86 26 50
Contact: Jerome Joliat

MULTIFIDUCIARE SA
45 Rue du Simplon, 1800 VEVEY
Tel: + *41* (21) 52 75 21
Contact: Pierre-Antoine Morard

Total Number of Offices: 4

NEUTRA GRUPPE

Löwenstrasse 56, 8023 ZURICH
Tel: + *41* (1) 211 29 90
Fax: + *41* (1) 221 38 81

European Affiliation: BDO Binder

International Contact: Beat Röthlisberger

Partners:	72
Professional staff:	225
Non-professional staff:	89
Total Staff:	**386**

FEE INCOME

Year End: 31.12.90	SFr	%
Accountancy & Audit:	37,100,000	72.0
Consultancy:	5,700,000	11.0
Tax:	5,700,000	11.0
Other:	3,100,000	6.0
Total:	**51,600,000**	

CONTACT INFORMATION

Chairman: Peter Bühler
Chairman: Hermann Trostel
Chairman: Viktor Fischer

CLIENT SERVICES

All Services

Industry Specialisations: Banking, Manufacturing

MAJOR CLIENTS

Schindler, Sika, Swiss Bank Corporation, Swiss Volksbank, Telekurs

OTHER OFFICES

GESELLSCHAFT FÜR BANKENREVISION (GBR)
Centralbahnstrasse 7, 4051 BASLE
Tel: + *41* (61) 271 87 55 *Fax:* + *41* (61) 271 80 03
Contact: Hermann Trostel

GESELLSCHAFT FÜR BANKENREVISION (GBR)
Kapellenstrasse 5, Postfach 7435, 3011 BERN
Tel: + *41* (31) 26 06 26 *Fax:* + *41* (31) 26 15 32
Contact: Peter Bühler

GESELLSCHAFT FÜR BANKENREVISION (GBR)
Glärnischstrasse 34/36, 8022 ZURICH
Tel: + *41* (1) 202 04 35 *Fax:* + *41* (1) 202 68 40
Contact: Richard Keller

NEUTRA FIDUCIAIRE SA
15 Boulevard des Philosophes, Case postale 266, 1211 GENEVA 4
Tel: + *41* (22) 20 32 11 *Fax:* + *41* (22) 20 48 62
Contact: Beat Röthlisberger

NEUTRA FIDUCIAIRE SA
Chemin des Charmettes 9, Case postale 3433, 1002 LAUSANNE
Tel: + *41* (21) 23 06 24 *Fax:* + *41* (21) 312 07 96
Contact: René Fischer

NEUTRA FIDUCIARIA SA
Via Pretorio 20, Casella postale 2915, 6901 LUGANO
Tel: + *41* (91) 23 56 51 *Fax:* + *41* (91) 22 65 10
Contact: Gabriele Gandolfi

NEUTRA TREUHAND AG
Kapellenstrasse 5, 3011 BERN
Tel: + *41* (31) 26 06 21 *Fax:* + *41* (31) 26 15 32
Contact: Peter Bühler

NEUTRA TREUHAND AG
Poststrasse 11, 9000 ST GALLEN
Tel: + *41* (71) 22 60 88 *Fax:* + *41* (71) 23 54 08
Contact: Herbert Wettstein

NEUTRA TREUHAND AG
Bundesstrasse 3, Postfach 4523, 6304 ZUG
Tel: + *41* (42) 21 61 61 *Fax:* + *41* (42) 21 47 12
Contact: Armin Landtwing

NEUTRA TREUHAND AG
Löwenstrasse 53, Postfach 6633, 8023 ZURICH
Tel: + *41* (1) 211 29 90 *Fax:* + *41* (1) 211 29 23
Contact: Beat Röthlisberger

SOCIETA DI REVISIONE BANCARIA SRB
Via Pretorio 20, Case postale 2915, 6901 LUGANO
Tel: + *41* (91) 23 56 53 *Fax:* + *41* (91) 22 65 10
Contact: Gabriele Gandolfi

SOCIÉTÉ DE RÉVISION BANCAIRE SRB
Boulevard des Philosophes 14, Case Postale 568, 1211 GENEVA 4
Tel: + *41* (22) 20 60 30 *Fax:* + *41* (22) 20 67 00
Contact: Jean-Pierre Vaucher

SOCIÉTÉ DE RÉVISION BANCAIRE SRB
Place Chauderon 4, Case postale 314, 1000 LAUSANNE 9
Tel: + *41* (21) 3 12 15 31 *Fax:* + *41* (21) 20 86 37
Contact: Henri Bonvin

ASSOCIATED FIRMS

FIDUCIAIRE FISCHER SA
Rue Neuve 8, 2800 DELÉMONT
Tel: + *41* (66) 22 98 83 *Fax:* + *41* (66) 22 09 86
Contact: Jean-Claude Courtet

FIDUCIAIRE FISCHER SA
62 Route de Frontenex, Case postale 274, 1211 GENEVA 6
Tel: + *41* (22) 735 42 05 *Fax:* + *41* (22) 735 55 16
Contact: Victor Fischer

FIDUCIAIRE FISCHER SA
45 Rue de la Gare, 1260 NYON
Tel: + *41* (22) 62 23 55 *Fax:* + *41* (22) 61 68 36
Contact: Jean-Pierre Heller

FIDUCIAIRE FISCHER SA
16 Chemin de la Gare, 2900 PORRENTRUY
Tel: + *41* (66) 66 54 61 *Fax:* + *41* (66) 66 54 64
Contact: Michel Duval

F.F. FISCHER TREUHAND AG
23 Boulevard de Pérolles, 1700 FRIBOURG
Tel: + *41* (37) 81 51 91 *Fax:* + *41* (37) 22 49 41
Contact: Martin Mueller

F.F. FISCHER TREUHAND AG
Flughofstrasse 39, 8152 GLATTBRUGG
Tel: + *41* (1) 810 15 45 *Fax:* + *41* (1) 810 89 00
Contact: Arthur Maag

NEOFIDARIA AG/NEOFIDARIA SA
Kapellenstrasse 5, Postfach 7435, 3011 BERN
Tel: + *41* (31) 26 06 28 *Fax:* + *41* (31) 26 15 32
Contact: Rolf Mauerhofer

NEOFIDARIA AG/NEOFIDARIA SA
Boulevard des Philosophes, 1204 GENEVA 11
Tel: + *41* (22) 20 32 11 *Fax:* + *41* (22) 20 48 62
Contact: Beat Röthlisberger

NEOFIDARIA AG/NEOFIDARIA SA
Chemin des Charmettes 9, 1002 LAUSANNE
Tel: + *41* (21) 20 00 42 *Fax:* + *41* (21) 312 07 96
Contact: Philippe Rubin

NEOFIDARIA AG/NEOFIDARIA SA
Bundesstrasse 3, 6304 ZUG
Tel: + *41* (42) 21 60 15 *Fax:* + *41* (42) 21 98 44
Contact: Willy Huber

NEOFIDARIA AG/NEOFIDARIA SA
Heinrichstrasse 147, 8031 ZURICH
Tel: + *41* (1) 271 39 02 *Fax:* + *41* (1) 272 06 26
Contact: Hans-Rudolf Küenzel

NEUTRA EDV-REVISION UND-BERATUNG AG
Kapellenstrasse 5, 3011 BERN
Tel: + *41* (31) 26 06 21 *Fax:* + *41* (31) 26 15 32
Contact: Walter Muster

NEUTRA EDV-REVISION UND-BERATUNG AG
Bundesstrasse 3, 6304 ZUG
Tel: + *41* (42) 21 60 15 *Fax:* + *41* (42) 21 98 44
Contact: Willy Huber

NEUTRA RÉVISON ET CONSEILS EN INFORMATIQUE SA
15 Boulevard des Philosophes, Case Postale 266, 1204 GENEVA 11
Tel: + *41* (22) 20 32 11 *Fax:* + *41* (22) 20 48 62
Contact: Jean Bloch

OFFICE COMPTABLE W. WANNIER SA
5 Quai de la Sorne, 2800 DELÉMONT
Tel: + *41* (66) 22 20 57 *Fax:* + *41* (66) 22 00 08
Contact: Albert Jubin

Total Number of Offices: 34

OBT TREUHAND AG

Rorschacher Strasse 63, 9003 ST GALLEN
Tel: + *41* (71) 26 31 31
Fax: + *41* (71) 25 83 05

European Affiliation: Summit International Associates Inc

International Contact: Jules Wick

Partners:	14
Professional staff:	266
Non-professional staff:	55
Total Staff:	**335**

FEE INCOME

Year End: 31.12.91	**SFr**
Total:	**34,600,000**

▷

CONTACT INFORMATION
Chairman: Artur Buergi
Managing Partner: Jules Wick
Accountancy & Administration: Walter Lengwiler
Audit: Mauro Palazzesi
Management Consultancy: Hans Lindauer
Public Sector: Hans Lindauer
Corporate Finance & Insolvency: Mauro Palazzesi
Tax (Corporate & International): Stefan Dietrich
Informatics: Richard Ritter
Mergers & Acquisitions: Urs Hasler

CLIENT SERVICES
Accountancy (General), Audit, Computer Installation, Corporate Finance Advice, Insolvency & Corporate Restructuring, Litigation/Legal Services, Management & Business Advice, Management Buy-outs, Mergers & Acquisitions, Pensions Planning, Value for Money Studies, Taxation (Corporate), Taxation (International), Trust Settlement & Estates

Industry Specialisations: Apparel, Construction, Electricity, Forest Products, Real Estate, Legal, Transportation, Hospitals

OTHER OFFICES
OBT TREUHAND AG
Eigerplatz 5, 3007 BERN
Tel: + *41* (31) 45 38 88 *Fax:* + *41* (31) 46 20 52
Contact: Artur Buergi

OBT TREUHAND AG
Paradiesstrasse 15, 5200 BRUGG
Tel: + *41* (56) 41 82 21 *Fax:* + *41* (56) 41 82 81
Contact: Markus Fehr

OBT TREUHAND AG
Bahnhofstrasse 8, 7000 CHUR
Tel: + *41* (81) 22 31 84 *Fax:* + *41* (81) 22 84 92
Contact: Jules Wick

OBT TREUHAND AG
Bahnhofstrasse 3, 8570 WEINFELDEN
Tel: + *41* (72) 22 10 10 *Fax:* + *41* (72) 22 35 68
Contact: Jules Wick

OBT TREUHAND AG
Industriestrasse 9, 6301 ZUG
Tel: + *41* (42) 21 64 44 *Fax:* + *41* (42) 21 43 69
Contact: Jules Wick

OBT TREUHAND AG
Weinbergstrasse 137/139, 8042 ZURICH
Tel: + *41* (1) 363 25 50 *Fax:* + *41* (1) 363 41 32
Contact: Peter Langenauer

OBT TRUEHAND AG
Bruoel 16, 6430 SCHWYZ
Tel: + *41* (43) 21 57 93 *Fax:* + *41* (43) 21 55 61
Contact: Jules Wick

Total Number of Offices: 8

OFISA
Chemin des Charmettes 7, 1003 LAUSANNE
Tel: + *41* (21) 20 77 81
Fax: + *41* (21) 311 13 51
Mailing Address: Case postale 3453, 1002 LAUSANNE

European Affiliation: Clark Kenneth Leventhal

International Contact: Françoise Golay

Partners:	5
Professional staff:	37
Non-professional staff:	45
Total Staff:	**87**

FEE INCOME
Year End: 1990	%
Accountancy & Audit:	25.0
Tax:	10.0
Other:	65.0

CLIENT SERVICES
Accountancy (General), Audit, Corporate Finance Advice, Insolvency & Corporate Restructuring, Management & Business Advice, Taxation (Corporate), Taxation (International)

OTHER OFFICES
OFISA
Rue du Marché 7, 1204 GENEVA
Tel: + *41* (22) 21 24 66 *Fax:* + *41* (22) 28 56 46
Contact: Casimir Bossy

Total Number of Offices: 2

OFOR RÉVISION BANCAIRE SA
Place Saint-Gervais 1, 1201 GENEVA
Tel: + *41* (22) 732 13 50
Fax: + *41* (22) 732 20 48
Mailing Address: Case postale 1832, 1211 GENEVA 1

Partners:	3
Professional staff:	20
Total Staff:	**23**

CONTACT INFORMATION
Chairman: Carl Helbling
Managing Partner: Daniel Wanner
Accountancy (General): Jacques Girardin
Tax (International): Van Thanh Bui

CLIENT SERVICES
Audit, Litigation/Legal Services, Management & Business Advice, Mergers & Acquisitions, Taxation (Corporate), Taxation (International), Management Consultancy

Industry Specialisations: Banking

MAJOR CLIENTS
Banque du Gothard, Banque Indosuez, Banque Pallas, Crédit Lyonnais, Discount Bank & Trust Co, Lombard, Odier & Co, Pictet & Co

---

OSTSCHWEIZERISCHE TREUHANDGESELLSCHAFT AG
Selnaustrasse 15, 8002 ZURICH
Tel: + *41* (1) 202 37 05
Fax: + *41* (1) 202 37 08
Mailing Address: Postfach 719, 8039 ZURICH

European Affiliation: HLB International

International Contact: Edwin Weibel

Partners:	4
Professional staff:	7
Non-professional staff:	5
Total Staff:	**16**

OTHER OFFICES
OSTSCHWEIZERISCHE TREUHANDGESELLSCHAFT AG
Alte Bahnhofstrasse 3, 9100 HERISAU
Tel: + *41* (71) 51 14 83

OSTSCHWEIZERISCHE TREUHANDGESELLSCHAFT AG
Burggraben 18, 9004 ST GALLEN
Tel: + *41* (71) 22 51 72

Total Number of Offices: 3

PANNELL KERR FORSTER AG

Postfach 375, 8027 ZURICH
Tel: + *41* (1) 202 58 87
Fax: + *41* (1) 201 46 60

European Affiliation: Pannell Kerr Forster Worldwide

International Contact: Wolfgang Heilmann

OTHER OFFICES

PANNELL KERR FORSTER AG
Via San Salvatore 10, 6902 LUGANO
Mailing Address: Postfach 44, 6902 LUGANO
Tel: + *41* (91) 55 10 30 *Fax:* + *41* (91) 55 11 88
Contact: Diego Colombo

Total Number of Offices: 4

REVISUISSE PRICE WATERHOUSE

Stampfenbachstrasse 109, 8035 ZURICH
Tel: + *41* (1) 365 65 65
Fax: + *41* (1) 365 63 60
Mailing Address: Postfach, 8035 ZURICH

European Affiliation: Price Waterhouse

Partners:	71
Professional staff:	690
Non-professional staff:	250
Total Staff:	**1,011**

FEE INCOME

Year End: 30.06.91	**SFr**	**%**
Accountancy & Audit:	72,504,000	50.0
Insolvency:		15.0
Consultancy:	26,102,000	18.0
Tax:	24,652,000	17.0
Other:	21,751,000	
Total:	**145,009,000**	

CONTACT INFORMATION

Managing Partner: Dr. Peter F. Weibel
Accountancy (General): Kurt Schmidinger
Audit: Dr. Reto Weber
Corporate Finance: Dr. Jakob Bär
Management Consultancy: Peter Ehrensperger
Tax: Hans Jäggi
Fiduciary Services: Anton H. Bleisch
Information Technology: Dr. Bruno Gloor

CLIENT SERVICES

Accountancy (General), Audit, Computer Installation, Corporate Finance Advice, Insolvency & Corporate Restructuring, Litigation/Legal Services, Management & Business Advice, Management Buy-outs, Mergers & Acquisitions, Pensions Planning, Value for Money Studies, Taxation (Corporate), Taxation (International), Management Consultancy

Industry Specialisations: Mutinational Companies, Banking, Insurance, Public Sector, Emerging Businesses

MAJOR CLIENTS

Amag-Group, Bank for International Settlements, Bank Leumi, Chase Manhattan Corp, Credit Suisse-Group, Dar-Al-Maal Al-Islami Trust, Inter Finance SA, Jacobs Suchard-Group, Lloyds Bank International Ltd, Manufacturers Hanover Trust Co, Nomura Securities Ltd, Sony Corporation, Steinbeck-Group, Sulzer-Group, UBS-Group

OTHER OFFICES

REVISUISSE PRICE WATERHOUSE
Bahnhofstrasse 17, 5001 AARAU
Tel: + *41* (64) 24 04 04 *Fax:* + *41* (64) 22 38 75
Contact: Christoph Hochstrasser

REVISUISSE PRICE WATERHOUSE
Steinengraben 5, 4003 BASLE
Tel: + *41* (61) 278 78 78 *Fax:* + *41* (61) 278 78 77
Contact: Franz Bürgisser

REVISUISSE PRICE WATERHOUSE
Spitalgasse 33, 3001 BERN
Tel: + *41* (31) 22 34 72 *Fax:* + *41* (31) 22 44 81
Contact: Dr. Gabriel Heldner

REVISUISSE PRICE WATERHOUSE
Hugistrasse 3, 2501 BIEL
Tel: + *41* (32) 23 63 43 *Fax:* + *41* (32) 22 61 54
Contact: Hansjorg Sägesser

REVISUISSE PRICE WATERHOUSE
Grünaustrasse 21, 3402 BURGDORF
Tel: + *41* (34) 22 78 89 *Fax:* + *41* (34) 22 84 92
Contact: Heinz Brönnimann

REVISUISSE PRICE WATERHOUSE
Hartbertstrasse 9, 7000 CHUR
Tel: + *41* (81) 22 86 83 *Fax:* + *41* (81) 22 86 54
Contact: Hansjürg Bollhalder

REVISUISSE PRICE WATERHOUSE
8 Rue St Pierre, 1701 FRIBOURG
Tel: + *41* (37) 81 15 15 *Fax:* + *41* (37) 22 33 07

REVISUISSE PRICE WATERHOUSE
5 Rue Pedro-Meylan, 1211 GENEVA
Tel: + *41* (22) 786 08 44 *Fax:* + *41* (22) 786 31 13
Contact: Anthony W. Travis

REVISUISSE PRICE WATERHOUSE
Chalet les Arcades, Hauptstrasse, 3780 GSTAAD
Tel: + *41* (30) 462 22 *Fax:* + *41* (30) 464 13
Contact: Silvia Henchoz

REVISUISSE PRICE WATERHOUSE
Murbacherstrasse 3, 6003 LUCERNE
Tel: + *41* (41) 23 85 66 *Fax:* + *41* (41) 23 47 06
Contact: Urs Renggli

REVISUISSE PRICE WATERHOUSE
Via Cattori 3, 6902 LUGANO-PARADISO
Tel: + *41* (91) 55 07 07 *Fax:* + *41* (91) 54 38 18
Contact: Giorgio Della Santa

REVISUISSE PRICE WATERHOUSE
Belpbergstrasse 29, 3110 MÜNSINGEN
Tel: + *41* (31) 721 60 11 *Fax:* + *41* (31) 721 62 20
Contact: Jurg Kummer

REVISUISSE PRICE WATERHOUSE
10 Rue St Honoré, 2001 NEUCHATEL
Tel: + *41* (38) 25 83 33 *Fax:* + *41* (38) 24 67 44
Contact: Frédéderic Gesissbuhler

REVISUISSE PRICE WATERHOUSE
Oberer Graben 31, 9000 ST GALLEN
Tel: + *41* (71) 20 71 91 *Fax:* + *41* (71) 23 38 13
Contact: Rudolf Schiapfer

REVISUISSE PRICE WATERHOUSE
Niesenstrasse 1, 3601 THUN
Tel: + *41* (33) 21 42 14 *Fax:* + *41* (33) 23 35 23
Contact: Peter Zeier

REVISUISSE PRICE WATERHOUSE
Menzbergstrasse 14, 6130 WILLISAU
Tel: + *41* (45) 81 33 41 *Fax:* + *41* (45) 81 40 13
Contact: Urs Renggli

REVISUISSE PRICE WATERHOUSE
Ackeretstrasse 13, 8400 WINTERTHUR
Tel: + *41* (52) 25 29 21 *Fax:* + *41* (52) 25 31 15
Contact: Rudolf Harlacher

▷

Switzerland

REVISUISSE PRICE WATERHOUSE
Baarerstrasse 94, 6302 ZUG
Tel: + *41* (42) 31 06 55 *Fax:* + *41* (42) 32 21 24
Contact: Werner Blatter

REVISUISSE PRICE WATERHOUSE
Chemin de Mornex 3, 1001 LAUSANNE
Tel: + *41* (21) 23 69 16 *Fax:* + *41* (21) 312 77 47
Contact: Peter Muther

REVISUISSE PRICE WATERHOUSE
Zelgliackerstrasse 4, 5200 WINDISCH
Tel: + *41* (56) 41 02 22 *Fax:* + *41* (56) 41 69 21
Contact: Hans Bachmann

REVISUISSE PRICE WATERHOUSE
Bahnhofstrasse 28, 3076 WORB
Tel: + *41* (31) 839 34 31 *Fax:* + *41* (31) 839 75 67
Contact: Dr. Gabriel Heldner

Total Number of Offices: 22

RFF REVISION FISCALITÉ FIDUCIAIRE SA

Chemin Rieu 12, 1211 GENEVA 17
Tel: + *41* (22) 47 47 87
Fax: + *41* (22) 47 82 96
Mailing Address: Case postale 241, 1211 GENEVA 17

European Affiliation: Alliott Peirson International

International Contact: Michel de Preux

RST REVISIONS AG

Peter Merian-Strasse 54, 4002 BASLE
Tel: + *41* (61) 272 24 24
Fax: + *41* (61) 272 29 85
Mailing Address: Postfach 3944, 4002 BASLE

European Affiliation: BKR International

International Contact: Marcel Durrer

Partners:	2
Professional staff:	7
Non-professional staff:	2
Total Staff:	**11**

FEE INCOME

Year End: 31.12.90	%
Accountancy & Audit:	22.0
Consultancy:	30.0
Tax:	10.0
Other:	38.0

CONTACT INFORMATION

Chairman: Peter Lecsko

CLIENT SERVICES

Accountancy (General), Audit, Corporate Finance Advice, Litigation/ Legal Services, Management & Business Advice, Management Buy-outs, Mergers & Acquisitions, Taxation (Corporate), Trust Settlement & Estates

OTHER OFFICES

RST REVISIONS AG
Quellenstrasse 10, 4310 RHEINFELDEN
Tel: + *41* (61) 831 48 28 *Fax:* + *41* (61) 272 29 85
Contact: Marcel Durrer

RST REVISIONS AG
Asylstrasse 17, 8032 ZURICH
Tel: + *41* (1) 262 08 88 *Fax:* + *41* (1) 262 11 10
Contact: Marcel Egli

Total Number of Offices: 3

SOCIÉTÉ DE CONTROLE FIDUCIAIRE SA

Rue Ami-Lullin 4, 1211 GENEVA 3
Tel: + *41* (22) 735 65 00
Fax: + *41* (22) 735 60 82
Mailing Address: Case Postale 801, 1211 GENEVA 3

European Affiliation: Summit International Associates Inc

International Contact: Roger Perrenoud

Partners:	8
Professional staff:	36
Non-professional staff:	12
Total Staff:	**56**

FEE INCOME

Year End: 31.12.90	%
Accountancy & Audit:	75.0
Consultancy:	5.0
Tax:	15.0
Other:	5.0

CONTACT INFORMATION

Chairman: Christian Reiser
Managing Partner: Roger Perrenoud
Accountancy (General): Jean Biedermann
Tax (Corporate): Nicole Stocker
Audit, Tax & Management Consultancy: Roger Perrenoud
Administration & Public Sector: Jean Biedermann

CLIENT SERVICES

Accountancy (General), Audit, Mergers & Acquisitions, Taxation (Corporate), Taxation (International), Trust Settlement & Estates

Industry Specialisations: Insurance, Public Sector

OTHER OFFICES

SOCIÉTÉ DE CONTROLE FIDUCIAIRE SA
Place Général-Guisan 16, 2502 BIENNE
Tel: + *41* (32) 22 72 30 *Fax:* + *41* (32) 22 91 05
Contact: Claude von Gunten

SOCIÉTÉ DE CONTROLE FIDUCIAIRE SA
Boulevard de Pérolles 22, 1701 FRIBOURG
Tel: + *41* (37) 22 21 12 *Fax:* + *41* (37) 23 12 20
Contact: Werner Spycher

SOCIÉTÉ DE CONTROLE FIDUCIAIRE SA
Avenue de la Gare 50, 1001 LAUSANNE
Tel: + *41* (21) 20 44 01 *Fax:* + *41* (21) 311 20 17
Contact: Jean Barre

SOCIÉTÉ DE CONTROLE FIDUCIAIRE SA
Avenue de la Gare 32, 1950 SION
Tel: + *41* (27) 22 05 55 *Fax:* + *41* (27) 22 05 57
Contact: Claude Nancoz

SOCIÉTÉ DE CONTROLE FIDUCIAIRE SA
Avenue de la Gare 16, 1800 VEVEY
Tel: + *41* (21) 921 55 35 *Fax:* + *41* (21) 922 53 58
Contact: Willy Delafontaine

Total Number of Offices: 6

TESTOR TREUHAND AG

Rittergasse 35, 4001 BASLE
Tel: + *41* (61) 272 50 18
Fax: + *41* (61) 272 83 61

European Affiliation: DRM Internationally

International Contact: F. Peter Staehelin

Partners:	10
Professional staff:	40
Non-professional staff:	10
Total Staff:	**60**

FEE INCOME

Year End: 1990	**SFr**	**%**
Accountancy & Audit:	3,300,000	55.0
Consultancy:	900,000	15.0
Tax:	900,000	15.0
Other:	900,000	15.0
Total:	**6,000,000**	

CONTACT INFORMATION
Chairman: Christoph Loew
Managing Partner: Peter Schroff
Accountancy (General): Peter Forrer
Corporate Finance: Peter Schroff
Management Consultancy: F. Peter Staehelin
Audit & EDP: Felix Zimmermann
Tax: Hans-U. Voellmy

CLIENT SERVICES
Accountancy (General), Audit, Corporate Finance Advice, Insolvency & Corporate Restructuring, Management & Business Advice, Management Buy-outs, Mergers & Acquisitions, Taxation (Corporate), Taxation (International), Trust Settlement & Estates

Industry Specialisations: Industry, Trade, Services

OTHER OFFICES
TESTOR TREUHAND AG
Bahnhofplatz 9, 8023 ZURICH
Tel: + *41* (1) 211 73 90 *Fax:* + *41* (1) 211 05 54
TESTOR TREUHAND AG
Rue des Pres 135, 2503 BIENNE
Tel: + *41* (32) 35 36 11 *Fax:* + *41* (32) 25 69 11
Contact: Jean-Paul Corbaz
TESTOR TREUHAND AG
Baarerstrasse 59, 6300 ZUG
Tel: + *41* (42) 211 73 90 *Fax:* + *41* (42) 211 05 54
Total Number of Offices: 4

TREFIMA INC
Atlantis Building, Zurcherstrasse 65, 9500 WIL 1, Zurich
Tel: + *41* (73) 20 33 88
Fax: + *41* (73) 22 63 53
Mailing Address: Postfach 737, 9500 WIL 1

European Affiliation: S & W International

International Contact: Werner Gramm

CLIENT SERVICES
Trust & Financial Management

OTHER OFFICES
TREFIMA INC
Muenchhaldenstrasse 10, 8034 ZURICH
Tel: + *41* (1) 55 64 19 *Fax:* + *41* (1) 382 22 19
Total Number of Offices: 2

TREUHANDVEREINIGUNG AG
Ziegelrain 29, 5001 AARAU
Tel: + *41* (64) 27 17 17
Fax: + *41* (64) 24 12 86

European Affiliation: Alliott Peirson International

International Contact: Arno Meyer

OTHER OFFICES
TREUHANDVEREINIGUNG AG
Winkelriedstrasse 58, 6003 LUCERNE
Tel: + *41* (41) 23 72 42 *Fax:* + *41* (41) 23 77 12
TREUHANDVEREINIGUNG AG
Bahnhofstrasse 7, 4600 OLTEN
Tel: + *41* (62) 26 33 41 *Fax:* + *41* (62) 26 76 20
Contact: Martin Fessler
TREUHANDVEREINIGUNG AG
Kaiserstrasse 9, 4310 RHEINFELDEN
Tel: + *41* (61) 87 65 65 *Fax:* + *41* (61) 87 61 13
Contact: Hans Keller
Total Number of Offices: 4

TREUHAND-UND REVISIONSGESELLSCHAFT ZURICH
Schaffhauserstrasse 18, 8023 ZURICH
Tel: + *41* (1) 362 36 65
Fax: + *41* (1) 362 44 23
Mailing Address: Postfach 6240, 8023 ZURICH

European Affiliation: Clark Kenneth Leventhal

International Contact: Peter Grote

Partners:	11
Professional staff:	23
Non-professional staff:	14
Total Staff:	**48**

FEE INCOME

Year End: 1990	**%**
Accountancy & Audit:	41.0
Tax:	43.0
Other:	16.0

CLIENT SERVICES
Accountancy (General), Audit, Corporate Finance Advice, Insolvency & Corporate Restructuring, Management & Business Advice, Taxation (Corporate), Taxation (International)

TREUREVA AG
Stampfenbachstrasse 153, 8035 ZURICH 6
Tel: + *41* (1) 362 63 63
Fax: + *41* (1) 362 11 20

European Affiliation: Independent Accountants International

International Contact: Pierre Schaerer
Maryann Rohner

Total Number of Offices: 3

TRIGEMA AG
Lessingstrasse 5, Postfach, 8059 ZURICH
Tel: + *41* (1) 202 36 69
Fax: + *41* (1) 202 22 43

European Affiliation: TGI International

International Contact: Kurt Briner

TUREVA TREUHAND AG
Splügenstrasse 10, 8002 ZURICH
Tel: + *41* (1) 202 47 42
Fax: + *41* (1) 202 47 44

European Affiliation: ATD International

International Contact: Samir Jarallah

Partners:	2
Professional staff:	5
Non-professional staff:	1
Total Staff:	**8**

FEE INCOME

Year End: 31.12.90	%
Accountancy & Audit:	45.0
Consultancy:	10.0
Tax:	30.0
Other:	15.0

CONTACT INFORMATION
Chairman: Duri Sulser
Managing Partner: Samir Jarallah
Managing Partner: Duri Sulser

CLIENT SERVICES
Accountancy (General), Audit, Corporate Finance Advice, Insolvency & Corporate Restructuring, Management & Business Advice, Management Buy-outs, Mergers & Acquisitions, Value for Money Studies, Taxation (Corporate), Taxation (International), Trust Settlement & Estates

Industry Specialisations: Finance Companies

OTHER OFFICES

DURI SULSER TREUHAND
Vazerolgasse 12, 7002 CHUR
Tel: + *41* (81) 22 52 12 *Fax:* + *41* (81) 22 99 86

Total Number of Offices: 2

USHER & CO

Place des Eaux Vives 6, 1207 GENEVA
Tel: + *41* (22) 786 14 44
Fax: + *41* (22) 786 18 46
Mailing Address: Case postale 408, 1211 GENEVA 3

European Affiliation: Moores Rowland International

International Contact: John Usher

Partners:	3
Professional staff:	12
Non-professional staff:	4
Total Staff:	**19**

FEE INCOME

Year End: 31.12.90	**SFr**	%
Accountancy & Audit:	1,547,000	48.4
Insolvency:	30,000	1.0
Consultancy:	200,000	6.2
Tax:	1,363,000	42.6
Other:	60,000	1.8
Total:	**3,200,000**	

CONTACT INFORMATION
Chairman: John Usher
Administration: Raj Nair
Insolvency & Tax: Kaloyan Stoyanov
Accountancy, Audit & Administration: Raj Nair
Public Sector & Trusts: John Usher
Corporate Finance & Consultancy: John Usher

CLIENT SERVICES
All Services

OTHER OFFICES

USHER & CO
12 via Pioda, 6900 LUGANO
Mailing Address: Casella postale 3453, 6900 LUGANO
Tel: + *41* (91) 23 57 76 *Fax:* + *41* (91) 23 53 25
Contact: Andrea Melera

Total Number of Offices: 2

VISURA TREUHAND-GESELLSCHAFT

Talstrasse 80, 8021 ZURICH
Tel: + *41* (1) 211 38 33
Fax: + *41* (1) 211 48 82
Mailing Address: Postfach 614, 8021 ZURICH

European Affiliation: Jeffreys Henry International

International Contact: Rudi Haefeli

OTHER OFFICES

VISURA TREUHAND GESELLSCHAFT
Jurastrasse 20, 4603 OLTEN
Tel: + *41* (62) 32 71 71 *Fax:* + *41* (62) 32 33 86
Contact: Martin Hulmann

VISURA TREUHAND-GESELLSCAHFT
Sandmattstrasse 2, 4501 SOLOTHURN
Tel: + *41* (65) 24 62 46 *Fax:* + *41* (65) 22 58 35
Contact: Josef Ingold

VISURA TREUHAND-GESELLSCHAFT
Entfelderstrasse 5, 5000 AARAU
Tel: + *41* (64) 25 55 66 *Fax:* + *41* (64) 24 58 59
Contact: Hans Roesch

VISURA TREUHAND-GESELLSCHAFT
Daetwylerstrasse 9, 6460 ALTDORF
Tel: + *41* (44) 283 83 *Fax:* + *41* (44) 2 89 39
Contact: Bruno Baumann

VISURA TREUHAND-GESELLSCHAFT
Taefernstrasse 16, 5405 BADEN-DAETTWIL
Tel: + *41* (56) 84 02 45 *Fax:* + *41* (56) 83 54 45
Contact: Kurt Haller

VISURA TREUHAND-GESELLSCHAFT
Rennweg 34, 4020 BASLE
Tel: + *41* (61) 312 66 61 *Fax:* + *41* (61) 312 56 06
Contact: Helmuth Disch

VISURA TREUHAND-GESELLSCHAFT
Kirchbergstrasse 215, 3401 BURGDORF
Tel: + *41* (34) 22 88 11 *Fax:* + *41* (34) 22 07 46
Contact: Urs Seiler

VISURA TREUHAND-GESELLSCHAFT
Dammstrasse 14, 2540 GRENCHEN
Tel: + *41* (65) 51 31 41 *Fax:* + *41* (65) 52 53 61
Contact: Peter Bachofner

VISURA TREUHAND-GESELLSCHAFT
Hauptstrasse 14, 8280 KREUZLINGEN
Tel: + *41* (72) 72 10 58 *Fax:* + *41* (72) 72 38 23
Contact: Roland Breutsch

VISURA TREUHAND-GESELLSCHAFT
Rue St Martin 9, 1002 LAUSANNE
Tel: + *41* (21) 20 89 71 *Fax:* + *41* (21) 20 02 36
Contact: Alphonse Staubli

VISURA TREUHAND-GESELLSCHAFT
Gestadeckplatz 2, 4410 LIESTAL
Tel: + *41* (61) 921 94 93 *Fax:* + *41* (61) 921 90 60
Contact: Reto Mueller

VISURA TREUHAND-GESELLSCHAFT
Landenbergstrasse 34, 6005 LUCERNE
Tel: + *41* (41) 40 44 88 *Fax:* + *41* (41) 44 03 30
Contact: Otto Wyss

VISURA TREUHAND-GESELLSCHAFT
Hauptstrasse 36, 4702 OENSINGEN
Tel: + *41* (62) 76 33 20 *Fax:* + *41* (62) 76 33 47
Contact: Kurt Zimmerli

VISURA TREUHAND-GESELLSCHAFT
Pilatusstrasse 5, 6060 SARNEN
Tel: + *41* (41) 66 28 42 *Fax:* + *41* (41) 66 82 06
Contact: Ruedi Riebli

VISURA TREUHAND-GESELLSCHAFT
Aemaettlistrasse 2, 6370 STANS
Tel: + 41 (41) 61 44 34 *Fax: + 41* (41) 61 32 25
Contact: Franz Stoeckli

VISURA TREUHAND-GESELLSCHAFT
Kornhausstrasse 3, 9001 ST GALLEN
Tel: + 41 (71) 22 73 83 *Fax: + 41* (71) 22 73 52
Contact: Felix Troesch

VISURA TREUHAND-GESELLSCHAFT
Pappelnstrasse 12, 8622 WETZIKON
Tel: + 41 (1) 930 38 32 *Fax: + 41* (1) 930 38 66
Contact: Jean-Jacques Wymann

VISURA TREUHAND-GESELLSHAFT
Chr. Schnyderstrasse, 6210 SURSEE
Tel: + 41 (45) 21 61 61 *Fax: + 41* (45) 21 72 78
Contact: Peter Aeschbacher

Total Number of Offices: 19

United Kingdom

Area: 244,103 sq km (94,249 sq miles)
Population: 56,763,300 (1986 estimate)
Density: 232.5 per sq km
Capital: London

GDP: £518 bn, US$922 bn
GDP per head: US$16,010
Inflation: 1990 - 9.3%
1991 - 6.4% (forecast)

Official and Spoken Language: English

Time: GMT (in Summer GMT + 1)
Telephone Dialling Code: + 44

Currency: Pound sterling (£) = 100 pence
Banking Hours: 0930-1530 Monday-Friday
Professional accountancy body: Institute of Chartered Accountants in England & Wales
Institute of Chartered accountants of Scotland
Chartered Association of Certified Accountants
Chartered Institute of Management Accountants
Chartered Institute of Public Finance and Accountancy

Corporate Tax Data

Information supplied by Richard Citron, international tax partner of Stoy Hayward.

The tax year; nature and rates of tax
The tax year is the year ending 31 March.

Corporation tax is levied at a rate of 33% on distributed and undistributed income. Taxable profits below £250,000 (proportionately reduced with the number of "associated" companies) are taxed at 25% (the "small companies rate") and profits between £250,000 and £1,250,000 are taxed at a marginal rate which has the effect of progressively increasing the average rate of tax between these limits to 33%.

The "small companies" rate of corporation tax does not apply to acompany which is a "close investment-holding company". This is, broadly speaking an investment company which has an entirely passive role (ie. it does not administer a group of trading companies or hold shares in a qualifying trading company or a company which makes investments in land etc) and is primarily family owned.

Residence and territoriality

UK resident companies are liable to corporation tax on their worldwide income and gains. A company is resident in the UK if it is incorporated in the UK or if central management and control abides in the UK.

The tax base

Method of computation. Taxable profits are based on the profit reported in the annual accounts.

Disallowable items. The major disallowable items are expenditure not incurred wholly and exclusively for the purposes of the trade, non-staff entertaining, capital expenditure, depreciation (for capital allowances, see below) and general provisions. ▷

Exempt income/special deductions. For dividends see below. Capital allowances are deductible in computing profits, see 'Depreciation' below.

Interest paid. Interest (other than interest paid to a UK bank for business purposes) is normally deductible on a paid rather than on an accruals basis. Where interest is paid other than to a UK bank or UK branch of an overseas bank, the company must deduct a withholding tax of 25% which is regularly reduced to zero under the terms of a tax treaty. Where interest is paid by a UK resident company to an overseas parent with 75% control, it is prima-facie, non-deductible and treated similarly to a dividend payment attracting ACT.

Stock. Stock and work in progress is valued at the lower of cost and market value ona FIFO basis.

Depreciation. Accounts depreciation is not deductible for tax purposes. There is instead a system of capital allowances for specified classes of assets including, inter-alia:

(1) Plant and machinery (other than private cars) are entitled to an annual allowance of 25% on the reducing balance basis.
(2) Private motor cars attract an allowance of 25% but this cannot exceed £3,000 pa where the car's cost is in excess of £12,000.
(3) Industrial buildings have an annual allowance of 4% based on original cost.
(4) Hotel buildings have a flat 4% annual allowance based on the original cost.
(5) Office and shop buildings do not generally qualify for capital allowances.
(6) An initial allowance of 100% is given for most industrial and commercial buildings (including offices and shops) located in an enterprise zone where the expenditure is incurred in the zone's first 10 years.
(7) Patent rights, industrial know-how, scientific research, dredging, mineworks and agricultural buildings all qualify for special rates of capital allowance.

The treatment of dividends

Dividends received from UK companies. Dividends received from UK companies are exempt from corporation tax. The tax credit attaching to them (25/75ths of the net dividend) may be used to reduce the advance corporation tax payable by the companyon its own dividend.

Dividends received from abroad. Liable to UK corporation tax. A foreign tax credit will be available for the amount of any withholding tax. Where the recipient company's holding is 10% or more, a foreign tax credit will also be available for the underlying tax.

Dividends paid to UK residents. Advance corporation tax (ACT) is payable at a rate of 25/75 of the net dividend and an equivalent tax credit is available to the recipient. ACT may be used (as reduced by the tax credit on incoming dividends) to reduce the company's corporation tax liability on its profits.

Dividends paid to non-residents. The company must still pay ACT but non-residents are not entitled to the tax credit represented by the ACT. Dividends paid to residents in certain countries with which the UK has a tax treaty will attract a refund of half the ACT paid (less a withholding tax). Other than where a half-ACT refund is available, there is no withholding tax on dividends paid.

Anti-avoidance measures

Transfer pricing legislation exists. There are also wide ranging measures to prevent avoidance by transfer of income abroad and also the accruing of capital gains to non-resident subsidiaries (the latter may be avoided by an appropriately worded double tax treaty). In addition, there are anti-avoidance provisions dealing with controlled foreign companies. These apply to treat the income (but not capital gains) of non-UK resident companies controlled by UK residents as accruing to the UK shareholders and subject to corporation tax in their hands. The provisions will apply if the foreign subsidiary company is subject to a lower level of taxation in its country of residence although there are fairly extensive exclusions.

There are no statutory thin capitalisation rules. However, although interest paid to an overseas parent with 75% control is prima facie non-deductible, if the recipient is resident in a country which has a tax treaty with the UK, the interest paid will be deductible to the extent that the interest rate and debt/equity ratios are within "arms length terms". The UK revenue authorities will normally regard a debt/equity ratio of 1:1 as being acceptable.

Treatment of losses

Current period. Trading losses may be set off against all income and gains of the same period.

Past periods. A trading loss may be carried back and set against all income and gains of the previous three accounting periods.

Future periods. To the extent that losses remain unrelieved in the current or preceding periods, trading losses may be carried forward indefinitely against profits from the same trade.

Treatment of Capital Gains

Treatment. A company's capital gains are assessable to corporation tax at the same rate as income.

Computation. Capital gains are computed by deducting the cost of an asset from its proceeds. Where an asset being sold was owned at 31 March 1982 its market value at that date may be substituted for cost. The cost of acquisition is adjusted for inflation.

Roll-over. Deferral of a gain by roll-over against the cost of replacement assets is possible in many situations.

Treatment of Groups

Group treatment is available whereby losses of the current period may be transferred to other companies in the group and assets may be transferred between group companies free of tax. Dividends and interest may be paid free of ACT or income (withholding) tax and surplus ACT may be surrendered within a group. A group consists of a holding company and its 51% subsidiaries (for dividend and interest payments) or its 75% subsidiaries (for loss and asset transfers).

Treatment of Branches.

The profits and gains of a UK branch of a non-resident company are computed in the same way as those of a UK resident company. There is no withholding tax and no ACT on remittances of profits from a branch.

Other Taxes

Local authority rates are charged on the occupier of commercial property.

Turnover taxes. A value added tax is charged on the supply of goods and services by UK business entities. There is a standard rate of 17.5%, a zero rate and also certain supplies can be exempted from the tax. The export of goods and certain services from the UK are zero rated.

Transaction taxes. A stamp duty will apply on the transfer of shares in UK incorporated companies and on UK properties (if of a value of £30,000 or more). The rate for the former is 1/2% and that for the latter 1%.

Payroll taxes. Social security contributions are payable by employers at 10.4% (lower rates apply for those earning less than £190 per week) and are payable by employees at 9% on salaries of up to £21,060 per annum. Lower rates apply to members of certain pension schemes.

Other taxes. A petroleum revenue tax applies to profits from oil and gas derived in the UK and there is also an inheritance tax.

United Kingdom

ALLEN, SYKES

1 Cockton Hill Road, BISHOP AUCKLAND, Co Durham DL14 6EN
Tel: + *44* (388) 603917
Fax: + *44* (388) 450427

European Affiliation: Moores Rowland International

International Contact: Michael J. Chipchase

ALLIOTT PEIRSON ASSOCIATES

5th Floor, 9 Kingsway, LONDON WC2B 6XF
Tel: + *44* (71) 240 9971
Fax: + *44* (71) 240 9692

European Affiliation: Alliott Peirson International

International Contact: David W. Almond

ASSOCIATED FIRMS

ALLIOTT BLOOM
7 Park Quadrant, GLASGOW G3 6BS
Tel: + *44* (41) 331 1977 *Fax:* + *44* (41) 331 2656
Contact: Charles S. Burton

ALLIOTT BLYTHE & CO
8 Green Lane, BELPER, Derbyshire DE5 1BY
Tel: + *44* (773) 825051
Contact: William A. Lane

ALLIOTT BLYTHE & CO
Georgian House, 66-66a Friar Gate, DERBY DE1 1DJ
Tel: + *44* (332) 48744
Contact: William A. Lane

ALLIOTT MILLAR
Kintyre House, 70 High Street, FAREHAM, Hampshire PO16 7BB
Tel: + *44* (329) 822232 *Fax:* + *44* (329) 822405
Contact: Michael Wingham

ALLIOTT MILLAR
23b High Street, SALISBURY SP1 2NL
Tel: + *44* (722) 337455 *Fax:* + *44* (722) 337194
Contact: Ronald N. Millar

ALLIOTT MILLAR
Manor House, 239 Manor Farm Road, Bitterne Park, SOUTHAMPTON SO2 4NZ
Tel: + *44* (703) 551311 *Fax:* + *44* (703) 584649
Contact: John H. Beale

ALLIOTTS
Canterbury House, Sydenham Road, CROYDON CR9 2DG
Tel: + *44* (81) 681 6926 *Fax:* + *44* (81) 680 3650
Contact: Peter J. Edwards

ALLIOTTS
96 High Street, GUILDFORD, Surrey GU1 3DL
Tel: + *44* (483) 33119 *Fax:* + *44* (483) 37339
Contact: David W. Almond

ALLIOTTS
10 College Road, HARROW, Middlesex HA1 1DA
Tel: + *44* (81) 861 1771 *Fax:* + *44* (81) 861 3759
Contact: Alan P. Wilson

ALLIOTT, RAWKINS & HOLDEN
263 Church Street, BLACKPOOL FY1 3PB
Tel: + *44* (253) 751515 *Fax:* + *44* (253) 751160
Contact: Andrew J.B. McDonald

ALLIOTT, RAWKINS & HOLDEN
88-96 Market Street West, PRESTON PR1 2EU
Tel: + *44* (772) 202655 *Fax:* + *44* (772) 202631
Contact: Robert M. Rawkins

ALLIOTT, RAWKINS & HOLDEN
52 Chorley New Road, BOLTON BL1 4AP
Tel: + *44* (204) 381124 *Fax:* + *44* (204) 364814
Contact: Peter Shaw

BARTFIELD & CO
Burley House, 12 Clarendon Road, LEEDS LS2 9NF
Tel: + *44* (532) 449051 *Fax:* + *44* (532) 420098
Contact: Kenneth Cope

BARTFIELD & CO
18 Commercial Street, Rothwell, LEEDS LS26 0AW
Tel: + *44* (532) 826542
Contact: Kenneth Cope

CHARLES BURROWS & CO
7 Palmerston Place, EDINBURGH EH12 5AH
Tel: + *44* (31) 225 1755 *Fax:* + *44* (31) 220 0048
Contact: Derek R.M. Wilson

HAMILTON-BURKE DUFAU
31/33 Heathfield Road, LIVERPOOL L15 9EX
Tel: + *44* (51) 733 0564 *Fax:* + *44* (51) 735 0370
Contact: Ian D. Hamilton-Burke

KENNETH HAYES & CO
1st Floor, City House, 2/4 Dam Street, LICHFIELD, Staffordshire WS13 6AA
Tel: + *44* (543) 268377 *Fax:* + *44* (543) 415234

KENNETH HAYES & CO
Lombard House, Great Charles Street, BIRMINGHAM B3 3NB
Tel: + *44* (21) 236 4111
Contact: John S. Matthewman

NELSON HALL & JOHNSON
Suite 3, Saville Office Suites, 5 North Street, NEWCASTLE-UPON-TYNE NE1 8DF
Tel: + *44* (91) 232 0713 *Fax:* + *44* (91) 232 2696
Contact: Bryan Nelson

NELSON HALL & JOHNSON
3 Lintonville Terrace, ASHINGTON, Northumberland NE63 9UN
Tel: + *44* (670) 818201

NELSON HALL & JOHNSON
32/34 Dudley Court, CRAMLINGTON, Northumberland NE23 6QW
Tel: + *44* (670) 737717 *Fax:* + *44* (670) 716231

NELSON HALL & JOHNSON
Serenig, Bridge Street, Rothbury, MORPETH, Northumberland NE65 6QW
Tel: + *44* (669) 20069
Contact: Bryan Nelson

Total Number of Offices: 23

ALLOTTS

1 South Terrace, Moorgate Street, ROTHERHAM, South Yorkshire S60 2EX
Tel: + *44* (709) 828400
Fax: + *44* (709) 829807

National Affiliation: The CharterGroup Partnership

Partners:	7
Professional staff:	50
Non-professional staff:	6
Total Staff:	**63**

CONTACT INFORMATION

Managing Partner: Peter W. Allot
Accountancy (General): Jonathan G. Woolley
Audit: Anthony E. Grice
Management Consultancy: Stephen G. Pepper
Tax (Corporate): J. David Welch
Computers: Alan Holloway
Chambers of Commerce: Jacqueline N. Saunders

CLIENT SERVICES
All Services

Industry Specialisations: Farming, Hotels

OTHER OFFICES

ALLOTTS
11/13 Thorne Road, DONCASTER, South Yorkshire DN1 2HR
Tel: + *44* (302) 349218 *Fax:* + *44* (302) 321739
Contact: Jonathan G. Woolley

Total Number of Offices: 2

ALLWOOD BAIRD HACK

White Friars, CHESTER CH1 1QD
Tel: + *44* (244) 312351
Fax: + *44* (244) 320881

National Affiliation: The UK 200 Group of Practising Accountants

Partners:	11
Professional staff:	42
Non-professional staff:	17
Total Staff:	**70**

CONTACT INFORMATION
Managing Partner: Gordon Glover
Accountancy (General): J.P. Bennion
Administration: Gordon Glover
Tax (Corporate): J.M. Arrowsmith
Audit & Corporate Finance: N.P.D. Jackson

CLIENT SERVICES
Accountancy (General), Audit, Corporate Finance Advice, Management & Business Advice, Taxation (Corporate), Trust Settlement & Estates

Industry Specialisations: Agriculture, Independent Schools, Charities

---

ARMSTRONG WATSON & CO

15 Victoria Place, CARLISLE CA1 1EW
Tel: + *44* (228) 27551
Fax: + *44* (228) 401760

European Affiliation: Independent Accountants International

International Contact: Robin Liddell

Total Number of Offices: 20

ARTHUR ANDERSEN & CO

1 Surrey Street, LONDON WC2R 2PS
Tel: + *44* (71) 438 3000
Fax: + *44* (71) 831 1133

European Affiliation: Arthur Andersen Worldwide

International Contact: Manuel Soto

Partners:	588
Professional staff:	12,915
Non-professional staff:	3,632
Total Staff:	**17,135**

FEE INCOME

Year End: 31.08.91	**US$**	**%**
Accountancy & Audit:	497,400,000	36.6
Consultancy:	662,800,000	48.8
Tax:	198,300,000	14.6
Total:	**1,358,500,000**	

CONTACT INFORMATION
Managing Partner: Manuel Soto
Marketing Director: Francis H. Quinlan

CLIENT SERVICES
All Services

OTHER OFFICES

ARTHUR ANDERSEN & CO
One Victoria Square, BIRMINGHAM B1 1BD
Tel: + *44* (21) 233 2101 *Fax:* + *44* (21) 233 2954
Contact: Anthony Timberlake

ARTHUR ANDERSEN & CO
Broad Quay House, Broad Quay, BRISTOL BS1 4DJ
Tel: + *44* (272) 277436 *Fax:* + *44* (272) 277507
Contact: David Perry

ARTHUR ANDERSEN & CO
Betjeman House, 104 Hills Road, CAMBRIDGE CB2 1LH
Tel: + *44* (223) 353906 *Fax:* + *44* (223) 66287
Contact: Nigel Pye

ARTHUR ANDERSEN & CO
18 Charlotte Square, EDINBURGH EH2 4DF
Tel: + *44* (31) 225 4554 *Fax:* + *44* (31) 226 3948
Contact: Eric M. Hagman

ARTHUR ANDERSEN & CO
199 St Vincent Street, GLASGOW G2 5QD
Tel: + *44* (41) 248 7941 *Fax:* + *44* (41) 248 6155
Contact: David Haxby

ARTHUR ANDERSEN & CO
St Paul's House, Park Square, LEEDS LS1 2PJ
Tel: + *44* (532) 438222 *Fax:* + *44* (532) 459240
Contact: David Haxby

ARTHUR ANDERSEN & CO
Bank House, 9 Charlotte Street, MANCHESTER M1 4EU
Tel: + *44* (61) 228 2121 *Fax:* + *44* (61) 228 1421
Contact: John Priestley

ARTHUR ANDERSEN & CO
Fothergill House, 16 King Street, NOTTINGHAM NG1 2AS
Tel: + *44* (602) 353900 *Fax:* + *44* (602) 353949
Contact: Anthony Timberlake

ARTHUR ANDERSEN & CO
Abbots House, Abbey Street, READING RG1 3BD
Tel: + *44* (734) 508141 *Fax:* + *44* (734) 508101
Contact: David Perry

Total Number of Offices: 10

AUCKLAND GODDARD HAMPSON & SWAIN

Hogarth House, 31 Sheet Street, WINDSOR, Berkshire SL4 1BY
Tel: + *44* (753) 831525
Fax: + *44* (753) 831352

European Affiliation: ATD International

International Contact: Martin Goddard

Partners:	8
Professional staff:	26
Non-professional staff:	13
Total Staff:	**47**

CONTACT INFORMATION
Chairman: Paul Hampson
Managing Partner: Martin Goddard
Accountancy (General): Philip Shepherd
Audit: Paul Hampson
Corporate Finance: Keith Auckland
Management Consultancy: Martin Goddard
Tax (Corporate): Tim O'Brien
Tax (Personal): Murray Gellatly

▷

CLIENT SERVICES

Accountancy (General), Audit, Computer Installation, Corporate Finance Advice, Management & Business Advice, Pensions Planning, Taxation (Corporate), New Ventures, Profit Forecasts, Added Value Audit, Viability Review, Cashflow Projects, Share Valuations

OTHER OFFICES

AUCKLAND GODDARD HAMPSON & SWAIN (LONDON)
2 Cromwell Place, LONDON SW7 2JE
Tel: + *44* (71) 823 9844 *Fax:* + *44* (71) 589 6685

Total Number of Offices: 2

BAKER TILLY

2 Bloomsbury Street, LONDON WC1B 3ST
Tel: + *44* (71) 413 5100
Fax: + *44* (71) 413 5101

European Affiliation: BKR International

International Contact: Charles Tucker

Partners:	50
Professional staff:	430
Non-professional staff:	100
Total Staff:	**580**

FEE INCOME

Year End: 31.08.90	**£**	**%**
Accountancy & Audit:	12,000,000	53.0
Insolvency:	1,000,000	4.0
Consultancy:	1,800,000	8.0
Tax:	6,000,000	26.0
Other:	2,000,000	9.0
Total:	**22,800,000**	

CONTACT INFORMATION

Chairman: Walter Hoffman
Managing Partner: Clive Parritt
Accountancy (General): Graham Tyler
Audit: Richard White
Corporate Finance: Tony Pierre
Insolvency: Peter Souster
Management Consultancy: Richard Spooner
Public Sector: Walter Hoffman
Tax: Bill Hogan

CLIENT SERVICES

All Services

OTHER OFFICES

BAKER TILLY
35A High Street, BILLINGSHURST, West Sussex RH14 9PP
Tel: + *44* (403) 783411 *Fax:* + *44* (403) 784167

BAKER TILLY
New Oxford House, 16 Waterloo Street, BIRMINGHAM B2 5UG
Tel: + *44* (21) 643 3451 *Fax:* + *44* (21) 643 3859
Contact: John Hall

BAKER TILLY
1A Manor Row, BRADFORD, West Yorkshire BD1 4NS
Tel: + *44* (274) 735311 *Fax:* + *44* (274) 370562
Contact: Chris Maslen

BAKER TILLY
2 Newman Road, BROMLEY, KENT BR1 1RJ
Tel: + *44* (81) 290 5522 *Fax:* + *44* (81) 460 9156
Contact: Ted Swaysland

BAKER TILLY
12 Gleneagles Court, Brighton Road, CRAWLEY, West Sussex RH10 6AD
Tel: + *44* (293) 565165 *Fax:* + *44* (293) 32695

BAKER TILLY
The Clockhouse, 140 London Road, GUILDFORD, Surrey GU1 1UW
Tel: + *44* (483) 503050 *Fax:* + *44* (483) 69281
Contact: Peter Bessler

BAKER TILLY
5 Windsor Court, Clarence Drive, HARROGATE,
North Yorkshire HG1 2PE
Tel: + *44* (423) 560160 *Fax:* + *44* (423) 569647

BAKER TILLY
Yorkshire House, Greek Street, LEEDS LS1 5SN
Tel: + *44* (532) 449912 *Fax:* + *44* (532) 436728
Contact: Bob Tilley

BAKER TILLY
Brazennose House, Lincoln Square, MANCHESTER M2 5BL
Tel: + *44* (61) 834 5777 *Fax:* + *44* (61) 835 3242
Contact: Alan Sutton

BAKER TILLY
Abbots Fee, Greenhill, SHERBORNE, Dorset DT9 4ET
Tel: + *44* (935) 812428 *Fax:* + *44* (935) 814004

BAKER TILLY
Lester House, 7 Bridge Street, STURMINSTER NEWTON, Dorset DT10 1AF
Tel: + *44* (258) 72543

BAKER TILLY
Redfern House, 29 Jury Street, WARWICK CV34 4EH
Tel: + *44* (926) 492347 *Fax:* + *44* (926) 410016

BAKER TILLY
Suites 22 and 24 The Courtyards, Croxley Business Centre, Hatters Lane, WATFORD WD1 8RR
Tel: + *44* (923) 816400 *Fax:* + *44* (923) 253402
Contact: Charles Tucker

BAKER TILLY
Old Sarum House, 49 Princes Street, YEOVIL, Somerset BA20 1EG
Tel: + *44* (935) 76266 *Fax:* + *44* (935) 706968

Total Number of Offices: 15

BARBER, HARRISON & PLATT

2 Rutland Park, SHEFFIELD S10 2PD
Tel: + *44* (742) 667171
Fax: + *44* (742) 669846

International Contact: Kim Staniforth

BARNES ROFFE

24 Bedford Row, LONDON WC1R 4HA
Tel: + *44* (71) 831 6393
Fax: + *44* (71) 405 1275

National Affiliation: The CharterGroup Partnership

International Contact: Neville Sassienie

OTHER OFFICES

BARNES ROFFE
Highbridge House, 93-96 Oxford Road, UXBRIDGE, Middlesex UB8 1LU
Tel: + *44* (895) 56423 *Fax:* + *44* (895) 74107

BARNES ROFFE
26 & 27 Copperfields, Spital Street, DARTFORD DA1 2DE
Tel: + *44* (322) 275335 *Fax:* + *44* (322) 287177

BARNES ROFFE
840-842 High Road, Leyton, LONDON E10 6AE
Tel: + *44* (81) 539 5033 *Fax:* + *44* (81) 539 1582

BARNES ROFFE
3 Brook Business Centre, Cowley Mill Road, UXBRIDGE,
Middlesex UB8 2FX
Tel: + *44* (895) 256423 *Fax:* + *44* (895) 274107

Total Number of Offices: 5

BARRIE SCOTT & CO

16-18 Weir Street, FALKIRK FK1 1RA
Tel: + 44 (324) 37654
Fax: + 44 (324) 35678

National Affiliation: The CharterGroup Partnership

International Contact: Clive Scott

Partners:	4
Professional staff:	25
Non-professional staff:	5
Total Staff:	**34**

FEE INCOME

Year End: 1990	%
Accountancy & Audit:	80.0
Consultancy:	3.0
Tax:	17.0

CONTACT INFORMATION

Managing Partner: Clive Scott
Accountancy (General): Alister McBride
Audit: James Coats
Tax: Margaret Smith
Business Services: John Cunningham

CLIENT SERVICES

Accountancy (General), Audit, Computer Installation, Life & Risk Assurance, Management & Business Advice, Pensions Planning, Taxation (Corporate)

OTHER OFFICES

BARRIE SCOTT & CO
18-20 Mid Street, BATHGATE, West Lothian EH48 1PT
Tel: + 44 (506) 56345 *Fax:* + 44 (506) 634696

Total Number of Offices: 2

BARRON & BARRON

Bathurst House, 86 Micklegate, YORK YO1 2HN
Tel: + 44 (904) 628551
Fax: + 44 (904) 623533

European Affiliation: INPACT - International Network of Professional Accountants

Partners:	4
Professional staff:	16
Non-professional staff:	12
Total Staff:	**32**

CONTACT INFORMATION

Managing Partner: Brian Taylor
Accountancy (General): Peter Skelton
Audit: Guy Ward
Administration: Brian Taylor
Tax (Corporate): Richard Bailey

CLIENT SERVICES

Accountancy (General), Audit, Taxation (Corporate)

OTHER OFFICES

BARRON & BARRON
Windross Square, Market Place, EASINGWOLD, North Yorkshire Y06 3AG
Tel: + 44 (347) 22055
Contact: Christopher Ramsay

BARRON & BARRON
21a Millgate, THIRSK, North Yorkshire Y07 1AA
Tel: + 44 (845) 523963
Contact: Margaret Flintoff

BARRON & BARRON
5 The Crescent, SELBY, North Yorkshire Y08 OPU
Tel: + 44 (757) 704904
Contact: Michael Brooks

Total Number of Offices: 4

BARTON, COTSEN

1st Floor, Dominions House North, Dominions Arcade, CARDIFF CF1 4AR
Tel: + 44 (222) 372641
Fax: + 44 (222) 220848

European Affiliation: Jeffreys Henry International

Partners:	4
Professional staff:	14
Non-professional staff:	7
Total Staff:	**25**

FEE INCOME

Year End: 30.11.90	£	%
Accountancy & Audit:	640,000	86.6
Consultancy:	30,000	4.0
Tax:	80,000	9.4
Total:	**750,000**	

CONTACT INFORMATION

Managing Partner: A. Haydn Cotsen
Accountancy (General): Brian Roberts
Audit: Susan Arthur
Administration: Nigel Morris
Audit & Accountancy: Gareth Williams
Audit & Accountancy: John Jones

CLIENT SERVICES

Accountancy (General), Audit, Computer Installation, Corporate Finance Advice, Life & Risk Assurance, Management & Business Advice, Mergers & Acquisitions, Pensions Planning, Taxation (Corporate)

Industry Specialisations: Leisure, Insurance Brokers

MAJOR CLIENTS

H.L. Bazaars (Wholesale) Ltd, B.A. Cash & Carry Ltd, F.J. Leisure, Chris Leach & Associates Ltd, Millar Cosens Group, Sabre Vehicle Contracts, Sun Valley Holdings Ltd, Villa Caterers Group, Western Permanent Housing Society

BDO BINDER HAMLYN

20 Old Bailey, LONDON EC4M 7BH
Tel: + 44 (71) 489 6261
Fax: + 44 (71) 489 6281

European Affiliation: BDO Binder

International Contact: Chris Swinson

Partners:	231
Professional staff:	2,042
Non-professional staff:	741
Total Staff:	**3,014**

FEE INCOME

Year End: 30.04.91	£	%
Accountancy & Audit:	63,440,000	53.0
Insolvency:	5,985,000	5.0
Consultancy:	5,985,000	5.0
Tax:	37,107,000	31.0
Other:	7,182,000	6.0
Total:	**119,699,000**	

CONTACT INFORMATION

Managing Partner: Chris Swinson
Senior Partner: Lord Lane of Horsell

▷

Corporate Finance: Rodney Graves
Insolvency: Peter Dubuisson
Management Consultancy: William Casey
Administration: Alistair Durie
Public Sector: Lord Lane of Horsell
Accountancy & Audit: David Hunt
Tax (Corporate & International): Paul Morris
Personal Financial Services: Frank Akers-Douglas
Investment Management: Paul G. Cattermull

CLIENT SERVICES

All Services, Personal Financial Planning, Advice for Individuals & Families, Investment Management

Industry Specialisations: Property Companies, Publishing, Banks & Finance Houses, Manufacturing, Public Services

MAJOR CLIENTS

AEG, Anglia Television, Attwoods, Automated Security Holdings, Babcock International, British Land, Cray Electronics, Eagletrust, Expedier Leisure, FKI, HP Bulmer Holdings, Michelin, Mountleigh Group, Nuclear Electric, Owners Abroad Group, Schering, Speyhawk, Strand VCI, United Newspapers, Wace Group

OTHER OFFICES

BDO BINDER HAMLYN
64 Dalblair Road, AYR KA7 1UH
Tel: + *44* (292) 263277 *Fax:* + *44* (292) 268852
Contact: Ian B. Valentine

BDO BINDER HAMLYN
7-9 Irwell Terrace, BACUP, Lancashire OL13 9AJ
Tel: + *44* (706) 873213 *Fax:* + *44* (706) 874211
Contact: R.D. Uttley

BDO BINDER HAMLYN
12 Malone Road, BELFAST BT9 5BP
Tel: + *44* (232) 381900 *Fax:* + *44* (232) 661772
Contact: Eric G. Bell

BDO BINDER HAMLYN
The Rotunda, 150 New Street, BIRMINGHAM B2 4PD
Tel: + *44* (21) 643 5544 *Fax:* + *44* (21) 643 4665
Contact: Michael Bolton

BDO BINDER HAMLYN
Narrow Quay House, Prince Street, BRISTOL BS1 4PQ
Tel: + *44* (272) 279936 *Fax:* + *44* (272) 225000
Contact: Nigel Belletty

BDO BINDER HAMLYN
87 Guildhall Street, BURY ST EDMUNDS, Suffolk IP33 1PU
Tel: + *44* (284) 763311 *Fax:* + *44* (284) 704203
Contact: Lyndon J. Mills

BDO BINDER HAMLYN
129 Cathedral Road, CARDIFF CF1 9UY
Tel: + *44* (222) 396916 *Fax:* + *44* (222) 399151
Contact: Michael Bishop

BDO BINDER HAMLYN
7-17 Lansdowne Road, CROYDON CR9 2PL
Tel: + *44* (81) 688 4422 *Fax:* + *44* (81) 681 8186
Contact: John M. Cholmeley

BDO BINDER HAMLYN
11 Manor Place, EDINBURGH EH3 7DP
Tel: + *44* (31) 225 6366 *Fax:* + *44* (31) 220 1041
Contact: Robert Clark

BDO BINDER HAMLYN
Ulster Bank Buildings, 16 Darling Street, ENNISKILLEN, Co Fermanagh BT74 7ER
Tel: + *44* (365) 323807 *Fax:* + *44* (365) 26158
Contact: W. Kenneth Rainey

BDO BINDER HAMLYN
Ballantine House, 168 West George Street, GLASGOW G2 2PT
Tel: + *44* (41) 248 3761 *Fax:* + *44* (41) 332 5467
Contact: A. Stewart Clark

BDO BINDER HAMLYN
Number Twenty One Queen Street, LEEDS LS1 2TW
Tel: + *44* (532) 440204 *Fax:* + *44* (532) 425938
Contact: John M. Stubbs

BDO BINDER HAMLYN
Scottish Provident House, 52 Brown Street, MANCHESTER M2 2AU
Tel: + *44* (61) 831 7121 *Fax:* + *44* (61) 833 0669
Contact: Anthony Leon

BDO BINDER HAMLYN
Sundial House, Cheap Street, NEWBURY, Berkshire RG14 5DH
Tel: + *44* (635) 550456 *Fax:* + *44* (635) 550366
Contact: C.P. Callen

BDO BINDER HAMLYN
Pearl Assurance House, 7 New Bridge Street, NEWCASTLE-UPON-TYNE NE1 8BQ
Tel: + *44* (91) 261 2481 *Fax:* + *44* (91) 232 0364
Contact: Arthur Wappat

BDO BINDER HAMLYN
Waterwitch House, 44 Exeter Road, NEWMARKET CB8 8LR
Tel: + *44* (638) 665718 *Fax:* + *44* (638) 662014
Contact: Henry R. Saltmarsh

BDO BINDER HAMLYN
7 The Close, NORWICH NR1 4DP
Tel: + *44* (603) 610181 *Fax:* + *44* (603) 633618
Contact: David J.B. Coventry

BDO BINDER HAMLYN
206 Derby Road, NOTTINGHAM NG7 1NQ
Tel: + *44* (602) 415312 *Fax:* + *44* (602) 410193
Contact: Peter Moore

BDO BINDER HAMLYN
Old Orchard, 39-61 High Street, POOLE, Dorset BH15 1AE
Tel: + *44* (202) 681221 *Fax:* + *44* (202) 687211
Contact: Brian Perryman

BDO BINDER HAMLYN
Lewis House, 12 Smith Street, ROCHDALE, Lancashire OL16 1TX
Tel: + *44* (706) 355505 *Fax:* + *44* (706) 59486
Contact: David Brierley

BDO BINDER HAMLYN
Victoria Square, Victoria Street, ST ALBANS, Hertfordshire AL1 5BB
Tel: + *44* (727) 836363 *Fax:* + *44* (727) 40993
Contact: Robert Clark

BDO BINDER HAMLYN
12 Hamilton Street, SALTCOATS, Ayrshire KA21 5DS
Tel: + *44* (294) 602491 *Fax:* + *44* (294) 604901
Contact: W. Findlay Turner

BDO BINDER HAMLYN
Suite 4b, Midland House, Trinity Street, Hanley, STOKE-ON-TRENT ST1 5RL
Tel: + *44* (782) 286037 *Fax:* + *44* (782) 285782
Contact: Malcolm Matravers

BDO BINDER HAMLYN
29 Hanover Street, STRANRAER, Wigtownshire DG9 7HZ
Tel: + *44* (776) 3536 *Fax:* + *44* (776) 5750
Contact: Peter McMahon

BDO BINDER HAMLYN
Mander House, Mander Centre, WOLVERHAMPTON WV1 3NF
Tel: + *44* (902) 714828 *Fax:* + *44* (902) 711475
Contact: Malcolm H. Gilbert

Total Number of Offices: 26

BEATONS
York House, 2-4 York Road, FELIXSTOWE, Suffolk IP11 7HX
Tel: + *44* (394) 279692
Fax: + *44* (394) 274661

International Contact: R.A. Beaton

Partners:	2
Professional staff:	2
Non-professional staff:	12
Total Staff:	**16**

FEE INCOME

Year End: 31.10.91	**£**	**%**
Accountancy & Audit:	212,000	53.0
Consultancy:	28,000	7.0
Tax:	120,000	30.0
Other:	40,000	10.0
Total:	**400,000**	

CONTACT INFORMATION
Managing Partner: R.A. Beaton
Partner: J.J. Oakley

CLIENT SERVICES
All Services

Industry Specialisations: Shipping, Haulage

BEAVIS WALKER
14 Southampton Place, LONDON WC1A 2AJ
Tel: + *44* (71) 430 1111
Fax: + *44* (71) 831 0439

European Affiliation: INPACT - International Network of Professional Accountants

International Contact: Simon Noakes

Partners:	6
Professional staff:	41
Non-professional staff:	9
Total Staff:	**56**

CONTACT INFORMATION
Chairman: Simon Hammerton
Corporate Finance: Peter Drown
Management Consultancy: Simon Hammerton
Administration: Simon Noakes
Accountancy & Audit: Peter Bennetts
Tax: John Handley
VAT: Richard Clark
Company Secretary: Rory Haines

CLIENT SERVICES
Accountancy (General), Audit, Computer Installation, Corporate Finance Advice, Litigation/Legal Services, Management & Business Advice, Management Buy-outs, Mergers & Acquisitions, Taxation (Corporate), Taxation (International), Trust Settlement & Estates, VAT Advice, Company Secretarial Work

BERLEY & CO
76 New Cavendish Street, LONDON W1M 7LB
Tel: + *44* (71) 636 9094
Fax: + *44* (71) 636 4115

National Affiliation: The CharterGroup Partnership

International Contact: Jeremy Berman

CLIENT SERVICES
Accountancy (General), Audit, Computer Installation, Corporate Finance Advice, Insolvency & Corporate Restructuring, Life & Risk Assurance, Management & Business Advice, Management Buy-outs, Mergers & Acquisitions, Pensions Planning, Value for Money Studies, Taxation (Corporate), Taxation (International), Trust Settlement & Estates

BILLIMORIA, BRACE, HAMBLIN, WILLIAMS
7th Floor, Queens House, 2 Holly Road, TWICKENHAM, Middlesex TW1 4EG
Tel: + *44* (81) 744 1177
Fax: + *44* (81) 744 2881

European Affiliation: IAG International

International Contact: Paul Williams

BLACKSTONE FRANKS
Barbican House, 26-34 Old Street, LONDON EC1V 9HL
Tel: + *44* (71) 250 3300
Fax: + *44* (71) 250 1402

European Affiliation: IAG International

International Contact: Lance R. Blackstone

Partners:	11
Professional staff:	40
Non-professional staff:	45
Total Staff:	**96**

FEE INCOME

Year End: 07.04.91	**%**
Accountancy & Audit:	35.0
Consultancy:	10.0
Tax:	35.0
Other:	10.0

CONTACT INFORMATION
Managing Partner: Lance Blackstone
Managing Partner: David Franks
Accountancy (General): Lance Blackstone
Audit: David Franks
Corporate Finance: Richard Coon
Management Consultancy: Richard Blood
Administration: Subash Thakraar
Tax (Corporate & International): Robert Maas
Company Administration: Jawis Pogson
Litigation Services: Subash Thakraar
Financial Services: William Blevins

CLIENT SERVICES
Accountancy (General), Audit, Corporate Finance Advice, Life & Risk Assurance, Litigation/Legal Services, Management & Business Advice, Management Buy-outs, Mergers & Acquisitions, Pensions Planning, Value for Money Studies, Taxation (Corporate), Taxation (International), Trust Settlement & Estates

Industry Specialisations: Lawyers, Clothing, Architects, Computer Services

OTHER OFFICES

BLACKSTONE FRANKS
Berkeley House, Walton Street, AYLESBURY, Buckinghamshire HP21 7DS
Tel: + *44* (296) 24242 *Fax:* + *44* (296) 393199
Contact: Christopher Smith

Total Number of Offices: 2

▷

United Kingdom

BLOOMER HEAVEN

33 Lionel Street, BIRMINGHAM B3 1AB
Tel: + 44 (21) 236 0465
Fax: + 44 (21) 236 1464

National Affiliation: The CharterGroup Partnership

International Contact: Peter Jones

Partners:	8
Professional staff:	82
Total Staff:	**90**

CONTACT INFORMATION

Chairman: Robert Varnisn
Managing Partner: Alan Whitehouse
Accountancy (General): Ron Crowdy
Audit: Peter Jones
Corporate Finance: Robert Billingham
Management Consultancy: Ross Griffiths
Administration: Alan Whitehouse
Tax (Corporate): Peter Higgs
Tax (International): Archie Gilmour

CLIENT SERVICES

Accountancy (General), Audit, Computer Installation, Corporate Finance Advice, Life & Risk Assurance, Management & Business Advice, Management Buy-outs, Mergers & Acquisitions, Pensions Planning, Value for Money Studies, Taxation (Corporate), Taxation (International), Trust Settlement & Estates, Human Resource Consultancy

BRACE WHINCUP

National Westminster Bank Buildings, 113 Bute Street, CARDIFF CF1 6EQ
Tel: + 44 (222) 493855
Fax: + 44 (222) 485342

European Affiliation: Moores Rowland International

International Contact: Brian Whincup

BREBNER, ALLEN & TRAPP

The Quadrangle, 180 Wardour Street, LONDON W1V 3AA
Tel: + 44 (71) 734 2244
Fax: + 44 (71) 287 5315

European Affiliation: Growth & Progress Challenge

International Contact: Peter Leonard Thomas

BRYDEN JOHNSON & CO

Kings Parade, Lower Coombe Street, CROYDON CR0 1AA
Tel: + 44 (81) 686 0255
Fax: + 44 (81) 688 5620

National Affiliation: The CharterGroup Partnership

International Contact: Donal Johnson

Partners:	4
Professional staff:	26
Non-professional staff:	8
Total Staff:	**38**

FEE INCOME

Year End: 31.03.91	**£**
Total:	**1,300,000**

CONTACT INFORMATION

Managing Partner: D.K. Johnson
Accountancy (General): G.R. Bull
Audit: N.F.K. Johnson
Corporate Finance & Insolvency: T.J. Negus
Tax: D.K. Johnson

CLIENT SERVICES

Accountancy (General), Audit, Computer Installation, Corporate Finance Advice, Insolvency & Corporate Restructuring, Management & Business Advice, Taxation (Corporate), Taxation (International), Trust Settlement & Estates, Company Secretarial

MAJOR CLIENTS

B.T.P. plc

BURNETT SWAYNE

Charter Court, Third Avenue, SOUTHAMPTON SO9 1QS
Tel: + 44 (703) 702345
Fax: + 44 (703) 702570

National Affiliation: The CharterGroup Partnership

International Contact: Michael Howson-Green

Partners:	9
Professional staff:	80
Non-professional staff:	20
Total Staff:	**109**

FEE INCOME

Year End: 31.12.90	%
Accountancy & Audit:	60.0
Consultancy:	10.0
Tax:	20.0
Other:	10.0

CONTACT INFORMATION

Chairman: Ken R. Ball
Accountancy (General): Peter G. Stone
Audit: David A. Hoare
Corporate Finance: Mike Richards
Management Consultancy: Jon E. Lisby
Administration: Brian M. Baxendale
Public Sector: Ken R. Ball
Tax (Corporate): N. John Chase
Tax (International): David L. Harper
Litigation Support: G.W. Porter
VAT: B.A. Atkinson

CLIENT SERVICES

Accountancy (General), Audit, Corporate Finance Advice, Litigation/Legal Services, Management & Business Advice, Management Buy-outs, Mergers & Acquisitions, Taxation (Corporate), Trust Settlement & Estates

Industry Specialisations: Property & Construction, Motor Vehicle Distribution & Sales, Agricultural Estates

BUZZACOTT & CO

4 Wood Street, LONDON EC2V 7JB
Tel: + 44 (71) 600 0336
Fax: + 44 (71) 606 3408

International Contact: Anthony de Lacey

Partners:	17
Professional staff:	90
Non-professional staff:	30
Total Staff:	**137**

FEE INCOME

Year End: 1990	%
Accountancy & Audit:	63.0
Consultancy:	3.0
Tax:	34.0

CONTACT INFORMATION

Chairman: Robert Vincent
Managing Partner: Mark Farmar
Accountancy (General): Anthony de Lacey

Audit: Peter Cousins
Administration: Mark Farmar
Public Sector: Ray Mayes
Tax (Corporate): John Boyton
Tax (International): Clifford Coxe
Corporate Finance & Charities: Robert Vincent
Computer Services: Stuart Defries
Education: John McNiff

CLIENT SERVICES

Accountancy (General), Audit, Computer Installation, Corporate Finance Advice, Life & Risk Assurance, Litigation/Legal Services, Management & Business Advice, Management Buy-outs, Mergers & Acquisitions, Pensions Planning, Value for Money Studies, Taxation (Corporate), Taxation (International), Trust Settlement & Estates

Industry Specialisations: Charities, Not for Profit Organisations, Schools, Hospitals

ASSOCIATED FIRMS

BUZZACOTT & CO
16a Falcon Street, IPSWICH IP1 1SL
Tel: + *44* (473) 259984 *Fax:* + *44* (473) 259988
Contact: G.R. Manning

Total Number of Offices: 2

CAPE & DALGLEISH

401 St John Street, LONDON EC1 4LH
Tel: + *44* (71) 833 2333
Fax: + *44* (71) 837 7347

International Contact: T.A.J. Back

OTHER OFFICES

CAPE & DALGLEISH
5 St George's Yard, Castle Street, FARNHAM, Surrey GU9 7LW
Tel: + *44* (252) 734345 *Fax:* + *44* (252) 734264

Total Number of Offices: 2

CARTER BACKER WINTER

Hill House, Highgate Hill, LONDON N19 5UU
Tel: + *44* (71) 263 7111
Fax: + *44* (71) 281 2166

National Affiliation: The CharterGroup Partnership

CASSON BECKMAN

Hobson House, 155 Gower Street, LONDON WC1E 6BJ
Tel: + *44* (71) 387 2888
Fax: + *44* (71) 388 0600

European Affiliation: Summit International Associates Inc

International Contact: Peter Catto
Mary Carroll

Partners:	25
Professional staff:	158
Non-professional staff:	61
Total Staff:	**244**

FEE INCOME

Year End: 31.05.91	**£**
Accountancy & Audit:	6,500,000
Insolvency:	800,000
Consultancy:	1,300,000
Tax:	2,300,000
Other:	400,000
Total:	**11,300,000**

CONTACT INFORMATION

Chairman: Geoff Barnes
Managing Partner: Peter Ohrenstein
Audit: Peter Ohrenstein
Corporate Finance: Chilton Taylor
Insolvency: Ian Holland
Management Consultancy: Ron Shashoua
Administration: Ian Frewer
Tax (Corporate): John Tipping
Tax (International): Martin Ben Nathan
Accountancy & Public Sector: Geoff Barnes
Entertainment: John Golding
Property: Colin Wagman
Hotel & Leisure: Geoff Barnes
Professional Partnerships: Richard Lampert

CLIENT SERVICES

Accountancy (General), Audit, Computer Installation, Corporate Finance Advice, Insolvency & Corporate Restructuring, Litigation/Legal Services, Management & Business Advice, Management Buy-outs, Mergers & Acquisitions, Pensions Planning, Taxation (Corporate), Taxation (International), Trust Settlement & Estates

Industry Specialisations: Entertainment, Hotel & Leisure, Property, Retail, Manufacturing, Professional Partnerships

OTHER OFFICES

J B LEVER
Bow Chambers, 8 Tib Lane, MANCHESTER M2 4JB
Tel: + *44* (61) 832 3074
Contact: Peter Catto

MACMILLAN & CO
98 West George Street, GLASGOW G2 1PJ
Tel: + *44* (41) 332 5906 *Fax:* + *44* (41) 332 2197

Total Number of Offices: 3

CAVELLS

Bridge House, 7-9 Church Road, Lawrence Hill, BRISTOL BS5 9JJ
Tel: + *44* (272) 558414
Fax: + *44* (272) 558407

European Affiliation: INPACT - International Network of Professional Accountants

International Contact: Roger Howells

Partners:	2
Professional staff:	10
Non-professional staff:	4
Total Staff:	**16**

FEE INCOME

Year End: 31.12.90	%
Accountancy & Audit:	80.0
Consultancy:	10.0
Tax:	10.0

CONTACT INFORMATION

Managing Partner: Chris Cave
Partner: Roger Howells
Tax Manager: Roy Clark
Insolvency Manager: Julienne Cotterell

CLIENT SERVICES
Accountancy (General), Audit, Computer Installation, Corporate Finance Advice, Insolvency & Corporate Restructuring, Life & Risk Assurance, Management & Business Advice, Pensions Planning, Value for Money Studies, Taxation (Corporate), Taxation (International), Trust Settlement & Estates

Industry Specialisations: Transport, Engineering, Licensed Trades, Construction, Clinical Waste

MAJOR CLIENTS
Atlas Contracts (UK) Ltd, Brandwells Ltd, A. Chard & Son Ltd, Colliers Mower Centre Ltd, G. Mead Scaffolding Ltd, L.C. Munded & Son Ltd, Sentinel Industrial Trading Ltd, Sirup Ltd, Solar Communications Ltd, South West Cleaners Ltd, South West Contractors Ltd, South West Decorating Ltd, South West Homes Ltd, Spraybarlow Ltd, J.T. Stafford Limited, Victoria Foods (Bristol) Ltd

CHADWICK & CO
Bridgewater House, 60 Whitworth Street, MANCHESTER M1 6LX
Tel: + *44* (51) 236 6262
Fax: + *44* (51) 236 6262

European Affiliation: INPACT - International Network of Professional Accountants

International Contact: Stephen Lawrence

Partners: 6

CONTACT INFORMATION
Accountancy (General): Jeremy W. Lowe
Audit: David J. Lowe
Management Consultancy: Stephen Lawrence
Tax (Corporate): Richard Burrows
Tax (International): Keith Pope
Corporate Finance & Administration: William Lowe

CLIENT SERVICES
Accountancy (General), Audit, Corporate Finance Advice, Management & Business Advice, Management Buy-outs, Mergers & Acquisitions, Pensions Planning, Taxation (Corporate), Taxation (International), Trust Settlement & Estates, Management Information Services

Industry Specialisations: Professional Practices, Builders, Motor Trade

Total Number of Offices: 2

CHANTREY VELLACOTT
Russell Square House, 10/12 Russell Square, LONDON WC1B 5LF
Tel: + *44* (71) 436 3666
Fax: + *44* (71) 436 8884

European Affiliation: DFK International

Partners:	39
Professional staff:	192
Non-professional staff:	85
Total Staff:	**316**

FEE INCOME

Year End: 31.07.91	%
Accountancy & Audit:	45.0
Tax:	35.0
Other:	20.0

CONTACT INFORMATION
Managing Partner: John Roberts
Accountancy (General): Geoff Lane
Audit: Howard Veglio
Corporate Finance: Jeremy Harris
Insolvency: Brian Callaghan
Management Consultancy: Mike Tovey
Administration: Christine Freshwater
Public Sector: Michael Wheeler
Tax (Corporate): Colin Heath
Tax (International): John Newman
Tax (Personal): Chris Jones
Tax (Business): John Keating
Personal Financial Planning: David Harris

CLIENT SERVICES
All Services

Industry Specialisations: Lawyers, Property Companies, Schools Charities, Pension Funds, Housing & Trade Associations

OTHER OFFICES

CHANTREY VELLACOTT
7 Dane John, CANTERBURY, Kent CT1 2QS
Tel: + *44* (227) 464195 *Fax:* + *44* (227) 762374
Contact: David Anning

CHANTREY VELLACOTT
75 Park Lane, CROYDON CR0 1JG
Tel: + *44* (81) 686 3915 *Fax:* + *44* (81) 681 4063
Contact: Ian Brodie

CHANTREY VELLACOTT
21 New Walk, LEICESTER LE1 6TE
Tel: + *44* (533) 471393
Contact: Elliot Harris

CHANTREY VELLACOTT
Derngate Mews, Derngate, NORTHAMPTON NN1 1UE
Tel: + *44* (604) 39257 *Fax:* + *44* (604) 231460
Contact: John Burdett

CHANTREY VELLACOTT
23-25 Castle Street, READING RG1 7SB
Tel: + *44* (734) 595432 *Fax:* + *44* (734) 598532
Contact: Graham Matthews

CHANTREY VELLACOTT
Gresham House, 53 Clarendon Road, WATFORD WD1 1LR
Tel: + *44* (923) 55111 *Fax:* + *44* (923) 241300
Contact: Peter Cox

Total Number of Offices: 7

THE CHARTERGROUP PARTNERSHIP LTD
Orbital House, 85 Croydon Road, CATERHAM, Surrey CR3 6PD
Tel: + *44* (883) 341341
Fax: + *44* (883) 340066

European Affiliation: Eura-Audit International

International Contact: Peter Collier

Partners: 250

CONTACT INFORMATION
Marketing Manager: Mary Porch

CHIENE & TAIT
3 Albyn Place, EDINBURGH EH2 4NQ
Tel: + *44* (31) 225 7515
Fax: + *44* (31) 220 1083

National Affiliation: The CharterGroup Partnership

International Contact: Martin Sinclair

Partners:	8
Professional staff:	34
Non-professional staff:	15
Total Staff:	57

CONTACT INFORMATION
Managing Partner: Robert Gordon
Accountancy (General): Bill Thomson
Audit: Martin Sinclair
Corporate Finance: Norman Lessels
Tax (Corporate): Gavin Morton

CLIENT SERVICES
Accountancy (General), Audit, Computer Installation, Corporate Finance Advice, Management Buy-outs, Mergers & Acquisitions, Taxation (Corporate), Trust Settlement & Estates

Industry Specialisations: Investment Trusts, Charities, Housing Associations, Education, Professional Partnerships

CITROEN WELLS
Devonshire House, 1 Devonshire Street, LONDON W1N 2DR
Tel: + *44* (71) 637 2841
Fax: + *44* (71) 637 1206

International Contact: Ray Pollock

Partners:	15
Professional staff:	70
Non-professional staff:	15
Total Staff:	**100**

CONTACT INFORMATION
Managing Partner: Eric Charles
Audit: Gordon Smith
Insolvency: Jimmy Mehta
Tax (Corporate): David Kidd
Tax (International): Eric Charles
Accountancy & Consultancy: Ray Pollock
Corporate Finance & Administration: Peter Emanuel
Data Processing: Fred Dorn
Financial Services: Chris Bryans

CLIENT SERVICES
All Services

Industry Specialisations: Commodity Dealers, Metal Traders, Authors, Property Investment, Advertising/PR Services, Trusts

CLARK WHITEHILL
25 New Street Square, LONDON EC4A 3LN
Tel: + *44* (71) 353 1577
Fax: + *44* (71) 583 1720

European Affiliation: Clark Kenneth Leventhal

International Contact: James Gemmell

Partners:	69
Professional staff:	401
Non-professional staff:	146
Total Staff:	**616**

CLIENT SERVICES
All Services

OTHER OFFICES

CLARK WHITEHILL
28 Paradise Circus, Queensway, BIRMINGHAM B1 2BY
Tel: + *44* (21) 632 4888 *Fax:* + *44* (21) 633 3765
Contact: Keith Porteous

CLARK WHITEHILL
Carrick House, Lypiatt Road, CHELTENHAM, Gloucestershire GL50 2QJ
Tel: + *44* (242) 234421 *Fax:* + *44* (242) 243921
Contact: Clive Astin

CLARK WHITEHILL
52 Perrymount Road, HAYWARDS HEATH, West Sussex RH16 3DS
Tel: + *44* (444) 459691 *Fax:* + *44* (444) 413643
Contact: David Langridge

CLARK WHITEHILL
4 Priory Road, HIGH WYCOMBE, Buckinghamshire HP13 6SE
Tel: + *44* (494) 462726 *Fax:* + *44* (494) 444080
Contact: John Stalker

CLARK WHITEHILL
Foley House, 123 Stourport Road, KIDDERMINSTER, Worcestershire DY11 7BW
Tel: + *44* (562) 60101 *Fax:* + *44* (562) 820196
Contact: Joseph Hancox

CLARK WHITEHILL
10 Palace Avenue, MAIDSTONE, Kent ME15 6NF
Tel: + *44* (622) 692122 *Fax:* + *44* (622) 691399
Contact: Michael Subert

CLARK WHITEHILL
6th Floor, Arkwright House, Parsonage Gardens, MANCHESTER M3 2LE
Tel: + *44* (61) 834 1654 *Fax:* + *44* (61) 839 0282
Contact: Damian Keeling

CLARK WHITEHILL
The Triangle, Station Road, NEWBURY, Berkshire RG14 7LP
Tel: + *44* (635) 529320 *Fax:* + *44* (635) 580048
Contact: Patrick O'Neill

CLARK WHITEHILL
37 Minster Street, READING RG1 2RY
Tel: + *44* (734) 597222 *Fax:* + *44* (734) 584640
Contact: John May

CLARK WHITEHILL
1st Floor, Norwich Union House, 17 Lichfield Street, WALSALL WS1 1TU
Tel: + *44* (922) 725590 *Fax:* + *44* (922) 25790
Contact: Keith Porteous

CLARK WHITEHILL JOSOLYNE
Cheapside Chambers, 43 Cheapside, BRADFORD, West Yorkshire BD1 4HP
Tel: + *44* (274) 732522 *Fax:* + *44* (274) 390154
Contact: Kenneth Fortune

CLARK WHITEHILL JOSOLYNE
Holly House, Spring Gardens Lane, KEIGHLEY, West Yorkshire BD20 6LE
Tel: + *44* (535) 607361 *Fax:* + *44* (535) 609761
Contact: David Eteson

CLARK WHITEHILL JOSOLYNE
North Lane House, 9B North Lane, Headingley, LEEDS LS6 3HG
Tel: + *44* (532) 740404 *Fax:* + *44* (532) 743780
Contact: Nicholas Marriner

Total Number of Offices: 14

ASSOCIATED FIRMS

BARLOW ANDREWS
74 Chorley New Road, BOLTON BL1 4BY
Tel: + *44* (204) 27451 *Fax:* + *44* (204) 364573
Contact: David L. Barlow

H.L. BARNES & SONS
Barclays Bank Chambers, STRATFORD-UPON-AVON, Warwickshire CV37 6AH
Tel: + *44* (789) 204185 *Fax:* + *44* (789) 414331
Contact: David J. Barnes

▷

United Kingdom

H.L. BARNES & SONS
22 Queens Road, COVENTRY CV1 3EG
Tel: + *44* (203) 256331 *Fax:* + *44* (203) 553551
Contact: Clive L. Barnes

BOOTH AINSWORTH
Ashfield House, Ashfield Road, CHEADLE, Cheshire SK8 1BE
Tel: + *44* (61) 491 0200 *Fax:* + *44* (61) 491 0660
Contact: E. Peter R. Ainsworth

BOOTH AINSWORTH
Burrough Chambers, St Petersgate, STOCKPORT, Cheshire SK1 1BE
Tel: + *44* (61) 427 0200 *Fax:* + *44* (61) 427 0660
Contact: Geoffrey K. Duckworth

DEXTER & CO
Rollestone House, Bridge Street, HORNCASTLE, Lincolnshire LN9 5HZ
Tel: + *44* (507) 526071 *Fax:* + *44* (507) 524423
Contact: David A. Dexter

F. GEEN & CO
68 Liverpool Road, STOKE-ON-TRENT ST4 1BG
Tel: + *44* (782) 47952 *Fax:* + *44* (782) 744357
Contact: Tony Middleton

HAYHOW & CO
19 King Street, KING'S LYNN, Norfolk PE30 1HB
Tel: + *44* (553) 764711 *Fax:* + *44* (553) 767152
Contact: Anthony W. Bruce

C.H. JEFFERSON & CO
108 Oswald Road, SCUNTHORPE, South Humberside DN15 7PA
Tel: + *44* (724) 282236 *Fax:* + *44* (724) 282037
Contact: Allan L. Clark

KENDALL WADLEY
Granta Lodge, 71 Graham Road, MALVERN, Worcestershire WR14 2JS
Tel: + *44* (684) 892666 *Fax:* + *44* (684) 892851
Contact: L. Barry Jones

KENDALL WADLEY
Merevale House, 27 Sansome Walk, WORCESTER WR1 1NU
Tel: + *44* (905) 26215 *Fax:* + *44* (905) 611706
Contact: W. Keith Martin

LANGTON MORLAND
Maritime House, 47/49 Paradise Street, LIVERPOOL L1 3BP
Tel: + *44* (51) 709 5925 *Fax:* + *44* (51) 709 1202
Contact: Christopher R. Morland

LANGTON MORLAND
81 High Street, RUNCORN, Cheshire WA7 1AH
Tel: + *44* (9285) 63111
Contact: Peter M. Unsworth

PETER LOBBENBERG & CO
74 Chancery Lane, LONDON WC2A 1AA
Tel: + *44* (71) 430 9300 *Fax:* + *44* (71) 430 9315
Contact: J. Peter Lobbenberg

LYON, GRIFFITHS & CO
63-67 Welsh Row, NANTWICH, Cheshire CW5 5EW
Tel: + *44* (270) 624445 *Fax:* + *44* (270) 623916
Contact: S. John Beech

MAPUS-SMITH & LEMMON
23 London Road, DOWNHAM MARKET, Norfolk PE38 9BJ
Tel: + *44* (366) 383300 *Fax:* + *44* (366) 385226
Contact: Robert N.W. Parker

MAPUS-SMITH & LEMMON
48 King Street, KING'S LYNN, Norfolk PE30 1HE
Tel: + *44* (553) 774761 *Fax:* + *44* (553) 768419
Contact: Colin J. Groom

MAPUS-SMITH & LEMMON
6 London Street, SWAFFHAM, Norfolk PE37 7DG
Tel: + *44* (760) 721728 *Fax:* + *44* (760) 725112
Contact: Robert N.W. Parker

ROBT A. PAGE & CO
16 Pelham Road, NOTTINGHAM NG5 1AR
Tel: + *44* (602) 622726 *Fax:* + *44* (602) 691461
Contact: Richard W. Bonnello

ROBT A. PAGE & CO
4 Marine Avenue, Sutton-on-Sea, MABLETHORPE, Lincolnshire LN12 2ND
Tel: + *44* (507) 441337 *Fax:* + *44* (602) 691461
Contact: Martin P. Mellor

PHILLIPS FRITH
9 Tregarne Terrace, ST AUSTELL, Cornwall PL25 4DD
Tel: + *44* (726) 75981 *Fax:* + *44* (726) 67489
Contact: Ian W. Chalmers

PRINCE, CROFT & BALL
3 Lorne Park Road, Lansdowne, BOURNEMOUTH BH1 1LD
Tel: + *44* (202) 558551 *Fax:* + *44* (202) 559186
Contact: David J. Robinson

PRINCE, CROFT & BALL
11 Church Road, Parkstone, POOLE, Dorset BH14 8UF
Tel: + *44* (202) 732255 *Fax:* + *44* (202) 733066
Contact: Anthony J. Raymond

PRINCE, CROFT & BALL
73 East Borough, WIMBORNE, Dorset BH21 1PJ
Tel: + *44* (202) 841173 *Fax:* + *44* (202) 883521
Contact: Terence Burrells

PRIOR & PALMER
56 High Pavement, NOTTINGHAM NG1 1HX
Tel: + *44* (602) 580212 *Fax:* + *44* (602) 588800
Contact: Nigel W. Turner

PULLEYN HESELTON
54 Bootham, YORK YO3 7BZ
Tel: + *44* (904) 611164 *Fax:* + *44* (904) 611596
Contact: Philip A. Thake

REYNOLDS & CO
3 Southernhay West, EXETER EX1 1JG
Tel: + *44* (392) 434654 *Fax:* + *44* (392) 421475
Contact: Alan R. Quantick

REYNOLDS & CO
11 Market Street, NEWTON ABBOTT, Devon TQ12 2RJ
Tel: + *44* (626) 333700 *Fax:* + *44* (626) 331014
Contact: Alan J. Bunn

ROSS, HOUGHTON & CO
37 Wilson Patten Street, WARRINGTON, Cheshire WA1 1PG
Tel: + *44* (925) 35353 *Fax:* + *44* (925) 444776

SAGAR CROUDSON
Station House, Station Road, KENDAL, Cumbria LA9 6RY
Tel: + *44* (539) 725032 *Fax:* + *44* (539) 740299
Contact: Alan R. Reed

SAGAR CROUDSON
Elizabeth House, Queen Street, LEEDS LS1 2TW
Tel: + *44* (532) 435402 *Fax:* + *44* (532) 424326
Contact: Roger Croudson

SCOTT ELLISON
35 Watling Street, CANTERBURY, Kent CT1 2UH
Tel: + *44* (227) 763500 *Fax:* + *44* (227) 762365

TORGERSEN, NICHOLSON & CO
Somerford Buildings, Norfolk Street, SUNDERLAND SR1 1EE
Tel: + *44* (91) 567 8611 *Fax:* + *44* (91) 567 2929
Contact: Stephen Torgersen

WAGSTAFFS
St Andrews Lodge, Southdown Road, HARPENDEN, Hertfordshire AL5 1PB
Tel: + 44 (582) 712836 *Fax:* + 44 (582) 461169
Contact: Andrew J. Wiggett

WAGSTAFFS
Portmill House, Portmill Lane, HITCHIN, Hertfordshire SG5 1DJ
Tel: + 44 (462) 420042 *Fax:* + 44 (462) 421043
Contact: Mark Hjertzen

WAGSTAFFS
Lines House, 78 High Street, STEVENAGE, Hertfordshire SG1 3DU
Tel: + 44 (438) 740074 *Fax:* + 44 (438) 741075
Contact: John A. Simmonds

WALKER, SMYTH & MARSHALL
11 The Avenue, LINCOLN LN1 1PA
Tel: + 44 (522) 545337
Contact: John Skinner

WALKER, SMYTH & MARSHALL
21/23 Algitha Road, SKEGNESS, Lincolnshire PE25 2AG
Tel: + 44 (754) 766991 *Fax:* + 44 (754) 769318
Contact: Alistair T. Smyth

WALTONS
Oakland House, 40 Victoria Road, HARTLEPOOL, Cleveland TS26 8DD
Tel: + 44 (429) 234414 *Fax:* + 44 (429) 231263

WALTONS
Erimus House, Queens Square, MIDDLESBROUGH, Cleveland TS2 1AA
Tel: + 44 (642) 228141 *Fax:* + 44 (642) 228142

WARNER MARSH
11 College Place, London Road, SOUTHAMPTON SO1 2FE
Tel: + 44 (703) 638237 *Fax:* + 44 (703) 211702
Contact: Terence G. Marsh

WHITMARSH STERLAND
62 Hills Road, CAMBRIDGE CB2 1LA
Tel: + 44 (223) 65816 *Fax:* + 44 (223) 66695
Contact: Michael C. Cherry

WHITMARSH STERLAND
Church Street, St Neots, HUNTINGDON, Cambridgeshire PE19 2HT
Tel: + 44 (480) 215755 *Fax:* + 44 (480) 406124
Contact: Trevor J. Crowe

Total Number of Offices: 44

CLAY SHAW THOMAS

Charter House, 46-48 Coity Road, BRIDGEND, Mid Glamorgan CF31 1LR
Tel: + 44 (656) 654271
Fax: + 44 (656) 667040

OTHER OFFICES

CLAY SHAW THOMAS
Ardmean House, 27-28 Blue Street, CARMARTHEN, Dyfed SA31 3LE
Tel: + 44 (267) 236026 *Fax:* + 44 (267) 237981

Total Number of Offices: 2

CLEMENT KEYS RABJOHNS

Nettleton House, Calthorpe Road, Edgbaston, BIRMINGHAM B15 1RL
Tel: + 44 (21) 456 4456
Fax: + 44 (21) 456 4510

European Affiliation: TGI International

International Contact: Michael Beardsmore

OTHER OFFICES

CLEMENT KEYS RABJOHNS
Swinford House, Albion Street, BRIERLY HILL, West Midlands DY5 3EL
Tel: + 44 (384) 75611 *Fax:* + 44 (384) 77592

CLEMENT KEYS RABJOHNS
1, 2 & 3 College Yard, WORCESTER WR1 2LB
Tel: + 44 (905) 26103 *Fax:* + 44 (905) 723279

CLEMENT KEYS RABJOHNS
111/113 High Street, EVESHAM, Worcestershire WR11 4EB
Tel: + 44 (386) 765567 *Fax:* + 44 (386) 49275

CLEMENT KEYS RABJOHNS
Dartmouth House, Sandwell Road, WEST BROMWICH, West Midlands B70 8TH
Tel: + 44 (21) 500 5567 *Fax:* + 44 (21) 500 5381
Contact: Michael J. Beardsmore

Total Number of Offices: 5

COMINS & CO

22 St Andrew Street, LONDON EC4A 3AN
Tel: + 44 (71) 353 5691
Fax: + 44 (71) 583 1296

European Affiliation: InterContinental Consultants (ICC)

International Contact: Roger C. Paine

Partners: 10

CONTACT INFORMATION

Partner: Keith A. Wilson
Partner: Brian Sturt
Partner: Paul F.M. Bouquet
Partner: Roger F. Cornish
Partner: Richard J.C. Jones
Partner: Keith R. Joiner
Partner: Michael B. Hearne
Partner: Jonathan E. Askew
Partner: Dale C. Taylor
Partner: Geoffrey J. Bedingfield

CLIENT SERVICES

Accountancy (General), Audit, Management & Business Advice, Mergers & Acquisitions, Taxation (Corporate), Taxation (International), Company Secretarial Services, Financial Forecasting, Payroll & Bookkeeping Services

OTHER OFFICES

COMINS & CO
1st Floor, East Wing, Charter House, ASHFORD, Kent TN24 8EZ
Tel: + 44 (233) 621501 *Fax:* + 44 (233) 620288
Contact: Roger C. Paine

Total Number of Offices: 2

CONDIE & CO

11 Alva Street, EDINBURGH EH2 4PH
Tel: + 44 (31) 226 5373
Fax: + 44 (383) 729865

European Affiliation: INPACT - International Network of Professional Accountants

International Contact: Ian Condie

Partners:	6
Professional staff:	6
Non-professional staff:	44
Total Staff:	**56**

▷

FEE INCOME

Year End: 30.06.91	**£**
Accountancy & Audit:	900,000
Tax:	150,000
Total:	**1,050,000**

CONTACT INFORMATION
Managing Partner: Ian Condie
Accountancy (General): David Terms
Tax (Corporate): Graham Pascall
Tax (International): Ann McDade
Audit & Corporate Finance: George Primrose
Public Sector & Administration: Ian Condie
Tax (Personal): Eileen Hunter

CLIENT SERVICES
Accountancy (General), Audit, Computer Installation, Corporate Finance Advice, Management & Business Advice, Management Buy-outs, Mergers & Acquisitions, Pensions Planning, Taxation (Corporate), Taxation (International)

OTHER OFFICES

CONDIE & CO
10 Abbey Park Place, DUNFERMLINE, Fife KY12 7NZ
Tel: + *44* (383) 721421 *Fax:* + *44* (383) 729865
Contact: Alan Condie

Total Number of Offices: 2

COOPER LANCASTER

Aldwych House, 79/91 Aldwych, LONDON WC2B 4HN
Tel: + *44* (71) 242 2444
Fax: + *44* (71) 242 1117

European Affiliation: TGI International

International Contact: Ken Clarke

OTHER OFFICES

COOPER LANCASTER
33-35 Bell Street, REIGATE, Surrey RH2 7AW
Tel: + *44* (737) 221311 *Fax:* + *44* (737) 222219
Contact: Martin Neve

COOPER LANCASTER
14 Wood Street, BOLTON BL1 1DZ
Tel: + *44* (204) 31573 *Fax:* + *44* (204) 361552
Contact: Michael Cliff

COOPER LANCASTER
Fleet House, New Road, LANCASTER LA1 1EZ
Tel: + *44* (524) 67722 *Fax:* + *44* (524) 841664
Contact: Rodney Ward

COOPER LANCASTER
Century House, 11 St. Peter's Square, MANCHESTER M2 3DN
Tel: + *44* (61) 228 6856 *Fax:* + *44* (61) 228 6606
Contact: Denis Robson

Total Number of Offices: 11

COOPERS & LYBRAND DELOITTE

Plumtree Court, LONDON EC4A 4HT
Tel: + *44* (71) 583 5000
Fax: + *44* (71) 822 4652

European Affiliation: Coopers & Lybrand Europe

International Contact: Brandon Gough
John Bullock

Partners:	735
Professional staff:	7,807
Non-professional staff:	2,951
Total Staff:	**11,493**

CONTACT INFORMATION
Chairman: Brandon Gough
Managing Partner: Alan McFeterich
Corporate Finance: Richard Stone
Insolvency: Chris Hughes
Management Consultancy: Malcolm Coster
Administration: Roger Reeves
Public Sector: Michael Roberts
Tax (Corporate): Bob White
Tax (International): Peter Dickinson
Accountancy & Audit: Roger Davis
Deputy Chairman: John Bullock

CLIENT SERVICES
All Services

OTHER OFFICES

COOPERS & LYBRAND DELOITTE
3-5 Market Street, ARMAGH BT61 7BW
Tel: + *44* (861) 522695 *Fax:* + *44* (861) 526820
Contact: Alan R. Wylie

COOPERS & LYBRAND DELOITTE
20 Hamilton Road, BANGOR, County Down BT20 4LE
Tel: + *44* (247) 466516 *Fax:* + *44* (247) 270603
Contact: John B. Hutcheson

COOPERS & LYBRAND DELOITTE
Fanum House, 108 Great Victoria Street, BELFAST BT2 7AX
Tel: + *44* (232) 245454 *Fax:* + *44* (232) 242416
Contact: Noel Stewart

COOPERS & LYBRAND DELOITTE
35 Newall Street, BIRMINGHAM B3 3DX
Tel: + *44* (21) 200 2828 *Fax:* + *44* (21) 200 2829
Contact: John R. Hawksley

COOPERS & LYBRAND DELOITTE
Hill House, Richmond Hill, BOURNEMOUTH BH2 6HS
Tel: + *44* (202) 294621 *Fax:* + *44* (202) 26978
Contact: Godfrey Whitehead

COOPERS & LYBRAND DELOITTE
66 Queen Square, BRISTOL BS1 4JP
Tel: + *44* (272) 292791 *Fax:* + *44* (272) 307008
Contact: Christopher J. Barlow

COOPERS & LYBRAND DELOITTE
Mount Pleasant House, Huntingdon Road, CAMBRIDGE CB3 0BL
Tel: + *44* (223) 460055 *Fax:* + *44* (223) 64036
Contact: Simon N. Anderson

COOPERS & LYBRAND DELOITTE
Churchill House, Churchill Way, CARDIFF CF1 4XQ
Tel: + *44* (222) 237000 *Fax:* + *44* (222) 223361
Contact: Hywel G. Jones

COOPERS & LYBRAND DELOITTE
16 Northland Row, DUNGANNON, County Tyrone BT71 6AP
Tel: + *44* (8687) 22726 *Fax:* + *44* (8687) 27324
Contact: J.J. Cavanagh

COOPERS & LYBRAND DELOITTE
Lennox House, Beaufort Buildings, Spa Road, GLOUCESTER GL1 1XD
Tel: + *44* (452) 423031 *Fax:* + *44* (452) 300699
Contact: Malcolm S.H. Bell

COOPERS & LYBRAND DELOITTE
20 Upper Main Street, LARNE, County Antrim BT40 1SX
Tel: + *44* (574) 75733 *Fax:* + *44* (574) 60038
Contact: Edward M. McClelland

COOPERS & LYBRAND DELOITTE
Albion Court, 5 Albion Place, LEEDS LS1 6JP
Tel: + *44* (532) 431343 *Fax:* + *44* (532) 424009
Contact: Barrie Cottingham

COOPERS & LYBRAND DELOITTE
Abacus House, 32 Friar Lane, LEICESTER LE1 5RA
Tel: + 44 (533) 518164 *Fax:* + 44 (533) 536929
Contact: Michael J. Kennedy

COOPERS & LYBRAND DELOITTE
Richmond House, 1 Rumford Place, LIVERPOOL L3 9QS
Tel: + 44 (51) 227 4242 *Fax:* + 44 (51) 227 4575
Contact: John C. Jeffrey

COOPERS & LYBRAND DELOITTE
P.O. Box 207, 128 Queen Victoria Street, LONDON EC4P 4JX
Tel: + 44 (71) 583 5000 *Fax:* + 44 (71) 248 3623
Contact: Brandon Gough

COOPERS & LYBRAND DELOITTE
Melrose House, 42 Dingwall Road, CROYDON CR0 2NE
Tel: + 44 (81) 681 5252 *Fax:* + 44 (81) 760 0897

COOPERS & LYBRAND DELOITTE
Harman House, 1 George Street, UXBRIDGE, Middlesex UB8 1QQ
Tel: + 44 (895) 73333 *Fax:* + 44 (895) 56413
Contact: David H.A.C. Caddy

COOPERS & LYBRAND DELOITTE
Orchard House, 10 Albion Place, MAIDSTONE, Kent ME14 5DZ
Tel: + 44 (622) 672961 *Fax:* + 44 (622) 758071
Contact: George A. Emmerson

COOPERS & LYBRAND DELOITTE
Abacus Court, 6 Minshull Street, MANCHESTER M1 3ED
Tel: + 44 (61) 236 9191 *Fax:* + 44 (61) 247 4000
Contact: John C. Jeffrey

COOPERS & LYBRAND DELOITTE
Church House, Grange Road, MIDDLESBOROUGH, Cleveland TS1 2LR
Tel: + 44 (642) 241001 *Fax:* + 44 (642) 222330
Contact: Lionel Davies

COOPERS & LYBRAND DELOITTE
Central Business Exchange, Midsummer Boulevard, CENTRAL MILTON KEYNES MK9 2DF
Tel: + 44 (908) 690064 *Fax:* + 44 (908) 690065
Contact: Alan G. Waller

COOPERS & LYBRAND DELOITTE
Hadrian House, Higham Place, NEWCASTLE-UPON-TYNE NE1 8BP
Tel: + 44 (91) 261 2121 *Fax:* + 44 (91) 281 7492
Contact: Lionel Davies

COOPERS & LYBRAND DELOITTE
Oriel House, 55 Sheep Street, NORTHAMPTON NN1 2NF
Tel: + 44 (604) 230770 *Fax:* + 44 (604) 238001
Contact: David B.A. Hirst

COOPERS & LYBRAND DELOITTE
The Atrium, St Georges Street, NORWICH NR3 1AG
Tel: + 44 (603) 615244 *Fax:* + 44 (603) 631060
Contact: Jonathan M. Sisson

COOPERS & LYBRAND DELOITTE
Cumberland House, 35 Park Row, NOTTINGHAM NG1 6FY
Tel: + 44 (602) 419066 *Fax:* + 44 (602) 470862
Contact: Hugh A. Sinclair

COOPERS & LYBRAND DELOITTE
43 Market Street, OMAGH, County Tyrone BT78 1EE
Tel: + 44 (662) 246100 *Fax:* + 44 (662) 246283
Contact: Francis M. McCarthy

COOPERS & LYBRAND DELOITTE
Mutley House, 23 Princess Street, PLYMOUTH PL1 2HE
Tel: + 44 (752) 267441 *Fax:* + 44 (752) 673514
Contact: Michael G. Pallot

COOPERS & LYBRAND DELOITTE
43 High Street, PORTADOWN, County Armagh BT62 1HY
Tel: + 44 (762) 333718 *Fax:* + 44 (762) 350201
Contact: Alan R. Wylie

COOPERS & LYBRAND DELOITTE
1 Port Way, Port Solent, PORTSMOUTH PO6 4TY
Tel: + 44 (705) 201888 *Fax:* + 44 (705) 201818
Contact: Godfrey Whitehead

COOPERS & LYBRAND DELOITTE
9 Greyfriars Road, READING RG1 1JG
Tel: + 44 (734) 597111 *Fax:* + 44 (734) 607700
Contact: John P. Belton

COOPERS & LYBRAND DELOITTE
1 East Parade, SHEFFIELD S1 2ET
Tel: + 44 (742) 729141 *Fax:* + 44 (742) 752573
Contact: Anthony J. Wood

COOPERS & LYBRAND DELOITTE
5 Town Quay, SOUTHAMPTON SO9 1ZG
Tel: + 44 (703) 632772 *Fax:* + 44 (703) 330493
Contact: Godfrey Whitehead

COOPERS & LYBRAND DELOITTE
Princess House, Princess Way, SWANSEA SA1 5LH
Tel: + 44 (792) 473691 *Fax:* + 44 (792) 476857
Contact: Hywel G. Jones

COOPERS & LYBRAND DELOITTE
The Vanguard Centre, University of Warwick Science Park, Sir William Lyons Road, WARWICK CV4 7EZ
Tel: + 44 (203) 417585 *Fax:* + 44 (203) 411151
Contact: Richard J. Platford

COOPERS & LYBRAND DELOITTE
32 Albyn Place, ABERDEEN AB1 1YL
Tel: + 44 (224) 210100 *Fax:* + 44 (224) 576183
Contact: Michael J. Stevenson

COOPERS & LYBRAND DELOITTE
Erskine House, P.O. Box 90, 68-73 Queen Street, EDINBURGH EH2 4NH
Tel: + 44 (31) 226 2595 *Fax:* + 44 (31) 226 2693

COOPERS & LYBRAND DELOITTE
George House, 126 George Street, EDINBURGH EH2 4JZ
Tel: + 44 (31) 226 2595 *Fax:* + 44 (31) 226 2692
Contact: Robin A.F. Wight

COOPERS & LYBRAND DELOITTE
Kintyre House, 209 West George Street, GLASGOW G2 2LW
Tel: + 44 (41) 248 2644 *Fax:* + 44 (41) 221 8256
Contact: Robert J.T. Glen

COOPERS & LYBRAND DELOITTE
Galt House, 31 Bank Street, IRVINE, Ayrshire KA12 OAJ
Tel: + 44 (294) 78046 *Fax:* + 44 (294) 75692
Contact: Robert J.T. Glen

CORK GULLY
Shelley House, 3 Noble Street, LONDON EC2V 7DQ
Tel: + 44 (71) 606 7700 *Fax:* + 44 (71) 606 9887
Contact: Brandon Gough

Total Number of Offices: 41

COOPER-PARRY, WATSON, SOWTER & CO

102 Friar Gate, DERBY DE1 1FH
Tel: + 44 (332) 295544
Fax: + 44 (332) 295600

European Affiliation: The International Group of Accounting Firms Ltd (IGAF)

International Contact: Alan Woods

Partners:	10
Professional staff:	93
Non-professional staff:	21
Total Staff:	**124**

▷

FEE INCOME

Year End: 30.04.91	**£**	**%**
Accountancy & Audit:	2,002,000	60.0
Insolvency:	467,000	14.0
Consultancy:	167,000	5.0
Tax:	501,000	15.0
Other:	200,000	6.0
Total:	**3,337,000**	

CONTACT INFORMATION

Chairman: David Moss
Managing Partner: Alan Woods
Accountancy (General): David Walker
Accountancy (General): Tony Harbron
Audit: Tony Moore
Corporate Finance: Alan Woods
Insolvency: Roger Leivers
Management Consultancy: Peter Colledge
Tax (Corporate): Ian Tedcastle
VAT: Steve Taylor
Receiver/Insolvency: Mike Ellingworth
Business Services: Derek McGowan
Business Services: Jeremy Bowler
Business Services: Paul Coxon

CLIENT SERVICES

Accountancy (General), Audit, Computer Installation, Corporate Finance Advice, Insolvency & Corporate Restructuring, Litigation/Legal Services, Management & Business Advice, Management Buy-outs, Mergers & Acquisitions, Taxation (Corporate), Trust Settlement & Estates, Specialist Services to Proprietors

Industry Specialisations: Manufacturing

OTHER OFFICES

COOPER-PARRY, WATSON, SOWTER & CO
26 The Ropewalk, NOTTINGHAM NG1 5DW
Tel: + *44* (602) 419046 *Fax:* + *44* (602) 483813

Total Number of Offices: 2

CRANE & PARTNERS

Rutland House, 44 Masons Hill, BROMLEY, Kent BR2 9EG
Tel: + *44* (81) 464 0131
Fax: + *44* (81) 464 6018

International Contact: Richard E. Lane

Partners:	7
Professional staff:	35
Non-professional staff:	25
Total Staff:	**67**

CONTACT INFORMATION

Managing Partner: Richard E. Lane

CLIENT SERVICES

All Services

Industry Specialisations: Trade Associations

OTHER OFFICES

CRANE & PARTNERS
20-21 Tooks Court, Cursitor Street, LONDON EC4A 1LB
Tel: + *44* (71) 405 5445

Total Number of Offices: 2

JEFFREY CRAWFORD & CO

25 Castle Terrace, EDINBURGH EH1 2ER
Tel: + *44* (31) 228 6606
Fax: + *44* (31) 228 4911

European Affiliation: The International Group of Accounting Firms Ltd (IGAF)

International Contact: Bob Crawford

Partners:	3
Professional staff:	14
Non-professional staff:	8
Total Staff:	**25**

CONTACT INFORMATION

Tax (Corporate): John Hume
Accountancy & Audit: Ron Smith
Corporate Finance & Tax: Bob Crawford
Tax: C. Herald

CLIENT SERVICES

Accountancy (General), Audit, Corporate Finance Advice, Management Buy-outs, Mergers & Acquisitions, Trust Settlement & Estates, Specialist Taxation Consultancy

Industry Specialisations: Property, Accountants, Solicitors, Motor Vehicle Dealers, Engineering, Insulation

---

CREASEYS

12 Lonsdale Gardens, TUNBRIDGE WELLS, Kent TN1 1PA
Tel: + *44* (892) 548211
Fax: + *44* (892) 511232

European Affiliation: The International Group of Accounting Firms Ltd (IGAF)

International Contact: Peter Clark

CRITCHLEYS

Boswell House, 1-5 Broad Street, OXFORD OX1 3AW
Tel: + *44* (865) 243155
Fax: + *44* (865) 790957

International Contact: Frank Collingwood

Partners:	19
Professional staff:	120
Non-professional staff:	30
Total Staff:	**169**

FEE INCOME

Year End: 31.05.91	%
Accountancy & Audit:	60.0
Consultancy:	5.0
Tax:	35.0

CONTACT INFORMATION

Chairman: Peter Barclay-Watt
Managing Partner: David Stew
Accountancy (General): David David
Audit: Michael Good
Corporate Finance: Jonathan Russell
Administration: Cyril Williams
Tax (Corporate): Len Payne
Tax (Personal) & Financial Planning: Frank Collingwood
Schools, Education & Charities: Peter Barclay-Watt

CLIENT SERVICES

Accountancy (General), Audit, Computer Installation, Corporate Finance Advice, Management & Business Advice, Mergers & Acquisitions, Pensions Planning, Value for Money Studies, Taxation (Corporate),

Taxation (International), Trust Settlement & Estates, Personal tax, Business Start Ups, Expatriate Advice, Inheritance, VAT, Capital Tax Planning, Health Checks

Industry Specialisations: Education, Farming, Publishing, Charities, Professional Practices, Taxation of Lloyds Underwriters

OTHER OFFICES

CRITCHLEYS
The Market Place, DIDCOT, Oxfordshire OX11 7LE
Tel: + 44 (235) 511555 *Fax:* + 44 (235) 813392
Contact: Tim Alder

CRITCHLEYS
10 Marlborough Street, FARINGDON, Oxfordshire SN7 7JP
Tel: + 44 (367) 240226 *Fax:* + 44 (367) 242747
Contact: Adam Stein

CRITCHLEYS
16 High Street, THAME, Oxfordshire OX9 2BZ
Tel: + 44 (84 421) 4151 *Fax:* + 44 (84 421) 4809
Contact: Nigel Pledger

CRITCHLEYS
37 Market Square, WITNEY, Oxfordshire OX8 6AD
Tel: + 44 (993) 702418 *Fax:* + 44 (993) 775099
Contact: David Stew

CRITCHLEYS
9 Sheep Street, BICESTER, Oxfordshire OX6 7JE
Tel: + 44 (869) 252405 *Fax:* + 44 (869) 320172
Contact: Alan Thornton

CRITCHLEYS
Avalon House, Marcham Road, ABINGDON, Oxfordshire OX14 1UD
Tel: + 44 (235) 553333 *Fax:* + 44 (235) 553587
Contact: Dennis Leen

Total Number of Offices: 7

DAFFERN & CO

Queens House, Queens Road, COVENTRY CV1 3DR
Tel: + 44 (203) 221046
Fax: + 44 (203) 631702

National Affiliation: The CharterGroup Partnership

International Contact: Ian Smedley

Partners:	8
Professional staff:	40
Non-professional staff:	20
Total Staff:	**68**

CONTACT INFORMATION

Managing Partner: Ian Smedley
Corporate Finance: Paul Varney
Accountancy & Audit: Ian Smedley
Tax: Andrew Jones

CLIENT SERVICES

Accountancy (General), Audit, Computer Installation, Corporate Finance Advice, Management & Business Advice, Management Buy-outs, Mergers & Acquisitions, Pensions Planning, Taxation (Corporate), Taxation (International), Trust Settlement & Estates

OTHER OFFICES

DAFFERN & CO
Warwick House, 32 Clarendon Street, LEAMINGTON SPA, Warwickshire CV32 4PG
Tel: + 44 (926) 330464 *Fax:* + 44 (926) 450264
Contact: David Boakes

Total Number of Offices: 2

DAIN & CO

St John's Court, Wiltell Road, LICHFIELD, Staffordshire WS14 9DS
Tel: + 44 (543) 263484
Fax: + 44 (543) 415465

National Affiliation: The CharterGroup Partnership

Partners:	11
Professional staff:	64
Non-professional staff:	28
Total Staff:	**103**

FEE INCOME

Year End: 31.12.90	**£**	**%**
Accountancy & Audit:	1,600,000	80.0
Consultancy:	60,000	3.0
Tax:	160,000	8.0
Other:	180,000	9.0
Total:	**2,000,000**	

CONTACT INFORMATION

Managing Partner: John Dain
Managing Partner: Kenneth Webb
Management Consultancy: Nigel Coghill
Administration: John Dain
Tax (Corporate): Nigel Smith
Accountancy & Audit: Chris Windsor
Computers: Bill Summ

CLIENT SERVICES

Accountancy (General), Audit, Computer Installation, Corporate Finance Advice, Management & Business Advice, Management Buy-outs, Mergers & Acquisitions, Taxation (Corporate), Trust Settlement & Estates

Industry Specialisations: Light Manufacturing Industry, Sub-contract Assembly, Professional Practices

OTHER OFFICES

DAIN & CO
Peel House, Lichfield Street, BURTON-ON-TRENT, Staffordshire DE14 3RU
Tel: + 44 (283) 37311 *Fax:* + 44 (283) 511592
Contact: David Gill

DAIN & CO
140 High Street, Coleshill, BIRMINGHAM B46 3BJ
Tel: + 44 (675) 462306 *Fax:* + 44 (675) 464994
Contact: Martin Anderson

DAIN & CO
2-6 Hill Street, Swadlincote, BURTON-ON-TRENT, Staffordshire DE11 8HL
Tel: + 44 (283) 214468 *Fax:* + 44 (283) 550484
Contact: Bill Summ

DAIN & CO
29-31 Upper Brook Street, RUGELEY, Staffordshire WS15 3DP
Tel: + 44 (889) 583878 *Fax:* + 44 (889) 579962
Contact: Andrew Massey

DAIN & CO
Bedford House, 22 Eastgate Street, STAFFORD ST16 2LZ
Tel: + 44 (785) 42379 *Fax:* + 44 (785) 224443
Contact: Nigel Coghill

Total Number of Offices: 6

DAVIES ROGERS & CO

45 Etnam Street, LEOMINSTER, Herefordshire HR6 8AE
Tel: + 44 (568) 612685
Fax: + 44 (568) 611970

National Affiliation: The UK 200 Group of Practising Accountants

International Contact: Peter Rogers

▷

Partners:	2
Professional staff:	3
Non-professional staff:	3
Total Staff:	**8**

FEE INCOME

Year End: 31.12.90	**£**	**%**
Accountancy & Audit:	120,000	86.0
Tax:	20,000	14.0
Total:	**140,000**	

CONTACT INFORMATION

Partner: P.M. Rogers

CLIENT SERVICES

All Services

Industry Specialisations: Agriculture-related Enterprises

DENDY NEVILLE GRADONS

1 Bower Mount Road, London Road, MAIDSTONE, Kent ME16 8AX
Tel: + *44* (622) 686441
Fax: + *44* (622) 690221
National Affiliation: The CharterGroup Partnership

International Contact: Peter Lee

Partners:	3
Professional staff:	15
Non-professional staff:	5
Total Staff:	**23**

FEE INCOME

Year End: 30.06.91	**%**
Accountancy & Audit:	70.0
Consultancy:	5.0
Tax:	20.0
Other:	5.0

CONTACT INFORMATION

Managing Partner: Peter Lee
Accountancy, Audit & Administration: David Williams
Corporate Finance & Consultancy: Graham Bough
Tax: Peter Lee
Tax (Lloyds Underwriters): David Felton
Tax (Personal): Gilly Wilford
Tax (Personal): Jackie Cole

CLIENT SERVICES

Accountancy (General), Audit, Computer Installation, Corporate Finance Advice, Management & Business Advice, Management Buy-outs, Mergers & Acquisitions, Pensions Planning, Taxation (Corporate), Taxation (International), Trust Settlement & Estates, Computer Bureau Service, Company Secretarial Service, VAT Advice & Planning

Industry Specialisations: FIMBRA Audits, Solicitors, Wholesale Distribution, Leisure & Tourism

---

DIXON WILSON

P.O. Box 900, Rotherwick House, 3 Thomas More Street,
LONDON E1 9YX
Tel: + *44* (71) 628 4321
Fax: + *44* (71) 702 9769

European Affiliation: TEG (The European Group of Accounting & Auditing Firms)

International Contact: John Godfrey

DOWNHAM TRAIN EPSTEIN

The Hollins, Hollins Lane, Unsworth, BURY, Lancashire BL9 8AT
Tel: + *44* (61) 953 9510
Fax: + *44* (61) 766 3685

European Affiliation: Independent Accountants International

International Contact: Gerald Epstein

DOWNHAM & CO

Northern Assurance Buildings, Albert Square, 9-21 Princess Street, MANCHESTER M2 4DN
Tel: + *44* (61) 832 6413
Fax: + *44* (61) 834 2230

European Affiliation: Jeffreys Henry International

International Contact: Yitz Jaffe

DUNCAN SHEARD GLASS

Castle Chambers, 43 Castle Street, LIVERPOOL L2 9TL
Tel: + *44* (51) 236 8813
Fax: + *44* (51) 236 1430

European Affiliation: Midsnell International

International Contact: Stanley Douglas

Total Number of Offices: 5

DYKE YAXLEY & COMPANY

Abbey House, Abbey Foregate, SHREWSBURY SY2 6BH
Tel: + *44* (743) 241281
Fax: + *44* (743) 235794

National Affiliation: The CharterGroup Partnership

International Contact: John Dodds

GERALD EDELMAN

25 Harley Street, LONDON W1N 2BR
Tel: + *44* (71) 637 8555
Fax: + *44* (71) 631 0917

European Affiliation: A.E.E. International

International Contact: Richard H. Kleiner

Partners:	11

CLIENT SERVICES

All Services, Non-corporate Audits, Flotations, Financial Services

OTHER OFFICES

EDELMANS
Edelman House, 1238 High Road, Whetstone, LONDON N20 0LH
Tel: + *44* (81) 446 5888 *Fax:* + *44* (81) 446 2670
Contact: B. Hoffman

Total Number of Offices: 2

EDWARDS LITTLE & COMPANY

All Saints Chambers, Eign Gate, HEREFORD HR4 0AE
Tel: + *44* (432) 272136
Fax: + *44* (432) 353751

National Affiliation: The CharterGroup Partnership

International Contact: Eddie Hunt

ERNEST FRANCIS & SON

Somerset House, Blagrave Street, READING RG1 1QB
Tel: + *44* (734) 581331
Fax: + *44* (734) 586922

National Affiliation: The CharterGroup Partnership

International Contact: Richard Rand

ERNST & YOUNG

Becket House, 1 Lambeth Palace Road, LONDON SE1 7EU
Tel: + *44* (71) 928 2000
Fax: + *44* (71) 928 1345

European Affiliation: Ernst & Young Europe

International Contact: Nigel Moore

Partners:	421
Professional staff:	5,550
Non-professional staff:	1,860
Total Staff:	**7,831**

FEE INCOME

Year End: 31.03.91	**£**	**%**
Accountancy & Audit:	168,300,000	47.0
Insolvency:	29,200,000	8.1
Consultancy:	57,900,000	16.2
Tax:	102,900,000	28.7
Total:	**358,300,000**	

CONTACT INFORMATION

Corporate Finance: Richard Mead
Insolvency: Nigel Hamilton
Senior Partner: Elwyn Eilledge
Insurance: Paul McNamara
UK Managing Partner: Harold Cottam
Accountancy (General Practice): Jock Lennox
Audit & Natural Resources: Michael Boyd
Banking & Financial Services: Howard Brown
Management Consultancy: Clive Williams
Manufacturing: David Essex
Public Sector: Bob Harris
Tax: Andrew Jones

CLIENT SERVICES

Accountancy (General), Audit, Corporate Finance Advice, Insolvency & Corporate Restructuring, Litigation/Legal Services, Management & Business Advice, Management Buy-outs, Mergers & Acquisitions, Pensions Planning, Value for Money Studies, Taxation (Corporate), Taxation (International), Trust Settlement & Estates, Consultancy, Internal Audit, Fraud Investigations & Prevention, Expatriate Tax, Taxation (Indirect)

Industry Specialisations: Eastern Europe, Banking & Finance, Media, Entertainment, Food & Drink, Retail, High Tech, Manufacturing, Property

MAJOR CLIENTS

ASDA, Bass, Blue Circle, Bowater Industries, British Airways, British Coal, British Petroleum, BTR, Burmah Castrol, Hanson, Ladbroke, LASMO, Lucas Industries, Next, NFC, Northern Foods, Post Office, Thorn EMI, United Biscuits, Whitbread

OTHER OFFICES

ERNST & YOUNG
50 Huntly Street, ABERDEEN AB9 1XN
Tel: + *44* (224) 640033 *Fax:* + *44* (224) 630753

ERNST & YOUNG
Bedford House, 16 Bedford Street, BELFAST BT2 7QT
Tel: + *44* (232) 246525 *Fax:* + *44* (232) 240920

ERNST & YOUNG
Pendragon House, Fitzalan Court, Fitzalan Road, CARDIFF CF2 1TF
Tel: + *44* (222) 484641 *Fax:* + *44* (222) 490156

ERNST & YOUNG
Ten Constitution Hill, DUNDEE DD1 9PN
Tel: + *44* (382) 313131 *Fax:* + *44* (382) 27177

ERNST & YOUNG
17 Abercromby Place, EDINBURGH EH3 6LT
Tel: + *44* (31) 556 8641 *Fax:* + *44* (31) 556 5156

ERNST & YOUNG
George House, 50 George Square, GLASGOW G2 1RR
Tel: + *44* (41) 552 3456 *Fax:* + *44* (41) 953 1812

ERNST & YOUNG
Moray House, 16 Bank Street, INVERNESS IV1 1QY
Tel: + *44* (463) 237581 *Fax:* + *44* (463) 226098
Contact: J.I. Ross Martin

ERNST & YOUNG
P.O. Box 1, 3 Colmore Row, BIRMINGHAM B3 2DB
Tel: + *44* (21) 626 6262 *Fax:* + *44* (21) 626 6363
Contact: Christopher R. Lunt

ERNST & YOUNG
Kenburgh House, Manor Row, BRADFORD, West Yorkshire BD1 4NB
Tel: + *44* (274) 737737 *Fax:* + *44* (274) 73778
Contact: Peter G. Meredith

ERNST & YOUNG
One Bridewell Street, BRISTOL BS1 2AA
Tel: + *44* (272) 290808 *Fax:* + *44* (272) 260162
Contact: A. Keith Bonham

ERNST & YOUNG
Compass House, 80 Newmarket Road, CAMBRIDGE CB5 8DZ
Tel: + *44* (223) 461200 *Fax:* + *44* (223) 324609
Contact: Brian W. Waters

ERNST & YOUNG
Broadwalk House, Southernhay West, EXETER EX1 1LF
Tel: + *44* (392) 433541 *Fax:* + *44* (392) 75175
Contact: David H.A. Peacock

ERNST & YOUNG
P.O. Box 3, Lowgate House, Lowgate, HULL HU1 1JJ
Tel: + *44* (482) 25531 *Fax:* + *44* (482) 20284
Contact: Iain R. Bryce

ERNST & YOUNG
Queen's House, Queen Street, IPSWICH IP1 1SW
Tel: + *44* (473) 217491 *Fax:* + *44* (473) 214484
Contact: John D. Mullett

ERNST & YOUNG
P.O. Box 61, Cloth Hall Court, 14 King Street, LEEDS LS1 2JN
Tel: + *44* (532) 431221 *Fax:* + *44* (532) 434195
Contact: Brian S. Atkinson

ERNST & YOUNG
Provincial House, 37 New Walk, LEICESTER LE1 6TU
Tel: + *44* (533) 549818 *Fax:* + *44* (533) 551357
Contact: Victor M. Green

ERNST & YOUNG
Silkhouse Court, Tithebarn Street, LIVERPOOL L2 2LE
Tel: + *44* (51) 236 8214 *Fax:* + *44* (51) 236 0258
Contact: Frank W. Taylor

ERNST & YOUNG
Rolls House, 7 Rolls Buildings, Fetter Lane, LONDON EC4A 1NH
Tel: + *44* (71) 928 2000 *Fax:* + *44* (71) 405 2147

ERNST & YOUNG
400 Capability Green, LUTON LU1 3LU
Tel: + *44* (582) 400700 *Fax:* + *44* (582) 484121
Contact: Richard G. Combes

▷

ERNST & YOUNG
Commercial Union House, Albert Square, MANCHESTER M2 6LP
Tel: + 44 (61) 953 9000 *Fax:* + 44 (61) 832 4124
Contact: Bernard J. Whewell

ERNST & YOUNG
Silbury Court, 188 Silbury Boulevard,
CENTRAL MILTON KEYNES MK9 3AS
Tel: + 44 (908) 672882 *Fax:* + 44 (908) 662119
Contact: Richard G. Combes

ERNST & YOUNG
Norham House, 12 New Bridge Street West,
NEWCASTLE-UPON-TYNE NE1 8AD
Tel: + 44 (91) 261 1063 *Fax:* + 44 (91) 261 7744
Contact: Geoff K. Norman

ERNST & YOUNG
Cambridge House, 26 Tombland, NORWICH NR3 1RH
Tel: + 44 (603) 660482 *Fax:* + 44 (603) 614430
Contact: Peter C. Forbes

ERNST & YOUNG
10-12 The Ropewalk, NOTTINGHAM NG1 5DT
Tel: + 44 (602) 411861 *Fax:* + 44 (602) 483369
Contact: Henry P.B. Clark

ERNST & YOUNG
New Priestgate House, 57 Priestgate, PETERBOROUGH PE1 1JX
Tel: + 44 (733) 60348 *Fax:* + 44 (733) 51717
Contact: Brian W. Waters

ERNST & YOUNG
St Andrew's Court, Notte Street, PLYMOUTH PL1 2AH
Tel: + 44 (752) 673567 *Fax:* + 44 (752) 660650
Contact: Jeremy W.E. White

ERNST & YOUNG
Apex Plaza, READING RG1 1YE
Tel: + 44 (734) 500611 *Fax:* + 44 (734) 507744
Contact: Gerald W. Russell

ERNST & YOUNG
Talbot Chambers, 2-6 North Church Street, SHEFFIELD S1 2DH
Tel: + 44 (742) 752929 *Fax:* + 44 (742) 754572
Contact: Michael Entract

ERNST & YOUNG
Wessex House, 19 Threefield Lane, SOUTHAMPTON S01 1TW
Tel: + 44 (703) 230230 *Fax:* + 44 (703) 227409
Contact: Brett R.J. Gill

ERNST & YOUNG
Old Town Court, 10-14 High Street, SWINDON SN1 3EP
Tel: + 44 (793) 618822 *Fax:* + 44 (793) 619198
Contact: John A. Rendell

Total Number of Offices: 31

EVANS & PARTNERS

The Old Manse, 9 Bank Road, Kingswood, BRISTOL BS15 2LS
Tel: + 44 (272) 675215
Fax: + 44 (272) 635088

National Affiliation: The CharterGroup Partnership

CONTACT INFORMATION

Managing Partner: M.R. Evans
Audit: D. Morland

CLIENT SERVICES

All Services

OTHER OFFICES

EVANS & PARTNERS
36 North Street, Bedminster, BRISTOL BS3 1HW
Tel: + 44 (272) 635088
Contact: Derek Morland

Total Number of Offices: 2

FAWCETTS

Windover House, St Ann Street, SALISBURY SP1 2DR
Tel: + 44 (722) 334251
Fax: + 44 (722) 411375

National Affiliation: The UK 200 Group of Practising Accountants

Partners:	4
Professional staff:	4
Non-professional staff:	30
Total Staff:	**38**

CONTACT INFORMATION

Partner: Michael Humby
Partner: Bryan Jones
Partner: Trevor Austreng
Partner: Richard Allen

CLIENT SERVICES

All Services

FINNIE & CO

Kreston House, 8 Gate Street, LONDON WC2A 3HJ
Tel: + 44 (71) 831 9100
Fax: + 44 (71) 831 2666

European Affiliation: Kreston International

International Contact: C.J.P. Benbow

Partners:	43
Professional staff:	232
Non-professional staff:	95
Total Staff:	**370**

FEE INCOME

Year End: 30.04.91	**£**
Total:	**14,000,000**

CONTACT INFORMATION

Audit: C.H. Clark
Corporate Finance: J. Ward
Insolvency: N. Harrison
Management Consultancy: J. Hall
Tax: P.T. Stevens

CLIENT SERVICES

All Services

Industry Specialisations: Owner-managed Businesses, Housing Associations

MAJOR CLIENTS

BEAMA Limited, Bennett & Fountain Group plc, The Bodyshop International plc, Burndene Investments plc, Cakebread Robey plc, Cosmos Air plc, Emess Plc, Haslemere Estates plc, Institute of Marine Engineers, International Business Communications Holdings plc, Monarch Airlines Limited, National Dairy Council, National Pharmaceutical Association, Queen's Park Rangers Football & Athletic Assn Ltd, Sucden (UK) Limited

OTHER OFFICES

FINNIE & CO
Hellenic House, 87 Bath Street, GLASGOW G2 2HL
Tel: + 44 (41) 332 8291 *Fax:* + 44 (41) 333 0963
Contact: David McIntyre

FINNIE & CO
46 Church Avenue, BECKENHAM, Kent BR3 1DT
Tel: + 44 (81) 658 7911 *Fax:* + 44 (81) 650 9227
Contact: John Clemence

FINNIE & CO
4-6 Swabys Yard, Dyer Lane, BEVERLEY, North Humberside HU17 9BZ
Tel: + *44* (482) 861919 *Fax:* + *44* (482) 861774
Contact: Michael Auton

FINNIE & CO
Kreston House, 66 Broomfield Road, CHELMSFORD CM1 1SW
Tel: + *44* (245) 264644 *Fax:* + *44* (245) 490682
Contact: Clive Clark

FINNIE & CO
70 High Street, Ewell, EPSOM, Surrey KT17 1RQ
Tel: + *44* (81) 394 0925 *Fax:* + *44* (81) 393 8091
Contact: Anthony Heath

FINNIE & CO
Oxford House, 12/20 Oxford Street, NEWBURY, Berkshire RG13 1JB
Tel: + *44* (635) 49699 *Fax:* + *44* (635) 521884
Contact: Michael Ross

FINNIE & CO
3/5 Sidmouth Street, READING RG1 4QX
Tel: + *44* (734) 576582 *Fax:* + *44* (734) 391943
Contact: Hugh Wates

FINNIE & CO
Corporate Recovery Office, 74 South Street, READING RG1 4RA
Tel: + *44* (734) 585466 *Fax:* + *44* (734) 567782
Contact: Neil Harrison

FINNIE & CO
Spencer House, 23 Sheen Road, RICHMOND-UPON-THAMES, Surrey TW9 1BN
Tel: + *44* (81) 332 2033 *Fax:* + *44* (81) 948 8611
Contact: John Fenton-Jones

FINNIE & CO
42 Kingfield Road, SHEFFIELD S11 9AT
Tel: + *44* (742) 556591 *Fax:* + *44* (742) 585104
Contact: Martin Venning

FINNIE & CO
York House, 45 Baldock Street, WARE, Hertfordshire SG12 9DH
Tel: + *44* (920) 460241 *Fax:* + *44* (920) 462521
Contact: Geoff Warren

FINNIE & CO
York House, Empire Way, WEMBLEY HA9 0PA
Tel: + *44* (81) 903 5522 *Fax:* + *44* (81) 903 3688
Contact: Victor Sopher

FINNIE & CO
1a The Old Yard, Rectory Lane, Brasted, WESTERHAM, Kent TN16 1JP
Tel: + *44* (959) 565555 *Fax:* + *44* (959) 565500
Contact: John Clemence

Total Number of Offices: 15

H.W. FISHER & COMPANY

11-15 William Road, LONDON NW1 3ER
Tel: + *44* (71) 388 7000
Fax: + *44* (71) 380 4900

European Affiliation: Affiliated Conference of Practising Accountants International (ACPA)

International Contact: Martin Kudlick

Partners: 16

CONTACT INFORMATION

Managing Partner: Martin Kudlick
Managing Partner: Paul Beer

CLIENT SERVICES

All Services

OTHER OFFICES

FISHER FINANCIAL
Acre House, 10-12 Victoria Street, NORTHAMPTON NN1 5ED
Tel: + *44* (604) 231555 *Fax:* + *44* (604) 234136
Contact: Brian Anderson

Total Number of Offices: 2

FORRESTER BOYD

26 South St Mary's Gate, GRIMSBY, South Humberside DN31 1LW
Tel: + *44* (472) 350601
Fax: + *44* (472) 241748

European Affiliation: Moores Rowland International

International Contact: Barrie N. Moore

OTHER OFFICES

FORRESTER BOYD
Waynflete House, 139 Eastgate, LOUTH, Lincolnshire LN11 9QQ
Tel: + *44* (507) 606111 *Fax:* + *44* (507) 607817
Contact: David R. Gelsthorpe

FORRESTER BOYD
74 Oswald Road, SCUNTHORPE, South Humberside DN15 7PG
Tel: + *44* (724) 863105 *Fax:* + *44* (724) 281325
Contact: David I. Clayton

Total Number of Offices: 3

FRANCIS CLARK

23 Devon Square, NEWTON ABBOT, Devon TQ12 2HU
Tel: + *44* (626) 331155
Fax: + *44* (626) 331451

European Affiliation: INPACT - International Network of Professional Accountants

International Contact: Anthony Golding

Partners:	20
Professional staff:	150
Non-professional staff:	70
Total Staff:	**240**

FEE INCOME

Year End: 30.04.91	**£**	**%**
Accountancy & Audit:	3,000,000	60.0
Insolvency:	100,000	2.0
Consultancy:	500,000	10.0
Tax:	1,000,000	20.0
Other:	300,000	8.0
Total:	**4,900,000**	

CONTACT INFORMATION

Chairman: Anthony William Pitkin
Insolvency: Derek Kenneth Swann
Accountancy & Audit: Jeffrey Carl Brown
Computer & Administration: Robert Morgan Beard
Tax: Steven Collins
Personnel: Peter Richards

CLIENT SERVICES

Accountancy (General), Audit, Computer Installation, Corporate Finance Advice, Insolvency & Corporate Restructuring, Life & Risk Assurance, Litigation/Legal Services, Management & Business Advice, Management Consultancy Only, Management Buy-outs, Mergers & Acquisitions, Pensions Planning, Value for Money Studies, Taxation (Corporate), Taxation (International), Trust Settlement & Estates, Taxation (Personal), Underwriters, VAT

Industry Specialisations: Motor Trade, Construction, Plant Hire, Schools, Medical Practices

▷

MAJOR CLIENTS
BAI (UK) Ltd (Brittany Ferries), Bennah Ltd, Bray Leino Ltd, Champion Chemicals Ltd, Clarity Copiers Ltd, Kencrete Ltd, Midas Construction Ltd, Symbol Services Ltd, B.H. Thompson Ltd, Torex Hire Plc, Trago Mills Ltd, Vospers of Plymouth Ltd, J. Wipple & Co Ltd

OTHER OFFICES

FRANCIS CLARK
31 St David's Hill, EXETER EX4 4DA
Tel: + *44* (392) 76226 *Fax:* + *44* (392) 412451
Contact: Patrick D. Degan

FRANCIS CLARK
31 Houndiscombe Road, PLYMOUTH PL4 6HA
Tel: + *44* (752) 669982 *Fax:* + *44* (752) 222430
Contact: Anthony Peter Golding

Total Number of Offices: 6

FRANK BROWN & WALFORD

314-316 Linthorpe Road, MIDDLESBROUGH, Cleveland TS1 3QX
Tel: + *44* (642) 225421
Fax: + *44* (642) 249251

National Affiliation: The CharterGroup Partnership

International Contact: Keith Thomas

Partners:	4
Professional staff:	34
Non-professional staff:	12
Total Staff:	**50**

FEE INCOME

Year End: 30.11.90	**£**	**%**
Accountancy & Audit:	750,000	75.0
Consultancy:	40,000	4.0
Tax:	210,000	21.0
Total:	**1,000,000**	

CONTACT INFORMATION
Chairman: David Otter
Managing Partner: Adrian Walker
Accountancy & Medical Practice: David Otter
Accountancy & Tax (Personal): Bill Milner
Corporate Finance, Tax & Consultancy: Keith Thomas
Audit, Tax & Administration: Adrian Walker

CLIENT SERVICES
Accountancy (General), Audit, Computer Installation, Corporate Finance Advice, Management & Business Advice, Management Buy-outs, Mergers & Acquisitions, Taxation (Corporate), Trust Settlement & Estates

Industry Specialisations: Medical Practices

OTHER OFFICES

FRANK BROWN & WALFORD
Suite 8, Municipal Buildings, Church Square, HARTLEPOOL, Cleveland TS24 7EQ
Tel: + *44* (429) 869148 *Fax:* + *44* (429) 863416

FRANK BROWN & WALFORD
Marblemand House, 25 Yarm Road, STOCKTON, Cleveland TS18 3NJ
Tel: + *44* (642) 607154 *Fax:* + *44* (642) 617147

Total Number of Offices: 3

FRASER GORDON & CO

Station House, 15 Station Road, ST IVES, Cambridgeshire PE17 4BH
Tel: + *44* (480) 66384
Fax: + *44* (480) 68538

European Affiliation: Midsnell International

International Contact: Ian F. Gordon

FREEDA, MILSTON, CEDAR, BAKER

Hathaway House, Popes Drive, Finchley, LONDON N3 1QF
Tel: + *44* (81) 346 6446
Fax: + *44* (81) 349 3990

European Affiliation: InterContinental Consultants (ICC)

International Contact: Raymond Freeda
Martin H. Stone

FREEDMAN ROSS & CO

9 Lisbon Square, LEEDS LS1 4LY
Tel: + *44* (532) 433022
Fax: + *44* (532) 422091

National Affiliation: The CharterGroup Partnership

International Contact: Malcolm Ross

Partners:	4
Professional staff:	30
Non-professional staff:	5
Total Staff:	**39**

CONTACT INFORMATION
Managing Partner: Michael Freedman
Accountancy (General): Ian North
Audit: Andrew King
Tax (Corporate): Derek Smith

CLIENT SERVICES
All Services

FREEMAN RICH

284 Clifton Drive South, St Annes, LYTHAM ST ANNES, Lancashire FY8 1LH
Tel: + *44* (253) 722246
Fax: + *44* (253) 722581

National Affiliation: The CharterGroup Partnership

International Contact: Robin Upton

OTHER OFFICES

FREEMAN RICH
10 Richmond Terrace, BLACKBURN BB1 7BD
Tel: + *44* (254) 580311 *Fax:* + *44* (254) 673979

FREEMAN RICH
London House, Primrose Hill, off London Road, PRESTON PR1 4BX
Tel: + *44* (772) 57596 *Fax:* + *44* (772) 58731

Total Number of Offices: 3

GARBUTT & ELLIOTT

Sherburn House, 41 Ings Road, LEEDS LS9 9EJ
Tel: + *44* (532) 488646
Fax: + *44* (532) 488620

European Affiliation: Moores Rowland International

International Contact: David J. Dickson

OTHER OFFICES

GARBUTT & ELLIOTT
Monkgate House, 44 Monkgate, YORK YO3 7HF
Tel: + *44* (904) 654656 *Fax:* + *44* (904) 610015
Contact: Bob Elliot

Total Number of Offices: 2

GARNERS

Haydon House, 14 Haydon Place, GUILDFORD, Surrey GU1 4LL
Tel: + *44* (483) 575218
Fax: + *44* (483) 63383

National Affiliation: The UK 200 Group of Practising Accountants

International Contact: Andrew Goodman

Partners:	6
Professional staff:	13
Non-professional staff:	3
Total Staff:	**22**

FEE INCOME

Year End: 31.05.91	**%**
Accountancy & Audit:	55.0
Consultancy:	10.0
Tax:	25.0
Other:	10.0

CONTACT INFORMATION
Managing Partner: Peter Hounslow
Partner: Andrew Goodman

CLIENT SERVICES
All Services

OTHER OFFICES

GARNERS
Bermuda House, 45 High Street, Hampton Wick, KINGSTON UPON THAMES, Surrey KT1 4EH
Tel: + *44* (81) 943 2191 *Fax:* + *44* (81) 977 9347
Contact: Graham Merricks

Total Number of Offices: 2

GERBER, LANDA & GEE

54/56 Berkeley Street, GLASGOW G3 7DS
Tel: + *44* (41) 221 7446
Fax: + *44* (41) 248 2469

European Affiliation: Jeffreys Henry International

International Contact: Thomas Hughes

GIBSON APPLEBY

Wenlock House, 41 North Street, BRIGHTON BN1 1RH
Tel: + *44* (273) 204661
Fax: + *44* (273) 204664

International Contact: David Povah

GILCHRIST, TASH

Cleveland Buildings, Queen's Square, MIDDLESBROUGH, Cleveland TS2 1PA
Tel: + *44* (642) 248387
Fax: + *44* (642) 232108

European Affiliation: Moores Rowland International

International Contact: Norman Bayley

ALBERT GOODMAN & CO

Mary Street House, Mary Street, TAUNTON, Somerset TA1 3NW
Tel: + *44* (823) 286096
Fax: + *44* (823) 257319

European Affiliation: Moores Rowland International

International Contact: John B. Hunt

OTHER OFFICES

ALBERT GOODMAN
Essex House, Fore Street, CHARD, Somerset TA20 1QA
Tel: + *44* (4606) 4646 *Fax:* + *44* (4606) 61648
Contact: Paul Hazell

Total Number of Offices: 2

JOHN GORDON, WALTON & COMPANY

Yorkshire House, Greek Street, LEEDS LS1 5ST
Tel: + *44* (532) 431007
Fax: + *44* (532) 422601

National Affiliation: The CharterGroup Partnership

GRANT THORNTON

Grant Thornton House, Melton Street, Euston Square, LONDON NW1 2EP
Tel: + *44* (71) 383 5100
Fax: + *44* (71) 383 4334

European Affiliation: Grant Thornton International

International Contact: Michael Timms

Partners:	230
Professional staff:	2,012
Non-professional staff:	864
Total Staff:	**3,106**

FEE INCOME

Year End: 30.06.90	**£**
Total:	**109,000,000**

CONTACT INFORMATION
Managing Partner: David McDonnell

CLIENT SERVICES
Accountancy (General), Audit, Corporate Finance Advice, Insolvency & Corporate Restructuring, Management & Business Advice, Management Buy-outs, Mergers & Acquisitions, Pensions Planning, Taxation (Corporate), Taxation (International), Trust Settlement & Estates, Company Formation & Administration

OTHER OFFICES

GRANT THORNTON
Ringwood House, Walton Street, AYLESBURY, Buckinghamshire HP21 7QP
Tel: + *44* (296) 434231 *Fax:* + *44* (296) 436166

GRANT THORNTON
Grant Thornton House, 46 West Bar, BANBURY, Oxfordshire OX16 9RZ
Tel: + *44* (295) 264343 *Fax:* + *44* (295) 270083

GRANT THORNTON
7 Old King Road, BATH BA1 2JW
Tel: + *44* (225) 336575 *Fax:* + *44* (225) 325717

GRANT THORNTON
49 Mill Street, BEDFORD MK40 3LB
Tel: + *44* (234) 211521 *Fax:* + *44* (234) 325717

GRANT THORNTON
Enterprise House, 115 Edmund Street, BIRMINGHAM B3 2HJ
Tel: + *44* (21) 212 4000 *Fax:* + *44* (21) 212 4012

GRANT THORNTON
Oxford House, Oxford Road, BOURNEMOUTH BH8 8HY
Tel: + *44* (202) 294551 *Fax:* + *44* (202) 294550

GRANT THORNTON
Eldon Lodge, Eldon Place, BRADFORD, West Yorkshire BD1 3AP
Tel: + *44* (274) 734341 *Fax:* + *44* (274) 390191

GRANT THORNTON
Lees House, 21 Dyke Road, BRIGHTON BN1 3GD
Tel: + *44* (273) 778955 *Fax:* + *44* (273) 739585

▷

United Kingdom

GRANT THORNTON
43 Queen Square, BRISTOL BS1 4QR
Tel: + *44* (272) 268901 *Fax:* + *44* (272) 265458

GRANT THORNTON
18 Langton Place, BURY ST EDMUNDS, Suffolk IP33 1NE
Tel: + *44* (284) 701271 *Fax:* + *44* (284) 762760

GRANT THORNTON
11-13 Penhill Road, CARDIFF CF1 9UP
Tel: + *44* (222) 235591 *Fax:* + *44* (222) 383803

GRANT THORNTON
The Quadrangle, Imperial Square, CHELTENHAM, Gloucestershire GL50 1PZ
Tel: + *44* (242) 222900 *Fax:* + *44* (242) 222330

GRANT THORNTON
Eildon, CLECKHEATON, West Yorkshire BD19 3LS
Tel: + *44* (274) 876701 *Fax:* + *44* (274) 851169

GRANT THORNTON
Whitecrook Centre, 78 Whitecrook Street, CLYDEBANK, Dunbartonshire G81 1QF
Tel: + *44* (41) 941 2010

GRANT THORNTON
2nd Floor, Douglas House, Queens Square, CORBY, Northamptonshire NN17 1PL
Tel: + *44* (536) 63657 *Fax:* + *44* (536) 400109

GRANT THORNTON
32-34 Queens Road, COVENTRY CV1 3FJ
Tel: + *44* (203) 257481 *Fax:* + *44* (203) 520590

GRANT THORNTON
Ashdown House, 125 High Street, CRAWLEY, West Sussex RH10 1DQ
Tel: + *44* (293) 561383 *Fax:* + *44* (293) 561392

GRANT THORNTON
1/4 Atholl Crescent, EDINBURGH EH3 8LQ
Tel: + *44* (31) 229 9181 *Fax:* + *44* (31) 229 4560

GRANT THORNTON
P.O. Box 151, 112 West George Street, GLASGOW G2 1QF
Tel: + *44* (41) 332 7484 *Fax:* + *44* (41) 333 0581

GRANT THORNTON
The Old Registry, Amersham Hill, HIGH WYCOMBE, Buckinghamshire HP13 6NA
Tel: + *44* (494) 450781 *Fax:* + *44* (494) 526550

GRANT THORNTON
Crown House, Crown Street, IPSWICH IP1 3HS
Tel: + *44* (473) 221491 *Fax:* + *44* (473) 230304

GRANT THORNTON
St John's Centre, 110 Albion Street, LEEDS LS2 8LA
Tel: + *44* (532) 455514 *Fax:* + *44* (532) 465055

GRANT THORNTON
8 West Walk, LEICESTER LE1 7NH
Tel: + *44* (533) 471234 *Fax:* + *44* (533) 471434

GRANT THORNTON
1 Stanley Street, LIVERPOOL L1 6AD
Tel: + *44* (51) 227 4211 *Fax:* + *44* (51) 236 3429

GRANT THORNTON
GT House, 24-26 Rothesay Road, LUTON LU1 1QX
Tel: + *44* (582) 27368 *Fax:* + *44* (582) 400130

GRANT THORNTON
Heron House, Albert Square, MANCHESTER M2 5HD
Tel: + *44* (61) 834 5414 *Fax:* + *44* (61) 832 6042

GRANT THORNTON
Grant Thornton House, 202 Silbury Boulevard, CENTRAL MILTON KEYNES MK9 1LW
Tel: + *44* (908) 660666 *Fax:* + *44* (908) 690180

GRANT THORNTON
4th Floor, Higham House, Higham Place, NEWCASTLE-UPON-TYNE NE1 8EE
Tel: + *44* (91) 261 2631 *Fax:* + *44* (91) 232 6903

GRANT THORNTON
Elgin House, Billing Road, NORTHAMPTON NN1 5AU
Tel: + *44* (604) 27811 *Fax:* + *44* (604) 230486

GRANT THORNTON
30 Hounds Gate, NOTTINGHAM NG1 7DH
Tel: + *44* (602) 483483 *Fax:* + *44* (602) 484504

GRANT THORNTON
1 Westminster Way, OXFORD OX2 0PZ
Tel: + *44* (865) 244977 *Fax:* + *44* (865) 724420

GRANT THORNTON
Walltree Court, St Peter's Road, PETERSFIELD, Hampshire GU32 3HY
Tel: + *44* (730) 66711 *Fax:* + *44* (730) 68763

GRANT THORNTON
Cobourg House, Mayflower Street, PLYMOUTH PL1 1LG
Tel: + *44* (752) 669911 *Fax:* + *44* (752) 665414

GRANT THORNTON
Towngate House, 2 Parkstone Road, POOLE, Dorset BH15 2PJ
Tel: + *44* (202) 683406 *Fax:* + *44* (202) 680826

GRANT THORNTON
Enterprise House, Isambard Brunel Road, PORTSMOUTH PO1 2RZ
Tel: + *44* (705) 753175 *Fax:* + *44* (705) 825356

GRANT THORNTON
20 Winckley Square, PRESTON PR1 3JJ
Tel: + *44* (772) 53883 *Fax:* + *44* (772) 202620

GRANT THORNTON
74 Wellingborough Road, RUSHDEN, Northamptonshire NN10 9TY
Tel: + *44* (933) 59227 *Fax:* + *44* (933) 410135

GRANT THORNTON
Charter House, 16 Melville Street, RYDE, Isle of Wight PO33 2AF
Tel: + *44* (983) 65135 *Fax:* + *44* (983) 616877

GRANT THORNTON
28 Kenwood Park Road, SHEFFIELD S7 1NG
Tel: + *44* (742) 553371 *Fax:* + *44* (742) 500294

GRANT THORNTON
31 Carlton Crescent, SOUTHAMPTON S01 2EW
Tel: + *44* (703) 221231 *Fax:* + *44* (703) 330443

GRANT THORNTON
Bold Street Chambers, 31 Bold Street, WARRINGTON WA1 1HL
Tel: + *44* (925) 31333 *Fax:* + *44* (925) 413899

GRANT THORNTON
Brooke House, Queen Street, WELLINGBOROUGH, Northamptonshire NN8 4RW
Tel: + *44* (933) 227666 *Fax:* + *44* (933) 229268

GRANT THORNTON
Grant Thornton House, 4 Witan Way, WITNEY, Oxfordshire OX8 6NT
Tel: + *44* (993) 71121 *Fax:* + *44* (993) 779021

GRANT THORNTON
Barclays Bank Building, 1 Chapel Road, WORTHING, West Sussex BN11 1SA
Tel: + *44* (903) 204511 *Fax:* + *44* (903) 820697

ASSOCIATED FIRMS

WITT THORNTON
Waterford House, 32 Lodge Road, COLERAINE, Co Londonderry BT52 1NB
Tel: + *44* (265) 52171 *Fax:* + *44* (265) 58419

WITT THORNTON
Sinclair House, 89 Royal Avenue, BELFAST BT1 1BP
Tel: + *44* (232) 329481 *Fax:* + *44* (232) 439185

WITT THORNTON
59-61 Main Street, LARNE, Co Antrim BT40 1JE
Tel: + *44* (574) 272698 *Fax:* + *44* (574) 277882

WITT THORNTON
5 Market Street, DOWNPATRICK, Co Down BT30 6LP
Tel: + *44* (396) 614017 *Fax:* + *44* (396) 616795

WITT THORNTON
2 Loy Street, COOKSTOWN, Co Tyrone BT80 8PE
Tel: + *44* (6487) 64007 *Fax:* + *44* (6487) 65788

WITT THORNTON
32a Main Street, LIMAVADY, Co Londonderry BT49 0EU
Tel: + *44* (504) 22189 *Fax:* + *44* (504) 45515

WITT THORNTON
40 Clooney Terrace, LONDONDERRY BT47 1AP
Tel: + *44* (504) 42920 *Fax:* + *44* (504) 45515

Total Number of Offices: 52

GREAVES JOSEPH & CO

Greaves Joseph House, No. 3 Pride Court, 80/82 White Lion Street, LONDON N1 9PF
Tel: + *44* (71) 278 6129
Fax: + *44* (71) 278 6264

International Contact: Bernard M. Joseph

Partners:	4
Professional staff:	7
Non-professional staff:	4
Total Staff:	**15**

CONTACT INFORMATION

Senior Partner: Bernard Joseph
Managing Partner: Claude Greaves
Accountancy & Insolvency: Anthony Letchumanan
Audit & Public Sector: Jerry Netto
Corporate Finance & Consultancy: Bernard Joseph
Tax & Administration: Claude Greaves
Senior Tax Assistant: Felix Tagert
Senior Audit Assistant: Gordon Ferguson

CLIENT SERVICES

All Services

Industry Specialisations: Legal Firms, Housing Associations, Entertainment

GRIFFIN STONE, MOSCROP & COMPANY

41 Welbeck Street, LONDON W1M 8HD
Tel: + *44* (71) 935 3793

National Affiliation: The CharterGroup Partnership

International Contact: Geoffrey Hill

GRIFFITH & MILES

24 Castle Street, SWANSEA SA1 1HY
Tel: + *44* (792) 654324
Fax: + *44* (792) 651742

National Affiliation: The CharterGroup Partnership

International Contact: Eric Davies

GRUBER LEVINSON FRANKS

Peter House, Oxford Street, MANCHESTER M1 5AB
Tel: + *44* (61) 236 8784
Fax: + *44* (61) 228 7350

European Affiliation: The International Group of Accounting Firms Ltd (IGAF)

Partners:	20
Professional staff:	160
Non-professional staff:	40
Total Staff:	**220**

CONTACT INFORMATION

Managing Partner: Will Kintish
Accountancy (General): Andrew Pearce
Accountancy (General): P.D. Levinson
Accountancy (General): Harold Franks
Accountancy (General): Alan Tranter
Accountancy (General): Russell Silverman
Accountancy (General): Colin Humphrey
Accountancy (General): Paul Roach
Accountancy (General): Elliot Simon
Accountancy (General): Michael Green
Accountancy (General): Christine Owen
Accountancy (General): Mitchell Crisp
Audit: Bob Theckston
Insolvency: Dermot Paver
Insolvency: David Swaden
Management Consultancy: Steve Carter
Administration: Will Kintish
Corporate Finance & Tax: Tony Tesciuba
Tax: Mike Longman
Tax: Simon Topperman

CLIENT SERVICES

Accountancy (General), Audit, Computer Installation, Corporate Finance Advice, Insolvency & Corporate Restructuring, Life & Risk Assurance, Management & Business Advice, Management Buy-outs, Mergers & Acquisitions, Pensions Planning, Value for Money Studies, Taxation (Corporate), Taxation (International), Trust Settlement & Estates, Marketing Consultancy

OTHER OFFICES

GRUBER LEVINSON FRANKS
46 Rodney Street, LIVERPOOL L1 9AA
Tel: + *44* (51) 709 3255 *Fax:* + *44* (51) 708 9564

GRUBER LEVINSON FRANKS
Fernden House, Chapel Lane, Stockton Heath, WARRINGTON WA4 6LL
Tel: + *44* (925) 265040 *Fax:* + *44* (925) 268055
Contact: Dermot Power

GRUBER LEVINSON FRANKS
Durwen House, 7 Stanley Place, CHESTER CH1 2LU
Tel: + *44* (244) 319904 *Fax:* + *44* (244) 314620
Contact: Mitchell Crisp

Total Number of Offices: 4

HACKER YOUNG

St Alphage House, 2 Fore Street, LONDON EC2Y 5DH
Tel: + *44* (71) 588 3611
Fax: + *44* (71) 638 2159

European Affiliation: Urbach Hacker Young International

International Contact: Arthur Harverd

▷

Partners:	49	
Professional staff:	233	
Non-professional staff:	99	
Total Staff:	**381**	

FEE INCOME

Year End: 30.04.91	**£**	**%**
Accountancy & Audit:	7,800,000	56.1
Insolvency:	750,000	5.4
Consultancy:	600,000	4.3
Tax:	4,300,000	31.0
Other:	450,000	3.2
Total:	**13,900,000**	

CONTACT INFORMATION

Accountancy (General): Ian Cohen
Audit: Peter Tegg
Corporate Finance: Jeffrey Nedas
Insolvency: Ladislav Hornan
Management Consultancy: Arthur Harverd
Administration: Brian Baldwin
Public Sector: Peter Luscombe
Tax (Corporate): Derek Murphy
Tax (International): Dudley Stebbings
Senior Partner: Frank Stansil
Joint Managing Partner: Jeffrey Nedas
Joint Managing Partner: Peter Tegg
Technical & Training: Jack Easton
Marketing: Howard Spencer
Computer Services: Edward Stothard
Company Secretarial: Michael Fiszzon
Business Development: Ian Cohen

CLIENT SERVICES

Accountancy (General), Audit, Computer Installation, Corporate Finance Advice, Insolvency & Corporate Restructuring, Litigation/Legal Services, Management & Business Advice, Management Buy-outs, Mergers & Acquisitions, Value for Money Studies, Taxation (Corporate), Taxation (International), Trust Settlement & Estates, Payroll Services, Management Consultancy, Housing Association Services, Company Secretarial Services

Industry Specialisations: Charities, Housing Assns, Leisure, Solicitors, Professional Firms, DIY, Textiles, Retail, Travel, Property

OTHER OFFICES

GODKIN & CO
Cobden House, 106 New Walk, LEICESTER LE1 7EA
Tel: + *44* (533) 557722 *Fax:* + *44* (533) 543163
Contact: Peter Cooney

GODKIN & CO
41 Biggin Street, LOUGHBOROUGH, Leicestershire LE11 1UA
Tel: + *44* (509) 214496 *Fax:* + *44* (509) 262881
Contact: Neil Murphy

HACKER YOUNG
Metropolitan House, 1 Hagley Road, Edgbaston, BIRMINGHAM B16 8TG
Tel: + *44* (21) 456 4010 *Fax:* + *44* (21) 456 3842
Contact: Gerald Nash

HACKER YOUNG
3 & 5 St Paul's Road, Clifton, BRISTOL BS8 1LX
Tel: + *44* (272) 738926 *Fax:* + *44* (272) 730872
Contact: Alan Vaughan

HACKER YOUNG
23/24 Royal Crescent, GLASGOW G3 7SL
Tel: + *44* (41) 333 9515 *Fax:* + *44* (41) 332 7929
Contact: Arthur Harverd

HACKER YOUNG
St James Building, 79 Oxford Street, MANCHESTER M1 6HT
Tel: + *44* (61) 236 6936 *Fax:* + *44* (61) 228 0117
Contact: David Sassoon

HACKER YOUNG
22 The Ropewalk, NOTTINGHAM NG1 5DT
Tel: + *44* (602) 410410 *Fax:* + *44* (602) 470628
Contact: Philip Oliver

LEGG & CO
St George's House, 103 Tonbridge Road, MAIDSTONE, Kent ME16 8JN
Tel: + *44* (622) 671717 *Fax:* + *44* (622) 691434
Contact: Tony Legg

MOREY SUGARMAN & CO
204 Church Road, HOVE, East Sussex BN3 2DJ
Tel: + *44* (273) 726445 *Fax:* + *44* (273) 731821
Contact: John Guest

Total Number of Offices: 10

HAGLEY KNIGHT & COMPANY

108 Guildford Street, CHERTSEY, Surrey KT16 9AH
Tel: + *44* (932) 567676
Fax: + *44* (932) 568865

National Affiliation: The CharterGroup Partnership

International Contact: Barry Hollands

OTHER OFFICES

HAGLEY KNIGHT & COMPANY
Estate House, 122 London Road, CAMBERLEY, Surrey GU15 3TJ
Tel: + *44* (276) 20143 *Fax:* + *44* (276) 20049

Total Number of Offices: 2

HARDY & CO

13 Rubislaw Terrace, ABERDEEN AB1 1XE
Tel: + *44* (224) 647490
Fax: + *44* (224) 640771

International Contact: Derek A.H. Hardy

FEE INCOME

Year End: 31.12.91	**£**	**%**
Accountancy & Audit:	144,000	80.0
Consultancy:	9,000	5.0
Tax:	27,000	15.0
Total:	**180,000**	

CONTACT INFORMATION

Managing Partner: Derek A.H. Hardy
Managing Partner: W.A.M. Gardner

CLIENT SERVICES

All Services

Industry Specialisations: Farming

OTHER OFFICES

HARDY & CO
33 Bogie Street, HUNTLY, Aberdeenshire AB5 5DX
Tel: + *44* (446) 784046
Contact: Julia Winsey

HARDY & CO
22 Commerce Street, INSCH, Aberdeenshire AB52 6HX
Tel: + *44* (464) 20258
Contact: Derek Hardy

HARDY & CO
Station Road, MAUD, Aberdeenshire AB4 8NE
Tel: + *44* (7714) 525
Contact: Bill Gardner

Total Number of Offices: 4

J.R. HAWORTH & CO

1 Stanley Street, ACCRINGTON, Lancashire BB5 6PD
Tel: + *44* (254) 32521
Fax: + *44* (254) 872459

European Affiliation: INPACT - International Network of Professional Accountants

International Contact: Peter Wilkinson

Partners:	6
Professional staff:	13
Non-professional staff:	7
Total Staff:	**26**

CONTACT INFORMATION
Managing Partner: Peter Wilkinson
Accountancy (General): Peter Wilkinson
Insolvency: James McLean
Audit & Tax: Mark Schofield
Corporate Finance & Consultancy: Peter Horrocks
Administration & Public Sector: Peter Robinson

CLIENT SERVICES
All Services

Industry Specialisations: Motor Trade, Textiles, Printing

HAWSONS

Pegasus House, 463a Glossop Road, SHEFFIELD S10 2QD
Tel: + *44* (742) 667141
Fax: + *44* (742) 661456

European Affiliation: Moores Rowland International

International Contact: Peter J. Flint

OTHER OFFICES

HAWSONS
Jubilee House, Billing Brook Road, NORTHAMPTON NN3 4NW
Tel: + *44* (604) 414500 *Fax:* + *44* (604) 411192
Contact: John Lister

Total Number of Offices: 2

HAYLES & PARTNERS

39 Castle Street, LEICESTER LE1 5WN
Tel: + *44* (533) 512215
Fax: + *44* (533) 510631

European Affiliation: INPACT - International Network of Professional Accountants

Partners:	4
Professional staff:	34
Non-professional staff:	12
Total Staff:	**50**

FEE INCOME

Year End: 31.12.90	**£**	**%**
Accountancy & Audit:		75.0
Tax:		20.0
Other:		5.0
Total:	**984,532**	

CONTACT INFORMATION
Managing Partner: Geoff Banks
Accountancy (General): Geoff Banks
Audit: Andrew West

CLIENT SERVICES
Accountancy (General), Audit, Taxation (Corporate)

OTHER OFFICES

HAYLES & PARTNERS
3 High Street, IBSTOCK, Leicestershire LE6 1L9
Tel: + *44* (530) 61518 *Fax:* + *44* (530) 63326
Contact: Barry Hayles

Total Number of Offices: 2

HAYS ALLAN

Southampton House, 317 High Holborn, LONDON WC1V 7NL
Tel: + *44* (71) 831 6233
Fax: + *44* (71) 831 2416

International Contact: John Rose

Partners:	29
Professional staff:	180
Non-professional staff:	53
Total Staff:	**262**

FEE INCOME

Year End: 30.04.90	**£**
Total:	**9,900,000**

CONTACT INFORMATION
Chairman: John Gordon
Managing Partner: John Rose
Accountancy (General): Jeremy Harding-Edgar
Audit: Bernie Watson
Corporate Finance: David Riley
Insolvency: John Rose
Tax: Nick Vaughton

CLIENT SERVICES
Accountancy (General), Audit, Corporate Finance Advice, Insolvency & Corporate Restructuring, Litigation/Legal Services, Management & Business Advice, Management Buy-outs, Mergers & Acquisitions, Value for Money Studies, Taxation (Corporate), Taxation (International), Trust Settlement & Estates, Taxation (Personal)

Industry Specialisations: Charities, Arts & Antiques Dealers, Insurance Brokers, Construction & Property, Professional Partnerships

OTHER OFFICES

HAYS ALLAN
Beech House, 4a Newmarket Road, CAMBRIDGE CB5 8DT
Tel: + *44* (223) 354233 *Fax:* + *44* (223) 460702
Contact: Bill Barnard

HAYS ALLAN
Culham House, 122 Castle Street, READING RG1 7RJ
Tel: + *44* (734) 574083 *Fax:* + *44* (734) 504529
Contact: Mike Procter

HAYS ALLAN
2 Barnfield Crescent, EXETER EX1 1QT
Tel: + *44* (392) 432774 *Fax:* + *44* (392) 51175
Contact: Stephen Reid

Total Number of Offices: 4

HAYSOM SILVERTON & PARTNERS

145 Queensway, Bletchley, MILTON KEYNES MK2 2DY
Tel: + *44* (908) 640601
Fax: + *44* (908) 270391

European Affiliation: Jeffreys Henry International

International Contact: Dennis Silverton

Partners:	4
Professional staff:	22
Non-professional staff:	5
Total Staff:	**31**

▷

FEE INCOME

Year End: 30.06.91	%
Accountancy & Audit:	65.0
Consultancy:	5.0
Tax:	20.0
Other:	10.0

CONTACT INFORMATION
Accountancy (General): Robert Haysom
Audit: Susan Apps
Management Consultancy: Paul Cudmore

CLIENT SERVICES
Accountancy (General), Audit, Corporate Finance Advice, Litigation/Legal Services, Management & Business Advice, Taxation (Corporate), Taxation (International)

Industry Specialisations: Construction, Franchisees

HAZLEMS FENTON
Palladium House, 1-4 Argyll Street, LONDON WIV 1AD
Tel: + *44* (71) 437 7666
Fax: + *44* (71) 734 0644

National Affiliation: The CharterGroup Partnership

International Contact: Michael Krieger

HAZLEWOODS
Windsor House, Bayshill Road, CHELTENHAM, Gloucestershire GL50 3AT
Tel: + *44* (242) 237661
Fax: + *44* (242) 584263

European Affiliation: Moores Rowland International

International Contact: Norman L. Webber

OTHER OFFICES

HAZLEWOODS
Staverton Court, Staverton, CHELTENHAM, Gloucestershire GL5 0UX
Tel: + *44* (242) 680000 *Fax:* + *44* (242) 680857
Contact: W.M. Riley

HAZLEWOODS
Windsor House, Brunswick Road, GLOUCESTER GL1 1JR
Tel: + *44* (452) 305551 *Fax:* + *44* (452) 300391
Contact: Harvey G.E. Grove

HAZLEWOODS
Stroud House, Station Approach, STROUD, Gloucestershire GL5 3AN
Tel: + *44* (453) 759826 *Fax:* + *44* (453) 751938
Contact: Peter Evans

HAZLEWOODS
40 High Street, TEWKESBURY, Gloucestershire GL20 5BB
Tel: + *44* (684) 297543 *Fax:* + *44* (684) 293942
Contact: Graham Jell

Total Number of Offices: 5

T.A. HEAL & CO
64 High Street, BIDEFORD, Devon EX39 2AN
Tel: + *44* (237) 472725
Fax: + *44* (237) 473187

National Affiliation: The UK 200 Group of Practising Accountants

Partners:	4
Professional staff:	30
Non-professional staff:	10
Total Staff:	**44**

CONTACT INFORMATION
Managing Partner: Colin Heal
Audit: Mark Ohlsen

CLIENT SERVICES
Accountancy (General), Audit, Corporate Finance Advice, Management & Business Advice, Pensions Planning, Value for Money Studies, Taxation (Corporate)

Industry Specialisations: Farming

OTHER OFFICES

T.A. HEAL & CO
4 Bodmin Street, HOLSWORTHY, Devonshire EX22 6BB
Tel: + *44* (409) 253297 *Fax:* + *44* (409) 254534
Contact: Mark Ohlsen

Total Number of Offices: 2

HENDERSON & LOGGIE (IN ASSOCIATION WITH PRINGLE & WATT)
11 Panmure Street, DUNDEE DD1 2BQ
Tel: + *44* (382) 200055
Fax: + *44* (382) 200764

National Affiliation: The CharterGroup Partnership

International Contact: Donald McIntosh

HILTON, SHARP & CLARKE
30 New Road, BRIGHTON BN1 1BN
Tel: + *44* (273) 24163
Fax: + *44* (273) 23983

European Affiliation: Moores Rowland International

International Contact: M.R. Benton

Partners:	5
Professional staff:	25
Non-professional staff:	5
Total Staff:	**35**

FEE INCOME

Year End: 31.03.91	£	%
Accountancy & Audit:		70.0
Tax:		30.0
Total:	**1,100,000**	

CONTACT INFORMATION
Managing Partner: Paul S. Savage

CLIENT SERVICES
All Services

HOBSON PHILLIPS & SHARPE
Alexandra House, 43 Alexandra Street, NOTTINGHAM NG5 1AY
Tel: + *44* (602) 621590
Fax: + *44* (602) 691071

National Affiliation: The CharterGroup Partnership

International Contact: Jim Scully

OTHER OFFICES

HOBSON PHILLIPS & SHARPE
Cheltermill House, 38 Lombard St, Newark, NOTTINGHAM NG24 1XP
Tel: + *44* (636) 702100 *Fax:* + *44* (636) 605246

Total Number of Offices: 2

HOMER GITTINS
402/403 Stourport Road, KIDDERMINSTER, Worcestershire DY11 7BG
Tel: + *44* (562) 66333
Fax: + *44* (562) 746982

European Affiliation: Midsnell International

International Contact: Mike L. Homer

Partners:	5
Professional staff:	25
Non-professional staff:	2
Total Staff:	**32**

CONTACT INFORMATION
Managing Partner: Mike L. Homer
Administration: Roger F. Sedgwick
Tax (Corporate): Mike L. Homer
Accountancy & Audit: John H. Wilkes

CLIENT SERVICES
Accountancy (General), Audit, Corporate Finance Advice, Management & Business Advice, Taxation (Corporate)

OTHER OFFICES
HOMER GITTINS
Charlton House, Priory Street, DUDLEY, West Midlands DY1 1HQ
Tel: + *44* (384) 252369 *Fax:* + *44* (384) 54707
Contact: David F. Hughes
Total Number of Offices: 2

HONEY BARRETT & CO
51-55 Gildredge Road, EASTBOURNE, East Sussex BN21 4SF
Tel: + *44* (323) 412277
Fax: + *44* (323) 412414

European Affiliation: Moores Rowland International

International Contact: Bill A. Honey
Charles W. House

OTHER OFFICES
HONEY BARRETT & CO
48 St Leonards Road, BEXHILL-ON-SEA, East Sussex TN40 1JB
Tel: + *44* (424) 730345 *Fax:* + *44* (424) 730330
Contact: Paul A.J. Knight
HONEY BARRETT & CO
2-3 St Andrew's Place, Southover Road, LEWES, East Sussex BN7 1UP
Tel: + *44* (273) 480255 *Fax:* + *44* (273) 480244
Contact: Geoff Davies
HONEY BARRETT & CO
122/124 High Street, UCKFIELD, East Sussex TN22 1PX
Tel: + *44* (825) 765077 *Fax:* + *44* (825) 765011
Contact: Mervyn P. Jones
Total Number of Offices: 4

HOWARD WORTH & CO
163 Chester Road, NORTHWICH, Cheshire CW8 4AQ
Tel: + *44* (606) 75338
Fax: + *44* (606) 783138

National Affiliation: The CharterGroup Partnership

International Contact: David V. Hubbard

Partners:	4
Professional staff:	24
Non-professional staff:	4
Total Staff:	**32**

FEE INCOME

Year End: 31.12.90	**£**	**%**
Accountancy & Audit:	240,000	40.0
Consultancy:	6,000	1.0
Tax:	240,000	40.0
Other:	114,000	19.0
Total:	**600,000**	

CONTACT INFORMATION
Chairman: Philip T. Proffit
Managing Partner: David V. Hubbard
Tax (Corporate): Ian R. Wright
Accountancy & Corporate Finance: Kevin Dickens
Audit & Management Consultancy: Ian R. Wright
Tax & Administration: Kevin Dickens

CLIENT SERVICES
All Services

Industry Specialisations: Building/Development, Farm/Estate, Management, Nursing/Retirement Care, Motor Main Dealer Franchises

HOWARTH HAWSONS
37 Stramongate, KENDAL, Cumbria LA9 4BH
Tel: + *44* (539) 721008
Fax: + *44* (539) 727774

European Affiliation: Moores Rowland International

International Contact: Giles W. Howarth

HUGHES ALLEN
Greenwood House, 4/7 Salisbury Court, LONDON EC4Y 8BT
Tel: + *44* (71) 583 7575
Fax: + *44* (71) 583 2081

European Affiliation: CPA Associates Inc

International Contact: Peter Scolding

Partners:	18
Professional staff:	80
Non-professional staff:	26
Total Staff:	**124**

CONTACT INFORMATION
Managing Partner: Peter J.C. Scolding
Senior Partner: Maurice E. Sargent

OTHER OFFICES
HUGHES ALLEN
9 Lower Brook Street, IPSWICH IP4 1AG
Tel: + *44* (473) 215927 *Fax:* + *44* (473) 221777
Contact: James B. McElhinney
HUGHES ALLEN
Waterman House, 101/107 Chertsey Road, WOKING, Surrey GU2 1LJ
Tel: + *44* (4837) 29924 *Fax:* + *44* (4837) 62683
Contact: A. John Groves
HUGHES ALLEN
102 The Thoroughfare, WOODBRIDGE, Suffolk IP2 1AR
Tel: + *44* (394) 385432 *Fax:* + *44* (394) 384034
Contact: Roy B. Brewster
HUGHES ALLEN
16/17 Lower Bridge Street, CANTERBURY, Kent CT1 2LQ
Tel: + *44* (227) 463527 *Fax:* + *44* (227) 463540
Contact: Stephen J. Taylor
Total Number of Offices: 5

HUGILL & CO
46 Museum Street, LONDON WC1A 1LY
Tel: + *44* (71) 242 8808
Fax: + *44* (71) 405 7566

International Contact: Terence B.L. Feller

▷

Partners:	9
Professional staff:	61
Non-professional staff:	30
Total Staff:	**100**

FEE INCOME

Year End: 30.04.91	**£**
Total:	**2,680,000**

CONTACT INFORMATION
Managing Partner: Philip A. Bayliss
Audit: David A. Preston
Management Consultancy: John W. Bayliss
Administration: Rohit Shastri
Tax (Corporate): Terence J. Brigden

CLIENT SERVICES
Accountancy (General), Audit, Computer Installation, Corporate Finance Advice, Management & Business Advice, Management Buy-outs, Mergers & Acquisitions, Pensions Planning, Taxation (Corporate), Trust Settlement & Estates

Industry Specialisations: Construction & Allied Trades, Including Suppliers, Solicitors

OTHER OFFICES

HUGILL & CO
Hugill House, Swanfield Road, WALTHAM CROSS, Hertfordshire EN8 7JR
Tel: + *44* (992) 29144 *Fax:* + *44* (992) 39961
Contact: Terence B.L. Feller

HUGILL & CO
Corbiere House, 21/23 New Road, BASINGSTOKE, Hampshire RG21 1PR
Tel: + *44* (256) 467369 *Fax:* + *44* (256) 840517
Contact: David A. Preston

HUGILL & CO
Pavilion Chambers, 1a South Street, ST NEOTS, Cambridgeshire PE19 2BW
Tel: + *44* (480) 213813 *Fax:* + *44* (480) 405661
Contact: Gordon Round

HUGILL & CO
Albany House, 73/79 Station Road, WEST DRAYTON, Middlesex UB7 7LT
Tel: + *44* (895) 444525 *Fax:* + *44* (895) 448593
Contact: Terence J. Brigden

Total Number of Offices: 5

JACKSON ANDREWS
Andras House, 60 Great Victoria Street, BELFAST BT2 7ET
Tel: + *44* (232) 233152
Fax: + *44* (232) 332757

European Affiliation: Moores Rowland International

Partners:	4
Professional staff:	12
Non-professional staff:	4
Total Staff:	**20**

FEE INCOME

Year End: 31.08.90	%
Accountancy & Audit:	80.0
Consultancy:	5.0
Tax:	15.0

CONTACT INFORMATION
Managing Partner: Tim C. Browne
Accountancy (General): N.A. Lawtmer
Audit: J.N. Greer
Management Consultancy & Tax: Tim C. Browne

CLIENT SERVICES
All Services

ALAN JAMES & CO
Shepperton Marina, Felix Lane, SHEPPERTON, Middlesex TW17 8NJ
Tel: + *44* (932) 240540
Fax: + *44* (932) 243152

International Contact: Alan James

Partners:	2
Professional staff:	10
Non-professional staff:	1
Total Staff:	**13**

FEE INCOME

Year End: 30.04.91	**£**	%
Accountancy & Audit:	120,000	70.0
Consultancy:	30,000	17.6
Tax:	20,000	12.4
Total:	**170,000**	

CLIENT SERVICES
Accountancy (General), Audit, Computer Installation, Corporate Finance Advice, Life & Risk Assurance, Management & Business Advice, Mergers & Acquisitions, Value for Money Studies, Taxation (Corporate), Taxation (International), International Consolidated Accounts

---

JEFFREYS HENRY
Finsgate, 5/7 Cranwood Street, LONDON EC1V 9EE
Tel: + *44* (71) 253 7064
Fax: + *44* (71) 608 1983

European Affiliation: Jeffreys Henry International

International Contact: Alan Bell

Partners:	9
Professional staff:	35
Non-professional staff:	10
Total Staff:	**54**

CONTACT INFORMATION
Managing Partner: Malcolm Coleman
Accountancy (General): Sidney Hirst
Audit: Nicholas Michaels
Corporate Finance: Michael Coleman
Insolvency: Mark Tenzer
Management Consultancy: Alan Bell
Administration: Neville Gamsu
Public Sector: David Fobel
Tax (Corporate): Denis Wanderer
Tax (International): Michael Stascewski

CLIENT SERVICES
All Services

W.D. JOHNSTON & CARMICHAEL
7-9 Commerce Street, ELGIN, Moray IV30 1BS
Tel: + *44* (343) 547492
Fax: + *44* (343) 548896

National Affiliation: The UK 200 Group of Practising Accountants

Partners:	16
Professional staff:	120
Non-professional staff:	80
Total Staff:	**216**

CONTACT INFORMATION
Chairman: G.S. Johnston
Managing Partner: P.L. Simpson
Managing Partner: D.G. Horn
Accountancy (General): R.M. Mackintosh

Audit: K. Ferguson
Insolvency: W.A.D. MacPhail
Management Consultancy: P.L. Simpson
Tax: N.H. Seligman

CLIENT SERVICES

Accountancy (General), Audit, Computer Installation, Insolvency & Corporate Restructuring, Management & Business Advice, Management Buy-outs, Pensions Planning, Taxation (Corporate), Taxation (International), Trust Settlement & Estates

OTHER OFFICES

W.D. JOHNSTON & CARMICHAEL
30 West High Street, INVERURIE, Aberdeenshire AB5 9QR
Tel: + *44* (467) 20178 *Fax:* + *44* (467) 24245

W.D. JOHNSTON & CARMICHAEL
158 Mid Street, KEITH, Banffshire AB5 3BJ
Tel: + *44* (5422) 6116 *Fax:* + *44* (5422) 6440

W.D. JOHNSTON & CARMICHAEL
25 Duke Street, HUNTLY, Aberdeenshire AB5 5DL
Tel: + *44* (446) 4148

W.D. JOHNSTON & CARMICHAEL
4 Gordon Street, NAIRN IV12 4AU
Tel: + *44* (667) 52355

W.D. JOHNSTON & CARMICHAEL
22 Carden Place, ABERDEEN AB1 1UQ
Tel: + *44* (224) 625500 *Fax:* + *44* (224) 626252

W.D. JOHNSTON & CARMICHAEL
Coutts Building, Main Street, ALFORD, Aberdeenshire AB3 8QA
Tel: + *44* (975) 562348

W.D. JOHNSTON & CARMICHAEL
8 Low Street, BANFF AB4 1AS
Tel: + *44* (2612) 8259

W.D. JOHNSTON & CARMICHAEL
51/53 High Street, TURRIFF, Aberdeenshire AB5 7EJ
Tel: + *44* (888) 62396 *Fax:* + *44* (888) 68919

Total Number of Offices: 9

JONES PETERS & COMPANY

6 Church Street, BANBRIDGE, Co Down BT32 4AA
Tel: + *44* (8206) 25427
Fax: + *44* (8206) 26102

European Affiliation: DRM Internationally

JUDKINS

14-20 Star Hill, ROCHESTER, Kent ME1 1UU
Tel: + *44* (634) 830321
Fax: + *44* (634) 830969

National Affiliation: The CharterGroup Partnership

International Contact: M.A. Cook

Partners:	4
Professional staff:	17
Non-professional staff:	13
Total Staff:	**34**

CONTACT INFORMATION

Managing Partner: K.A. Cook
Accountancy (General): Susan M. Robinson
Audit & Management Consultancy: M.A. Cook
Corporate Finance & Insolvency: K.A. Cook

CLIENT SERVICES

All Services

KANAS & PARTNERS

Bridgewater House, 60 Whitworth Street, MANCHESTER M1 6LX
Tel: + *44* (61) 228 1582
Fax: + *44* (61) 236 8090

European Affiliation: INPACT - International Network of Professional Accountants

International Contact: C.P. Bodimeade

Partners:	6
Professional staff:	19
Non-professional staff:	25
Total Staff:	**50**

FEE INCOME

Year End: 30.04.91	%
Accountancy & Audit:	50.0
Consultancy:	25.0
Tax:	25.0

CONTACT INFORMATION

Chairman: P.E. Kanas
Managing Partner: P. Johnson
Accountancy (General): A.G. Smith
Audit: J.T. Traynor
Corporate Finance: P.E. Kanas
Management Consultancy: C.P. Bodimeade
Administration: P. Johnson
Tax: S.C. Peters

CLIENT SERVICES

Accountancy (General), Audit, Computer Installation, Corporate Finance Advice, Management & Business Advice, Management Buy-outs, Mergers & Acquisitions, Taxation (Corporate), Taxation (International), Trust Settlement & Estates

Industry Specialisations: Entertainment, Construction, Motor Trade, Law, Insurance

Total Number of Offices: 2

KEENS SHAY KEENS

Christchurch House, Upper George Street, LUTON LU1 2RS
Tel: + *44* (582) 21571
Fax: + *44* (582) 414377
National Affiliation: The CharterGroup Partnership
International Contact: John Vincent

OTHER OFFICES

KEENS SHAY KEENS
10 Cambrdige Road, SANDY, Bedfordshire SG19 1JE
Tel: + *44* (767) 80527

KEENS SHAY KEENS
Victoria House, 42/44 Shortmead Street, BIGGLESWADE, Bedfordshire SG18 0AP
Tel: + *44* (767) 313765 *Fax:* + *44* (767) 600211

KEENS SHAY KEENS
25 Tilehouse Street, HITCHIN, Hertfordshire SG5 2DY
Tel: + *44* (462) 431266 *Fax:* + *44* (462) 421816

KEENS SHAY KEENS
2nd Floor, Exchange Building, 16 St Cuthberts Street, BEDFORD MK40 3JG
Tel: + *44* (234) 325981 *Fax:* + *44* (234) 210454

United Kingdom

KEENS SHAY KEENS
Norman House, 199 North Second Street, Grafton Gate Street, CENTRAL MILTON KEYNES MK9 1NJ
Tel: + *44* (908) 674484 *Fax:* + *44* (908) 690371

Total Number of Offices: 6

KIDSONS IMPEY

Spectrum House, 20/26 Cursitor Street, LONDON EC4A 1HY
Tel: + *44* (71) 405 2088
Fax: + *44* (71) 831 2206
Mailing Address: Peel House, Barttelot Road, HORSHAM, West Sussex RH12 1BQ

European Affiliation: HLB International

International Contact: Raymond E. Greatorex

Partners:	178
Professional staff:	1,227
Non-professional staff:	345
Total Staff:	**1,750**

CONTACT INFORMATION

Managing Partner: P.A. Douglas
Managing Partner: G. Burton
Corporate Finance: S. Gray
Insolvency: H.C. Brunt
Management Consultancy: W.J. Oates
Public Sector, Audit & Accountancy: K.A. Sherwood
Tax: F.H. Harris
International Matters: R.E. Greatorex
Grants & Regional Aid: W.J. Oates
Administration: T.J. Patten

CLIENT SERVICES

Accountancy (General), Audit, Computer Installation, Corporate Finance Advice, Insolvency & Corporate Restructuring, Life & Risk Assurance, Litigation/Legal Services, Management & Business Advice, Management Buy-outs, Mergers & Acquisitions, Pensions Planning, Value for Money Studies, Taxation (Corporate), Taxation (International), Trust Settlement & Estates, Personnel Selection & Recruitment, Management Consultancy

Industry Specialisations: Food, Engineering, Manufacturing, Motor, Property, Computer, Building, Horse Racing, Arts, Agriculture

OTHER OFFICES

KIDSONS IMPEY
Spectrum House, 20-26 Cursitor Street, LONDON EC4A 1HY
Tel: + *44* (71) 405 2088 *Fax:* + *44* (71) 831 2206
Contact: Ian Macfarlane

KIDSONS IMPEY
11 Albyn Place, ABERDEEN AB1 1YE
Tel: + *44* (224) 212222 *Fax:* + *44* (244) 210190
Contact: James Braid

KIDSONS IMPEY
2 The Downs, ALTRINCHAM, Cheshire WA14 2PX
Tel: + *44* (61) 928 4391 *Fax:* + *44* (61) 926 8169
Contact: Alan Ramsey

KIDSONS IMPEY
Clock and Chimes Courtyard, 2 Rickfords Hill, AYLESBURY, Buckinghamshire HP20 2RX
Tel: + *44* (296) 432755 *Fax:* + *44* (296) 433274
Contact: John Cook

KIDSONS IMPEY
Carmichael Chambers, 1 Wood Lane, North Bar Within, BEVERLEY, North Humberside HU17 8BS
Tel: + *44* (482) 867951 *Fax:* + *44* (482) 863577
Contact: Michael Holland

KIDSONS IMPEY
Bank House, 8 Cherry Street, BIRMINGHAM B2 5AD
Tel: + *44* (21) 631 2631 *Fax:* + *44* (21) 631 2632
Contact: Michael Gash

KIDSONS IMPEY
100 Wide Bargate, BOSTON, Lincolnshire PE21 6SE
Tel: + *44* (205) 362405 *Fax:* + *44* (205) 360529
Contact: David Hamshaw

KIDSONS IMPEY
51 Kirk Street, CAMPBELTOWN, Argyll PA28 6BW
Tel: + *44* (586) 52372 *Fax:* + *44* (586) 53486
Contact: Donnie Darroch

KIDSONS IMPEY
Carlton House, 31-34 Railway Street, CHELMSFORD CM1 1NJ
Tel: + *44* (245) 269595 *Fax:* + *44* (245) 354285
Contact: Derek Powell

KIDSONS IMPEY
2 George Street, CHESTER CH1 3EQ
Tel: + *44* (244) 327171 *Fax:* + *44* (244) 377648
Contact: Tom Lowndes

KIDSONS IMPEY
Clarendon House, 12 North Hill, COLCHESTER CO1 1DZ
Tel: + *44* (206) 578464 *Fax:* + *44* (206) 761927
Contact: Michael A. Wood

KIDSONS IMPEY
Park House, Station Square, COVENTRY CV1 2NS
Tel: + *44* (203) 256333 *Fax:* + *44* (203) 222101
Contact: John Coulson

KIDSONS IMPEY
217 High Street, COWDENBEATH, Fife KY4 9QF
Tel: + *44* (383) 513512 *Fax:* + *44* (383) 514093

KIDSONS IMPEY
6 Vernon Street, DERBY DE1 1FR
Tel: + *44* (332) 360808 *Fax:* + *44* (332) 384801
Contact: Philip Palfreyman

KIDSONS IMPEY
2 Victoria Road, DISS, Norfolk IP22 3EY
Tel: + *44* (379) 642504 *Fax:* + *44* (379) 651206
Contact: Tony Storer

KIDSONS IMPEY
23 Queen Street, EDINBURGH EH2 1JX
Tel: + *44* (31) 225 1134 *Fax:* + *44* (31) 220 1282
Contact: Ronald Ironside

KIDSONS IMPEY
Breckenridge House, 274 Sauchiehall Street, GLASGOW G2 3EH
Tel: + *44* (41) 307 5000 *Fax:* + *44* (41) 307 5005
Contact: Nick Robinson

KIDSONS IMPEY
3 Beaufort Buildings, Spa Road, GLOUCESTER GL1 1XB
Tel: + *44* (452) 527000 *Fax:* + *44* (452) 309314
Contact: Lord Kershaw

KIDSONS IMPEY
25 Chantry Lane, GRIMSBY, South Humberside DN31 2LP
Tel: + *44* (472) 348521 *Fax:* + *44* (472) 242988
Contact: Stuart Falconer

KIDSONS IMPEY
Elgar House, Holmer Road, HEREFORD HR4 9SF
Tel: + *44* (432) 352222 *Fax:* + *44* (432) 269367
Contact: Ann Sheldon

KIDSONS IMPEY
11 Downham Road South, Heswall, WIRRAL, Merseyside L60 5RG
Tel: + *44* (51) 342 6281 *Fax:* + *44* (51) 342 8745
Contact: Norman Pursglove

KIDSONS IMPEY
Enterprise House, 83a Western Road, HOVE, East Sussex BN3 1LJ
Tel: + 44 (273) 720311 *Fax:* + 44 (273) 205453
Contact: Chris Warne

KIDSONS IMPEY
Dunedin House, 45 Percy Street, HULL HU2 8HL
Tel: + 44 (482) 27406 *Fax:* + 44 (482) 26957
Contact: Norman Staveley

KIDSONS IMPEY
Friars Courtyard, 30 Princes Street, IPSWICH IP1 1RJ
Tel: + 44 (473) 216154 *Fax:* + 44 (473) 231586
Contact: Jonathan Penn

KIDSONS IMPEY
3 High Street, KINROSS KY13 7AW
Tel: + 44 (577) 63611 *Fax:* + 44 (577) 64801
Contact: David Birrell

KIDSONS IMPEY
Barclays House, 41 Park Cross Street, LEEDS LS1 2QH
Tel: + 44 (532) 422666 *Fax:* + 44 (532) 422038
Contact: Bob Crossey

KIDSONS IMPEY
122 Commercial Street, LERWICK, Shetland Isles ZE1 OHX
Tel: + 44 (595) 3384 *Fax:* + 44 (595) 5902
Contact: Bob Steele

KIDSONS IMPEY
Number One, Old Hall Street, LIVERPOOL L3 9SX
Tel: + 44 (51) 227 3671 *Fax:* + 44 (51) 236 4615
Contact: Trevor Mathew-Jones

KIDSONS IMPEY
Clydesdale Bank Buildings, Poltalloch Street, LOCHGILPHEAD, Argyll PA31 8LP
Tel: + 44 (546) 2180 *Fax:* + 44 (546) 2683
Contact: Stuart Ramsay

KIDSONS IMPEY
Devonshire House, 36 George Street, MANCHESTER M1 4HA
Tel: + 44 (61) 236 7733 *Fax:* + 44 (61) 236 7020
Contact: John Oates

KIDSONS IMPEY
Fulcrum House, 7 The Norwich Business Park, Whiting Road, NORWICH NR4 6DJ
Tel: + 44 (603) 628767 *Fax:* + 44 (603) 662077
Contact: Paul Muttitt

KIDSONS IMPEY
22 Regent Street, NOTTINGHAM N1 5DG
Tel: + 44 (602) 473002 *Fax:* + 44 (602) 473062
Contact: Anthony Grimley

KIDSONS IMPEY
26 Beaumont Street, OXFORD OX1 2NP
Tel: + 44 (865) 52996 *Fax:* + 44 (865) 310359
Contact: Frankie Ko

KIDSONS IMPEY
618 Warwick Road, SOLIHULL, West Midlands B91 1AA
Tel: + 44 (21) 711 3939 *Fax:* + 44 (21) 711 4151
Contact: Peter Hackett

KIDSONS IMPEY
Welland House, High Street, SPALDING, Lincolnshire PE11 1UB
Tel: + 44 (775) 766205 *Fax:* + 44 (775) 710512
Contact: John Lister

KIDSONS IMPEY
Marlborough House, 7 Billetfield, TAUNTON, Somerset TA1 3NN
Tel: + 44 (823) 331657 *Fax:* + 44 (823) 336830
Contact: Christopher Rimmer

KIDSONS IMPEY
Ruskin House, 14 St John's Road, TUNBRIDGE WELLS, Kent TN4 9NP
Tel: + 44 (892) 511944 *Fax:* + 44 (892) 515852
Contact: David Wilson

KIDSONS IMPEY
Waterside Court, Witan Way, WITNEY, Oxfordshire OX8 6EH
Tel: + 44 (993) 771438 *Fax:* + 44 (993) 776425
Contact: Clive Wilkinson

KIDSONS IMPEY
Hendford Manor, YEOVIL, Somerset BA20 1UN
Tel: + 44 (935) 23667 *Fax:* + 44 (935) 31875
Contact: Ken McIver

KIDSONS IMPEY
71 Preston New Road, BLACKBURN BB2 6AY
Tel: + 44 (254) 674222 *Fax:* + 44 (254) 674223
Contact: John Bury

KIDSONS IMPEY
10 Apsley Road, Clifton, BRISTOL BS8 2SP
Tel: + 44 (272) 730285 *Fax:* + 44 (272) 238456
Contact: Geoff Gollop

Total Number of Offices: 42

KILBY FOX & COMPANY

St Martin's House, 43-44 Billing Road, NORTHAMPTON NN1 5DA
Tel: + 44 (604) 233399
Fax: + 44 (604) 783138

National Affiliation: The CharterGroup Partnership

International Contact: David Ward

KING & TAYLOR

10-12 Wrotham Road, GRAVESEND, Kent DA11 OPE
Tel: + 44 (474) 569777
Fax: + 44 (474) 355623

National Affiliation: The UK 200 Group of Practising Accountants

International Contact: Trevor Climpson

Partners:	5
Professional staff:	9
Non-professional staff:	7
Total Staff:	**21**

CLIENT SERVICES

Accountancy (General), Audit, Computer Installation, Corporate Finance Advice, Management & Business Advice, Pensions Planning, Taxation (Corporate)

KINGSTON SMITH

Devonshire House, 146 Bishopsgate, LONDON EC2M 4JX
Tel: + 44 (71) 377 8888
Fax: + 44 (71) 247 7048

European Affiliation: K.S. International

International Contact: M.A. Burchmore

Partners:	24
Professional staff:	154
Non-professional staff:	59
Total Staff:	**237**

FEE INCOME

Year End: 30.04.91	**£**
Total:	**10,000,000**

CONTACT INFORMATION

Managing Partner: M.J. Snyder
Accountancy (General): B.J. Howe

Audit: P.J. Timms
Tax (Corporate): R.F. Wallis
Tax (International): A.G. McMichen
Corporate Finance & Consultancy: S. Neal
Administration & Consultancy: M.J. Snyder
VAT: A.J. Houstoun
Litigation Support & Expert Witness: E.H. Woolf

CLIENT SERVICES
Accountancy (General), Audit, Computer Installation, Corporate Finance Advice, Life & Risk Assurance, Litigation/Legal Services, Management & Business Advice, Management Buy-outs, Mergers & Acquisitions, Pensions Planning, Value for Money Studies, Taxation (Corporate), Taxation (International), Trust Settlement & Estates, Financial Presentations, Training, VAT, PAYE, NIC Advisory Service, Government Grants

Industry Specialisations: Medical, Advertising, Distribution, Shipping, Freight, Solicitors, Architects, Restaurants, Media

MAJOR CLIENTS
AGFA-Gevaert Ltd, ASSA Ltd, Bayer UK Ltd, BM Group plc, Hella Ltd, Kores (UK) Ltd, Malaya Group plc, Panalpina International Ltd, Seacon Holdings Ltd, T.R. City of London Trust plc

OTHER OFFICES

KINGSTON SMITH
Surrey House, Surrey Street, CROYDON CR0 1SZ
Tel: + *44* (81) 680 6033 *Fax:* + *44* (81) 681 0854
Contact: Parveen Chadda

KINGSTON SMITH
800 Uxbridge Road, HAYES, Middlesex UB4 0RS
Tel: + *44* (81) 573 8258 *Fax:* + *44* (81) 848 8747
Contact: Anthony Sansom

KINGSTON SMITH
105 St Peter's Street, ST ALBANS, Hertfordshire AL1 3EJ
Tel: + *44* (727) 832261 *Fax:* + *44* (727) 838916
Contact: David Goodridge

KINGSTON SMITH
Exchange House, 180-182 St Mary's Lane, UPMINSTER, Essex RM14 3BT
Tel: + *44* (4022) 21872 *Fax:* + *44* (4022) 24938
Contact: Graham Fildes

KINGSTON SMITH
15 Cavendish Square, LONDON W1M 9DA
Tel: + *44* (71) 580 4646 *Fax:* + *44* (71) 580 4955
Contact: Robert Willott

Total Number of Offices: 6

KNOX CROPPER
16 New Bridge Street, LONDON EC4V 6AX
Tel: + *44* (71) 583 8355
Fax: + *44* (71) 583 2944

Partners:	8
Professional staff:	35
Non-professional staff:	6
Total Staff:	**49**

FEE INCOME

Year End: 31.12.90	**£**	**%**
Accountancy & Audit:	1,254,700	87.0
Tax:	143,294	10.0
Other:	52,039	3.0
Total:	**1,450,033**	

CONTACT INFORMATION
Managing Partner: P.H. Grove
Administration: B.E. Gandee
Public Sector: R.O. Dulieu
Tax (Corporate): P.J. Ford
Accountancy & Audit: M.I. Hussein
Accountancy & Audit: B.E. Marshall
Accountancy & Audit: K.P. Lally
Accountancy & Audit: J.D. Jones

CLIENT SERVICES
Accountancy (General), Audit, Computer Installation, Corporate Finance Advice, Management & Business Advice, Pensions Planning, Value for Money Studies, Taxation (Corporate), Trust Settlement & Estates, Internal Audit

Industry Specialisations: Educational & General Charities, Housing Associations

MAJOR CLIENTS
Central Bureau for Educational Visits & Exchanges, Froebel Institute, Goldsmiths College, London School of Economics, National Union of Teachers, Richmond Fellowship, Royal Masonic Benevolent Institute, Salvation Army, St George's Hospital Medical School, Teachers Assurance Company, Teachers Building Society, Tidy Britain Group, University of London, National Federation of Womens' Institutes

OTHER OFFICES

KNOX CROPPER
24 Petworth Road, HASLEMERE, Surrey GU27 2HR
Tel: + *44* (428) 652788 *Fax:* + *44* (428) 61272
Contact: Peter Ford

Total Number of Offices: 2

KPMG

KPMG PEAT MARWICK
1 Puddle Dock, Blackfriars, LONDON EC4V 3PD
Tel: + *44* (71) 236 8000
Fax: + *44* (71) 248 6552

European Affiliation: KPMG

International Contact: C.G. Sneath

Partners:	606
Professional staff:	7,535
Non-professional staff:	2,171
Total Staff:	**10,312**

FEE INCOME

Year End: 30.09.91	**£**	**%**
Accountancy & Audit:	256,300,000	52.9
Insolvency:	44,500,000	9.1
Consultancy:	84,400,000	17.4
Tax:	98,800,000	20.4
Total:	**484,000,000**	

CONTACT INFORMATION
Chairman: P.J. Butler
Accountancy (General): T.W. Allen
Accountancy (General): M.Y.A. Hughes
Audit: E.S. Awty
Audit: W.M.T. Fowle
Corporate Finance: G. Archer
Insolvency: C.T.E. Hayward
Management Consultancy: R.J. Simm
Administration: N.W.M. May
Public Sector: M.J. Dron
Tax: R.J.G. White

CLIENT SERVICES
All Services

Industry Specialisations: Banking & Finance, Food & Drink, Construction & Property, High Tech, Leisure & Tourism, Petroleum

MAJOR CLIENTS

Allied-Lyons, AMEC, Beazer, Boots, British Aerospace, Cable & Wireless, Co-Operative Wholesale Society, General Accident, Grand Metropolitan, Hillsdown Holdings, Imperial Chemical Industries, Lex Service, Lonrho, National Westminster Bank, P & O Steam Navigation, Rolls-Royce, Saatchi & Saatchi, Standard Life Assurance, Tarmac, Unigate

OTHER OFFICES

KPMG PEAT MARWICK
Royfold House, Hill of Rubislaw, Anderson Drive, ABERDEEN AB9 1JE
Tel: + 44 (224) 208888 *Fax:* + 44 (224) 208027
Contact: J.L. Athol Munro

KPMG PEAT MARWICK
Verum House, New Street, BASINGSTOKE, Hampshire RG21 1DN
Tel: + 44 (256) 473811 *Fax:* + 44 (256) 475296
Contact: David G. Brooks

KPMG PEAT MARWICK
Peat House, 2 Cornwall Street, BIRMINGHAM B3 2DL
Tel: + 44 (21) 233 1666 *Fax:* + 44 (21) 233 4390
Contact: J. David Leake

KPMG PEAT MARWICK
Peat House, 1 Commercial Street, Forster Square, BRADFORD, West Yorkshire BD1 4AS
Tel: + 44 (274) 725546 *Fax:* + 44 (274) 735039
Contact: David R. Jones

KPMG PEAT MARWICK
Queen Square House, Queen Square, BRIGHTON BN1 3FD
Tel: + 44 (273) 820042 *Fax:* + 44 (273) 23723
Contact: Michael A. Pitts

KPMG PEAT MARWICK
Richmond Park House, 15 Pembroke Road, Clifton, BRISTOL BS8 3BG
Tel: + 44 (272) 732291 *Fax:* + 44 (272) 732191
Contact: Greg K. Cairns

KPMG PEAT MARWICK
Chater House, 37 Hills Road, CAMBRIDGE CB2 1XL
Tel: + 44 (223) 66692 *Fax:* + 44 (223) 460701
Contact: David R. Walter

KPMG PEAT MARWICK
16-17 Lower Bridge Street, CANTERBURY, Kent CT1 2LG
Tel: + 44 (227) 762800 *Fax:* + 44 (227) 762810
Contact: Keith Nicholson

KPMG PEAT MARWICK
Marlborough House, Fitzalan Court, Fitzalan Road, CARDIFF CF2 1TE
Tel: + 44 (222) 462463 *Fax:* + 44 (222) 462188
Contact: T. David Snowden

KPMG PEAT MARWICK
Peat House, Lansdown Road, CHELTENHAM, Gloucestershire NP6 5LN
Tel: + 44 (242) 222020 *Fax:* + 44 (242) 221970
Contact: Austin P. Knight

KPMG PEAT MARWICK
Welsh Street Chambers, CHEPSTOW, Gwent NP6 5LN
Tel: + 44 (291) 620126 *Fax:* + 44 (291) 624864
Contact: Martyn C. Llewwllin

KPMG PEAT MARWICK
Northgate House, St Augustines Way, DARLINGTON, Co Durham DL1 1UZ
Tel: + 44 (325) 381400 *Fax:* + 44 (325) 381184
Contact: Tony M. Dennett

KPMG PEAT MARWICK
Peat House, Smart Street, DERBY DE1 2EQ
Tel: + 44 (332) 49268 *Fax:* + 44 (332) 49163
Contact: Roger K. Pedley

KPMG PEAT MARWICK
Royal Exchange, DUNDEE DD1 1DZ
Tel: + 44 (382) 201234 *Fax:* + 44 (382) 21240
Contact: Ronald W. Gibson

KPMG PEAT MARWICK
Saltire Court, 20 Castle Terrace, EDINBURGH EH1 2EG
Tel: + 44 (31) 222 2000 *Fax:* + 44 (31) 222 2020
Contact: Simon H. Ingall

KPMG PEAT MARWICK
Linacre House, Southernhay East, EXETER EX1 1UG
Tel: + 44 (392) 211654 *Fax:* + 44 (392) 221654
Contact: Gerald A. Sturtidge

KPMG PEAT MARWICK
24 Blythswood Square, GLASGOW G2 4Q5
Tel: + 44 (41) 226 5511 *Fax:* + 44 (41) 204 1584
Contact: Archie S. Hunter

KPMG PEAT MARWICK
Eastgate Court, GUILDFORD, Surrey GU1 3AE
Tel: + 44 (483) 303000 *Fax:* + 44 (483) 68732
Contact: Richald L. Spalding

KPMG PEAT MARWICK
Station Street Buildings, HUDDERSFIELD HD1 1LZ
Tel: + 44 (484) 421433 *Fax:* + 44 (484) 518447
Contact: Peter B. Scaman

KPMG PEAT MARWICK
Essex House, Manor Street, HULL HU1 1YW
Tel: + 44 (482) 27011 *Fax:* + 44 (482) 25696
Contact: John D. Coish

KPMG PEAT MARWICK
6 Lower Brook Street, IPSWICH 1P4 1AP
Tel: + 44 (473) 233499 *Fax:* + 44 (473) 230131
Contact: Barry J.J. Peek

KPMG PEAT MARWICK
1 The Embankment, Neville Street, LEEDS LS1 4DW
Tel: + 44 (532) 313000 *Fax:* + 44 (532) 313200
Contact: Harold North

KPMG PEAT MARWICK
Peat House, 1 Waterloo Way, LEICESTER LE1 6LP
Tel: + 44 (533) 471122 *Fax:* + 44 (533) 547626
Contact: Michael A. Chamberlain

KPMG PEAT MARWICK
Richmond House, 1 Rumford Place, LIVERPOOL L3 9QY
Tel: + 44 (51) 236 5052 *Fax:* + 44 (51) 236 1882
Contact: Tim J. Beer

KPMG PEAT MARWICK
Barham Court, Teston, MAIDSTONE, Kent ME18 5BZ
Tel: + 44 (622) 814814 *Fax:* + 44 (622) 814888
Contact: Peter Chadwick

KPMG PEAT MARWICK
7 Tib Lane, MANCHESTER M2 6DS
Tel: + 44 (61) 832 4221 *Fax:* + 44 (61) 832 7265
Contact: Hubert W.E. Thompson

KPMG PEAT MARWICK
St James House, 139 Albert Road, MIDDLESBROUGH, Cleveland TS1 2PP
Tel: + 44 (642) 242651 *Fax:* + 44 (642) 240680
Contact: John R. Kirton

KPMG PEAT MARWICK
Norfolk House, 499 Silbury Boulevard, CENTRAL MILTON KEYNES MK9 2HA
Tel: + 44 (908) 661881 *Fax:* + 44 (908) 664363
Contact: David J.F. Winks

KPMG PEAT MARWICK
Maybrook House, 27 Grainger Street, NEWCASTLE-UPON-TYNE NE1 5JT
Tel: + 44 (91) 232 8815 *Fax:* + 44 (91) 232 8615
Contact: Ian E.M. Farquhar

▷

KPMG PEAT MARWICK
Spencer House, Cliftonville Road, NORTHAMPTON NN1 5BU
Tel: + *44* (604) 34480 *Fax:* + *44* (604) 32297
Contact: Alastair Gray

KPMG PEAT MARWICK
Holland Court, The Close, NORWICH NR1 4DY
Tel: + *44* (603) 620481 *Fax:* + *44* (603) 623078
Contact: Harry G. Hornor

KPMG PEAT MARWICK
St Nicholas House, 31 Park Row, NOTTINGHAM NG1 6GR
Tel: + *44* (602) 483444 *Fax:* + *44* (602) 483401
Contact: Fred C. Marks

KPMG PEAT MARWICK
Chamberlain House, St Aldates Courtyard, 38 St Aldates, OXFORD OX1 1BN
Tel: + *44* (865) 791911 *Fax:* + *44* (865) 790919
Contact: E.C.F. Gerard Hodge

KPMG PEAT MARWICK
Phoenix House, Notte Street, PLYMOUTH PL1 2RT
Tel: + *44* (752) 225381 *Fax:* + *44* (752) 266800
Contact: Roger J. Harris

KPMG PEAT MARWICK
Old Orchard, 39-61 High Street, POOLE, Dorset BH15 1AE
Tel: + *44* (202) 684606 *Fax:* + *44* (202) 6806697
Contact: A. Crawford McKinlay

KPMG PEAT MARWICK
Edward VII Quay, Navigation Way, Ashton-on-Ribble, PRESTON PR2 2YF
Tel: + *44* (772) 722822 *Fax:* + *44* (772) 736777
Contact: Peter T. Masterson

KPMG PEAT MARWICK
Abbots House, Abbey Street, READING RG1 3BD
Tel: + *44* (734) 505555 *Fax:* + *44* (734) 589285
Contact: A. Jim Kerevan

KPMG PEAT MARWICK
The Fountain Precinct, 1 Balm Green, SHEFFIELD S1 3AF
Tel: + *44* (742) 766789 *Fax:* + *44* (742) 766213
Contact: Christopher E. Druce

KPMG PEAT MARWICK
Dukes Keep, Marsh Lane, SOUTHAMPTON S01 1EX
Tel: + *44* (703) 631465 *Fax:* + *44* (703) 223547
Contact: Mike S. Killingley

KPMG PEAT MARWICK
Aquis Court, 31 Fishpool Street, ST ALBANS, Hertfordshire AL3 4RF
Tel: + *44* (727) 43000 *Fax:* + *44* (727) 41005
Contact: Wm. M. Tannett

KPMG PEAT MARWICK
Festival Way, Festival Park, STOKE-ON-TRENT ST1 5TA
Tel: + *44* (782) 216000 *Fax:* + *44* (782) 216050
Contact: Don P. Johnstone

KPMG PEAT MARWICK
Grove House, Grove Place, SWANSEA SA1 5DE
Tel: + *44* (792) 456868 *Fax:* + *44* (792) 456869
Contact: Barry Jones

KPMG PEAT MARWICK
1 Cricklade Court, Cricklade Street, Old Town, SWINDON SN1 3EB
Tel: + *44* (793) 512522 *Fax:* + *44* (793) 488808
Contact: Adrian J. Bligh

KPMG PEAT MARWICK
Peat House, Newham Road, TRURO, Cornwall TR1 2DP
Tel: + *44* (872) 76116 *Fax:* + *44* (872) 222172
Contact: Tony A. Hill

KPMG PEAT MARWICK
121 The Mount, YORK YO2 2DA
Tel: + *44* (904) 610565 *Fax:* + *44* (904) 630744
Contact: Christopher J. Adams

Total Number of Offices: 49

LAMONT PRIDMORE

Milburn House, 3 Oxford Street, WORKINGTON, Cumbria CA14 2AL
Tel: + *44* (900) 65955
Fax: + *44* (900) 65999

National Affiliation: The CharterGroup Partnership

International Contact: Graham Lamont

OTHER OFFICES

LAMONT PRIDMORE
8 Stanger Street, Keswick, CUMBRIA CA12 5JU
Tel: + *44* (7687) 72182 *Fax:* + *44* (7687) 71388

Total Number of Offices: 2

LANHAM & FRANCIS

60 Princes Street, YEOVIL, Somerset BA20 1HL
Tel: + *44* (935) 76401
Fax: + *44* (935) 33534

European Affiliation: Midsnell International

International Contact: Stephen J. Guppy

Total Number of Offices: 7

LARKINGS

31 St George's Place, CANTERBURY, Kent CT1 1XD
Tel: + *44* (227) 464991
Fax: + *44* (227) 451796

National Affiliation: The UK 200 Group of Practising Accountants

International Contact: Roger J. Clarke

Partners:	8
Professional staff:	43
Non-professional staff:	16
Total Staff:	**67**

CONTACT INFORMATION

Managing Partner: Roger J. Clarke
Accountancy & Administration: Roger J. Clarke
Audit: Michael J. Moore
Corporate Finance: Geoffrey D. Smith
Management Consultancy: Jake H. Davies
Tax: John S. Penrose

CLIENT SERVICES

Accountancy (General), Audit, Computer Installation, Corporate Finance Advice, Management & Business Advice, Management Buy-outs, Mergers & Acquisitions, Pensions Planning, Taxation (Corporate), Taxation (International), Trust Settlement & Estates

Industry Specialisations: Farming, Building

OTHER OFFICES

LARKINGS
The Clergy House, Churchyard, ASHFORD, Kent TN23 1QG
Tel: + *44* (233) 621271 *Fax:* + *44* (233) 610528
Contact: Peter J.C. Canney

LARKINGS
Cornwallis House, Pudding Lane, MAIDSTONE, Kent ME14 1NH
Tel: + *44* (622) 754033 *Fax:* + *44* (622) 679732
Contact: John S. Penrose

LARKINGS
82a Sandgate High Street, SANDGATE, Kent CT20 3BX
Tel: + 44 (303) 48485 *Fax:* + 44 (303) 49339
Contact: Martin Ades

LARKINGS
7 Park Road, SITTINGBOURNE, Kent ME10 1DR
Tel: + 44 (795) 472265 *Fax:* + 44 (795) 470928
Contact: John C. Selwood

Total Number of Offices: 5

LATHAM CROSSLEY & DAVIS

Arkwright House, Parsonage Gardens, MANCHESTER M3 2LE
Tel: + 44 (61) 834 3313
Fax: + 44 (61) 835 3480

International Contact: David Wood

Partners:	16
Professional staff:	160
Non-professional staff:	90
Total Staff:	**266**

CONTACT INFORMATION

Managing Partner: Keith Seeley
Audit: Derek Warren
Corporate Finance: Helen Ashcroft
Insolvency: David Wood
Insolvency: Peter Dunn
Insolvency: Michael Appleby
Management Consultancy: Martin Kirby
Accountancy & Audit: Ian Simmonds
Tax: Mike Cochrane

CLIENT SERVICES

All Services

Industry Specialisations: Construction, Agriculture, Privately-owned Manufacturing

OTHER OFFICES

LATHAM CROSSLEY & DAVIS
Sumner House, St Thomas's Road, CHORLEY, Lancashire PR7 1HP
Tel: + 44 (257) 272441 *Fax:* + 44 (257) 261754
Contact: Keith Seeley

LATHAM CROSSLEY & DAVIS
152 Wigan Lane, WIGAN, Lancashire WN1 2LA
Tel: + 44 (942) 41854 *Fax:* + 44 (942) 497826
Contact: Martin Kirby

LATHAM CROSSLEY & DAVIS
45 Conduit Sreet, LONDON W1R 9FB
Tel: + 44 (71) 408 1868 *Fax:* + 44 (71) 287 1045
Contact: Peter Dunn

LATHAM CROSSLEY & DAVIS
7-9 Crow Lane, ROCHESTER, Kent ME1 1RF
Tel: + 44 (634) 848334

LATHAM CROSSLEY & DAVIS
Suite 203, Winpenny House, 135-137 High Street, YARM, Cleveland TS15 8AY

LATHAM CROSSLEY & DAVIS
57a Fawcett Street, SUNDERLAND SR1 1SR
Tel: + 44 (91) 565 2767

LATHAM CROSSLEY & DAVIS
5th Floor, Cale Cross House, Pilgrim Street, NEWCASTLE-UPON-TYNE NE1 6SU

Total Number of Offices: 8

LEIGH CARR

27-31 Blandford Street, LONDON W1H 3AD
Tel: + 44 (71) 935 7755
Fax: + 44 (71) 935 9172

European Affiliation: The Channel International Association

International Contact: Peter Galloway

Partners:	20
Professional staff:	100
Non-professional staff:	15
Total Staff:	**135**

FEE INCOME

Year End: 30.04.91	%
Accountancy & Audit:	76.0
Insolvency:	2.0
Consultancy:	2.0
Tax:	10.0
Other:	10.0

CONTACT INFORMATION

Managing Partner: Andrew Kaye
Corporate Finance: Laurence Sacker
Management Consultancy: Derek Levy
Tax (Corporate): Howard Shelter
Tax (International): Martin Miller
Litigation, Accountancy & Audit: Rakesh Kapila
Insolvency & Administration: Andrew Kaye

CLIENT SERVICES

Accountancy (General), Audit, Computer Installation, Corporate Finance Advice, Insolvency & Corporate Restructuring, Litigation/Legal Services, Management & Business Advice, Management Buy-outs, Mergers & Acquisitions, Taxation (Corporate), Taxation (International), Trust Settlement & Estates

Industry Specialisations: Property, Leisure

MAJOR CLIENTS

The Brent Walker Group plc

LEVY GEE

100 Chalk Farm Road, LONDON NW1 8EH
Tel: + 44 (71) 267 4477
Fax: + 44 (71) 267 1028

European Affiliation: The International Group of Accounting Firms Ltd (IGAF)

International Contact: Leon Nahon

Partners:	27
Professional staff:	143
Non-professional staff:	58
Total Staff:	**228**

FEE INCOME

Year End: 30.04.91	£	%
Accountancy & Audit:	4,700,000	42.0
Insolvency:	3,200,000	29.0
Consultancy:	1,000,000	9.0
Tax:	1,600,000	13.0
Other:	700,000	7.0
Total:	**11,200,000**	

CONTACT INFORMATION

Chairman: Malcolm Gee
Managing Partner: Stephen Raznick
Accountancy (General): Jonathan Hoffman
Audit: Tony Simons
Insolvency: Derrick Woolf
Administration: Stephen Raznick

▷

Tax (Corporate): Paul Belsman
Tax (International): Colin Barratt
Corporate Finance & Consultancy: Graham Woolfman

CLIENT SERVICES
All Services

Industry Specialisations: Professional Partnerships, Gaming, Leisure

LEVY GEE & PARTNERS

4th Floor, Southfield House, 11 Liverpool Gardens, WORTHING, West Sussex BN11 1RY
Tel: + *44* (903) 206841
Fax: + *44* (903) 207009

National Affiliation: The CharterGroup Partnership

International Contact: Ivor Richards

OTHER OFFICES

LEVY GEE & PARTNERS
7th Floor, Wettern House, 56 Dingwall Road, CROYDON CR9 2PN
Tel: + *44* (81) 681 8389 *Fax:* + *44* (81) 681 8402

Total Number of Offices: 2

LEWIS, ALEXANDER & COLLINS

103 Portland Street, MANCHESTER M1 6DF
Tel: + *44* (61) 236 5175
Fax: + *44* (61) 228 6297

National Affiliation: The CharterGroup Partnership

International Contact: S. Hoffman

FEE INCOME

Year End: 30.06.91	**£**	**%**
Accountancy & Audit:	440,000	79.0
Insolvency:	30,000	6.0
Consultancy:	55,000	10.0
Tax:	25,000	5.0
Total:	**550,000**	

CONTACT INFORMATION
Managing Partner: Michael D. Alexander

LISHMAN, SIDWELL, CAMPBELL & PRICE

Becket's House, 34 Market Place, RIPON, North Yorkshire HG4 1BZ
Tel: + *44* (765) 600681
Fax: + *44* (765) 601658
National Affiliation: The CharterGroup Partnership

Partners:	9
Professional staff:	5
Non-professional staff:	45
Total Staff:	**59**

CONTACT INFORMATION
Managing Partner: Barrie Price
Audit: D. Randles
Corporate Finance: L. Mason
Management Consultancy: B. Price
Accountancy & Farming: B. Elsworth
Tax & Administration: I. Jones

CLIENT SERVICES
All Services

Industry Specialisations: Farming

OTHER OFFICES

LISHMAN, SIDWELL, CAMPBELL & PRICE
8 York Place, KNARESBOROUGH, North Yorkshire HG5 0AA
Tel: + *44* (423) 864964
Contact: John Darnbrough

LISHMAN, SIDWELL, CAMPBELL & PRICE
Fountain Court, 8 St James Square, Boroughbridge, YORK YO5 9AR
Tel: + *44* (423) 323757
Contact: David Randles

LISHMAN, SIDWELL, CAMPBELL & PRICE
80-81 High Street, NORTHALLERTON, North Yorkshire DL7 8EG
Tel: + *44* (609) 779400
Contact: Peter Tarren

LISHMAN, SIDWELL, CAMPBELL & PRICE
73 Duke Street, DARLINGTON, Co Durham DL3 7SD
Tel: + *44* (325) 465797 *Fax:* + *44* (325) 467063
Contact: Ken Jowett

LISHMAN, SIDWELL, CAMPBELL & PRICE
9 York Place, LEEDS LS1 2DS
Tel: + *44* (532) 444411 *Fax:* + *44* (532) 448416
Contact: Tim Jones

LISHMAN, SIDWELL, CAMPBELL & PRICE
26 High Street, WETHERBY, West Yorkshire LS22 4LT
Tel: + *44* (937) 63939
Contact: Nick Price

LISHMAN, SIDWELL, CAMPBELL & PRICE
29 Blossom Street, YORK YO2 2AQ
Tel: + *44* (904) 630221 *Fax:* + *44* (904) 623056
Contact: Justin Williams

LISHMAN, SIDWELL, CAMPBELL & PRICE
5a Finkle Street, THIRSK, North Yorkshire YO7 1DA
Tel: + *44* (845) 523621
Contact: John Darnbrough

LISHMAN, SIDWELL, CAMPBELL & PRICE
Marlborough House, Marlborough Road, off Manning Lane, BRADFORD, West Yorkshire BD8 7LD
Tel: + *44* (274) 481240
Contact: Les Mason

LISHMAN, SIDWELL, CAMPBELL & PRICE
Lishman Chambers, 12 Princes Square, HARROGATE, North Yorkshire HG1 1LY
Tel: + *44* (423) 568888 *Fax:* + *44* (423) 505522
Contact: Richard Pugh

Total Number of Offices: 11

LITTLEJOHN FRAZER

1 Park Place, Canary Wharf, LONDON E14 4HJ
Tel: + *44* (71) 987 5030
Fax: + *44* (71) 987 9707

European Affiliation: Independent Accountants International

International Contact: I. Frazer

Partners:	30
Professional staff:	145
Non-professional staff:	78
Total Staff:	**253**

FEE INCOME

Year End: 31.08.91	**£**	**%**
Accountancy & Audit:	5,600,000	52.3
Consultancy:	600,000	5.6
Tax:	4,100,000	38.3
Other:	400,000	3.8
Total:	**10,700,000**	

CONTACT INFORMATION
Managing Partner: Alastair Campbell
Accountancy (General): Melvin Crutchley
Audit: Mary Stenson
Corporate Finance: Ian Frazer
Management Consultancy: Graham Matthews
Administration: Roland Hitchcock
Public Sector: David Roberts
Tax: Debbie Annells

CLIENT SERVICES
Accountancy (General), Audit, Computer Installation, Corporate Finance Advice, Litigation/Legal Services, Management & Business Advice, Management Buy-outs, Mergers & Acquisitions, Taxation (Corporate), Taxation (International), Trust Settlement & Estates, Lloyds of London

Industry Specialisations: Wine & Spirits, Transport & Distribution, Professional Practices

LONGCROFTS
Longcroft House, Victoria Avenue, Bishopsgate, LONDON EC2M 4NS
Tel: +44 (71) 623 6626
Fax: +44 (71) 623 4997

International Contact: James Longcroft

Total Number of Offices: 3

LONSDALE & PARTNERS
Priory Close, St Mary's Gate, LANCASTER LA1 1XB
Tel: +44 (524) 62801
Fax: +44 (524) 37764

National Affiliation: The CharterGroup Partnership

Partners:	6
Professional staff:	55
Non-professional staff:	10
Total Staff:	**71**

FEE INCOME
Year End: 30.04.91	**£**	**%**
Accountancy & Audit:		60.0
Tax:		30.0
Other:		10.0
Total:	**1,500,000**	

CONTACT INFORMATION
Managing Partner: Chris Oddie

CLIENT SERVICES
All Services

OTHER OFFICES
LONSDALE & PARTNERS
11 Northumberland Street, MORECAMBE, Lancashire LA4 4AU
Tel: +44 (524) 410311 *Fax:* +44 (524) 832279
Contact: Warwick Wilson

LONSDALE & PARTNERS
53 Highgate, KENDAL, Cumbria LA9 4ED
Tel: +44 (539) 729727 *Fax:* +44 (539) 740929
Contact: Michael Proudfoot

LONSDALE & PARTNERS
55 Main Street, Kirkby Lonsdale, CARNFORTH, Lancashire LA6 2AH
Tel: +44 (5242) 71402 *Fax:* +44 (5242) 72318
Contact: Ian MacGregor

Total Number of Offices: 4

LOVEWELL BLAKE
102 Prince of Wales Road, NORWICH NR1 1NY
Tel: +44 (603) 663300
Fax: +44 (603) 619459

European Affiliation: Moores Rowland International

International Contact: George J.R. Isbell

OTHER OFFICES
LOVEWELL BLAKE
Cedar House, White Hart Street, AYLESHAM, Norfolk NR11 6HG
Tel: +44 (263) 732151 *Fax:* +44 (263) 732302

LOVEWELL BLAKE
49 Smallgate, BECCLES, Suffolk NR34 9AE
Tel: +44 (502) 713251 *Fax:* +44 (232) 713148

LOVEWELL BLAKE
Havenbridge House, North Quay, GREAT YARMOUTH, Norfolk NR30 1HE
Tel: +44 (493) 858131 *Fax:* +44 (493) 850408

LOVEWELL BLAKE
16 Bridge Street, HALESWORTH, Suffolk IP19 8AG
Tel: +44 (9867) 3163 *Fax:* +44 (9867) 4523

LOVEWELL BLAKE
Old Market Street, THETFORD, Norfolk IP24 2EN
Tel: +44 (842) 755032 *Fax:* +44 (842) 762753

LOVEWELL BLAKE
Ocean View, 30 Suffolk Road, LOWESTOFT, Suffolk NR3 1DW
Tel: +44 (502) 563921 *Fax:* +44 (502) 584630

LOVEWELL BLAKE
Brentnall House, Vicarage Street, NORTH WALSHAM, Norfolk NR28 9DQ
Tel: +44 (5308) 5399

Total Number of Offices: 8

LUBBOCK FINE
Russell Bedford House, City Forum, 250 City Road, LONDON EC1V 2QQ
Tel: +44 (71) 490 7766
Fax: +44 (71) 490 5102

European Affiliation: Russell Bedford International

International Contact: Geoffrey Goodyear

McCRACKENS
Hanover House, 117-119 Cleethorpe Road, GRIMSBY,
South Humberside DN31 3ET
Tel: +44 (472) 355215
Fax: +44 (472) 242600

European Affiliation: INPACT - International Network of Professional Accountants

Partners:	2
Professional staff:	6
Non-professional staff:	22
Total Staff:	**30**

CONTACT INFORMATION
Managing Partner: Douglas P. Everitt
Accountancy (General): David R. Hatford
Tax: Peter Wilkinson

CLIENT SERVICES
Accountancy (General), Audit, Computer Installation, Corporate Finance Advice, Management & Business Advice, Mergers & Acquisitions, Pensions Planning, Taxation (Corporate), Trust Settlement & Estates ▷

McKENZIE & COMPANY

14a Station Road West, OXTED, Surrey RH8 9EP
Tel: + *44* (883) 717077
Fax: + *44* (883) 712243

National Affiliation: The CharterGroup Partnership

International Contact: Bernard J. McKenzie

Partners:	2
Professional staff:	16
Non-professional staff:	4
Total Staff:	**22**

FEE INCOME

Year End: 31.12.90	%
Accountancy & Audit:	50.0
Consultancy:	25.0
Tax:	25.0

CONTACT INFORMATION
Accountancy, Tax & Administration: Bernard J. McKenzie
Audit, Corporate Finance & Consultancy: P.S. Baker
Management Consultancy: T. Horsfall
Tax: J. Pullinger

CLIENT SERVICES
All Services

MANN, JUDD, GORDON

26 Lewis Street, STORNOWAY, Isle of Lewis PA87 2JF
Tel: + *44* (851) 702335
Fax: + *44* (851) 706132

European Affiliation: Moores Rowland International

International Contact: Jack Kernahan

Partners:	2
Professional staff:	4
Non-professional staff:	4
Total Staff:	**10**

FEE INCOME

Year End: 30.04.91	£	%
Accountancy & Audit:	156,707	76.0
Other:	49,487	24.0
Total:	**206,194**	

CONTACT INFORMATION
Managing Partner: Jack Kernahan
Accountancy (General): R.H. MacLeod
Accountancy, Audit & Tax: Jack Kernahan

CLIENT SERVICES
Accountancy (General), Audit, Taxation (Corporate), Computer Book-keeping Bureau

McPHERSON & PARTNERS

23 St Leonards Road, BEXHILL-ON-SEA, East Sussex TN40 1HH
Tel: + *44* (424) 730000
Fax: + *44* (424) 730489

National Affiliation: The UK 200 Group of Practising Accountants

International Contact: Keith McPherson

CONTACT INFORMATION
Partner: Keith McPherson
Partner: Alan G. Buontempo
Partner: Nigel S.G. Harper

OTHER OFFICES

McPHERSON & PARTNERS
49 Havelock Road, HASTINGS, East Sussex TN34 1BE

THORP & CO
45 High Street, BATTLE, East Sussex TN33 0EE

Total Number of Offices: 3

MENZIES

Sandringham, Guildford Road, WOKING, Surrey GU22 7QL
Tel: + *44* (483) 755000
Fax: + *44* (483) 756661

International Contact: Richard Dodd

Partners:	17
Professional staff:	113
Non-professional staff:	39
Total Staff:	**169**

FEE INCOME

Year End: 30.06.90	£	%
Accountancy & Audit:	3,630,000	55.0
Consultancy:	1,320,000	20.0
Tax:	1,650,000	25.0
Total:	**6,600,000**	

CONTACT INFORMATION
Managing Partner: Maurice Tate
Accountancy (General): Terence Gale
Audit: Andrew Denley
Corporate Finance: Andrew Day
Management Consultancy: Michael Sands
Administration: Trevor Ansell
Tax (Corporate & International): Barry Gay

CLIENT SERVICES
All Services, Personnel recruitment

OTHER OFFICES

MENZIES
The Chestnuts, 18 East Street, FARNHAM, Surrey GU9 7SD
Tel: + *44* (252) 712828 *Fax:* + *44* (252) 733670
Contact: Colin F. Bonner

MENZIES
116 Richmond Road, KINGSTON-UPON-THAMES, Surrey KT2 5EP
Tel: + *44* (81) 546 4441 *Fax:* + *44* (81) 541 5820
Contact: Maurice S. Tate

MENZIES
1 The Quadrangle, Church Street, SLOUGH, Berkshire SL1 1PH
Tel: + *44* (753) 20175 *Fax:* + *44* (252) 733670
Contact: Terence Gale

MENZIES
57 Church Street, STAINES, Middlesex TW18 4XS
Tel: + *44* (784) 462121 *Fax:* + *44* (784) 460237
Contact: Julie B. Adams

MENZIES
Ashby House, 64 High Street, WALTON-ON-THAMES, Surrey KT12 1BW
Tel: + *44* (932) 247611 *Fax:* + *44* (932) 246457
Contact: Andrew J. Day

Total Number of Offices: 6

MIDGLEY, SNELLING & CO

6th Floor, 9 Kingsway, LONDON WC2B 6XF
Tel: + *44* (71) 836 9671
Fax: + *44* (71) 836 0573

European Affiliation: Midsnell International

International Contact: Stephen Yeates

Partners:	8

CONTACT INFORMATION
Managing Partner: Chris Snelling
Accountancy (General): James Midgley
Audit: Martyn Cayless
Insolvency: Chris Britten
Tax (Corporate): Paul Chamberlain
Tax (International): Robin Sewell
Tax (International): Andrew Grout

CLIENT SERVICES
Accountancy (General), Audit, Computer Installation, Insolvency & Corporate Restructuring, Management & Business Advice, Taxation (Corporate), Taxation (International), Trust Settlement & Estates, International Fiscal Planning

Industry Specialisations: Film & Entertainment

OTHER OFFICES
MIDGLEY, SNELLING & CO
Ibex House, Baker Street, WEYBRIDGE, Surrey KT13 8AH
Tel: + *44* (932) 853393 *Fax:* + *44* (932) 854323
Contact: Stephen Yeates

Total Number of Offices: 2

R.F. MILLER & COMPANY
102 Duke Street, BARROW-IN-FURNESS, Cumbria LA14 1RD
Tel: + *44* (229) 820003
Fax: + *44* (229) 870116

National Affiliation: The CharterGroup Partnership

International Contact: Terry Crossley

OTHER OFFICES
R.F. MILLER & COMPANY
Central Buildings, 9 Brogden Street, ULVERSTON, Cumbria LA12 7AH
Tel: + *44* (229) 52149

Total Number of Offices: 2

MILNE ROSS
Chapel House, 24 Nutford Place, LONDON W1H 6AE
Tel: + *44* (71) 262 7788
Fax: + *44* (71) 724 6953

National Affiliation: ASSOCIATION OF PRACTISING ACCOUNTANTS

Partners:	20
Professional staff:	83
Non-professional staff:	38
Total Staff:	**141**

FEE INCOME

Year End: 31.05.91	**£**	**%**
Accountancy & Audit:	6,000,000	60.0
Consultancy:	500,000	6.0
Tax:	1,750,000	34.0
Total:	**8,250,000**	

CONTACT INFORMATION
Managing Partner: Roger Alexander
Corporate Finance: David McSweeney
Administration: Nigel Tristem
Tax (Corporate): Tom Dean
Tax (International): Alan Stroud
Accountancy & Audit: Terry Saunders
Marketing: Keith Humphrey

CLIENT SERVICES
Accountancy (General), Audit, Corporate Finance Advice, Management & Business Advice, Management Buy-outs, Mergers & Acquisitions, Pensions Planning, Taxation (Corporate), Taxation (International), Trust Settlement & Estates

Industry Specialisations: Engineering Consultancy, Architects, Dentists

MAJOR CLIENTS
W.S. Atkins Group Ltd, Securicor plc

OTHER OFFICES
MILNE ROSS
Chapel House, Westmead Drive, Westlea, SWINDON SN5 7UW
Tel: + *44* (793) 511300 *Fax:* + *44* (793) 51123
Contact: Richard Casling

MILNE ROSS
Neville House, 55 Eden Street, KINGSTON-UPON-THAMES, Surrey KT1 1BW
Tel: + *44* (81) 541 0144 *Fax:* + *44* (81) 541 5165
Contact: Keith Humphrey

Total Number of Offices: 3

MITCHELL CHARLESWORTH
Chavasse Court, 24 Lord Street, LIVERPOOL L2 1TA
Tel: + *44* (51) 707 1177
Fax: + *44* (51) 707 1777

International Contact: C.H. Plummer

Partners:	10
Professional staff:	62
Non-professional staff:	27
Total Staff:	**99**

CONTACT INFORMATION
Chairman: T. Morris
Managing Partner: D. Darlington
Accountancy (General): R.A.K. Hopping
Insolvency: G.M. Weisgard
Management Consultancy: C.B. Mitchell
Administration: D. Darlington
Public Sector & Tax: D.J. Antonia
Audit & Housing Associations: Paul N. Wainwright
Corporate Finance & Tax: C.H. Plummer

CLIENT SERVICES
Accountancy (General), Audit, Computer Installation, Corporate Finance Advice, Insolvency & Corporate Restructuring, Life & Risk Assurance, Litigation/Legal Services, Management & Business Advice, Management Buy-outs, Mergers & Acquisitions, Pensions Planning, Taxation (Corporate), Taxation (International), Trust Settlement & Estates, Taxation (Personal)

Industry Specialisations: Tanneries, Housing Associations, Construction, Larger Family Companies

MAJOR CLIENTS
Edward Billington & Son Ltd, British Leather Ltd, Kirby Tyres Ltd, Liverpool Tanning Ltd, Portgrade Ltd, Spencer Holdings plc, Trafford Chemicals Ltd, Walker Property plc, Ward, Ashcroft & Parkman Ltd

OTHER OFFICES
MITCHELL CHARLESWORTH
Fountain Court, 68 Fountain Street, MANCHESTER M2 2FB
Tel: + *44* (61) 228 7883 *Fax:* + *44* (61) 236 3268
Contact: David Frangleton

MITCHELL CHARLESWORTH
Victoria House, 488 Knutsford Road, Latchford, WARRINGTON WA4 1DX
Tel: + *44* (925) 35141 *Fax:* + *44* (925) 55839
Contact: C.B. Mitchell

▷

MITCHELL CHARLESWORTH
101 Albert Road, WIDNES, Cheshire WA8 6LD
Tel: + *44* (51) 423 2557 *Fax:* + *44* (51) 495 2557
Contact: David Antonia

MITCHELL CHARLESWORTH
107a Main Street, Frodsham, WARRINGTON WA6 7AB
Tel: + *44* (928) 33220
Contact: Richard A.K. Hopping

Total Number of Offices: 5

MOFFAT & CO

5 Clarendon Place, LEAMINGTON SPA, Warwickshire CV32 5QL
Tel: + *44* (926) 334373
Fax: + *44* (926) 881464

European Affiliation: INPACT - International Network of Professional Accountants

International Contact: Sheilagh Moffat

Partners:	3
Professional staff:	8
Non-professional staff:	2
Total Staff:	**13**

FEE INCOME

Year End: 30.06.91	%
Accountancy & Audit:	70.0
Tax:	25.0
Other:	5.0

CONTACT INFORMATION

Chairman: David C. Moffat
Managing Partner: Sheilagh Moffat
Accountancy, Audit & Administration: Sheilagh Moffat
Accountancy & Audit: Greg Smout
Tax: David C. Moffat

CLIENT SERVICES

Accountancy (General), Audit, Corporate Finance Advice, Management & Business Advice, Management Buy-outs, Mergers & Acquisitions, Pensions Planning, Value for Money Studies, Taxation (Corporate), Taxation (International), Trust Settlement & Estates, Payroll Bureau

Industry Specialisations: Building, Property Developement

MOORE FLETCHER & CO

26 Paradise Square, SHEFFIELD S1 1TU
Tel: + *44* (742) 768491
Fax: + *44* (742) 739935

European Affiliation: INPACT - International Network of Professional Accountants

International Contact: John E. Moore

Partners:	4
Professional staff:	4
Non-professional staff:	10
Total Staff:	**18**

FEE INCOME

Year End: 1990	%
Accountancy & Audit:	75.0
Consultancy:	5.0
Tax:	20.0

CONTACT INFORMATION

Senior Partner: John E. Moore
Accountancy (General): Robert Matthews
Corporate Finance: John Elston
Tax (Corporate): Christopher Rawlins

CLIENT SERVICES

Accountancy (General), Audit, Computer Installation, Corporate Finance Advice, Management & Business Advice, Management Buy-outs, Mergers & Acquisitions, Pensions Planning, Value for Money Studies, Taxation (Corporate), Taxation (International), Trust Settlement & Estates, Corporate Restructuring

Industry Specialisations: Engineering, Steel, Iron Foundries, Wholesale Distribution, Motor Trade

MOORE STEPHENS

St Paul's House, Warwick Lane, LONDON EC4P 4BN
Tel: + *44* (71) 248 4499
Fax: + *44* (71) 248 3408

European Affiliation: Moore Stephens

International Contact: Paul Stockton

Partners:	123
Professional staff:	698
Non-professional staff:	264
Total Staff:	**1,085**

FEE INCOME

Year End: 31.12.90	**£**	%
Accountancy & Audit:	15,400,000	44.5
Insolvency:	300,000	1.0
Consultancy:	6,300,000	18.3
Tax:	10,800,000	31.3
Other:	1,800,000	6.0
Total:	**34,600,000**	

CONTACT INFORMATION

Chairman: Michael Hathorn
Managing Partner: Richard Moore
Corporate Finance: Arthur Davy
Insolvency: David Rolph
Management Consultancy: Alan Cox
Administration: John Baylis
Public Sector: Gervase Hulbert
Accountancy & Audit: Richard Moore
Tax: Stephen Hogg
Marketing: Nicholas Hilton

CLIENT SERVICES

All Services, Project Management, Company Secretarial Services

Industry Specialisations: Shipping, Insurance

OTHER OFFICES

MOORE STEPHENS
30 Gay Street, BATH BA1 2PA
Tel: + *44* (225) 424281 *Fax:* + *44* (225) 448198
Contact: Nicholas Brown

MOORE STEPHENS
St Philips House, St Philips Place, BIRMINGHAM B3 2PP
Tel: + *44* (21) 200 3077 *Fax:* + *44* (21) 200 2454
Contact: Peter R. Moore

MOORE STEPHENS
Cross Lane House, Crown Street, CLEAKHEATON, West Yorkshire BD19 3NF
Tel: + *44* (274) 874867 *Fax:* + *44* (274) 851242
Contact: Philip Broomhead

MOORE STEPHENS
Stuart House, Elizabeth Street, CORBY, Northamptonshire NN17 1SN
Tel: + *44* (536) 200999 *Fax:* + *44* (536) 204494
Contact: Fred Murphy

MOORE STEPHENS
Trafalgar House, King Street, DUDLEY, West Midlands DY2 8PS
Tel: + *44* (384) 239996 *Fax:* + *44* (384) 456145
Contact: David Barrett

MOORE STEPHENS
17 Melville Street, EDINBURGH EH3 7PH
Tel: + 44 (31) 225 3820 *Fax:* + 44 (31) 225 9829
Contact: Michael Hathorn

MOORE STEPHENS
Ross House, Windmill Hill, ENFIELD, Middlesex EN2 6SW
Tel: + 44 (81) 366 4331 *Fax:* + 44 (81) 367 8246
Contact: Douglas Fussell

MOORE STEPHENS
Lister House, Lord Street, HALIFAX HX1 5AE
Tel: + 44 (422) 341881 *Fax:* + 44 (422) 349517
Contact: Michael J. Addy

MOORE STEPHENS
Norwich Union House, High Street, HUDDERSFIELD HD1 2LN
Tel: + 44 (484) 538351 *Fax:* + 44 (484) 513522
Contact: Roger S. Armitage

MOORE STEPHENS
Aspen House, 14 Station Road, KETTERING, Northamptonshire NN15 7HE
Tel: + 44 (536) 517636 *Fax:* + 44 (536) 513562
Contact: David E. Sharp

MOORE STEPHENS
Airedale House, 77 Albion Street, LEEDS LS1 5HT
Tel: + 44 (532) 451483 *Fax:* + 44 (532) 426124
Contact: N. Christopher Makin

MOORE STEPHENS
42 Castle Street, LIVERPOOL L2 7TJ
Tel: + 44 (51) 236 9044 *Fax:* + 44 (51) 231 1267
Contact: Brian McGain

MOORE STEPHENS
The Old Bank, 10 High Street, MALMESBURY, Wiltshire SN16 9AU
Tel: + 44 (666) 823201 *Fax:* + 44 (666) 825295
Contact: John Glasby

MOORE STEPHENS
50-51 Hungate, PICKERING, North Yorkshire YO18 7DG
Tel: + 44 (751) 72949 *Fax:* + 44 (723) 500564
Contact: Stephen Clough

MOORE STEPHENS
65 New Street, SALISBURY SP1 2PH
Tel: + 44 (722) 335182 *Fax:* + 44 (722) 412154
Contact: Graham J. Tate

MOORE STEPHENS
12/13 Alma Square, SCARBOROUGH, North Yorkshire YO11 1JU
Tel: + 44 (723) 260361 *Fax:* + 44 (723) 500564
Contact: Stephen Watson

MOORE STEPHENS
The Grey House, 3 Broad Street, STAMFORD, Lincolnshire PE9 1PB
Tel: + 44 (780) 63855
Contact: O.N.N. Hart

MOORE STEPHENS
38 High Street West, UPPINGHAM, Leicestershire LE15 9QD
Tel: + 44 (572) 823291 *Fax:* + 44 (572) 823241
Contact: R.W. Foster

MOORE STEPHENS
33 Sayce Street, WIDNES, Cheshire WA8 6EE
Tel: + 44 (51) 423 5265
Contact: Stephen Jones

MOORE STEPHENS
2nd Floor, Wotton Chambers, 6 Market Street, WOTTON-UNDER-EDGE, Gloucestershire GL12 7AE
Tel: + 44 (453) 845146 *Fax:* + 44 (453) 845095
Contact: Alan Cavill

MOORE STEPHENS
Charter House, Watercombe Lane, Lynx West, YEOVIL, Somerset BA20 1QD
Tel: + 44 (935) 22362 *Fax:* + 44 (935) 32604
Contact: David Whalley

MOORE STEPHENS
Steward House, Sydenham Road, GUILDFORD, Surrey GU1 3SR
Tel: + 44 (483) 38881 *Fax:* + 44 (483) 37331
Contact: Ian Spring

MOORE STEPHENS
Pride Hill House, 23 St Mary's Street, SHREWSBURY SY1 1ED
Tel: + 44 (743) 235276 *Fax:* + 44 (743) 66502
Contact: Peter Forrester

ASSOCIATED FIRMS

BLYTHENS
Haydn House, 309-329 Haydn Road, Sherwood, NOTTINGHAM NG5 1HG
Tel: + 44 (602) 607111 *Fax:* + 44 (602) 691313
Contact: John Foxon

Total Number of Offices: 37

MOORES ROWLAND

Clifford's Inn, Fetter Lane, LONDON EC4A 1AS
Tel: + 44 (71) 831 2345
Fax: + 44 (71) 831 6123

European Affiliation: Moores Rowland International

International Contact: Joe M. Michaelson

OTHER OFFICES

MOORES ROWLAND
Nile House, Nile Street, BRIGHTON BN1 1JB
Mailing Address: P.O. Box 1034, BRIGHTON BN1 1JB
Tel: + 44 (273) 24411 *Fax:* + 44 (273) 779172
Contact: Alan H. Morris

MOORES ROWLAND
11 Langton Place, Hatter Street, BURY ST EDMUNDS, Suffolk IP33 1NE
Tel: + 44 (284) 752042 *Fax:* + 44 (284) 769592
Contact: Roger A.G. Luckin

MOORES ROWLAND
115 New London Road, CHELMSFORD CM2 0QT
Tel: + 44 (245) 265777 *Fax:* + 44 (245) 260258
Contact: Noel E.B. Swan

MOORES ROWLAND
9 Bedford Park, CROYDON CR0 2AP
Tel: + 44 (81) 686 9281 *Fax:* + 44 (81) 760 0411
Contact: Ron Saunders

MOORES ROWLAND
7 Melville Crescent, EDINBURGH EH3 7NA
Tel: + 44 (31) 225 2041 *Fax:* + 44 (31) 225 6488
Contact: Ronnie Ludwig

MOORES ROWLAND
171/173 High Street, EPPING, Essex CM16 4BL
Tel: + 44 (378) 560060 *Fax:* + 44 (378) 73678
Contact: John A. Whittaker

MOORES ROWLAND
Allan House, 25 Bothwell Street, GLASGOW G2 6NL
Tel: + 44 (41) 221 6991 *Fax:* + 44 (41) 221 2685
Contact: Iain A. Paterson

MOORES ROWLAND
50 St Andrew Street, HERTFORD SG14 1JA
Tel: + 44 (992) 589321 *Fax:* + 44 (992) 582616
Contact: L.A.G. Berry

▷

MOORES ROWLAND
Applemarket House, 17 Union Street, KINGSTON-UPON-THAMES, Surrey KT1 1RP
Tel: + *44* (81) 549 6399 *Fax:* + *44* (81) 549 6209
Contact: Alan K. Skinner

MOORES ROWLAND
Hesketh House, Alderley Road, WILMSLOW, Cheshire SK9 1NX
Tel: + *44* (625) 532741 *Fax:* + *44* (625) 539951
Contact: Tony Webley

MOORES ROWLAND
Folk House, Church Street, READING RG1 2SB
Tel: + *44* (734) 594424 *Fax:* + *44* (734) 589155
Contact: Richard W. Garner

MOORES ROWLAND
7 St Botolph's Road, SEVENOAKS, Kent TN13 3AJ
Tel: + *44* (732) 460808 *Fax:* + *44* (732) 456184
Contact: Chris M. Gandon

MOORES ROWLAND
Tameway Tower, Bridge Street, WALSALL, West Midlands WS1 1QX
Mailing Address: P.O. Box 30, WALSALL, West Midlands WS1 1QX
Tel: + *44* (922) 720100 *Fax:* + *44* (922) 645775
Contact: Keith J. Ellis

MOORES ROWLAND
7/8 Bishop's Wharf, 109 South Street, BISHOP'S STORTFORD, Hertfordshire CM23 3AR
Tel: + *44* (279) 755511 *Fax:* + *44* (279) 755799
Contact: Jeremy D.B. Mitchell

MOORES ROWLAND
3rd Floor, Belgrave House, Station Way, CRAWLEY, West Sussex RH10 1HU
Tel: + *44* (293) 516099 *Fax:* + *44* (293) 516129
Contact: Geoff M. Peck

Total Number of Offices: 16

MORISON STONEHAM

805 Salisbury House, 31 Finsbury Circus, LONDON EC2M 5SQ
Tel: + *44* (71) 628 2040
Fax: + *44* (71) 628 7531

European Affiliation: Morison International

International Contact: Martin Silverman

Partners:	17
Professional staff:	81
Non-professional staff:	48
Total Staff:	**146**

FEE INCOME

Year End: 30.04.91	**£**
Total:	**6,100,000**

CONTACT INFORMATION

Managing Partner: Stephen Chang
Accountancy (General): Elaine Oddie
Audit: Richard Kennett
Insolvency: Grant Jones
Management Consultancy: Stephen Chang
Senior Partner & Corporate Finance: Martin Silverman
Tax: Jay Sanghrajka
Marketing: Gillian Angel
Litigation Support: Perry Lewis
Personnel & Recruitment: Michael Leaney
Systems & Computers: Barnie Davies

CLIENT SERVICES

All Services

Industry Specialisations: Manufacturing, Distribution, Financial Services, Retail, Leisure, Entertainment, Real Estate

MAJOR CLIENTS

A & P Roberts (Holdings) Ltd, Colt International Ltd, Dwyer plc, General Council of British Shipping, Robert Dyas Limited, Specialeyes plc, TRMS Insurance

OTHER OFFICES

MORISON STONEHAM
75 Springfield Road, CHELMSFORD CM2 6JB
Tel: + *44* (245) 492920 *Fax:* + *44* (245) 490841
Contact: Richard Harvey

MORISON STONEHAM
1 Cricklade Street, SWINDON SN1 3LP
Tel: + *44* (793) 616169 *Fax:* + *44* (793) 511944
Contact: Robin Platt

Total Number of Offices: 3

HENRY MURRAY & CO

23 Church Place, LURGAN, Co Armagh
Tel: + *44* (762) 327744
Fax: + *44* (762) 326585

European Affiliation: INPACT - International Network of Professional Accountants

International Contact: Peter Gogarty
Paul Kennedy

NASH BROAD WESSON

42 Upper Berkeley Street, LONDON W1H 8AB
Tel: + *44* (71) 723 7293
Fax: + *44* (71) 724 3488

European Affiliation: GMN International

International Contact: Michael J. Cannon

Partners:	18
Professional staff:	65
Non-professional staff:	29
Total Staff:	**112**

FEE INCOME

Year End: 30.06.91	**%**
Accountancy & Audit:	40.0
Consultancy:	20.0
Tax:	35.0
Other:	5.0

CONTACT INFORMATION

Chairman: Peter Parr-Head
Managing Partner: Michael J. Cannon
Accountancy (General): David Hull
Audit: Nicholas Morgan
Administration: Keith D. Blaxhill
Tax (Corporate): John A. Garden
Tax (International): Bryan Tarttelin
Finance & Administration Director: Simon G. Nickols

CLIENT SERVICES

Industry Specialisations: Trade Unions, Entertainment, Professional Services

ASSOCIATED FIRMS

ALEXANDER SLOAN & CO
142 St Vincent Street, GLASGOW G2 5LB
Tel: + *44* (41) 248 6976 *Fax:* + *44* (41) 221 7904
Contact: J. Willoughby

ANDERSON BURROWS
Griffin House, Digbeth Street, STOW-ON-WOLD, Gloucestershire GL54 1BS
Tel: + *44* (451) 30202
Contact: James Calver-Jones

BROWN & BUTLER & CO
Yorkshire Bank Chambers, Infirmary Street, LEEDS LS1 2JT
Tel: + *44* (532) 461234 *Fax:* + *44* (532) 423714
Contact: T.R. Gurney

DUNELL, WYCHERLEY & PARTNERS
15/17 High Street, BEDFORD MK40 1RU
Tel: + *44* (234) 349616 *Fax:* + *44* (234) 360645
Contact: Ted J. Dunnell

GRAY, McDONALD & DINNIE
7 Albert Street, ABERDEEN AB1 1XX
Tel: + *44* (224) 649494 *Fax:* + *44* (224) 644672
Contact: Ian R. Mcdonald

GRIFFIN TANNER & PARTNERS
152 Church Road, HOVE, East Sussex BN3 2DL
Tel: + *44* (273) 720316
Contact: T. Tanner

GRIFFIN & PARTNERS
38 Grosvenor Gardens, LONDON SW1W 0EB
Tel: + *44* (71) 730 6171 *Fax:* + *44* (71) 824 8685
Contact: T.A. Griffin

GRIFFIN, SUTTON & PARTNERS
207-215 High Street, ORPINGTON, Kent BR6 OPF
Tel: + *44* (689) 825731
Contact: Alan Sutton

HEATHCOTE & COLEMAN
Heathcote House, 136 Hagley Road, Edgbaston, BIRMINGHAM B16 9PN
Tel: + *44* (21) 454 4141 *Fax:* + *44* (21) 454 4949
Contact: Steven Heathcote

JAMES & CO
8 Fairfax Mansions, Finchley Road, Swiss Cottage, LONDON NW3 6JY
Tel: + *44* (71) 372 1144 *Fax:* + *44* (71) 372 0485
Contact: Peter Levey

McGUINNESS & CO
46/48 Southbourne Grove, Southbourne, BOURNEMOUTH BH6 3RB
Tel: + *44* (202) 431968 *Fax:* + *44* (202) 425530
Contact: Bill McGuinness

NASH BROAD
Queensway Chambers, 58 Queensway, STEVENAGE, Hertfordshire
SG1 1EG
Tel: + *44* (438) 312233 *Fax:* + *44* (438) 741337
Contact: Mark Stevens

PETER NICHOLAS
3 Chapel Street, CHICHESTER, West Sussex PO19 1BU
Tel: + *44* (243) 775722
Contact: P.N. Nicholas

W.H. PAYNE & CO
Sandringham House, 199 Southwark Bridge Road, LONDON SE1 OHA
Tel: + *44* (71) 407 7752 *Fax:* + *44* (71) 407 1254
Contact: Ron Smith

ROYCE, PEELING, GREEN
Hilton Chambers, 15 Hilton Street, MANCHESTER M1 1JL
Tel: + *44* (61) 236 7792 *Fax:* + *44* (61) 228 0173
Contact: John Hall

Total Number of Offices: 16

NEVILLE RUSSELL
246 Bishopsgate, LONDON EC2M 4PB
Tel: + *44* (71) 377 1000
Fax: + *44* (71) 377 8931

European Affiliation: Nexia International

International Contact: John S. Mellows

Partners:	87
Professional staff:	609
Non-professional staff:	228
Total Staff:	**924**

FEE INCOME

Year End: 30.04.91	**£**	**%**
Accountancy & Audit:	20,200,000	58.1
Insolvency:	2,000,000	5.7
Consultancy:	3,600,000	10.3
Tax:	9,000,000	25.9
Total:	**34,800,000**	

CONTACT INFORMATION
Chairman: Glyn F. Macaulay
Managing Partner: Glyn F. Macaulay
Accountancy (General): George E. Bull
Insolvency: Barry Davis
Management Consultancy: Derek G. Smith
Administration: Nicholas H. Holmes
Public Sector: John G. Chastney
Tax (Corporate): David R.B. Ingmire
Tax (International): David Ross
Audit & Corporate Finance: John S. Mellows
Personal Financial Planning: Andrew C. Burgess

CLIENT SERVICES
All Services

Industry Specialisations: Insurance & Lloyds, Housing Assns, Building Societies, Charities, Education, Professnal. Partnerships

OTHER OFFICES

NEVILLE RUSSELL
19 Goldington Road, BEDFORD MK40 3JY
Tel: + *44* (234) 273500 *Fax:* + *44* (234) 273600

NEVILLE RUSSELL
Britannia House, 50 Great Charles Street, Queensway, BIRMINGHAM B3 2LY
Tel: + *44* (21) 236 7711 *Fax:* + *44* (21) 236 2778

NEVILLE RUSSELL
37 Frederick Place, BRIGHTON BN1 4EA
Tel: + *44* (273) 206788 *Fax:* + *44* (273) 820901

NEVILLE RUSSELL
Clifton Down House, Beaufort Buildings, Clifton Down, Clifton, BRISTOL BS8 4AN
Tel: + *44* (272) 734481 *Fax:* + *44* (272) 745203

NEVILLE RUSSELL
Russell House, 1 The Inhedge, DUDLEY, West Midlands DY1 1RR
Tel: + *44* (384) 230432 *Fax:* + *44* (384) 239635

NEVILLE RUSSELL
90 St Vincent Street, GLASGOW G2 5UB
Tel: + *44* (41) 226 4924 *Fax:* + *44* (41) 204 1338

NEVILLE RUSSELL
Spencer House, 29 Grove Hill Road, HARROW, Middlesex HA1 3UP
Tel: + *44* (81) 427 8868 *Fax:* + *44* (81) 427 2341

NEVILLE RUSSELL
City House, 9 Cranbrook Road, ILFORD, Essex IG1 4EA
Tel: + *44* (81) 553 0623 *Fax:* + *44* (81) 553 0729

▷

NEVILLE RUSSELL
Oxford House, 2 Oxford Row, LEEDS LS1 3BE
Tel: + *44* (532) 459637 *Fax:* + *44* (532) 448310

NEVILLE RUSSELL
Aquis House, Clasketgate, LINCOLN LN2 IJN
Tel: + *44* (522) 543051 *Fax:* + *44* (522) 543073

NEVILLE RUSSELL
1 Telford Way, LUTON LU1 1HT
Tel: + *44* (582) 23401 *Fax:* + *44* (582) 413315

NEVILLE RUSSELL
Sovereign Court, 202 Upper Fifth Street, Silbury Boulevard, CENTRAL MILTON KEYNES MK9 2JB
Tel: + *44* (908) 664466 *Fax:* + *44* (908) 690567

NEVILLE RUSSELL
9/11 Clarendon Street, NOTTINGHAM NG1 5HR
Tel: + *44* (602) 417408 *Fax:* + *44* (602) 475131

NEVILLE RUSSELL
Prama House, 267 Banbury Road, OXFORD OX2 7YA
Tel: + *44* (865) 53241 *Fax:* + *44* (865) 514833

NEVILLE RUSSELL
5 Winchester Place, North Street, POOLE, Dorset BH15 1NX
Tel: + *44* (202) 680777 *Fax:* + *44* (202) 682671

NEVILLE RUSSELL
46 Algitha Road, SKEGNESS, Lincolnshire PE25 2AJ
Tel: + *44* (754) 68313 *Fax:* + *44* (754) 4760

NEVILLE RUSSELL
Regent House, Heaton Lane, STOCKPORT, Cheshire SK4 IBS
Tel: + *44* (61) 477 4750 *Fax:* + *44* (61) 476 0533

NEVILLE RUSSELL
Raffety House, 2-4 Sutton Court Road, SUTTON, Surrey SM1 4TN
Tel: + *44* (81) 661 1826 *Fax:* + *44* (81) 643 5058

NEVILLE RUSSELL
Pearl Assurance House, Queen Street, WAKEFIELD, West Yorkshire WF1 1LE
Tel: + *44* (924) 360101 *Fax:* + *44* (924) 373840

Total Number of Offices: 20

NEWBY CASTLEMAN

110 Regent Road, LEICESTER LE1 7LT
Tel: + *44* (533) 549262
Fax: + *44* (533) 470021

National Affiliation: The UK 200 Group of Practising Accountants

International Contact: C.J. Castleman

Partners:	12
Professional staff:	90
Non-professional staff:	60
Total Staff:	**162**

CONTACT INFORMATION

Managing Partner: J.D. Castleman
Accountancy (General): J.C. Soars
Audit: M.D. Castleman
Corporate Finance: C.J. Castleman
Tax (Corporate): K.R. Harkness
Tax (International): B.W. Austin
Consultancy & Administration: S.D. Castleman
Tax (General): I.R. Fawcett

CLIENT SERVICES

All Services

OTHER OFFICES

NEWBY CASTLEMAN
Eltham House, 6 Forest Road, LOUGHBOROUGH, Leicestershire LE11 3NP
Tel: + *44* (509) 263500 *Fax:* + *44* (509) 234811
Contact: David Hastings

NEWBY CASTLEMAN
22 Park Road, MELTON MOWBRAY, Leicestershire LE13 1TT
Tel: + *44* (664) 63084 *Fax:* + *44* (664) 410013
Contact: Ian Pattinson

NEWBY CASTLEMAN
3 Pelham Court, Pelham Road, NOTTINGHAM NG5 1AP
Tel: + *44* (602) 606078 *Fax:* + *44* (602) 609879
Contact: Bryan Buck

NEWBY CASTLEMAN
23 Sttion Road, HINCKLEY, Leicestershire LE10 1AW
Tel: + *44* (455) 251150
Contact: John Soars

Total Number of Offices: 5

NICHOLS FULFORD & CO

7 Donegal Square East, BELFAST BT1 5HD
Tel: + *44* (232) 231822
Fax: + *44* (232) 438664

European Affiliation: The International Group of Accounting Firms Ltd (IGAF)

International Contact: James Fulford

Partners:	2
Professional staff:	1
Non-professional staff:	1
Total Staff:	**4**

CONTACT INFORMATION

Partner: James Fulford
Partner: Richard Nicholls

CLIENT SERVICES

Accountancy (General), Audit, Corporate Finance Advice, Life & Risk Assurance, Management & Business Advice, Pensions Planning, Taxation (Corporate)

NOTTS

1 Union Street, LUTON LU1 3AN
Tel: + *44* (582) 458777
Fax: + *44* (582) 22765

National Affiliation: The UK 200 Group of Practising Accountants

International Contact: Clive Nott

Partners:	3
Professional staff:	12
Non-professional staff:	4
Total Staff:	**19**

FEE INCOME

Year End: 31.12.90	**£**	**%**
Accountancy & Audit:	560,000	70.0
Consultancy:	40,000	5.0
Tax:	200,000	25.0
Total:	**800,000**	

CONTACT INFORMATION

Managing Partner: C.G. Nott
Audit: R.J. Philpot
Corporate Finance & Tax: C.G. Nott
Consultancy & Administration: R.D. Munday
Tax Manager: D. Kirk

CLIENT SERVICES
All Services

Industry Specialisations: Medical/Health Care

O'BRIEN & JAMES

Llanover Road, PONTYPRIDD, Mid Glamorgan CF37 4LB
Tel: + *44* (443) 400325
Fax: + *44* (443) 400375

European Affiliation: Midsnell International

International Contact: Russell de Frias

Partners:	4
Professional staff:	2
Non-professional staff:	15
Total Staff:	**21**

FEE INCOME

Year End: 31.12.90	**£**	**%**
Accountancy & Audit:		70.0
Consultancy:		5.0
Tax:		20.0
Other:		5.0
Total:	**630,000**	

CONTACT INFORMATION
Managing Partner: Mike J. O'Brien
Accountancy (General): Adrian James
Audit: Russell de Frias
Corporate Finance: Mike O'Brien
Tax (Corporate): Ken Doel
Consultancy & Administration: Adrian James
VAT: Brian Appleton

CLIENT SERVICES
Accountancy (General), Audit, Computer Installation, Corporate Finance Advice, Litigation/Legal Services, Management & Business Advice, Mergers & Acquisitions, Pensions Planning, Taxation (Corporate), Trust Settlement & Estates, Tax Investigation, VAT Specialist Advice & Services

Total Number of Offices: 2

C. O'HARA & CO.

Radleigh House, 1 Golf Road, Clarkston, GLASGOW G76 7HU
Tel: + *44* (41) 638 8216
Fax: + *44* (41) 620 0151

International Contact: C. O'Hara

Partners:	3
Professional staff:	12
Non-professional staff:	5
Total Staff:	**20**

CONTACT INFORMATION
Chairman: C. O'Hara
Accountancy & Audit: J. A'Hara
Partner: J. O'Hara
Corporate Tax Manager: Lynne Doak

CLIENT SERVICES
Accountancy (General), Audit, Computer Installation, Corporate Finance Advice, Life & Risk Assurance, Management & Business Advice, Management Buy-outs, Mergers & Acquisitions, Pensions Planning, Taxation (Corporate), Trust Settlement & Estates, Business Start-Up Advice, Grant Assistance Advice

Industry Specialisations: Construction, Charities, Property Development, Civil Engineering

PANNELL KERR FORSTER

New Garden House, 78 Hatton Garden, LONDON EC1N 8JA
Tel: + *44* (71) 831 7393
Fax: + *44* (71) 405 6736

European Affiliation: Pannell Kerr Forster Worldwide

International Contact: Claude Brown

Partners:	220
Professional staff:	1,835
Non-professional staff:	339
Total Staff:	**2,394**

FEE INCOME

Year End: 30.04.91	**£**	**%**
Accountancy & Audit:		54.5
Insolvency:		10.7
Consultancy:		4.5
Tax:		26.0
Other:		4.3
Total:	**84,600,000**	

CONTACT INFORMATION
Chairman: Richard Pearson
Managing Partner: Timothy Richmond
Corporate Finance: Steven Bruck
Insolvency: Philip Long
Management Consultancy: Michael Whelan
Administration: Anthony Butcher
Tax (Corporate): Ronald McBurnie
Tax (International): Dan Snyder
Accountancy & Audit: Anthony J. Cornelius

CLIENT SERVICES
All Services

OTHER OFFICES

PANNELL KERR FORSTER
38 Albyn Place, ABERDEEN AB9 1US
Tel: + *44* (224) 589195 *Fax:* + *44* (224) 581529
Contact: P.J. Campbell

PANNELL KERR FORSTER
8 Churchfield Court, BARNSLEY, South Yorkshire S70 OJT
Tel: + *44* (226) 282807 *Fax:* + *44* (226) 730234
Contact: William Salt

PANNELL KERR FORSTER
Pannell House, 6-7 Litfield Place, The Promenade, Clifton, BRISTOL BS8 3LX
Tel: + *44* (272) 736841 *Fax:* + *44* (272) 741238

PANNELL KERR FORSTER
18 Park Place, CARDIFF CF1 3PD
Tel: + *44* (222) 378781 *Fax:* + *44* (222) 388455

PANNELL KERR FORSTER
Jardine House, 6 Laird Street, COATBRIDGE, Lanarkshire ML5 3LJ
Tel: + *44* (236) 23144 *Fax:* + *44* (236) 28306
Contact: John Crawford

PANNELL KERR FORSTER
Norfolk House, 23 Southway, COLCHESTER CO1 1DY
Tel: + *44* (206) 563131 *Fax:* + *44* (206) 41947
Contact: Antony R. James

PANNELL KERR FORSTER
Harbourne House, 7-9 Victoria Road, DARLINGTON, County Durham DL1 5SN
Tel: + *44* (325) 382828 *Fax:* + *44* (325) 489446

PANNELL KERR FORSTER
Wilmot House, St James' Court, Friar Gate, DERBY DE1 1BT
Tel: + *44* (332) 372936 *Fax:* + *44* (332) 371449
Contact: Anthony Howell

▷

PANNELL KERR FORSTER
4 South Parade, DONCASTER, South Yorkshire DN1 2DY
Tel: + *44* (302) 340333 *Fax:* + *44* (302) 340334
Contact: E. Michael Shepherd

PANNELL KERR FORSTER
16 Rothesay Place, EDINBURGH EH3 7SQ
Tel: + *44* (31) 225 3688 *Fax:* + *44* (31) 225 6017

PANNELL KERR FORSTER
40 Wellington Street, GLASGOW G2 6RL
Tel: + *44* (41) 221 3512 *Fax:* + *44* (41) 221 9546

PANNELL KERR FORSTER
141 King Street, GREAT YARMOUTH, Norfolk NR30 2PQ
Tel: + *44* (493) 842281 *Fax:* + *44* (483) 330075
Contact: M.J. Muskett

PANNELL KERR FORSTER
Pannell House, Park Street, GUILDFORD, Surrey GU1 4HN
Tel: + *44* (483) 64646 *Fax:* + *44* (483) 578880

PANNELL KERR FORSTER
Princes House, 31 Princes Street, IPSWICH 1P1 1PU
Tel: + *44* (473) 217691 *Fax:* + *44* (473) 217691
Contact: M. Martin

PANNELL KERR FORSTER
Pannell House, 6 Queen Street, LEEDS LS1 2TW
Tel: + *44* (532) 443541 *Fax:* + *44* (532) 445560
Contact: O.T. Morton

PANNELL KERR FORSTER
Horsefair House, 3 Horsefair Street, LEICESTER LE1 5BA
Tel: + *44* (533) 625334 *Fax:* + *44* (533) 620105
Contact: Brian J. Hamblin

PANNELL KERR FORSTER
Becor House, Green Lane, LINCOLN LN6 7DL
Tel: + *44* (522) 531441 *Fax:* + *44* (522) 510185
Contact: N. Gray

PANNELL KERR FORSTER
52 Mount Pleasant, LIVERPOOL L3 5UN
Tel: + *44* (51) 708 8232 *Fax:* + *44* (51) 708 8169
Contact: J.H.H. Mounsey

PANNELL KERR FORSTER
10 Regent Road, LOWESTOFT, Suffolk NR32 1PA
Tel: + *44* (502) 574663 *Fax:* + *44* (502) 514620
Contact: D.N. Bailey

PANNELL KERR FORSTER
Christchurch House, 40 Upper George Street, LUTON LU1 2RD
Tel: + *44* (582) 22262 *Fax:* + *44* (582) 37260
Contact: John L. Wosner

PANNELL KERR FORSTER
Sovereign House, Queen Street, MANCHESTER M2 5HR
Tel: + *44* (61) 832 5481 *Fax:* + *44* (61) 832 3849
Contact: D.N. Bailey

PANNELL KERR FORSTER
16 Thorpe Road, NORWICH NR1 1RY
Tel: + *44* (603) 615914 *Fax:* + *44* (603) 661626
Contact: Graham R. Woodford

PANNELL KERR FORSTER
Regent House, Clinton Avenue, NOTTINGHAM NG5 1AZ
Tel: + *44* (602) 608171 *Fax:* + *44* (602) 603665
Contact: Anthony Howell

PANNELL KERR FORSTER
Knowle House, 4 Norfolk Park Road, SHEFFIELD S2 2QE
Tel: + *44* (742) 767991 *Fax:* + *44* (742) 753538
Contact: B.E. Smith

PANNELL KERR FORSTER
St George's Chambers, Merrial Street, NEWCASTLE-UNDER-LYME, Staffordshire ST5 2BG
Tel: + *44* (782) 632111 *Fax:* + *44* (782) 711202
Contact: Noel Fryer

PANNELL KERR FORSTER
1 St John's Street, WOODBRIDGE, Suffolk 1P12 1EB
Tel: + *44* (394) 380801 *Fax:* + *44* (3943) 2214
Contact: Marilyn Martin

PANNELL KERR FORSTER
Virginia House, The Butts, WORCESTER WR1 3PA
Tel: + *44* (905) 24437 *Fax:* + *44* (905) 29006
Contact: R.L.F. Hudson

PANNELL KERR FORSTER
3rd Floor, Northumberland House, Princess Square, NEWCASTLE-UPON-TYNE NE1 8ER
Tel: + *44* (91) 261 2214 *Fax:* + *44* (91) 261 2226
Contact: J. Stephen Askey

PANNELL KERR FORSTER
New Guild House, 45 Great Charles Street, Queensway, BIRMINGHAM B3 2LX
Tel: + *44* (21) 212 2222 *Fax:* + *44* (21) 212 2300
Contact: M.R.G. Cook

PANNELL KERR FORSTER
Central Administration, Harby Lodge, 13 Pelham Road, NOTTINGHAM NG5 1AP
Tel: + *44* (602) 606260 *Fax:* + *44* (602) 622229
Contact: Anthony Butcher

Total Number of Offices: 33

THE PARKER PARTNERSHIP

Cornelius House, 178-180 Church Road, HOVE, East Sussex BN3 2DJ
Tel: + *44* (273) 722505
Fax: + *44* (273) 204773

National Affiliation: The CharterGroup Partnership

International Contact: Stephen Monk

ROGER PEACHEY & PARTNERS

22 Chepstow Road, NEWPORT, Gwent NP9 8EA
Tel: + *44* (633) 213318
Fax: + *44* (633) 259584

National Affiliation: The CharterGroup Partnership

International Contact: Roger Peachey

OTHER OFFICES

ROGER PEACHEY & PARTNERS
21 Nevill Street, ABERGAVENNY, Gwent NP7 5AA
Tel: + *44* (873) 2124 *Fax:* + *44* (873) 6615

Total Number of Offices: 2

PETERS, ELWORTHY & MOORE

Salisbury House, Station Road, CAMBRIDGE CB1 2LA
Tel: + *44* (223) 62333
Fax: + *44* (223) 461424

National Affiliation: The CharterGroup Partnership

International Contact: David Collison

Partners:	12
Professional staff:	55
Non-professional staff:	45
Total Staff:	**112**

CONTACT INFORMATION
Managing Partner: Roy Guy
Accountancy (General): Roger Webster
Audit: Mark Thomas
Corporate Finance: John Parry
Management Consultancy: Paul Chapman
Administration: Alison Counsell
Tax: David Collison

CLIENT SERVICES
Accountancy (General), Audit, Computer Installation, Corporate Finance Advice, Life & Risk Assurance, Management & Business Advice, Management Buy-outs, Mergers & Acquisitions, Pensions Planning, Value for Money Studies, Taxation (Corporate), Taxation (International), Trust Settlement & Estates

OTHER OFFICES
PETERS, ELWORTHY & MOORE
17 Church Street, SAFFRON WALDEN, Essex CB10 1JW
Tel: + *44* (799) 22285 *Fax:* + *44* (799) 513619

Total Number of Offices: 2

PICKLES WALTHAM & CO

20/24 Park Street, SELBY, North Yorkshire YO8 0PW
Tel: + *44* (757) 703731
Fax: + *44* (757) 210358

National Affiliation: The UK 200 Group of Practising Accountants

International Contact: Robert Pickles

Partners:	6
Professional staff:	20
Non-professional staff:	40
Total Staff:	**66**

CLIENT SERVICES
Accountancy (General), Audit, Computer Installation, Corporate Finance Advice, Life & Risk Assurance, Management & Business Advice, Management Buy-outs, Mergers & Acquisitions, Pensions Planning, Value for Money Studies, Taxation (Corporate), Trust Settlement & Estates

Industry Specialisations: Agriculture

OTHER OFFICES
PICKLES WALTHAM & CO
66 Aire Street, GOOLE, North Humberside DN14 5QS

Total Number of Offices: 2

POLE ARNOLD

Stoughton House, Harborough Road, OADBY, Leicestershire LE2 4LP
Tel: + *44* (533) 717551
Fax: + *44* (533) 710597

National Affiliation: The CharterGroup Partnership

Partners:	10
Professional staff:	66
Non-professional staff:	14
Total Staff:	**90**

CONTACT INFORMATION
Managing Partner: Leslie Pole
Managing Partner: John Newton
Accountancy (General): Patric Phelan
Audit: Ian Monk
Corporate Finance: Dan Desmond
Administration: Robert Cant
Tax (Corporate & International): Martin Hume

CLIENT SERVICES
Accountancy (General), Audit, Computer Installation, Corporate Finance Advice, Management & Business Advice, Management Buy-outs, Pensions Planning, Taxation (Corporate), Taxation (International), Trust Settlement & Estates

PORTER, MATTHEWS & MARSDEN

Oakmount, 6 East Park Road, BLACKBURN BB1 8BW
Tel: + *44* (254) 679131
Fax: + *44* (254) 681759

European Affiliation: Moores Rowland International

International Contact: Michael H. Townend

OTHER OFFICES
PORTER, MATTHEWS & MARSDEN
83 Bank Parade, BURNLEY, Lancashire BB11 1UG
Tel: + *44* (282) 38035 *Fax:* + *44* (282) 27021
Contact: David P. Bradley

Total Number of Offices: 2

PRB MARTIN POLLINS

5 Bridge Road Business Park, HAYWARDS HEATH, West Sussex RH16 1TX
Tel: + *44* (444) 458252
Fax: + *44* (444) 458184

National Affiliation: The CharterGroup Partnership

International Contact: Martin Pollins

Partners:	1
Professional staff:	5
Non-professional staff:	8
Total Staff:	**14**

CONTACT INFORMATION
Managing Partner: Martin Pollins
Accountancy (General): John Forgham
Audit: Chris Whitley-Jones
Administration: Debbie Short
Tax (Corporate): Simon Power
Corporate Finance & Consultancy: Martin Pollins
BES Issues & Venture Capital: Martin Pollins

CLIENT SERVICES
All Services

PRICE BAILEY & PARTNERS

Causeway House, 1 Dane Street, BISHOP'S STORTFORD, Hertforshire CM23 3BT
Tel: + *44* (279) 755888
Fax: + *44* (279) 755417

National Affiliation: The UK 200 Group of Practising Accountants

International Contact: Graham Savage

CONTACT INFORMATION
Managing Partner: Graham Savage

PRICE WATERHOUSE

Southwark Towers, 32 London Bridge Street, LONDON SE1 9SY
Tel: + *44* (71) 939 3000
Fax: + *44* (71) 378 0647

European Affiliation: Price Waterhouse

International Contact: Sir Jeffery Bowman

▷

United Kingdom

Partners:	493
Professional staff:	4,880
Non-professional staff:	2,104
Total Staff:	**7,477**

FEE INCOME

Year End: 31.03.91	**£**	**%**
Accountancy & Audit:	151,300,000	40.1
Insolvency:	27,600,000	7.3
Consultancy:	103,000,000	27.3
Tax:	95,500,000	25.3
Total:	**377,400,000**	

CONTACT INFORMATION

Chairman: Sir Jeffery Bowman
Managing Partner: Ian Brindle
Corporate Finance: Tom Wilson
Insolvency: Mark Homan
Management Consultancy: Eric Hetherington
Administration: Geoffrey Johnson
Public Sector: Bob Eames
Accountancy & Audit: David Morris
Tax: John Barnsley
Privatisation: Richard Gledhill

CLIENT SERVICES

Accountancy (General), Audit, Corporate Finance Advice, Insolvency & Corporate Restructuring, Litigation/Legal Services, Management & Business Advice, Management Buy-outs, Mergers & Acquisitions, Pensions Planning, Value for Money Studies, Taxation (Corporate), Taxation (International), Trust Settlement & Estates, Joint Ventures, Inbound Investment, Management Consultancy

Industry Specialisations: Communication, Financial Services, Government, Hotels, Leisure, Health, Insurance, Retail FMCG, Utilities

MAJOR CLIENTS

Barclays Bank plc, British Gas plc, British Railways Board, The Burton Group plc, Courtaulds plc, Dalgety plc, Forte plc, Guardian Royal Exchange plc, Guinness plc, Harrisons & Crosfield plc, Hawker Siddeley Group plc, John Lewis Group plc, Land Securities plc, Legal & General Group plc, Lloyds Bank plc, Nationwide Building Society, Prudential Corporation plc, Sears plc, SmithKline Beecham plc, Tesco plc

OTHER OFFICES

PRICE WATERHOUSE
Kings Close, 62 Huntly Street, ABERDEEN AB1 1RS
Tel: + *44* (224) 636940 *Fax:* + *44* (224) 634105
Contact: Kenneth Murray

PRICE WATERHOUSE
Beaver House, Butcher Row, BEVERLEY, North Humberside HU17 OAA
Tel: + *44* (482) 861578 *Fax:* + *44* (482) 872331
Contact: Keith Usher

PRICE WATERHOUSE
Livery House, 169 Edmund Street, BIRMINGHAM B3 2JB
Tel: + *44* (21) 200 3000 *Fax:* + *44* (21) 200 2464
Contact: George Carter

PRICE WATERHOUSE
31 Great George Street, BRISTOL BS1 5QD
Tel: + *44* (272) 293701 *Fax:* + *44* (272) 290519
Contact: Peter McIlwraith

PRICE WATERHOUSE
Haywood House, Dumfries Place, CARDIFF CF1 4BA
Tel: + *44* (222) 376255 *Fax:* + *44* (222) 374124
Contact: Hugh Thomas

PRICE WATERHOUSE
Albany House, 58 Albany Street, EDINBURGH EH1 3QR
Tel: + *44* (31) 557 9900 *Fax:* + *44* (31) 225 5352
Contact: Ian Adam

PRICE WATERHOUSE
1 Blythswood Square, GLASGOW G2 4AD
Tel: + *44* (41) 226 4593 *Fax:* + *44* (41) 221 6970
Contact: Ian Adam

PRICE WATERHOUSE
Queen Victoria House, P.O. Box 88, Guildhall Road, HULL HU1 1HH
Tel: + *44* (482) 224111 *Fax:* + *44* (482) 27479
Contact: William Galleway

PRICE WATERHOUSE
Sun Alliance House, 9 Bond Court, LEEDS LS1 2SN
Tel: + *44* (532) 442044 *Fax:* + *44* (532) 441401
Contact: Ronald McMillian

PRICE WATERHOUSE
Southgate House, 61 Millstone Lane, LEICESTER LE1 5QA
Tel: + *44* (533) 531981 *Fax:* + *44* (533) 532697
Contact: Derek Trendell

PRICE WATERHOUSE
Silkhouse Court, Tithebarn Street, LIVERPOOL L2 2LJ
Tel: + *44* (51) 236 7862 *Fax:* + *44* (51) 236 3203
Contact: John Teare

PRICE WATERHOUSE
York House, York Street, MANCHESTER M2 4WS
Tel: + *44* (61) 228 6541 *Fax:* + *44* (61) 228 1429
Contact: Rodger Hughes

PRICE WATERHOUSE
Corporation House, Albert Road, MIDDLESBROUGH, Cleveland TS1 2RU
Tel: + *44* (642) 231222 *Fax:* + *44* (642) 225464
Contact: Peter Wilkin

PRICE WATERHOUSE
89 Sandyford Road, NEWCASTLE-UPON-TYNE NE99 1PL
Tel: + *44* (91) 232 8493 *Fax:* + *44* (91) 261 9490
Contact: Derek Booth

PRICE WATERHOUSE
Victoria House, 76 Milton Street, NOTTINGHAM NG1 3QY
Tel: + *44* (602) 419321 *Fax:* + *44* (602) 472660
Contact: Norman Deakin

PRICE WATERHOUSE
Bridge Gate, 55/57 High Street, REDHILL, Surrey RH1 1RX
Tel: + *44* (737) 766300 *Fax:* + *44* (737) 772342
Contact: Simon Bruce-Smythe

PRICE WATERHOUSE
The Quay, 30 Channel Way, Ocean Village, SOUTHAMPTON SO1 1XF
Tel: + *44* (703) 330077 *Fax:* + *44* (703) 223473
Contact: Robert Niddrie

PRICE WATERHOUSE
10 Bricket Road, ST ALBANS, Hertfordshire AL1 3JX
Tel: + *44* (727) 44155 *Fax:* + *44* (727) 45039
Contact: Robert Clark

PRICE WATERHOUSE
Thames Court, 1 Victoria Street, WINDSOR, Berkshire SL4 1HB
Tel: + *44* (753) 868202 *Fax:* + *44* (753) 864826
Contact: Christopher Burley

PRICE WATERHOUSE
200 Churchill Square, Kings Hill, WEST MALLING, Kent ME19 6AZ
Tel: + *44* (732) 872137 *Fax:* + *44* (732) 872138
Contact: Simon Bruce-Smythe

Total Number of Offices: 21

PRICE & COMPANY

30-32 Gildredge Road, EASTBOURNE, East Sussex BN21 4SH
Tel: + *44* (323) 639661
Fax: + *44* (323) 38198
National Affiliation: The CharterGroup Partnership
International Contact: Tim Firth

RAFTERY & CO

Marlborough House, 679 Warwick Road, SOLIHULL, West Midlands B91 3DA
Tel: + 44 (21) 711 2468
Fax: + 44 (21) 711 1701

National Affiliation: The UK 200 Group of Practising Accountants

International Contact: Patrick Raftery

Partners:	4
Professional staff:	18
Non-professional staff:	8
Total Staff:	**30**

CONTACT INFORMATION

Managing Partner: Patrick Raftery
Corporate Finance: Roger Edmonds
Tax (Corporate): B.M. Noble
Accountancy, Tax & Audit: Michael Williams
Administration, Tax & Consultancy: Patrick Raftery
Practice Administration: R. Cotton

CLIENT SERVICES

Accountancy (General), Audit, Computer Installation, Corporate Finance Advice, Management & Business Advice, Management Buy-outs, Mergers & Acquisitions, Pensions Planning, Value for Money Studies, Taxation (Corporate), Taxation (International), Trust Settlement & Estates, Business Start-Ups, Payroll, Company Secretarial, Share Valuations & Disposals

Industry Specialisations: Building Industry, Doctors, Dentists, Retail

JAS. HENRY REID & SON

4 West Craibstone Street, ABERDEEN AB9 1YL
Tel: + 44 (224) 590227
Fax: + 44 (224) 575409

National Affiliation: The CharterGroup Partnership

Partners:	4
Professional staff:	25
Non-professional staff:	4
Total Staff:	**33**

CLIENT SERVICES

Accountancy (General), Audit, Computer Installation, Corporate Finance Advice, Management & Business Advice, Pensions Planning, Taxation (Corporate), Taxation (International)

RICKARD KEEN & CO

9 Nelson Street, SOUTHEND-ON-SEA, Essex SS1 1EH
Tel: + 44 (702) 347771
Fax: + 44 (702) 330951

European Affiliation: Midsnell International

Partners:	10
Professional staff:	40
Non-professional staff:	20
Total Staff:	**70**

CONTACT INFORMATION

Managing Partner: Noel Kelleway

CLIENT SERVICES

Accountancy (General), Audit, Computer Installation, Corporate Finance Advice, Management & Business Advice, Management Buy-outs, Pensions Planning, Taxation (Corporate), Trust Settlement & Estates

OTHER OFFICES

RICKARD KEEN & CO
9 Kingsway, LONDON WC2B 6XF
Tel: + 44 (71) 836 1712 *Fax:* + 44 (71) 836 0573
Contact: Edward Hughes

Total Number of Offices: 3

PETER RILEY & CO

Britannic House, 51 North Hill, PLYMOUTH PL4 8HZ
Tel: + 44 (752) 260451
Fax: + 44 (752) 226154

National Affiliation: The CharterGroup Partnership

International Contact: David Powell

Partners:	2
Professional staff:	10
Non-professional staff:	4
Total Staff:	**16**

FEE INCOME

Year End: 30.04.91	%
Accountancy & Audit:	65.0
Consultancy:	10.0
Tax:	15.0
Other:	10.0

CONTACT INFORMATION

Managing Partner: Peter Riley
Accountancy & Audit: David Powell
Corporate Finance & Tax: Peter Riley

CLIENT SERVICES

All Services

Industry Specialisations: Food Manufacturing, Motor Trade, Leisure

RITSON, SMITH & PARTNERS

16 Carden Place, ABERDEEN AB9 1XF
Tel: + 44 (224) 643311
Fax: + 44 (224) 624359

European Affiliation: Moores Rowland International

International Contact: George C. Leadley

Partners:	6
Professional staff:	40
Non-professional staff:	16
Total Staff:	**62**

FEE INCOME

Year End: 1990	%
Accountancy & Audit:	70.0
Insolvency:	5.0
Consultancy:	5.0
Tax:	20.0

CONTACT INFORMATION

Managing Partner: George C. Leadley
Accountancy (General): N.E. Harper
Audit: N.A. Farquharson
Insolvency: I.M. Smith
Management Consultancy: C.J. Edmond
Information Technology: Ian Thomson

CLIENT SERVICES

Accountancy (General), Audit, Computer Installation, Corporate Finance Advice, Insolvency & Corporate Restructuring, Management & Business Advice, Pensions Planning, Taxation (Corporate), Taxation (Personal) ▷

Industry Specialisations: Farming, Oil Industry Support Firms, Medical Groups

OTHER OFFICES

RITSON, SMITH & PARTNERS
42 Market Street, ELLON, Aberdeenshire AB41 9JD
Tel: + 44 (358) 20712
Contact: Ian Baker

RITSON, SMITH & PARTNERS
Worlds End, FRASERBURGH, Aberdeenshire AB43 5BH
Tel: + 44 (346) 25709

RITSON, SMITH & PARTNERS
Aboyne Business Centre, ABOYNE, Aberdeenshire AB34 5HE
Tel: + 44 (3398) 86189

Total Number of Offices: 4

ROBSON RHODES

186 City Road, LONDON EC1V 2NU
Tel: + 44 (71) 251 1644
Fax: + 44 (71) 250 0801

European Affiliation: DRM Internationally

International Contact: Frank Attwood

Partners:	69
Professional staff:	566
Non-professional staff:	213
Total Staff:	**848**

FEE INCOME

Year End: 30.04.91	**£**	**%**
Accountancy & Audit:	13,900,000	39.7
Insolvency:	6,200,000	17.8
Consultancy:	2,000,000	5.7
Tax:	8,800,000	25.1
Other:	4,100,000	11.7
Total:	**35,000,000**	

CONTACT INFORMATION
Managing Partner: Hugh Aldous
Corporate Finance: Robert Hale
Insolvency: Neil Cooper
Management Consultancy: Jim Sloane
Public Sector: Eugene Sullivan
Tax (Corporate): Frank Smith
Tax (International): Peter Bryan
Accountancy & Audit: William Smith

CLIENT SERVICES
All Services

OTHER OFFICES

ROBSON RHODES
Data Centre, Old Wakefield Road, DEWSBURY, West Yorkshire WF12 8DF
Tel: + 44 (924) 458854 *Fax:* + 44 (924) 455488

ROBSON RHODES
10 Queen Square, BRISTOL BS1 4NT
Tel: + 44 (272) 260066 *Fax:* + 44 (272) 225759
Contact: Bill Dascombe

ROBSON RHODES
Daedalus House, 26-30 Station Road, CAMBRIDGE CB1 2RE
Tel: + 44 (223) 68020 *Fax:* + 44 (223) 65436
Contact: Jeremy Francis

ROBSON RHODES
The Galleria, Station Road, CRAWLEY, West Sussex RH10 1HY
Tel: + 44 (293) 560211 *Fax:* + 44 (293) 521737
Contact: John Rayer

ROBSON RHODES
Bryanston Court, HEMEL HEMPSTEAD, Hertfordshire HP2 4TN
Tel: + 44 (442) 60200 *Fax:* + 44 (422) 236294
Contact: Michael Biles

ROBSON RHODES
St George House, 40 Great George Street, LEEDS LS1 3DQ
Tel: + 44 (532) 459631 *Fax:* + 44 (532) 452823
Contact: Chris Connor

ROBSON RHODES
132 New Walk, LEICESTER LE1 7JA
Tel: + 44 (533) 544548 *Fax:* + 44 (533) 551858
Contact: Bill Smith

ROBSON RHODES
Invicta Chambers, Pudding Lane, MAIDSTONE, Kent ME14 1NX
Tel: + 44 (622) 671962 *Fax:* + 44 (622) 671954
Contact: John Rayer

ROBSON RHODES
Bernard House, Piccadilly Plaza, MANCHESTER M1 4DJ
Tel: + 44 (61) 236 4702 *Fax:* + 44 (61) 236 1152
Contact: Chris Bell

ROBSON RHODES
52 St Margaret's Street, ROCHESTER, Kent ME1 1TU
Tel: + 44 (634) 829300 *Fax:* + 44 (634) 829082
Contact: John Rayer

ASSOCIATED FIRMS

READS & CO
71 Mark Lane, LONDON EC3R 7RD
Tel: + 44 (71) 929 5715

Total Number of Offices: 12

ROWLANDS

5 West Lane, CHESTER-LE-STREET, County Durham DL15 9ED
Tel: + 44 (91) 388 6268
Fax: + 44 (91) 387 1431

National Affiliation: The CharterGroup Partnership

International Contact: Mark Scott

OTHER OFFICES

ROWLANDS
Gladstone House, Gladstone Street, CROOK, County Durham DL15 9ED
Tel: + 44 (388) 762478 *Fax:* + 44 (388) 762695

Total Number of Offices: 2

RUSHTONS

Starkie House, Winckley Square, PRESTON PR1 3JJ
Tel: + 44 (772) 51502
Fax: + 44 (772) 563257

National Affiliation: The UK 200 Group of Practising Accountants

International Contact: Stephen W. Valentine

Partners:	4
Professional staff:	12
Non-professional staff:	4
Total Staff:	**20**

CONTACT INFORMATION
Football Club Accounts & Taxation: Colin Foster
Partner: Brian Willacy
Partner: Neil M. Calvert

Partner: Stephen W. Valentine

CLIENT SERVICES
All Services

Industry Specialisations: Football Clubs

RUTHERFORD MANSON DOWDS

9 Great Stuart Sreet, EDINBURGH EH3 7TP
Tel: + *44* (31) 225 4727
Fax: + *44* (31) 220 1663

International Contact: Colin Rutherford

Partners:	8
Professional staff:	48
Non-professional staff:	18
Total Staff:	**74**

FEE INCOME

Year End: 30.04.91	**£**	**%**
Accountancy & Audit:	1,017,500	37.0
Tax:	687,500	25.0
Other:	1,045,000	38.0
Total:	**2,750,000**	

CONTACT INFORMATION
Accountancy (General): Cahal Dowds
Accountancy (General): Steven Cowie
Accountancy (General): William Skene
Corporate Finance: Colin Rutherford
Corporate Finance: Colin Welsh
Corporate Finance: John Craib
Corporate Finance: Iain A. Reid
Tax: A. Graeme Manson

CLIENT SERVICES
Accountancy (General), Audit, Computer Installation, Corporate Finance Advice, Litigation/Legal Services, Management & Business Advice, Management Buy-outs, Mergers & Acquisitions, Taxation (Corporate), Taxation (International), Trust Settlement & Estates

Industry Specialisations: Property, Advertising, Engineering, Vehicle Franchising, Retail, Food, Waste Management, Textiles, Leisure

OTHER OFFICES

RUTHERFORD MANSON DOWDS
2 Queens Terrace, ABERDEEN AB1 1XL
Tel: + *44* (224) 625888 *Fax:* + *44* (224) 625025
Contact: Colin Welsh

RUTHERFORD MANSON DOWDS
223/225 West George Street, GLASGOW G2 2ND
Tel: + *44* (41) 248 5532 *Fax:* + *44* (41) 248 6001
Contact: John Craib

Total Number of Offices: 3

SAFFERY CHAMPNESS

Fairfax House, Fulwood Place, Gray's Inn, LONDON EC1V 6UB
Tel: + *44* (71) 405 2828
Fax: + *44* (71) 405 7887

European Affiliation: SC International

International Contact: Nicholas Kelsey

OTHER OFFICES

SAFFERY CHAMPNESS
40 Melville Street, EDINBURGH EH3 7TW
Tel: + *44* (31) 225 2741 *Fax:* + *44* (31) 225 5376
Contact: Max Floydd

SAFFREY CHAMPNESS
Fox House, 26 Temple End, HIGH WYCOMBE, Buckinghamshire HP1 5DR

SAFFREY CHAMPNESS
Lloyds Bank Chambers, 34 High Street, MARCH, Cambridgeshire PE15 0JD
Tel: + *44* (354) 53900

SAFFREY CHAMPNESS
Commercial House, Chapel Street, WOKING, Surrey GU21 1YQ

SAFFREY CHAMPNESS
Hill Place House, INVERNESS, Highland IV2 3AD
Tel: + *44* (463) 224660

SAFFREY CHAMPNESS
10 Windsor Court, Clarence Drive, HARROGATE, West Yorkshire HG1 2PE
Tel: + *44* (423) 568012 *Fax:* + *44* (423) 501798
Contact: Keith Weston

Total Number of Offices: 7

SCOTT OSWALD & CO

1 Royal Terrace, EDINBURGH EH7 5AD
Tel: + *44* (31) 557 4455
Fax: + *44* (31) 556 0662

European Affiliation: DRM Internationally

International Contact: M.J. Gilbert

Partners:	24
Professional staff:	125
Non-professional staff:	50
Total Staff:	**199**

CONTACT INFORMATION
Chairman: William L.R. Scott
Managing Partner: W.L.R. Scott
Accountancy & Public Sector: W.C. Davidson
Insolvency: C.D. Gray
Tax: M.H. Eckersall
Audit & Corporate Finance: M.J. Gilbert
Consultancy & Administration: N.J. Vestey

CLIENT SERVICES
Accountancy (General), Audit, Computer Installation, Corporate Finance Advice, Insolvency & Corporate Restructuring, Management & Business Advice, Management Buy-outs, Mergers & Acquisitions, Pensions Planning, Value for Money Studies, Taxation (Corporate), Taxation (International), Trust Settlement & Estates

OTHER OFFICES

SCOTT OSWALD & CO
480 Union Street, ABERDEEN AB1 1TS
Tel: + *44* (224) 624033 *Fax:* + *44* (224) 624047
Contact: Alexander Duthie

SCOTT OSWALD & CO
Waverley House, DUNDEE DD1 1JU
Tel: + *44* (382) 25301 *Fax:* + *44* (382) 202059
Contact: Thomas Dyer

SCOTT OSWALD & CO
37 Wellside Place, FALKIRK FK1 5RL
Tel: + *44* (324) 611234 *Fax:* + *44* (324) 612187
Contact: Robin Jack

▷

SCOTT OSWALD & CO
St Vincent Chambers, 41 St Vincent Place, GLASGOW G1 2ER
Tel: + *44* (41) 226 3241 *Fax:* + *44* (41) 204 3609

SCOTT OSWALD & CO
10 Ardross Street, INVERNESS IV3 4NS
Tel: + *44* (463) 235321 *Fax:* + *44* (463) 231040
Contact: Ian Fraser

SCOTT OSWALD & CO
13 Kirk Wynd, KIRKCALDY, Fife KY1 1EH
Tel: + *44* (592) 263212 *Fax:* + *44* (592) 641180
Contact: David Gill

SCOTT OSWALD & CO
7 Atholl Place, PERTH PE1 5NE
Tel: + *44* (738) 36069 *Fax:* + *44* (738) 441700
Contact: David Garrick

SCOTT OSWALD & CO
16 Park Terrace, STIRLING FK8 2JT
Tel: + *44* (786) 63336 *Fax:* + *44* (786) 50014
Contact: Peter Moodie

Total Number of Offices: 9

SEYMOUR, TAYLOR & CO

57 London Road, HIGH WYCOMBE, Buckinghamshire HP11 1BS
Tel: + *44* (494) 523254
Fax: + *44* (494) 461157

International Contact: Bill Johnston

Partners:	8
Professional staff:	55
Non-professional staff:	20
Total Staff:	**83**

FEE INCOME

Year End: 30.04.91	**£**	**%**
Accountancy & Audit:	2,481,688	84.0
Consultancy:	88,632	3.0
Tax:	354,527	12.0
Other:	29,543	1.0
Total:	**2,954,390**	

CONTACT INFORMATION

Managing Partner: Gary Francis
Accountancy (General): Colin Hornabrook
Accountancy (General): Edward Baker
Audit: Richard Parsons
Corporate Finance: Gary Francis
Management Consultancy: Peter Allen
Administration: Clifford Baker
Financial Services: David Madeley
Tax: Peter Beedham

CLIENT SERVICES

Accountancy (General), Audit, Corporate Finance Advice, Life & Risk Assurance, Management & Business Advice, Management Buy-outs, Mergers & Acquisitions, Pensions Planning, Value for Money Studies, Taxation (Corporate), Taxation (International), Trust Settlement & Estates

OTHER OFFICES

SEYMOUR, TAYLOR & CO
60 High Street, CHESHAM, Buckinghamshire HP5 1EG
Tel: + *44* (494) 782648 *Fax:* + *44* (494) 791567
Contact: Bill Johnston

Total Number of Offices: 2

SHARLES

29 Brandon Street, HAMILTON, Lanarkshire ML3 6AB
Tel: + *44* (698) 282062
Fax: + *44* (698) 425840
National Affiliation: The CharterGroup Partnership

International Contact: James W. Watson

Partners:	5
Professional staff:	10
Non-professional staff:	5
Total Staff:	**20**

CONTACT INFORMATION

Managing Partner: James W. Watson
Accountancy (General): John Gowans
Audit: R.J. McGurk
Corporate Finance: George Rice
Management Consultancy: Evelyn Grierson
Tax (Corporate): Peter Lavelle
Computer Installation: Patricia Flannigan

CLIENT SERVICES

Accountancy (General), Audit, Computer Installation, Corporate Finance Advice, Management & Business Advice, Management Buy-outs, Mergers & Acquisitions, Value for Money Studies, Taxation (Corporate), Taxation (International), Trust Settlement & Estates, Wages, Grants & Financial Assistance

Industry Specialisations: Engineering & Wholesale Engineering, Construction, Property Development

MAJOR CLIENTS

Akura International Ltd, Alexander Holdings plc, A.A. Brothers Ltd, BBI Associates, A. Borland & Co (Glaziers) Ltd, Botterills of Blantyre, Cadzow Heavy Haulage Ltd, Findlay Campbell Blacksmiths, Flamingoland Ltd, Hamilton Engineering Development Company, H.T. Electrical Ltd, Kilmarnock Engineers, Luks UK Ltd, McGregor Flooring Ltd, M.B. Techniques Ltd, Nissan Ltd, Preston Components Ltd, J. Steper Ltd, Strathclyde Fabricators Ltd, Swissmatic Ltd

OTHER OFFICES

SHARLES
18 Sandyford Place, GLASGOW G3 7NB
Tel: + *44* (41) 248 6195
Contact: Jim Watson

Total Number of Offices: 2

SHARLES & PARTNERS

100 Wigmore Street, LONDON W1H 0AE
Tel: + *44* (71) 486 0431
Fax: + *44* (71) 487 5561
National Affiliation: The CharterGroup Partnership

International Contact: J. Wise

Partners:	8
Professional staff:	35
Non-professional staff:	6
Total Staff:	**49**

FEE INCOME

Year End: 30.09.91	**£**	**%**
Accountancy & Audit:	900,000	75.0
Consultancy:	50,000	5.0
Tax:	250,000	20.0
Total:	**1,200,000**	

CONTACT INFORMATION

Managing Partner: J. Wise
Corporate Finance: J. Wise
Public Sector: C. Waters

Accountancy & Consultancy: M. Davis
Audit & Administration: J. Hadjinicocady
Tax: R. Maher
Computer: P. Batten
Pensions & Investment: P. Ruddy

CLIENT SERVICES
Accountancy (General), Audit, Computer Installation, Corporate Finance Advice, Life & Risk Assurance, Management & Business Advice, Management Buy-outs, Mergers & Acquisitions, Pensions Planning, Value for Money Studies, Taxation (Corporate), Taxation (International), Trust Settlement & Estates

---

SHIPLEY BLACKBURN

14-16 Regent Street, LONDON SW1Y 4PS
Tel: + *44* (71) 839 4311
Fax: + *44* (71) 930 6602

International Contact: R.B. Lyle

Partners:	12
Professional staff:	75
Non-professional staff:	25
Total Staff:	**112**

CONTACT INFORMATION
Chairman: C.J. Langrish
Accountancy (General): E.M. Oliver
Audit: J.S. McCuin
Corporate Finance: G.N. Fisher
Insolvency: M. Moore
Administration: R.B. Lyle
Tax (Corporate): R.B. Magill
Tax (International): P.J. Squires
Consultancy & Public Sector: E.S. Tully
Trusts: A.J. Allen

CLIENT SERVICES
All Services

Industry Specialisations: Financial Services, Collective Investment Schemes, Film & Entertainment, Law

---

S.E. SHORT & CO

6 Fairfield Road, CHESTERFIELD, Derbyshire S40 4TP
Tel: + *44* (246) 208282
Fax: + *44* (246) 208282

National Affiliation: The CharterGroup Partnership

International Contact: Peter Freeman

Partners:	4
Professional staff:	40
Non-professional staff:	6
Total Staff:	**50**

CONTACT INFORMATION
Managing Partner: J.A. Brier
Accountancy (General): P.E. Freeman
Audit: P.D. Beeson
Corporate Finance: J.A. Bown
Tax: C.J. Chambers

CLIENT SERVICES
Accountancy (General), Audit, Computer Installation, Corporate Finance Advice, Life & Risk Assurance, Management & Business Advice, Mergers & Acquisitions, Pensions Planning, Taxation (Corporate), Trust Settlement & Estates

---

SMITH & LUDKIN

Canterbury House, Market Place, DEREHAM, Norfolk NR19 2AY
Tel: + *44* (362) 692101

National Affiliation: The UK 200 Group of Practising Accountants

International Contact: K.V. Ludkin

Partners:	2
Non-professional staff:	10
Total Staff:	**12**

CONTACT INFORMATION
Managing Partner: Kerry Ludkin
Audit: C.M. Richardson

CLIENT SERVICES
All Services

Industry Specialisations: Agriculture

SMITH & WILLIAMSON

No. 1 Riding House Street, LONDON W1A 3AS
Tel: + *44* (71) 637 5377
Fax: + *44* (71) 631 0741

European Affiliation: S & W International

International Contact: John McCagney

CONTACT INFORMATION
EC Contact Partner: Ian M. Buckley

OTHER OFFICES

SMITH & WILLIAMSON
Onslow Bridge Chambers, Bridge Street, GUILDFORD, Surrey GU1 4RA
Tel: + *44* (483) 302200 *Fax:* + *44* (483) 301232

SMITH & WILLIAMSON
Old Library Chambers, 21 Chipper Lane, SALISBURY SP1 1BG
Tel: + *44* (722) 411881 *Fax:* + *44* (722) 411438

ASSOCIATED FIRMS

MALPAS SIMMONS
Lime Tree House, The Plocks, BLANDFORD FORUM, Dorset DT11 7AA
Tel: + *44* (258) 452383 *Fax:* + *44* (258) 459245

MALPAS SIMMONS
Wootton Grange, Wootton Mount, BOURNEMOUTH BH1 1PJ
Tel: + *44* (202) 553474 *Fax:* + *44* (202) 295036
Contact: Alan F. Simmons

MALPAS SIMMONS
The Old Rectory, South Walks Road, DORCHESTER, Dorset DT1 1DT
Tel: + *44* (305) 266236 *Fax:* + *44* (305) 251064

Total Number of Offices: 6

SPAIN BROTHERS & CO

Falcon House, 73 College Road, MAIDSTONE, Kent ME15 6RW
Tel: + *44* (622) 692255
Fax: + *44* (622) 690993

European Affiliation: Moores Rowland International

International Contact: Peter J. Sutton

Partners:	22
Professional staff:	120
Non-professional staff:	60
Total Staff:	**204**

CONTACT INFORMATION
Chairman: John C. Davidson
Managing Partner: Martin C. Beck
Audit: Anthony D. Brand

▷

Corporate Finance: Barry Mortimer
Administration: Jeremy U. Cope
Tax (Corporate): Paul Woodward

CLIENT SERVICES
Accountancy (General), Audit, Computer Installation, Corporate Finance Advice, Life & Risk Assurance, Management & Business Advice, Management Buy-outs, Mergers & Acquisitions, Pensions Planning, Value for Money Studies, Taxation (Corporate), Trust Settlement & Estates

OTHER OFFICES

SPAIN BROTHERS & CO
19 North Street, ASHFORD, Kent TN24 8LF
Tel: + *44* (233) 628848 *Fax:* + *44* (233) 646439
Contact: Michael A. Wood

SPAIN BROTHERS & CO
Westgate House, 87 St Dunstan's Street, CANTERBURY, Kent CT2 8AE
Tel: + *44* (227) 769321 *Fax:* + *44* (227) 464169
Contact: John C. Davidson

SPAIN BROTHERS & CO
5 St James's Street, DOVER, Kent CT16 1QD
Tel: + *44* (304) 201994 *Fax:* + *44* (304) 240117
Contact: Raymond C. Coop

SPAIN BROTHERS & CO
29 Manor Road, FOLKESTONE, Kent CT20 2SE
Tel: + *44* (303) 52207 *Fax:* + *44* (303) 56679
Contact: Barry J. Booth

SPAIN BROTHERS & CO
Thames House, Roman Square, SITTINGBOURNE, Kent ME10 4BJ
Tel: + *44* (795) 475363 *Fax:* + *44* (795) 426017
Contact: Barry Mortimer

SPAIN BROTHERS & CO
Olwen House, 8-12 Quarry Hill Road, TONBRIDGE, Kent TN9 2SZ
Tel: + *44* (732) 366366 *Fax:* + *44* (732) 770254
Contact: Robert J. Bursey

SPAIN BROTHERS & CO
16 Lonsdale Gardens, TUNBRIDGE WELLS, Kent TN1 1NU
Tel: + *44* (892) 546546 *Fax:* + *44* (892) 511334
Contact: Drummond E. Abrams

Total Number of Offices: 8

F.W. STEPHENS & CO

10 Charterhouse Square, LONDON EC1M 6LQ
Tel: + *44* (71) 251 4434
Fax: + *44* (71) 608 3555

National Affiliation: The UK 200 Group of Practising Accountants

International Contact: Peter Laley

Partners:	11
Professional staff:	40
Non-professional staff:	16
Total Staff:	**67**

FEE INCOME

Year End: 30.04.90	%
Accountancy & Audit:	65.0
Tax:	35.0

CONTACT INFORMATION
Chairman: Roger Coulson
Managing Partner: Hugh Taylor
Accountancy & Audit: Richard Stevens
Corporate Finance & Administration: Hugh Taylor
Tax: Peter Laley
Tax (Personal): James McCarthy

CLIENT SERVICES
Accountancy (General), Audit, Computer Installation, Corporate Finance Advice, Management & Business Advice, Management Buy-outs, Mergers & Acquisitions, Taxation (Corporate), Taxation (International), Trust Settlement & Estates

Industry Specialisations: Solicitors, Property, Construction, Family Companies

STEPHENSON SMART & CO

80a Oswald Road, SCUNTHORPE, South Humberside DN15 7PA
Tel: + *44* (724) 843361
Fax: + *44* (724) 270262

National Affiliation: The UK 200 Group of Practising Accountants

International Contact: A.P. Pratt

Partners:	3
Professional staff:	25
Non-professional staff:	4
Total Staff:	**32**

CONTACT INFORMATION
Managing Partner: A.P. Pratt
Partner: D.S. Lynaugh
Partner: K.D. Cross

CLIENT SERVICES
All Services

STOY HAYWARD

8 Baker Street, LONDON W1M 1DA
Tel: + *44* (71) 486 5888
Fax: + *44* (71) 487 3686

European Affiliation: Horwath International

International Contact: David Shrimpton

Total Staff: **1,700**

FEE INCOME

Year End: 31.03.91	**£**
Accountancy & Audit:	34,400,000
Insolvency:	9,000,000
Consultancy:	10,200,000
Tax:	13,000,000
Total:	**66,600,000**

CONTACT INFORMATION
Chairman: Paul A. Hipps
Managing Partner: Adrian Martin
Corporate Finance: Paul Smith
Insolvency: George Auger
Management Consultancy: Michael Grunberg
Administration: Brian Udell
Public Sector: Bob Stubbs
Tax (Corporate): Barry Stillerman
Tax (International): Allan Cinnamon
Accountancy & Audit: Michael Haan
Hotel Consultancy: Geoff Parkinson

CLIENT SERVICES
Accountancy (General), Audit, Computer Installation, Corporate Finance Advice, Insolvency & Corporate Restructuring, Litigation/Legal Services, Management & Business Advice, Management Buy-outs, Mergers & Acquisitions, Pensions Planning, Value for Money Studies, Taxation (Corporate), Taxation (International), Trust Settlement & Estates

OTHER OFFICES

STOY HAYWARD
Franklin House, 12 Brunswick Street, BELFAST BT2 7GE
Tel: + 44 (232) 439009 *Fax:* + 44 (232) 439010
Contact: Stephen Prenter

STOY HAYWARD
Waterloo House, 20 Waterloo Street, BIRMINGHAM B2 5TF
Tel: + 44 (21) 643 4024 *Fax:* + 44 (21) 631 2400
Contact: Stephen Craig

STOY HAYWARD
Oakfield House, Oakfield Grove, Clifton, BRISTOL BS8 2BN
Tel: + 44 (272) 237000 *Fax:* + 44 (272) 732741
Contact: Philip E. Moody

STOY HAYWARD
James Sellars House, 144 West George Street, GLASGOW G2 2HG
Tel: + 44 (41) 331 2811 *Fax:* + 44 (41) 332 6148
Contact: James G. Wylie

STOY HAYWARD
Peter House, St Peter's Square, MANCHESTER M1 5BH
Tel: + 44 (61) 228 6791 *Fax:* + 44 (61) 228 1545
Contact: Grahame N. Elliot

STOY HAYWARD
58 Thorpe Road, NORWICH NR1 1RY
Tel: + 44 (603) 620241 *Fax:* + 44 (603) 630224
Contact: Michael R. Parish

STOY HAYWARD
Foxhall Lodge, Gregory Boulevard, NOTTINGHAM NG7 6LH
Tel: + 44 (602) 626578 *Fax:* + 44 (602) 691043
Contact: Roger F.J. Graham

STOY HAYWARD
Garrick House, 76-80 High Street, Old Fletton, PETERBOROUGH PE2 8DR
Tel: + 44 (733) 342444 *Fax:* + 44 (733) 54704
Contact: Paul Temple

STOY HAYWARD
19 Borough Road, SUNDERLAND SR1 1LA
Tel: + 44 (91) 565 0565 *Fax:* + 44 (91) 514 2083
Contact: David W. Wrightson

Total Number of Offices: 10

TAYLOR HAWSONS

Albion House, 6 Albion Place, South Parade, DONCASTER, South Yorkshire DN1 2EG
Tel: + 44 (302) 367262

European Affiliation: Moores Rowland International

International Contact: D.J. Aldred

THICKBROOM COVENTRY

147a High Street, WALTHAM CROSS, Hertfordshire EN8 7LN
Tel: + 44 (992) 36454
Fax: + 44 (992) 36557

National Affiliation: The CharterGroup Partnership

International Contact: Mark Payne

THOBURN & CHAPMAN

Milburn House, Dean Street, NEWCASTLE-UPON-TYNE NE1 1NR
Tel: + 44 (91) 261 4804
Fax: + 44 (91) 261 4842

European Affiliation: INPACT - International Network of Professional Accountants

International Contact: Ralph Thoburn Jr.

Partners:	3
Professional staff:	34
Non-professional staff:	8
Total Staff:	**45**

FEE INCOME

Year End: 30.04.91	**£**	**%**
Accountancy & Audit:	700,000	87.5
Insolvency:	50,000	6.2
Consultancy:	30,000	3.7
Tax:	20,000	2.5
Total:	**800,000**	

CONTACT INFORMATION

Managing Partner: Ralph Thoburn Sr.
Audit: Ralph Thoburn Jr.
Tax: Mark Charlton
Tax: Andrea Williamson
Trusts & Tax: Ian Montgomerie
Insolvency Manager: Hillary Nicholson

CLIENT SERVICES

Accountancy (General), Audit, Corporate Finance Advice, Insolvency & Corporate Restructuring, Life & Risk Assurance, Litigation/Legal Services, Management & Business Advice, Management Buy-outs, Mergers & Acquisitions, Pensions Planning, Taxation (Corporate), Taxation (International), Trust Settlement & Estates

OTHER OFFICES

CHAPMAN AND PARTNERS
14 Barrington Street, SOUTH SHIELDS, Tyne & Wear NE33 1AJ
Tel: + 44 (91) 456 2425 *Fax:* + 44 (91) 454 7382
Contact: Peter Brumby

THOBURN & CHARLTON
Coronation Building, 2 Charlotte Terrace, SOUTH SHIELDS, Tyne & Wear NE33 1QQ
Tel: + 44 (91) 456 8021 *Fax:* + 44 (91) 427 0246
Contact: Mark Charlton

Total Number of Offices: 3

THOMAS, WESTCOTT & GILLARD

42 New Street, HONITON, Devon EX14 8BU
Tel: + 44 (404) 44616
Fax: + 44 (404) 45830

European Affiliation: The International Group of Accounting Firms Ltd (IGAF)

International Contact: Richard Thomas

TIFFIN GREEN

11 Queens Road, BRENTWOOD, Essex CM14 4HE
Tel: + 44 (277) 224422
Fax: + 44 (277) 262863

National Affiliation: The CharterGroup Partnership

International Contact: Nigel Tidbury

Partners:	5
Professional staff:	22
Non-professional staff:	6
Total Staff:	**33**

FEE INCOME

Year End: 31.05.91	**£**	**%**
Accountancy & Audit:		76.0
Tax:		23.0
Other:		1.0
Total:	**1,092,485**	

▷

CONTACT INFORMATION
Accountancy (General): Martin Churchill
Audit: Martyn Rust
Corporate Finance & Administration: Colin Tiffin
Tax: Nigel Tidbury
Computers: Brian Hill-Cottingham

CLIENT SERVICES
Accountancy (General), Audit, Corporate Finance Advice, Management & Business Advice, Management Buy-outs, Pensions Planning, Taxation (Corporate), Taxation (International), Trust Settlement & Estates

TOUCHE ROSS & CO

Peterborough Court, 133 Fleet Street, LONDON EC4A 2TR
Tel: + *44* (71) 936 3000
Fax: + *44* (71) 583 1198

European Affiliation: DRT International

International Contact: D. John S. Roques

Total Staff: **6,700**

CLIENT SERVICES
All Services

MAJOR CLIENTS
Amstrad, BAA, BASF (UK), Coats Viyella, Dixons, First National Finance, GEC, Hammersons, Hays Group, King & Shaxson, Kleinwort Benson, LEP, Marsh & McLennan, Racal Electronics, W.H. Smith & Son, Taylor Woodrow, Trafalgar House, U.P.S., Wellcome

Total Number of Offices: 27

THE UK 200 GROUP OF PRACTISING CHARTERED ACCOUNTANTS

7th Floor, Victoria House, Victoria Road, ALDERSHOT, Hampshire GU11 1JJ
Tel: + *44* (252) 27666
Fax: + *44* (252) 310890

European Affiliation: International Association of Practising Accountants (IAPA)
National Affiliation: The UK 200 Group of Practising Accountants

International Contact: David A. Turnbull

F.L. WALKER & COMPANY

Gordon Chambers, 82 Mitchell Street, GLASGOW G1 3PX
Tel: + *44* (41) 248 4211
Fax: + *44* (41) 248 3224

National Affiliation: The CharterGroup Partnership

International Contact: John Park

WALTER WRIGHT & CO

89 High Street, HADLEIGH, Suffolk 1P7 5EA
Tel: + *44* (473) 822145
Fax: + *44* (473) 827656

National Affiliation: The UK 200 Group of Practising Accountants

International Contact: James Walter

Partners:	5
Professional staff:	6
Non-professional staff:	14
Total Staff:	**25**

FEE INCOME

Year End: 30.09.91	**£**	**%**
Accountancy & Audit:	430,000	78.0
Consultancy:	50,000	9.0
Tax:	50,000	9.0
Other:	20,000	4.0
Total:	**550,000**	

CONTACT INFORMATION
Accountancy (General): Paul Garrard
Audit: David Simcox
Management Consultancy: James Walter
Tax (Corporate): Alain Harris
New Business Start-Ups: James Walter

CLIENT SERVICES
Accountancy (General), Audit, Computer Installation, Corporate Finance Advice, Life & Risk Assurance, Management & Business Advice, Management Buy-outs, Mergers & Acquisitions, Pensions Planning, Value for Money Studies, Taxation (Corporate), Trust Settlement & Estates, Corporate Planning & Forecasting, Management Consultancy

MAJOR CLIENTS
Elgar Euroblaze (UK) Ltd, Gainsborough Silk Ltd, Haverhill Generators Ltd, Kendrick Hire plc, Plescon Ltd

WATERWORTH, RUDD & HARE

Central Buildings, Richmond Terrace, BLACKBURN BB1 7AP
Tel: + *44* (254) 51123
Fax: + *44* (254) 682483

National Affiliation: The CharterGroup Partnership

International Contact: Simon Westhead

Partners:	5
Professional staff:	25
Non-professional staff:	10
Total Staff:	**40**

CONTACT INFORMATION
Managing Partner: J. Simon Westhead
Accountancy (General): Peter J. Bridge
Audit: Graham M. Wilson
Insolvency: J. Simon Westhead
Administration: David Fielding
Tax (Corporate): Alan T. Rowntree

CLIENT SERVICES
All Services

WATSON WOOD

York House, 249 Manningham Lane, BRADFORD, West Yorkshire BD8 7EW
Tel: + *44* (274) 495581
Fax: + *44* (274) 547204

European Affiliation: Midsnell International

International Contact: Philip V. Smith

WEEKS GREEN

College Keep, 4-12 Terminus Terrace, SOUTHAMPTON SO1 1XJ
Tel: + *44* (703) 632023
Fax: + *44* (703) 638220

European Affiliation: Independent Accountants International

International Contact: Nicholas Parker

Partners:	9
Professional staff:	52
Non-professional staff:	13
Total Staff:	74

CONTACT INFORMATION
Managing Partner: Barrie Gay
Accountancy (General): Barrie Gay
Corporate Finance & Audit: David Griffiths
Tax: Nicholas Parker

CLIENT SERVICES
Accountancy (General), Audit, Corporate Finance Advice, Management & Business Advice, Management Buy-outs, Mergers & Acquisitions, Pensions Planning, Taxation (Corporate), Taxation (International), Trust Settlement & Estates

Industry Specialisations: Medical Practices, Construction

OTHER OFFICES
WEEKS GREEN
Cooper House, New Road, Hythe, SOUTHAMPTON SO4 6BR
Tel: + *44* (703) 843136 *Fax:* + *44* (703) 207091
Contact: Michael Wilkinson

Total Number of Offices: 2

WENHAM MAJOR
89 Cornwall Street, BIRMINGHAM B3 3BY
Tel: + *44* (21) 236 1866
Fax: + *44* (21) 200 1389

European Affiliation: Midsnell International

International Contact: Michael A. Stokes

WHEAWILL & SUDWORTH
35 Westgate, HUDDERSFIELD HD1 1PA
Tel: + *44* (484) 423691
Fax: + *44* (484) 518803

Partners:	10
Professional staff:	52
Non-professional staff:	13
Total Staff:	75

CONTACT INFORMATION
Managing Partner: Richard Warrington
Accountancy (General): John Ardley
Audit: Roger Womersley
Corporate Finance: Richard Warrington
Administration: John Black
Tax (Corporate): David Butterworth
Tax (International): Andrew Frape

CLIENT SERVICES
Accountancy (General), Audit, Corporate Finance Advice, Litigation/Legal Services, Management & Business Advice, Management Buy-outs, Mergers & Acquisitions, Pensions Planning, Taxation (Corporate), Taxation (International), Trust Settlement & Estates, Company Secretarial, Business Start-Up, Feasibility Studies

G.A. WHEELER & COMPANY
30 Old Market, WISBECH, Cambridgeshire PE13 1NE
Tel: + *44* (945) 582547
Fax: + *44* (945) 585575

National Affiliation: The CharterGroup Partnership

International Contact: Michael Bell

OTHER OFFICES
G.A. WHEELER & COMPANY
16 Market Place, Long Sutton, SPALDING, Lincolnshire PE12 9JF
Tel: + *44* (406) 362367

G.A. WHEELER & COMPANY
11 King Street, KING'S LYNN, Norfolk PE20 1ET
Tel: + *44* (553) 761316 *Fax:* + *44* (553) 766454

Total Number of Offices: 3

WHITLEY, STIMPSON & PARTNERS
Penrose House, Oxford Road, BANBURY, Oxfordshire OX16 7AB
Tel: + *44* (295) 270200
Fax: + *44* (295) 271784

European Affiliation: Moores Rowland International

International Contact: Roger M. Hancock

J. WILD & CO
Lancaster House, Blackburn Street, Radcliffe, MANCHESTER M26 9TS
Tel: + *44* (61) 723 3211
Fax: + *44* (61) 725 9162

European Affiliation: Midsnell International

International Contact: M.J. Hulme

Partners:	6
Professional staff:	26
Non-professional staff:	7
Total Staff:	**39**

CONTACT INFORMATION
Administration: D.H. Taylor
Tax (Corporate): R.H. Pilkington
Accountancy & Audit: M.J. Hulme

CLIENT SERVICES
Accountancy (General), Audit, Computer Installation, Corporate Finance Advice, Life & Risk Assurance, Management & Business Advice, Pensions Planning, Taxation (Corporate), Taxation (International), Trust Settlement & Estates, International Tax Planning

OTHER OFFICES
J. WILD & CO
11 Peel Street, Farnworth, BOLTON BL4 8AA
Tel: + *44* (204) 792182 *Fax:* + *44* (61) 725 9162
Contact: John Leyland

Total Number of Offices: 2

WILLIAMS ALLAN
8-10 William Street, WINDSOR, Berkshire SL4 1BA
Tel: + *44* (753) 840605
Fax: + *44* (753) 840762
National Affiliation: The CharterGroup Partnership

International Contact: Ross Wilson

Partners:	5
FEE INCOME	
Year End: 30.04.91	**£**
Accountancy & Audit:	650,000
Consultancy:	150,000
Tax:	450,000
Other:	250,000
Total:	**1,500,000**

CONTACT INFORMATION
Managing Partner: Ross Wilson

▷

Audit: Billy Mills
Corporate Finance: Ross Wilson
Management Consultancy: Sandy Kerr
Tax: Alan Ross
Computers: Jenny Nicholls

CLIENT SERVICES
Accountancy (General), Audit, Computer Installation, Corporate Finance Advice, Management & Business Advice, Management Buy-outs, Mergers & Acquisitions, Pensions Planning, Taxation (Corporate), Taxation (International)

WILSON KINNAIR
Hutton House, Sandyford Road, NEWCASTLE-UPON-TYNE NE2 1QU
Tel: + *44* (91) 281 5837
Fax: + *44* (91) 281 5274

European Affiliation: The International Group of Accounting Firms Ltd (IGAF)

International Contact: Brian Wilson

WOOLFORD & COMPANY
Suite 22, Bridge House, Bridge Street, WALTON-ON-THAMES, Surrey KT12 1AL
Tel: + *44* (932) 253133
Fax: + *44* (932) 254135

European Affiliation: The International Group of Accounting Firms Ltd (IGAF)

International Contact: Peter Wilman

ISLE OF MAN

BDO BINDER
Ragnall House, 18 Peel Road, DOUGLAS
Tel: + *44* (624) 620711
Fax: + *44* (624) 672446

European Affiliation: BDO Binder

Partners:	2
Professional staff:	5
Non-professional staff:	3
Total Staff:	**10**

FEE INCOME

Year End: 1990	%
Accountancy & Audit:	64.0
Consultancy:	1.0
Tax:	3.0
Other:	32.0

CONTACT INFORMATION
Managing Partner: John David Clarke
Accountancy (General): John David Clarke
Audit: Zbyszek Bernard Galka

CLIENT SERVICES
Accountancy (General), Audit, Computer Installation, Corporate Finance Advice, Insolvency & Corporate Restructuring, Life & Risk Assurance, Litigation/Legal Services, Management & Business Advice, Management Buy-outs, Mergers & Acquisitions, Pensions Planning, Value for Money Studies, Taxation (Corporate), Taxation (International), Trust Settlement & Estates, Corporate Management

Industry Specialisations: Captive Insurance, Shipping, Retailing, Trusts

BENNETT ROY & CO
Viking House, Nelson Street, DOUGLAS
Tel: + *44* (624) 627434
Fax: + *44* (624) 624497

European Affiliation: InterContinental Consultants (ICC)

International Contact: William L. Bennett
Andrew S. Roy
Richard L.D. Tucker

Total Number of Offices: 2

BROWNE CRAINE & CO
Burleigh Manor, Peel Road, DOUGLAS
Tel: + *44* (624) 629369
Fax: + *44* (624) 673827

European Affiliation: INPACT - International Network of Professional Accountants

Partners:	2
Professional staff:	7
Non-professional staff:	3
Total Staff:	**12**

CONTACT INFORMATION
Managing Partner: Maurice Singer
Managing Partner: David Craine
Accountancy & Audit: David Craine
Tax: Maurice Singer

CLIENT SERVICES
All Services including Offshore Company Formation

Industry Specialisations: International Trading, Trusts & Trustee Services

CLARK WHITEHILL
7th Floor, Victory House, Prospect Hill, DOUGLAS
Tel: + *44* (624) 627335
Fax: + *44* (624) 677225

European Affiliation: Clark Kenneth Leventhal

International Contact: Roger Barrs

Partners:	2
Professional staff:	9
Non-professional staff:	4
Total Staff:	**15**

FEE INCOME

Year End: 1990	%
Accountancy & Audit:	35.0
Tax:	40.0
Other:	25.0

CLIENT SERVICES
Accountancy (General), Audit, Corporate Finance Advice, Insolvency & Corporate Restructuring, Management & Business Advice, Taxation (Corporate), Taxation (International)

COOPERS & LYBRAND
12 Finch Road, DOUGLAS
Tel: + *44* (624) 626711
Fax: + *44* (624) 626712

European Affiliation: Coopers & Lybrand Europe

International Contact: Stephen Moorhouse

Partners: 4
Professional staff: 40
Non-professional staff: 5
Total Staff: **49**

CONTACT INFORMATION
Managing Partner: Roger Breadner
Accountancy & Corporate Finance: John Cannell
Audit & Public Sector: Chris Talavera
Consultancy & Administration: Roger Breadner
Tax (Corporate & International): Stephen Moorhouse
Trusts: Michael McBain

CLIENT SERVICES
All Services

Industry Specialisations: Insurance, Banking, Communications, Shipping, Pharmaceuticals, Food & Drink, Automotive

---

ERNST & YOUNG
Derby House, Athol Street, DOUGLAS
Tel: + 44 (624) 626661
Fax: + 44 (624) 626375

European Affiliation: Ernst & Young Europe

International Contact: Larry Kearns

Partners: 5
Professional staff: 14
Non-professional staff: 33
Total Staff: **52**

CONTACT INFORMATION
Chairman: Jim Cowell
Managing Partner: Larry Kearns
Public Sector & Consultancy: Jim Cowell
Tax (Corporate): Peter Horsthuis
Tax (International): Larry Kearns
Audit & Administration: Martin Callister
Corporate Finance & Insolvency: Jim Cowell

CLIENT SERVICES
Accountancy (General), Audit, Corporate Finance Advice, Insolvency & Corporate Restructuring, Management & Business Advice, Pensions Planning, Taxation (Corporate), Taxation (International), Trust Settlement & Estates

Industry Specialisations: Banking, Insurance, Financial Services

OTHER OFFICES

ERNST & YOUNG
Shannon Court, Bowring Road, RAMSAY
Tel: + 44 (624) 812343 *Fax:* + 44 (624) 626375

ERNST & YOUNG
5 The Parade, CASTLETOWN
Tel: + 44 (624) 822015 *Fax:* + 44 (624) 626375

Total Number of Offices: 3

FINNIE & CO
Kreston House, 6 Goldie Terrace, DOUGLAS
Tel: + 44 (624) 621523
Fax: + 44 (624) 625712

European Affiliation: Kreston International

International Contact: David McPhee

KPMG

KPMG PEAT MARWICK
Heritage Court, 41 Athol Street, DOUGLAS
Tel: + 44 (624) 623008
Fax: + 44 (624) 672768

European Affiliation: KPMG

International Contact: Peter Pell-Hiley

Partners: 5
Professional staff: 51
Non-professional staff: 17
Total Staff: **73**

CONTACT INFORMATION
Managing Partner: Peter Pell-Hiley
Accountancy (General): Mike Gardner
Management Consultancy: Peter Pell-Hiley
Public Sector: Mike Fayle
Audit & Corporate Finance: David McGarry
Insolvency & Administration: Peter Pell-Hiley
Tax: Nigel Scott

CLIENT SERVICES
Accountancy (General), Audit, Corporate Finance Advice, Insolvency & Corporate Restructuring, Management & Business Advice, Management Buy-outs, Mergers & Acquisitions, Pensions Planning, Value for Money Studies, Taxation (Corporate), Taxation (International), Trust Settlement & Estates, Management Consultancy

---

MOORE SNELLING
Victory House, Prospect Hill, DOUGLAS
Tel: + 44 (624) 623911
Fax: + 44 (624) 672901
Mailing Address: P.O. Box 23, DOUGLAS

European Affiliation: Midsnell International

International Contact: David Snelling

MOORE STEPHENS
P.O. Box 25, Clinch's House, Lord Street, DOUGLAS
Tel: + 44 (624) 662020
Fax: + 44 (624) 662430

European Affiliation: Moore Stephens

International Contact: Clive Dixon

Partners: 2
Professional staff: 4
Non-professional staff: 4
Total Staff: **10**

FEE INCOME

Year End: 31.12.90	%
Accountancy & Audit:	55.0
Insolvency:	5.0
Consultancy:	20.0
Tax:	10.0
Other:	10.0

CONTACT INFORMATION
Managing Partner: Clive Barton
Accountancy, Audit & Administration: Clive Dixon
Insolvency, Public Sector & Tax: Mark Solly

CLIENT SERVICES
All Services, Offshore Trust, Financial Services, Company Administration, Captive Insurance

MOORES ROWLAND
Finch House, 24 Finch Road, DOUGLAS
Tel: + 44 (624) 628006
Fax: + 44 (624) 674520

European Affiliation: Moores Rowland International

International Contact: W.T. (Will) Tickle

NOBLE & CO
Abacus House, Mona Street, DOUGLAS
Tel: + 44 (624) 628978
Fax: + 44 (624) 627215

European Affiliation: Summit International Associates Inc

International Contact: George C. Noble

Partners:	1
Professional staff:	2
Non-professional staff:	3
Total Staff:	**6**

FEE INCOME

Year End: 31.03.91	%
Accountancy & Audit:	44.0
Insolvency:	15.0
Other:	41.0

CONTACT INFORMATION
Company Formation Trustee Services: George C. Noble

CLIENT SERVICES
Accountancy (General), Audit, Insolvency & Corporate Restructuring, Management & Business Advice, Taxation (Corporate), Taxation (International), Trust Settlement & Estates, Company Formation & Management, Offshore Trusts & Taxation, Liquidations

PANNELL KERR FORSTER
Exchange House, 54-58 Athol Street, DOUGLAS
Tel: + 44 (624) 673811
Fax: + 44 (624) 629983
Mailing Address: P.O. Box 16, DOUGLAS

European Affiliation: Pannell Kerr Forster Worldwide

CONTACT INFORMATION
Managing Partner: Roger C. Rawcliffe

OTHER OFFICES

PANNELL KERR FORSTER
10 Auckland Terrace, RAMSEY
Tel: + 44 (624) 812270 *Fax:* + 44 (624) 815878

PANNELL KERR FORSTER
Eaglehurst Business Centre, Belmont Hill, DOUGLAS
Mailing Address: P.O. Box 155, DOUGLAS
Tel: + 44 (624) 628800 *Fax:* + 44 (624) 629329

Total Number of Offices: 3

PRICE WATERHOUSE
Target House, 1 & 3 Upper Church Street, DOUGLAS
Tel: + 44 (624) 662550
Fax: + 44 (624) 673113
Mailing Address: P.O. Box 213, DOUGLAS

European Affiliation: Price Waterhouse

Partners:	1
Professional staff:	6
Non-professional staff:	3
Total Staff:	**10**

CONTACT INFORMATION
Managing Partner: Graham H. Bolton

CLIENT SERVICES
Accountancy (General), Audit, Insolvency & Corporate Restructuring, Taxation (Corporate), Taxation (International), Trust Settlement & Estates

Industry Specialisations: Financial Sevices

READS & CO
Meghraj Centre, Upper Church Street, DOUGLAS
Tel: + 44 (624) 662250
Fax: + 44 (624) 662249
Mailing Address: P.O. Box 142, DOUGLAS

European Affiliation: DRM Internationally

K.J. ROSIER ASSOCIATES
1 Crosby Terrace, DOUGLAS
Tel: + 44 (624) 620857
Fax: + 44 (624) 673236

European Affiliation: TGI International

International Contact: Kelvyn J. Rosier

L. THOMPSON & CO
First Floor, Wellington House, Market Street, DOUGLAS
Tel: + 44 (624) 620793
Fax: + 44 (624) 629143

European Affiliation: Jeffreys Henry International

International Contact: L. Thompson

TOUCHE ROSS & CO
Bank of Scotland House, Prospect Hill, DOUGLAS
Tel: + 44 (624) 672332
Fax: + 44 (624) 672334

European Affiliation: DRT International

International Contact: Geoffrey Davies

Total Staff: 39

CLIENT SERVICES
All Services

FIDUCIAIRE TYRRELL HIGHAM LTD
P.O. Box 35, Derby Road, DOUGLAS
Tel: + 44 (624) 629615
Fax: + 44 (624) 629676

International Contact: Jan Katz

HORWATH ANDORRA SA

Bonaventura Armengol 15, 5º 3º, ANDORRA LA VELLA
Tel: + *33* 628 22081
Fax: + *33* 628 60978

European Affiliation: Horwath International

International Contact: Daniel Mestre

Partners:	4
Professional staff:	2
Non-professional staff:	3
Total Staff:	**9**

FEE INCOME

Year End: 31.12.90	%
Accountancy & Audit:	20.0
Consultancy:	10.0
Tax:	70.0

CLIENT SERVICES

Audit, Corporate Finance Advice, Management & Business Advice, Taxation (Corporate), Taxation (International)

Industry Specialisations: General Investment, Real Estate, Tobacco

---

NORMAN ALLPORT & CO

P.O. Box 781, ST HELIER, Jersey JE4 8ZZ
Tel: + *44* (534) 80321
Fax: + *44* (534) 69249

European Affiliation: ATD International

ARTHUR ANDERSEN & CO

40 The Esplanade, ST HELIER, Jersey JE4 8NN
Tel: + *44* (534) 89944
Fax: + *44* (534) 89945

European Affiliation: Arthur Andersen Worldwide

International Contact: Roy J. Chapman

MARTIN BATTY & PARTNERS

Hugo Chambers, 36 Hilgrove Street, ST HELIER, Jersey JE2 4SL
Tel: + *44* (534) 26573
Fax: + *44* (534) 68612

International Contact: Peter Wilton

Partners:	2
Professional staff:	5
Non-professional staff:	4
Total Staff:	**11**

CONTACT INFORMATION

Managing Partner: Martin Batty
Trust & Company Formation: Peter Wilton

CLIENT SERVICES

Accountancy (General), Corporate Finance Advice, Management & Business Advice, Taxation (International), Trust Settlement & Estates, Offshore Set Up & Administration

---

BDO CARNABY BARRETT

Seaton House, Seaton Place, ST HELIER, Jersey
Tel: + *44* (534) 21565
Fax: + *44* (534) 21987

European Affiliation: BDO Binder

International Contact: J. Barrett

BDO READS

Commerce House, ST PETER PORT, Guernsey
Tel: + *44* (481) 724561
Fax: + *44* (481) 711657
Mailing Address: P.O. Box 119, ST PETER PORT, Guernsey

European Affiliation: BDO Binder

International Contact: John Rowe

Partners:	11
Professional staff:	120
Non-professional staff:	19
Total Staff:	**150**

FEE INCOME

Year End: 30.06.91	£	%
Accountancy & Audit:	1,430,000	22.0
Insolvency:	65,000	1.0
Tax:	325,000	5.0
Other:	4,680,000	72.0
Total:	**6,500,000**	

CONTACT INFORMATION

Managing Partner: Kevin Lycett
Audit: Michael Quarrington
Insolvency: Stephen J. Ball
Administration: Steven Parrott
Tax (Corporate): Anthony C. Rogers
Tax (International): Alan Donaldson

CLIENT SERVICES

Accountancy (General), Audit, Computer Installation, Insolvency & Corporate Restructuring, Litigation/Legal Services, Management & Business Advice, Taxation (Corporate), Taxation (International), Trust Settlement & Estates, Trusteeship, Investment Advice

Industry Specialisations: Trusts & Trusteeship, Captive Insurance

---

CHANNEL TRUST LIMITED

Albert House, South Esplanade, ST PETER PORT, Guernsey
Tel: + *44* (481) 721896
Fax: + *44* (481) 724500
Mailing Address: P.O. Box 203, ST PETER PORT, Guernsey

European Affiliation: InterContinental Consultants (ICC)

International Contact: Richard G. Rowe

CLARK WHITEHILL LONG

Borough House, Rue du Pré, ST PETER PORT, Guernsey
Tel: + *44* (481) 721686
Fax: + *44* (481) 724831

European Affiliation: Clark Kenneth Leventhal
National Affiliation: Clark Whitehill Associates

International Contact: Simon Chandler

Partners:	3
Professional staff:	3
Non-professional staff:	6
Total Staff:	**12**

FEE INCOME

Year End: 1990	%
Accountancy & Audit:	50.0
Other:	50.0

CLIENT SERVICES

Accountancy (General), Audit, Corporate Finance Advice, Insolvency & Corporate Restructuring, Taxation (Corporate), Taxation (International), Trust Settlement & Estates

▷

COOPERS & LYBRAND DELOITTE
La Motte Chambers, ST HELIER, Jersey JE2 4SY
Tel: + *44* (534) 602000
Fax: + *44* (534) 602002

European Affiliation: Coopers & Lybrand Europe

International Contact: Geoffrey J. Grime

Partners:	26
Professional staff:	400
Total Staff:	**426**

CONTACT INFORMATION
Chairman: Geoffrey J. Grime
Tax (International): P.E. Giddings
Accountancy & Audit: D.H.C. Hill
Insolvency & Tax (Corporate): W.J. Perchard
Corporate Finance & Public Sector: D.H.C. Hill
Company & Trust Consultancy: M.P. Pinchard

CLIENT SERVICES
Accountancy (General), Audit, Corporate Finance Advice, Insolvency & Corporate Restructuring, Management & Business Advice, Management Buy-outs, Mergers & Acquisitions, Taxation (Corporate), Taxation (International), Trust Settlement & Estates, Secretarial Services

Industry Specialisations: Financial Sector, Automotive, CI-based Funds, Trust Companies, Pharmaceuticals, Food & Drink

OTHER OFFICES
COOPERS & LYBRAND DELOITTE
P.O. Box 626, National Westminster House, Le Truchot, ST PETER PORT, Guernsey
Tel: + *44* (481) 726921 *Fax:* + *44* (481) 711075
Contact: John E. Hallam

Total Number of Offices: 2

CRICHTON ASSOCIATES
P.O. Box 218, Equity & Law House, La Motte Street, ST HELIER, Jersey
Tel: + *44* (534) 74633
Fax: + *44* (534) 27349

National Affiliation: The CharterGroup Partnership

International Contact: John M. Scarborough

ERNST & YOUNG
14 New Street, ST PETER PORT, Guernsey
Tel: + *44* (481) 723232
Fax: + *44* (481) 710091

European Affiliation: Ernst & Young Europe

International Contact: Stephen J. Harlow

ERNST & YOUNG
Le Gallais Chambers, 54 Bath Street, ST HELIER, Jersey JE4 8YD
Tel: + *44* (534) 501000
Fax: + *44* (534) 23265

European Affiliation: Ernst & Young Europe

International Contact: John de Veulle

FEATHERSTONE TOOLE & CO
16 Dumaresq Street, ST HELIER, Jersey
Tel: + *44* (534) 59372
Fax: + *44* (534) 22630

European Affiliation: Horwath International

International Contact: Ian C. Toole

MICHAEL FORREST & PARTNERS
Langtry House, 40 La Motte Street, ST HELIER, Jersey
Tel: + *44* (534) 73921
Fax: + *44* (534) 24668
Mailing Address: P.O. Box 124, ST HELIER, Jersey

European Affiliation: Nexia International

International Contact: Michael Weston

Partners:	6
Professional staff:	5
Non-professional staff:	11

CONTACT INFORMATION
Managing Partner: Michael Forrest
Administration: John Pierce
Trustee Services: Gerry Smith
Corporate Planning & Administration: Margaret Lenaghan
Legal Services: Patricia Forbes

CLIENT SERVICES
Accountancy (General), Corporate Finance Advice, Taxation (International), Trust Settlement & Estates, Multi-jurisdictional Companies, Formation & Administration

---

HORLOCK & CO
P.O. Box 134, Town Mills, Trinity Square, ST PETER PORT, Guernsey
Tel: + *44* (481) 728228
Fax: + *44* (481) 711335

International Contact: Gordon Snelling

Partners:	2
Professional staff:	3
Non-professional staff:	27
Total Staff:	**32**

CONTACT INFORMATION
Partner: Martin Wright
Partner: Gordon Snelling

CLIENT SERVICES
Accountancy (General), Audit, Corporate Finance Advice, Management & Business Advice, Taxation (International), Company Administration

---

JACKSON FOX
Union House, Union Street, ST HELIER, Jersey JE4 8TZ
Tel: + *44* (534) 23352
Fax: + *44* (534) 74578
Mailing Address: P.O. Box 264, ST HELIER, Jersey JE4 8TZ

European Affiliation: HLB International

International Contact: Roger King

Partners:	5
Professional staff:	22
Non-professional staff:	13
Total Staff:	**40**

CONTACT INFORMATION
Managing Partner: Roger Maddock

CLIENT SERVICES
Accountancy (General), Audit, Computer Installation, Corporate Finance Advice, Insolvency & Corporate Restructuring, Life & Risk Assurance, Litigation/Legal Services, Management & Business Advice, Management Buy-outs, Mergers & Acquisitions, Pensions Planning, Value for Money Studies, Taxation (Corporate), Taxation (International), Trust Settlement & Estates, International Offshore Services

Industry Specialisations: Trustee Services

KPMG PEAT MARWICK

10 Lefebvre Street, ST PETER PORT, Guernsey
Tel: + 44 (481) 721000
Fax: + 44 (481) 722373

European Affiliation: KPMG

International Contact: M.J. Wilson

Partners:	13
Professional staff:	105
Non-professional staff:	25
Total Staff:	**143**

CONTACT INFORMATION

Chairman: M.J. Wilson
Accountancy (General): A.G. Sutherland
Audit & Offshore Funds: D. Farrimond
Partner: S.A. Matheson
Tax: M.S. Dean
Banking: S.F. Carnegie
Insurance: E.J.D. MacDonald

CLIENT SERVICES

Accountancy (General), Audit, Computer Installation, Corporate Finance Advice, Insolvency & Corporate Restructuring, Litigation/Legal Services, Management & Business Advice, Management Buy-outs, Mergers & Acquisitions, Pensions Planning, Value for Money Studies, Taxation (Corporate), Taxation (International), Trust Settlement & Estates, Forensic Accounting, International Tax Planning

Industry Specialisations: Banking, Insurance, Offshore Funds, Trust & Company Administration, Local Government

OTHER OFFICES

KPMG PEAT MARWICK - CHANNEL ISLANDS
Equity & Law House, La Motte Street, ST HELIER, Jersey JE4 8WQ
Tel: + 44 (534) 27225 *Fax:* + 44 (534) 39487

Total Number of Offices: 2

GRAEME LE ROSSIGNOL & CO

6 Hilgrove Street, ST HELIER, Jersey
Tel: + 44 (534) 75178
Fax: + 44 (534) 26391

European Affiliation: INPACT - International Network of Professional Accountants

International Contact: Graham Journeaux
Peter Ingram

LE SUEUR, IRESON & CO

Portman House, Hue Street, ST HELIER, Jersey
Tel: + 44 (534) 72190
Fax: + 44 (534) 24773

International Contact: Terry Le Sueur

Partners:	3
Professional staff:	9
Non-professional staff:	8
Total Staff:	**20**

FEE INCOME

Year End: 28.02.90	**US$**
Total:	**1,333,000**

CONTACT INFORMATION

Accountancy (General): James Colclough
Audit: Richard Ireson

CLIENT SERVICES

Accountancy (General), Audit, Taxation (Corporate), Taxation (International), Trust Settlement & Estates

LINCE SALISBURY

Avenue House, St Julian's Avenue, ST PETER PORT, Guernsey
Tel: + 44 (481) 723071
Fax: + 44 (481) 720499

European Affiliation: Moores Rowland International

International Contact: Ray R. Salisbury

LUBBOCK FINE

Suite 11, Queensway House, Queen Street, ST HELIER, Jersey JE4 8TZ
Tel: + 44 (534) 74707
Fax: + 44 (534) 34703
Mailing Address: P.O. Box 258, ST HELIER, Jersey JE4 9TZ

European Affiliation: Russell Bedford International

International Contact: Andrew Crichton

McFADYEN, SCOTT-WARREN & MORRIS

Broadcasting House, Rouge Bouillon, ST HELIER, Jersey
Tel: + 44 (534) 37236

European Affiliation: CPA Associates Inc

International Contact: C.A. McFadyen

MOORE STEPHENS

First Island House, Peter Street, ST HELIER, Jersey JE4 8SG
Tel: + 44 (534) 80088
Fax: + 44 (534) 80099
Mailing Address: P.O. Box 236, ST HELIER, Jersey JE4 8SG

European Affiliation: Moore Stephens

International Contact: Clive Barton

Partners:	5
Professional staff:	10
Non-professional staff:	60
Total Staff:	**75**

FEE INCOME

Year End: 31.12.91	**%**
Accountancy & Audit:	60.0
Insolvency:	2.0
Consultancy:	18.0
Tax:	10.0
Other:	10.0

CONTACT INFORMATION

Managing Partner: Clive Barton
Audit: Stephen Milsom
Administration: David Croxford
Accountancy & Insolvency: David Croxford
Tax & Management Consultancy: Clive Barton
Corporate Finance & Administration: James Y. Bowman

CLIENT SERVICES
Accountancy (General), Audit, Corporate Finance Advice, Insolvency & Corporate Restructuring, Litigation/Legal Services, Management & Business Advice, Taxation (International), Trust Settlement & Estates, Offshore Trust, Company Administration Service

Total Number of Offices: 2

MOORE STEPHENS

Town Mills South, La Rue du Pré, ST PETER PORT, Guernsey
Tel: + *44* (481) 721769
Fax: + *44* (481) 724657
Mailing Address: P.O. Box 146, Rue du Pré, ST PETER PORT, Guernsey

European Affiliation: Moore Stephens

International Contact: George T. Shaw

MOORES ROWLAND

Broadcasting House, Rouge Bouillon, ST HELIER, Jersey
Tel: + *44* (534) 37235
Fax: + *44* (534) 39143

European Affiliation: Moores Rowland International

International Contact: Chris McFadyen

MOORES ROWLAND

Barclays Bank Chambers, Grand Rue, ST MARTIN, Guernsey
Tel: + *44* (481) 35448
Fax: + *44* (481) 35627

European Affiliation: Moores Rowland International

International Contact: Mark Gill

PANNELL KERR FORSTER

Suites 13 & 15, Sarnia House, Le Truchot, ST PETER PORT, Guernsey
Tel: + *44* (481) 727927
Fax: + *44* (481) 710511
Mailing Address: P.O. Box 296, ST PETER PORT, Guernsey

European Affiliation: Pannell Kerr Forster Worldwide

CONTACT INFORMATION
Managing Partner: C.P. Spencer

ALEX PICOT & CO

Paragon House, 95-97 Halkett Place, ST HELIER, Jersey JE1 1BX
Tel: + *44* (534) 21311
Fax: + *44* (534) 66832

European Affiliation: GMN International

International Contact: Rod Amy

PRICE WATERHOUSE

Eagle House, Don Road, ST HELIER, Jersey
Tel: + *44* (534) 74222
Fax: + *44* (534) 36790

European Affiliation: Price Waterhouse

Partners:	4
Professional staff:	42
Non-professional staff:	11
Total Staff:	**57**

CONTACT INFORMATION
Insolvency: J.L. Warry
Management Consultancy: I.D. Wright
Senior Partner: J.L. Warry
Accountancy & Audit: L.P.C. Taylor
Tax: R.M. Ingram

CLIENT SERVICES
Accountancy (General), Audit, Insolvency & Corporate Restructuring, Taxation (Corporate), Taxation (International), Trust Settlement & Estates

Industry Specialisations: Offshore Financial Services

READS & CO

Wellington House, Union Street, ST HELIER, Jersey
Tel: + *44* (534) 73377
Fax: + *44* (534) 38946
Mailing Address: P.O. Box 641, ST HELIER, Jersey JE4 8YJ

European Affiliation: DRM Internationally

International Contact: Brian Pierce

Partners:	5
Professional staff:	30
Non-professional staff:	65
Total Staff:	**100**

FEE INCOME

Year End: 30.06.91	%
Accountancy & Audit:	30.0
Consultancy:	10.0
Tax:	60.0

CONTACT INFORMATION
Managing Partner: Harry Craig
Accountancy (General): Ian Richardson
Audit: Jim Bennett
Management Consultancy: Tony Grimes
Management Consultancy: Ian Dove
Administration: Brian Pierce
Tax (International): Peter Newbala

CLIENT SERVICES
Accountancy (General), Audit, Computer Installation, Corporate Finance Advice, Management & Business Advice, Management Buy-outs, Mergers & Acquisitions, Taxation (International), Trust Settlement & Estates, Offshore Collective Investment Fund

Industry Specialisations: Offshore Finance, Tourism

MAJOR CLIENTS
BHF Bank (Jersey) Ltd, Cater Allen Bank (Jersey) Ltd, Hambros Bank (Jersey) Ltd, Lloyds Bank Finance Ltd, Morgan Grenfell Ltd

OTHER OFFICES

READS & CO
P.O. Box 191, Commerce House, Les Banques, ST PETER PORT, Guernsey
Tel: + *44* (481) 724561 *Fax:* + *44* (481) 711657
Contact: Alan C.J. Donaldson

Total Number of Offices: 2

SAFFERY CHAMPNESS

La Tonnelle House, Les Banques, ST SAMPSON, Guernsey
Tel: + *44* (481) 721374
Fax: + *44* (481) 722046
Mailing Address: P.O. Box 141, ST SAMPSON, Guernsey

European Affiliation: SC International

International Contact: Robert A.G. Sinclair

STRACHANS

Sommerville House, Phillips Street, ST HELIER, Jersey
Tel: +44 (534) 71505
Fax: +44 (534) 23902

European Affiliation: BKR International

International Contact: Terry A. Jehan

CONTACT INFORMATION
Partner: Richard J. Egglishaw

TOUCHE ROSS & CO

66-68 Esplanade, ST HELIER, Jersey JE2 3QB
Tel: +44 (534) 37770
Fax: +44 (534) 34037
Mailing Address: P.O. Box 403, ST HELIER, Jersey JE2 3QB

European Affiliation: DRT International

International Contact: Geoffrey Davies

Total Staff: **172**

CLIENT SERVICES
All Services

Total Number of Offices: 2

WOOLFORD & CO

Dixcart House, Sir William Place, ST PETER PORT, Guernsey
Tel: +44 (481) 23996
Fax: +44 (481) 27417

European Affiliation: The International Group of Accounting Firms Ltd (IGAF)

International Contact: Robert P. Woolford

AFXENTIOU & PHILLIPPIDES

Afemia House, 3rd Floor, 70 Makarios Avenue, NICOSIA
Tel: +357 (2) 455706
Fax: +357 (2) 444489
Mailing Address: P.O. Box 7171, NICOSIA

European Affiliation: Clark Kenneth Leventhal

International Contact: George Philippides

Partners:	2
Professional staff:	13
Non-professional staff:	5
Total Staff:	**20**

FEE INCOME

Year End: 1990	%
Accountancy & Audit:	67.0
Tax:	11.0
Other:	22.0

CLIENT SERVICES
Accountancy (General), Audit, Corporate Finance Advice, Insolvency & Corporate Restructuring, Management & Business Advice, Taxation (Corporate), Taxation (International)

BDO IOANNOU & CHRISTODOULIDES

Office 403, Galaxias Comm Cntr, 4th Floor, Corner of 33 Makarios III Avenue & 36 Ayias Elenis Street, NICOSIA
Tel: +357 (2) 442797
Fax: +357 (2) 446308
Mailing Address: P.O. Box 2283, NICOSIA

European Affiliation: BDO Binder

International Contact: Minas Ioannou

Partners:	2
Professional staff:	20
Non-professional staff:	8
Total Staff:	**30**

FEE INCOME

Year End: 31.12.90	**C£**	%
Accountancy & Audit:	264,970	51.0
Consultancy:	25,330	5.0
Tax:	207,480	40.0
Other:	20,840	4.0
Total:	**518,620**	

CONTACT INFORMATION
Chairman: Minas Ioannou
Managing Partner: Andreas Christodoulides
Audit: Angelos Christodoulides
Audit: Christakis Ioannou
MAS/Offshore Companies: Nicos Gavrielides

CLIENT SERVICES
All Services

Industry Specialisations: Retailing, Offshore Companies, Building, Hotels & Tourism, Car Hire, Light Industry

MAJOR CLIENTS
Achellec Electronics Ltd, Alaska Refrigerators Ltd, Avenita Tourist Enterprises Ltd, Chapo Holdings Ltd, Charilaos Apostolides & Company Ltd, Elijela Travel Ltd, Glyfades Tourist & Development Ltd, Kennedy Hotels Ltd, Kestrel (Cyprus) Ltd, Laos Bros Ltd, M.C. General Flooring Company Ltd, Petousis Bros Ltd, Spie Capag Equipment (Cyprus) Ltd, Technotel Trading Ltd, Ttofis Kyriacou & Sons Ltd, U.A. Automotive Dealers Ltd, Varosiotis Supermarkets Ltd, Vassos Eliades Ltd, Viometal Ltd, Wellgoods Ltd

OTHER OFFICES

BDO IOANNOU & CHRISTODOULIDES
Meliza Court, 5th Floor, 229 Archbishop Makarios III Avenue, LIMASSOL
Mailing Address: P.O. Box 4844, LIMASSOL
Tel: +357 (5) 358800 *Fax:* +357 (5) 374342
Contact: Andreas Christodoulides

Total Number of Offices: 2

CHRYSANTHOU & CHRISTOFOROU

3 Homer Avenue, Flat 310, NICOSIA
Tel: +357 (2) 475181
Fax: +375 (2) 473909
Mailing Address: P.O. Box 1675, NICOSIA

European Affiliation: Arthur Andersen Worldwide

International Contact: Michael Christoforou

Partners:	7
Professional staff:	20
Non-professional staff:	6
Total Staff:	**33**

FEE INCOME

Year End: 31.12.90	%
Accountancy & Audit:	60.0
Consultancy:	10.0
Tax:	25.0
Other:	5.0

CONTACT INFORMATION
Chairman: Michael Christoforou
Corporate Finance: Nicos Papakyriacou

▷

Insolvency: Chr. Chrysanthou
Management Consultancy: Christis Christoforou
Accountancy & Audit: Michael Christoforou

CLIENT SERVICES
All Services

A. CHRYSANTHOU & CO

El Greco House, 20 Queen Frederica Street, Office 303, NICOSIA
Tel: +357 (2) 455900
Fax: +357 (2) 450498
Mailing Address: P.O. Box 5316, NICOSIA

European Affiliation: DFK International

International Contact: T. Chrysanthou

N. CONSTANTINOU & CO

Rega Ferou Street, Limassol Centre, Block B, Office 508, LIMASSOL
Tel: +357 (5) 368823
Fax: +357 (5) 375173
Mailing Address: P.O. Box 4039, LIMASSOL

European Affiliation: DFK International

International Contact: N.A. Constantinou

COOPERS & LYBRAND/IOANNOU ZAMPELAS & CO

Julia House, 3 Themistocles Dervis Street, NICOSIA
Tel: +357 (2) 453053
Fax: +357 (2) 475194
Mailing Address: P.O. Box 1612, NICOSIA

European Affiliation: Coopers & Lybrand Europe

International Contact: Michael H. Zampelas

Partners:	14
Professional staff:	200
Non-professional staff:	60
Total Staff:	**274**

CONTACT INFORMATION
Chairman: Michael H. Zampelas
Audit: Dinos N. Papadopoulos
Management Consultancy: Nicos C. Nicolaides
Offshore: Anthony Haji Roussos
Tax: Panikos N. Tsiailis
Computer Software: Kyriakos Fiakkas

CLIENT SERVICES
Accountancy (General), Audit, Computer Installation, Corporate Finance Advice, Insolvency & Corporate Restructuring, Life & Risk Assurance, Litigation/Legal Services, Management & Business Advice, Management Buy-outs, Mergers & Acquisitions, Pensions Planning, Value for Money Studies, Taxation (Corporate), Taxation (International), Trust Settlement & Estates, Offshore Companies Services, Trusts

Industry Specialisations: Offshore, Shipping, Pharmaceuticals, Banking, Automotive, Food & Drink, Captive Insurance, Communications

OTHER OFFICES

COOPERS & LYBRAND/IOANNOU ZAMPELAS & CO
Abacus House, 3a Artemidos Avenue, P.O. Box 450, LARNACA
Tel: +357 (4) 627070 *Fax:* +357 (4) 627072
Contact: Loizos Shakallis

COOPERS & LYBRAND/IOANNOU ZAMPELAS & CO
P.O. Box 3034, Nora Court, Athinon Street, LIMASSOL
Tel: +357 (5) 372603 *Fax:* +357 (5) 370946
Contact: Tassos Televantides

COOPERS & LYBRAND/IOANNOU ZAMPELAS & CO
P.O. Box 479, Panayiotis Centre, 63 Makarios Avenue, PAPHOS
Tel: +357 (6) 237134 *Fax:* +357 (6) 242868
Contact: Angelos Loizou

COOPERS & LYBRAND/IOANNOU ZAMPELAS & CO
P.O. Box 170, 15 Ayios Georgios Street, PARALIMNI
Tel: +357 (3) 822311 *Fax:* +357 (3) 820514

Total Number of Offices: 5

COSTOURIS, MICHAELIDES & CO

"Cosmo" Building, Corner Grivas Dighenis & Dem Severis Av., NICOSIA
Tel: +357 (2) 448868
Fax: +357 (2) 477849
Mailing Address: P.O. Box 1392, NICOSIA

European Affiliation: Grant Thornton International

International Contact: George Michaelides

FEE INCOME

Year End: 31.12.90	**Dr (million)**
Total:	**714,066**

CONTACT INFORMATION
Managing Partner: Michalakis Costouris

CLIENT SERVICES
Accountancy (General), Audit, Computer Installation, Insolvency & Corporate Restructuring, Management & Business Advice, Mergers & Acquisitions, Pensions Planning, Taxation (Corporate), Taxation (International), Computer Consultancy, Company Formation

OTHER OFFICES

COSTOURIS, MICHAELIDES & CO
Panayides Building 4th Floor, Grivas Deighenis Avenue, LIMASSOL
Mailing Address: P.O. Box 493, LIMASSOL
Tel: +357 (5) 363316 *Fax:* +357 (5) 363453

Total Number of Offices: 2

DAMIANOU & CO

5 Hitron Street, NICOSIA
Tel: +357 (2) 459299
Fax: +357 (2) 461754

European Affiliation: BKR International

International Contact: Chris Damianou

DELOITTE & TOUCHE

256 Makarios Avenue, LIMASSOL
Tel: +357 (5) 355644
Fax: +357 (5) 356010
Mailing Address: P.O. Box 3180, LIMASSOL

European Affiliation: DRT International

International Contact: J.D. Ioannides

Partners:	6
Professional staff:	58
Non-professional staff:	14
Total Staff:	**78**

CLIENT SERVICES
Accountancy (General), Audit, Computer Installation, Corporate Finance Advice, Insolvency & Corporate Restructuring, Management & Business

Advice, Management Buy-outs, Mergers & Acquisitions, Taxation (Corporate), Taxation (International), Management Consultancy

MAJOR CLIENTS

Arab Bank, C.C.C. Holdings & Investments, Columbia Shipmanagement, Covotsos Textiles, Cyprus Popular Bank, C.F. Ahrienkel, DSR Shipping, Françoudi & Stephanou, Hanseatic Shipping, Harmstorff, Intership, Lanitis Group, Le Meridien, Navigo Management, Klaus E. Oldendorff, Scandia

Total Number of Offices: 3

L. DEMETRIOU

4-6 Romanos Street, Office 103, NICOSIA
Tel: +357 (2) 456933
Fax: +357 (2) 467564
Mailing Address: P.O. Box 5540, NICOSIA

European Affiliation: GMN International

International Contact: Louis Demetriou

Partners:	1
Professional staff:	1
Non-professional staff:	3
Total Staff:	**5**

CLIENT SERVICES

All Services

Industry Specialisations: Real Estate, Hotels, Professionals

P.G. ECONOMIDES & CO

Doma Building, 227 Archbishop Makarios III Avenue, LIMASSOL
Tel: +357 (5) 342301
Fax: +357 (5) 370687
Mailing Address: P.O. Box 3117, LIMASSOL

European Affiliation: Independent Accountants International

International Contact: Peter G. Economides

Partners:	3
Professional staff:	16
Non-professional staff:	7
Total Staff:	**26**

FEE INCOME

Year End: 31.12.90	%
Accountancy & Audit:	60.0
Consultancy:	5.0
Tax:	10.0
Other:	25.0

CONTACT INFORMATION

Managing Partner: Peter G. Economides
Accountancy & Tax (Corporate): Michael Michaelides
Audit & Management Consultancy: Panayiotis Constantinou
Management Offshore Entities: Elena Pirilli

CLIENT SERVICES

All Services including Offshore Formation & Management

ERNST & YOUNG

Nicosia Tower Centre, 36 Byron Avenue, 162 NICOSIA
Tel: +357 (2) 467000
Fax: +357 (2) 476613
Mailing Address: P.O. Box 1656, 162 NICOSIA

European Affiliation: Ernst & Young Europe

International Contact: Nicos Lakoufis

OTHER OFFICES

ERNST & YOUNG
Nicolaou Pendadromos Centre, Office 908, Block A, 205 LIMASSOL
Mailing Address: P.O. Box 123, 205 LIMASSOL
Tel: +357 (5) 362580 *Fax:* +357 (5) 365174

Total Number of Offices: 2

GREGORIOU & CO

Greg Tower, 7 Florina Street, NICOSIA
Tel: +357 (2) 447507
Fax: +357 (2) 447601
Mailing Address: P.O. Box 4854, NICOSIA

European Affiliation: Midsnell International

International Contact: Andreas N. Gregoriou

EMILIOS KALLENOS

Demitas Tower, 14 Michalakopoulou, NICOSIA
Tel: +357 (2) 474301
Fax: +357 (2) 367644
Mailing Address: P.O. Box 7050, NICOSIA

European Affiliation: INPACT - International Network of Professional Accountants

Partners:	1
Professional staff:	7
Non-professional staff:	3
Total Staff:	**11**

FEE INCOME

Year End: 31.12.90	%
Accountancy & Audit:	85.0
Consultancy:	5.0
Tax:	10.0

CONTACT INFORMATION

Managing Partner: Emilios Kallenos

CLIENT SERVICES

All Services

P. KALOPETRIDES & CO

2 Christ Sozos Street, Eiffel Tower, 3rd & 6th Floors, NICOSIA
Tel: +357 (2) 477017
Fax: +357 (2) 451297
Mailing Address: P.O. Box 1855, NICOSIA

European Affiliation: Horwath International

International Contact: Petros Kalopetrides

OTHER OFFICES

P. KALOPETRIDES & CO
32 Archbishop Makarios III Avenue, LARNACA
Mailing Address: P.O. Box 369, LARNACA
Tel: +357 (4) 653555

P. KALOPETRIDES & CO
Corner Gladstone 69 & Aristophanes Street, Acropolis Centre, LIMASSOL
Mailing Address: P.O. Box 6383, LIMASSOL
Tel: +357 (5) 364368

Total Number of Offices: 3

KITTIS-TROKOUDES

Anemomylos Offices, Suite 104, 8M Karaolis Street, 162 NICOSIA
Tel: +357 (2) 365085
Fax: +357 (2) 445577
Mailing Address: P.O. Box 3957, 162 NICOSIA

▷

European Affiliation: SC International

International Contact: Anthoulis Trokoudes
Dinos Kittis

KPMG PEAT MARWICK

10 Mnasiadou Street, NICOSIA
Tel: +357 (2) 448700
Fax: +357 (2) 365336
Mailing Address: P.O. Box 1121, NICOSIA

European Affiliation: KPMG

International Contact: A. Michaelides

OTHER OFFICES

KPMG PEAT MARWICK
Berengaria Building, 25 Spyrou Araouzou Street, LIMASSOL
Mailing Address: P.O. Box 161, LIMASSOL
Tel: +357 (5) 163251 *Fax:* +357 (5) 163842
Contact: A.M. Lozides

KPMG PEAT MARWICK
8 Saint Paul Street, LARNACA
Mailing Address: P.O. Box 75, LARNACA
Tel: +357 (4) 151158 *Fax:* +357 (4) 120975
Contact: C.C. Christofides

KPMG PEAT MARWICK
Paphos Popular Bank Building, Apostolos Pavlos Avenue, PAPHOS
Mailing Address: P.O. Box 288, PAPHOS
Tel: +357 (6) 143050 *Fax:* +357 (6) 143062
Contact: A.A. Demetriou

KPMG PEAT MARWICK
37 1st April Street, Office 4, PARALIMNI
Mailing Address: P.O. Box 200, PARALIMNI
Tel: +357 (3) 120080 *Fax:* +357 (3) 120084
Contact: A.M. Gregoriades

Total Number of Offices: 5

KYPRIANIDES & STYLIANOU

6 Ayas Elenis Street, Saint Helen Tower, 2nd Floor, No. 21, NICOSIA
Tel: +357 (2) 448305
Fax: +357 (2) 452119
Mailing Address: P.O. Box 1950, NICOSIA

European Affiliation: HLB International

International Contact: B. Stylianou

Partners:	2
Professional staff:	2
Non-professional staff:	11
Total Staff:	**15**

CONTACT INFORMATION
Managing Partner: B. Stylianou
Partner: P. Kyprianides

CLIENT SERVICES
All Services

MOORE STEPHENS

Iris Tower, 6th Floor, Makarios Avenue & Agapinor Street, NICOSIA
Tel: +357 (2) 462906
Fax: +357 (2) 442021
Mailing Address: P.O. Box 4656, NICOSIA

European Affiliation: Moore Stephens

International Contact: Panayiotis P. Stylianou

PAVLOU, POYIADJIS & CO

2 Sophouli Street, Chanteclair House, NICOSIA
Tel: +357 (2) 453406
Fax: +357 (2) 453276
Mailing Address: P.O. Box 1814, NICOSIA

European Affiliation: Nexia International

International Contact: John P. Poyiadjis

Partners:	2
Professional staff:	9
Non-professional staff:	4
Total Staff:	**15**

FEE INCOME

Year End: 31.12.90	**C£**	**%**
Accountancy & Audit:		80.0
Insolvency:		5.0
Tax:		10.0
Other:		5.0
Total:	**180,000**	

CONTACT INFORMATION
Managing Partner: John P. Poyiadjis
Accountancy (General): Stelios Malekkos
Audit: Raffi Boyadjian
Insolvency: John P. Poyiadjis
Administration: Andreas Demosthenous

CLIENT SERVICES
All Services

Industry Specialisations: Offshore Business, Fashion

PETRIDES & MODINOS

3rd Floor, Loucaides Building, St Andrew & Archbishop Kyprianou, LIMASSOL
Tel: +357 (5) 369295
Fax: +357 (5) 367007
Mailing Address: P.O. Box 11, LIMASSOL

European Affiliation: Moores Rowland International

International Contact: Demetrios Petrides

PRICE WATERHOUSE

Kermia House, 4 Diagoras Street, NICOSIA
Tel: +357 (2) 463800
Fax: +357 (2) 449473
Mailing Address: P.O. Box 1687, NICOSIA

European Affiliation: Price Waterhouse

Partners:	4
Professional staff:	40
Non-professional staff:	11
Total Staff:	**55**

FEE INCOME

Year End: 30.06.91	**C£**	**%**
Accountancy & Audit:	410,000	63.0
Insolvency:	20,000	3.0
Consultancy:	60,000	9.0
Tax:	60,000	9.0
Other:	100,000	16.0
Total:	**650,000**	

CONTACT INFORMATION
Managing Partner: Theodoros Philippou
Accountancy (General): Theodoros Philippou
Tax: Nicos Ionides

CLIENT SERVICES
All Services

MAJOR CLIENTS
Bank for Foreign Economic Affairs USSR, BAT (Cyprus) Ltd, Alexander Demetriou & Son, Electricity Authority of Cyprus, Esso Cyprus Incorporated, Etko Ltd, Grecian Hotel Enterprises Ltd, Hawaii Constructions Ltd, Iacovos P. Iacovou Ltd, IBM - Cyprus Branch, Lord Jeans Ltd, Lordos Hotels (Holdings) Ltd, George D. Lordos & Sons Ltd, A. Loutsios Ltd, Reuters Ltd, Shell Cyprus Ltd, Tetra Pak (Near East) Ltd, Tricomitis Ltd, United Plastics Ltd, F.W. Woolworth & Co (Cyprus) Ltd

OTHER OFFICES
PRICE WATERHOUSE
1 April Street 66, PARALIMNI
Mailing Address: P.O. Box 187, PARALIMNI
Tel: +357 (3) 822966 *Fax:* +357 (3) 820733

PRICE WATERHOUSE
Elpa Building, 8 Greg. Afxentiou Avenue, LARNACA
Mailing Address: P.O. Box 863, LARNACA
Tel: +357 (4) 653878 *Fax:* +357 (4) 629008
Contact: Takis C. Christofides

PRICE WATERHOUSE
Helios Court, 221 Chr. Haggipavlou Street, LIMASSOL
Mailing Address: P.O. Box 1631, LIMASSOL
Tel: +357 (5) 373200 *Fax:* +357 (5) 373737
Contact: Costas Tsielepis

Total Number of Offices: 4

PROIOS & CO
6 Neoptolemos Street, NICOSIA
Tel: +357 (2) 490094
Fax: +357 (2) 490494
Mailing Address: P.O. Box 8530, NICOSIA

European Affiliation: Summit International Associates Inc

Partners:	3
Professional staff:	7
Non-professional staff:	3
Total Staff:	**13**

FEE INCOME

Year End: 1990	%
Accountancy & Audit:	40.0
Insolvency:	5.0
Consultancy:	20.0
Tax:	20.0
Other:	15.0

CLIENT SERVICES
Accountancy (General), Audit, Corporate Finance Advice, Insolvency & Corporate Restructuring, Management & Business Advice, Mergers & Acquisitions, Pensions Planning, Value for Money Studies, Taxation (Corporate), Taxation (International), Trust Settlement & Estates

SAVVIDES & PARTNERS/PANNELL KERR FORSTER
4th, 5th & 7th Floor Meliza Court, 229 Archbishop Makarios III Avenue, 255 LIMASSOL
Tel: +357 (5) 369404
Fax: +357 (5) 377871
Mailing Address: P.O. Box 1263, LIMASSOL

European Affiliation: Pannell Kerr Forster Worldwide

International Contact: Frixos Savvides
Mehran Eftekhar

Partners:	6
Professional staff:	38
Non-professional staff:	16
Total Staff:	**60**

FEE INCOME

Year End: 1990	%
Accountancy & Audit:	50.0
Insolvency:	5.0
Consultancy:	30.0
Tax:	10.0
Other:	5.0

CONTACT INFORMATION
Managing Partner: Frixos Savvides
Accountancy (General): Pavlos Meletiou
Accountancy & Audit: Christos Antoniou
Corporate Finance & Consultancy: Frixos Savvides
Insolvency & Administration: Mehran Eftekhar
Public Sector & Tax: Mehran Eftekhar
Information Technology: Angelos Christodoulides

CLIENT SERVICES
Accountancy (General), Audit, Computer Installation, Corporate Finance Advice, Insolvency & Corporate Restructuring, Management & Business Advice, Mergers & Acquisitions, Pensions Planning, Value for Money Studies, Taxation (Corporate), Taxation (International), Trust Settlement & Estates, Shipping & Ship Management, Secretarial Services, Offshore Companies

Industry Specialisations: Aerospace, Shipping, Media, Banks, Insurance, Hospitality, Distillers, Fish Farms, Construction, Bookshops

OTHER OFFICES
SAVVIDES & PARTNERS/PANNELL KERR FORSTER
64 Kennedy Avenue, NICOSIA
Mailing Address: P.O. Box 8584, NICOSIA
Tel: +357 (2) 313066 *Fax:* +357 (2) 312514
Contact: Pavlos Meletiou

SAVVIDES & PARTNERS/PANNELL KERR FORSTER
5th Floor, Office 52, 81 Archbishop Makarios III Avenue, LARNACA
Mailing Address: P.O. Box 962, LARNACA
Tel: +357 (4) 624005 *Fax:* +357 (4) 623989
Contact: Stavros Stavrou

Total Number of Offices: 3

T.C. SHAKALLIS & CO
Acropolis Centre, 3rd Floor, Gladstone Street, LIMASSOL
Tel: +357 (5) 362252
Fax: +357 (5) 362407
Mailing Address: P.O. Box 4428, LIMASSOL

European Affiliation: DRM Internationally

International Contact: Tonis Skakallis

Partners:	3
Professional staff:	7
Non-professional staff:	3
Total Staff:	**13**

▷

FEE INCOME

Year End: 31.12.90	**%**
Accountancy & Audit:	56.0
Consultancy:	13.0
Tax:	7.0
Other:	24.0

CONTACT INFORMATION
Managing Partner: Tonis Shakallis
Public Sector & Consultancy: George Savvides
Tax (Corporate): Louis Loizou
Administration & Tax: Tonis Shakallis
Corporate Finance & Insolvency: Tonis Shakallis

CLIENT SERVICES
Accountancy (General), Audit, Computer Installation, Corporate Finance Advice, Insolvency & Corporate Restructuring, Life & Risk Assurance, Litigation/Legal Services, Management & Business Advice, Management Buy-outs, Mergers & Acquisitions, Pensions Planning, Value for Money Studies, Taxation (Corporate), Taxation (International), Trust Settlement & Estates, Offshore Activities

---

TIMENIDES & EVANGELI
10 Dimitsanis, NICOSIA
Tel: +*357* (2) 442621
Fax: +*357* (2) 360691
Mailing Address: P.O. Box 1560, NICOSIA

European Affiliation: K.S. International

International Contact: Evangelos Evangelou

Partners:	2
Professional staff:	1
Non-professional staff:	3
Total Staff:	6

CONTACT INFORMATION
Management Consultancy: Evi Timenidou
Accountancy, Audit & Insolvency: Evi Timenidou
Tax, Public Sector & Administration: Evangelos Evangelou

CLIENT SERVICES
Accountancy (General), Audit, Computer Installation, Corporate Finance Advice, Insolvency & Corporate Restructuring, Management & Business Advice, Mergers & Acquisitions, Taxation (Corporate), Taxation (International)

Industry Specialisations: Insurance, Manufacturing, Trading

N. A. YAMAKIS
Regaena House, Regaena Street 4, P.O. Box 1082, NICOSIA
Tel: +*357* (2) 463510
Fax: +*357* (2) 475143

European Affiliation: TGI International

International Contact: Ninos A. Yamakis

BROWNE CRAINE & CO
Don House, 37 Line Wall Road, GIBRALTAR

European Affiliation: INPACT - International Network of Professional Accountants

International Contact: Maurice Singer

CLIENT SERVICES
All Services

CARUANA & CO
Imossi House, 1/5 Irish Town, GIBRALTAR
Tel: +*350* 41200
Fax: +*350* 41201
Mailing Address: P.O. Box 758, GIBRALTAR
European Affiliation: Urbach Hacker Young International

CHALBRIDGE MANAGEMENT LTD
Suite G, Second Floor, Eurolife Building, 1 Corral Road, GIBRALTAR
Tel: +*350* 78978
Fax: +*350* 70498

European Affiliation: InterContinental Consultants (ICC)

International Contact: Roydon J. Tucker

CLINTONS
Units 2 & 3 (2nd floor), Gibraltar Heights, 215 Main Street, GIBRALTAR
Tel: +*350* 74100
Fax: +*350* 78081
Mailing Address: P.O. Box 239, GIBRALTAR

European Affiliation: Grant Thornton International

International Contact: Arthur G. Clinton

Partners:	2
Professional staff:	0
Non-professional staff:	5
Total Staff:	7

FEE INCOME

Year End: 1990	**US$**
Total:	**564,000**

CONTACT INFORMATION
Managing Partner: Arthur Clinton

COOPERS & LYBRAND
ICC Building, Casemates Square, GIBRALTAR
Tel: +*350* 73520
Fax: +*350* 76689
Mailing Address: P.O. Box 559, GIBRALTAR

European Affiliation: Coopers & Lybrand Europe

International Contact: Kenneth Cappie-Wood

Partners:	3
Professional staff:	12
Non-professional staff:	28
Total Staff:	43

CONTACT INFORMATION
Accountancy (General): J.P. Galliano
Audit & Insolvency: R.A. Hooper
Management Consultancy & Tax: Kenneth Cappie-Wood
Trust & Company Administration: J.A. Welham

CLIENT SERVICES
Accountancy (General), Audit, Corporate Finance Advice, Insolvency & Corporate Restructuring, Management & Business Advice, Taxation (Corporate), Taxation (International), Trust Settlement & Estates, Company Secretarial

Industry Specialisations: Trust & Company Administration, Offshore Clients

ERNST & YOUNG
Suite 5, International House, Bell Lane, GIBRALTAR
Tel: +*350* 79799
Fax: +*350* 75141
Mailing Address: P.O. Box 178, GIBRALTAR
European Affiliation: Ernst & Young Europe
International Contact: Kenneth A. Robinson

KPMG PEAT MARWICK
Suite C, 3rd Floor, Regal House, Queensway, GIBRALTAR
Tel: +*350* 74015
Fax: +*350* 74016
Mailing Address: P.O. Box 191, GIBRALTAR
European Affiliation: KPMG
International Contact: F.A. Isola

Partners:	2
Total Staff:	**32**

CLIENT SERVICES
Accountancy (General), Audit, Corporate Finance Advice, Insolvency & Corporate Restructuring, Management & Business Advice, Pensions Planning, Taxation (Corporate), Taxation (International), Trust Settlement & Estates

Industry Specialisations: Banking & Financial Services, Insurance, Construction,, Hotels & Tourism

MAJOR CLIENTS
Banco Bilbao Vizcaya, Bank of Credit and Commerce, Credit Suisse Finance, Gibcomponents Factory Ltd, Gibraltar Building Society, Gibraltar Government, Gibraltar Homes Ltd, Gibraltar Tourism Agency, Hojgaard & Schultz, Holiday Inn Gibraltar, Marina Bay Complex Ltd, National Westminister Bank Plc, The New Harbours Industrial Park, Newcastle Building Society, Norwich Union Fire Insurance (Gib) Ltd, Omrod Electricity Supply Co Ltd, Republic National Bank of New York (Gib) Ltd, Scamp Ltd, Volker Stevin Ltd, White Shield Insurance Co Ltd

OTHER OFFICES
ORBIS ACCOUNTING SERVICES LIMITED
Montague Building, Queensway, GIBRALTAR
Tel: +*350* 72035 *Fax:* +*350* 42607
Contact: Freddie White

Total Number of Offices: 2

MOORE STEPHENS
Suite 34, Victoria House, 26 Main Street, GIBRALTAR
Tel: +*350* 74518
Fax: +*350* 70189
Mailing Address: P.O. Box 743, GIBRALTAR
European Affiliation: Moore Stephens
International Contact: Bernard Hazell

OLIVERO & DODWELL
12/3 George's Lane, P.O. Box 417, GIBRALTAR
Tel: +*350* 78440
Fax: +*350* 74716
European Affiliation: Moores Rowland International
International Contact: Arthur Olivero

PRICE WATERHOUSE
9th, Floor Suite 6, International Commercial Centre, Casemates Square, GIBRALTAR
Tel: +*350* 41992
Fax: +*350* 41996
Mailing Address: P.O. Box 615, GIBRALTAR
European Affiliation: Price Waterhouse
International Contact: Steven Knight

Partners:	2
Professional staff:	10
Non-professional staff:	4
Total Staff:	**16**

CONTACT INFORMATION
Managing Partner: Peter Farrar
Tax (Senior Manager): Steven Knight
Tax: Michael Maskall
Senior Manager: Adrian Bourne
Insolvency (Manager): Jill Barker

CLIENT SERVICES
Accountancy (General), Audit, Insolvency & Corporate Restructuring, Management & Business Advice, Taxation (Corporate), Taxation (International), Trust Settlement & Estates

Industry Specialisations: Financial Services, Banking & Fund Manangement

---

ENDURSKODUN & RADGJOF HF
Skeifan 11a, 108 REYKJAVIK
Tel: +*354* (1) 685511
Fax: +*354* (1) 689585
European Affiliation: Ernst & Young Europe
International Contact: Erna Halldorsdottir

ENDURSKODUNARMIDSTÖDIN HF - N. MANSCHER/COOPERS & LYBRAND
Höfdabakki 9, 112 REYKJAVIK
Tel: +*354* (1) 685455
Fax: +*354* (1) 673256
Mailing Address: P.O. Box 12370, 132 REYKJAVIK
European Affiliation: Coopers & Lybrand Europe
International Contact: Valdimar Olafsson

Partners:	12
Professional staff:	24
Non-professional staff:	5
Total Staff:	**41**

CLIENT SERVICES
Accountancy (General), Audit, Management & Business Advice, Mergers & Acquisitions, Taxation (Corporate)

OTHER OFFICES
ENDURSKODUNARMIDSTÖDIN HF - N. MANSCHER/COOPERS & LYBRAND
Gránufélagsgötu 4, 600 AKUREYRI
Tel: +*354* (6) 25609 *Fax:* +*354* (6) 27386
Contact: Thorir Olafsson

ENDURSKODUNARMIDSTÖDIN HF - N. MANSCHER/COOPERS & LYBRAND
Lagaras 4, 700 EGILSSTADIR
Tel: +*354* (7) 11379 *Fax:* +*354* (7) 11679
Contact: Gisli Bjarnason

▷

ENDURSKODUNARMIDSTÖDIN HF - N. MANSCHER/COOPERS & LYBRAND
Gardarsbraut 17, 640 HUSAVIK
Tel: + *354* (6) 41865 *Fax:* + *354* (6) 41832
Contact: Björn St. Haraldsson

ENDURSKODUNARMIDSTÖDIN HF - N. MANSCHER/COOPERS & LYBRAND
Hafnargötu 37A, 230 KEFLAVIK
Tel: + *354* (2) 13219 *Fax:* + *354* (2) 15788
Contact: David Einarsson

Total Number of Offices: 5

HAGSKIL H.F.

Furugerdi 5, 108 REYKJAVIK
Tel: + *354* (1) 685420
Fax: + *354* (1) 84790

European Affiliation: Independent Accountants International

International Contact: Ragnar Gislason

OTHER OFFICES

HAGSKIL H.F.
Strandvegur 63, 900 VESTMANNAEYJAR
Tel: + *354* (8) 12200 *Fax:* + *354* (8) 73243

HAGSKIL H.F.
Vatnsnesvegur 14, 230 KEFLAVIK
Tel: + *354* (2) 12100

Total Number of Offices: 3

KPMG

KPMG ENDURSKODUN HF

Sudurlandsbraut 18, 108 REYKJAVIK
Tel: + *354* (1) 686533
Fax: + *354* (1) 689725

European Affiliation: KPMG

International Contact: Tryggvi Jonsson

Partners:	13
Professional staff:	70
Non-professional staff:	10
Total Staff:	**93**

FEE INCOME

Year End: 31.12.90	%
Accountancy & Audit:	62.0
Insolvency:	3.0
Consultancy:	10.0
Tax:	15.0
Other:	10.0

CONTACT INFORMATION

Managing Partner: Olafur Nilsson
Corporate Finance: Tryggvi Jonsson
Insolvency: Helgi V. Jonsson
Management Consultancy: Ronar B. Johannson
Administration: Gudni S. Gustafsson
Public Sector: Halldor Sigurdsson
Accountancy & Audit: Jon Eirikson
Tax: Olafur Nilsson

CLIENT SERVICES

Accountancy (General), Audit, Corporate Finance Advice, Insolvency & Corporate Restructuring, Life & Risk Assurance, Management & Business Advice, Mergers & Acquisitions, Taxation (Corporate), Taxation (International)

Industry Specialisations: Financial Institutions, Banking, Thrifts, Insurance, Investment, Air Transportation, Municipalities

MAJOR CLIENTS

The Agricultural Bank of Iceland, Association of Municipalities, Byko, Glitnir HF, Grandi HF, Hewlett Packard, Hitaveita Sudurnesja, IBM, Icelandair, Icelandic Investment Co, Idunn, Industrial Loan Fund of Iceland, Islandsbanki, Islenska Auglysingastofan, Oliuverslun Islands HF, Rafmagnsveitur Rikisins, Sildaverksmidjur Rikisins, Skeljungur HF, Urval-Utsyn, Verbrefasjodurinn HF

OTHER OFFICES

KPMG ENDURSKODUN HF
Glerårgata 24, 600 AKUREYRI
Tel: + *354* (6) 26600 *Fax:* + *354* (6) 26601

KPMG ENDURSKODUN HF
Eyravegur 37, SELFOSS

KPMG ENDURSKODUN HF
Bjarnarbraut 8, BORGARNES

KPMG ENDURSKODUN HF
Rádhústorg, DALVIK

KPMG ENDURSKODUN HF
Borgarmyri 1, SAUDARKROKUR

KPMG ENDURSKODUN HF
Baejarhraun 12, HAFNARFJÖRDUR

KPMG ENDURSKODUN HF
Laufás 3, EGILSSTADIR

Total Number of Offices: 8

LÖGGILTIR ENDURSKODENDUR HF

Suóurlandsbraut 32, 108 REYKJAVIK
Tel: + *354* (1) 686377
Fax: + *354* (1) 689379
Mailing Address: P.O. Box 8191, 128 REYKJAVIK

European Affiliation: Horwath International

International Contact: Ingi R. Johannsson

SAMEINADA ENDURSKODUNARSKRIFSTOFAN H/F

Armuli 10, 108 REYKJAVIK
Tel: + *354* (1) 687210
Fax: + *354* (1) 688352

European Affiliation: DFK International

International Contact: Sigurdur B. Arnthorsson

ADVISA TREUHAND-ANSTALT

Heiligkreuz 42, 9490 VADUZ
Tel: + *4175* 28755
Fax: + *4175* 20132
Mailing Address: Postfach 1117, 9490 VADUZ

European Affiliation: Midsnell International

International Contact: Georg Vogt

CONFIDA TRUSTEE & AUDITING COMPANY

Heilligkreuz 8, Postfach 40, 9490 VADUZ
Tel: + *4175* 58800
Fax: + *4175* 28263

European Affiliation: Alliott Peirson International

International Contact: Heinrich Schwaegler

COOPERS & LYBRAND AKTIENGESELLSCHAFT

Pflugstrasse 20, VADUZ
Tel: *+4175* 29080
Fax: *+4175* 29079
Mailing Address: Postfach 1113, 9490 VADUZ

European Affiliation: Coopers & Lybrand Europe

International Contact: Reto H. Silvani

Partners:	3
Professional staff:	3
Non-professional staff:	4
Total Staff:	**10**

CONTACT INFORMATION
Managing Partner: Reto H. Silvani
Corporate Finance: E. Hilti
Partner: Günter R. Meier

CLIENT SERVICES
Accountancy (General), Audit, Corporate Finance Advice, Insolvency & Corporate Restructuring, Life & Risk Assurance, Management & Business Advice, Pensions Planning, Value for Money Studies, Taxation (Corporate), Taxation (International), Trust Settlement & Estates, Captive Insurance Management, Offshore Funds Management, Trust Administration

EUROCOUNT WIRTSCHAFTSBERATUNG ANSTALT

Altenbach 8, 9490 VADUZ
Tel: *+4175* 22135
Fax: *+4175* 28357

European Affiliation: BKR International

International Contact: Albert Meyer

INDUSTRIE-UND-FINANZKONTOR ETABLISSEMENT

Altenbach 8, 9490 VADUZ
Tel: *+4175* 22135
Fax: *+4175* 28357

Partners:	3
Professional staff:	8
Non-professional staff:	10
Total Staff:	**21**

CONTACT INFORMATION
Chairman: Prinz Michael von Liechtenstein
Managing Partner: Dr. Albert Mayer
Managing Partner: Dr. Hans-Peter Brüllmann
Accountancy (General): Erich Strub
Audit: Bruno Caldonazzi

CLIENT SERVICES
Accountancy (General), Audit, Insolvency & Corporate Restructuring, Taxation (Corporate), Taxation (International), Trust Settlement & Estates, Incorporation of Legal Structures, Management of Legal Structures

ERNST NIGG

Lettstrasse 10, 9490 VADUZ
Tel: *+4175* 23344
Fax: *+4175* 28265
Mailing Address: Postfach 525, 9490 VADUZ

European Affiliation: Grant Thornton International

International Contact: Ernst Nigg

Partners:	2
Professional staff:	3
Non-professional staff:	6
Total Staff:	**11**

FEE INCOME

Year End: 1990	**SwF**
Total:	**1,491,000,000**

CONTACT INFORMATION
Managing Partner: Ernst Nigg

CLIENT SERVICES
Accountancy (General), Audit, Taxation (Corporate), Taxation (International), Trust Settlement & Estates, Company Formation & Administration

REVIKON REVISIONS-UND BERATUNGS AG

Städtle 35, 9490 VADUZ
Tel: *+4175* 27070
Fax: *+4175* 20804

European Affiliation: BDO Binder

International Contact: Carl von Seemann

R.S. ATTARD & CO

P.O. Box 324, 46 Timber Wharf, MARSA
Tel: *+356* 233664
Fax: *+356* 339354

European Affiliation: Moore Stephens

International Contact: Reginald Attard

OTHER OFFICES
R.S. ATTARD & CO
67 Sir Arturo Mercieca Street, SLIEMA
Total Number of Offices: 2

BDO ATTARD BUTTIGIEG PSAILA & CO

136 St Christopher Street, VALLETTA
Tel: *+356* 221242
Fax: *+356* 243219

European Affiliation: BDO Binder

International Contact: Lino Buttigieg

Partners:	3
Professional staff:	10
Non-professional staff:	24
Total Staff:	**37**

FEE INCOME

Year End: 1990	%
Accountancy & Audit:	50.0
Consultancy:	28.0
Tax:	5.0
Other:	17.0

▷

CONTACT INFORMATION
Managing Partner: John Attard
Audit: John Attard
Corporate Finance: Lino Buttigieg
Tax (International): John Psaila

CLIENT SERVICES
Industry Specialisations: Manufacturing, Retailing, Hotels, Catering, Travel & Shipping, Tax Planning & Offshore Services

---

BONELLO, GAUCI & MICALLEF

Grant Thornton House, Princess Elizabeth Street, TA'XBIEX
Tel: *+356* 344751
Fax: *+356* 331161

European Affiliation: Grant Thornton International

International Contact: Martin Bonello-Cole

FEE INCOME

Year End: 1990	**Lm**
Total:	**209,000,000**

CONTACT INFORMATION
Managing Partner: Martin Bonello-Cole

CLIENT SERVICES
Accountancy (General), Audit, Management & Business Advice, Taxation (Corporate), Taxation (International), Computer Consultancy

---

ANTON CHETCUTI-GANADO

2 Merchants Street, VALLETTA 5
Tel: *+356* 222097
Fax: *+356* 234941

European Affiliation: Moores Rowland International

International Contact: Anton Chetcuti-Ganado

COOPERS & LYBRAND/ZAMMIT TABONA BONELLO & CO

167 Merchants Street, VALLETTA
Tel: *+356* 233648
Fax: *+356* 244768
Mailing Address: P.O. Box 61, VALLETTA

European Affiliation: Coopers & Lybrand Europe

International Contact: John Bonello

Partners:	5
Professional staff:	60
Non-professional staff:	15
Total Staff:	**80**

CONTACT INFORMATION
Managing Partner: John Bonello
Corporate Finance: Joseph Zammit Tabona
Management Consultancy: John Bonello
Tax (International): Kevin Valanzia
Accountancy & Insolvency: Alan Camilleri
Audit & Public Sector: John Zarb
Administration & Tax (Corporate): Joseph Zammit Tabona

CLIENT SERVICES
Accountancy (General), Audit, Computer Installation, Corporate Finance Advice, Insolvency & Corporate Restructuring, Management & Business Advice, Mergers & Acquisitions, Value for Money Studies, Taxation (Corporate), Taxation (International), Trust Settlement & Estates

Industry Specialisations: Banking, Insurance, Airlines, Soft Drinks Manufacturing, Automotive (Retail), Offshore

DIAMANTINO, MIZZO & CO

Valletta Buildings, South Street, VALLETTA
Tel: *+356* 243258
Fax: *+356* 242232
Mailing Address: P.O. Box 472, VALLETTA

European Affiliation: DRM Internationally

International Contact: Guido Mizzi

FALZON & FALZON

Casa Floriana, Pietro Floriani Street, FLORIANA
Tel: *+356* 233026
Fax: *+356* 239113

European Affiliation: HLB International

International Contact: Godwin Falzon

Partners:	3
Professional staff:	10
Non-professional staff:	17
Total Staff:	**30**

CONTACT INFORMATION
Chairman: John Falzon
Managing Partner: Alfred Falzon
Partner: John Falzon
Partner: Godwin Falzon

CLIENT SERVICES
Accountancy (General), Audit, Computer Installation, Corporate Finance Advice, Insolvency & Corporate Restructuring, Management & Business Advice, Management Buy-outs, Mergers & Acquisitions, Taxation (Corporate), Taxation (International), Management Consultancy

Industry Specialisations: Building & Construction

OTHER OFFICES

FALZON & FALZON
Mgorr Road, XEW RIJA I GOZO
Tel: *+356* 233026 *Fax:* *+356* 239113

Total Number of Offices: 2

MANDUCA, MERCIECA & CO

21 Archbishop Street, VALLETTA
Tel: *+356* 236231
Fax: *+356* 220386

European Affiliation: DRT International

International Contact: Andrew Manduca

Partners:	6
Professional staff:	45
Non-professional staff:	9
Total Staff:	**60**

CLIENT SERVICES
All Services

Total Number of Offices: 2

MANGION MERCIECA & CO

21 Mannario Road, BIRKIRKARA
Tel: *+356* 484373
Fax: *+356* 441718

European Affiliation: BKR International

International Contact: George Mangion

MERCIECA & ASSOCIATES

International House, Naxxar road, SAN GWANN
Tel: *+356* 371995
Fax: *+356* 340145

European Affiliation: Summit International Associates Inc

International Contact: Ray Mercieca

Partners:	2
Professional staff:	2
Non-professional staff:	1
Total Staff:	**5**

CONTACT INFORMATION
Managing Partner: Peter Mamo
Accountancy (General): Ray Mercieca
Tax (International): Peter Mamo

CLIENT SERVICES
Accountancy (General), Audit, Corporate Finance Advice, Management & Business Advice, Taxation (Corporate), Taxation (International), Offshore Company Registrations

Industry Specialisations: International Offshore Taxation

MIZZI SCERRI SAID & CO

Fifth Floor, Airways House, 6-10 High Street, SLIEMA
Tel: *+356* 341857
Fax: *+356* 336296

European Affiliation: Nexia International

International Contact: Michael Scerri

Partners:	3
Professional staff:	10
Non-professional staff:	1
Total Staff:	**14**

CONTACT INFORMATION
Accountancy (General): Martin Said
Audit & Public Sector: Michael Scerri
Administration: Lino Mizzi
Tax: Martin Said

CLIENT SERVICES
All Services

NAUDI, GIORGIO, LEONE GANADO & CO

Villa Mauramy, Mgr A. Mifsud Street, TA'XBIEX
Tel: *+356* 344360
Fax: *+356* 343958

European Affiliation: Price Waterhouse

Partners:	6
Professional staff:	44
Non-professional staff:	11
Total Staff:	**61**

CONTACT INFORMATION
Managing Partner: Major Francis Naudi
Audit: Frederick Mifsud Bonnici
Corporate Finance: Peter Paris
Management Consultancy: Richard Giorgio
Insolvency & Administration: Godfrey Leone Ganado
Tax: Major Francis Naudi
Offshore: Edwin Vella

CLIENT SERVICES
All Services

Industry Specialisations: Offshore Nominee & Trustee Function, Tax Planning, Financial Services

OTHER OFFICES
NAUDI, GIORGIO, LEONE GANADO & CO
President J.F. Kennedy Square, Victoria, GOZA
Tel: *+356* 560473 *Fax:* *+356* 343958
Contact: Godfrey Leone Ganado

Total Number of Offices: 2

FRANÇOIS JEAN BRYCH

2 avenue Saint Charles, 98000 MONTE CARLO
Tel: *+3393* 50 46 60
Fax: *+3393* 50 44 25

European Affiliation: INPACT - International Network of Professional Accountants

Partners:	1
Professional staff:	7
Non-professional staff:	2
Total Staff:	**10**

CONTACT INFORMATION
Chairman: F.J. Brych
Accountancy (General): Joel Varetto
Audit: J.P. Maurice
Management Consultancy: Philip Coulamb
Computer Installation: José Miralles

CLIENT SERVICES
Accountancy (General), Audit, Computer Installation, Management & Business Advice, Taxation (Corporate)

CORPORATE DATA SERVICES

18 boulevard des Moulins, 98000 MONACO
Tel: *+3393* 30 30 37
Fax: *+3393* 50 51 55

European Affiliation: IAG International

International Contact: Tony van Vurren

HOOGEWERF & CO

57 rue Grimaldi, 98000 MONACO
Tel: *+3393* 30 26 55
Fax: *+3393* 25 85 22

International Contact: Francis Hoogewerf

MOORE STEPHENS SERVICES SAM

L'Estoril, avenue Princesse Grace, 98000 MONTE CARLO
Tel: *+3393* 30 81 52
Fax: *+3393* 25 62 70

European Affiliation: Moore Stephens

International Contact: David U. Tugman

Monaco

MOORES ROWLAND CORPORATE SERVICES

2 avenue de Monte-Carlo, B.P. 343, 98006 MONACO
Tel: +*3393* 50 08 20
Fax: +*3393* 25 24 12

European Affiliation: Moores Rowland International

International Contact: Eamonn McGregor

SOMODECO

Immeuble Les Lys, 3 rue Louis Aurèglia, 98000 MONACO
Tel: +*3393* 25 00 52
Fax: +*3393* 25 58 92

European Affiliation: Ernst & Young Europe

CLAUDE L.R. TOMATIS

7 rue de l'Industrie, 98000 MONACO
Tel: +*3393* 05 71 00
Fax: +*3393* 05 90 60

European Affiliation: SC International

International Contact: Claude Tomatis

AUSTRIA

INSTITUT ÖSTERREICHISCHER WIRTSCHAFTSPRÜFER (IWP)/KAMMER DER WIRTSCHAFTSTREUHÄNDER

Bennoplatz 4, 1081 VIENNA
Tel: + *43* (1) 40 19 00
Fax: + *43* (1) 19 02 55

Secretary General: Dr. Helmut Samer
Stubenring 18, 1010 VIENNA
Tel: + *43* (1) 51 23 26 3
Fax: + *43* (1) 51 38 59 0

MEMBERSHIP

Professional Title: beeideter Wirtschaftsprüfer (und Steuerberater) – WP/Stb

Number of Members
Total: **420**

LEGAL FORM OF ENTITY

Sole practitioners, partnerships and limited companies permitted.

SERVICES AUTHORISED

Statutory audit not compatible with general accountancy services – other restrictions included in 271 HGB (commercial code). General accountancy services and taxation advice authorised.

GENERAL RESTRICTIONS

Liability insurance and recognition by the professional body Kammer der Wirtschaftstreuhänder required. Partners/shareholders and directors must be professionals.

BELGIUM

INSTITUT DES EXPERTS-COMPTABLES (IEC)/INSTITUUT DER ACCOUNTANTS (IDAC)

Rue Blanche 25, 1050 BRUSSELS
Tel: + *32* (2) 53 76 73 5
Fax: + *32* (2) 53 75 36 3

Director General: Benôit Vanderstichelen

MEMBERSHIP

Professional Title: Accountant/Expert Comptable

Number of Members

Registered:	3,644
Non-registered:	3,252
Companies Non-nationals:	734
Total:	**7,630**

SERVICES AUTHORISED

General accountancy and tax advice, non-statutory audit of smaller companies authorised.

LEGAL FORM OF ENTITY

Sole practitioners and limited companies permited.

GENERAL RESTRICTIONS

Companies are restricted to professional activities; shareholders and majority of directors must be members of the Institute. All activities must be supervised by Institute members. Statutory audit is restricted to members of IRE/IBR (see below). Advertising is not permitted.

INSTITUUT DER ACCOUNTANTS

(See Institut des Experts Comptables)

INSTITUTE DES RÉVISEURS D'ENTERPRISES (IRE)/INSTITUUT DER BEDRIJFSREVISOREN (IBR)

Avenue Marnix 22, 1050 BRUSSELS
Tel: + *32* (2) 51 25 13 6
Fax: + *32* (2) 51 27 88 6

Director General: Henri Olivier

MEMBERSHIP

Professional Title: Réviseur d'entreprises/Bedrijfsrevisoren

Number of Members
Total: **700** (Approx)

SERVICES AUTHORISED

Authorisation from the supervisory public authorities is required for statutory audit of banks and insurance companies. General accountancy services and taxation advice permitted, but audit services must form a major part of the firm's activity (around 85% or more). No right of appearance at hearings of the tax authorities.

LEGAL FORM OF ENTITY

Sole practitioners, partnerships and limited companies permitted. In Belgian limited companies, the majority of directors must be Belgian nationals. Non-Belgian firms must have a professional office in Belgium. The "Société Anonyme" is not permitted.

THE ACCOUNTANCY PROFESSION IN BELGIUM

The European directives concerning the qualification of auditors and the mutual recognition of accounting qualifications are fully enforced in Belgium. Nevertheless, three aspects of the current situation are still under discussion by government. These include the opportunity to organise a separate profession of tax advisers, the scope for a firm of auditors to provide additional services to an audit client and the field of activities for accountants and auditors.

CYPRUS

THE INSTITUTE OF CERTIFIED PUBLIC ACCOUNTANTS IN CYPRUS

Hawaii Nicosia Tower, 5th Floor 503/504, 41 Them. Dervis Street, NICOSIA

DENMARK

FORENINGEN AF STATSAUTORISEREDE REVISORER (FSR)

Kronprinsessegade 8, 1306 COPENHAGEN K
Tel: + *45* 33 93 91 91
Fax: + *45* 33 11 09 13

Management Secretary: Jens Nuchel

MEMBERSHIP

Professional Title: Statsautoriserede Revisorer (SR)

Number of Members
Total: **2,400** (approx)

SERVICES AUTHORISED

The Statsautoriserede Revisorer qualification is granted by the Ministry of Trade and Industry's Revisorkommission, and voluntary membership of FSR is held by about 90% of SRs. They are licensed by the Revisorkommission to audit all sizes of company. Quoted companies must have two auditors from different firms, at least one of whom must hold the SR qualification. General accountancy and particularly taxation services are provided, but not insolvency.

FORENINGEN AF REGISTRERERDE REVISORER (FRR)

Flint Alle 8, 2000 FREDERIKSBERG
Tel: + *45* 31 86 44 22
Fax: + *45* 38 33 13 18

MEMBERSHIP

Professional Title: Registrerede Revisorer (RR)

Number of Members
Total: **3,300** (approx)

SERVICES AUTHORISED

Formerly authorised to audit public and private unquoted companies but following implementation of the EC company law directives the qualification is under review; RRs who qualified after 1990 may not now audit the largest unquoted companies.

FINLAND

KHT – YHDISTYS FÖRENINGEN CGR RY (KHT-YHDISTYS)/FINNISH INSTITUTE OF AUTHORISED PUBLIC ACCOUNTANTS

Fredrikinkatu 61 A 39, 00100 HELSINKI 10
Tel: + *358* 0 694 2255
Fax: + *358* 0 693 1567

Executive Director: Jouko Ilola

MEMBERSHIP

Professional Title: KHT-tilintarkastaja/Authorised Public Accountant (KHT) or Certified Public Account (CPA)

Number of Members
Total: **453**

FRANCE

COMPAGNIE NATIONALE DES COMMISSAIRES AUX COMPTES (CNCC)

8 rue de l'Amiral de Coligny, 75001 PARIS
Tel: + *33* (1) 42 96 16 12
Fax: + *33* (1) 42 61 37 73

President: Bernard-Pierre Germond
Secretary General: M. Napoleon Susini

MEMBERSHIP

Professional Title: Commissaire aux Comptes

Number of Members
Total: **12,243**

SERVICES AUTHORISED

Statutory audit is authorised, but strict rules apply to safeguard independence (see below). General accountancy services and taxation advice are permitted but not if acting as a Commissaire aux Comptes of the same company.

LEGAL FORM OF ENTITY

Sole practitioners must be a member of Compagnie Nationale des Commissaires aux Comptes. In partnerships, all partners must be registered as members of CNCC. In limited companies 75% of the capital of the company must be held by members of CNCC (for statutory audit).

GENERAL RESTRICTIONS

The company law of 24 July 1966 prohibits a statutory auditor from taking part in the management or accounting functions of the company to which he is appointed as auditor, or from being a shareholder in that company. Members must have professional indemnity insurance, must not advertise and are subject to a regular practice review.

THE ACCOUNTANCY PROFESSION IN FRANCE

The French accountancy profession is organised for historical reasons into two institutes: the Ordre des Experts Comptables et des Comptables Agréés and the Compagnie Nationale des Commissaires aux Comptes. About 85% of professional practitioners are members of the two institutes and exercise both professions simultaneously either in individual auditing firms or within a company. Commissaires aux Comptes are responsible for statutory audit. The Commissaire aux Comptes must avoid being in a position which might jeopardise his freedom of judgement or prevent the proper execution of his engagement. The Compagnie Nationale des Commissaires aux Comptes has a strong technical and legal service and operates an effective quality control/practice review system. There is a continuing study of international professional standards which are considered in the formulation of professional practice standards.

ORDRE DES EXPERTS COMPTABLES ET DES COMPTABLES AGRÉÉS

109 boulevard Malesherbes, 75008 PARIS
Tel: + *33* (1) 45 63 05 44
Fax: + *33* (1) 45 63 90 93

President: F. Fournet
Secretary General: Bernard Zuber
Joint Secretary General: Jean-Pierre Littardi

MEMBERSHIP

Professoinal Title: Expert Comptable

SERVICES AUTHORISED

As Compagnie Nationale des Commissaires aux Comptes (above)

GENERAL RESTRICTIONS

As Compagnie Nationale des Commissaires Aux Comptes (above)

GERMANY

WIRTSCHAFTSPRÜFERKAMMER KÖRPERSCHAFT DES ÖFFENTLICHEN RECHTS (WPK)

Tersteegenstrasse 14, 4000 DUSSELDORF 30
Tel: + *49* (221) 4 56 10
Fax: + *49* (221) 4 56 11 93

Director: Rolf Lichtner

MEMBERSHIP

Professional Titles: Wirtschaftsprüfer (WP), Wirtschaftsprüfungsellschaften (WPG), vereidigter Buchprüfer (vBP), Buchprüfungsgellschaften (BPG)

Number of Members

Full/Fellow:	12,632
Associate:	29
Total:	**12,661**

SERVICES AUTHORISED

Statutory audit: no restrictions for Wirtschaftsprüfer but vereidigter Buchprüfer restricted to audit of small and medium-sized companies (excluding banks, insurance companies etc.). General accountancy services: no restrictions for Wirtschtsprüfer but vereidigter Buchprüfer restricted to small and medium-sized companies. Tax advice: no restrictions apply.

LEGAL FORM OF ENTITY

Sole practitioners, partnerships and private and public limited companies. Limited and unlimited partnerships can be recognised if they are entered as trading companies in the trade Register by reason of their trusteeship work.

GENERAL RESTRICTIONS
No Wirtschaftsprüfer may carry on any other business activity or in fact any activity based on an employment contract with a few exceptions or based on a civil servant relationship or acting as a judge on other than honorary basis. Limited private and public companies must have share capital of at least DM 50,000.

THE ACCOUNTANCY PROFESSION IN GERMANY
A highly recommended profession in Germany, recognised as a profession with one of the highest qualification standards among the German professions with emphasis on law or business matters. The number of professionals is slowy but steadily increasing. The relatively small number of professionals in comparison to other European countries mainly results from the long and hard theoretical and practical training which leads to the high professional quality already mentioned. There is a separate Steuerberater (StB) qualification for professional tax advisers and a Rechtsanwälte (RA) qualification for lawyers also giving tax advice; some 3,500 of these professionals have gained the vBP qualification allowing them to audit small and medium-sized companies.

INSTITUT DER WIRTSCHAFTSPRÜFER IN DEUTSCHLAND (IDW)
Tersteegenstrasse 14, Postfach 32 05 80, 4000 DUSSELDORF 30
Tel: +*49* (211) 45 61 0
Fax: +*49* (211) 4 54 10 97

Director: Rolf Lichtner

MEMBERSHIP
Professional Title: Wirtschaftsprüfer (see below)

Number of Members

Individuals:	5,600 (approx)
Firms:	600 (approx)
Total:	**6,200** (approx)

SERVICES AUTHORISED
Membership of the Institute is voluntary for professionals enrolled as WPs on the professional register of the WPK (see above); about 85 % of WPs are also members of the IDW.

GREECE

ASSOCIATION OF CERTIFIED ACCOUNTANTS & AUDITORS OF GREECE (SELE)
Appollon Tower, 64 Avenue Riankour, Ponorhou Square, 11523 ATHENS
Tel: +*30* (1) 69 12 294
Fax: +*30* (1) 69 12 294

MEMBERSHIP
Professional Title: Certified Accountant

Number of Members

Full:	200
Total:	**200**

SERVICES AUTHORISED
General accountancy and independent audit (non-statutory).

LEGAL FORM OF ENTITY
Audit: two or more members practising as a partnership with unlimited liabiity (under review).

GENERAL RESTRICTIONS
Not currently recognised by the Greek Government for the statutory audit of companies.

THE INSTITUTE OF CERTIFIED PUBLIC ACCOUNTANTS OF GREECE (SOL)
Fokionos Negri Street 3, 11257 ATHENS
Tel: +*30* (1) 862 9835
Fax: +*30* (1) 861 8016

MEMBERSHIP
Professional Title: Certified Public Accountant

Number of Members

Total:	**600**

GENERAL RESTRICTIONS
Members are authorised by the Greek ministry of finance to conduct statutory audit; they have a monopoly of statutory audit of larger public limited companies and are restricted to audit only, working as salaried staff of SOL and appointed to the audit client by SOL.

THE ACCOUNTANCY PROFESSION IN GREECE
Smaller limited companies must be audited either by SOL or by two non-SOL auditors, who must have an appropriate degree and at least five years experience, and are usually members of the Chamber of Economists and Commercial Graduates, a government-sponsored organisation. SELE members act mainly for foreign-owned companies and smaller businesses which require independent audit to attract investment.

ICELAND

FÉLAG LÖGGILTRA ENDURSKODENDA
P.O. Box 1546, 121 Reykjavik Island

President: Arni Tomasson
Secretary: Bryndis Helgadottir

IRELAND (REPUBLIC OF)

THE INSTITUTE OF CHARTERED ACCOUNTANTS IN IRELAND (ICAI)
Chartered Accountants House, 87/89 Pembroke Road, Ballsbridge, DUBLIN 4
Tel: +*353* (1) 680400
Fax: +*353* (1) 680342

Director: Roger Hussey

MEMBERSHIP
Professional Titles: Chartered Accountant (CA), Associate Member (ACA) and Fellow of the Institute (FCA)

Number of Members

Full/Fellow:	3,726
Associate:	3,877
Student:	2,500
Total:	**10,103**

SERVICES AUTHORISED
Statutory audit, financial services and insolvency in great Britain and Northern Ireland require specific authorisation (registration). No restriction on general accountancy services or taxation advice.

LEGAL FORM OF ENTITY
Sole practitioners, partnerships, limited companies and some practices incorporated but without limited liability. Insurance cover for incapacity or death required for sole practitioners authorised under UK financial services act, and advised for all others. In partnerships, 75 % (number and votes) must be Chartered Accountants for the firm to be so described. For registration as an auditor, 75 % of votes must be held by qualified partners. For limited company members in Northern Ireland, ▷

restriction on auditing registration si as for partnerships. In Republic of Ireland, no limited company may be an auditor.

GENERAL RESTRICTIONS

All members in practice, regardless of type, must comply with professional indemnity insurance regulations.

ITALY

CONSIGLIO NAZIONALE DEI DOTTORI COMMERCIALISTI (CRDC)

Via Poli 29, 00187 ROME
Tel: + *39* (6) 679 6600
Fax: + *39* (6) 678 1392

MEMBERSHIP

Professional Title: Dottori Commercialisti

Number of Members

Practising:	13,000
Other:	7,000
Total:	**20,000 (approx)**

SERVICES AUTHORISED

Statutory audit, general accountancy services, business management, insolvency and taxation advice.

GENERAL RESTRICTIONS

Audit and general accountancy services are incompatible. auditors of quoted companies must be registered with the stock exchange (CONSOB). Indemnity insurance is not compulsory. Direct or indirect promotion is not permitted.

CONSIGLIO NAZIONALE RAGIONIERI (CNR)

Via Paisiello 24, 00198 ROME
Tel: + *39* (6) 854 1354
Fax: + *39* (6) 841 7829

Secretary General: Emilio Nataloni

MEMBERSHIP

Professional Title: Ragionieri Commercialisti (RAG)

Number of Members

Practising:	15,000 (approx)
Other full:	9,500 (approx)
Associate:	1,800
Total:	**26,300**

SERVICES AUTHORISED

Statutory audit, general accountancy services, business management, insolvency and taxation advice.

GENERAL RESTRICTIONS

Audit and general accountancy services are incompatible. Auditors of quoted companies must be registered with the stock exchange (CONSOB). Indemnity insurance is not compulsory. Direct or indirect promotion is not permitted.

THE ACCOUNTING PROFESSION IN ITALY

Undergoing major change after adoption of the EC fourth and eighth company law directives. Professional qualification now requires a degree qualification and three years' practical training. New regulations from January 1992 require the names of professionals conducting statutory audit to be registered as Revisori Contabili on a special list kept by the Ministry of Justice (existing members of CNDC and CNR are automatically eligible).

LUXEMBOURG

INSTITUT DES RÉVISEURS D'ENTREPRISES (IRE)

7 rue Alcide de Casperi, 1615 LUXEMBOURG
Tel: + *352* 43 74 84
Fax: + *352* 43 83 26

Secretary: Jean-Jaques Soisson

MEMBERSHIP

Professional Title: Réviseur d'Entreprises

Number of Members

Full:	252
Student:	300
Total:	**552**

SERVICES AUTHORISED

The annual accounts of public companies, public limited partnerships and limited companies other than credit institutions and insurance companies must be independently audited if they exceed balance sheet total of 77m Francs, net turnover of 160m Francs and average number of full-time employees 50 + . Other services include consolidated accounts, examination of non-cash consideration for the issue of shares by a public company, undertakings for collective investment, supervision of co-operatives and the examination of merger and demerger proposals. Accountancy and statutory audit services for the same client are not permitted.

LEGAL FORM OF ENTITY

There is no prescribed legal form for these entities but they must have a separate legal personality. An individual may not practise under a pseudonym or name other than his own. In partnerships, the majority of directors or partners must meet the conditions for authorisation.

GENERAL RESTRICTIONS

Any reports and opinions issued on behalf of a legal entity must be signed by an individual who meets the conditions for authorisation as an independent auditor.

THE ACCOUNTING PROFESSION IN LUXEMBOURG

In Luxembourg, audits may only be carried out by independent auditors (Réviseurs d'Entreprises), who operate in public practice and may not be employed in any capacity by audit clients, nor pursue any activity that might impinge on professional independence.

ORDRE DES EXPERTS COMPTABLES LUXEMBOURGEOIS

B.P. 1362, 7 rue Alcide de Gasperi, 1615 LUXEMBOURG
Tel: + *352* 43 74 84
Fax: + *352* 43 83 26

MALTA

THE INSTITUTE OF ACCOUNTANTS

1 Wilga Street, Paceville, ST JULIANS
Tel: + *356* 33 88 51
Fax: + *356* 33 61 32

MONACO

CONSEIL DE L'ORDRE DES EXPERTS COMPTABLES DE MONACO

boulevard Princesse Charlotte 30, MONTE CARLO
Tel: + *33* (93) 30 15 15
Fax: + *33* (93) 25 80 30

NETHERLANDS

NEDERLANDS INSTITUUT VAN REGISTERACCOUNTANTS (NIVRA)

A. J. Ernsztstraat 55, 1083 GR AMSTERDAM
Tel: + *31* (20) 646 4046
Fax: + *31* (20) 644 3131

Director General: Wim P. Moleveld

MEMBERSHIP

Professional Title: Registeraccountant (RA)

Number of Members
Total: **7,800**

LEGAL FORM OF ENTITY

Neither sole practitioners nor partnerships permitted. All shareholders and directors of limited companies must be Registeraccountants practising in the company.

THE ACCOUNTING PROFESSION IN THE NETHERLANDS

Implementation of the EC Eighth directive and the mutual recognition directive has been delayed by discussion over whether the second tier of accountants in the Netherlands, the accountants-administratie-consulenten (AAs), should be given the right to statutory audit. A particular problem is what additional knowledge is required from the present AAs who have not enough audit experience to fulfil the requirements of the Eighth directive. there are two bills pending with parliament. A government bill proposes to join the two tiers of accountant and creates a new type of accountant with the professional title of Certified Accountant (CA) with sole right to carry out statutory audits. The bill contains onerous transitional measures for AAs. The second bill, introduced as a private member's bill, leaves the two tiers of accountatns in place, but restricts AAs to statutory audits for small and medium-sized companies only. The transitional requirements for AAs are considerably less onerous. A decision on which bill will become law was expected soon at the time of going to press.

NEDERLANDSE ORDE VAN ACCOUNTANTS-ADMINISTRATIECONSULENTEN (NOVAA)

Nieuwe Parklaan 69, 2597 LB THE HAGUE
Tel: + *31* (70) 352 1424
Fax: + *31* (70) 351 2836

MEMBERSHIP

Professional Title: Accountants - Administratieconsulenten (AA)

Number of Members
Total: **2,800**

GENERAL RESTRICTIONS

Not currently permitted to carry out statutory audit or make 'fairness statements' on financial matters. See commentary above on the profession in the Netherlands. AAs need not be paid-up members of NOVAA provided they have obtained the necessary qualifications.

NORWAY

NORGES REGISTRERTE REVISORERS FORENING

Gyldenl Ves Gate 44, 0260 OSLO 2
Tel: + *47* (2) 44 60 70
Fax: + *47* (2) 55 13 29

NORGES STATSAUTORISERTE REVISORERS FORENING (NSRF)

Revisorenes Hus, Uranienborg Terrasse 9, 0351 OSLO 3
Tel: + *47* (2) 69 59 10
Fax: + *47* (2) 69 05 55

Secretary-General: Børre Rognlien

MEMBERSHIP

Professional Title: Statsautorisert Revisor

Number of Members
Total: **1,303**

SERVICES AUTHORISED

Participation in general accountancy functions of a statutory audit client is not allowed. Taxation advice is limited to assistance with tax returns and related information, complaints and other contact with tax authorities.

LEGAL FORM OF ENTITY

No restrictions as to legal form of entity. In a partnership, a majority of partners must be Statsautorisert Revisors; other partners must be Registrert Revisors. A majority of board of directors of a limited company must be Statsautoriserte Revisorers and must hold the majority of the shares.

GENERAL RESTRICTIONS

No licence is required.

PORTUGAL

CAMARA DOS REVISORES OFICIAIS DE CONTAS

Rue Filipe Folque 26, 4 piso, 1000 LISBON
Tel: + *351* (1) 352 9085
Fax: + *351* (1) 525 592

MEMBERSHIP

Professional Title: Revisores Oficiais de Contas

Number of Members
Total: **600 (approx)**

SERVICES AUTHORISED

Statutory audit of public and major private companies is authorised (and restricted to members of the Camara).

SPAIN

INSTITUTO DE CENSORES JURADOS DE CUENTAS DE ESPAÑA

General Arrando 9, 28010 MADRID
Tel: + *34* (1) 446 0354
Fax: + *34* (1) 447 1162

President: Jesùs Peregrina
General Secretary: Aquilino Pravia Suarez

MEMBERSHIP

Professional Title: Censor Jurados de Cuentas

Number of Members
Practising: 3,000
Management/public finance 6,000
Total: **9,000**

GENERAL RESTRICTIONS

Statutory audit: auditors of quoted and larger unquoted companies must be listed in the offficial Registro Oficial de Auditores de Cuentas held by the Instituto de Contabilidad y Auditoria de Cuentas (see below). General ▷

accountancy and taxation services: no restrictions. Insolvency work: not permitted.

REGISTRO DE ECONOMISTAS AUDITORES SA

Pedro Muguruza 3, 28036 MADRID
Tel: + *34* (1) 458 0448

MEMBERSHIP
Professional Title: Economistas Auditor

Number of Members
Total: **3,100**

GENERAL RESTRICTIONS
As Censores Jurados (see above).

INSTITUTO DE CONTABILIDAD Y AUDITORIA DE CUENTAS

Paso de la Castellana 160, 28046 MADRID
Tel: + *24* (1) 458 8010

MEMBERSHIP
Professional Title: Auditor de Cuentas

Number of Members
Total: **14,000 (approx)**

SERVICES AUTHORISED
Following implementation of the EC company law directives, the Instituto, reporting to the ministry of economy and trade, maintains the official register of persons approved to conduct statutory audits. They will normally belong to one of the Spanish professional bodies, to whom the Instituto has delegated its authority to set professional accounting and audit examinations.

SWEDEN

FÖRENINGEN AUKTORISERADE REVISORER (FAR)

Norrtullsgatan 6, Box 6417, 113 82 STOCKHOLM
Tel: + *46* (8) 23 41 30
Fax: + *46* (8) 34 14 61

Secretary General: Björn Markland

MEMBERSHIP
Professional Title: Auktoriserad Revisor

Number of Members
Total: **2,000**

SERVICES AUTHORISED
Statutory audit, taxation advice and general accountancy authorised. Other services may not be combined with statutory audit assignments for the same client.

LEGAL FORM OF ENTITY
In sole practitioners and partnerships, all partners must be auktoriserade Revisorers. In limited companies, only Auktoriserade Revisorers can be shareholders or directors.

GENRAL RESTRICTIONS
Mandatory insurance. Auktoriserade Revisorers are prohibited from taking part in the management of business activities.

THE ACCOUNTANCY PROFESSION IN SWEDEN
The Swedish application for full membership of EC has created a need for harmonisation of some central legislation with the EC directives. Committees and Royal Commissions are currently working or planning to start working with the accounting act and the companies act (fourth, seventh and eleventh directives) and the decree on auditors (eighth directive). Likely results of the work are new examination procedures for the qualification as Auktoriserade Revisor, relaxed rules for the ownership of accounting firms (allowing foreign professionals to join as partners) and a wider definition of the area of compatible business.

SWITZERLAND

TREUHAND-KAMMER/CHAMBRE FIDUCAIRE/CAMERA FIDUCIARIA

Postfach 892, Limmatquai 120, 8001 ZURICH
Tel: + *41* (1) 252 32 12
Fax: + *41* (1) 252 39 11

President: G. Schultz
Director: A. Guntle

MEMBERSHIP
Professional Titles: Bücherexperte/Expert-Comptable Diplome/Perito Contabile Diplomato (Swiss Certified Accountant), Steuerexperte/Expert Fiscal Diplome/Perito Fiscale Diplomato (Swiss Certified Tax Consultant), Treuhandexperte/Expert Fiduciaire Diplome/Perito Fiduciario Diplomato (Swiss Certified Fiduciary).

Number of Members

Members:	2,700
Firms:	650
Internal Auditors:	130
#Total:	**3,480**

SERVICES AUTHORISED
There are no restrictions on general accountancy services, taxation advice or statutory audit at present except bank audits (see below).

LEGAL FORM OF ENTITY
Sole practitioners and limited companies permitted. Partnerships very rarely used.

GENERAL RESTRICTIONS
Bank audits need Certified Accountants licensed by the Federal Banking Commission. New corporate law in 1992/1993 will increase qualification requirement.

THE ACCOUNTING PROFESSION IN SWITZERLAND
The accounting profession is dominated by three large accounting/consulting companies (ATAG Ernst & Young, STG Coopers & Lybrand and KPMG Fides Peat) and a middle-sized company, Revisuisse Price Waterhouse. STG, Fides and Revisuisse recently became independent from their parent companies, the three largest Swiss Banks, Swiss Bank Corporation, Credit Suisse and Union Bank of Switzerland respectively. The profession is well organised through the Swiss Institute which also includes sections for internal auditors and tax consultants. The profession is striving to adjust to European and international accounting principles and auditing standards.

UNITED KINGDOM

THE CHARTERED ASSOCIATION OF CERTIFIED ACCOUNTANTS

29 Lincoln's Inn Fields, LONDON WC2A 3EE
Tel: + *44* (71) 242 6855
Fax: + *44* (71) 831 8054

Chief Executive and Secretary: Andrew Sansom

MEMBERSHIP
Professional Title: Certified Accountant (FCCA – Fellow of the Association; ACCA – Associate); Registered Auditor (if practising certificate held).

Number of Members

Fellow/Associate:	37,765
Students:	78,000
Total:	**115,765**

SERVICES AUTHORISED

Statutory audit, general accountancy services and taxation advice authorised (general accountancy and tax advice are not regulated services in the UK, but members providing general accountancy must hold a practising certificate). Audit firms (including sole practitioners) must be controlled by registered auditors eg FCCA/ACCAs holding valid practising certificate or equivalent. There are no incompatibilities in the UK between audit and general accounting activities.

LEGAL FORM OF ENTITY

Sole practitioners, partnerships, limited companies. Any of these entities practising as Certified Accountants or Chartered Accountants in the UK must be controlled by registered auditors (see above).

GENERAL RESTRICTIONS

Registered auditors must have professional indemnity insurance ('PII'), practice continuity arrangements, undertake continuous professional development ('CPD') and be monitored by the appropriate professional body (eg by the ACCA's practice regulation department).

THE ACCOUNTING PROFESSION IN THE UK

The EC eighth directive was implemented in the UK in the form of the companies act 1989 which brought about increased government regulation of the audit profession. The companies act 1989 has, in turn, been incorporated into the ACCA's internal byelaws in the form of the qualification and audit regulations. The main by-products of this increased regulation have been: obligatory 'CPD', 'PII', approved training practices, etc. A further development has been the implementation in the UK of the EC mutual recognition directive, which allows the holders of other EC accountancy qualifications to sit the ACCA's mutual recognition aptitude test and become a fully-qualified Certified Accountant – and if appropriate a registered auditor – without having to requalify from scratch.

THE CHARTERED INSTITUTE OF MANAGEMENT ACCOUNTANTS (CIMA)

63 Portland Place, LONDON W1N 4AB
Tel: + *44* (71) 637 2311
Fax: + *44* (71) 631 5309

Secretary: Sir George Vallings

MEMBERSHIP

Professional Titles: Fellow of the Chartered Institute of Management Accountants (FCMA); Member of the Chartered Institute of Management Accountants (ACMA).

Number of Members

Fellows:	8,228
Associates:	23,361
Students:	52,056
Total:	**83,645**

SERVICES AUTHORISED

General accountancy services and taxation advice – chiefly business taxation.

LEGAL FORM OF ENTITY

Sole practitioners, partnerships, limited companies. Most members work in industry, commerce and government. Only about 6 % are in practice.

GENERAL RESTRICTIONS

Ethical restrictions apply. Professional indemnity insurance advised. Registration likely to be compulsory from 1 January 1993.

THE CHARTERED INSTITUTE OF PUBLIC FINANCE & ACCOUNTANCY (CIPFA)

3 Robert Street, LONDON WC2N 6BH
Tel: + *44* (71) 895 8823
Fax: + *44* (71) 895 8825

Director: Noel P. Hepworth

MEMBERSHIP

Professional Title: Institute of Public Finance & Accountancy (IPFA)

Number of Members

Full:	11,087
Student:	3,442
Honorary Fellows:	5
Total:	**14,534**

SERVICES AUTHORISED

General accountancy services.

LEGAL FORM OF ENTITY

Sole practitioners, partnerships, limited companies, public service organisations.

GENERAL RESTRICTIONS

Not authorised to sign off accounts udner companies act 1989.

THE ACCOUNTANCY PROFESSION IN THE UK

The CIPFA is concerned with accounting and audit in the public sector. All the changes which have occurred over the last decade in the UK pubic sector have tended to place greater emphasis upon improved financial management. This has resulted in a strong growth in the demand for accountants by public sector institutions. The Financial Reporting Council, the UK standard-setting body, has established a public sector committee to which the profession submits proposals for accounting standards and guidelines.

THE INSTITUTE OF CHARTERED ACCOUNTANTS IN ENGLAND & WALES (ICAEW)

P.O. Box 433, Chartered Accountants' Hall, Moorgate Place, London EC2P 2BJ
Tel: + *44* (71) 628 7060
Fax: + *44* (71) 920 0547

Secretary & Chief Executive: Andrew Colquhoun

MEMBERSHIP

Professional Title: Chartered Accountant (ACA, FCA)

Number of Members

Fellows & Associates:	96,603
Students:	13,342
Total:	**109,945**

SERVICES AUTHORISED

Auditors must be approved to conduct statutory audit, registered by ICAEW and are subject to monitoring. General accountancy services and taxation advice are authorised.

LEGAL FORM OF ENTITY

Sole practitioners and partnerships only. In 'Chartered Accountant' partnerships, 75 % of partners must be Chartered Accountants.

GENERAL RESTRICTIONS

Compliance with the ICAEW byelaws, ethical guidelines and regulations.

THE ACCOUNTANCY PROFESSION IN ENGLAND & WALES

The accountancy profession in the UK has undergone some very radical changes in the recent past. Following the review of the process of setting accounting standards initiated by the profession, the new Financial Reporting Council was established on 1 August 1991, and the Accounting Standards Board was set up at the same time to replace the Accounting ▷

Standards Committee. The work of these independent bodies is aimed at raising corporate reporting standards. In addition, the Auditing Practices Board, which includes outside representtives, replaced the Auditing Practices Committee in April 1991. Audit regulation under the Companies Act 1989 came into effect on 1 October 1991 when the ICAEW became a recognised supervisory body and a recognised qualifying body. Compliance with the new audit regulations will be monitored by the joint monitoring unit (operated on behalf of ICAEW, the Scottish and Irish Institutes).

THE INSTITUTE OF CHARTERED ACCOUNTANTS OF SCOTLAND (ICAS)

27 Queen Street, EDINBURGH EH2 1LA
Tel: + *44* (31) 225 5673
Fax: + *44* (31) 225 3813

Chief Executive & Secretary: Peter W. Johnston

MEMBERSHIP

Professional Title: Chartered Accountant (CA)

Number of Members	
Full:	13,022
Students:	1,460
Total:	**14,482**

SERVICES AUTHORISED

Statutory audit authorised if a registered auditor. General accountancy services and/or taxation advice authorised if an Institute practising certificate is held. Insolvency work or investment business require authorisation by the Institute or another recognised body.

LEGAL FORM OF ENTITY

Sole practitioners and partnerships may be described as Chartered Accountants only if 75% of the partners and 75% of the voting rights are held by Chartered Accountants. Limited companies require that 75% control of the company must be held by Chartered Accountants.

GENERAL RESTRICTIONS

Practising members must have professional indemnity insurance in accordance with the Institute's byelaws.

THE ACCOUNTING PROFESSION IN SCOTLAND

In the UK accounting profession a number of trends are apparent: recognition of the need to reassess the present model of corporate governance in the UK and the role, responsibilities and liabilities of the auditor in that model; movement towards a greater emphasis on good, informative financial reporting thus moving away from 'creative accounting'; recognition that standard-setting does not involve just preparers/auditors but that user groups have to be an integral part of the standard-setting process; and progress towards increased self-regulation of the profession stemming from legislatory requirements to set up such regimes eg audit, financial services.

Acknowledgements

The Editors wish to extend their thanks to the following individuals for their co-operation and help in compiling this directory.

Jens Chr. Aarup (IGAF), Jérôme Adam (Moores Rowland International), Martine Agopian (Nexia International), David Almond (Alliott Pierson International), Nicholas C. Blake (Clark Kenneth Leventhal), Robert Bruce, Martin Burchmore (K. S. International), Peter Catto (Summit International Associates), Brenda Dale (Alliott Pierson International), Janine Daniel, Sarah Donne (Morison International), Agnes Dupre (Eura-Audit International), Robert Emery (Arthur Andersen Worldwide Organisation), Ian Fraser (Independent Accountants International), Lynn Gabbatiss (Grant Thornton International), Peter Galloway (The Channel International Association), Martin Goddard (ATD International), Vanessa Gunn (UHY International), Suzanne Harris (Coopers & Lybrand), Rene Harwood (DFK International), Nova Hastings (Arthur Andersen Worldwide), John Hegarty (FEE), Anton Hume (Stoy Hayward), Tina Humphreys (Price Waterhouse), Sue Hurley (Price Waterhouse), Deirdre Hynes (Kreston International), Fi Inchbald (Stoy Hayward), Barry Jackson (Arthur Andersen Worldwide Organisation), Deirdre Jones (ICC Inter-Continental Consultants), Nicholas Kelsey (SC International), Denzil Kennedy (HLB International), Richard Kleiner (A.E.E. International), Martin Kudlick (ACPA International Inc), Richard Lane (Crane & Partners), Ricky Lawrence (Grant Thornton International), Roger Lyle (Intercontinental Accounting Associates), John McCagney (S. & W. International), Richard Moore (Moore Stephens International), Dan Newman (Ernst & Young), Moji Oduwole, Hervé Pierret (DRM Europe), Mary Porch (The CharterGroup Partnership), Peter Quick (Jeffreys Henry International), David Read (DRT International), Claire Richards, Peter J. C. Scolding (CPA Associates Inc), Alison Seabrook (ACCA), Martin Silverman (Morison International), Phillip Soper (Horwath International), Hilary Stevens, Eric Tait (Pannell Kerr Forster Worldwide), Elisabeth Tham (GMN International), Claire Tizzard (Summit International), Claude Trolliet (FEE), Charles Tucker (BKR International), Sally-Ann Whittaker (INPACT International Ltd), Richard van Eekelen (KPMG International), Paul W. M. van Elten (BDO International), Ricardo van Winegarden (Arthur Andersen Worldwide Organisation), Doug Vickers (ACPA International), Katrin Voss (Russell Beford International), Stephen Yeates (Midsnell International) and the many more who spent hours compiling and checking information.